PL/I: Structured Programming and Problem Solving

Rama N. Reddy
University of Arkansas–Little Rock

Carol A. Ziegler
University of Arkansas–Little Rock

West Publishing Company

St. Paul New York San Francisco Los Angeles

Copyediting Sheryl Rose
Composition Science Press
Cover graphic Flowchart generated
by Bob Anderson of Computer Arts, Inc.

50 West Kellogg Boulevard
P.O. Box 64526
St. Paul, MN 55164–1003

Printed in the United States of America

Library of Congress Cataloging-in-Publication Data

Reddy, Rama N.
PL/I : structured programming and problem solving.

Includes index.
1. PL/I (Computer program language) 2. Structured programming. I. Ziegler, Carol A. II. Title.
QA76.73.P25R43 1986 005.13'3 85–26633
ISBN 0–314–93915–6

Contents

Preface

Despite the continual development of new programming languages, there are a few languages that have withstood the test of time. PL/I is the only one of these well-established languages that is truly a general-purpose language in that it contains most of the high-level language features used for scientific, and also for business applications. In addition, its designers were foresighted enough to include features that meet the needs of text-processing and systems applications.

PL/I is very modern in its approach to program structuring, having had from the beginning such features as the standard control structures, modularity, strong exception handling capabilities, flexible data structures, and options for concurrent processing. Although the complete language is often considered large and complex, it contains an easily learnable nucleus providing numeric and character manipulation instructions and program structures which reflect the basic principles of high-level programming languages. The procedural nature of the language makes it possible to write functional modules designed after the principles of software engineering. The powerful input/output facilities provide capabilities not found in any other commonly used or commonly taught programming language.

The choice of PL/I as a teaching language ensures that the student is introduced to all of the concepts available in other basic teaching languages, as well as provided with a tool that can be used throughout the curriculum and a language that is of practical use outside the educational environment.

This book was written to fulfill the needs of a two-semester course in programming. It attempts to present the features of PL/I most commonly found in production compilers. These include the complete ANSI Subset G, and such additional features as are supported by the majority of vendors. No attempt is made at comprehensive coverage of the full ANSI language. Unfortunately this means that decisions have been made to include some features and exclude others. We apologize to any reader whose favorites are missing.

This book has been used successfully by the authors and their colleagues in a number of different classes following the two-semester sequence. It is organized into eighteen chapters. The first nine chapters are intended to be covered in the first programming course. Chapters 9 through 17 are used by us in the second course. In practice we find that chapter 9 is covered quickly in the first course and more comprehensively in the second. Chapter 18 is included when the computer system being used provides a PL/I compiler with concurrent processing capabilities.

Used for a single-semester class, it would be necessary to omit either some of the more technical parts of each chapter, or those topics which are of lesser use to the students. One or more of the chapters on file processing should be included.

Once a structure, instruction, concept, or example has been introduced, it has been used freely in the book wherever appropriate. Nevertheless, many of the topics are semi-independent and chapters could be studied in several different orders. Various possible paths through the text are shown in the following figure.

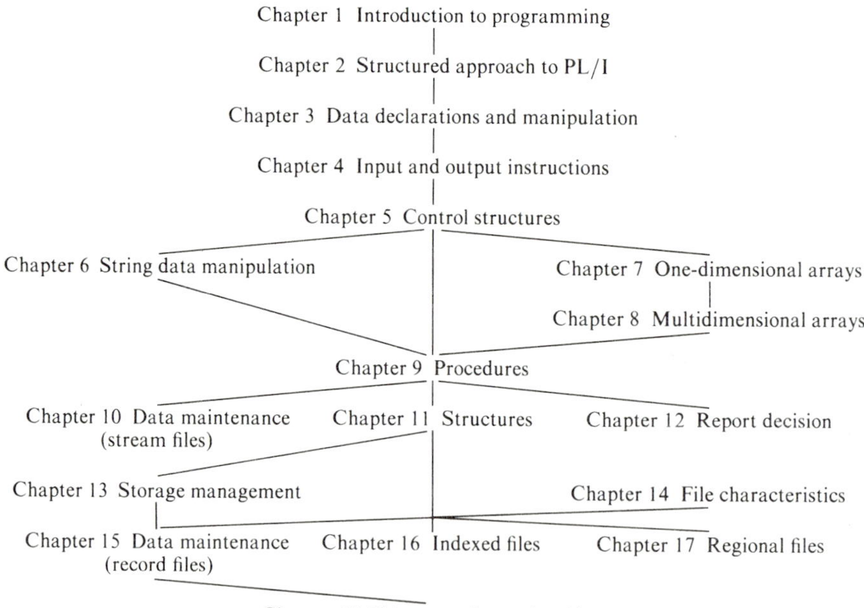

When students entering the programming course have already had an introduction to computers, algorithms, and programming, most of the topics of the first two chapters may be omitted. However, these chapters introduce techniques of algorithm design which are used throughout the book. Chapters 6 and 12 will be of less interest to those interested in scientific computing. However, chapter 12 should not be ignored entirely as it contains some useful hints for all programmers who are concerned with readable output. Chapter 13 will primarily be of interest to those interested in complex data structures and system programming. Parts of it should be studied prior to the discussion of locate mode processing in chapter 15. Chapters 15, 16, and 17 have been written in such a way that they may be approached in any order.

Throughout the book there is an emphasis on program design and implementation techniques which aid in the development of efficient and reliable software. Careful planning and top-down development is stressed through the use of hierarchy charts, structured flowcharts, and decision tables. The relationship between program modules and the modules of hierarchy charts is emphasized. The importance of standardization and documentation is shown by precept and example. As a pedagogical device, key concepts, rules, hints, and cautions are set off in such a way as to catch the student's attention.

Each section of the book is followed by a short set of review questions that checks the student's comprehension of the section. Answers to the odd-numbered review questions can be found in Appendix E. It is hoped that these questions will stimulate discussion as well as send the student back to reread portions of the text. Amplified answers to all of the review questions can be found in the Instructor's Manual.

Each chapter of the book is followed by a brief summary which highlights the most important information presented in the chapter and organizes it in a concise, meaningful way. A set of programming exercises is also presented. These exercises are closely connected to the material presented in the chapter. To some extent they are graduated from the very simple, to the more difficult. The exercises have been selected from the areas of computer science and mathematics, the sciences and engineering, text processing, and business. The exercise problems at the end of each chapter which are marked by an asterisk are implementation dependent.

Acknowledgments

The authors wish to express their sincere thanks to the editors, Jerry Westby and Pamela Barnard of West Publishing Company for their interest, enthusiasm, and the many fruitful discussions that led to the final form of this book. We also wish to express our thanks to the following reviewers:

Jessie Bethly, Southern University
Jane Brown, Danville Area Community College
Robert Crawford, Western Kentucky University
Kay Duffy, Marshall University
Michael Henry, West Virginia University
Jerald Kabell, Central Michigan University
Bhagat Singh, University of Wisconsin–Manitowoc Center

whose constructive criticism and suggestions improved the book's content and organization.

Finally, we wish to express our sincere thanks to our students for their willingness to serve as subjects of our pedagogical experiments and to learn from an unfinished manuscript, for their many suggestions and assistance in a multitude of ways. Last but not least of all, thanks to our colleagues in the Department of Computer Science and the College of Science at the

University of Arkansas at Little Rock for their encouragement, and to our families without whose support and longsuffering forbearance we would have been unable to complete this book.

Rama N. Reddy
Carol A. Ziegler

1
Introduction to programming

OBJECTIVE: To understand a computer's hardware configuration and functioning, and its software capabilities.

COMPUTERS AND COMPUTER PROGRAMMING have become an essential part of everyday activity in modern society. The computer is a tool for solving problems more accurately and more efficiently than could be done by hand. Computers are used in scientific research, daily business, as teaching aids, in industry and manufacturing, in medicine, space technology, the exploration of natural resources, and many other areas. The enhancement of industry and business in response to modern-day needs is primarily due to the development of computer technology.

1.1 Overview of computer systems

Computer systems are classified broadly as mainframe computers, minicomputers, and microcomputers. This classification is based on memory capacity, word size, processing power, number of peripherals, amount of software support, and most of all on types of applications. However, the distinction is less important today than in the past. In general the only sure way of determining a computer's category is to ask how it is marketed: as a mainframe, a minicomputer, or a microcomputer.

Mainframe machines store and transmit information in groups of four or more characters (usually given as a word size of twenty-four or more bits). They have more processing power and large amounts of memory, and therefore can support a great many remote job entry and time-sharing terminals and data storage devices. They have the capacity for teleprocessing, database management, and other large software environments. The mainframe systems are used for a variety of applications, primarily handling large amounts of data.

Minicomputers are medium-size machines storing and transmitting data in groups of two or more characters (word size of sixteen or more bits). They have enough memory and processing power to support the terminals and software sufficient for a single organization, such as a research institution or a medium-size business.

Microcomputers are small machines with a word size of eight or more bits. They have limited memory compared to mainframes, reasonable processing power, and a limited amount of software, usually designed for a single user such as a small business. Microcomputers are often called desktop machines.

It is difficult to make a clear distinction between mainframes, minicomputers, and microcomputers based on their technical differences because of the broad range of computer systems. It is easier to base the distinction on the different types of applications.

1.1.1 Hardware

A computer system contains electronic and mechanical components. These components are called *hardware,* a general term used to refer to the physical parts of a computer system. The primary hardware components of a typical computer system are the input/output devices, storage devices (primary memory and secondary memory), and the central processing unit (CPU). Figure 1–1 shows the components needed in any computer system.

The *input devices* are used to supply information to the computer in the form of instructions or data. The most common types of input devices are card readers and key-entry terminals. Magnetic storage devices such as magnetic tapes and magnetic disks are also used as input devices.

The *output devices* are used for presenting processed information to users, either in the form of printed material or as a visual display. The most common types of output devices are printers and CRT terminals (also called VDT terminals). Magnetic storage devices such as magnetic tape and magnetic disk are used as output devices to store processed information in machine-readable form.

The *CPU* is the most heavily used component of a computer system. It consists of two functional parts, the arithmetic/logic unit and the control

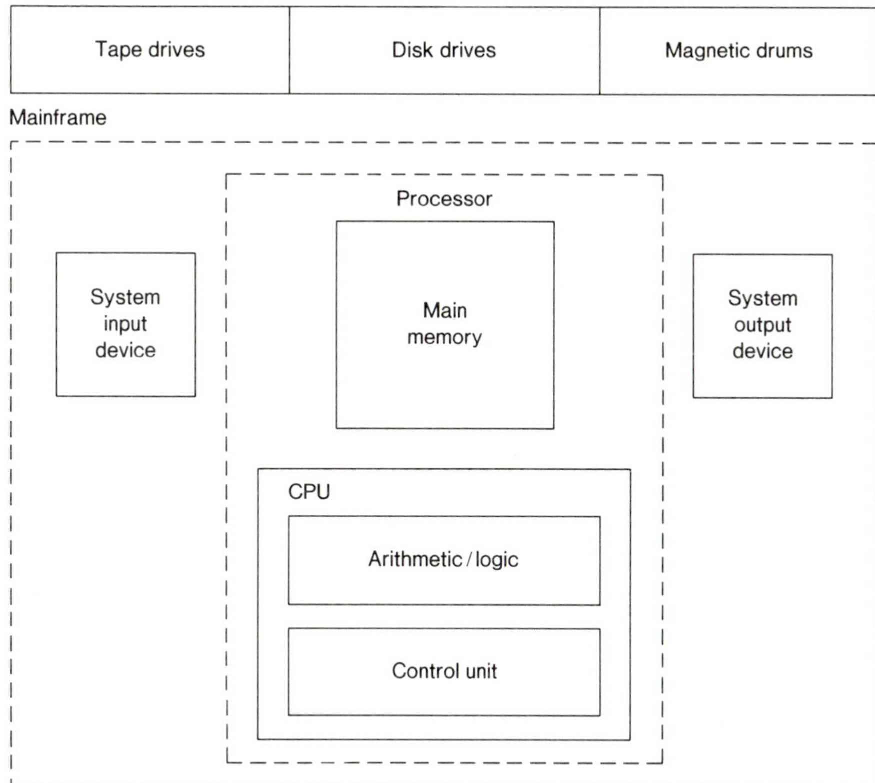

Figure 1–1

unit. The *arithmetic unit* performs all of the arithmetical operations and the *logic unit* compares data. The *control unit* generates commands to fetch instructions and data from memory, carry out the instructions, and store the results back in memory. The control unit also generates commands that control the activities of other components of the system.

The *memory* of a computer is the place where information is stored. It contains both instructions and data. These are supplied to the machine by the input devices in the form of symbols, words, and keyboard codes. These symbols are converted to binary zeros and ones according to a selected code, then stored internally in memory cells known as core. The memory of a computer is a collection of organized addressable locations which can hold symbolic information in binary form. Each memory location is like a post office box. Its address is unique, but its contents can be different at different times.

Computer memory has two important characteristics. First, the contents of each memory location can be retrieved at any time without being erased. Second, the contents can be changed by erasing old data and storing new values. Figure 1–2 shows the organization of memory with separate storage of program instructions and data.

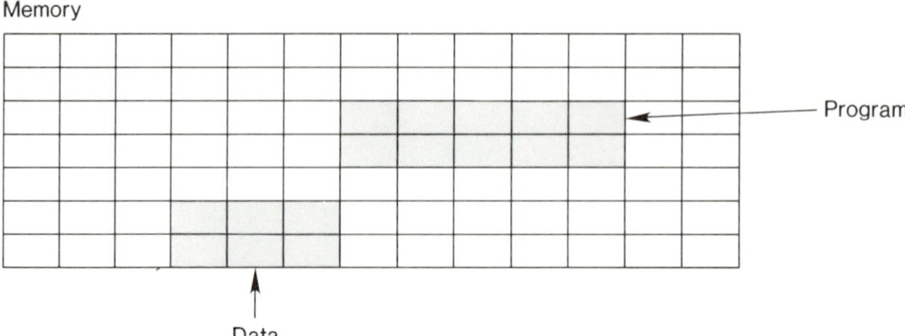

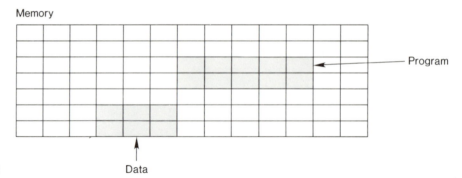

Figure 1–2

The hardware components of the computer that are outside the mainframe are called *peripherals*. These consist of such devices as tape drives, disk drives, magnetic drums, on-line card punches, and on-line plotters. The memory is the *primary storage device*, and the peripherals are input/output devices used as *secondary storage devices*.

1.1.2 Software

The programs that control the computer are known as *software*. They consist of sequences of instructions written in a low-level programming language. The software that supports a computer system is known as *system software*, while the software that users develop to solve specific problems is known as *application software*. Software is generally divided into operating systems, compilers, system utilities, and application programs.

The *operating system* is a collection of software modules which manages the hardware and software resources of the computer system. The operating system provides all of the facilities needed in the system to run user programs without user intervention. System resources such as memory, processor, and devices are supervised and allocated by the operating system. The primary goals of the operating system are to optimize system performance, to provide equitable access to all the users of the system, and to maintain a balance between input/output and processing.

Compilers are programs that process other programs. They translate a program from the symbolic code that people can comfortably use to one more suitable for computers, known as machine language. Languages that are people-oriented and must be translated for computer use are called *high-level languages*. Machine language and similar machine-oriented languages are called *low-level languages*.

The computer system provides software to assist the user in writing and running programs. These user tools are divided into utility programs and system library routines. *System utilities* include data management and device management routines. *System library routines* include mathematical packages, statistical packages, database management systems, and teleprocessing software.

Application programs are developed by users for such jobs as processing bank transactions, updating inventory records, designing buildings, analyzing chemicals, calculating payroll information, keeping track of student enrollment, and counting stars.

1.1.3 Firmware

The distinction between hardware and software is not always easy to make. It is possible to design the hardware circuits of a computer to carry out complicated functions that are usually part of the software. This is done with specialized military and space computers. It is also done with computers such as database machines, which specialize in storing information for fast retrieval.

It is also possible to build very general, limited hardware and provide most of the functions, such as multiplication, which is usually thought of as a hardware function, through the software. A compromise adopted for most computer systems is to build general hardware circuits, but then to build in permanent programs to do such things as multiplication. This type of program built into the hardware is known as *firmware.*

1.1.4 Program environment

The way the computer is used by a program determines the *program environment.* Programs may run without human intervention, calculating answers from data stored in the computer and printing reports. Such programs operate in a *batch environment.* Other programs run in an *interactive environment,* communicating with terminals where users enter data and request answers. Still other programs run in a *real-time environment,* receiving data as it is produced by attached equipment and sending the results of calculations to other equipment. Computers working in a real-time environment are used to machine parts, manage warehouses, guide rockets, and control assembly lines.

The environment of a program can also be characterized as single job, multiprogramming, or multiprocessing. In a *single-job environment,* only one program at a time is loaded into the computer. This may be a batch, interactive, or real-time job. All of the facilities of the computer are available to that job until it has finished executing. Most mainframe computers and minicomputers, and some microcomputers, support a *time-sharing environment,* in which several users can have access to the computer at the same time, running different programs. Multiprogramming and multiprocessing are two forms of time-sharing. In a *multiprogramming environment* several programs are loaded into memory at the same time, but only one is executed at a time. In a *multiprocessing environment,* there is more than one CPU. This makes it possible to execute several programs at the same time, or to execute parts of a single program on several different processors. The computer allocates the system resources to the programs according to a formula designed to increase efficiency. Time-sharing jobs may be batch, interactive, or real-time.

The environment can be designed to maximize turnaround, maximize throughput, or balance them so as to best satisfy the users. *Turnaround* is the time it takes a user to obtain output from a program after submitting it to a computer. It is fastest in a single-job environment. *Throughput* is the number of programs that can be executed in a given time period. It is often largest in a multiprocessing environment.

Review questions

1. What are the major hardware components of a computer system?
2. Name one device used only for input.
3. Name one device used only for output.
4. ____________ and ____________ can be used for both input and output.
5. What is the function of computer memory?
6. What is the function of the CPU?
7. What is the difference between system software and application software?
8. The ____________ is the software that manages the resources of a computer system.
9. Why does the computer use a compiler for PL/I?
10. What is the difference between batch processing and interactive processing?
11. What is the difference between multiprogramming and multiprocessing?
12. Would a computer center manager be more interested in throughput or turnaround? A computer user?

1.2 Concept of a program

To solve a problem by using a computer, a program must be written. A *program* is a sequence of instructions to a computer written in a programming language suitable for solving the particular problem. Programming languages are like other languages in having a set of symbols (alphabet), a syntax (grammar), and semantics (meaning).

PL/I is one of the more flexible, general-purpose programming languages through which users can communicate with the computer. It combines elements of English and mathematics. First the problem solution is written, possibly in English, as a sequence of steps called an *algorithm*. The algorithm is then translated into a logic diagram, such as a flowchart, and the flowchart is translated into a sequence of programming language instructions. Then the computer interprets the instructions and carries them out to solve the problem. This is called *program execution*. During the execution of the instructions, the computer performs certain fundamental hardware operations.

1.2.1 Fundamental operations (hardware, firmware)

A computer's basic operations are data transmission (input/output), arithmetic operations, control operations, and logic operations. Specific hardware, firmware, and software components in the computer are designed to perform these operations. They are carried out under the supervision of the operating system, which monitors all activities to check that everything is running smoothly.

The word "input" can be used for both an operation and the information that is supplied to the computer. This information can be program instructions and data, or commands directed to the operating system. Input devices are capable of accepting information and channeling it to memory for storage. Information entered into a computer is stored in main memory or on a peripheral storage device until it is needed.

The word "output" can also be used for both an operation and information. The output information is the processed data as it is formatted to suit the user. Output devices can retrieve the processed information from memory and either print it on paper, display it on a CRT screen, or occasionally put it on microfilm or microfiche.

Computers can move data or manipulate it much faster than people can. They can handle large amounts of data efficiently. *Arithmetic operations* such as addition, subtraction, multiplication, and division are very fast and accurate because they are built into the computer.

The *control operations* performed by a computer divert it from one sequence of instructions to another, based on the contents of a memory location higher than, lower than, or equal to zero. These comparisons are logic operations. *Logic operations* are carried out by comparing the contents of one memory location to the contents of another memory location. This type of comparison produces the equivalent of a true or false answer.

1.2.2 Fundamental instructions (software)

Most programming languages have a set of fundamental instructions based on the fundamental computer operations. This set contains move instructions, input/output instructions, arithmetic/logic instructions, and control instructions.

Move instructions are used to copy the contents of one memory location to another without altering the contents of the first memory location. If the instruction is

Move A to B

the results are

	Before		*After*
A	385	A	385
B	460	B	385

In this example, the contents of memory location A are moved to location B. The contents of A remain unaltered and the original contents of B are replaced.

Input instructions are used to enter information into the computer memory. This information is stored in memory by the input hardware without any alteration during the input process. The input software may then convert it to a more machine-usable form. *Output instructions* are used to retrieve information from the computer memory. This information is not altered by the output hardware during the output process but may be converted to a different form by the output software before it is retrieved by the hardware.

In higher level computer languages such as PL/I, the ordinary arithmetic operators are used for addition, subtraction, and division. Multiplication is indicated by an asterisk. Since superscripts are not available, a new symbol is introduced for exponentiation. The *arithmetic operation instructions* are shown in the following example.

```
addition          A + B
subtraction       A - B
multiplication    A * B
division          A / B
exponentiation    A ** B
```

There are four types of *control structures:* sequence, repetition, selection, and change of environment. (These will be explained in detail in a later chapter.) Basically, a sequence of instructions, one after the other, is called a *sequence structure. Repetition structures* contain instructions to be repeated. *Selection structures* present alternate sequences of instructions; which sequence is selected depends on the result of a comparison. *Change of environment structures* divert the processing from one set of instructions to another.

Review questions

1. Describe the differences among hardware, firmware, and software.

2. What is the difference between an algorithm and a program?

3. What three fundamental types of operations are built into the computer?

4. What are the four fundamental types of instructions in any programming language?

5. Give an English example of each of the fundamental types of instructions.

6. What are the four types of control structures in a programming language?

7. Give an English example of each of the types of control structures.

1.3 Concept of data

The collection of information to be processed under the control of a computer program is known as *data*. The data can be in the form of numbers (integers, real, and complex numbers), alphanumeric strings (character data), or bit strings (binary data). The following examples show these different data types.

integer numbers	380	650	−27	0
real numbers	326.62	−15.7	0.02	0.0
complex numbers	21+5I	−2.37−.08I	17.6	−8I
alphanumeric strings	'THIS IS A STRING'	'138764'		
bit strings	'101101'	'011000111'		

1.3.1 Input data

The data values that the computer obtains from the outside world are called *input data* because they come into the computer proper. The arrangement and type of representation of the input data must be known. Input data can be organized and punched on cards as a *card file* and then stored in the computer memory, or it can be keyed directly into a memory file, called a *data file*. When the data values are needed, they are read from the data file. The end of the input data can be recognized by special end-of-file symbols. The proper formatting and arrangement of data is one of the most important aspects of data processing.

Since it is easy to make typographical errors, input data must be validated. *Data validation* is the process of checking the data for correct form and values. The validation of input data is done in the computer by the program that processes the data. Having correct input data under the control of a correct computer program produces correct output.

PROGRAMMING HINT: Always validate input data.

1.3.2 Output data

The information generated or processed by a computer under the control of a computer program and then communicated to the outside world is known as *output data.* Usually it is printed on paper or displayed on terminals; occasionally other media are used. Many people handle computer output, so it must be readable, with proper spacing and labeling of values. Pages must be numbered, dated, and titled. The number of lines per page and horizontal and vertical spacing may be specified. With some output devices letter-quality copy can be produced for important and permanent records.

PROGRAMMING HINT: Make output visually attractive.

1.3.3 Internal control data

Besides the input and output data, a computer program may have *internal data.* Some of the internal data values are working values, intermediate stages in calculations, tallies, and counts that are needed to obtain the output values from the input values. If the input data consists of a list of numbers and the output data includes the average of the numbers in the list, the internal data includes a count of the numbers and their sum.

Internal data also includes values that keep track of the status of the various pieces of computer equipment. When a printer is out of paper, a terminal is turned off, or a card reader runs out of cards, a signal is stored in the computer. The programmer can use this information to control part of the program.

Review questions

1. What is the information called that is entered into a computer?
2. Describe two methods of entering information into a computer.
3. What is the information called that leaves a computer?
4. Describe the differences in form of real numbers and integers.
5. Why is data validation important?
6. Explain the saying "garbage in, garbage out" as it applies to computer use.
7. Give an example of internal data.
8. Give an example of internal control data.

1.4 Solution design

Computers are not superbrains. They can only do what they are told to do. Therefore they can only solve problems that people understand well enough to be able to describe the steps to the solution. A computer can do many things more quickly and accurately than people. It can sort lists faster, calculate faster, look up information in large collections of data faster, and do all of these operations without making mistakes. But it cannot solve problems in any true sense. When we talk about using a computer to solve a problem, we mean that the computer has been told exactly what to do. All it has to do is follow the detailed set of instructions provided in the form of a program.

Scientific problems usually involve complex mathematical computations. Scientific applications include such things as engineering design and development, space navigation, numerical solutions to mathematical models of fluid flow and heat transfer, models of chemical compounds, and mathematical models of problems in physics and astronomy.

Business problems include processing business data and producing reports, billing customers for purchases, preparing payment schedules for financial institutions, controlling inventory, keeping track of airline reservations, and many others.

There are also miscellaneous applications such as text processing, computer-aided instruction, computer-aided process control, microprocessor-controlled equipment, graphics, computer-controlled CAT scan, and other medical and technical uses.

1.4.1 Design

The first step in using a computer to solve a problem is to obtain a clear description of the problem.

PROGRAMMING RULE: DESIGN STEP Define the problem clearly.

In some instances, a clear definition of the problem may not be possible, but a trial and error approach may be attempted. Once the problem is defined, a solution must be developed.

PROGRAMMING RULE: DESIGN STEP Develop an algorithm.

The solution can be described narratively or graphically. It can be in the form of mathematical equations for scientific problems, or simple arithmetic operations and text processing in the case of business-oriented problems. Once the solution has been outlined, a computer program can be written to solve the problem.

The algorithm can be represented by a hierarchy chart and flowchart diagrams using standard symbols to represent the different operations.

PROGRAMMING RULE: DESIGN STEP Draw diagrams.

At this stage of the design, studying the diagrams will suggest modifications to the algorithm which will in turn suggest changes to the diagrams. Eventually a final design will be obtained. The design phase is a very important part of the development of software systems.

1.4.2 Implementation

Once the algorithm, hierarchy charts, and flowcharts have been developed, the computer code can be written. *Computer code* is simply instructions in a programming language that express the steps in a flowchart or algorithm. Before the code has been completely written, the input data formats must be designed and the proper output formats must be developed. Coding forms are available for these. As the output (the information the user wants) is the desired result, the output formats must be carefully designed. Both horizontal and vertical spacing must be described in the code. The proper margins, headings, and subheadings must be implemented.

PROGRAMMING RULE: DESIGN STEP Describe the data.

When the coding is finished, the code must be transferred to a machine-readable medium.

PROGRAMMING RULE: IMPLEMENTATION STEP Write the program code.

Both instructions and data can be entered directly, or they can be punched on cards and read by a card reader. The input data and code need not be entered the same way, or at the same time.

With some computer operating systems, job control statements must be added before the program can be run. The *job control statements* supply the operating system with information about the data and program.

PROGRAMMING RULE: IMPLEMENTATION STEP Provide job control statements.

PL/I programs are written in a symbolic code known as PL/I *source code.* The symbolic source code is processed by a compiler which translates it into machine code, which is more directly understandable by the machine.

PROGRAMMING RULE: IMPLEMENTATION STEP Compile the program.

The machine code generated during compilation is known as *object code.* The compilation process is shown in figure 1–3.

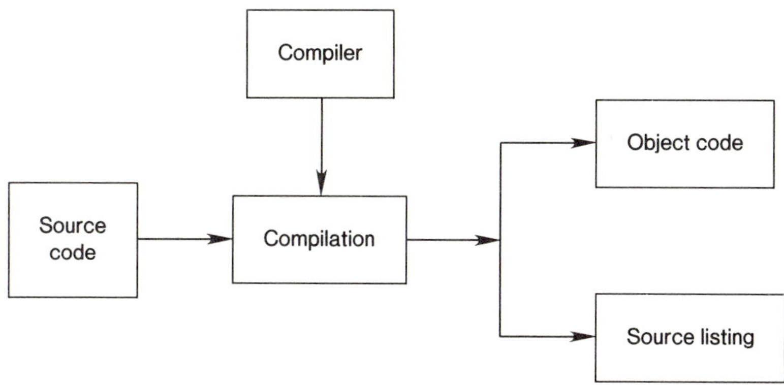

Figure 1–3

The object code generated is loaded into memory and executed by the computer to produce the desired output. There are additional system outputs designed to help the programmer. These include error messages and a source listing produced during program compilation.

A program will almost never execute properly the first time. It will not produce the desired results until it is free from error.

PROGRAMMING RULE: IMPLEMENTATION STEP Test the program.

The errors that are detected and diagnosed during compilation are called *compilation errors.* Most of these are caused by typing mistakes or incorrect use of the computer language. Once all of the compilation errors are corrected, the program must be executed using test data, to make sure that there are no logic errors in the design of the program. The logic errors that are detected and diagnosed during execution are called *execution errors.* Other logic errors will not be detected by the computer, but will cause the answers to be wrong. It is up to the programmer to discover these errors. If there are any logic errors, they must be corrected and the code rewritten.

PROGRAMMING RULE: IMPLEMENTATION STEP Debug the program.

Gradually the errors will be eliminated and finally the correct answers will be obtained. The process of correcting the program is known as *debugging.* This may include changes in the problem definition and design as well as in the code. Debugging aids are usually built into programming languages. System software also helps with debugging.

When the program finally produces accurate answers, there remains one last step: completing the documentation of the program.

PROGRAMMING RULE: IMPLEMENTATION STEP Complete the program documentation.

Documentation of the program is carried on along with the development of the design. The documentation includes all phases of the program development: a description of the problem, a glossary of input and output variables, a description of the functional modules of the program, any error messages the program may produce, and any security measures to be taken for the protection of the program and the data. Anything that a user needs to know about the program should be included in the documentation. Additional documentation is included in the program with the code. Some of it, along with flowcharts and operating instructions, becomes part of the guide to using and maintaining the program.

During the life of a production program, further modifications will be needed to meet changing situations and to correct previously undetected errors.

PROGRAMMING RULE: IMPLEMENTATION STEP Have maintenance ease as an objective.

Review questions

1. Explain the terms "source code" and "object code."

2. What is the purpose of the job control statement?

3. When a program is tested, it is important to try it with data that contain errors. Why?

4. Each of the following arithmetic expressions contains an error. Would each error most likely be detected by the compiler or during execution?
(a) 125.3.7 + 69
(b) 41 – 2 * – 16
(c) (–5) ** .5
(d) 436 / 0.0

5. Two different classes of people who make use of program documentation are ________________ and ________________.

1.5 Concept of structured programming

The programming process should be approached systematically. The purpose of the program should be expressed functionally as a short declarative sentence. Applied to a nonprogramming problem, this might be

Assemble the bicycle

This can then be expressed as a sequence of very general steps, also described functionally. These steps can be arranged as modules in a hierarchical diagram. Figure 1–4 shows the steps in assembling a bicycle. Some of the steps are divided into smaller steps. A module with other modules under it describes the result of those lower modules. In hierarchical design, the tasks of the lower level modules are carried out first, controlled by the higher level modules. The lowest level contains the most detailed modules.

A hierarchy chart can be developed for both procedures and data. Figure 1–5 shows the organization of the "data" making up the bicycle kit. The organization of the procedure for solving the problem, in this case assembling the bicycle, is related to the organization of the data. Analyzing the structure of the process and the data to a high level of detail makes it easy and straightforward to give instructions for the functional modules.

Structured design is a systematic approach to software development. The basic concept of the structured approach is "top-down" design, then

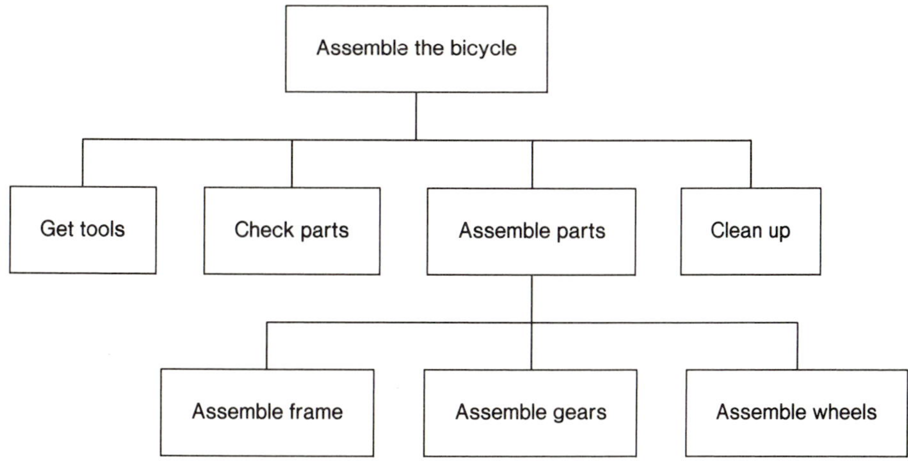

Figure 1–4

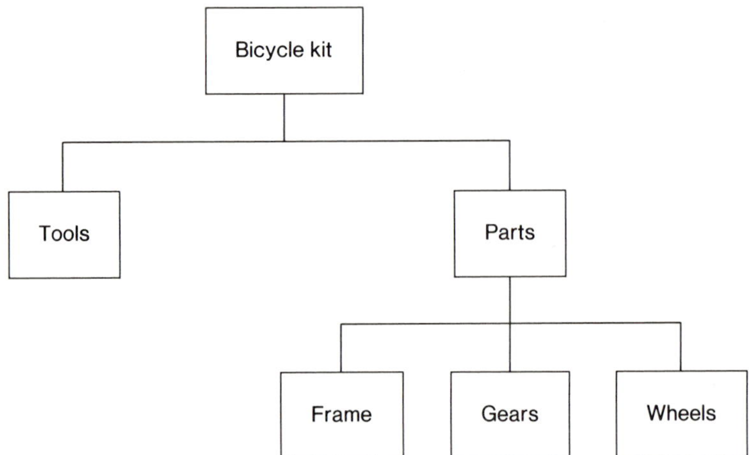

Figure 1–5

structured programming using standard program structures. The design is often implemented using top-down program implementation. The control flow for assembling the bicycle would be as shown in figure 1–6. Each box represents a standard step in the procedure. It has one entry at the top and one exit at the bottom. The concept of one entry at the top and one exit at the bottom is basic to all well-designed program structures.

Each control structure of a programming language will produce a module of code in the program. The resulting modules of code can follow each other, as in the sequence of steps for assembling a bicycle, or they can be nested, as in the diagrams of figure 1–7. In either case, the entry to the module is at the top and the exit is at the bottom. This design requirement makes it easy to read, correct, update, and maintain software. The "try bicycle" module of figure 1–7*a* is the entire loop of figure 1–7*b*.

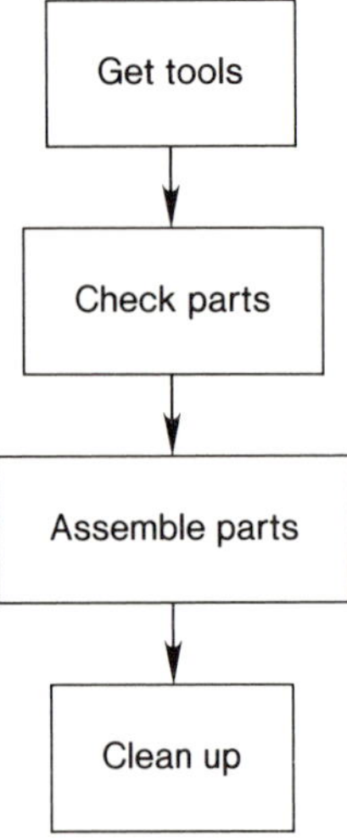

Figure 1–6

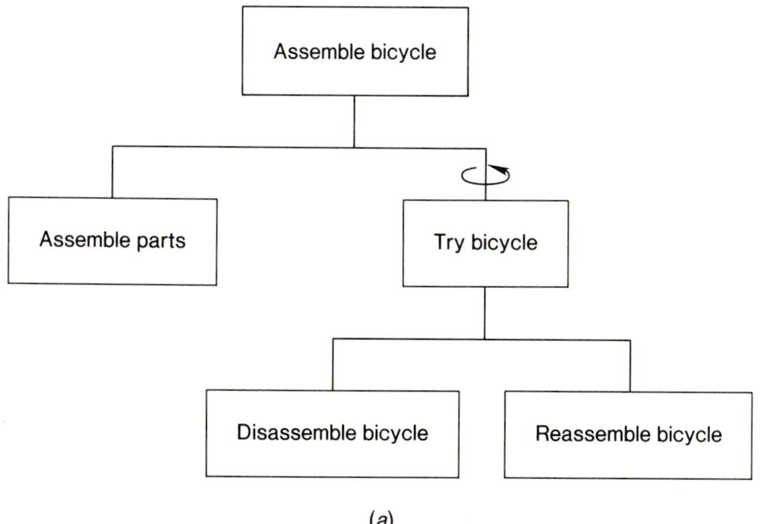

(*a*)

Figure 1–7a

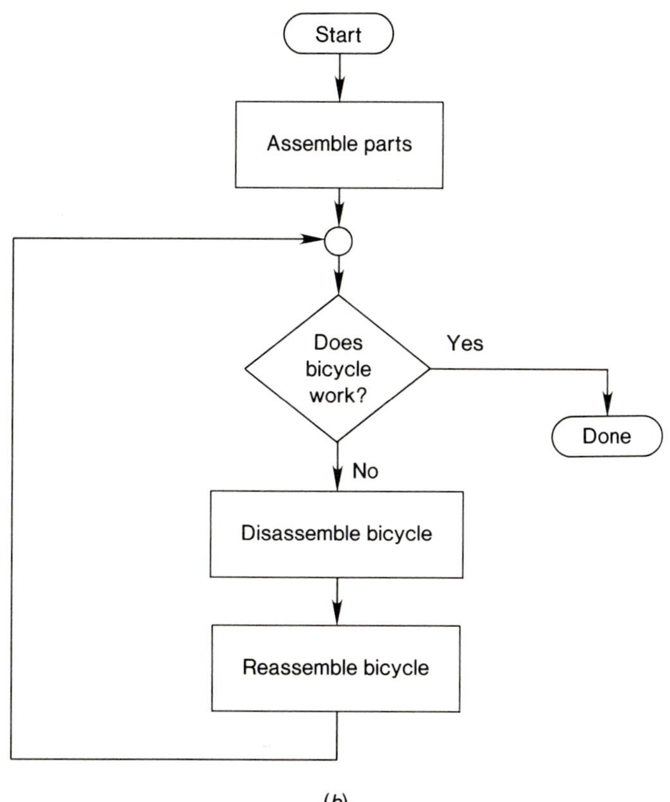

(*b*)

Figure 1–7b

Once the bicycle has been assembled, it cannot be neglected but will need periodic maintenance as long as it is in use. The same is true of a computer program.

METHODS OF STRUCTURING

The structure of the input data for a program depends on the type of environment in which the program is run. The main data structure for batch processing is the *file;* the program must be designed around processing entire files. Files are made up of records which in turn are made up of fields. If the program as a whole processes files, the smaller modules at the lower levels process records. The lowest and smallest modules process fields.

The main data structure of interactive programming is the *message,* which is made up of words. An interactive program must be built around the processing needed for a single message, with the lower levels processing the words.

Many programming languages, such as PL/I, PASCAL, ADA, and FORTRAN-77, are structured languages. They contain standard structures such as loops, which make it easy to write structured programs. The present trend in the software industry is toward improved design, structuring, and modularization. With the need for increased programmer productivity, the emphasis on structured programming will continue.

ADVANTAGES OF STRUCTURED PROGRAMMING

Through the use of structured techniques, programmers become more productive, and the programs they write are more cost effective. The structured techniques result in:

1. Integrated systems.
2. Standardized program modules.
3. Programs that are readable because of top-down design.
4. Programs that are correct because of careful development.
5. Programs that are reliable because of careful testing.
6. Programs that are easy to maintain because of the clarity and simplicity of the standard control structures.

Writing a computer program is like any type of writing. Content is important, and so is style. Structured programming along with "pretty printing" (indenting nested structures) and careful choice of vocabulary produces attractive self-documenting programs. The basic structures and their implementation will be discussed in detail in later chapters.

Review questions

1. What is meant by saying that a module of a hierarchy chart is functional?

2. What is the relationship between a module of a hierarchy chart and the modules below it?

3. In what sense can the development of a hierarchy chart be said to be top-down?

4. How could the development of a computer program from a hierarchy chart be said to be top-down?

5. What features must a programming language have to make it suitable for structured programming?

1.6 Summary

Computers are modern-day tools that can solve some types of problems faster and more accurately than people can. They consist of hardware, firmware, and software. The main hardware components of a computer system are the input/output devices and the processor. The input devices are used to enter data and programs into computers; the output devices are used to obtain answers and reports from computers. The processor contains memory where data is stored and circuitry for performing calculations and making decisions.

The main software components are the operating system, the system utilities and library routines, including the file management routines, and the compilers. These control the operation of the computer and facilitate the writing and running of application programs. Application software consists of programs that process data, written by computer programmers. Application programs may be designed to run in either batch, interactive, time-sharing, or real-time environments. A program environment may also be thought of as a single-job, multiprogramming, or multiprocessing environment.

Programs consist of step by step instructions to the computer, directing it during the input, processing, and output of data. A program has a lifespan containing three stages: design, implementation, and maintenance. Provided that a program is developed carefully and documented clearly, it will outlast the hardware on which it is initially developed.

1.7 Exercises

1. Draw a diagram showing the hardware configuration of the computer you are using.

2. List the software programs used in the process of writing a program and running it on the computer you are using.

3. List some of the computer languages available on the computer you are using. What are their basic differences?

4. What types of documentation are available for the PL/I compiler you are using?

5. What types of output are produced by the PL/I compiler you are using?

6. Design a hierarchy chart showing the steps in baking a cake.

7. Design a hierarchy chart showing your activities in the course of a school day.

8. Design a hierarchy chart showing how to calculate the amount of paint needed to paint the interior of a house if one gallon of paint covers 250 square feet.

9. Design a hierarchy chart showing the calculation of the volume of water that can be poured into a cylindrical jar of radius R and height H that has a sphere of radius R inside it. (Volume of cylinder = $3.1416\ R^2H$. Volume of sphere = $4/3 \times 3.1416\ R^3$).

2
Structured approach to PL/I

OBJECTIVE: To analyze the steps in solving a problem with a computer.

PL/I STANDS FOR "PROGRAMMING language/one." It was not the first programming language, but it was the first comprehensive one. Its developers intended it to include all the features available at that time in other programming languages. PL/I includes almost all of the original features of FORTRAN and COBOL, the earlier high-level computer languages developed for scientific and business applications. In addition, it contains some useful features they lacked. PL/I is capable of processing both the complicated numeric data needed for scientific computing and the alphanumeric data (character data) necessary for business applications. It can also be used for text processing and systems programming. It is a comprehensive general-purpose language with structured control organization and structured data types. PL/I has efficient and versatile processing capabilities and file organization.

Although the language was developed by IBM, most of the major computer vendors provide PL/I compilers, either the full *ANSI* (American National Standards Institute) version or the standard general-purpose subset known as Subset G. Most versions of the language on small computers or non-IBM computers are extensions of Subset G. A smaller subset, PL/C, is available in many university computer installations. The standardization of PL/I compilers makes the language highly independent of the particular computer system on which it is run. Software developed by using PL/I on one machine can be run on another machine with minimum modification.

PROGRAMMING HINT: PORTABILITY Use only standard PL/I features.

Portability is an important quality of computer application programs, which usually have a longer lifespan than the computers that run them. Programs are rarely completely portable, but the more standard the language used, the fewer changes necessary when hardware is changed. In this book we will attempt to avoid system-dependent features of the language. Where that is not possible, we will identify the features as being nonstandard. Features that belong to the full language but are not part of Subset G will also be identified. When you need a nonstandard feature, consult a language manual for the particular computer you are using.

There are PL/I compilers designed to produce application software for scientific, business, and industrial use. These compilers are sometimes called *production compilers*. One form of production compiler, the *optimizing compiler,* emphasizes the production of efficient machine language code. Other compilers, such as PL/C, are developed for instructional use in teaching institutions. These *student compilers* are specially designed to provide better diagnostic messages to aid students in *debugging* (finding the errors in) programs.

2.1 Overview of PL/I

PL/I is a high-level, procedural, modular, strongly typed, block-structured language. A *high-level* language is like any natural language in that it uses symbols and has its own syntax and semantics. The basic symbols of PL/I are chosen from mathematics, from business practices, and from ordinary English to make it easy for users to read and write programs and to make up additional symbols appropriate to the application. Some of the symbols are meaningful to the computer, others make programs easier for people to read. Besides discussing the language itself, we will look at styles of program design and writing that make programs readable, for readability is an important quality of computer programs.

PROGRAMMING HINT: READABILITY Develop a consistent programming style.

A *procedural* language is one that instructs the computer how to solve a problem in a step-by-step fashion. A program in such a language reads much like a set of instructions in a cookbook or product assembly manual.

A *modular* language is one that allows a problem solution to be developed in increments. In practice, a modular program often reads much like a book such as this which has footnotes, references to later sections, and appendices. Although this may seem awkward, it helps make the program easy to modify, and ease of maintenance is an important quality of computer programs. During its lifespan, a program usually must be modified many times as needs change.

PROGRAMMING HINT: MAINTAINABILITY Keep program modules short.

A *typed* language is one that tells the computer what type of data is to be processed before it begins carrying out the instructions. Providing the computer with advance information on data types helps it detect programmer and data entry errors. It also makes a program run more efficiently. Accuracy and efficiency are important qualities of computer programs.

PL/I is a *block-structured* language using the basic theoretical control structures as building blocks. The control structures may be nested to form complex structures. These blocks and procedures in turn are nested to form programs. There are four basic control structures: sequence, selection, repetition, and change of environment. Using these structures contributes to program modularity and ease of maintenance. These individual structures will be explained in detail later in this chapter.

PL/I is a *compiled* language. The compiler takes the PL/I source code and translates it to machine code. It produces a block of machine code from each of the control structures. This machine code can be saved for later use, or executed immediately. The small blocks of nested code are easy for the computer to manipulate.

PL/I is *comprehensive*. Because of its extensive numeric and alphanumeric data processing capabilities it can be used for all kinds of applications. Editing tools and characters are available to produce well-formatted, readable, edited output. There is a library of built-in functions, including all the common mathematical functions and many functions to manipulate character data. Table manipulation facilities are available for handling both one-dimensional and multidimensional arrays. Other facilities link together separately written programs, which may be compiled separately or at the same time.

PL/I is a versatile language, equally adapted to the beginner and to the skilled programmer. The beginner can learn a few basic statements in PL/I and start writing simple programs. Once the basic principles of the language are understood, additional data structures and application areas can be added. Any computer algorithm can be implemented in PL/I. Its extensive specialized features and the flexibility of its rules allow the experienced programmer to access most of the underlying capabilities of the computer system and develop new ways of solving complicated problems.

Review questions

1. Why is it important for a computer language to be standardized?

2. Why do some computer systems have more than one PL/I compiler?

3. What does it mean to say that PL/I is a compiled, high-level language?

4. What does it mean to say that PL/I is a modular, block-structured language?

5. The PL/I compiler translate PL/I source code into ______________.

2.2 Elements of PL/I

Studying PL/I is like studying any foreign language. The beginner must start with the alphabet, vocabulary, basic statement structure, and simple control structures (the paragraphs of the language).

2.2.1 Alphabet

Like any other language (natural or otherwise), PL/I uses a set of symbols (an alphabet), often called a *character set.* Three sets of characters are available: the ANSI character set, the 60-character set, and the 48-character set. The latter two are the most common, and the 60-character set is more often used than the 48-character set because it has all the common typewriter and teletype symbols. In general, the characters are grouped as alphabetic, numeric, and special characters. Some of the special characters, may be further identified as arithmetic operators, logic operators, relational operators, or PL/I punctuation characters.

When a 48-character set is used, the symbols from the 60-character set that are not available in the 48-character set may still be used under certain circumstances. However, when the 60-character set is used, some of the special symbols of the 48-character set (abbreviations such as LT) may not be used.

60-CHARACTER SET

Alphabetic characters These are letters and the extra symbols making up the twenty-nine-character extended alphabet. They are based on the English alphabet.

A B C D E F G H I J K L M N O P Q R S T U V W X Y Z

plus the symbols

$ # @

Numeric characters These are the numeric digits of the decimal number system.

0 1 2 3 4 5 6 7 8 9

Special characters These are further grouped as follows:

Arithmetic operators	+ − / *	
Logical operators	¬ | &	
Relational operators	= > <	
Punctuation	. , : ;	
Assignment	=	(has two uses)
Grouping	( ) '	
Blank		(sometimes handwritten as b̸)
Break (underscore)	_	
Percent	%	
Question	?	

There are twenty-nine alphabetic, ten numeric, and twenty-one special characters.

ADDITIONAL OPERATORS OF THE 60-CHARACTER SET

Besides the individual characters, we should be familiar with a few additional operators of the 60-character set which use multiple characters. The additional operators can be represented as follows:

Relational operators

"Not greater than"	¬>
"Not less than"	¬<
"Not equal to"	¬=
"Less than or equal to"	<=
"Greater than or equal to"	>=

Special operators

Exponential	**
Concatenation	||
"Points to"	−>
Comment grouping	/* */

When such double characters are used, no blank spaces is allowed between them. Therefore, when syntax errors occur in a statement that uses a double character, one of the possible errors could be a blank space between the symbols. In general PL/I ignores blank spaces, but not in this situation.

48-CHARACTER SET

Alphabetic characters These are the letters of the English alphabet and one additional character.

A B C D E F G H I J K L M N O P Q R S T U V W X Y Z

plus the symbol

$

Numeric characters These are the digits of the decimal number system.

0 1 2 3 4 5 6 7 8 9

Special characters These are grouped as follows:

Arithmetic operators	+ − / *
Punctuation	, .
Assignment	=
Grouping	( ) '
Blank	(sometimes handwritten as ƀ)

There are twenty-seven alphabetic letters, ten numeric digits, and eleven special characters.

ADDITIONAL OPERATORS OF THE 48-CHARACTER SET

There are a few additional operators of the 48-character set which use multiple characters. In this set, certain special characters are not available to represent common operators. Instead they are represented by using combinations of characters of the set or by using PL/I keywords.

Punctuation symbols

Semicolon	,.
Colon	..
Percent	//

Relational operators

"Greater than"	GT
"Less than"	LT
"Not greater than"	NG
"Not less than"	NL
"Not equal to"	NE
"Less than or equal to"	LE
"Greater than or equal to"	GE

Logical operators

"Or"	OR
"And"	AND
"Not"	NOT

Special operators

Exponentiation	**
Concatenation	CAT
"Points to"	PT
Comment grouping	/* */

When characters are combined to form a symbol, no blank spaces are allowed between them. The abbreviations and words used as symbols that appear in the list above must have one or more blanks on each side when they are used in a statement. For instance,

```
IF X LE 5 AND X GT 0 THEN Y = 1,.
```

Using the 60-character set, this would be written as

```
IF X <= 5 & X > 0 THEN Y = 1;
```

A PROCESS statement can be used to specify the character set wanted.

```
*PROCESS CHARSET(48);
```

The * must be in column 1 of the statement line. This statement specifies the 48-character set. The 60-character set is the default alphabet.

2.2.2 Vocabulary

The vocabulary of PL/I consists of keywords, user-defined words, numbers, other literals, and special characters and operators.

Keywords are built into the language. They have specific meanings and invoke software functions. They are not reserved; they can be used for other purposes, but this should be avoided as it makes a program harder to read. Some of the keywords instruct the computer to do something, such as DECLARE or GET. Others explain something, such as CHARACTER. Still others are identifiers, naming something known to the system, such as DATE.

PROGRAMMING HINT: READABILITY Do not use keywords for other purposes.

User-defined words are identifiers invented by the programmer. These identifiers are used to name data and parts of programs. PL/I *numbers* are ordinary numbers. Other *literals* are written as strings of characters inside single quotation marks.

Special characters and operators are those given with the character sets. Besides improving readability, the punctuation symbols have special meanings. The semicolon (;) indicates the end of a statement. The colon (:) marks a place in the program, and the comma (,) separates the items in a list. The blank, although usually ignored in PL/I, is a symbol like any other. It may be inserted between keywords, identifiers, and other vocabulary items in a statement, to improve the appearance of a PL/I program and make it more readable. However, when it is inside quotation marks, it is as important as any other quoted character. As already noted, the blank is required next to certain abbreviations of the 48-character set.

The lexical rules used to form identifiers and literals and their use in a program will be discussed in chapter 3. However, we give an example here of several simple statements using keywords, identifiers, and punctuation symbols.

```
PUT SKIP LIST ('VALUES ARE',W,X,Y,Z);
GET DATA (NAME,AMOUNT);
```

The words PUT, SKIP, LIST, GET, and DATA are keywords. They tell the computer what to do with the data values. 'VALUES ARE' is a literal. The words W, X, Y, Z, NAME, and AMOUNT are user-defined identifiers, which name the data values.

2.2.3 Statement structure

A statement in PL/I may consist of a label followed by a colon, keywords, identifiers, and constants or literals. The general form of a statement is

[label:] instruction;

For example:

```
CALC_AREA: A = B * H/2;
```

or

```
VOLUME = LENGTH * WIDTH * HEIGHT;
```

Every statement must end with a semicolon, but the label part (label and colon) is optional. Statement labels, identifiers, and constants are defined by the programmer. Labels are used to name procedures, entry points, places in a program, and remote formats for edited input and output.

Statements in PL/I are free-format. A statement can be punched on a card or typed on a line anywhere between column 2 and column 72 inclusive. Colume 1 is sometimes reserved for job control statements required by the operating system and for special compiler directives such as specifying a character set. Columns 73 through 80 are sometimes used for numbering or otherwise identifying the lines of a program, but some compilers simply ignore these columns. Any information beyond column 72 appears in the source code printout, but is not part of the object code in an ANSI standard compiler. More than one statement can be placed on a line, since the compiler recognizes the end of a statement by a semicolon, but this should be avoided as it reduces clarity and readability, and makes debugging more difficult. A statement can extend to more than one line if it is too long to fit on a single line, but each part should be placed between columns 2 and 72 inclusive. The compiler ignores line boundaries when processing a statement.

PROGRAMMING HINT: STYLE Place each PL/I statement on a separate line.

A *comment statement,* a nonexecutable statement used for documentation, is set apart by starting it with the symbol /* and ending it with */. The entire comment should be placed between columns 2 through 72 inclusive. No semicolon is needed at the end of a comment.

```
/* THIS IS A COMMENT STATEMENT */
```

A comment statement can stand alone or be used at the end of an executable statement to explain the function of the statement, as in

```
A = L * W; /* CALCULATE THE AREA OF THE RECTANGLE */
```

It may extend over several lines if necessary.

```
/* A PROGRAM CONSISTS OF INPUT DATA
                         INSTRUCTIONS
                         OUTPUT DATA */
```

For readability comments are often enclosed in boxes.

```
/**********************************************************/
/*                                                        */
/*   THIS PROGRAM CONSISTS OF INPUT DATA: NAMES           */
/*                            INSTRUCTIONS TO SORT THEM   */
/*                            OUTPUT DATA: SORTED NAMES   */
/*                                                        */
/**********************************************************/
```

Executable statements are instructions to the computer, such as

```
A = B * C - D * E;
AREA = LENGTH * WIDTH;
GET LIST (W,X,Y,Z);
PUT SKIP LIST (A,B,C);
IF X < 0 THEN Y = -X; ELSE Y = X;
```

Such statements tell the computer to do something that involves the basic operations of calculating, making decisions, or moving data. Control structures and blocks can also be thought of as executable statements. They are very complex statements but they have the same form: an optional label at the beginning, a semicolon at the end.

Nonexecutable statements include statements that provide information to someone reading the program, for example, comments; and statements that provide information to the computer, such as

```
DECLARE TEXT CHARACTER;
```

Nonexecutable statements do not have labels.

Following is a simple PL/I program to calculate the volume of a rectangular box. It contains both executable and nonexecutable statements. The lines have been numbered for easy reference, but the numbers are not part of the program.

```
1    BOX: PROCEDURE OPTIONS (MAIN);
2    /****************************************************/
3    /*                                                  */
4    /* PROGRAM: VOLUME OF BOX                           */
5    /* AUTHOR:  R REDDY                                 */
6    /* VERSION: 07/17/84                                */
7    /*                                                  */
8    /* PROGRAM DESCRIPTION:                             */
9    /* ------------------------------------------------ */
10   /* THIS PROGRAM CALCULATES THE VOLUME OF A BOX.     */
```

```
11   /*                                                  */
12   /* INPUT: LENGTH, WIDTH, AND HEIGHT OF BOX          */
13   /*                                                  */
14   /* OUTPUT: LENGTH, WIDTH, HEIGHT, AND VOLUME        */
15   /*                                                  */
16   /****************************************************/
17   DECLARE (LENGTH,WIDTH,HEIGHT) FIXED BINARY,
18           VOLUME                FIXED BINARY;
19
20   GET LIST (LENGTH,WIDTH,HEIGHT);
21   VOLUME = LENGTH * WIDTH * HEIGHT;
22   PUT LIST (LENGTH,WIDTH,HEIGHT,VOLUME);
23   END BOX;
```

Lines 2–19 contain nonexecutable statements. Lines 1 and 20–23 contain executable statements.

Line 1 is a header statement that names the program BOX, a user-defined name. The rest of the statement consists of required words and symbols. PROCEDURE is the PL/I word for program or program module. The clause OPTIONS (MAIN) is required for a main procedure. Every PL/I program must start with a header similar to this.

Lines 2–16 form a comment box that describes the program, identifies the programmer, and indicates what input and output are involved.

Lines 17–18 describe the data values being used. The computer uses these descriptions in setting aside space for the values. Measurements that are integers are declared as FIXED BINARY. As a matter of style, the input is described separately from the output.

Line 19 is left blank as a matter of style so that the reader may visually separate the nonexecutable statements of lines 2–18 from the executable statements of lines 20–23.

Line 20 is an input statement that obtains the values for the variables LENGTH, WIDTH, and HEIGHT from a standard system input device, either a card reader or a terminal. GET LIST is the keyword phrase instructing the computer to obtain input. The values must be typed, separated by spaces or a comma. When the computer executes this statement, it stores a value in each computer memory space associated with a variable name in the input list.

Line 21 is the formula for volume. In a computer language this is known as an *assignment statement,* because the computer calculates the value indicated by the expression on the right side of the equal sign and assigns the result to the name on the left side. The calculated value is stored in the memory space associated with the name VOLUME.

Line 22 is an output statement. PUT LIST is the keyword phrase instructing the computer to display or print the values for LENGTH, WIDTH, HEIGHT, and VOLUME on the standard system output device.

Line 23 is the final statement of the BOX program. Every PL/I program must have an END statement.

In this sample program, only the names BOX, LENGTH, WIDTH, HEIGHT, and VOLUME are user-defined names. All the other words are keywords with specific meanings to the computer. The user-defined data names were selected to be appropriate for their use.

2.2.4 Control structures/flowcharts

The statements in procedural languages such as PL/I are normally executed one after the other in the order in which they are written. This is called *sequential execution.* However, instead of executing every statement in order, it is sometimes necessary to select from alternate statements or to execute a group of statements repeatedly. These three situations are implemented as the sequential, selection, and repetition control structures.

The PL/I forms of the structures are known as the sequence, the IFTHENELSE and SELECT forms of branching, and the DOWHILE and DOUNTIL forms of repetition. There is an additional control structure available in PL/I, CALLRETURN, which provides a change of environment, a level of abstraction, and a link between separate procedures. These structures and their relationships can be represented schematically by flowchart diagrams.

Flowcharts may be used as an aid in the planning stages when a program is being designed. Often they are included in the final description of a complete program as an aid to understanding its logic.

STRUCTURED FLOWCHART SYMBOLS

Each flowchart symbol represents part of an algorithm or program. When flowcharts are used in a structured way, symbols are grouped together to form single-entry, single-exit structures.

Process box This is a rectangular symbol with one control line leading into it and one leading out of it. At the lowest level it represents a single instruction, which is a computation, performs input or output, moves data from one place to another, or carries out some other type of data manipulation. At a higher level it represents a sequence of instructions, which jointly implement a step in the program.

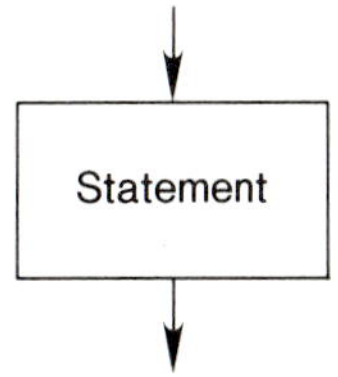

A process box can also represent a single control structure or a sequence of nested control structures.

Decision box A diamond-shaped symbol is used for the comparison of quantities for equality or inequality. The comparison generates either a true or a false answer, which is the basis for a decision.

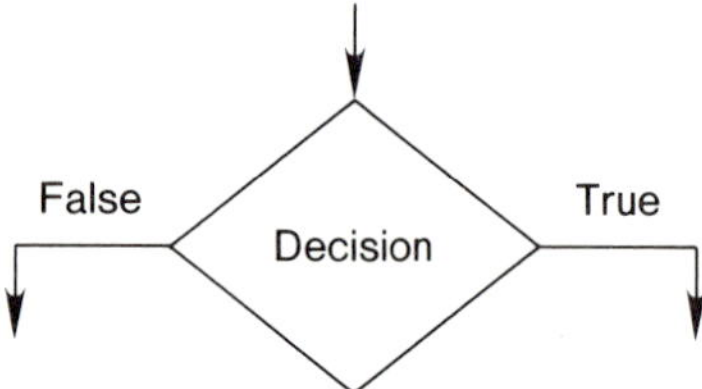

Execution follows either the path on the true branch or the path on the false branch, but not both paths.

The multiple-choice decision used in the SELECT statement is drawn as

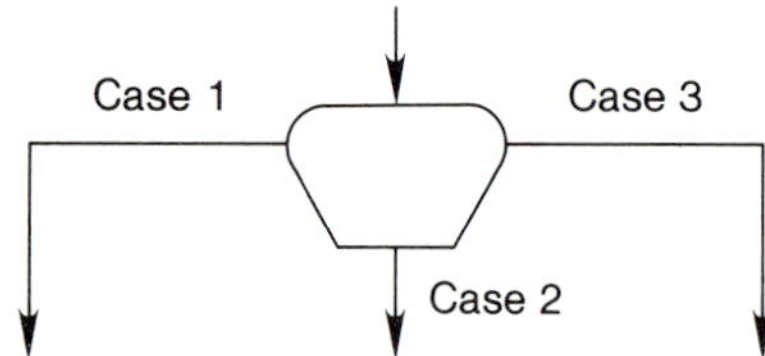

if there are three choices, with more branches if there are more choices.

Connector A circle is used as a connector when two flowlines are to be shown coming together. Two lines are drawn into the circle and a single line drawn out of it. A connector is also used when a flowchart is too large to fit on a single page or too complicated for all the lines to be drawn completely. In this case, the circle has only a single line in or a single line out and is labeled to show which parts of the flowchart are connected.

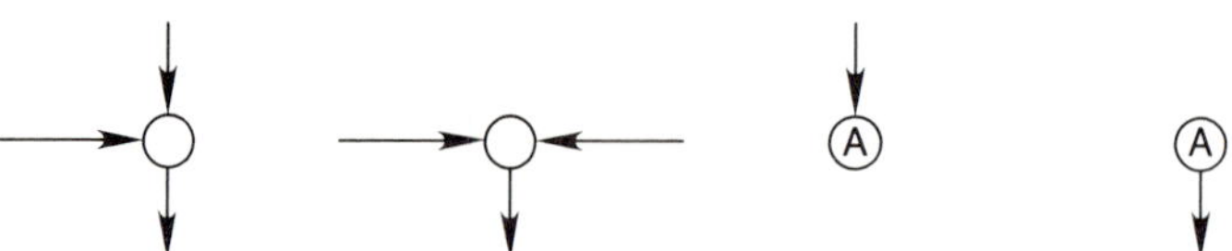

Flowlines These lines are used to connect process boxes and decision symbols in the order of the logic and control flow of the program. An arrowhead is used to indicate the direction of the logic flow.

There are other ANSI standard symbols used in writing conventional flowcharts. You can refer to them in an ANSI publication. For structured flowcharts, we will restrict ourselves to the symbols given above.

STRUCTURED FLOWCHARTS

By using these few flowchart symbols, we can draw the flowcharts for each one of the control structures used in structured PL/I programming.

Sequence structure

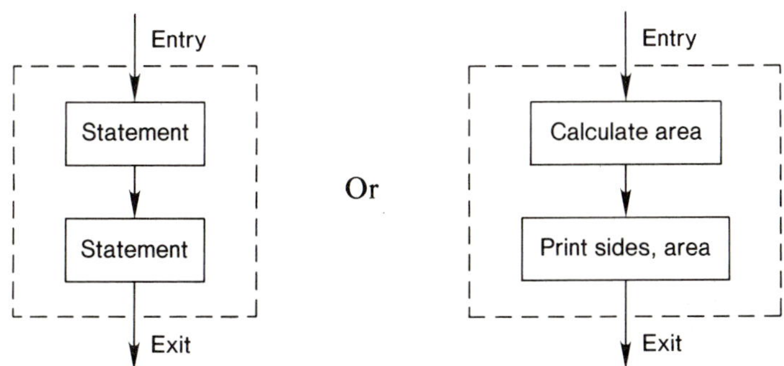

The sequence structure has one or more process boxes, one after the other in order. There is only one entry at the top and one exit at the bottom. The inside process boxes can each represent a single executable statement, a control structure such as a sequence, selection, or repetition structure, or a block. Any control structure can be reduced to a sequence structure with a top entry and a bottom exit by placing it in a process box. The sequence structure is itself shown as a process box. In PL/I the sequence has two forms. It may be written as

```
statement;
statement;
...
statement;
```

or as

```
DO;
  statement;
  statement;
  ...
  statement;
END;
```

Either form may be preceded by a label. Examples of this are

```
GET LIST (LENGTH,WIDTH,HEIGHT);
VOLUME = LENGTH * WIDTH * HEIGHT;
PUT SKIP LIST (LENGTH,WIDTH,HEIGHT,VOLUME);
```

and

```
DO;
  GET LIST (BASE,HEIGHT);
  AREA = BASE * HEIGHT / 2;
  PUT SKIP LIST (BASE,HEIGHT,AREA);
END;
```

The first of these examples calculates the volume and prints the length, width, height, and volume of a rectangular solid. The second calculates the area and prints the base, height, and area of a triangle.

SELECTION STRUCTURES

Decision structure This is a flowchart of a two-valued selection structure, also known as an IFTHENELSE structure. In PL/I it takes the form

```
IF condition
  THEN
    statement;
  ELSE
    statement;
```

The flowchart for this takes the form

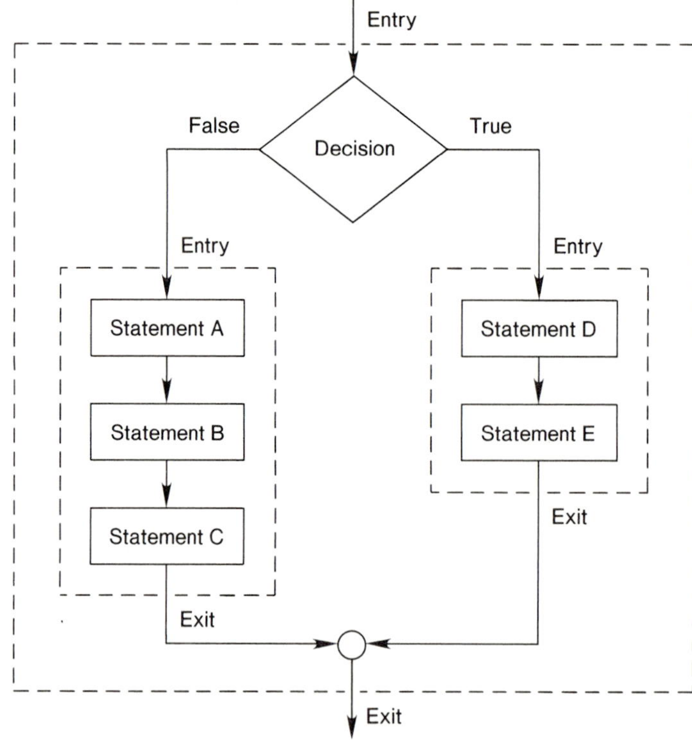

For example:

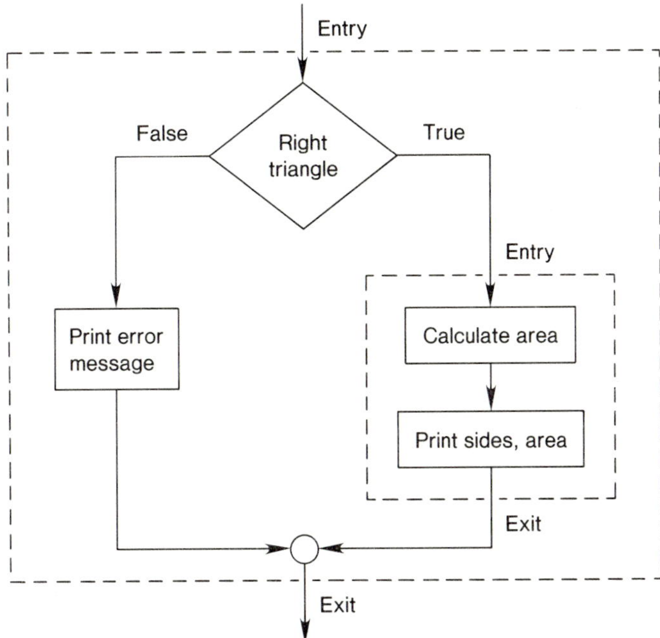

The condition in the decision box will be tested during execution. Based on the test, either a true or a false logical value is produced. The control follows the branch marked true if the logical value is true and executes the sequence on the right, ignoring the false branch. If the condition generates a logical value of false, the control follows the false branch and executes the sequence on the left, ignoring the true branch. Notice that the junction of the two flowlines at the bottom is indicated by a connector. The sequence along each branch of the decision can contain a single statement or a group of statements, or any other control structure such as another decision, a repetition, or a case structure.

Notice also that the entry to the decision flowchart structure is at the top and the exit is at the bottom. The right and left branch sequences each have an entry at the top and exit at the bottom. This convention of top-down flow makes the diagrams easy to read. The entire decision structure is enclosed in a process box to indicate that it is a sequence structure itself.

The specifications for a decision structure may be written as a decision table:

Condition	Y	N
A		X
B		X
C		X
D	X	
E	X	

The four parts of a decision table are:

Condition stub	Condition entry
Action stub	Action entry

The condition stub asks questions, which are answered in the condition entry quadrant. Each column of the condition entry indicates a different situation. There should be enough columns to cover all possible situations. The action stub lists actions, and the action entry quadrant indicates which actions are to be carried out for each set of conditions. The conditions need not be checked in order, but the actions of a decision table must be carried out in order, from top to bottom. Each vertical column can be implemented as a sequence. For example:

Right triangle	Y	N
Calculate area	X	
Print sides,area	X	
Print error message		X

Case structure (not in Subset G) The IFTHENELSE structure is a selection structure that provides only two choices; if more than two choices are needed, we use the SELECT structure. This is a multiple-choice structure, the PL/I version of the case structure. Only one of the choices may be selected. This structure takes the form

```
SELECT;
  WHEN (condition)
    statement;
  WHEN (condition)
    statement;
  . . .
  OTHERWISE
    statement;
END;
```

The general form of the flowchart is

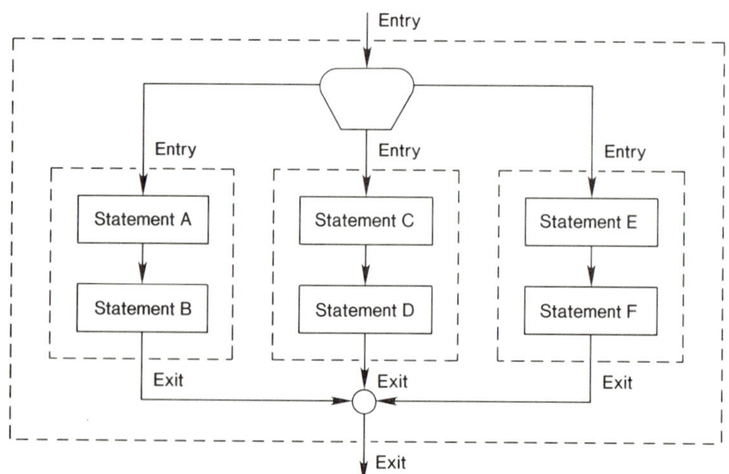

which represents the decision table

Condition	Case 1	Case 2	Case 3
Statement A	X		
Statement B	X		
Statement C		X	
Statement D		X	
Statement E			X
Statement F			X

An example of this is

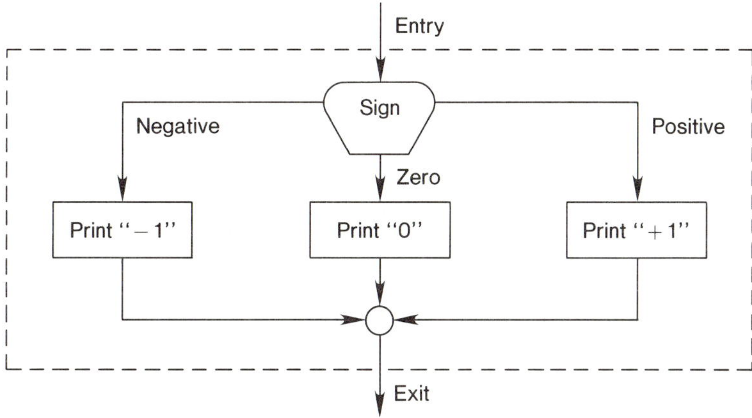

This diagram shows a case structure with three choices, but there could be four, five, or more choices. The sequence on each branch can contain single statements or other structures. Notice that the entire structure is enclosed in a process box, with one entry and one exit.

The specifications for this case structure, written as a multiple-choice decision table, are

Sign	Negative	Zero	Positive
Print "– 1"	X		
Print "0"		X	
Print "+ 1"			X

or

Sign	Negative	Zero	Positive
Print	"– 1"	"0"	"+ 1"

REPETITION STRUCTURES

DOWHILE structure The DOWHILE structure controls the execution of a group of statements repeated a finite number of times. The DOWHILE statement is the first statement of the structure. It always expresses the condition under which the loop is to be repeated. The range of the loop is indicated by an END statement. If the condition tested in the DOWHILE is true, the statements in the body of the loop are executed. If the condition is false, the control will skip the loop body and pass from the DOWHILE statement to the statement following the END. In PL/I this takes the form

```
DO WHILE (condition);
  sequence
END;
```

The condition tested can ask whether an end-of-file has been found, whether a counter has reached a predetermined value, whether a particular data value has been input, or whether the loop has been executed a predetermined number of times. In a DOWHILE loop, if the condition tests false the very first time, the statements in the loop are not executed at all. Therefore, DOWHILE begins by testing the value of the condition. Using flowchart symbols, this is drawn as

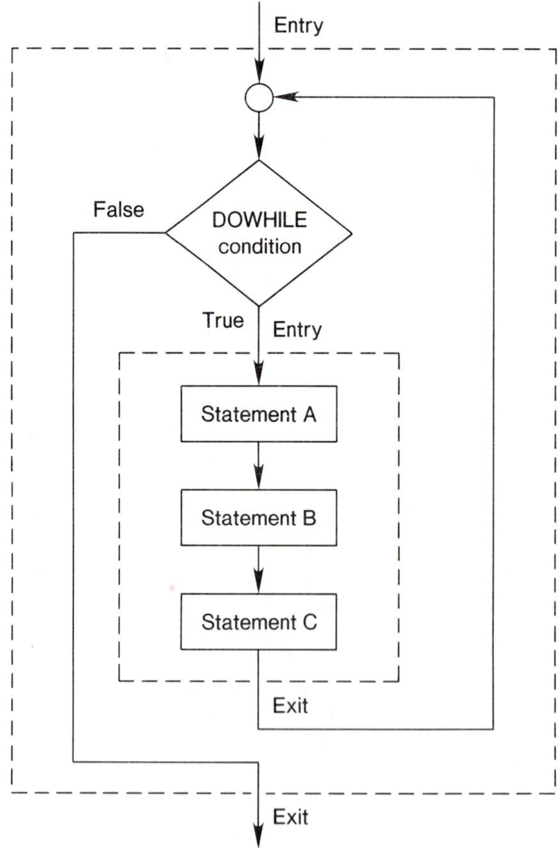

Notice that the entry to the loop is at the top and the exit is at the bottom. The entire loop can be enclosed in a process box with entry and exit at the top and

bottom respectively. The sequence of statements in the loop body can be any sequence of single statements or structures such as a selection, a case, or another repetition. An example of this is

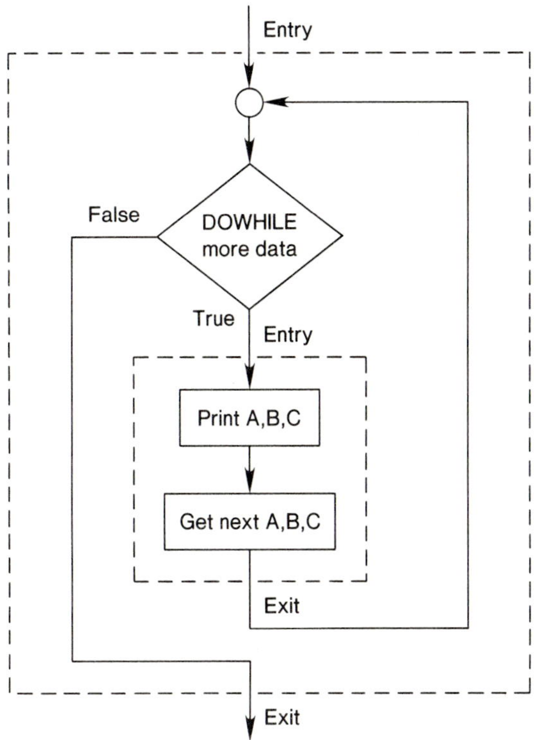

In this example it is assumed that the first values of A, B, and C are already available. This is a general rule of PL/I programming.

PROGRAMMING RULE: STYLE The first data values must already be available before a DOWHILE loop is entered.

The specifications for a DOWHILE loop may be written as a decision table. For example:

More data	Y	N
Print A,B,C	X	
Get next A,B,C	X	
Repeat	X	
Exit		X

Normally the actions of a decision table are carried out in order as selected by the Xs in the action stub. With a loop structure, one of the actions, Repeat, repeats the entire process specified by the decision table. The Exit action takes place when the condition for continuing the loop has not been satisfied.

DOUNTIL structure In this repetition structure, the condition is tested at the end of the loop. In PL/I this takes the form of

```
DO UNTIL (condition);
  sequence
END;
```

The general form of the flowchart for this structure is

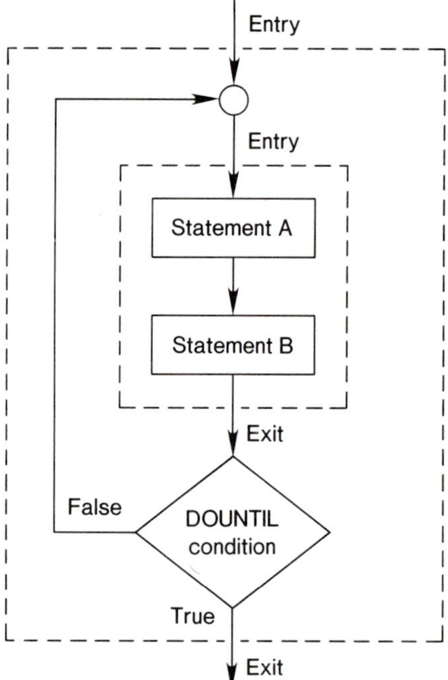

If the condition tested is true, the loop is terminated. If the condition is false, the control returns to the top of the loop, repeating the body of the loop until the condition is true. In a flowchart the condition is shown at the bottom. This repetition structure can also be enclosed in a process box as shown by the outside dotted line. The entry to the loop is at the top and the exit at the bottom. The statements inside the loop can be single statements in a sequence, or other structures such as a selection, a case, or another loop. Since the condition tested is at the end of the loop, the body of the loop is executed at least once. For example:

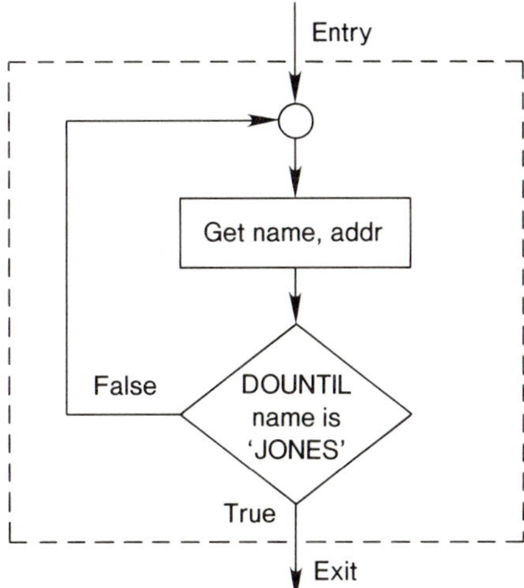

This repetition searches through a list of names and addresses for a specific name.

The specifications of a DOUNTIL loop can be given in a decision table only by making a special case of the first entry into the body of the structure, as in

First time	Y	N	N
'JONES'	—	Y	N
Get name,addr	X		X
Repeat	X		X
Exit		X	

The dash (—) as a condition entry of the decision table means that that condition is irrelevant. In fact, the computer will not test the condition the first time it reaches the body of the loop. With two condition entries in a decision table, there may be as many as four different sequences of actions; here there are only three.

DOUNTIL is used primarily for searching through data for a specific value, but it is rarely used in PL/I. If there is a chance that there is no data, DOWHILE should be used instead.

The following sample program illustrates the use of the sequence structure, the DOWHILE loop, and the IFTHENELSE. In this example the IFTHENELSE is nested inside the DOWHILE. There is a sequence on the true branch of the IFTHENELSE. The DOWHILE is nested inside another sequence.

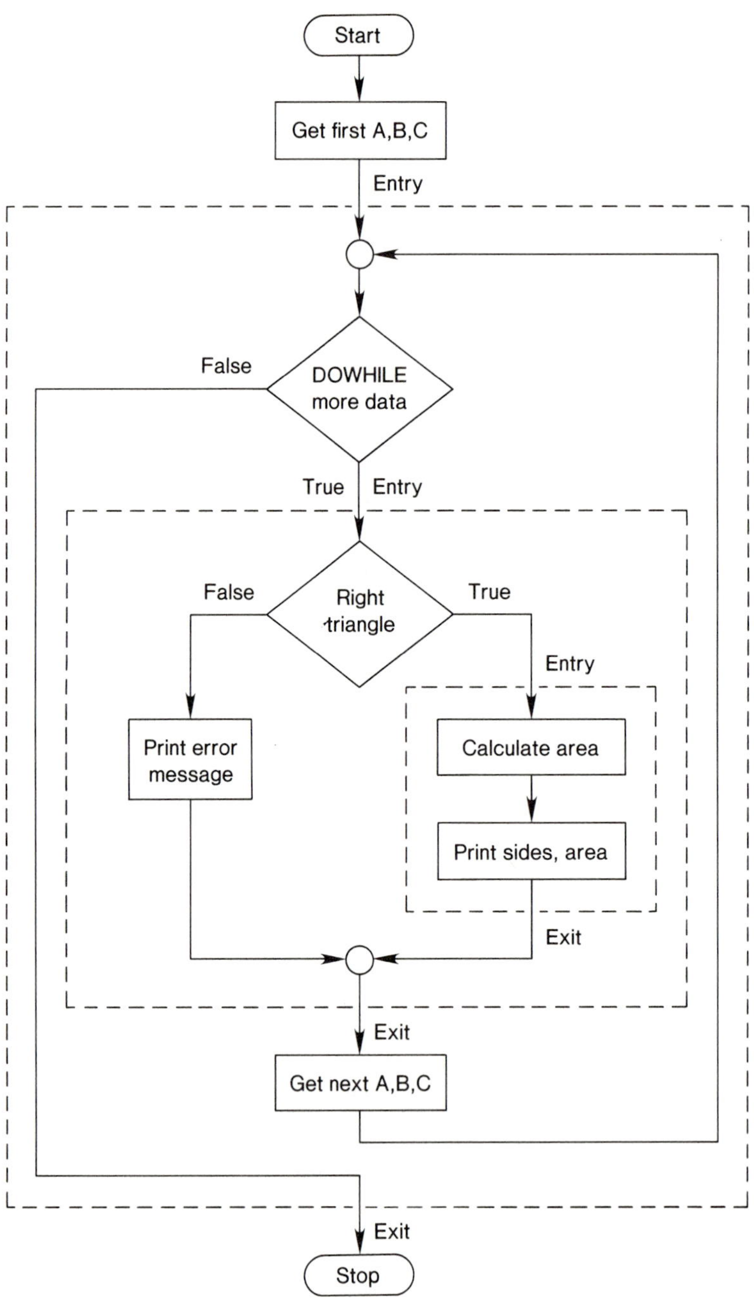

The PL/I code for this is found on the next page.

```
1   TRIAREA: PROCEDURE OPTIONS (MAIN);
2   /*******************************************************/
3   /*                                                     */
4   /* PROGRAM: AREA OF RIGHT TRIANGLES                    */
5   /* AUTHOR:  R REDDY                                    */
6   /* VERSION: 07/17/84                                   */
7   /*                                                     */
8   /* PROGRAM DESCRIPTION:                                */
9   /* --------------------------------------------------- */
10  /* THIS PROGRAM CALCULATES THE AREAS OF RIGHT          */
11  /* TRIANGLES.  THE END OF THE DATA IS INDICATED        */
12  /* BY ENTERING 0,0,0 FOR A, B, AND C.  IF A            */
13  /* TRIANGLE IS NOT A RIGHT TRIANGLE, AN ERROR          */
14  /* MESSAGE IS PRINTED.                                 */
15  /*                                                     */
16  /* INPUT: A,B,C THE SIDES OF A TRIANGLE                */
17  /*              C IS THE LONGEST SIDE                  */
18  /*                                                     */
19  /* OUTPUT: A,B,C, AREA OF EACH TRIANGLE                */
20  /*                                                     */
21  /*******************************************************/
22  DECLARE (A,B,C) FLOAT BINARY,
23          AREA    FLOAT BINARY;
24
25  GET LIST (A,B,C);
26  DO WHILE (A > 0);          /* FOR EACH A,B,C                   */
27    IF C*C = A*A + B*B      /*CHECK IF IT IS A RIGHT TRIANGLE */
28      THEN
29        DO;
30          AREA = A* B/2;
31          PUT SKIP LIST (A,B,C,AREA);
32        END;
33      ELSE
34        PUT SKIP LIST (A,B,C,'IS NOT A RIGHT TRIANGLE');
35    GET LIST (A,B,C);
36  END;
37  END TRIAREA;
```

This program begins with the program header and a descriptive comment box. Following the comment box are the descriptions of the data.

Lines 22–23 describe the data. Values representing measurements are FLOAT BINARY if not all of the values are integers.

Line 25 is an input statement that obtains the values for the variables A, B, and C.

Lines 26–36 form the DOWHILE loop. The contents of this loop are repeated as long as the A value is greater than zero.

Lines 27–34 form the IFTHENELSE structure, which is nested in the DOWHILE loop. The values of A, B, and C may or may not form a right triangle. The true branch consists of a nested sequence.

Line 30 calculates and stores the area of the right triangle.

Line 31 is an output statement that prints the input values and the area of the triangle. The keyword SKIP indicates to the computer that the output is to be placed on a new line.

Line 34 is an output statement that prints the input values and an error message if the triangle is not a right triangle. It is important to print appropriate messages when data errors are found, and to identify incorrect data.

Line 35 is the input statement that obtains the next set of values for A, B, and C. Because the DOWHILE statement checks the condition at the beginning of the repetition, the first set of values must be obtained ahead of the DOWHILE statement and the next set of values obtained just before it is repeated.

Line 36 marks the end of the DOWHILE loop.

Line 37 indicates the end of the entire TRIAREA program.

This would be a better program if the data were validated to make sure that C is the longest side, as the documentation indicated.

CHANGE OF ENVIRONMENT

CALLRETURN statement The CALLRETURN structure moves control from one procedure block to another on a temporary basis. This is usually shown as nested process boxes.

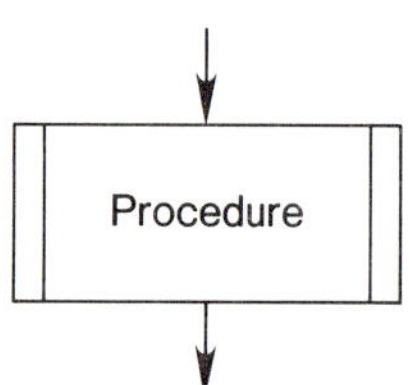

Control passes "in" on the call and "out" again on the return. The nested or striped process box is shown from the point of view of the "calling" block. A completely separate flowchart would be needed to show the structure of the procedure that is called.

Since there are no decisions to be made in a CALLRETURN, there is no decision table equivalent.

Block structure A block or procedure differs from a control structure in that it contains data as well as instructions. It provides a complete environment for carrying out a step in the processing. In PL/I this takes the form of

```
PROC;
  sequence
END;
```

or

```
BEGIN;
  sequence
END;
```

Control flowing from one block to another is like your stepping from one room into another. The objects in the new environment are different except for those you take with you. The relationships between blocks and their entrances and exits can be best represented by hierarchy charts, discussed in the following sections.

Review questions

1. The PL/I alphabet is the same as the English alphabet. True or false?

2. Which PL/I character set is available on your computer?

3. Which of the following belong to a PL/I character set?
(a) <=
(b) * *
(c) LE
(d) .EQ.
(e) ||
(f) G T

4. User-defined words name ____________________ and ____________________.

5. Keywords tell the computer ____________________, ____________________, and ____________________.

6. The compiler recognizes a PL/I comment by the symbols __________ and __________.

7. The compiler recognizes the end of a PL/I statement by the __________ symbol.

8. The compiler recognizes the end of a keyword by the __________ or __________ symbol.

9. Nonexecutable statements are used to provide information to the ____________________ and the ____________________.

10. The keyword phrases GET LIST and PUT LIST instruct the computer to ____________________ and ____________________, respectively.

11. How do an IFTHENELSE structure and a SELECT structure differ?

12. How do a DOWHILE structure and a DOUNTIL structure differ?

13. A DO . . . END structure and a BEGIN . . . END structure differ in that there may be a change in the ____________________ in a BEGIN . . . END block, but not in a DO . . . END group.

14. Draw a decision table for lines 27-34 of the TRIAREA program on p. 43.

15. Draw a decision table for the entire DOWHILE loop of the TRIAREA program on p. 43.

16. (a) Draw a flowchart for the BOX program on pp. 29-30.
(b) Draw a flowchart showing the steps needed to calculate the volumes of ten boxes.
(c) Draw a flowchart showing the steps needed to calculate the volumes of many boxes assuming the end of the data is indicated by input values of 0,0,0.

17. Draw decision tables for the three algorithms of Question 16.

2.3 Algorithm design

The solution of a problem must be developed in logical steps. This development includes the specification of proper input data, the description of the arithmetical and logical manipulation of the data, and the design of the input and output formats. These steps are the first stage in the development of a computer program to solve a problem. Additional stages are coding the program, developing test data, testing the program, and maintaining the program. In the development stage, special forms are available for use in specifying the input data and formatting the output.

A description of data manipulation to solve a problem is an *algorithm*. An algorithm may be expressed as a diagram, a verbal description of a problem solution, or a set of computer instructions for manipulating data.

The general description of a problem solution is usually *functional* in nature; that is, it starts with a verb and describes an action. Thus we have descriptions such as "count the number of men and women in the class," "solve a set of simultaneous equations," and so forth. Flowcharts are used to describe an algorithm in great detail. The process boxes of flowcharts are given functional descriptions; for example, "input a,b,c," "DOWHILE F <= 150." Different boxes are used for different types of functions.

2.3.1 Hierarchy charts

Sometimes we are interested in looking at the structure of an algorithm rather than at the details as they are given in a flowchart. The process boxes that contain control structures are not usually given functional descriptions in a flowchart but they represent processes such as "validate data," "print report," and so forth. These more general functional modules are the basis of a different type of diagram, a module or *hierarchy chart*. When flowchart structures are nested, the hierarchy chart has many levels. The top level represents the functional description of the entire algorithm. The boxes in the lower levels represent control structures or blocks containing only simple statements. Control structures and blocks are not distinguished in the chart, as what may be a block in one implementation of an algorithm may be a control structure in another.

The second level of the chart usually has three parts: the initialization of the variables, a loop to process the data, and some final instructions. The third level of the chart may represent the processing of a single data value.

HIERARCHY CHART SYMBOLS

A module that appears only once in a hierarchy chart is shown as a rectangular box.

A duplicated module is represented by a banded rectangular box after the first time it occurs.

Looping is indicated by a circular arrow at the top of the box to be repeated.

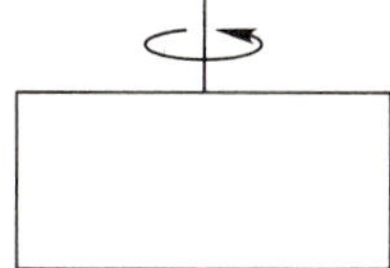

Conditional execution is indicated by a diamond.

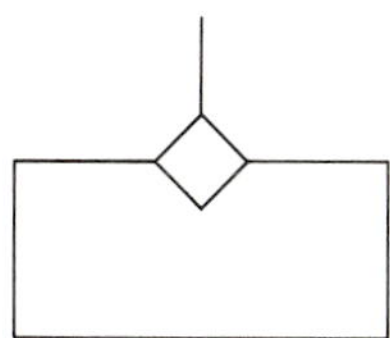

Figure 2–1 is an example of a hierarchy chart showing the steps in processing a company payroll. The main module controls the processing of all the paychecks and the printing of a report. The second-level modules make the preparations necessary before employee records can be processed, then process the records, and do the final job of printing the report. The middle module at this level controls the processing of the records, one at a time. The third and fourth levels give the processing of a single record in more detail, explaining the steps necessary to convert the information from a single input record into output. There is one record for each employee.

The top-level module is the main module. It is a driver module for the rest

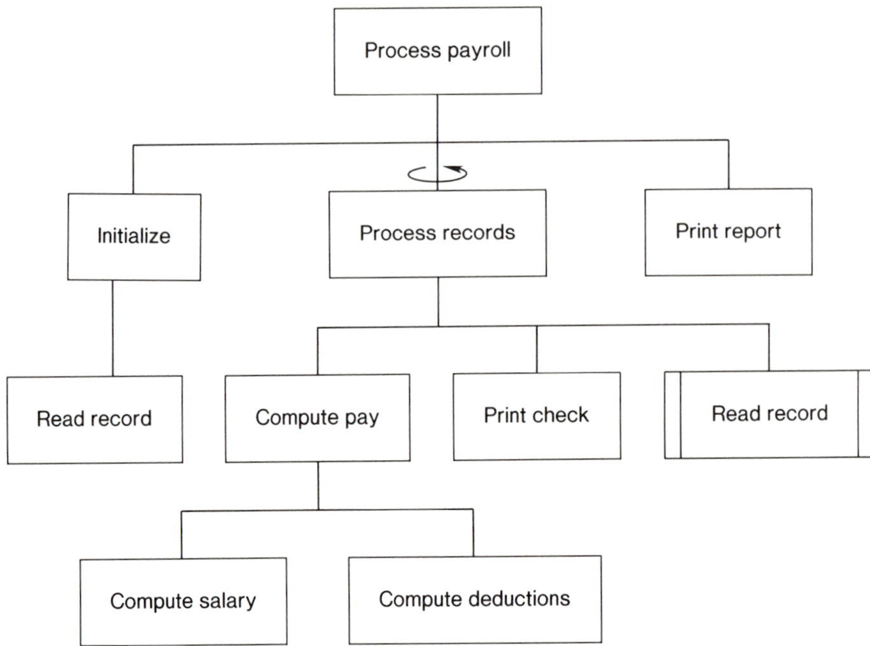

Figure 2–1

of the program. A hierarchy chart is like an industrial assembly line. The actual manufacturing of parts is represented at the lowest level, the subassemblies that use these parts are at the next higher level, the major assemblies at the next higher level, and the final product at the highest level. There may be any number of levels, depending on the complexity of the final product. Most of the data processing takes place in the lowest modules, which are the equivalent of the flowchart process boxes.

Using hierarchy charts and flowcharts makes it easier to follow program logic and make modifications before the program actually exists. Modifications are usually restricted to a single module or just a few modules, so that the overall logic design of the program does not have to be reworked. Errors in the overall logic are hard to correct after a program has been written, but often can be detected by studying the design diagrams.

Hierarchy charts show the functional parts, the structure of the algorithm. Flowcharts show the various steps making up one or more of the blocks. Decision tables clarify the logic of complex parts of the process. Flowcharts, hierarchy charts, and decision tables are simply visual aids in the development and understanding of the logic of an algorithm. Other types of diagrams are used to show the scheduling of parts of the processing or the flow of data.

An algorithm can also be described in English or in a computer language. In fact, a computer program is an algorithm described in a form a computer can understand. English is not a precise enough language to be used by a computer. Languages such as PL/I are designed to be unambiguous.

2.3.2 Top-down design

Starting algorithm design with a hierarchy chart (in complicated cases) rather than a flowchart or a decision table assists in identifying the various subfunctions of the algorithm and in determining the order in which they are to be performed.

Hierarchy charts are built little by little as the problem to be solved is analyzed. First versions of a chart may contain only a few functions. Other functions are added as they are identified. This is known as *top-down design.* For a complex problem, such as computing a company's payroll, the first and least detailed version of the hierarchy chart might be the one shown in figure 2–2. This box states the function of the algorithm. The function must then be analyzed and steps identified to accomplish the job.

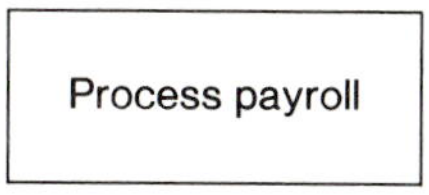

Process payroll

Figure 2–2

A hierarchy chart shows the nesting of the structures. It is like an outline of a program. Each level gives a more detailed explanation of the level above. A module at a higher level can be thought of as a process box containing all of the modules below it in the chart. The process boxes representing the substructures are labeled functionally and are nested according to the hierarchy. The top module can usually be subdivided into three parts: preparing to do the processing, repeatedly processing the data records, and doing any final printing. This stage of analysis is shown in figure 2–3. Here each step represents a fairly complicated process, one of the three parts of the algorithm.

Lower-level modules may be implemented as control structures in a single procedure, or they may be separate procedures invoked by the higher-level module. What this means is that at the time of execution of the program, control is passed from a higher-level module to the invoked lower-level module, even when it is a separate program. This is the way programs are linked together. When the lower-level module completes its work, control is returned to the higher-level module. When there are more than two levels to

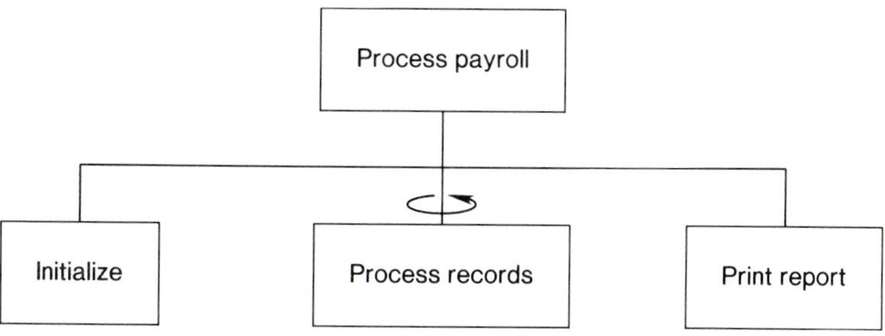

Figure 2–3

the hierarchy chart, control will pass through many modules and many levels before returning to the main module at the highest level of the chart. Whether modules are implemented as procedures or as control structures depends on the amount of PL/I code involved. In general, a procedure should contain 10 to 100 lines of code. It may be shorter if the module appears in more than one place in the hierarchy chart.

To preserve the vertical lines of control (invocation and return) of a hierarchy chart, it is sometimes necessary to show a module more than once, at the same level, or at different levels in the hierarchy.

The third level contains a detailed description of the processing. The basic steps of handling each employee record are placed here. These steps are to obtain the record, to calculate the pay, and to print the paycheck. They are shown in figure 2–4 under the middle box of the second level, because they are an expansion of the function of that box.

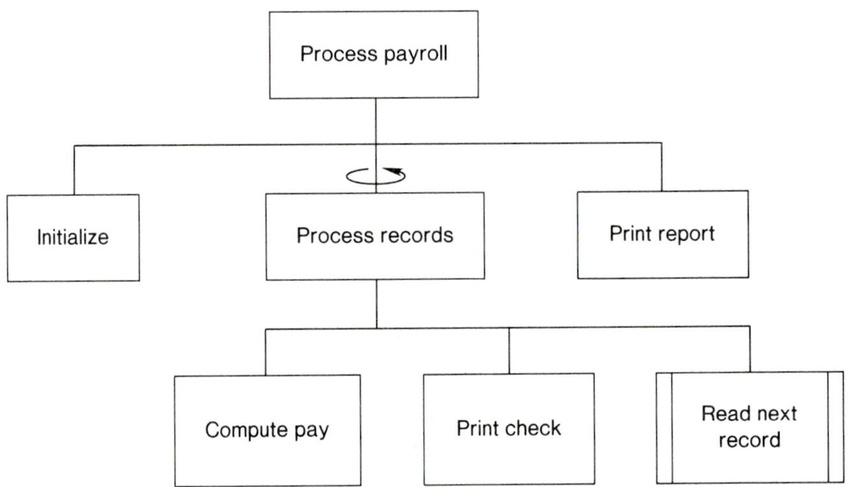

Figure 2–4

Rather than showing the reading of the record being processed, it is assumed that a record is already present. This is done because of the way computers handle input.

In order to be ready to process the next record in the same way, the steps in processing a record conclude with the reading of the next record. A banded box is used for getting the next record because the procedure involved is the same as for getting the first record.

Reading the first record is part of the initialization. This is known as a *priming read.* An expanded version of the payroll hierarchy chart appears in figure 2–1. It shows the priming read along with an elaboration of the steps needed to compute the pay.

At this point the program designer would begin to develop flowcharts of the individual modules.

Review questions

1. A descriptive procedure to solve a problem is called an ______.

2. What does it mean to say that a box in a hierarchy chart or a flowchart should be given a functional label?

3. If module B is below module A in a hierarchy chart, then the flowchart structure corresponding to module B is ______ the structure corresponding to module A.

4. A repetition in a flowchart is represented as a box with ______ in a hierarchy chart.

5. A decision in a flowchart is represented as a box with ______ in a hierarchy chart.

6. Describe the order of execution of the modules in a hierarchy chart.

7. When can a module of a hierarchy chart be implemented as a PL/I control structure?

8. When can a module of a hierarchy chart be implemented as a PL/I procedure?

2.4 Examples of algorithms

The following examples illustrate the development of computer algorithms. They show the different types of diagrams and, in some cases, the completed PL/I programs.

2.4.1 Compound interest

The mathematical formula for calculating accumulated investments involving compound interest is

$$A = P(1 + r/c)^{cn}$$

where A is the amount accumulated, p is the principal, r is the annual rate, c is the number of compounding periods per year, and n is the number of years of the investment. The steps in the computer algorithm are:

1. Get the values of P, r, c, and n.
2. Calculate the accumulated amount.
3. Display the answer.

The flowchart of this process is shown in figure 2–5.

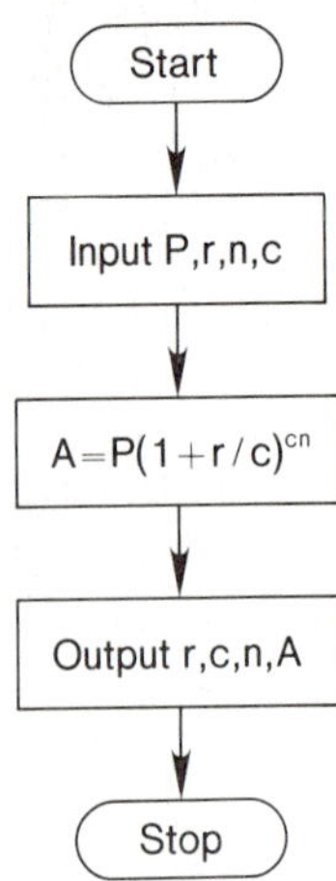

Figure 2–5

This is not an accurate way to calculate compound interest on a computer, but if the formula is to be used in this form, the flowchart clearly expresses the steps needed to do the calculation. These same three steps are given in the hierarchy chart of figure 2–6. No repetition is involved here. Nevertheless, the hierarchy chart has three parts, the first to obtain the first (and only) set of values, the second to calculate the answer, and the third to finish by printing the input values and the accumulated amount.

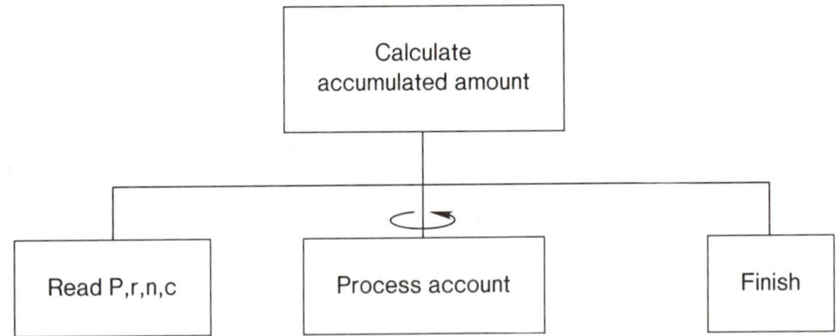

Figure 2–6

If this calculation were to be carried out for more than one set of input values, the hierarchy chart would first be developed as in figure 2–7a, then expanded as in figure 2–7b and 2–7c. The Process accounts module controls the repetition. The third level shows the calculations that are carried out for a single set of input values.

The only processing that might be needed in the Finish box is to indicate that the data processing has been completed successfully. Output values are calculated for each set of input data, so the output is shown at the third level, inside the repetition.

If increased accuracy is needed, a different formula would have to be used. With computers, as with people, using exponents is slower and less accurate than doing other types of calculations.

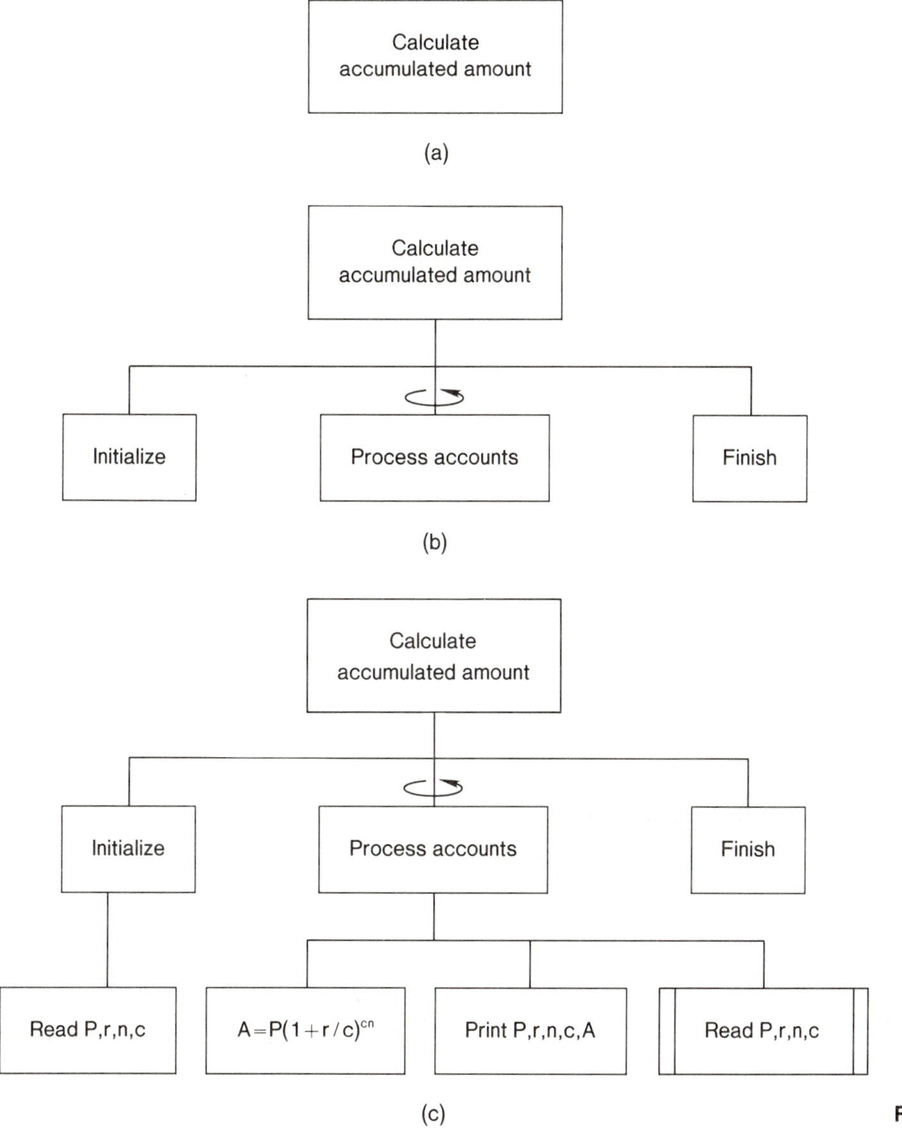

Figure 2–7

2.4.2 Temperature conversion

Printing a table of temperature conversions from Fahrenheit to Celsius (centigrade) is another example of a calculation done repeatedly. If such a table is needed for temperatures ranging from −50°F through 150°F, the steps of the algorithm might be originally developed as

1. Start with F = −50°.
2. Calculate and print Celsius temperatures for all values of F through 150°.

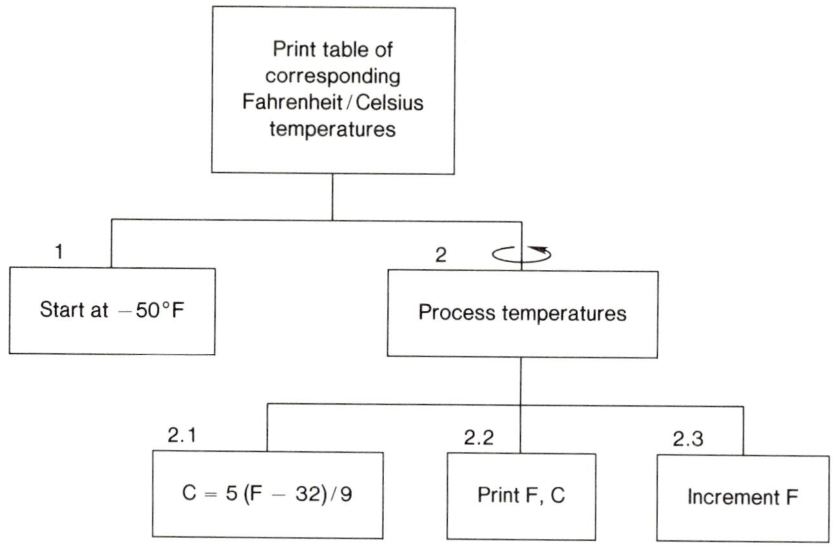

Figure 2–8

These steps are the first two levels of the hierarchy chart of figure 2–8. If details of step 2 are given, the steps of the algorithm become

1. Start with F = −50°.
2. Repeat steps 2.1 through 2.3 while F is less than or equal to 150°, then stop.
   2.1 Calculate C = 5(F − 32)/9.
   2.2 Print F and C.
   2.3 Increase F by 1.

The decision table specification of this is

F <= 150°	Y	N
Calculate C	X	
Print F,C	X	
F = F+1	X	
Repeat	X	
End		X

Notice that the decision table does not show the initialization of F, only the loop control and the steps inside the loop.

Step 1 of the algorithm describes the initialization. Step 2 describes the repetition. Steps 2.1, 2.2, and 2.3 are the steps being repeated. The hierarchy chart is shown in figure 2–8 with numbered modules. No "finish" box is needed if there are no totals or summaries to be printed after the data has been processed.

The flowchart representation of this algorithm is given in figure 2–9. The statement F = F + 1 is not a formula in the usual sense. It is an abbreviation for the formula

$$F_{new} = F_{old} + 1$$

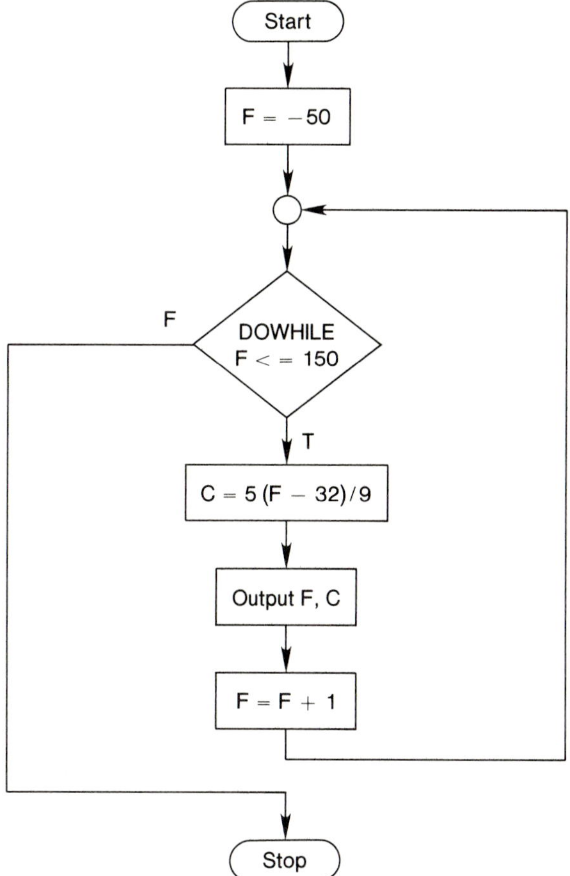

Figure 2-9

which indicates that one is to be added to F to obtain a new value for F. The repeated calculations are controlled by a DOWHILE loop with the repeating condition of F <= 150. This example shows that sometimes data values are generated by the algorithm rather than being input to the computer. With either method, obtaining the first value is part of the initialization, and the steps being repeated end with the next value being obtained.

The PL/I program to generate the conversion table for Fahrenheit temperatures follows.

```
TEMPCON: PROCEDURE OPTIONS (MAIN);
/*******************************************************/
/*                                                     */
/* PROGRAM: TEMPERATURE CONVERSION                     */
/* AUTHOR:   R REDDY                                   */
/* VERSION: 07/17/84                                   */
/*                                                     */
/* PROGRAM DESCRIPTION:                                */
/* ------------------------------------------------    */
```

```
10   /* THIS PROGRAM PRODUCES A TABLE OF CONVERSIONS    */
11   /* OF FAHRENHEIT TEMPERATURES TO CELSIUS.  THE     */
12   /* FAHRENHEIT TEMPERATURES RANGE FROM -50 DEGREES  */
13   /* TO 150 DEGREES.                                 */
14   /*                                                 */
15   /* INPUT: NONE                                     */
16   /*                                                 */
17   /* OUTPUT: FAHRENHEIT AND CELSIUS TEMPERATURES     */
18   /*                                                 */
19   /***************************************************/
20   DECLARE (C,F) FLOAT BINARY;
21
22   PUT SKIP LIST ('FAHRENHEIT', 'CELSIUS');
23   F = -50;
24   DO WHILE (F <=150);      /* FOR EACH FAHRENHEIT VALUE */
25     C= 5 * (F - 32)/ 9;    /* CALCULATE CELSIUS VALUE   */
26     PUT SKIP LIST (F,C);
27     F = F + 1;
28   END;
29   END TEMPCON;
```

The new features of this program are the printing of column headings in line 22, and the generation of data values in lines 23 and 27, rather than obtaining them from input.

2.4.3 Counting data

Suppose we want to count the number of men and the number of women in a group of students. Assume furthermore that student records are available coded "M" for male students and "F" for female students, with other information about the students. The computer can be asked to look only at the codes, ignoring the other information, and to tally the number of students in each category. The steps in the algorithm might be as follows:

1. Assume a total of zero male and zero female students is possible (MSUM = 0 and FSUM = 0) and get the first student record.
2. Repeat steps 2.1 and 2.2 as long as there are more records, then go to step 3.
   2.1 If the code is "M", add 1 to MSUM.
   2.2 If the code is "F", add 1 to FSUM.
3. Display MSUM and FSUM.

The decision table specifications are:

More data Code	Y "M"	Y "F"	N *
MSUM = MSUM+1	X		
FSUM = FSUM+1		X	
Get next record	X	X	
Repeat	X	X	
End			X

This decision table mixes true/false answers with multiple-choice answers. The asterisk (*) means that the question cannot be asked if there is no more data. Some of the actions to be taken in the "M" and "F" columns are the same. These actions may be included in both branches of the case statement or may follow the closing of the case statement; the latter is more efficient. Again, initialization of the variables including a priming read of the data is assumed rather than shown.

The hierarchy chart for this procedure is given in figure 2–10.

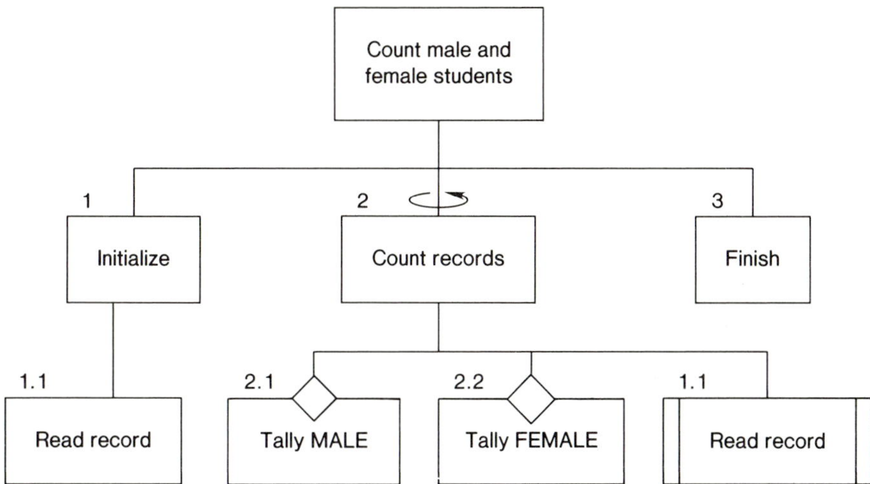

Figure 2–10

The initialization module is responsible for clearing the tallies as well as obtaining the first input record. The Tally MALE and Tally FEMALE boxes are alternate choices. This is shown by the small decision boxes that connect them to the chart. The counts cannot be printed until all the records have been processed. Therefore, there is no output box in the loop; the only output occurs at the Finish. Notice that a module is given the same number everywhere it appears.

A flowchart for this algorithm is shown in figure 2–11. Its PL/I program follows:

```
MFSUM: PROCEDURE OPTIONS (MAIN);
/*******************************************************/
/*                                                     */
/* PROGRAM: MALE-FEMALE COUNT                          */
/* AUTHOR:   R REDDY                                   */
/* VERSION: 07/17/84                                   */
/*                                                     */
/* PROGRAM DESCRIPTION:                                */
/* --------------------------------------------------- */
/* THIS PROGRAM COUNTS THE NUMBER OF MALE AND THE      */
/* NUMBER OF FEMALE STUDENTS IN A CLASS.  THE          */
/* DATA IS FOLLOWED BY THE WORDS 'THE END'.            */
```

```
/*                                                       */
/* INPUT: NAME, SEX OF STUDENT                           */
/*                                                       */
/* OUTPUT: NUMBER OF MALE AND FEMALE STUDENTS            */
/*                                                       */
/*********************************************************/
DECLARE NAME    CHARARTER(25),
        CODE    CHARACTER(1),
        MSUM    FIXED BINARY,
        FSUM    FIXED BINARY;
DECLARE MALE    CHARACTER(1)  INIT('M'),
        FEMALE  CHARACTER(1)  INIT('F');

MSUM = 0;
FSUM = 0;
GET LIST (CODE,NAME);
DO WHILE (NAME ¬= 'THE END');
  SELECT;
    WHEN (CODE = MALE)
      MSUM = MSUM + 1;
    WHEN (CODE = FEMALE)
      FSUM = FSUM + 1;
    OTHERWISE
      PUT SKIP LIST (CODE,NAME,'INVALID CODE');
  END;
  GET LIST (CODE,NAME);
END;
PUT LIST (MSUM,'MEN',FSUM,'WOMEN');
END MFSUM;
```

Notice that in this program there is a SELECT statement nested inside the DOWHILE. This structure is used rather than an IFTHENELSE to allow validation of the input CODE. Notice also that the variables MSUM and FSUM are initialized ahead of the repetition structure and printed after the repetition structure, since their values depend on the entire set of data. But the output statement for the error message is inside the repetition structure, since it only refers to a single value of CODE.

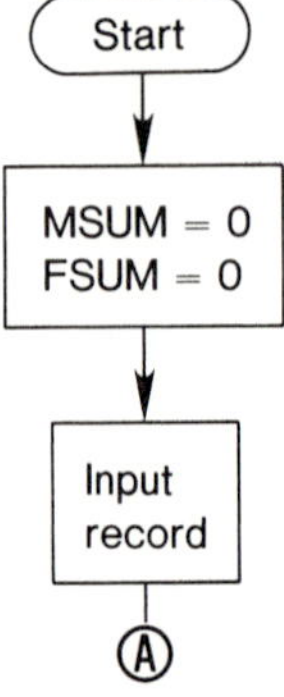

Figure 2–11

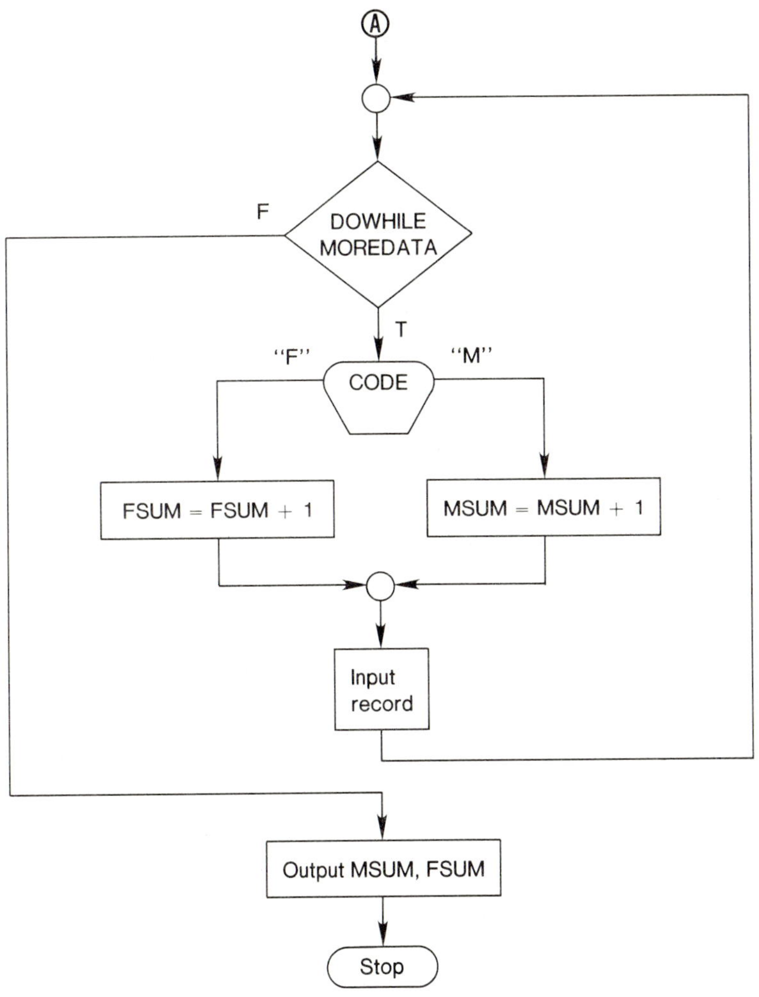

Figure 2–11 *continued*

2.4.4 Simultaneous equations

In the set of simultaneous equations

$$AX + BY = C$$

$$DX + EY = F$$

X and Y are the variables and A, B, C, D, E, and F are constant coefficients. The values of X and Y can be computed from the values of the constants as follows:

$$X = \frac{CE - BF}{AF - BD} \qquad Y = \frac{AF - CD}{AE - BD}$$

The steps of the solution algorithm are:

1. Input the values of A,B,C,D,E, and F.
2. Compute AE − BD.
3. If AE − BD is not zero, then do steps 4 and 5; otherwise, print message and stop.
4. Calculate X and Y.
5. Display the values of X and Y.

The decision table form of the specification is:

More data	Y	Y	N
A*E − B*D = 0	Y	N	*
Print "No solution"	X		
Calculate X, Y		X	
Print X, Y		X	
Repeat	X	X	
End			X

The quantity AE − BD must be computed first and tested to avoid division by zero. An error such as attempting division by zero will make the computer terminate the program.

Data validation is an important part of every program. Unusual situations should be detected and diagnostic messages written by the program so that

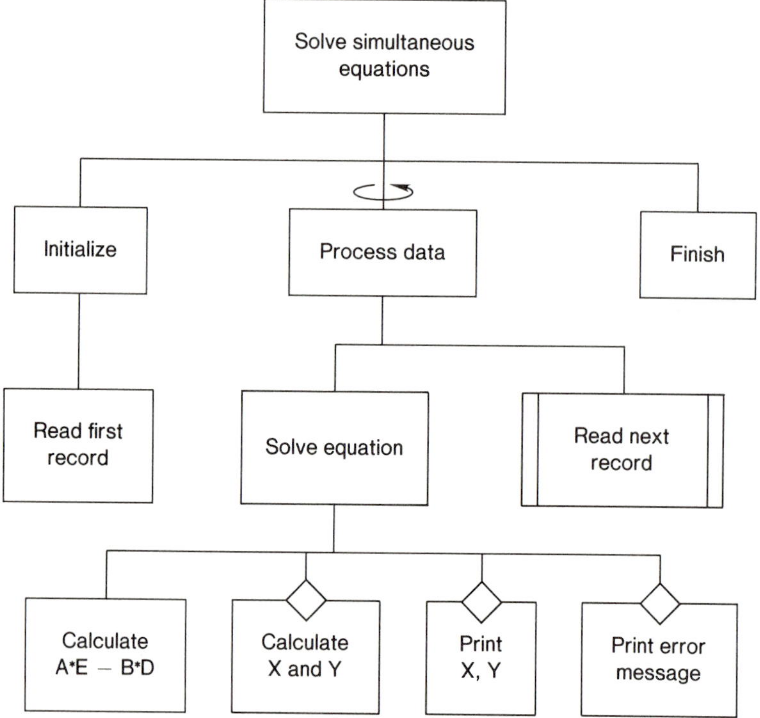

Figure 2–12

the computer will not stop the processing abnormally. Mathematically, if AE − BD is zero, there is no error. The set of equations simply does not have a solution. It would be misleading to have the computer stop with a system error message as though there were an error. The values of X and Y can be computed only if AE − BD is not zero.

The hierarchy chart for this is shown in figure 2–12. The steps of this algorithm are generalized by using symbolic coefficients rather than

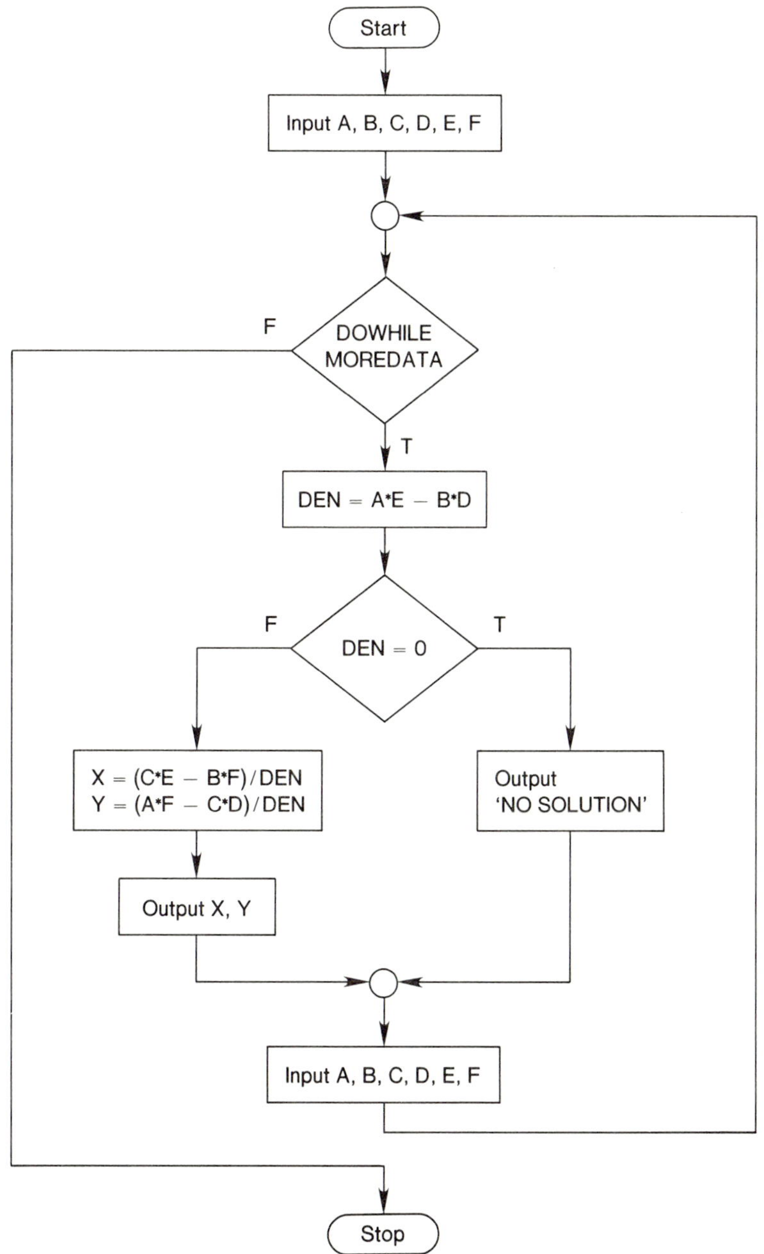

Figure 2–13

numbers. They are further generalized in the hierarchy chart and in the flowchart of figure 2–13 by including a loop so that several sets of simultaneous equations can be solved.

PROGRAMMING HINT: UTILITY Generalize algorithms.

Generality is an important quality of computer programs.

In figure 2–13, the asterisk has been used to indicate multiplication. Otherwise, in an equation such as DEN = A*E − B*D, which uses both single letters as identifiers and the character string DEN as an identifier, it would not be clear whether DEN was meant as a product, or AE and BD were meant as single identifiers. PL/I always requires the asterisk when multiplication is intended. The program for this algorithm is given in chapter 3, section 3.6.1.

2.4.5 Quadratic equations

The quadratic equation

$$AX^2 + BX + C = 0$$

where A, B, and C are constant coefficients, has two roots. The roots can be complex, can be real and identical, or can be real and distinct. The roots X_1 and X_2 are given by the formulas

$$X_1 = \frac{-B + \sqrt{B^2 - 4AC}}{2A}$$

$$X_2 = \frac{-B - \sqrt{B^2 - 4AC}}{2A}$$

The input values A, B, and C must be validated. If A is zero, then there is an error and the equation is not really quadratic. If A is not zero, then the types of roots can be found as follows:

$B^2 - 4AC < 0$ (Two complex roots)

$B^2 - 4AC = 0$ (Two identical real roots)

$B^2 - 4AC > 0$ (Two distinct real roots)

PROGRAMMING HINT: UTILITY Consider all possible situations.

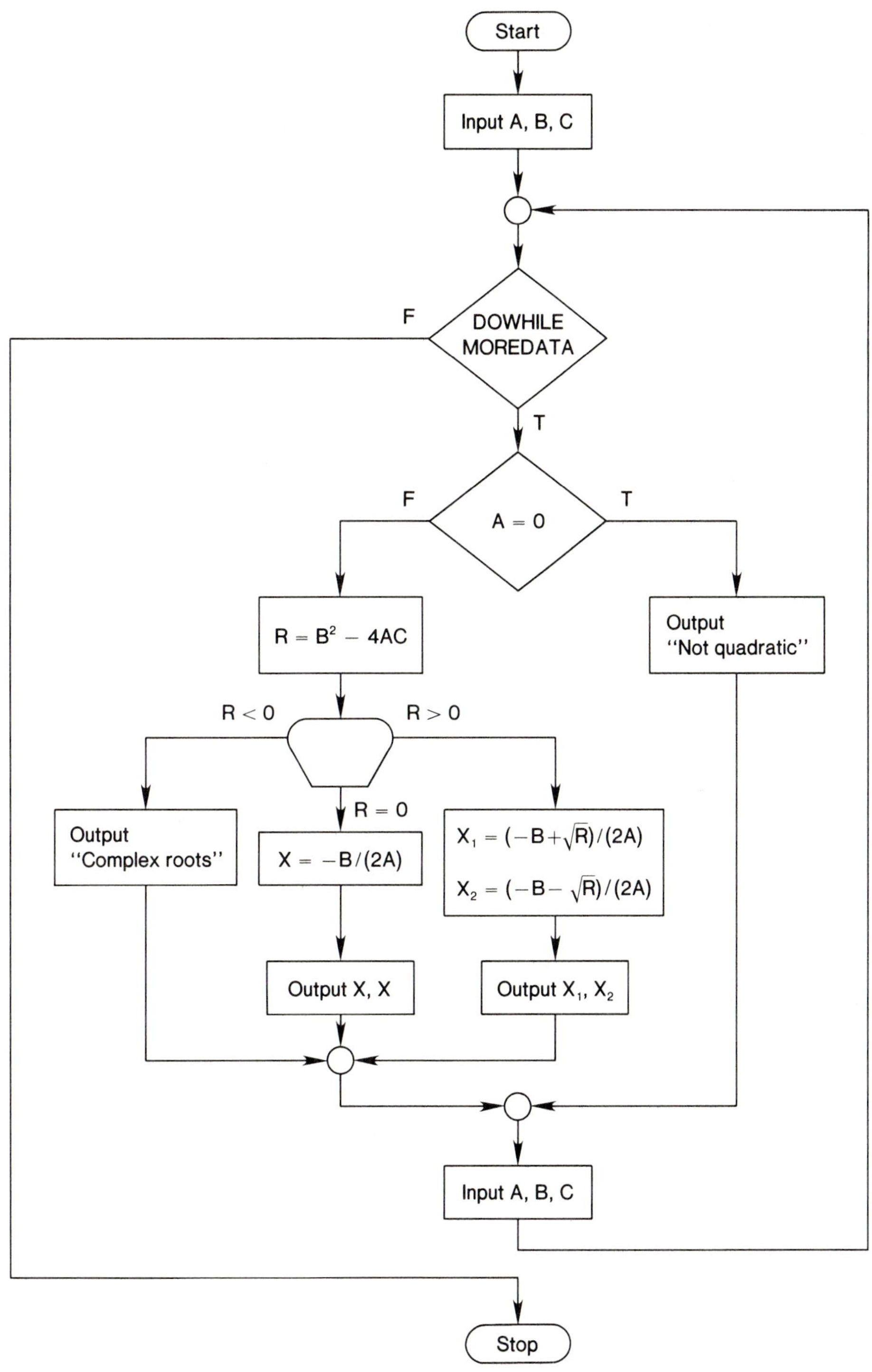
Start
Input A, B, C
DOWHILE MOREDATA
F
T
A = 0
F
T
R = B² − 4AC
Output "Not quadratic"
R < 0
R > 0
R = 0
Output "Complex roots"
X = −B/(2A)
X₁ = (−B+√R)/(2A)
X₂ = (−B− √R)/(2A)
Output X, X
Output X₁, X₂
Input A, B, C
Stop

Figure 2–14

The decision table specifications for this are:

More data	Y	Y	Y	Y	N
A = 0	Y	N	N	N	*
$B^2 - 4AC$	—	>0	$=0$	<0	*
Print "Complex roots"				X	
Print "Not quadratic"	X				
Calculate X_1 and X_2		X			
Print X_1 and X_2		X			
Calculate X			X		
Print X			X		
Read A,B,C	X	X	X	X	
Repeat	X	X	X	X	
End					X

PL/I has facilities for computing complex roots. However, at this time, if the roots are complex, we will simply put out a message to that effect. The two types of real roots will be calculated separately for efficiency.

Figure 2–14 is a flowchart of the algorithm. Its hierarchy chart is shown in figure 2–15. A similar PL/I program is given in chapter 3, section 3.6.2.

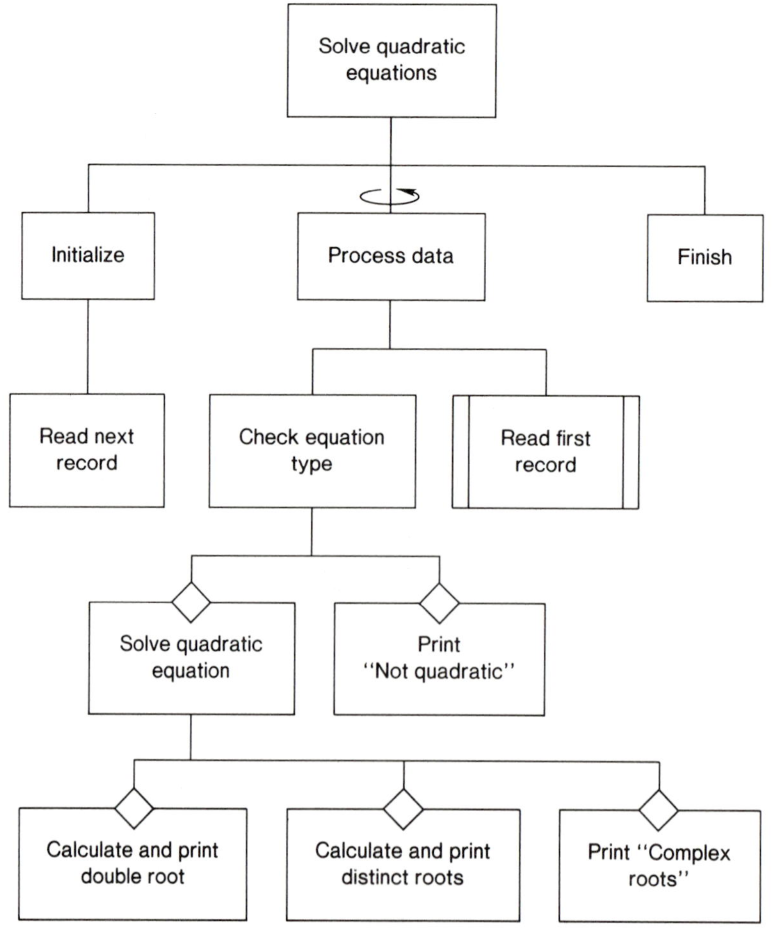

Figure 2–15

2.5 Summary

PL/I is a high-level, procedural, modular, strongly typed, block-structured language. Three character sets are available: ANSI, 60-character, and 48-character. The 60-character set is the most common. PL/I is a highly structured language with well-designed sequence, selection, and repetition structures. It is a comprehensive language that can be used for business, science, text processing, and other applications.

Programs are more easily read and maintained if they are well designed and well documented. Decision tables, hierarchy charts, and flowcharts are tools for the design and development of algorithms. They are language-independent, but programs can be implemented from them. They also serve as part of the documentation needed for every program. Top-down design proceeds in steps from a very general description of the algorithm to increasing levels of detail. The hierarchy chart most clearly reflects this progression. Flowcharts clarify the flow of control through the modules. Decision tables display the details of complex logical situations. These are complementary diagrams which provide different views of the same situation.

2.6 Exercises

1. Draw a hierarchy chart and a flowchart for an algorithm that computes the moment of inertia of a rectangle around its axis. The formula for moment of inertia is

$$I = bd^3 / 12$$

where b is the breadth and d is the depth of the rectangle. The algorithm should compute I for many sets of values of b and d.

2. Assume that a car salesman sells four different models of cars, M_1, M_2, M_3, and M_4, which are priced at P_1, P_2, P_3, and P_4, respectively. During one month he sells N_1 cars of model M_1, N_2 cars of model M_2, and so forth. Draw a hierarchy chart and a flowchart for an algorithm that calculates the total number of cars sold during the month, the total amount of money involved, and the salesman's commission at 6 percent.

3. The *modulo 11 check digit* method is a common way of checking an ID number or account number for accuracy (the numbers must have been especially selected for this method to work). Multiply the first digit by one, the second digit by two, the third digit by three, and so forth. Add the results of the multiplications. If the total is evenly divisible by eleven, the number is accurate. Draw a flowchart for an algorithm to check the accuracy of a number by this method.

4. Let a, b, and c represent three numbers. A certain computer-controlled machine will cut pieces of metal in a, b, and c lengths if they can be used to form a triangle. Use a decision table to express an algorithm that determines whether these numbers can be used as the lengths of sides of a triangle. Express the same thing with a flowchart.

5. Student records are being entered into a computer. For each student, an ID number, the student's name, age, address, and telephone number are being entered. Each item entered must be validated to make sure that it is alphabetic, numeric, or alphanumeric, whichever is appropriate. Also, the numbers entered must all be positive and have the right numbers of digits. None of the information can be missing. Use a decision table to show how the data validation would be done and what error messages would be appropriate.

6. Numbers being entered from a terminal are to be added and both the numbers and their sum are to be printed on a line printer. Draw a flowchart for the algorithm if the end of the input is indicated by CTL/Z. Do the same if the last number is supposed to be zero (but it may be missing). Give the decision tables for these.

3
Data declarations and manipulation

OBJECTIVE: To tell the computer how to process data.

IN THIS CHAPTER THE basics of the PL/I program and the types of PL/I instructions needed to manipulate data are introduced. At the lowest level, data consist of numbers and character strings. The basic data types of PL/I are numbers, logical values, and strings, including character strings. The primary operations in the manipulation of data are the arithmetic and logic operations. (Manipulation of character data will be discussed in chapter 6.) All the ordinary mathematical operations are available in PL/I, some using the symbols introduced in chapter 2, and some using procedures available in the PL/I library. String manipulations are carried out using library routines. The basic arithmetic instructions are addition, subtraction, multiplication, division, and exponentiation. As we have seen, these do not always use the ordinary, everyday symbols. The logic instructions use Boolean operations and comparisons.

3.1 Structure of a PL/I program

PL/I is a procedural language. A *procedure* is a program module that itself has the form of a program. There are *external procedures* (procedures that are compiled separately and are known by name to the operating system) and *internal procedures* (procedures that are compiled together). The *main procedure,* where the execution starts, is an external procedure. It should have the following structure:

```
label: PROCEDURE OPTIONS(MAIN);
declarations of data needed
definitions of exception handlers
body of the procedure
END label;
```

The parts of the structure shown in capital letters are keywords, required in every main procedure. The parts shown in lowercase are to be provided by the programmer. We will follow this convention throughout the book. In simple examples of main procedures such as

```
TRIAREA: PROCEDURE OPTIONS(MAIN);
DECLARE (AREA,BASE,HEIGHT) FLOAT BINARY;
GET LIST (BASE,HEIGHT);
AREA = .5*BASE*HEIGHT;
PUT LIST ('AREA=',AREA);
END TRIAREA;
```

and

```
HYPOT: PROC OPTIONS(MAIN);
DECLARE (A,B,C) FLOAT BINARY;
GET LIST (A,B);
C = SQRT (A*A+B*B);
PUT LIST ('HYPOTENUSE=',C);
END HYPOT;
```

some of the words are the same in both since they are required. Others are selected by the programmer for use as data names. The programmer may call the data anything that is appropriate for the application, in this case, the standard letters and names used in geometry.

Everything in a program should have a name, including the procedures that make up the program. The first statement of a procedure is called the *header.* Its label provides a name by which the procedure is known. The selection of this name follows rules explained in section 3.2. The label must be followed by a colon (:), which identifies it to the compiler as a label. PROCEDURE (abbreviated PROC) is a keyword that explains what type of object is to follow. The attribute OPTIONS(MAIN) identifies the procedure as a main procedure. Since the entire header is a statement in the PL/I language, it must be followed by a semicolon (;).

At the end of the procedure there must be an END statement. Although PL/I does not require it, we will always use the name of the procedure in the END statement. This helps make the procedure readable. Since end statements are used to mark the ends of other structures besides procedures, using the label to show that this is the end of the procedure rather than the end of some other structure avoids confusion.

Although in many situations the declaration of data is not needed or required in PL/I, we will consider it mandatory in well-written programs. The DECLARE statement (abbreviated DCL) provides names for the data, specifies the type of data being used, and provides information needed to reserve space in memory to store the data values. Declarations can be placed anywhere in the program between the PROCEDURE statement and the matching END statement; however, we will always place them immediately after the procedure header, before the body of the procedure, so that they are available for quick reference.

PROGRAMMING HINT: MODULARITY Explicitly declare all variables.

Besides data declarations, procedures usually contain definitions of small nameless internal procedures which are invoked under unusual circumstances. These are known as *exception handlers*. They are used to print error messages or to send signals to the main procedure when normal processing fails. This can occur when a program tries to read data when none is available, or tries to divide by zero.

The *body of the procedure* is made up of executable instructions, which are needed to solve the problem. These are the arithmetic instructions, input/output instructions, and control instructions implementing the flowchart of the problem-solving algorithm. Comments may be included at any place in a procedure.

Review questions

1. What do the parts of the header of a PL/I program mean?

2. Why is it a good idea to place the declarations ahead of the executable statements even though PL/I does not require that?

3. What are exception handlers?

4. Why is it a good idea to use the name of a procedure in the END statement for the procedure?

5. The abbreviation for PROCEDURE is ________________.

6. The abbreviation for DECLARE is ________________.

3.2 Identifiers

Identifiers are the symbolic names given by the system or the programmer to data, formats, and procedures. There are specific rules for the construction of user-defined identifiers.

3.2.1 External names and labels

An *external identifier* provides access to procedures or data from outside the program. It is used by the operating system or by other programs. The standard rules for construction of external identifiers are as follows:

1. A maximum of seven characters is permitted.
2. The first character can be only A through Z or $.
3. For the remaining characters, only A through Z, 0 through 9, and $ may be used.
4. No embedded blanks or break characters are allowed.

For example:

Valid names	*Invalid names*
PROJ1B	1B
PROBLEM5	PROB_5
SHELSRT	SHELLSORT
INFOR5A	#5A
MP	MAIN PROGRAM

3.2.2 Internal names

Internal names are used for internal procedures, data, entry points and formats. They can only be referenced inside the program module where they are declared. The standard rules for their construction are as follows:

1. A maximum of thirty-one characters is permitted.
2. The first character must be A through Z, $, #, or @.
3. For the remaining characters, only A through Z, 0 through 9, $, #, @, and the break character may be used.
4. The break character must be between two other characters; no embedded blanks are allowed.

For example:

Valid names	*Invalid names*
BANK_BALANCE	BANK BALANCE
AMOUNT_OF_DEPOSIT	AMOUNT_DEPOSIT
STATE_TAX	STATE_TAX_ON_GROSS_RECEIPTS_FROM_BUSINESS
STELLAR_VELOCITY	15.CC3P7
@CHANGE	%CHANGE

3.2.3 Selection of names

The data names selected by the programmer must be unique (except in particular complex circumstances to be discussed in chapters 9 and 11). It would be confusing if the same name were given to different elements of the same program. Names should be descriptive of the quantities or situations they represent. If common formulas are being used, it makes sense to use the same names in the PL/I program that are commonly used in the formulas. Selecting good names is an art that is developed with experience.

PROGRAMMING HINT: STYLE **Use meaningful names.**

Using names that are meaningful and descriptive helps to document the program, making it easier to understand. This is accomplished by using the break character (_) where a blank or hyphen, both illegal in names, would ordinarily be used. The difference between names that are simply valid and names that are meaningful is shown in the following examples.

Quantity	*Valid name*	*Meaningful name*
State tax	ST	STATE_TAX
Bank balance	REM	BANK_BALANCE
Grade point average	AVG	GPA
Store number 5	ST5	STORE_NUM_5
Present interest	PI	CURRENT_INTEREST

Review questions

1. The symbolic names given to data, remote formats, and procedures are called ____________________.

2. An identifier must be external if it is to be used ____________________.

3. An external name has a maximum of __________ characters while an internal name has a maximum of __________ characters.

4. An internal name can have the symbols __________, __________, and __________, which cannot be used in external names.

5. Which of the following are valid external or internal names?

NASA150	SHELL SORT
COST_IN_$	$_PER_DOZEN
MAXIMUMVAL	PROCEDURE
$VALUE	AN5VA1
MAX_VAL	TOP.RATE
FLOW_	BASE_QUANTITY
7O'CLOCK	BANK_DEPOSIT
@COST	COST_OF_MATERIAL

6. Which name of each pair is better? Why?

ACCT or ACCT_NUM
INT or INTEREST
LIST_OF_NAMES or LIST
QRT or QT

3.3 Declarations

A *declaration* statement is used to specify the attributes of the data and the storage space needed for values. There are many different possible attributes. The declaration statement has the general form

```
DECLARE data-name attributes;
```

or

```
DCL data-name attributes;
```

The full set of possible attributes is given in Appendix B.

3.3.1 Numeric data

The type attributes of numeric data are classified as mode, scale, and base; the storage space needed is specified by the precision. Both constants and variables can be declared. *Constants* are data objects that have a single value throughout a program. They are usually given as literals, but, when appropriate, can be named and declared like variables. *Variables* are data objects that have different values at different times.

The four basic types of numeric data in PL/I are fixed decimal, float decimal, fixed binary, and float binary. These may be declared in either the real or the complex mode. The attributes and their options are:

Attribute	*Options*
Mode	REAL/COMPLEX
Scale	FIXED/FLOAT
Base	DECIMAL/BINARY

Any combination of these options may be used. Those that are selected depend on the types of values being stored.

CONSTANTS

Fixed-decimal constants All ordinary numbers used for calculations, such as 15, −37.6, and +.02, are stored as fixed-decimal constants. If there is a decimal point, the constant is further classified as real; if there is no decimal point, it is an integer. Both real numbers and integer numbers have the mode

REAL. Some examples of fixed-decimal constants are:

Integer constant	*Real constant*
685	483.754
−750	−304.76
75	0.0765
+1032	+580.
0	0.0

Float-decimal constants Float-decimal constants are usually numbers that are too large or too small to be represented in anything other than scientific notation. However, any real constant can be written as a float-decimal constant. To be float decimal, a constant must have a decimal point and an exponent. The number 385.645 can be represented as a float-decimal constant by any of the following:

0.385645E03
3.85645E02
38.5645E01
385.645E00
3856.45E-01
38564.5E-02

Internally, float-decimal numbers are stored in a different form from fixed-decimal numbers. Of the two, the internal representation of fixed-decimal numbers is the more accurate. However, numbers that are very large or very close to zero cannot be stored as fixed-decimal numbers. For business applications, fixed decimal is usually used. For scientific applications, float decimal is used.

To convert a float-decimal number to its equivalent fixed-decimal number, if the exponent is positive, the decimal point is shifted to the right by the number of places equal to the exponent. If the exponent is negative, the decimal point is shifted to the left by the number of places equal to the exponent. This can be seen in the following examples.

Exponential form	*Nonexponential form*	*Comment*
0.2854E02	28.54	Right shift
38.654E01	386.54	Right shift
145.423-02	1.4542	Left shift
86.32E-04	.008632	Left shift
.654E05	65400.0	Right shift
−1.32E00	−1.32	No shift

Fixed-binary constants Fixed-binary constants are the binary equivalent of decimal numbers. They are real if they have a binary point, integer if they do not. The following are examples of fixed-binary constants and their decimal equivalents.

Fixed-binary integer	*Decimal*	*Fixed-binary real*	*Decimal*
1111011B	123	11101.00B	29.0
1101011B	107	110011.101B	51.625
010101B	21	0.1011B	.6875

Binary/decimal equivalents up through 256 are shown in Appendix A. This type of constant is the closest to the actual internal representation of numbers. These numbers are handled efficiently by the computer but are very rarely used as constants in programs, because they are not very readable.

Float-binary constants The float-binary representation is not often used for constants and is included here only for completeness. It is an exponential form having a binary number as the mantissa, but a decimal number as the exponent. The exponent represents a power of two. Some float-binary constants and their fixed-binary and decimal equivalents are:

Float-binary	*Fixed-binary*	*Decimal*
0.1101E01B	1.101B	1.625
11.101E-01B	1.1101B	1.8125
1.11011E02B	111.011B	7.375

NUMERIC VARIABLES

The general form of a declaration for numeric variables is

```
DECLARE variable mode scale base precision;
```

or

```
DCL variable mode scale base precision;
```

The attributes are customarily written in this order, but any order is acceptable to the computer. Attribute declarations are optional.

Mode There are two modes, COMPLEX and REAL. COMPLEX mode is used if the values stored in the variable are complex numbers such as

$3.8 + 6.5i$
$64 + 72i$
$-129 + 13i$

Complex numbers are used only in specialized scientific applications. The variable X might be declared to be complex by

```
DCL X COMPLEX;
```

REAL mode is used for all other numbers, both real and integer. If the mode is not specified, the compiler assumes that a numeric variable is REAL. REAL is the default value for the mode attribute. The variable X might be declared to be real by

```
DCL X;
```

or

```
DCL X REAL;
```

Scale The scale attribute specifies either fixed or float. FIXED is used if the values stored in the variable are fixed-point real or integer numbers. The location of the point in the numeric value is known in advance for fixed-point numbers. The scale attribute is FLOAT if the values to be stored are floating-point numbers. FLOAT simply means that the numbers are to be stored in exponential form and that the position of the point, rather than being known in advance, is determined from the exponent. If X is to be declared a fixed-point number and Y is to be a floating-point number, their declarations might be

```
DCL X FIXED;
```

and

```
DCL Y FLOAT;
```

Both of these have REAL mode.

Base There are two types of bases, DECIMAL (abbreviated DEC) and BINARY (abbreviated BIN). When the base is DECIMAL and the scale is FIXED, the value is stored as a decimal number, with each decimal digit represented separately in internal storage. When the base is BINARY and the scale is FIXED, the value is stored as a binary number. FLOAT DECIMAL is a misleading combination of attributes, because a FLOAT DECIMAL number and a FLOAT BINARY number are both stored as float binary in many computers. For the programmer, however, FLOAT DECIMAL is easier to work with than FLOAT BINARY, because the precision attribute and the constants are in a convenient form. Adding the base attribute to our declarations we have the combinations

```
DCL X FIXED BINARY;
DCL Y FIXED DECIMAL;
DCL A FLOAT BINARY;
DCL B FLOAT DECIMAL;
```

The default values for base and scale depend on the first letter of the name of the variable. If the first letter of the name is A through H, O through Z, or any of the special characters $, #, or @, the compiler assigns the attributes FLOAT DECIMAL to the variable. If the first letter of the name is I through N, the compiler assigns FIXED BINARY to the variable. If a variable is not declared, the compiler uses these default rules to assign a type to it. The rules of structured programming require that variables be explicitly declared.

Precision The precision attribute specifies the amount of space needed to store the number by indicating the total number of digits the number will contain, and the number of digits to the right of the point, if any. Precision is meaningless unless the scale and base of the number are known. The precision of a decimal number specifies the number of decimal digits; the precision of a binary number specifies the number of binary digits.

The precision attribute is written (w, d) where w is the field width (the total number of digits) and d is the number of digits to the right of the decimal or binary point. If the number is a decimal or binary integer, the precision can be given either as (w) or as (w, 0). The relationship between the precision of the variable and the form of the number stored is shown as follows:

Precision	*Form*
(5, 2)	xxx.xx
(8, 3)	xxxxx.xxx
(4, 0)	xxxx
(4)	xxxx
(3, 3)	.xxx
(4, 3)	x.xxx

The point is not actually stored, but it would appear as shown if the number were printed.

The precision of a variable does not have to fit the value of the number stored in it exactly. It tells the computer how much space to allocate and where to align the point. When a number is stored, extra space is filled with zeros. If the number is too large, it is made to fit by truncating digits. The actual storage for decimal numbers is as follows:

Number	*Precision*	*Storage*	*Comment*
385.65	(5, 2)	385 65	Exact specification
"	(6, 2)	0385 65	Overspecification
"	(6, 3)	385 650	Overspecification
"	(4, 2)	85 65	Loss of significance
"	(4, 1)	385 6	Truncation of fraction
"	(3, 0)	385	Conversion to integer
4856	(4, 0)	4856	
"	(4)	4856	
"	(5, 0)	04856	
"	(5)	04856	
"	(5, 1)	4856 0	
"	(3, 0)	856	Loss of Significance
"	(3)	856	Loss of Significance

The precision must always be specified carefully to avoid loss of significance when the high-order digits are truncated. The computer considers this an error and stops the processing. If the precision attribute is not declared, the default precisions are usually (5, 0) for fixed decimal variables and (15, 0) for fixed binary variables.

To avoid errors in a program, it is usually advisable to adopt a standard precision for the numbers. For business applications in which fixed-decimal numbers are used, the size of the values anticipated in the application will determine the precision. With fixed-binary numbers two standard sizes are used. The smaller permits numbers to fit exactly into two bytes (a half-word) of computer memory. The larger uses four bytes (an entire word) of memory. These precisions are hardware-dependent. On a machine that has a 32-bit word, a common size, the standard binary precisions are (15) and (31). Each of these leaves one bit of storage for use as the sign of the number.

The precision of fixed-binary numbers is specified as follows:

Precision	*Storage*	*Comment*
(15)	xxxxxxxxxxxxxxx	15 binary digits
(31)	xxxxxxxxxxxxxxxxxxxxxxxxxxxxxxx	31 binary digits
(15, 3)	xxxxxxxxxxxx xxx	15 binary digits
(31, 4)	xxxxxxxxxxxxxxxxxxxxxxxxxxx xxxx	31 binary digits

Following are some examples of fixed-decimal and fixed-binary declarations.

```
DECLARE VALUE FIXED DECIMAL (6,2);
```

A decimal number in the range −9999.99 through 9999.99 can be stored in the variable VALUE.

```
DECLARE VAR FIXED DECIMAL (6,0);
```

A decimal number in the range −999999 through 999999 can be stored in the variable VAR.

```
DECLARE INTEREST FIXED DECIMAL (2,2);
```

A decimal number in the range of −.99 through .99 can be stored in the variable INTEREST.

```
DECLARE INTR FIXED BINARY (15);
```

A binary number in the range of −111111111111111B through +111111111111111B can be stored in the variable INTR. This has the same value as a decimal number in the range −32767 through 32767.

```
DECLARE JMAX FIXED BIN (31);
```

A binary number with a value in the decimal range between -2^{31} and $+2^{31}$ can be stored in the variable JMAX.

Floating-point numbers Very large numbers and numbers very close to zero can best be stored as floating-point numbers. With these numbers, the field width of the precision specification gives the number of significant digits in the number. The exponent of the value controls where the point is with respect to the significant digits. Therefore the field width is the only value in the specification. A precision of (w) indicates that a number with w significant digits, written in scientific notation, can be stored in the variable.

```
DECLARE RATE FLOAT DECIMAL (6);
```

The number stored in the variable RATE has six significant decimal digits. Any of the values shown below can be stored in RATE.

Normal form	*Exponential form*
38.6547	.386547E02
.000125436	.125436E-03
837253000	.837253E09
−2.43564	−.243564E01

The default precision is (6) for FLOAT DECIMAL variables. The range of possible positive values for all FLOAT DECIMAL variables is the same, approximately 10^{-78} to 10^{78} depending on the implementation.

With FLOAT BINARY numbers, the precision specifies the number of significant binary digits. In

```
DCL BVAL FLOAT BIN (10);
```

BVAL has ten significant binary digits. It can hold any of the values shown below:

Normal form	*Exponential form*
1011101011.00B	.1011101011E10B
0.01110110101B	.1110110101E-01B
.0001111111111B	.1111111111E-03B
1010000001000B	.1010000001E13B

The default precision for FLOAT BIN numbers is (21) depending on the implementation. Positive values will be in the range of 2^{-260} to 2^{260}. This is equivalent to the default precision and range of values for floating-point decimal numbers.

Default specifications Any of the numeric data attributes may be omittted and the default values used, except that if precision is specified, then scale or

Table 3–1

Declared type	*Default specification*
FIXED DECIMAL	(5, 0)
FLOAT DECIMAL	(6)
FIXED BINARY	(15, 0)
FLOAT BINARY	(21)
DECIMAL	FLOAT(6)
BINARY	FLOAT(21)
FIXED	DECIMAL(5, 0)
FLOAT	DECIMAL (6)
Undeclared	
name starts with	
A-H	FLOAT DECIMAL(6)
I-N	FIXED BINARY(15)
O-Z	FLOAT DECIMAL(6)
@, #, $	FLOAT DECIMAL(6)

base, or both, must also be specified. The meaning of the precision depends on the scale and base of the variable. The default values used for the numeric attributes on a 32-bit machine are shown in table 3–1.

Every numeric variable has mode, scale, base, and precision. If the programmer does not specify all of these attributes explicitly, the compiler uses the default values for the attributes that are not declared. The default value of mode is REAL. Complex variables must be specifically declared. If the programmer specifies only FIXED, then the compiler assumes a default base of DECIMAL and default precision of (5, 0). The entire set of attributes is FIXED DECIMAL (5, 0). Default mode and precision should be used with BINARY variables, but scale and base should be explicitly declared. With DECIMAL variables, precision, scale, and base should all be explicitly declared. In any case, the programmer must be aware of the range of potential values to be stored and leave sufficient space for them.

The most common uses of these various specifications are:

FIXED DECIMAL	Business data, particularly dollars and cents
FIXED BINARY	Indices, counters, other internal data
FLOAT BINARY	Scientific applications, measurements
FLOAT DECIMAL	Occasional business or scientific applications when significance must be controlled

Fixed-point numbers are always more accurate and more efficient than floating-point numbers. Floating-point numbers are useful when the size of the values cannot be foreseen, when the values are very large or very close to zero, or when the values are inexact to begin with. Binary numbers are handled more efficiently than decimal numbers. As we will see in the next section, ordinary decimal values can be stored in all four types of variables. The computer automatically converts the value to the correct storage representation.

Initialization If it is appropriate to name a constant, it can be declared as though it were a variable and given its value in the declaration. The general form for initializing a constant is

```
DECLARE name type INITIAL (value);
```

Only under rare circumstances should a true variable be given a value in a declaration.

PROGRAMMING HINT: MAINTENANCE Do not initialize variables in declarations.

A variable differs from a constant in that the value of a variable is intended to be different at different times during program execution while the value of a constant remains unchanged. To give a value to a variable in a declaration would be misleading. The declaration of a variable should only establish storage space and provide a description of the form of representation of values to be stored there. The space is not empty, but it does not contain anything of use to the programmer. Often some kind of background pattern is used to fill all the declared storage space. Until a value has been stored, the variable is said to be *undefined.* Actually storing a numeric value can be done in one of four ways: the compiler can put the value in (*initialization*), the value can be read in as input under program control, the value can be moved from some other storage location, or the value can be the result of a calculation.

Constants (and variables) can be initialized by using the INITIAL option of the declaration. This tells the compiler to store a value in the space that has been set aside. The keyword INITIAL (abbreviated INIT) is used to introduce the value, as shown in the following examples.

```
DECLARE RATE     FIXED DECIMAL (5,2) INIT (.16);
DECLARE PI       FLOAT BINARY        INIT (3.14159);
DECLARE DOZEN    FIXED BINARY        INIT (12);
DECLARE INACTIVE FIXED BINARY        INIT (1111111B);
```

The value provided for initialization need not match the type specified. When necessary, the compiler converts the initialization value to the proper form. The decimal value .16 is stored in RATE by the compiler. The decimal value 3.14159 is converted to FLOAT BINARY and stored in PI. The decimal value 12 is converted to FIXED BINARY and stored in DOZEN. Fixed-binary variables may be initialized using either decimal or binary constants. Values stored in the variables by using the INITIAL attribute may have signs and decimal points. Their size must be appropriate for the precision used.

The decimal point given in the INIT clause is not actually stored. A sign is stored with each value, whether or not one is given. An unsigned number is stored as positive. Note that the precision does not include space for the sign; extra space for it is always available.

If the value given does not fit, the compiler truncates digits at the left or right, or pads with zeros at the left or right, until the value has the correct form. This truncation and padding is shown in the following examples:

Declaration	*Storage*	*Comment*
DCL X FIXED DEC(6, 2) INIT (1234.56);	1234 56	Exact fit
DCL Y FIXED DEC(5, 2) INIT (1234.56);	234 56	Truncated (error)
DCL Z FIXED DEC(7, 2) INIT (1234.56);	01234 56	Padded
DCL V FIXED DEC(5, 1) INIT (1234.56);	1234 5	Truncated
DCL W FIXED DEC(7, 3) INIT (1234.56);	1234 560	Padded

When several variables have the same attributes of scale, base, and precision, they can be *factored.* If they are to be initialized to the same value, that can be factored too. For example:

```
DCL (X,Y,Z)                FLOAT BINARY;
DCL (AMOUNT,BALANCE)       FIXED DECIMAL (8,2);
DCL (A_CNT,B_CNT,C_CNT)    FIXED BINARY(15) INIT (0);
```

The parentheses group the variables that have the same declaration. X, Y, and Z are all float-binary variables of default precision. AMOUNT and BALANCE are both fixed-decimal variables having eight digits, two of them to the right of the decimal point. A_CNT, B_CNT, and C_CNT are all fixed-binary variables with the initial value of zero.

If some but not all of the attributes are to be the same, as in the following,

```
DCL (VAL1    INIT (10),
     VAL2    INIT (25),
     VAL3    INIT (4))        FIXED DEC (2,0);

DCL (TOTAL   FIXED DEC(6,2),
     CNT     FIXED BIN)       INIT (0);

DCL (((X     FLOAT,
       K     FIXED) BINARY),
       SIZE FIXED  DEC(4) ) INIT (10);
```

the attributes themselves are factored. VAL1, VAL2, VAL3 have different initial values, but the same scale and base. TOTAL and CNT are of different types, but are initialized to the same value. X and K are both binary and all three, X, K, and SIZE, are initialized to ten. It can be seen from these complicated examples that factoring the attributes makes the declarations difficult to read, even with careful alignment of parallel constructs. The programmer should always try to make the program readable. For this reason it is often best not to factor attributes. The last example, above, would be more readable written as

```
DCL X    FLOAT BINARY INIT (10),
    K    FIXED BINARY INIT (10),
    SIZE FIXED DEC(4) INIT (10);
```

Here all three variables are being included in a single declaration. They are separated by commas, and the declaration ends with a semicolon. It is appropriate to group variables in a single declaration when they represent similar types of things. For example, a business program calculating mortgage payments might have several different values, which are calculated and then summed. The declarations could be grouped as

```
DCL AMOUNT     FIXED DEC (8,2),
    INTEREST   FIXED DEC (8,2),
    TAXES      FIXED DEC (6,2),
    PRINCIPAL  FIXED DEC (8,2);
DCL TOT_AMT    FIXED DEC (10,2),
    TOT_INT    FIXED DEC (10,2),
    TOT_TAX    FIXED DEC (8,2);
DCL NEW_PRINC  FIXED DEC (8,2);
```

PROGRAMMING HINT: STYLE Group variables according to use.

3.3.2 String data

PL/I has two string data types: character strings and bit strings. A character string is composed of characters from the PL/I character set. A bit string resembles binary numbers in that it is composed only of the binary digits zero and one. However, it is a distinct data type, and is not used for arithmetic.

DECLARATIONS OF CHARACTER DATA

Character string constants are written with single quotation marks.

Character constants	*Comment*
'ABC'	An alphabetic character constant
'12307'	Not numeric data (treated as characters)
'$#%*/|'	Any characters are allowed
'ƀƀƀƀ'	Four blanks
'IT''S'	A quotation mark is quoted by repeating it

Character string variables are declared using the keyword CHARACTER (abbreviated CHAR). Since character strings may contain as many as 32,767 characters, depending on the computer system, the anticipated length of the value of the variable must be declared. The following example,

```
DECLARE STRN CHARACTER (10);
```

sets aside ten locations (bytes) for the variable STRN.

STRN

If the value contains exactly ten characters, it will just fill the storage space. If its length is less than ten characters, blanks are added at the right end to pad it to ten. If the length is greater than ten characters, the least significant characters, those at the right end, are truncated. This can be seen in the following example:

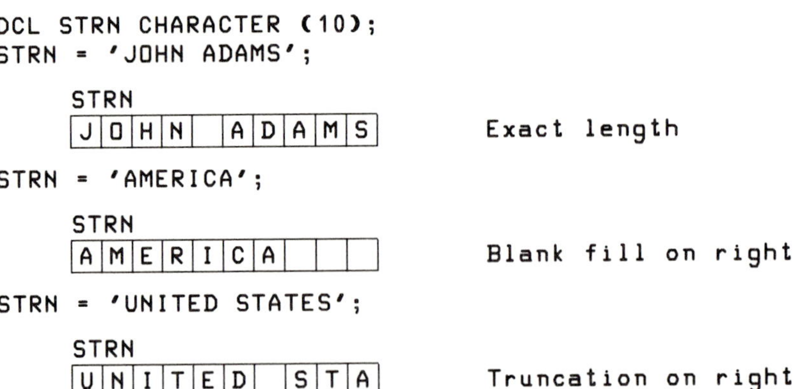

In the first of these assignments, the length specified for the character variable is exactly the same as the length of the character constant. In the second, the variable has more storage allocated to it than is needed for the constant, so the value is *left-justified* (aligned at the left end and padded with blanks on the right). The third declaration sets aside too little space. Again the value is left-justified, but the right end has to be truncated, and the characters that do not fit are lost.

At times character values of different lengths are to be stored in the same variable, but the trailing blanks provided by the padding are not wanted. The VARYING (abbreviated VAR) attribute allows this type of storage. If a variable is declared with the maximum storage needed, character strings of any shorter length may be stored in it without padding.

```
DCL STRN CHARACTER (15) VARYING;
STRN = 'JOHN ADAMS';

    STRN
    |J|O|H|N| |A|D|A|M|S|/|/|/|/|/|        Length is 10

STRN = 'AMERICA';

    STRN
    |A|M|E|R|I|C|A|/|/|/|/|/|/|/|/|        Length is 7

STRN = 'UNITED STATES';

    STRN
    |U|N|I|T|E|D| |S|T|A|T|E|S|/|/|        Length is 13

STRN = '';

    STRN
    |/|/|/|/|/|/|/|/|/|/|/|/|/|/|/|        Length is 0
```

A storage area of length 15 is allocated for the variable, but only the number of positions needed are used. The character value is left-justified in the storage area. The unused part of the storage is not accessible. Notice that a null character string having length zero may be stored.

Character variables are used primarily to hold nonnumeric data. They are also used for strings of digits that are not intended to be computed, such as account numbers and dates.

DECLARATION OF BIT DATA

Bit string constants are strings of zeros and ones written with single quotation marks and the letter B.

Bit constants

'0'B
'1'B
'1010'B
'001111'B

The declaration of bit string variables is similar to that of character strings. The amount of storage needed is specified and the value is left-justified with the right end padded or truncated as needed. Since only bit values, binary zeros and ones, can be stored, the padding consists of zeros.

```
DECLARE MAXIM BIT(5);
```

Here the keyword BIT indicates the variable type and the (5) specifies the number of bit locations allocated to the variable MAXIM. The storage for the declaration is

```
MAXIM
| | | | | |          5 binary (0 or 1) bits can be stored
```

When a bit value is stored, if the declared length of the bit string is the same as the length of the bit value, the value will occupy the entire storage location. If the declared length of the bit string is longer than the length of the constant, the extra positions are filled with zeros. If the declared length is shorter than the length of the constant, truncation occurs on the right and the extra bits are lost. This can be seen in the following examples:

```
DECLARE BSTRN BIT(10);

BSTRN = '0111011101'B;

BSTRN
|0|1|1|1|0|1|1|1|0|1|     Exact length

BSTRN = '10011011'B;

BSTRN
|1|0|0|1|1|0|1|1|0|0|     Zero fill on right

BSTRN = '1100111011011'B;

BSTRN
|1|1|0|0|1|1|1|0|1|1|     Truncation of 011 on right
```

Bit strings may be declared with the VARYING attribute. When this is done, the value is left-justified in the storage and any unused bit positions are inaccessible.

```
DECLARE BSTRN BIT(10) VARYING;

BSTRN = '0111011101'B;

BSTRN
|0|1|1|1|0|1|1|1|0|1|     Length is 10

BSTRN = '10011011'B;

BSTRN
|1|0|0|1|1|0|1|1|/|/|     Length is 8

BSTRN = '11'B;

BSTRN
|1|1|/|/|/|/|/|/|/|/|     Length is 2
```

Bit strings are most commonly used to store flags and switches; that is, to keep track of the condition of the data or the status of the processing. For example:

```
DECLARE MORE_DATA BIT(1);
DECLARE TRUE      BIT(1) INIT('1'B);
DECLARE FALSE     BIT(1) INIT('0'B);
```

Initialization of strings A character constant can be stored in the space set aside for a character variable by using the INITIAL attribute. For example:

```
DECLARE STRN CHARACTER (10) INIT ('HEADING');
```

STRN

H	E	A	D	I	N	G			

```
DECLARE STRN CHARACTER (10) INIT ('FIRST SECTION');
```

STRN

F	I	R	S	T		S	E	C	T

The value is left-justified with truncation or padding on the right as needed. Blank fill is used.

The initialization of bit strings is similar. The bit value is stored left-justified with truncation or padding on the right. Zero fill padding is used, as in the following example:

```
DECLARE BSTRN BIT(10) INIT ('11011101'B);
```

BSTRN

1	1	0	1	1	1	0	1	0	0

Repetition factor If some of the characters or bits in a string constant are to be repeated, rather than writing them out in full, a *repetition factor* may be used. The following are equivalent strings.

```
STRN = 'XXXXXXX';
STRN = (7)'X';              7 is the repetition factor

RSTN = 'XYXYXYXY';
RSTN = (4)'XY';             4 is the repetition factor

BSTRN = '10101010'B;
BSTRN = (4)'10'B;           4 is the repetition factor
```

The string constant after the repetition factor occurs the number of times specified by the repetition factor. Repetition factors may be used in assignments or in the initialization of variables.

```
DECLARE STRN    CHAR(7) INIT ((7)'X');
DECLARE RSTN    CHAR(8) INIT ((4)'XY');
DECLARE ABSTRN BIT(8)   INIT ((4)'10'B);
```

All of these strings used for initialization fit exactly.

Review questions

1. A declaration tells the compiler the ____________ and ____________ for the values to be stored.

2. What is the difference in the values being stored for a REAL and a COMPLEX variable?

3. What is the difference in the representation of the values being stored for a FIXED and a FLOAT variable?

4. What is the difference in the representation of the values being stored for a BINARY and a DECIMAL variable?

5. The precision attribute is used to indicate ____________ and ____________.

6. What are the default attributes for a numeric constant such as 25?

7. Are the constants 1, '1', 1B, and '1'B the same to the computer?

8. What are the default attributes for a numeric variable declared as DCL X? Declared as DCL K?

9. Show how the value 1234.5678 would be stored using each of the following declarations. (If the computer would detect an error, indicate that.)
   (a) FIXED DECIMAL (4, 0)
   (b) FIXED DECIMAL (4, 1)
   (c) FIXED DECIMAL (6, 2)
   (d) FIXED DECIMAL (6, 3)
   (e) FIXED DECIMAL (7, 3)
   (f) FIXED DECIMAL (8, 4)
   (g) FIXED DECIMAL (9, 5)

10. Give the smallest value and the largest value that may be stored in each of the following.
    (a) FIXED DECIMAL (4, 2)
    (b) FIXED BINARY (8)
    (c) FLOAT DECIMAL (3)
    (d) FLOAT BINARY (5)

11. Does the precision of a FIXED BINARY number include space for a sign? A FIXED DECIMAL number?

12. Does the precision of a FIXED BINARY number include space for a point? A FIXED DECIMAL number?

13. FIXED BINARY numbers are sometimes better than FIXED DECIMAL numbers. Why?

14. FIXED DECIMAL numbers are sometimes better than FIXED BINARY numbers. Why?

15. FLOAT numbers are sometimes better than FIXED numbers. Why?

16. FIXED numbers are sometimes better than FLOAT numbers. Why?

17. Give an appropriate declaration for an interest rate of 7.5 percent.

18. Give an appropriate declaration for the gravitational acceleration of 9.8 meters / $sec.^2$

19. Give an appropriate declaration for the number 100.

20. Give an appropriate declaration for your telephone number.

21. Show how the character value 'ABCDEFG' would be stored using each of the following declarations.
(a) CHAR(10)
(b) CHAR(5)
(c) CHAR(10) VARYING

22. What value would be stored by each of the following declarations?
(a) DCL STRNG CHAR(10) INIT('HEADING');
(b) DCL STR CHAR(10) INIT((5)'AX');
(c) DCL (STR1,STR2) CHAR (10) INIT ((5)'AX');
(d) DCL (STR1,STR2) CHAR(10) INIT((2)'AX');

3.4 Arithmetic operations and expressions

Arithmetic operations in PL/I can be performed only on numeric values. However, the internal representation may be of any type. The result of an arithmetic operation is a number of a type dependent on the types of the operands.

3.4.1 Arithmetic operators

The five arithmetic operations are addition, subtraction, multiplication, division, and exponentiation. Their symbols are:

Arithmetic operation	*PL/I symbol*	*Comment*
Addition	+	Used in ordinary arithmetic
Subtraction	−	Used in ordinary arithmetic
Multiplication	*	Different from ordinary use
Division	/	Used in ordinary arithmetic
Exponentiation	**	Different from ordinary use

The following examples show the use of these binary operators.

Arithmetic operation	*Ordinary arithmetic*	*PL/I*
Addition	$a + b$	A+B
	$5 + x$	5+X
Subtraction	$a - b$	A–B
Multiplication	$a \times b$	A*B
	$a \cdot b$	A*B
	$3X$	3*X
Division	$\frac{a}{b}$	A/B
	$x \div y$	X/Y
	$1/2$	1/2
Exponentiation	a^2	A**2
	3^X	3**X

In addition, the plus and minus signs are used as unary operators and as signs, as in the following examples:

Unary operator	*Sign*
+X	+5
–Y	–17

Arithmetic expressions in ordinary arithmetic and algebra use variables, constants, and arithmetic operators. Parentheses should be used in PL/I to emphasize the grouping of the symbols. The following examples show some algebraic expressions and their PL/I equivalents.

Algebraic expression	*PL/I expression*	
$a \cdot b - c \div d + e$	A*B–C/D+E	or (A*B) – (C/D) +E
$a + b - c^2 + d \cdot e$	A+B–C**2+D*E	or A+B–(C**2)+(D*E)
$w - x + y \div z + r^2$	W–X+Y/Z+R**2	or W–Y+(Y/Z)+(R**2)
b^2h	B**2*H	or (B**2)*H
$l \cdot w \cdot h$	L*W*H	
$l \cdot w \cdot h$	LENGTH*WIDTH*HEIGHT	

Where the algebraic variables are standard symbols, it is appropriate to use the same letters in PL/I. Where they are completely abstract and meaningless, the choice of letters in PL/I is unimportant, except that O (oh) should be avoided as it is hard to distinguish from zero. When the letters stand for a meaningful quantity, it is appropriate to use a meaningful name.

The above examples can be written as parentheses-free expressions. There is a specific order in both algebra and PL/I to evaluate these expressions. The order in which the arithmetic operations are carried out is called the hierarchical order of operators.

3.4.2 Order of arithmetic operations

In a parentheses-free expression, the arithmetic operations are carried out in the following order:

1. All the exponentiations are performed first, from left to right, with the exception of a double exponentiation, which is performed right to left.

   3**3 + 5**2 is 27 + 5**2
   is 27 + 25
   is 52

   but X**2**3 is X^{2^3}
   is X^8

   The 2**3 is computed first, then the power of X.

2. All multiplications and/or divisions are performed next, from left to right.

   6/2/3 is 3/3
   is 1

   6/2*3 is 3*3
   is 9

   2*3*6 is 6*6
   is 36

   2*3/6 is 6/6
   is 1

3. All additions and/or subtractions are performed next, from left to right.

   8−2−4 is 6−4
   is 2

   8−2+4 is 6+4
   is 10

   8+2−4 is 10−4
   is 6

These rules are an oversimplification of what actually takes place, but they are sufficiently accurate for programming needs. A more thorough discussion is beyond the scope of this book.

The following example demonstrates step by step evaluation of an expression as performed by the computer.

	$a \cdot b + c - \frac{d}{e} + f^2 + g$	Algebraic expression
	A * B + C − D / E + F ** 2 + G	PL/I expression
Step 1	A * B + C − D / E + R_1 + G	Where R_1 is F**2
Step 2	R_2 + C − R_3 + R_1 + G	Where R_2 is A*B and R_3 is D/E
Step 3	R_4 − R_3 + R_1 + G	Where R_4 is R_2 + C
	R_5 + R_1 + G	Where R_5 is R_4 − R_3
	R_6 + G	Where R_6 = R_5 + R_1
	R_7	Where R_7 = R_6 + G

Each R is the result of a computation from the line above, and R_7 is the final result, the value of the entire expression. Substitute numeric values for the variables A, B, C, D, E, F, and G and repeat the step-by-step evaluation.

USE OF PARENTHESES

The order of evaluation indicated above is the natural order of the hierarchy of operations. In some expressions it is essential to change the natural order by using parentheses. For example, the algebraic expression

$$\frac{a + b}{c + d}$$

when coded in PL/I requires parentheses around both the numerator and denominator.

Algebraic equivalent	*PL/I expression*
$\frac{a + b}{c + d}$	(A+B)/(C+D)
$a + \frac{b}{c} + d$	A+B/C+D
$\frac{a + b}{c} + d$	(A+B)/C+D
$a + \frac{b}{c + d}$	A+B/(C+D)

In general, parentheses will be needed whenever there is a fraction with more than a single number or variable in either the numerator or denominator. Parentheses will also be needed whenever there is an exponent with more than a single number or variable, or when the exponent is negative. Parentheses should be used whenever they make the meaning of an expression clearer. They should also be used wherever they are needed in algebra.

Algebraic equivalent	*PL/I expression*
$x^{1/2}$	X**(1/2)
a^{-2}	A**(−2)
$(-2)^6$	(−2)**6
-2^6	−2**6 or −(2**6)
$(-3) \times (-5)$	(−3)*(−5)

When parentheses are nested, the expression inside the inner parentheses is evaluated first, which results in the removal of the inner parentheses. Then the resulting expression inside the outer parentheses is computed, which also results in the removal of parentheses. Finally the parentheses-free expression is evaluated. When there are parentheses, they are evaluated from inside out, from left to right. The order of evaluation of an expression inside parentheses is the same as it it were a parentheses-free expression.

The following example demonstrates the evaluation of an algebraic expression containing parentheses.

$$\frac{a + b}{c + \frac{d + e}{f + g}}$$ Algebraic expression

(A + B)/(C + (D + E)/(F + G)) PL/I expression

Step 1	R_1/(C + R_2/R_3)	Where R_1 is A+B R_2 is D+E R_3 is F+G
Step 2	R_1/(C + R_4)	R_4 is R_2/R_3
Step 3	R_1/R_5 R_6	R_5 is C + R_4 R_6 is R_1/R_5

In this example, all the parentheses are essential. This is the minimum number of parentheses that must be used for the expression to be correct. Extra parentheses could be used with caution if they made the expression easier to read. Blank spaces can be inserted anywhere except inside single symbols, such as the exponentiation symbol. They should be used whenever they improve the readability of an expression.

Caution must be used when an expression includes the division operator. Division by zero is undefined. It causes divide overflow and results in program termination. When this happens, the program must be rewritten to include a check that the divisor is not zero.

3.4.3 Assignment statement

The assignment statement, one of the basic statements of PL/I, is used to assign the computed result of an expression to a variable. It is used without computation to copy data from one memory location to another. It is also used to store numeric or string constants in variables. The symbol used for assignment is the equal sign (=). However, it does not mean that two values are equal. It represents the dynamic process of placing a particular value in a storage area. The name of the storage area appears on the left side of the equal sign; the right side provides the value. The resulting value will be identical to the original value only if they have the same attributes. Following are examples of assignment statements.

```
A = B + C - D + E ** F;          Assign result to a variable
A = .5 * B * H;                    "
X = X + 1;                         "
NEW_BALANCE = OLD_BALANCE;       Copy a value
N = Z;                             "
D = 5;                           Store a value
PRICE = 8.54;                      "
TITLE = 'GRADE REPORT';            "
```

The first two statements above are arithmetic assignment statements. In each, the expression on the right-hand side of the equal sign is evaluated by using the values of the operands, and the resulting value is assigned to the variable A, which is to the left of the equal sign. The second statement is a formula from geometry. In PL/I, the equal sign means the same thing that it means in a formula.

The third statement is also an arithmetic assignment statement, but it has the meaning "increase the value of X by 1." The value of X is picked up and one added to it, as shown by the expression on the right of the equal sign. The resulting value is then stored back in X, the variable X which appears to the left of the equal sign.

The next two statements cause the copying of data values from OLD_BALANCE to NEW_BALANCE and from Z to N. After each value is copied, it can be found under both names.

The last three statements store constants in the storage locations attached to variables. These differ from using initialization in a declaration in that the constant in the INITIAL clause of a declaration is already in storage when the program execution starts, while the constant in an assignment statement is stored during execution. The variable may have previously held a different value, or no value at all.

In all these assignment statements, any previous value of the variable to the left of the equal sign is lost. The new value is stored, provided that the receiving variable is of an appropriate type to hold it. In the last assignment statement, the receiving variable must have been declared type CHARACTER or the computer will detect a fatal error, and processing will terminate abnormally.

In all but the last example, the receiving variable probably should be numeric, with proper base, scale, and precision to hold the assigned value without losing any important digits. However, the PL/I compiler will try to do what a programmer asks, whether it makes sense or not, and regardless of what the programmer may have intended. If the type of the right side of an assignment statement does not match the type of the left side, adjustments and conversions will be made if at all possible so that the value can be stored successfully.

TYPE CONVERSIONS

The arithmetic and logical operations can be carried out efficiently only when the data types are the same. Each operation requires two operands. For the arithmetic operations, these operands must be numbers. They must have the same scale and base. If the scales are different (FIXED and FLOAT), then the fixed point number is automatically converted to floating point. If the bases are different (DECIMAL and BINARY), then the decimal number is automatically converted to binary. When the result is stored it may be converted again to the type of the variable receiving it. If the variable does not have enough storage space for the value, the SIZE error condition is raised. In the program segment

```
DCL FB   FIXED BIN,
    FD1  FIXED DEC,
    FD2  FIXED DEC;
FD2 = FB * FD1;
```

the variable FD1 is converted to binary before the multiplication takes place.

The result is converted back to decimal for storage. In the program segment

```
DCL XD1 FIXED DEC,
    LD  FLOAT DEC,
    XD2 FIXED DEC;
XD2 = LD + XD1;
```

the variable XD1 is converted to floating-point decimal and the addition is carried out. After the addition, the result is converted back to fixed-decimal for storage. Accuracy may be lost on the conversion from FIXED DECIMAL to FLOAT DECIMAL. When mixed types are used in arithmetic, the type with the smaller range of values is converted to the type with the larger range of values. Otherwise the conversion might not be possible.

When both character strings and bit strings are used in an operation, the bit string is converted to character. A bit 1 becomes a character 1, and a bit 0 becomes the character 0. The conversion could not be done in the opposite direction, as all bit strings can be converted to character, but not all character strings can be converted to bit.

Character strings can be converted to numeric if the value of the character string can be interpreted as a number. In the following example,

```
DCL STR  CHAR(5),
    X    FIXED DEC(5,2);
STR = '-25.39';
X = 17 + STR;
```

the character string can be interpreted as a number. The value −8.39 is stored in X. Conversions in the other direction, from numeric to character, are error prone and should not be attempted.

MULTIPLE ASSIGNMENTS (not in Subset G)

In each of the assignment statements we have looked at so far, there was only one variable to the left of the equal sign. In PL/I several variables may be given a value at once by putting them on the left of the same equal sign. If more than one variable is used, they must be given as a list, separated by commas. The following multiple assignment statements show this.

```
A, B, C = 5.0;
W, X, Y, Z = 0;
P, Q, R = P + 5;
ASTR, BSTR = 'XYZ';
FLAG, SWITCH = '1'B;
```

In the first statement, the same value 5.0 is assigned to the three variables A, B, and C. If the variables are not all of the same type with the same precision, the results can be unpredictable. In the next statement each of the variables is cleared to zero. In the third statement, the value of P is picked up and used in the calculation; then the result is stored in P, Q, and R. Multiple assignment statements may be used with any data type.

SEQUENCE OF ASSIGNMENT STATEMENTS

The following example shows the execution of a sequence of assignment statements. The numeric values shown under each variable in each line are the values stored in the variable after the execution of the statement on that line has been completed. These statements have a cumulative effect, each starting with the values as they were after the previous assignment statement was executed. It is assumed that at the beginning, none of the variables has been initialized.

	W	*X*	*Y*	*Z*
W = 2;	2	—	—	—
X = 2 * W;	2	4	—	—
Y = W + 2 * X;	2	4	10	—
Y = X ** 3;	2	4	64	—
Z = W + X +Y;	2	4	64	70
X = Z / 2 + 5;	2	40	64	70
W = 2 * X + y;	144	40	64	70
Y = W − Y + X;	144	40	120	70
X, Y = 0;	144	0	0	70

After execution of all the statements in sequence, the values stored in the variables are

W [144] X [0] Y [0] Z [70]

3.4.4 Built-in numeric functions

Built-in functions are subprograms, which are stored in a PL/I library where they are available to everyone using the language. Most of the common arithmetic and mathematical functions are included in the library. The available functions are listed in Appendix B.

Each built-in function has a unique name, which should not be used by the programmer for anything else. The name is followed by one or more arguments enclosed in parentheses. For example:

`SQRT (2.16)` Square root function

When more than one argument is needed, the arguments must be separated by commas.

`MAX(X,Y,Z)` Maximum of X, Y, and Z

This is standard mathematical notation and the result is the same as in mathematics. However, the meaning is slightly different. The arguments are sent as data to the library function and the result of the function is sent back. The user program provides input to and accepts output from the library program.

There are other built-in functions in PL/I that do not require arguments, such as

```
DATE()
```

and

```
TIME()
```

Such functions must be either written with an empty argument list as shown here or declared, as in

```
DECLARE (DATE, TIME)  BUILTIN;
```

The DATE and TIME functions will be discussed in chapter 6.

The general form of reference of a built-in function for arithmetic and mathematical operations is:

```
function_name(arg1,arg2,arg3,. . .,argn)
```

The arguments must have numeric values, but they do not need to be of any specific type. They can be variables, constants, or even arithmetic expressions. For instance,

```
F(5)
F(X)
F(2*X+7.25)
```

Library functions may be used anywhere the value of a variable may be used. For example:

```
Y = SQRT(X);               In an assignment statement
W = X - SQRT(Y - 7);                 "
Z = SQRT(MAX(X,Y));        As a function argument
PUT LIST (X,SQRT(X));      In an output list
```

SQRT FUNCTION

The SQRT function calculates the positive square root of a nonnegative number. The general form of the function is:

`SQRT(arg1)` Where arg1 $\geq$ 0

there is an example of its use:

```
X = 25;
Y = SQRT(X);
```

The value 5 is returned and stored in Y. The SQRT function always returns a floating point number. The calling program should check that the argument is not negative, or the SQRT function will produce an error message and halt.

SIN FUNCTION

The SIN function is a trignometric function that calculates the sine of its argument. The argument must be in radians. The general form of the function is

```
SIN(arg1)
```

If the sine of an angle measured in degrees is wanted, it must first be converted to radians, as shown in the following example.

```
X = 15;                              The angle measures 15 degrees
Y = SIN(X*3.14159/180);
```

The result is a floating point number. All the common trigonometric functions are available in PL/I.

Review questions

1. The PL/I symbols for arithmetic operators are: addition ________, subtraction ________, multiplication ________, division ________, and exponentiation ________.

2. Write the PL/I expression for each of the following algebraic expressions.

(a) $x - z \cdot w + \frac{h}{y}$

(b) $a + \frac{b}{c - d}$

(c) $\frac{2xy}{3z} - 7$

(d) $3x^2y^3$

(e) e^{x^3}

3. If X=5, Y=2, and Z=3, what is the value of each of the following PL/I expressions?
(a) X ** Y + Z ** Y
(b) −2 ** X
(c) X ** Y ** Z

4. If A=12, B=3, and C=4, what is the value of each of the following PL/I expressions?
(a) A / C / B
(b) A /B * C
(c) A * B / C

5. In each of the following expressions, the computer computes an intermediate result. If X=10, Y=5, and Z=2, what is the intermediate result?
(a) X + Y − Z
(b) X − Y * Z
(c) X + (Y − Z)

6. Given the following algebraic expressions, write the corresponding PL/I expression.

(a) $\frac{\dfrac{x + y + z}{w + k + m + n}}{p + q}$

(b) $ax^2 + bx + c$

7. If B=5, C=2, D=10, L=5, and M=6, and A is declared a FIXED DECIMAL(5,2), what is the value of A after each of these assignment statements?
   (a) A = B * C − D / L + M;
   (b) A = D ** 2 + B / C;
   (c) A = B − (C − (D − M));

8. Indicate whether each of the following statements is true or false.
   (a) An arithmetic expression may not contain mixed types.
   (b) Character variables can sometimes be added.
   (c) If FLOAT and FIXED variables are added, the result is FLOAT.
   (d) If BINARY and DECIMAL variables are added, the result is BINARY.
   (e) A FLOAT value cannot be assigned to a FIXED variable.
   (f) A DECIMAL value can be assigned to a BINARY variable.
   (g) A negative number can be raised only to an integer power.
   (h) If a DECIMAL number with precision (6, 3) is assigned to a DECIMAL variable with precision (6, 2), it is rounded.

3.5 Relational operations and expressions

3.5.1 Relational operators

The relational operators are used in PL/I to compare values. When these operators are used, the result is the logical value of true or false.

	Symbols	
Operations	*48-Character set*	*60-Character set*
Greater than	GT	>
Less than	LT	<
Equal to	=	=
Greater than or equal to	GE	>=
Less than or equal to	LE	<=
Not equal to	NE	¬=
Not greater than	NG	¬>
Not less than	NL	¬<

Blank spaces are not allowed between the characters in any of the double symbols. When the double symbols of the 48-character set are used, they must be preceded by a blank and followed by a blank.

The comparison operators are used to compare values. The result of true is represented internally as the bit value '1'B. The result of false is represented as the value '0'B.

Three types of data can be compared. First, numeric data can be compared for ordinary algebraic equality or inequality. The more positive number is the larger. Each of the following is true.

```
  23 < 37
 -21 < 15
-108 < -62
```

Variables, constants, and expressions may be compared:

```
C < A+B
X >= SQRT(Y)-25
Z = 0
```

However, it is not a good idea to compare computed values for equality because of the way numbers are stored in a computer.

```
SQRT(1.21) = 1.1          May be false
```

Instead, check for approximate equality, as in

```
ABS(SQRT(1.21)-1.1) < .00001    Will be true
```

PROGRAMMING HINT: ACCURACY Compare computed values for approximate equality.

Second, character data can be compared according to the order defined in the collating sequence used by the computer. In this sequence, alphabetic data is compared for alphabetic order. Characters that are digits are compared for numeric order. But mixed character strings with letters, digits, and punctuation symbols do not always have a meaningful order, as their order varies from computer to computer. Character data comparisons involve left-to-right, character-by-character comparisons. If one character string is identical with the beginning of another, the shorter is considered to be less than the longer provided that the longer string has additional nonblank characters. If the longer string has only additional blanks, the two strings are considered to be equal. The shorter string is compared as though it were padded with blanks to make it the same length. Each of the following comparisons is true.

```
'ADAMS' < 'JONES'
'MACDOUGAL' < 'MCDOUGAL'
'BROWN' < 'BROWNING'
'JAMES A SMITH' < 'JAMES E SMITH'
'ANN BROWNING' < 'ANNE BROWN'
'BILL GREEN' = 'BILL GREEN
```

The blank has a place in the collating sequence ahead of the letters of the English alphabet. This results in accurate alphabetical comparisons.

Third, bit string data is compared from left to right, bit by bit. When a position is found where the bits are not the same, the string with the zero bit is considered to be the lesser. Each of the following are true.

```
'010110111'B < '010111'B
'0'B < '1'B
'1100110'B < '1101110101'B
'101'B < '10101'B
'101'B = '101000'B
```

If one bit string is identical to the beginning of the other bit string, the shorter string is the lesser if the longer string has additional ones. If the longer string has only additional zeros, the strings are considered to be the same value. Data types may be mixed in a comparison, for example, '003' = 3.0, but the rules for type conversion are complicated and the result may be unpredictable.

3.5.2 Order of operations

The relational operators are used in IFTHENELSE, DOWHILE, and DOUNTIL statements to control the logic flow. They can also be used as expressions and their values assigned to BIT(1) variables. In the assignment

```
X = W < Y;
```

if W is less than Y, then '1'B is assigned to X. If W is not less than Y, than '0'B is assigned to X. In

```
X = W = Y;
```

the left equal sign is an assignment operator and the right equal sign is a relational operator. The variables W and Y are compared for equality, and either '1'B or '0'B is assigned to X. Consider the following:

```
X = A * B - C < D + E;
```

This example illustrates the position of the relational operators in the hierarchy of operators. All arithmetic operators take precedence over the relational operators. The arithmetic expression A * B – C is evaluated first. Next the arithmetic expression D + E is evaluated. Then the results of these two calculations are compared. The resulting value of '1'B or '0'B is assigned to the variable X.

When a relational expression contains arithmetic expressions, the arithmetic expressions are evaluated first, according to the order of evaluation of arithmetic operators. Then the resulting values are compared to obtain the logical result. If more than one relational operator is present, the relational operators are evaluated from left to right. For example:

```
A = 5;
B = 3;
C = '1'B;
D = A < B < C;
```

D is assigned the value '1'B by the following process: A and B are compared, resulting in '0'B, which is then compared with '1'B, resulting in '1'B. In this example A and B must be numeric variables and C and D must be BIT(1) variables.

The relative precedences of the arithmetic, logic, relational, and string operators are

	Operator
Highest	**, unary +, unary –, ¬
	*, /
	binary +, binary –
	<, ¬<, <=, =, ¬=, >, ¬>, >=
	&
Lowest	|

Review questions

1. Indicate whether each of the following statements is true or false.
   (a) Numeric values being compared must be of the same type.
   (b) Variables may be compared with expressions.
   (c) In general, computed expressions should not be compared for equality.
   (d) To be compared, character strings must have the same length.
   (e) A blank character 'ƀ' is the same as a zero character '0'.
   (f) PL/I allows numbers to be compared with character strings, but it is not generally meaningful.
   (g) When bit strings are compared, the shorter string is the lesser.

2. If A=5, B=6, C=2, and D=3, give the result of each of the following comparisons.
   (a) A * C + B > A + B − C * D
   (b) A * C <= B * D
   (c) A < B & C > D
   (d) A − B ¬= C − D

3. What is the result of each of the following comparisons?
   (a) 'SMITHSONIAN' > 'SMYTHE'
   (b) 'JAMES' = 'JAMES   '
   (c) 'MARY SMITH' <= 'MARY S JONES'
   (d) '1101'B < '11'B
   (e) '00101'B = '101'B
   (f) '10110'B <= '1011'B

4. What is the result of each of the following comparisons?
   (a) '101'B < '11'B < '10'B
   (b) '101'B = '100'B & '10'B > '1'B
   (c) '2+3' ¬= '5'
   (d) 'ABC' <'123'

3.6 Examples of simple programs

The following examples give complete PL/I programs showing the use of declarations and arithmetic. The output statements

```
PUT DATA;
```

or

```
PUT SKIP LIST (output list);
```

are used in all of them so that they may be run on a computer and the results observed. The PUT DATA statement causes all the variable names and the associated values to be printed. The PUT SKIP LIST statement causes the variables in the output list to be printed. Some of these examples are adapted from problems discussed in chapters 2 and 3. Others were selected to illustrate topics from this chapter.

3.6.1 Simultaneous equations

This program is adapted from the algorithm of section 2.4.4. Unlike the algorithm, it calculates only the solution of a single pair of simultaneous linear equations.

```
EQS: PROC OPTIONS(MAIN);
/***************************************************************/
/*                                                             */
/*  PROGRAM: SIMULTANEOUS EQUATIONS                            */
/*  AUTHOR:  R REDDY                                           */
/*  VERSION: 07/27/84                                          */
/*                                                             */
/*  PROGRAM DESCRIPTION:                                       */
/*  ---------------------------------------------------------- */
/*  THIS PROGRAM COMPUTES THE SOLUTION TO PAIRS OF             */
/*  SIMULTANEOUS EQUATIONS  AX + BY = C                        */
/*                          DX + EY = F                        */
/*                                                             */
/*  INPUT: A,B,C,D,E,F                                         */
/*                                                             */
/*  OUTPUT: A,B,C,D,E,F,X,Y                                    */
/*                                                             */
/***************************************************************/

DCL (A,B,C,D,E,F) FLOAT BIN,
    DEN           FLOAT BIN,
    (X,Y)         FLOAT BIN;
DCL K             FIXED BIN;


GET LIST (A,B,C,D,E,F);
DEN = A * E - B * D;
IF DEN = 0
  THEN
    PUT SKIP LIST (A,B,C,D,E,F, 'NO SOLUTION');
  ELSE
    DO;
      X = (C * E - B * F)/DEN;
      Y = (A * F - C * D)/DEN;
      PUT SKIP LIST (A,B,C,D,E,F,X,Y);
    END;
END EQS;
```

3.6.2 Hypotenuse of triangle

This program illustrates the use of the SQRT library function to calculate the hypotenuse of a right triangle. The program is given in two forms. The first calculates the hypotenuse of a single triangle.

```
HYPOT: PROC OPTIONS(MAIN);
/**************************************************************/
/*                                                            */
/*   PROGRAM: HYPOTENUSE OF A TRIANGLE                        */
/*   AUTHOR:  C ZIEGLER                                       */
/*   VERSION: 07/27/84                                        */
/*                                                            */
/*   PROGRAM DESCRIPTION:                                     */
/*   -------------------------------------------------------  */
/*   THIS PROGRAM PRINTS THE HYPOTENUSE OF A RIGHT            */
/*   TRIANGLE HAVING                                          */
/*                                                            */
/*            LEG A  = 6                                      */
/*            LEG B  = 8                                      */
/*                                                            */
/*   INPUT: NONE                                              */
/*                                                            */
/*   OUTPUT: A, B, C THE HYPOTENUSE                           */
/*                                                            */
/**************************************************************/

DCL (A, B) FIXED BIN,
    C      FLOAT BIN;

A = 6;
B = 8;
C = SQRT (A*A + B*B);
PUT DATA;
END HYPOT;
```

The second calculates the hypotenuse for each of a set of input values representing the lengths of the legs of triangles. It stops when values of zero are given for the legs.

```
HYPOT: PROC OPTIONS(MAIN);
/**************************************************************/
/*                                                            */
/*   PROGRAM: HYPOTENUSE OF A TRIANGLE                        */
/*   AUTHOR:  C ZIEGLER                                       */
/*   VERSION: 07/27/84                                        */
/*                                                            */
/*   PROGRAM DESCRIPTION:                                     */
/*   -------------------------------------------------------  */
/*   THIS PROGRAM PRINTS THE HYPOTENUSE OF EACH OF A SET      */
/*   OF RIGHT TRIANGLES HAVING                                */
/*                                                            */
/*   INPUT: A, B  LEGS OF A TRIANGLE                          */
/*                                                            */
/*   OUTPUT: A, B, C THE HYPOTENUSE                           */
/*                                                            */
/**************************************************************/
```

```
DCL (A, B) FIXED BIN,
    C      FLOAT BIN;

GET LIST (A,B);                   /* GET FIRST SET OF DATA   */
DO WHILE (A ¬= 0);                /* REPEAT WHILE MORE DATA */
  C = SQRT(A*A + B*B);
  PUT DATA;
  GET LIST (A,B);                 /* GET NEXT SET OF DATA    */
END;
END HYPOT;
```

3.6.3 Compound interest

This program, calculating compound interest, is adapted from the algorithm of section 2.4.1. The program is given in two forms. The first calculates compound interest for a single principal, rate, and time. The second calculates compound interest for many sets of data. It stops when the data sets have been exhausted.

```
COMPINT: PROC OPTIONS(MAIN);
/*****************************************************************/
/*                                                               */
/*   PROGRAM: COMPOUND INTEREST                                  */
/*   AUTHOR:  C ZIEGLER                                          */
/*   VERSION: 07/27/84                                           */
/*                                                               */
/*   PROGRAM DESCRIPTION:                                        */
/*   -------------------------------------------------------     */
/*   THIS PROGRAM CALCULATES COMPOUND INTEREST USING THE         */
/*   FORMULA                                                     */
/*                            CN                                 */
/*            A = P(1+R/C)                                       */
/*                                                               */
/*   USING    PRINCIPAL (P) = $10,000                            */
/*            INTEREST RATE (R) = 12%                            */
/*            TIME (N)          = 5 YEARS                        */
/*            # OF COMPOUND PERIODS PER YEAR (C) = 365           */
/*                                                               */
/*   INPUT: NONE                                                 */
/*                                                               */
/*   OUTPUT: A, P, R, C, N                                       */
/*                                                               */
/*****************************************************************/

DCL A  FIXED DEC (8,2),                    /* ACCUMULATED AMOUNT*/
    P  FIXED DEC (7,2),                    /* PRINCIPAL         */
    R  FIXED DEC (3,2)  INIT (.12),        /* INTEREST RATE     */
    C  FIXED DEC (3)    INIT (365),        /* # OF PERIODS/YEAR */
    N  FIXED DEC (3);                      /* # OF YEARS        */
```

```
P = 10000;
N = 5;
A = P*(1+R/C)**(C*N);
PUT DATA;
END COMPINT;
```

```
COMPINT: PROC OPTIONS(MAIN);
/**************************************************************/
/*                                                            */
/*  PROGRAM: COMPOUND INTEREST                                */
/*  AUTHOR:  R REDDY                                          */
/*  VERSION: 07/27/84                                         */
/*                                                            */
/*  PROGRAM DESCRIPTION:                                      */
/*  ------------------------------------------------------    */
/*  THIS PROGRAM CALCULATES COMPOUND INTEREST USING THE       */
/*  FORMULA                                                   */
/*                           CN                               */
/*              A = P(1+R/C)                                  */
/*                                                            */
/*  INPUT:      PRINCIPAL (P)                                 */
/*              INTEREST RATE (R)                             */
/*              TIME (N)                                      */
/*              # OF COMPOUND PERIODS PER YEAR (C)            */
/*                                                            */
/*  OUTPUT: A, P, R, C, N                                     */
/*                                                            */
/**************************************************************/

DCL A           FIXED DEC (8,2),    /* ACCUMULATED AMOUNT */
    P           FIXED DEC (7,2),    /* PRINCIPAL          */
    R           FIXED DEC (3,2),    /* INTEREST RATE      */
    C           FIXED DEC (3),      /* # OF PERIODS/YEAR  */
    N           FIXED DEC (3);      /* # OF YEARS         */
DCL MORE_DATA   BIT(1),             /* DATA STATUS FLAG   */
    TRUE        BIT(1)  INIT('1'B),
    FALSE       BIT(1)  INIT('0'B);

ON ENDFILE(SYSIN)                /* CHECK FOR END OF DATA */
  MORE_DATA = FALSE;

  MORE_DATA = TRUE;              /* ASSUME THERE IS DATA  */
GET LIST (P,R,C,N);
DO WHILE (MORE_DATA);            /* PROCESS EACH DATA SET */
  A = P*(1+R/C)**(C*N);
  PUT DATA;
  GET LIST (P,R,C,N);
END;
END COMPINT;
```

The statement

```
ON ENDFILE(SYSIN) MORE_DATA = FALSE;
```

is an exception handler. It checks whether there are more data values present on the standard system input device SYSIN.

3.6.4 Mailing label

This program prints mailing labels. It stops when there are no more data values.

```
MAILTAG: PROC OPTIONS(MAIN);
/*************************************************************/
/*                                                           */
/*   PROGRAM: MAILING LABEL                                  */
/*   AUTHOR:  C ZIEGLER                                      */
/*   VERSION: 07/27/84                                       */
/*                                                           */
/*   PROGRAM DESCRIPTION:                                    */
/*   ------------------------------------------------------  */
/*   THIS PROGRAM PRINTS A MAILING LABEL FOR EACH PERSON     */
/*                                                           */
/*   INPUT: NAME, STREET, CITY_STATE_ZIP                     */
/*                                                           */
/*   OUTPUT: NAME, STREET, CITY_STATE_ZIP                    */
/*                                                           */
/*************************************************************/

DCL DIVIDER          CHAR(25)  INIT ((25)'_');
DCL NAME             CHAR(20),
    STREET           CHAR(20),
    CITY_STATE_ZIP   CHAR (20);
DCL MORE_DATA        BIT(1),
    TRUE             BIT(1)    INIT ('1'B),
    FALSE            BIT(1)    INIT ('0'B);
ON ENDFILE(SYSIN)              /* CHECK FOR END OF DATA */
  MORE_DATA = FALSE;

MORE_DATA = TRUE;
GET LIST (NAME,STREET,CITY_STATE_ZIP);
DO WHILE (MORE_DATA);
  PUT SKIP LIST (DIVIDER);
  PUT SKIP LIST (NAME);
  PUT SKIP LIST (STREET);
  PUT SKIP LIST (CITY_STATE_ZIP);
  GET LIST (NAME,STREET,CITY_STATE_ZIP);
END;
END MAILTAG;
```

3.6.5 Picture

In the programs on the previous page, a bit flag has been used to indicate the status of the input data. This program shows one way bit strings can be used to store data compactly. The declarations contain a large digit 1 in an eight by eight bit pattern which, when printed, forms a crude picture.

```
PICTURE: PROC OPTIONS(MAIN);
/**************************************************************/
/*                                                            */
/*   PROGRAM: PICTURE                                         */
/*   AUTHOR:  C ZIEGLER                                       */
/*   VERSION: 07/27/84                                        */
/*                                                            */
/*   PROGRAM DESCRIPTION:                                     */
/*   --------------------------------------------------       */
/*   THIS PROGRAM USES BIT STRINGS TO STORE A SIMPLE          */
/*   PICTURE                                                  */
/*                                                            */
/*   INPUT: NONE                                              */
/*                                                            */
/*   OUTPUT: THE PICTURE                                      */
/*                                                            */
/**************************************************************/

DCL BSTR1  BIT(8) INIT ('00001000'B),
    BSTR2  BIT(8) INIT ('00011000'B),
    BSTR3  BIT(8) INIT ('00001000'B),
    BSTR4  BIT(8) INIT ('00001000'B),
    BSTR5  BIT(8) INIT ('00001000'B),
    BSTR6  BIT(8) INIT ('00011100'B);

PUT SKIP LIST (BSTR1);
PUT SKIP LIST (BSTR2);
PUT SKIP LIST (BSTR3);
PUT SKIP LIST (BSTR4);
PUT SKIP LIST (BSTR5);
PUT SKIP LIST (BSTR6);
END PICTURE;
```

3.7 Summary

A PL/I program consists of a PROCEDURE statement followed by declarations of variables, exception handlers, executable statements, and an END statement. The programmer provides a name for the procedure and names for the data variables. These names should be meaningful and appropriate to their use.

The declarations should include all the numeric variables and must include all the string variables. Constants are data items whose values will not be changed in the course of processing. These may be written as literals or given names and declared using the INITIAL clause. Variables are data items whose values are expected to change. In general, they should not be initialized in the declarations.

The most basic type of executable statement is the assignment statement. This can be used to name and store a computed value, to copy a value, or to store a constant. Arithmetic calculations follow the rules and notation of algebra. There are built-in library routines to calculate the standard mathematical functions, such as square root and sine.

Besides the arithmetic operators there are relational operators used to compare values. The results of the comparisons can be used in assignment statements or to control repeated execution of part of a program. All types of data may be compared. The result of the comparison of character data depends on the collating sequence used by the computer.

3.8 Exercises

1. Given two points (X_1, Y_1) and (X_2, Y_2), the formula for the slope of a line between them is

$$M = \frac{Y_2 - Y_1}{X_2 - X_1}$$

Write a program that calculates the slopes for a single set of points. If the denominator of the formula is zero, the line is vertical.

2. Using the straight-line method of depreciation, a piece of equipment that is purchased for P dollars, with an expected life of T years and a projected scrap value of S dollars, is depreciated $(P - S)/T$ dollars each year. Write a program that prints the amount of depreciation and the resultant value for each of the first three years of the life of this piece of equipment.

3. Without using the data type COMPLEX, write a program that reads the values a, b, and n and calculates

$(a + bi)^n$ where $(a + bi)^n = r^n(\cos(nt) + \sin(nt))$
and $r = (a + b)^{1/2}$ and $t = \text{arc}\tan(b/a)$

printing the two parts of the answer. See Appendix C for the built-in functions.

4. Write a program that finds the average of all the data values supplied to it.

5. A set of data contains the names of students, each followed by three test scores; for example,

```
'JOHN JONES'   95  92  94
'ANN SMITH'    87  91  89
```

Write a program that prints the average score for each student and also the class average.

4
Input and output instructions

OBJECTIVE: To tell the computer what data to process and what to do with the results.

FOR PL/I TO BE useful in its wide range of application areas, the programs must be able to communicate with their users. There must be ways to enter data and print the different data values. For a program to be worth the development effort, it must be possible to use it more than once, with different sets of data. Input and output data can take many forms. It may consist of numbers, character strings, or true and false values. It may be arranged as single items or groups of items. The arrangement must be controllable and predictable. Above all, input must be easy to enter and output must be easy to use.

4.1 Concepts of input and output

The information to be processed by a computer program is called *input*. It is entered into the computer by means of an input device such as a card reader or the keyboard of a CRT terminal. The information produced by the computer program is called *output.* It is sent to the user by means of an output device such as a printer or a CRT screen. Input and output can be as simple or as complex as the programmer desires. The programmer may have full control over the appearance of the input and output, or let the computer determine the arrangement of data.

There are two major classes of input and output: stream-oriented I/O and record-oriented I/O. In *stream input,* the data items are selected one after the other from a continuous stream of characters coming from outside the program. The characters in the stream are grouped under program control to form numbers and words, converted to internal form, and assigned to the variables specified in the input instruction. For example, under program control the input stream

```
15  2.76 'JONES' '145 CENTER ST'
```

would be grouped as characters forming an integer, a real number, a name, and an address. The intervening blanks are also characters of the input stream, but the programmer has the option of ignoring them. In *stream output,* the data items are converted one after the other from internal form into characters, and the characters transmitted one by one to the external device.

Record input/output handles collections of items called records, rather than individual items. In general a record corresponds to a keypunched card or a line typed at a terminal. The records are transmitted without being converted. Therefore, as records coming from a card reader or keyboard contain characters, they are stored internally as characters. Record I/O will be discussed in chapters 15–17. For now, it is enough to know that record I/O is efficient, since the data is transmitted without conversion, but the resulting data is more difficult to use. Stream I/O is less efficient because it takes time and extra steps to convert the items to internal form, but it is easier to use. Also, stream I/O is more machine-independent than record I/O. It is preferred for use with CRT terminals and printers.

PROGRAMMING RULE: Use stream I/O with terminals and printer.

Often stream I/O handles an input or output stream that has been broken into logical records for hardware convenience. When we talk about records with stream I/O, we are referring to a section of a larger data stream, such as a line from a terminal. With stream I/O, record boundaries are usually ignored.

4.1.1 Data movement

The input/output statements cause the movement of data between internal storage and an external device or between two places in internal storage; the

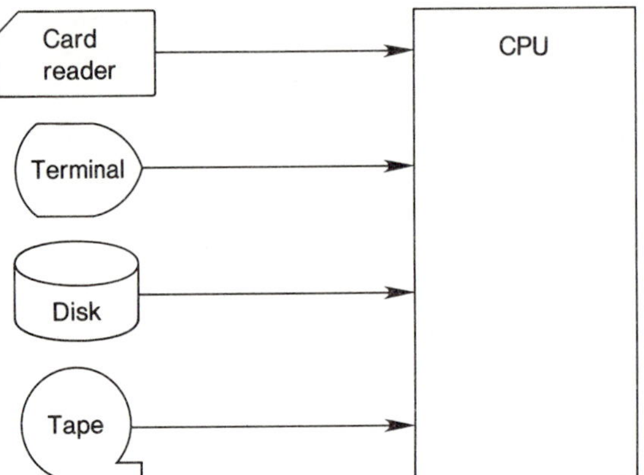

Figure 4-1

latter point will be considered in chapter 6. Input statements cause data to be transmitted into the computer from an external device to internal storage, as shown in figure 4-1. Output statements cause data to be transmitted from internal storage to an external output device, as shown in figure 4-2. The keywords that initiate all forms of stream I/O are GET for input and PUT for output.

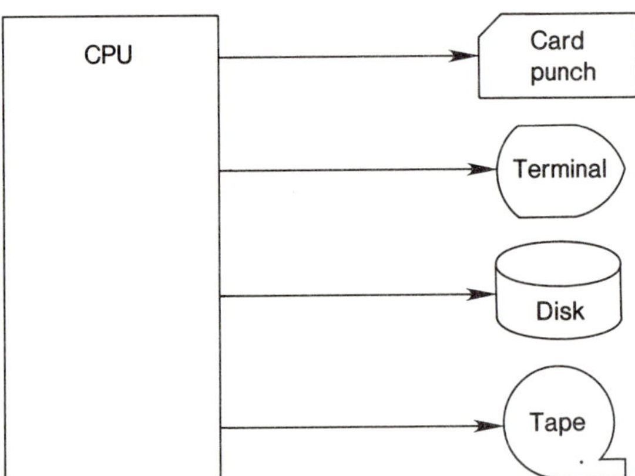

Figure 4-2

An external storage area is called a *file*. Data can be directed to or from a specific file. For the time being we will move data only between internal storage and the standard external files, which have names known to the operating system. These files are SYSIN, the standard system input file; SYSOUT, the standard system output file; and SYSPRINT, the standard system output file for printed output. Other files will be discussed in chapter 10.

4.1.2 Data organization

Three types of input/output statements are used in stream I/O: data-directed, list-directed, and edit-directed statements. The organization of the input data depends on the choice of input statement. In data-directed and list-directed input, the data organization is free-format. The computer searches for and locates the data. In data-directed and list-directed output, a system-dependent standard arrangement is used. In edit-directed input and output, the data format is specified by the programmer and the data must be arranged in accordance with it. Data-directed and list-directed I/O are primarily used for debugging programs and for quick results. Edit-directed I/O is used when attractive, readable output is to be produced, especially when input and output data are being handled by someone other than the programmer.

PROGRAMMING HINT: READABILITY Use edit-directed output.

The following examples show the basic differences among these types of I/O.

1. Input:

```
GET DATA (STR,NUM);                    /* Data-directed */
```

```
STR='ABC', NUM=15;
```

Data includes variable names; format is free.

```
GET LIST (STR,NUM);                    /* List-directed */
```

```
'ABC', 15
```

Input statement determines order; format is free.

```
GET EDIT (STR,NUM) (A(3),F(2));        /* Edit-directed */
```

```
ABC | 15|
```

Input statement determines order; input statement determines format.

2. Output:

```
PUT DATA (STR,NUM);                    /* Data-directed */
```

```
STR='ABC'      NUM=15;
```

Output statement determines order; data includes variable names; format is standard.

```
PUT LIST (STR,NUM);                    /* List-directed */
```

```
ABC           15
```

Output statement determines order; format is standard.

```
PUT EDIT (STR,NUM) (A(5),F(2));        /* Edit-directed */
```

```
ABCbb | 15 |
```

Output statement determines order; output statement determines format.

In this chapter we will discuss stream I/O of individual data items. Input and output of data records will be discussed in chapters 15, 16, and 17.

4.1.3 Data error conditions

A number of error conditions can occur during input and output. The following conditions can be raised by errors in stream processing.

CONVERSION ERROR

Data coming from or moving to a card reader, a terminal, or a printer is in the form of characters. During input it is converted to the internal form specified for the variables; during output it is converted from the internal form to characters. The computer will carry out whatever conversions are required, if they are possible. A string of digits such as '34264' can be converted to decimal or binary, fixed or float, or can be left as characters. A string of zeros and ones such as '10011' can be converted to any numeric representation, or to a bit string or character string. If an impossible conversion is attempted, such as trying to store the input string '17X8' as a numeric value, a fatal CONVERSION error is raised.

During output, any legitimate value can be converted to character form for printing or display. If, however, a variable has not been assigned a value, it may contain a bit pattern that does not represent any actual value. For example, a character variable may contain a bit pattern other than the sixty patterns that represent the PL/I character set. Attempting to print or display such a variable raises the fatal CONVERSION error condition.

ENDFILE CONDITION

An attempt to GET data from an input stream that has been exhausted raises the ENDFILE condition. This is a fatal error condition if the programmer does not define an exception handler for it. The examples of section 3.6.3 and 3.6.4 show how the programmer may take advantage of this condition and use it to recognize the end of a set of data. The ENDFILE condition will be discussed more fully in chapters 15–17.

ENDPAGE CONDITION

An attempt to PUT data into an output stream destined for a printer may raise the ENDPAGE condition when the page being printed is full. This condition is discussed in section 4.5.3.

ERROR CONDITION

The ERROR condition is raised when a fatal error has occurred.

NAME CONDITION

The NAME condition can be raised only during data-directed input. It is discussed in section 4.2.1.

Review questions

1. Data is arranged for input/output in either __________ or __________ form.

2. __________ input data is transmitted and stored without conversion.

3. __________ input data is transmitted and converted before being stored.

4. The three types of I/O used with stream files are __________, __________, and __________.

5. The programmer controls the arrangement of the output data with __________ I/O.

6. The system controls the arrangement of the output data with __________ and __________ I/O.

7. The programmer controls the order of the input data with __________ and __________ I/O.

8. The user controls the order of the data with __________ I/O.

9. How do files SYSIN, SYSOUT, and SYSPRINT differ?

4.2 Data-directed input/output (not in Subset G)

In *data-directed* I/O, the names of the data items are provided in the external file along with their values. The data items to be input are recognized by their names rather than by their order or position. The data items to be output are labeled with their names.

4.2.1 Data-directed input

Data-directed input can be requested in two forms. One specifies which items are to be input, the other does not. The general form of the input statement is

```
GET DATA [(var1, var2, var3, ..., varn)];
```

The input list is optional. When it is not present, all data values in the input file are transmitted, ending when a semicolon is found. Given the input statement

```
GET DATA;
```

and the data

```
W=18,X=-15, Y=7.5,Z='HI';
```

One line of data

or

```
W=18          Y=7.5   Z='HI'
```

```
      X=-15 ;
```

Several lines of data

then W has the value 18, X has the value −15, Y has the value 7.5, and Z has the value 'HI', provided the declarations of W, X, Y, and Z are suitable. The data items can be typed on one line or on several. Line boundaries are ignored and all the input treated as a single stream of characters. The semicolon indicates the end of a set of data. The values in the input stream are written as numeric constants or string literals separated by commas or blank spaces. The numeric constants may have signs, a decimal point, and an exponent. The string literals are enclosed in quotation marks. The order of the data has no significance.

When a list of input variables is given, only those variables are transmitted from the input file. They are identified by name. The order of the variables in the list need not be the same as the order of the data values. If some of the variables in the list do not match names in the data, those variables are not given new values. If some of the names in the data do not match the input list, a fatal error condition is raised.

Given the declaration and input statements

```
DCL (A,B,C)  FIXED DEC(8,5);
GET DATA (A,B,C);
GET DATA (A,B,C);
```

and the data

```
A=12.8, B=-182.5,  C=1; C=.073 A=17.092E-5;
```

then after the first input statement,

A contains	+012 80000	Value is padded
B contains	−182 50000	" " "
C contains	+001 00000	" " "

The position in the input stream is remembered. After the second input statement,

A contains	+000 00017	Value is truncated
B contains	−182 50000	Value is not changed
C contains	+000 07300	Value is padded

The type of variables A, B, and C is unimportant, as character digits from the input stream can be converted to any numeric type and truncated or padded as needed. After the second input statement, the value of B is unchanged since there is no B value in the second set of data. This will not raise any error condition.

Given the declaration and input statement

```
DCL (P,Q) FIXED DEC(5,2),
    R    FIXED BIN;
GET DATA (P,Q,R);
```

and the data

```
P=18.5, Q=6.8,    R=11.3,   S=7.5;
```

then the NAME condition is raised.

There is a data item S that is not in the list of input variables. This will cause a NAME error condition to be raised. Later, when ON conditions have been discussed, it will be possible to have the computer check for this condition and print a warning message. Meanwhile, it may be considered a fatal error that causes the processing to terminate abnormally.

The input of character strings and bit strings is as follows. Given the declaration and input statement

```
DCL CHV CHAR(10),
    BST BIT(8);
GET DATA (CHV,BST);
```

and the data

```
CHV='HEADING',BST='101101'B;
```

then CHV contains 'HEADINGbbb' and BST contains '10110100'B. The character string and the bit string data must have the form of character and bit constants. The variable CHV should be a declared character variable large enough to contain the value 'HEADING'. The bit variable BST should be large enough to contain '101101'B. If the variable sizes are not exact, the values will be handled the same way they would be handled in an initialization or assignment statement, left-justified with truncation or padding on the right as needed.

COPY OPTION (not in Subset G)

A COPY option used in a GET DATA statement,

```
GET DATA [(input-list)] COPY;
```

causes the "echo" printing of the input data. On some systems this echoing of the input preserves the original spacing so that the arrangement of the input can be checked for accuracy. On other systems standard spacing is used.

4.2.2 Data-directed output

The general form of the data-directed output statement is

```
PUT DATA [(var1, var2, var3, ..., varn)];
```

Again the variable list is optional. This statement sends output data to the printer. Only variable names are allowed in the output list. If a list is given, only those variables specified will be printed. If no list is given, all the variables known to the program at the time the statement is executed will be printed. This form of the output statement is particularly useful in debugging programs.

Both the names of the variables and their current values are printed. The output spacing is standard with the values aligned at preset tab positions. Given the declaration, current values of the variables, and the output statement

```
DCL A   FIXED BIN,
    B   FLOAT BIN,
    C   CHAR(10);
A=18; B=12.5; C='THE END';
PUT DATA (A,B,C);
```

then the output is printed as

```
1
A=   18          B=  1.25000E+01     C='THE END   ';
```

The exact spacing is implementation-dependent. The values are labeled, separated by blanks, and the set of output values concludes with a semicolon.

When necessary, the output is continued on another line. Given the declaration, current values of the variables, and output statement

```
DCL (A,B,C,D,E,F)   FIXED DEC(5);
A=10; B=-15; C=12; D=130; E=18; F=12.0;
PUT DATA (A,B,C,D,E,F);
```

then the output is printed as

```
1
A=   10        B=   -15        C=   12        D=   130        E=   18
F=   12;
```

Line boundaries are ignored in stream I/O; therefore as much output is placed on a single line as will fit. Given the declarations, current values of the variables, and the output statements

```
DCL (A,B,C,D)  FIXED BIN;
A=10; B=-15; C=3712; D=25;
PUT DATA (A,B);
PUT DATA (C,D);
```

then the output is printed as

```
1
A=   10        B=   -15;        C=   3712        D=   25;
```

The first output statement does not fill the line, so the second output statement continues with the same line.

The SKIP, LINE, and PAGE page formatting options are available with DATA-directed input and output. These are discussed in section 4.4.

PROGRAMMING HINT: DEBUGGING Use PUT SKIP DATA; to check on values of variables.

The SKIP option is the most useful with data-directed I/O as it forces the output to start on a new line. Given the declarations, current values of the variables, and the output statements

```
DCL (A,B,C,D) FIXED BIN;
A=10; B=-15; C=3712; D=25;
PUT DATA (A,B);
PUT SKIP DATA (C,D);
```

then the output is printed as

```
1
A=     10      B=   -15;

C=   3712      D=    25;
```

Review questions

1. Indicate whether each of the following statements is true or false.

(a) In data-directed input the data items must be written in the form of assignment statements.

(b) The GET DATA statement can be used without an input list.

(c) The semicolon is used as a data separator for data-directed I/O.

(d) The input list for a GET DATA statement and the data must match as to order of variables and number of variables.

(e) The main use of the PUT DATA statement is during debugging.

2. Show the output for the following program segment.

```
DCL A  CHAR(3),
    B  FLOAT BIN,
    C  FIXED DEC (5,2);
A = 'XYZ';
B = 12.5;
C = -15;
PUT DATA (A,B,C);
```

3. Show the output for the following program segment.

```
DCL A  CHAR(3),
    B  FLOAT BIN,
    C  FIXED DEC (5,2);
A = 'XYZ';
B = 12.5;
C = -15;
PUT DATA (A,B);
PUT DATA (C,A);
```

4.3 List-directed input/output

With *list-directed* I/O standard formatting is provided by the system. The data is transmitted in the order indicated by the I/O list, being converted from character on input and to character on output. Line boundaries are ignored.

4.3.1 List-directed input

The general form of the list-directed input statement is

```
GET LIST (var1, var2, var3, . . . , varn);
```

The values for the variables var1, var2, var3, . . . , varn, must be punched on a card or entered through a terminal in the order in which the variables are listed. The values may be numeric constants or string literals. The input list must be compatible with the data, because it controls the input and determines the number of values to be read. The data values must be separated by commas or one or more blanks. When it reaches the end of the input list, the computer stops reading data. It retains a pointer to the position in the input stream where the transmission stopped. If there is another input statement, it continues from that point. Line boundaries are ignored.

Given the declaration and input statement

```
DCL (X,Y,Z) FIXED DEC(5,2),
    S        CHAR(10);
GET LIST (X,S,Y,Z);
```

and the data

```
   18,'ABC',7.5,-26.827
```

One line of data

or

```
   18          'ABC'    7.5
```

```
       -26.827
```

Several lines of data

or

```
   18  'ABC'  7.5  -26.827  'SPQR'
```

Part of a line of data

then X contains +018 00, S contains 'ABCbbbbbbb', Y contains +007 50, and Z contains −026 82.

The data items may be on one line or on more than one. They may be separated by commas or by blanks. The computer keeps track of the current position in the input stream. Any data remaining in a line will be obtained by the next input statement. Given the declarations and input statements

```
DCL (A,B,C) FIXED DEC(5,2),
    (D,E,F) FIXED DEC(3,0),
    G       FIXED DEC(8,0);
GET LIST (A,B,C,D);
GET LIST (E,F,G);
```

and the data

```
  18 -35 47.9 15 .06 7.5 1.5E6
```

Input continues with the next value

then A contains +018 00, B contains −035 00, C contains +047 90, D contains +015, E contains +000, F contains +007, and G contains +01500000.

In practice it makes sense to keep the data lists short, to put all the data values for one input statement on the same card, and to put data values for separate input statements on separate lines.

PROGRAMMING HINT: CLARITY AND ACCURACY Put the input values for a single input statement in a single line of data. End each data line with a blank or comma.

In some implementations, each line of data must end with a blank or comma because the end of line is not a separator.

Blanks must not be embedded in numeric data items, but they may be part of character data items. For this reason character data must usually be enclosed in quotation marks. Character and bit data are written in the form used for literals. Given the declaration and input statement

```
DCL NAME CHAR(15),
    FLAG BIT(8);
GET LIST (NAME,FLAG);
```

and the data

```
  'JAMES L WALKER', '1011'B
```

then NAME contains 'JAMES̸bL̸bWALKER̸b' and FLAG contains '10110000'B.

As we have seen, numeric data and character data can be input by the same statement. If, however, the types of the variables and data values are mismatched and the computer attempts to read a character value into a numeric variable, a CONVERSION condition is raised.

When the input stream contains fewer data values than are requested by the GET LIST statement, an ENDFILE condition is raised. When the input stream contains more data values than are requested, the extra values are available to the next input statement. If there are none, they are ignored.

COPY OPTION (not in Subset G)

The COPY option used in a GET LIST statement

```
GET LIST (input-list) COPY;
```

causes the "echo" printing of the input data. On some systems this echoing preserves the original spacing so that the arrangement of the input can be checked for accuracy. On other systems standard spacing is used.

PROGRAMMING HINT: DEBUGGING   Use GET LIST (. . .) COPY; to check input formatting.

4.3.2 List-directed output

List-directed output statements are used to print unlabeled values. Both numeric and character constants can be printed and the programmer can provide any headings and labels that are needed. The general form of a list-directed output statement is

```
PUT LIST(output list);
```

The output list may contain constants, variables, or expressions. Given the output statement

```
PUT LIST (80,90,'WXYZ',-17);
```

the output is printed as

```
1
80                 90                 WXYZ               -17
```

This is an example of the printing of constants. The spacing is standard but implementation-dependent. Character strings are printed without quotation marks. Notice that the values are printed left-justified in standard-width fields, and that only the values are printed, not the names of the variables. The order of the values is the order of the variables as given in the output statement.

Expressions of all types can appear in the output list. Given the following statements

```
A = 10;
B = 8.0;
C = 12;
D = 6;
E = 5;
PUT LIST (A,SQRT(B),C,D*E-2*B);
```

the output is printed as

```
1
10                 2.82843E+00        12                 14
```

Notice that the square root is calculated and a floating-point value returned, and that D*E−2*B is evaluated before the values are printed.

Character constants can be used to label the output. Given the following statements

```
A = 15;
B = 18.5;
PUT LIST (A, B, 'TOTAL =',A+B);
```

the output is printed as

```
1
 15              18.5             TOTAL =              33.5
```

Quoted blanks can be used to increase the spacing, as in

```
A = 5;
B = 15;
C = 12;
PUT LIST (' ',A,B,' ',C);
```

which is printed as

```
1
                5             15                            12
```

Quoted blanks can also be used to adjust the spacing. The tab position can be overridden by a character variable that contains enough characters to span several fields. Given the following statements

```
X = 128596.00;
PUT LIST('         THE TOTAL COST OF EQUIPMENT IS',X);
```

the output is printed as

```
1
          THE TOTAL COST OF EQUIPMENT IS 128596.00
```

Review questions

1. Indicate whether each of the following statements is true or false.

- **(a)** The names are not part of the output in list-directed I/O.
- **(b)** In list-directed input, the input list must match the data as to type, number, and order.
- **(c)** Data values must be separated by commas in list-directed I/O.
- **(d)** Line boundaries are ignored in list-directed I/O.
- **(e)** An input statement may obtain data from several lines.
- **(f)** Character data that has blanks must be quoted.
- **(g)** A list for list-directed output may include literals, but it must not include expressions.

2. Show the output for the following program segment:

```
DCL A   CHAR(3),
        B   FLOAT BIN,
        C   FIXED DEC (5,2);
A = 'XYZ';
B = 12.5;
C = -15;
PUT LIST (A,B,C);
```

3. Show the output for the following program segment:

```
DCL A   CHAR(3),
        B   FLOAT BIN,
        C   FIXED DEC (5,2);
A = 'XYZ';
B = 12.5;
C = -15;
PUT LIST (A,B);
PUT LIST (C,A);
```

4. Show the output for the following program segment:

```
DCL A   FIXED BIN,
        B   FIXED DEC(5,2);
A = -256;
B = 14.75;
PUT LIST (A/16,B-7,SQRT(25));
```

4.4 Page-formatting options

Stream output wraps around to the next line only when a line is full. A PUT LIST or PUT DATA statement does not cause values to be printed directly. It transmits them to a line buffer where they are collected until all the fields of the line have been filled. Since line printers print an entire line at once, the line actually is printed only when the buffer is full. Any output left in the print buffer at the time a program terminates is printed at that time. If the program terminates abnormally, the final print buffer may not be printed.

4.4.1 SKIP option

The SKIP option is available to force the printing of the output buffer. This has the effect of starting the next output on a new line. Given the statements

```
A=10; B=-15; C=3712; D=25;

PUT LIST (A,B);
PUT SKIP LIST (C,D);
```

or

```
PUT LIST (A,B);
PUT SKIP;
PUT LIST (C,D);
```

the output is printed as

```
1
10          -15
3712        25
```

The SKIP option results in C and D being printed at the beginning of the second line. It actually causes the A and B values to be printed and the C and D values to be placed in the output buffer. The second line is printed when another SKIP is executed or when the end of the program is reached. The SKIP can be used by itself to force the printing of the buffer and the relocating of the current output position to the beginning of the line.

The SKIP takes effect before the placement of the C and D values. It does not cause a line to be skipped, but has the effect of a carriage return and line feed.

It is possible actually to skip one or more lines on the paper by providing a line count with the SKIP option. Given the statements

```
A=10; B=-15; C=3712; D=25; E=64;
PUT LIST (A,B,C);
PUT SKIP(3) LIST (D,E);
```

the output is printed as

```
1
10          -15          3712
                      Blank line
                      Blank line
25          64
```

The number of blank lines is always one less than the number specified in the SKIP option. In this case, SKIP(3) prints two blank lines before the variables D and E are printed. Printing two blank lines is the same as advancing to the third line with three carriage returns and line feeds.

If a SKIP option of zero is used, the effect is that of a carriage return without a line feed. This is known as *overprinting*. It is used for underlining headings and subheadings, for emphasizing words, or for printing pictures, as it causes a second line to be printed on top of the first. Given the output statements

```
PUT LIST('BANK BALANCE SHEET');
PUT SKIP(0) LIST('__________________');
```

or

```
PUT LIST('BANK BALANCE SHEET');
PUT SKIP(0) LIST((18)'_');           Repetition factor
```

then the output is printed as

```
1
BANK BALANCE SHEET
```

with the title underlined.

The SKIP option is used in input to move the input pointer to the next line. Given the declaration and input statements

```
DCL (A,B,C) FIXED BIN;
GET LIST (A,B);
GET SKIP LIST (C);
```

or

```
GET LIST (A,B);
GET SKIP;
GET LIST (C);
```

and the data

```
25        -17        'ABC'
```

```
296
```

then A has the value 25, B has the value −17, and C has the value 296. The character string 'ABC' is not read, because the SKIP option causes the computer to advance to the next line after reading the first two values.

4.4.2 PAGE option

The PAGE option is used in output statements to print the output at the top of a new page. This is used to control paging so that page breaks are made at appropriate places, report titles are placed on separate pages, and page numbers are placed on the first or last line of a page. Given the current values of the variables and the output statements

```
H = 'STATUS REPORT';
S = ' '; P = 'PAGE 1';
A=10; B=-15; C=3712;
PUT LIST (H);
PUT PAGE LIST (S,S,S,P);
PUT SKIP(2) LIST (A,B,C);
```

then the output is printed on two pages as

```
1
STATUS REPORT
```

```
1
                                                  PAGE 1
                              Blank line
  10          -15          3712
```

Notice that the variables S and P are printed on the second page. The effect of printing the blanks is to space across the page.

4.4.3 LINE option

The LINE option is used to specify the line on which the output is to be printed. Since a printer cannot backspace, if the line specified has already been printed, the printer advances to that position on the next page. Given the current values of the variables and the output statements

```
H = 'STATUS REPORT';
S = ' '; P = 'PAGE 1';
A=10; B=-15; C=3712;
PUT LIST (H);
PUT PAGE LIST (S,S,S,P);
PUT LINE(3) LIST (A,B,C);
```

then the output is again printed as

```
1
STATUS REPORT
```

```
1
                                                          PAGE 1
                                    Blank line
    10          -15            3712
```

The line option and the page option can be used together. The various options may be specified in any order, but they will always be executed in the order

1. PAGE option
2. LINE option or SKIP option
3. Output of data

Thus the following statements produce the same output.

```
PUT PAGE LINE(5) LIST (H);
PUT LINE(5) PAGE LIST (H);
```

Likewise, the following statements produce the same output.

```
PUT SKIP(3) LIST (A,B,C);
PUT LIST (A,B,C) SKIP(3);
```

The PAGE and LINE options can be used to skip to a new page and to a specified line. Given the current values of the variables and the output statements

```
M1 = 12.8;
M2 = 16.5;
M3 = 14.7;
PUT LIST(' ','QUARTERLY REPORT');
PUT PAGE LINE(5) LIST('JANUARY','FEBRUARY','MARCH');
PUT LINE(8) LIST(M1, M2, M3);
```

then the output is printed as

```
1
                        QUARTERLY REPORT

1
              Blank line
              Blank line
              Blank line
              Blank line
 JANUARY                      FEBRUARY                      MARCH
              Blank line
              Blank line
   12.8                         16.5                         14.7
```

Notice that the second output statement places the column headings on the fifth line of the next page. The last output statement places the numbers on the eighth line.

Review questions

1. Indicate whether each of the following statements is true or false.

(a) The SKIP option causes a blank line to be output.

(b) The keyword SKIP means the same thing no matter where it is placed in an output statement.

(c) The SKIP option is used only for output.

2. Show the output for the following program segment:

```
PUT LIST (25,-17);
PUT SKIP LIST('ABC',49);
```

3. Show the output for the following program segment:

```
PUT LIST (25,-17);
PUT SKIP(2) LIST('ABC',49);
```

4. Show the output for the following program segment:

```
PUT LIST (25,-17);
PUT PAGE;
PUT LIST('ABC',49)SKIP;
```

4.5 Edit-directed input/output

Edit-directed I/O gives the programmer full control over the format of both input and output. This is the most flexible and powerful of the three kinds of stream I/O. At the same time, it is the most exacting, requiring that the user enter the data spaced to the exact format specifications described in the program. Edited I/O is used in production programs or other situations in which control is needed over the appearance of the output.

Two lists are associated with the edit-directed input or output statement. One specifies the data to be transmitted in the order it is to be accessed. The other specifies the horizontal and vertical spacing. The general forms of the edit-directed I/O statements are

```
GET EDIT (input-list) (format-list);
```

for input and

```
PUT EDIT (output-list) (format-list);
```

for output. The input list is a list of variables. The output list is a list of variables, constants, and expressions. For each entry in the input or output list there must be a format specification of an appropriate type.

There are three classes of format items. Data format items describe the form in which the data is to be printed. Control format items such as PAGE, LINE, SKIP, and COLUMN describe the spacing. Remote formats name a format placed elsewhere in the program so it can be used in more than one I/O statement.

Data specification	*Type of data*
A	Character strings
B	Bit strings
C	Complex numbers
E	Floating-point numbers
F	Fixed-point numbers
P	Picture data

Control specification	*Effect*
X	Ignore specified number of positions
COL	Resume at specified position
LINE	Resume at specified line
PAGE	Resume at top of next page
SKIP	Advance specified number of lines

Remote specification	*Situation*
R	Format is referenced by name

4.5.1 Edit-directed input

The edit-directed input statement is used to input data values for the variables specified in the data list. The characteristics of each data value are specified in the format list. The use of the different types of input data specifications is as follows:

A(w)	Most types of processing
B(w)	Rare
C(w,d)	Scientific applications
E(w,d)	Scientific applications
F(w,d)	Most types of processing
P	Business applications

The format specification is selected to match the form and use of the data being read.

With edit-directed I/O, the input is usually organized in tabular form on cards or on a CRT screen. It is necessary to know the exact spacing of the input data, but not the total length of the line.

With edit-directed I/O, quotation marks are not used around strings and separators are not used between data items. The data items may be packed together. The edit format list indicates to the computer exactly where to find each item. With the input statement

```
GET EDIT (N,STR,K) (F(5),A(6),F(3));
```

and the data

```
1    6      12  15
24316|ABCDEF|519|
```

which matches the input list and format thus

```
1    6      12  15
24316|ABCDEF|519|

 F(5)   A(6)  F(3)
  N     STR    K
```

then N has the value 24316 from the first five columns; STR has the value 'ABCDEF' from the next six columns; and K has the value 519 from the next three columns.

When data extends to a second line, either a SKIP option or a COL(1) specification can be used to direct the computer to the second line. Given the input statements

```
GET EDIT (N,STR) (F(5),A(6));
GET SKIP EDIT (K) (F(3));
```

or

```
GET EDIT (N,STR) (F(5),A(6));
GET EDIT (K) (COL(1),F(3));
```

or

```
GET EDIT (N,STR) (COL(1),F(5),A(6));     (Best)
GET EDIT (K) (COL(1),F(3));
```

and the data

```
1    6     12
24316 ABCDEF
```

```
1  4
519
```

then N has the value 24316 from the first five columns; STR has the value 'ABCDEF' from the next six columns; and K has the value 519 from the next line.

The SKIP option explicitly directs the computer to the next line. The COL(1) specification directs the computer to advance to the first column of a line unless it is already at the first column of a line. Since the position pointer cannot back up, the COL(1) option of the second input statement advances the position pointer to the second line of input data. The example that uses the COL(1) specification in both input statements is the best because it is standardized and least likely to need changing if the program is modified.

PROGRAMMING HINT: STYLE AND ACCURACY Start each format with a column specification.

INPUT OF FIXED-POINT DECIMAL DATA

Fixed-point decimal values are simply numbers with or without a decimal point and without an exponent, punched on a card or entered from a terminal. They may be stored in any type of numeric variable, FIXED or FLOAT, DECIMAL or BINARY. The F format is used. The general form of this format is

```
F(w,d)
```

where the d is optional. The (w) or (w,d) specifies the precision of the value as found in the input, provided that neither a sign nor a decimal point explicitly appears in the input data. If there is a decimal point in the data, it overrides the value of d specified in the format. The w indicates the *field width,* that is, the total number of columns occupied by the value including any sign or decimal point and leading or trailing blanks. F(w) is the same as F(w,0). Storage of the value is determined by the declaration of the variable.

The following examples show the use of the F format specification.

```
DCL X FIXED DEC(6,3);
GET EDIT (X) (F(5,2));
```

Format	*Input data*	*Value stored*	*Contents of storage*
F(5,2)	12345	123.45	+123 450
	+1234	12.34	+012 340
	−1234	−12.34	−012 340
	ƀƀ123	1.23	+001 230
	ƀ.123	.123	+000 120
	1234.	Size error	?
	1234ƀ	12.34	+012 340

Notice that the precision specified in the declaration of X is sufficiently large that no error can occur when the value is stored. In fact, the precision is larger than necessary so the value is padded on the right. After the format specification is used to obtain the value, the value is converted to the type and precision specified by the declaration.

Given the declaration and input statement

```
DCL (A,B,C,D) FIXED DEC (8,3);
GET EDIT (A,B,C,D) (COL(1),F(5,2),F(6,3),F(4,1),F(4));
```

and the data

```
1    6     12  16  20
28936|832754|-135|5432|
```

then A contains +00289 360 with the value 289.36, B contains +00832 754 with the value 832.754, C contains −00013 500 with the value −13.5, and D contains +05432 000 with the value 5432. The fields are as shown in the diagram, the first five columns being accessed for the value of A, the next six for the value of B, then four for C, and finally four for D. The data items do not need to be separated by blanks or commas as the format specifies the exact position of each value.

For data entered from a terminal, it is often preferable to use a standard field specification large enough to accommodate any of the values. Leading blanks can be included to make the data easier to inspect visually. Given the declaration and input statement with standard field specification of F(8,3),

```
DCL (A,B,C,D) FIXED DEC(8,3);
GET EDIT (A,B,C,D) (COL(1),F(8,3),F(8,3),F(8,3),F(8,3));
```

or

```
GET EDIT (A,B,C,D) (COL(1),(4)F(8,3));        (Preferred)
```

and the data

```
1       9       17      25      33
bb289360|b832754b|bb-13500|b5432000|
```

then A contains +00289 360, B contains +00832 754, C contains −00013 500, and D contains +05432 000.

Notice that there may be leading or trailing blanks in the data, but no embedded blanks. With data stored on a disk or magnetic tape, it may be more efficient to condense the data to avoid leading and trailing blanks. Since no decimal point appears in the data, the specification (8,3) permits five leading digits or a sign and four leading digits, plus three digits to the right of the point. The preferred form contains the repetition factor (4) which indicates that the F(8,3) format is used four times. Values without explicit decimal points, read with a format of F(8,3), should be stored in variables of precision at least (8,3) if no significance is to be lost.

PROGRAMMING HINT: ACCURACY Numeric input formats for FIXED DECIMAL variables should not have greater precision than the declarations of the variables.

The following example shows how explicit decimal points override the format specification of the decimal position. Given the declaration and input statement

```
DCL (A,B,C,D)  FIXED DEC (8,3);
GET EDIT (A,B,C,D) (COL(1),F(8,3),F(8,3),F(8,3),F(8,3)
```

or

```
GET EDIT (A,B,C,D) (COL(1),(4)F(8,0));
```

or

```
GET EDIT (A,B,C,D) (COL(1),(4)F(8));        (Preferred)
```

and the data

```
1       9       17      25      33
bb289.36|b832.754|bbb-13.5|bb5432.b|
```

then A contains +00289 360, B contains +00832 754, C contains −00013 500, and D contains +05432 000. Each field width is again eight, but the decimal points do not occupy a fixed position within the field. Each value is picked up, converted to the proper form, then stored. For easy maintenance of a program, either exact specifications should be used in formats or, if the decimal point is recorded in the data, only the field width should be given.

PROGRAMMING HINT: CLARITY When the input has a decimal point, the format should only specify the field width.

If numbers are spaced farther apart, the field width can be increased to include the extra spaces. Given the declaration and input statement

```
DCL (A,B,C,D)  FIXED DEC(8,3);
GET EDIT (A,B,C,D) (COL(1), (4)F(12,0));
```

and the data

```
1           13          25          37          49
bbbbbb289.36 |bbbbb832.754|bbbbbbb-13.5 |bbbbbb5432.0|
```

then A contains +00289 360, B contains +00832 754, C contains −00013 500, and D contains +05432 000. The field width simply tells where on the card to search for the number.

The repetition factor can apply to a single field specification or to a group of specifications referring to a larger unit of the input. When the repetition factor applies to a group, the group is enclosed in parentheses.

INPUT OF FLOATING-POINT DECIMAL DATA

The E format specification is used to input floating-point decimal data. The general form of the specification is

```
E(w,d)
```

where d is optional, w is the total number of characters in the input field, and d is the number of decimal digits to the right of the decimal point. E(w) is the same as E(w,0). The following examples show the use of the E format specification.

```
DCL  X  FLOAT BIN;
GET EDIT (X) (E(7,2));
```

Format	*Input data*	*Value stored*		
E(7,2)	12345 ƀƀ	123.45	or	1.2345E2
	1234E–4	.001234	or	1.234E–3
	–1234 E2	–1234.	or	–1.234E3
	ƀƀ123 .4	123.4	or	1.234E2
	ƀ .123 4ƀ	.1234	or	1.234E–1

The input data may or may not have a decimal point. It may or may not be in exponential form. The input value is converted first to floating point, then to the form required for storage.

The following example shows the input of floating-point data without an explicit decimal point. The format controls the placement of the decimal point. Given the declaration and input statement

```
DCL (A,B)    FLOAT DEC,
    C        FLOAT BIN,
    D        FIXED DEC (8,3);
GET EDIT (A,B,C,D) (COL(1),E(7,3),E(9,4),E(9,2),E(8,3));
```

and the data

```
1       8        17       26       34
3854E01|-48756E02|28551E-02|-2325E02|
```

then A has the value 3.854E01, B has the value –4.8756E02, C has the value 285.51E–02, and D has the value is –2.325E02, stored as –00232.500.

When the decimal point is actually in the data, it overrides the d of the specification. The position of the point in the value stored is the same as the position of the point in the data. Given the declaration and input statement

```
DCL (A,B)   FLOAT DECIMAL,
    C       FLOAT BIN,
    D       FIXED DEC(8,3);

GET EDIT (A,B,C,D)
(COL(1),E(8,3),E(10,4),E(10,2),E(9,3));
```

or

```
GET EDIT (A,B,C,D) (COL(1),E(8),E(10),E(10),E(9));
```

and the data

```
1        9         19        29        38
3.854E01|-487.56bbb|285.51E-02|-2.3250E2|
```

then A has the value 3.854E01, B has the value −4.8756E02, C has the value 285.51E−02, and D has the value −2.325E02, stored as −00232 500.

The numbers may appear anywhere within the field specified, in either fixed-point or floating-point notation. Embedded blanks are not permitted, but there may be leading and trailing blanks. Therefore, the field width usually is standardized and a single specification used for all the values. The specification must be large enough to contain the largest possible value of the data. Given the declaration and input statement

```
DCL (A,B)  FLOAT DECIMAL,
    C      FLOAT BIN,
    D      FIXED DEC(8,3);

GET EDIT (A,B,C,D) (COL(1),E(12,0),E(12,0),E(12,0),E(12,0));
```

or

```
GET EDIT (A,B,C,D) (COL(1),(4)E(12,0));
```

and the data

```
1           13          25          37          49
bb3.854E01bb|bb-4.8756E02|b285.51E-02b|bb-232.5bbbb|
```

then A has the value 3.854E01, B has the value −4.8756E02, C has the value 285.51E−02, and D has the value is −2.325E02, stored as −00232.500.

Whenever the exponent part of the value is missing, an exponent of zero is assumed. If an entire field is blank, the CONVERSION condition is raised.

INPUT OF CHARACTER STRINGS

The format specification A is used to input character data. The general form of the specification is

```
A(w)
```

where w is the field width, the number of character positions in the input stream which provide the value. This specification controls the input. No quotation marks are needed in the data, even when there are blanks in part of the field. The following examples show the use of the A format specification.

```
DCL  X  CHAR(6);
GET EDIT (X) (A(6));
```

Format	*Input data*	*Contents of storage*
A(6)	1 2345b	'1 2345b'
	A BCbbb	'A BCbbb'
	bWXYZ4	'bWXYZ4'
	b−35bb	'b−35bb'
	A BCbYZ	'A BCbYZ'
	AB CDEFG	'A BCDEF'

```
DCL   X   CHAR(10) VARYING;
GET EDIT (X) (A(6));
```

Format	*Input data*	*Contents of storage*
A(6)	A BCbbb	'A BCbbb'
	bWXYZ4	'bWXYZ4'

The blanks in the input data are considered to be part of the value. The VARYING attribute of the second data declaration keeps the value from being padded with additional trailing blanks, but the length is determined by the edit format, not by the data. The VARYING attribute is only useful for list-directed or data-directed input.

PROGRAMMING HINT: CAUTION Do not use CHAR VARYING for edit-directed input.

Given the declaration and input statement

```
DCL NAME     CHAR(15),
    STREET   CHAR(12),
    CITY     CHAR(5),
    ST_ZIP   CHAR(8);
GET EDIT (NAME, STREET, CITY, ST_ZIP)
         (COL(1),A(15),A(12),A(5),A(8));
```

and the data

```
1              16          28   33      41
 JAMES M. WALKER|8 LINCOLN ST |OMAHA|NBb85932 |
```

then NAME contains 'JAMES M. WALKER', STREET contains '8 LINCOLN ST', CITY contains 'OMAHA', and ST_ZIP contains 'NB 85932'.

If the field width is overspecified, the data must be left-justified in the field. Given the declaration and input statement

```
DCL NAME     CHAR(15),
    STREET   CHAR(12),
    CITY     CHAR(5),
    ST_ZIP   CHAR(8);
GET EDIT (NAME, STREET, CITY, ST_ZIP)
         (COL(1),A(20),A(12),A(10),A(10));
```

and the data

```
1                   21          33        43        53
 JAMES M. WALKERbbbbb|8 LINCOLN ST |OMAHAbbbbb|NB 85932bb|
```

then NAME contains 'JAMES M. WALKER', STREET contains '8 LINCOLN ST', CITY contains 'OMAHA', and ST_ZIP contains 'NB 85932'.

When many records having the same type of information are to be read, the declarations and field specifications should be selected to fit all the likely data values. Extra spacing should be included in the data for legibility.

PROGRAMMING HINT: GENERALITY Use standard data formatting.

The following data is readable because the values are aligned in columns wide enough to provide blanks between even the largest values.

```
1                   21             36           49        59
JAMES M. WALKERbbbbb|8 LINCOLN STbbb|OMAHAbbbbbbbb|NB 85932bb|
MARY LOU THOMPSONbbb|14 ELM BLVDbbbb|LITTLE ROCKb|AR 72204bb|
W. D. ANDERSONbbbbbb|APT 10 SOUTH ST|PHOENIXbbbbb|AZ 21365bb|
LUCRETIA SANDERSbbbb|8 LINCOLN STbbb|BAKERSFIELDb|CA 91106bb|
```

INPUT OF BIT STRINGS

The B format specification is used for bit strings. The general form of the specification is

```
B(w)
```

where w is the field width. Other than leading and trailing blanks, the only characters that may appear in the field are zeros and ones. The data does not take the form of a bit constant. The following examples show the use of the B format specification.

```
DCL X BIT(6);
GET EDIT (X) (B(6));
```

Format	*Input data*	*Contents of storage*
B(6)	10101b	'101010'B
	b11bbb	'110000'B
	10101010	'101010'B

```
DCL X BIT(10) VARYING;
GET EDIT (X) (B(6));
```

Format	*Input data*	*Contents of storage*
B(6)	1011bb	'101100'B
	b10100	'010100'B

As with character strings, the value is left-justified when it is stored in the variable. The B format can be used only with variables that have been declared to be bit strings. The VARYING attribute has no effect.

Given the declaration and input statement

```
DCL BST1  BIT(7),
    BST2  BIT(6),
    BST3  BIT(12);
GET EDIT (BST1,BST2,BST3) (COL(1), B(7), B(6), B(12));
```

and the data

```
1      8     14          26
1011011 011101 111001011010
```

then BST1 contains '1011011'B, BST2 contains '011101'B, and BST3 contains '111001011010'B.

As with other data types, the field width may be overspecified and the extra places filled with blanks. Given the declaration and input statement

```
DCL BST1 BIT(7),
    BST2 BIT(6),
    BST3 BIT(12);

GET EDIT(BST1,BST2,BST3) (COL(1),B(15),B(15), B(15));
```

or

```
GET EDIT (BST1,BST2,BST3) (COL(1),(3)B(15));
```

and the data

```
1              16             31             46
ƀƀƀƀ1011011ƀƀƀƀ ƀƀƀƀƀ011101ƀƀƀƀ ƀƀ111001011010
```

then BST1 contains '1011011'B, BST2 contains '011101'B, and BST3 contains '111001011010'B.

INPUT OF MIXED DATA TYPES

Since stream input actually consists of characters, all stream input could use the A format. However, we often want data consisting of digits to be stored as a numeric value rather than a character string. Data types may be mixed in an input list as long as the format specifications, data types, and values are compatible. Given the declaration and input statement

```
DCL SSNO              CHAR(11),
    NAME              CHAR(20),
    (T1,T2,T3,T4)     FIXED BIN;
GET EDIT (SSNO,NAME,T1,T2,T3,T4)
         (COL(1),A(11), A(20),(4)F(3));
```

and the data

```
1          12                  32 35 38 41 44
123-45-6789 JOHN K. WILSONƀƀƀƀƀƀ ƀƀ5 ƀ98 -74 ƀ86
```

then SSNO contains '123-45-6789', NAME contains 'JOHN K. WILSONƀƀƀƀƀƀ', T1 has the value 5, T2 has the value 98, T3 has the value −74, and T4 has the value 86. The social security number and name are both read as character strings even though one contains digits and the other letters. Identification numbers such as social security numbers, account numbers, telephone numbers, and zip codes should be read using A format and stored in character string variables. The last four fields are read as fixed-point numbers.

PROGRAMMING HINT: PROCESSING EFFICIENCY Non-computational numbers should be stored as character strings.

Numbers to be used in arithmetic should be read with E or F format and stored in numeric variables.

MATCHING OF INPUT AND FORMAT LISTS

The format specifications must be compatible with the input list as to type. If the formats do not match the input list as to number, any extra format specifications are ignored. If there are fewer format specifications than variables in the input list, the format is repeated as many times as needed.

PROGRAMMING HINT: CAUTION Any unmatched edit format is ignored.

Given the declaration and input statement

```
DCL  (A,B,C)   FIXED DEC(5,3),
     STR       CHAR(5);

GET EDIT (A,B,STR,C) (COL(1),F(5,3),F(5,3),A(5));
```

or

```
GET EDIT (A,B,STR) (COL(1),F(5,3),F(5,3),A(5));
GET EDIT (C) (COL(1),F(5,3));
```

or

```
GET EDIT (A,B,STR,C) ((2)(COL(1),F(5,3),F(5,3),A(5));
```

or

```
GET EDIT (A,B,STR,C) (COL(1),F(5,3),F(5,3),A(5));
```

(Format is repeated)

and the data

```
 1     6     11    16
|38526|58763|VWXYZ|

|-2781|bb833|     |
```

then A contains +38 526, B contains +58 763, STR contains 'VWXYZ', and C contains −02 781.

Given the declaration and input statement

```
DCL (A,B,C,D)     FIXED DEC(5,3),
    (STR1,STR2)   CHAR(5);
GET EDIT (A,B,STR1,C,D,STR2)
          ((2)(COL(1),F(5,3) F(5,3),A(5)));
```

or

```
GET EDIT (A,B,STR1,C,D,STR2) ((COL(1),F(5,3),F(5,3),A(5)));
```

(Format is repeated)

and the data

```
 1    6     11    16
 38526 58763 VWXYZ

 -2781 bb833 bbbbb
```

then A contains +38 526, B contains +58 763, STR1 contains 'VWXYZ', C contains −02 781, D contains +00 833, and STR2 contains 'bbbbb' (note this value). A repeat factor may be used with any combination of format specifications.

4.5.2 Edit-directed output

Edit-directed output allows the programmer the greatest amount of control over the placement and the appearance of the output. It should be used whenever the output is to be printed and its appearance is important or when the output is to be read by people other than the programmer. With edit-directed output the programmer has complete control over both the horizontal and vertical spacing of the data and the ability to provide titles and column headings.

The format specifications for edit-directed output are nearly the same as for edit-directed input:

A(w)	Most types of processing
B(w)	Debugging
C(w, d)	Scientific applications
E(w, d)	Scientific applications
F(w, d)	Most types of processing
P	Business applications

The output list may include constants, variables, and expressions of all types, separated by commas. The format list must be compatible with the output list.

OUTPUT IN FIXED-POINT FORM

Any type of numeric data may be printed in ordinary decimal notation using the F format specification. The use of the F(w, d) specification for output differs slightly from its use for input. The field width w must be large enough to print the d fractional digits, the decimal point, any digits to the left of the point, and a sign. In general w must be at least as large as d+2.

PROGRAMMING HINT: ACCURACY Output format F(w, d) must have $w > d+1$.

If the field specification is too small, the SIZE error condition is raised. If too few digits are specified to the right of the decimal point, the value is automatically rounded or truncated (depending on the implementation) to the nearest value that meets the specification. In general, the output format specified for a variable must be larger than the declared precision, as space is needed for the sign and the decimal point. It must be possible to print both the smallest and the largest possible values of the variable. For example, output using the format F(6,2) takes the form 'xxx.xx' for positive numbers, '–xx.xx' for negative numbers. The smallest value that can be printed with this format is –99.99; the largest is 999.99.

The effect of F format output specifications is as follows:

Stored value	*Format specification*	*Output*	*Comment*
48563	F(5)	48563	Exact
48563	F(4)	****	SIZE error
48563	F(6)	ƀ48563	Padded
–48563	F(6)	–48563	Exact
–48563	F(5)	****	SIZE error
325.648	F(7,3)	325.648	Exact
–325.648	F(8,3)	–325.648	Exact
325.648	F(8,3)	ƀ325.648	Padded
325.648	F(7,2)	ƀ325.65	Rounded
325.648	F(6,1)	ƀ325.6	Rounded
325.648	F(5,0)	ƀƀ326	Rounded
325.648	F(6,3)	******	SIZE error
325.648	F(9,5)	325.64800	Padded

When a numeric value is printed, it is aligned with the position of the decimal point. If necessary, the left end is padded with blanks. If the number of decimal digits to the right of the point is overspecified, extra zeros are printed.

Given the following statements,

```
A = 135.62;
B = 97.5;
C = -625.72;
PUT EDIT (A,B,C) (COL(1),F(6,2),F(4,1),F(7,2));
```

the output is printed as

```
1      7    11     18
|135.62|97.5|-625.72|                                  |
```

The values exactly fit the format specifications. Because of this, the numbers are printed without any spacing between them. The numbers can be spaced apart by overspecifying the field width in the format. Given the following statements,

```
A = 135.62;
B = 97.5;
C = -625.72;

PUT EDIT (A,B,C) (COL(1),F(10,2),F(10,2),F(10,2));
```

the output is printed as

```
1           11           21           31
|ƀƀƀƀ135.62|ƀƀƀƀƀ97.50|ƀƀƀ-625.72|                    |
```

(One output line)

With the statements

```
PUT EDIT (A,B,C) (COL(1),(2)F(10,2),COL(1),F(10,2));
```

or

```
PUT EDIT (A,B,C) (COL(1),(2)F(10,2));
```

the output is printed as

```
1           11           21
|ƀƀƀƀ135.62|ƀƀƀƀƀ97.50|                               |

1           11
|ƀƀƀ-625.72|                                          |
```

(Two output lines)

Constants and expressions may be included in the output line. Given the statements

```
A = 5;
B = 2.25;
C = 12;
D = 1.5;
PUT EDIT (A*B+C,2*D-B) (COL(1),(2)F(10,3));
```

the output is printed as

```
1           11           22
|ƀƀƀƀ23.250|ƀƀƀƀƀ0.750|                               |
```

An output list may contain function calls. The functions are evaluated and the returned values placed in the print buffer. Given the following statements

```
DCL (X,Y) FIXED BIN;
X = 25;
Y = 64;
PUT EDIT (SQRT(X),MAX(X,Y)) (COL(1),(2)F(5,1));
```

the output is printed as

```
1     6     11
|ƀƀ5.0|ƀ64.0|                                         |
```

Notice that the square root function that returns a floating-point number can have its value printed using a fixed-point format. The MAX function returns the same type as its arguments. The fixed-point format can be used for any type of numeric value provided that the specification is adequate for the value.

Using a fixed-point format for floating-point values can lead to errors. If the field width is not large enough to print the sign or all the digits to the left of the decimal point, the SIZE error condition is raised.

OUTPUT IN FLOATING-POINT FORM

Any numeric data to be printed in floating-point form is output using the E specification. The general form of the specification is

```
E(w,d,s) or E(w,d)
```

where d specifies the number of decimal digits to be printed to the right of the decimal point, w specifies the total field width, and s, specifying the total number of digits, is optional. The value of w must be at least as large as d+7.

PROGRAMMING HINT: ACCURACY Output format E(w,d) must have w> d+6.

The value of w must include space for d digits to the right of the decimal point, at least one digit to the left of the point, a two-digit signed exponent, the letter E, and the sign of the number if it is negative. For example, output using the format E(10, 2) takes the form 'ƀƀx.xxExxx' for positive numbers, 'ƀ−x.xxExxx' for negative numbers.

If the field specification is too small, the SIZE error condition is raised. The effect of the E format is as follows:

Values stored	*Format*	*Printed form*	*Comment*
825.62	E(10, 4)	8.2562Eb02	Exact
825.62	E(9, 3)	8.256Eb02	Rounded
−0.003562	E(10, 3)	−3.562E−03	Exact
0.003562	E(12, 3)	bbb3.562E−03	Padded
0.003562	E(11, 5)	3.56200E−03	Padded
−3762.26	E(12, 6)	************	SIZE error
−3762.26	E(13, 6)	−3.762260E 03	Exact
−3762.26	E(12,4, 6)	−37.6226E 02	Scaled
−3762.26	E(12,3, 6)	−376.226E 01	Scaled

The last two examples show the use of the E(w, d, s) form of the floating-point format. The default value of s is d+1. This form of the format calls for the position of the decimal point to be adjusted so that there are d digits to the right of the point and s−d digits to the left of the point. The number is said to be *scaled*. The exponent is adjusted so that the value of the number is not changed.

Given the statements

```
W = 135.62;
X = -360.754;
Y = -0.00852;
PUT EDIT (W,X,Y) (COL(1),E(11,4),E(12,5),E(9,2));
```

the output is printed as

```
1          12          24       33
|b1.3562E+02 |-3.60754E+02|-8.52E-03 |                    |
```

With the output statement

```
PUT EDIT (W,X,Y) (COL(1),E(15,4),E(15,5),E(15,2));
```

the output is printed with standard spacing as

```
1              16             31             46
|bbbbb1.3562E+02|bbb-3.60754E+02|bbbbbb-8.52E-03|     |
```

The field widths are overspecified to produce leading blanks, but the number of decimal places are not. Given the statements

```
W = 135.62;
X = -360.754;
Y = -0.00852;
PUT EDIT (W,X,Y) (COL(1),E(15,5),E(15,6),E(15,4));
```

the output is printed with leading blanks and zero fill as

```
1              16             31             46
|bbbb1.35620E+02 |bb-3.607540E+02|bbbb-8.5200E-03|     |
```

Both the field widths and the number of decimal places are overspecified. Given the statements

```
W = 135.62;
X = -360.754;
Y = -0.00852;
PUT EDIT (W,X,Y) (COL(1),E(15,2),E(15,3),E(15,1));
```

the output is printed with leading blanks, but rounded as

```
1              16             31             46
|bbbbbbb1.36E+02|bbbbb-3.608E+02 |bbbbbbb-8.5E-03|     |
```

The field widths are overspecified, but the number of decimal digits is underspecified. The same values with underspecification of field width raise the SIZE condition.

OUTPUT IN CHARACTER FORM

Character strings are printed using the A format. The general form of the specification is

```
A(w)
```

where w specifies the field width for the output and is optional. Just as character strings are stored left-justified in memory, they are positioned left-justified in the print field. If the specification w is not large enough, the characters on the right are truncated. If the field is overspecified, the extra positions on the right are filled with blanks. When the field specification is not used, the field width defaults to the length of the variable to be printed.

The use of the A format for output is as follows:

Storage value	*Format*	*Output*	*Comment*
WXYZ	A(4)	WXYZ	Exact
WXYZ	A	WXYZ	Exact
WXYZ	A(3)	WXY	Truncated
WXYZ	A(5)	WXYZb̸	Padded
WXYZ	A(8)	WXYZb̸b̸b̸b̸	Padded
WXYZb̸b̸	A(5)	WXYZb̸	Truncated
b̸WXYZ	A(5)	b̸WXYZ	Exact
b̸WXYZ	A(4)	b̸WXY	Truncated
b̸WXYZ	A(6)	b̸WXYZb̸	Padded

The following examples show the spacing of character data on the output line. Given the following statements

```
DCL (NAME,STREET,CITY,ST_ZIP) CHAR(20) VARYING;
NAME = 'JOHN K JACOBS';
STREET = '1028 HARRINGTON';
CITY = 'MADISON';
ST_ZIP = 'WIS 39854';

PUT EDIT (NAME,STREET,CITY,ST_ZIP)
         (COL(1),A(13),A(15),A(7),A(9));
```

or

```
PUT EDIT (NAME,STREET,CITY,ST_ZIP) (COL(1),A,A,A,A);
```

or

```
PUT EDIT (NAME,STREET,CITY,ST_ZIP) (COL(1),(4)A);
```

the output is printed as

```
1             14             29     36       45
|JOHN K JACOBS|1028 HARRINGTON|MADISON|WIS 39854|     |
```

Notice that there is no space between data items as all the specifications are exact. In addition, the repetition factor is an abbreviated way of indicating four As without implying that the field widths are the same. Each field width depends on the length of the data value.

By changing the column specifications, the same character data can be printed in the form of a mailing label. Given the following statements

```
DCL (NAME,STREET,CITY,ST_ZIP) CHAR(20) VARYING;
NAME = 'JOHN K JACOBS';
STREET = '1028 HARRINGTON';
CITY = 'MADISON';
ST_ZIP = 'WIS 39854';

PUT EDIT (NAME,STREET,CITY,' ',ST_ZIP)
         (COL(1),A,COL(1),A,COL(1),A,A,A));
```

or

```
PUT EDIT (NAME,STREET,CITY,' ',ST_ZIP)
         ((3) (COL(1),A),A,A);
```

or

```
PUT EDIT (NAME) (COL(1),A);                          (Best)
PUT EDIT (STREET) (COL(1),A);
PUT EDIT (CITY,' ',ST_ZIP) (COL(1),A,A,A);
```

the output is printed as

```
JOHN K JACOBS
1028 HARRINGTON
MADISON WIS 39854
```

Notice the use of the character literal, the quoted blank, to separate the city and state.

PROGRAMMING HINT: SIMPLICITY Use the A format without field width specification for character output.

OUTPUT OF BIT DATA

The B format is used for the output of bit strings. The general form of the specification is

```
B(w)
```

The field width is optional. If it is not used, the actual width of the value being printed is taken as the default field width. If the field width is specified, using the form B(w), the bit string is left-justified in the field specification is too small, the right end of the value is truncated. If the specification is larger than necessary, the right end of the field is padded with blanks. The use of the B specification is as follows:

Storage value	*Format*	*Output*	*Comment*
101101	B(6)	101101	Exact
101101	B	101101	Exact
101101	B(5)	10110	Truncated
101101	B(8)	101101bb	Padded

The following example shows the use of the B format. Given the statements

```
DCL BST1  BIT(6),
    BST2  BIT(7),
    BST3  BIT(4);
BST1 = '101011'B;
BST2 = '1110111'B;
BST3 = '1110'B;
```

and the output statement

```
PUT EDIT (BST1,BST2,BST3) (COL(1),B(6),B(7),B(4);
```

or

```
PUT EDIT (BST1,BST2,BST3) (COL(1),(3)B);
```

the output is printed as

```
1     7      14  18
|101011|1110111|1110 |                                    |
```

As the bit strings are not separated by blanks, the output is unreadable. The strings are spaced apart if the fields are overspecified. Given the statements

```
DCL BST1  BIT(6),
    BST2  BIT(7),
    BST3  BIT(4);
BST1 = '101011'B;
BST2 = '1110111'B;
BST3 = '1110'B;
PUT EDIT (BST1,BST2,BST3) (COL(1),B(11),B(12),B(4));
```

the output is printed as

```
1          12          24  28
|101011     |1110111    |1110|                            |
```

Bit string data is not used very often in application programming. However, it can be useful in debugging programs. The library function UNSPEC takes a variable of any type as argument and returns a bit string showing how the value is stored inside the computer. At times the programmer may need to know this information, so output statements such as the following may be useful. Given the declaration and statements

```
DCL X FIXED BIN(15);
X = 13;
PUT EDIT ('X =', X, '    ', UNSPEC(X))
         (COL(1),A,F(5,0),A,B);
```

the output is printed as

```
1  4    9    14              30
|X =|   13|    |0000000000001101 |                        |
```

The output includes the name of the variable, its value, and the internal representation of the value as it appears in the binary number system. (On some computers, the bit value would appear reversed.) A FIXED BIN(15) value actually occupies sixteen bit positions in the computer's memory: the extra position is for the number's sign. When the leftmost bit is zero, the sign is positive. When the leftmost bit is one, the sign is negative.

This example shows how output may be labeled and mixed data types printed in the same line by using an appropriate specification for each value.

4.5.3 Page control

Within the edit format both horizontal and vertical spacing of output data can be controlled. To some extent the spacing of input data can be controlled as well.

HORIZONTAL SPACE CONTROL

The two horizontal print control formats are the COLUMN and X formats. X format specification is used to skip columns. In output, this leaves blank spaces between data items in the output. The specification X(n) leaves n blank spaces. In input, it skips n columns, which need not be blank. If an X specification is the last specification in an edit format, it is ignored. The COLUMN format is used to specify the starting print position of the data item to be read or printed.

Horizontal spacing of output An entire output line is set up in the print buffer before printing. It is initialized to blanks, then filled according to the output instructions. The line is transmitted to the printer only when the buffer is full, when COLUMN, LINE, or SKIP specifications indicate the start of a new line, or when processing stops. Given the statements

```
A = 135.62;
B = 97.5;
C = -625.72;
PUT EDIT (A,B,C) (COL(1),X(5),F(6,2),X(5),F(5,2),
                  X(5),F(7,2));
```

the output is printed as

```
1     6      12    17   22    27      34
|bbbbb|135.62|bbbbb|97.50|bbbbb|-625.72|        |
```

while with

```
PUT EDIT (A,B,C) (COL(6),F(6,2),COL(17),F(5,2),
                  COL(27),F(7,2));
```

the output is printed as

```
1     6      12    17   22    27      34
|     |135.62|     |97.50|     |-625.72|        |
```

If the column option specifies a column that has already been used, the output is forced to the next line as in the following example. Given the following statements

```
A = 6.75;
B = 18.325;
C = 17.95;
D = -145.6;
PUT EDIT (A,B,C,D) (COL(1),F(5,2),COL(11),F(6,3),
                    COL(1),F(5,2),COL(21),F(6,1));
```

the output is printed as

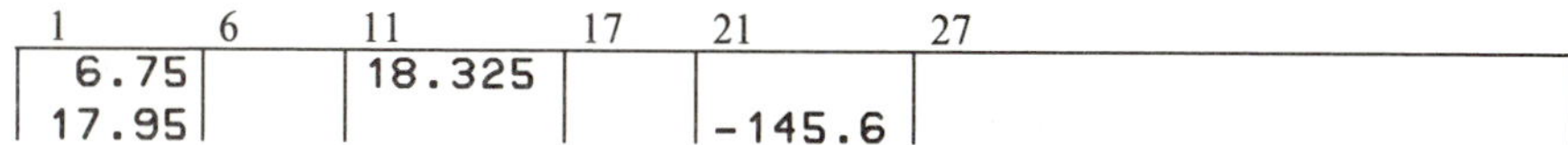

```
1    6    11    17  21    27
 6.75      18.325
17.95                -145.6
```

If the fields of the output are to be spaced apart for better readability, the fields may be overspecified, an X format may be used, or the COL option may be used. Given the following statements

```
NAME = 'JOHN K JACOBS';
STREET = '1028 HARRINGTON';
CITY = 'MADISON';
ST_ZIP = 'WIS 39854';

PUT EDIT (NAME,STREET,CITY,ST_ZIP)
         (COL(1),A(18), A(20),A(12),A(9));
```

or

```
PUT EDIT (NAME,STREET,CITY,ST_ZIP)
         (COL(1),A,X(5),A,X(5),A,X(5),A);
```

or

```
PUT EDIT (NAME,STREET,CITY,ST_ZIP)
         (COL(1),A,COL(19),A,COL(39),A,COL(51),A);
```

the output is printed as

```
1             14   19             34   39     46   51       60
 JOHN K JACOBS     1028 HARRINGTON     MADISON     WIS 39854
```

Horizontal spacing of input The X specification can be used in an input format for skipping a specified number of positions in the input stream. The COLUMN option can be used to skip to a particular position in the input stream. So far we have only used it to skip to the first position of a card or input line. It can also be used as a tab character. X(n) specifies that n positions are to be skipped. COL(n) specifies that the pointer is to be moved to the *nth* position. Given the declaration and input statement

```
DCL (A,B,C,D) FIXED DEC(6,2);
GET EDIT (A,B,C,D)
         (COL(1),F(5,3),X(5),F(6,2),X(5),F(2),COL(31),F(4,1));
```

and the data

```
1     6     11     17   22  24     31   35
38526 bbbX= 587639      91         -325
```

then A contains +0038 52, B contains +5876 39, C contains +0091 00, and D contains −0032 50. Columns 6 through 10, 17 through 21, and 24 through 30 are ignored. The character string 'X=' in positions 9 and 10 is not read by the computer. The value for A is read from a field starting in column 1. B starts in columns 11, C occupies columns 22 and 23, and D starts in columns 31.

VERTICAL SPACE CONTROL

The page formatting options PAGE, SKIP, and LINE were discussed in section 4.4. With these options, character literals may be used to print all types of headings. The following group of statements shows the formatting that can go into a report. It includes a report heading, a page heading, and column headings.

```
M1 = 21366.25;
M2 = 7978.84;
M3 = 10458.66;
PUT PAGE;
PUT SKIP EDIT ('P. 1')(COL(60),A);
PUT EDIT ('QUARTERLY REPORT') (COL(15),A);
PUT LINE(6) ('JANUARY','FEBRUARY','MARCH')
            (COL(1), (3)(X(6),A));
PUT SKIP(2);
PUT EDIT (M1,M2,M3) (COL(1),(3)F(13,2));
```

The output is printed as

```
                                                    P. 1
              QUARTERLY REPORT



      JANUARY        FEBRUARY        MARCH
     21366.25        7978.84      10458.66
```

SKIP and LINE options are used within a page. The PAGE option is used to change pages. These options may be placed either inside or outside the format list. If they are outside, they may be placed in any order. Regardless of the order, if the PAGE option is present, it is used first. The SKIP and LINE options are used in the order in which they are written. When these options are within the format, they are used in the order in which they are encountered as the format list is interpreted from left to right. When the same options are used both inside and outside the format list, the outside options are executed before the format list is used.

The following sets of options for each line of the headings are equivalent. Given the output statements

```
PUT PAGE EDIT ('PAYROLL REPORT',(14)'_')
             (COL(60),A,SKIP(0),COL(60),A);
```

or

```
PUT EDIT ('PAYROLL REPORT',(14)'_')
        (PAGE,(2)(COL(60),A,SKIP(0)));
```

or

```
PUT EDIT ('PAYROLL REPORT') (COL(60),A) PAGE;
```

or

```
PUT EDIT ('______________') (SKIP(0),COL(60),A);
```

the output is printed as

```
                          60
                          PAYROLL REPORT
                          --------------
```

with 'PAYROLL REPORT' printed in the middle of the top line of a page and underlined.

Given the output statements

```
PUT LINE(3) PAGE EDIT ('BANK BALANCE SHEET')
(COL(50),A);
```

or

```
PUT PAGE EDIT ('BANK BALANCE SHEET')
              (LINE(3), COL(50),A);
```

or

```
PUT EDIT ('BANK BALANCE SHEET')
         (PAGE,LINE(3), COL(50),A);
```

or

```
PUT EDIT ('BANK BALANCE SHEET')
         (LINE(3),COL(50),A) PAGE;
```

the output is printed as

```
                      50
                      (2 blank lines)
                      BANK BALANCE SHEET
```

with 'BANK BALANCE SHEET' printed on the third line of the next page.

Given the statements

```
PUT SKIP(5) EDIT ('PART 1') (COL(20),A);
```

or

```
PUT EDIT ('PART 1') (SKIP(5),COL(20),A);
```

or

```
PUT EDIT ('PART 1') (COL(20),A) SKIP(5);
```

the output is printed as

```
                          20
                          (4 blank lines)
          PART 1
```

with 'PART 1' on the fifth line of the same page. The report heading would be printed on just the first page; the other two headings might be printed on every page. All pages of an output report should be numbered and contain identification. Together the output statements

```
PUT PAGE EDIT ('PAYROLL REPORT') (COL(60),A);

PUT EDIT ('______________') (SKIP(0),COL(60),A);
PUT PAGE EDIT ('BANK BALANCE SHEET') (LINE(3),COL(50),A);
PUT EDIT ('PART 1') (SKIP(5),COL(20),A);
```

print the output on two pages as

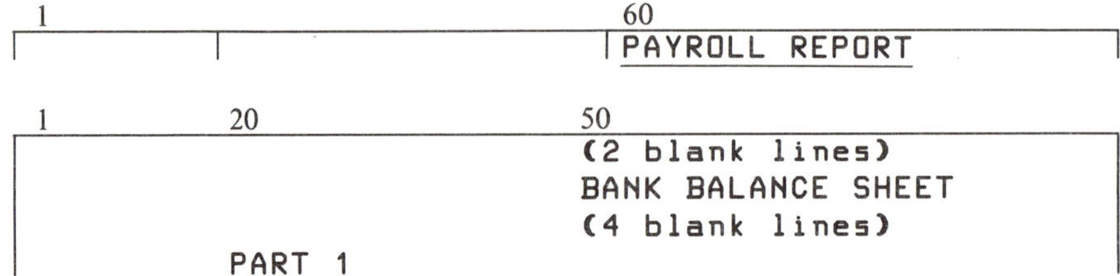

OUTPUT DESIGN

Output coding forms are available to plan the output format. The character positions in each line are marked on the form. Printer paper comes in different widths, 80-column, 120-column, and 132-column being the most popular. The titles, headings, and columns of data are planned on these sheets. Then the edit formats are written based on the layout on the output coding sheet. Given the following data layout,

```
1                        57                   77
                          ACME MATERIAL REPORT
```

we assume the title is in the middle of a 132-character line with 56 blanks on each side. This is coded as

```
PUT PAGE EDIT ('ACME MATERIAL REPORT')
              (COL(1),X(56),A);

PUT SKIP(0) EDIT ('___________________')
                 (COL(1),X(56),A);
```

The first output statement prints the heading at the center of the lines at the top of the page; the second output statement underlines the heading. The output statements shown above also can be coded using the column option for spacing rather than the X specification.

```
PUT PAGE EDIT ('ACME MATERIAL REPORT')(COL(57),A);

PUT SKIP(0) EDIT ('___________________')(COL(57),A);
```

Since both output statements use the same format, a remote format may be used. A remote format is named using a FORMAT statement. It is customarily placed just before the end of the procedure and is referred to by name, as in the following examples.

```
PUT PAGE EDIT ('ACME MATERIAL REPORT')(R(REFOR));

PUT SKIP(0) EDIT ('___________________')(R(REFOR));
. . .
REFOR: FORMAT (COL(57),A);
```

The following example shows a report title, headings, and subheadings. Given the statements

```
PUT PAGE EDIT ('ACME MATERIAL REPORT') (R(TITLE));

PUT SKIP(0) EDIT ('____________________') (R(TITLE));
PUT LINE(4) EDIT ('CAST IRON','STEEL','ALUMINUM',
                  'COPPER','ZINC')(R(HEADING));
PUT SKIP(0) EDIT ('__________','_____','_________',
                  '______','____')(R(HEADING));
. . .
TITLE: FORMAT (COL(57),A);
HEADING: FORMAT (COL(11),(5)(A,X(20)));
```

the output is printed as

```
1                     57                      77
                  ACME MATERIALS REPORT
                     (2 blank lines)
    CASTIRON     STEEL     ALUMINUM     COPPER     ZINC
```

Notice that LINE(4) prints on the fourth line of the page. The remote format TITLE prints the main title, and the format HEADING prints the column heading.

If the output is being sent to a printer file, PAGE and LINE options may be used; otherwise SKIP is the only option for vertical spacing. The X and COL specifications control horizontal spacing.

Behind the scenes there is a page counter that counts the number of times the PAGE option is carried out during execution. This can be used to number pages by including it in the output list, as in

```
PUT PAGE EDIT ('PAGE',PAGENO(SYSPRINT))
              (COL(100),A,A);
```

PAGENO is a library function that returns the value of the internal page counter for the file which is its argument, in this case the standard system printer file.

PAGING

Paging can be either automatic or controlled by the programmer. A library function, LINENO, returns the value of the internal line counter for the file that is its argument. With the ENDPAGE condition, this line counter can automatically interrupt the processing whenever there is an attempt to write beyond the end of a page. Through the explicit use of the line counter and the SIGNAL statement, the programmer can raise the ENDPAGE condition whenever a new page is desired.

ENDPAGE condition The ENDPAGE condition is an exception raised when the printer recognizes that the last line of a page has been printed.

Normally the printer automatically continues to the next page, without incrementing the page counter or reinitializing the internal line counter. If the ON ENDPAGE exception handler has been established by the program, page headings and column headings can be placed on each page. This exception handler takes the form

```
ON ENDPAGE(SYSPRINT)
  statement;
```

or

```
ON ENDPAGE(SYSPRINT)
  BEGIN;
    sequence
  END;
```

When the end of the page is reached and there is an attempt to print a line that will not fit on the page, control passes to the statement or sequence of statements following ON ENDPAGE. After these statements have been executed, control returns to the output statement that could not be carried out before. It is then used to print a line on the new page.

A program to print a heading on each page of output has the following structure:

```
. . .
ON ENDPAGE (SYSPRINT)           /* PRINT NEXT HEADING   */
  BEGIN;
    PUT PAGE;
    . . .
  END;

PUT PAGE EDIT ('...') (...); /* PRINT FIRST HEADING */
GET EDIT (...) (...);         /* GET FIRST DATA       */
DO WHILE (...);               /* PROCESS ALL DATA     */
  . . .
  PUT SKIP EDIT (...) (...); /* PRINT DETAIL LINE    */
  GET EDIT (...) (...);       /* GET NEXT DATA        */
END;
 . . .
```

The example in section 4.6.4 has this structure. Notice that the command to print the heading for the first page precedes the DOWHILE loop that contains the calculations. This sequence of instructions is used whenever the first page contains a title that is not used on the other pages. The headings for successive pages are produced automatically.

The ON ENDPAGE statement is an executable command, but executing it at the beginning of the program simply sets up an internal check for the end of the page. This is said to *establish* the *ON unit*. The block following ON ENDPAGE is executed automatically when the PUT SKIP EDIT statement is attempted but the page is full. Attempting to print beyond the end of the page *raises* the exception.

The ON condition is *enabled* automatically at the beginning of every program. After it has been invoked the first time, it will not be raised again unless the PAGE option is used in an output statement. The PAGE option initializes and reinitializes the internal line counter. The ENDPAGE condition is raised when the line counter becomes too large.

SIGNAL statement If there are to be titles on the first page of the output, or if page lengths other than the system default length are needed, the SIGNAL instruction can be used to explicitly raise the exception. In the following program segment the exception is raised at the beginning of the program for the first page, then afterward, whenever the value of the control field changes.

```
. . .
ON ENDPAGE (SYSPRINT)      /* PRINT PAGE HEADING                */
  BEGIN;
    PUT PAGE;
    PUT EDIT (...) (...);
    OLD_VALUE = NEW_VALUE;
  END;
. . .
GET EDIT (...) (...);      /* GET FIRST DATA                    */
OLD_VALUE = NEW_VALUE;
SIGNAL ENDPAGE(SYSPRINT); /* PRINT FIRST HEADING               */
DO WHILE (...);
  IF OLD_VALUE ¬= NEW_VALUE
    THEN
      SIGNAL ENDPAGE(SYSPRINT); /* PRINT HEADING ON NEW PAGE */
  PUT EDIT (...) (...);          /* PRINT DETAIL LINE         */
  GET EDIT (...) (...);          /* GET NEXT DATA             */
END;
. . .
```

Notice that it is assumed that the data is grouped by a control field, for example a department name, or day of the week. If all the data for a group fits on one page, the page break will come when the group changes, activated by the SIGNAL instruction. If there is more data for a group than fits on a single page, the automatic page break will occur when the page is full.

4.5.4 Remote formats

A remote format is to be used in several input or output statements by referring to it by its name. Generally, remote formats are placed either at the beginning or at the end of a program. Their definitions are not executable instructions. A remote format is defined by a PL/I statement having the form

```
label: FORMAT(format list);
```

A remote format is referred to by I/O statements in the forms

```
GET EDIT (input list) (R(remote format label));
PUT EDIT (output list) (R(remote format label));
```

An example would be

```
GET EDIT (A,B,C) (R(FORM_1));
PUT EDIT (A,B,C) (R(FORM_1));
FORM_1: FORMAT(COL(1),F(5,2),E(10,3),X(5),F(7));
```

The same format is being used for both the input and output statements. This is not always possible. The value of A has at most four digits if A is positive and three if it is negative; B has at most five digits if it is positive and four if it is negative; and C has at most six or seven digits. With this format, larger numbers could be used as input, but could not be used as output.

Review questions

1. Indicate whether each of the following statements is true or false.
   - **(a)** In edit-directed input each field specification must include the field width.
   - **(b)** In edit-directed output each field specification must include the field width.
   - **(c)** Floating-point format must be used only with variables declared to be floating point.
   - **(d)** Fixed-point format may be used with variables declared to be either fixed or float.
   - **(e)** The character format may be used for input of any data.
   - **(f)** A character value is printed left-justified in its field.
   - **(g)** A numeric value is printed left-justified in its field.
   - **(h)** The PAGE condition is raised when the last line of a page is printed.
   - **(i)** The ENDFILE condition is raised when an attempt to get data fails.
   - **(j)** The COLUMN format can be used to advance to the next line.

2. Horizontal spacing is controlled by the ____________________ and the ____________________ specifications.

3. Vertical spacing is controlled by the ____________________, ____________________, and ____________________ specifications.

4. Give the largest and smallest values that may be read with a format of F(5, 2).

5. Give the largest and smallest values that may be read with a format of E(5, 2).

6. Give the largest and smallest values that may be printed with a format of F(5, 2).

7. Give the largest and smallest values that may be printed with a format of E(9, 2).

8. What input format should be used with each of the following?
(a) 12.34
(b) −27E6
(c) 10110
(d) (315)270-5194
(e) JOHNbJONES

9. Write an edit-directed input statement to read the following data:

```
1                   21        31         41   46
JAMES L. MADISON    8 WOODSON DES MOINES IOWA 38601
```

10. Give the ouput for each of the following values, given that the output specification is F(6, 2).
(a) 123.45
(b) 123.4567
(c) 1.234
(d) −123.456
(e) −12.3456

11. For each of the following variables, give an output format that will not lose significant digits.

(a) A FIXED BIN(15)
(b) B FIXED DEC(10, 4)
(c) C FLOAT BIN
(d) D FLOAT DEC(5)
(e) E BIT(8)

12. Which of the following formats produce the same output as

```
PUT EDIT (STR1,N1,STR2,N2)
         (COL(1),A(10),X(4),F(5,2));
```

(a) ((2) (COL(1), A(10), F(9, 2)))
(b) (COL(1), A(14), F(5,2), COL(1), A(10), F(9, 2))
(c) (COL(1), A(14), F(9, 2))
(d) (COL(1), A(14), F(5, 2))

13. Using an input format of F(6, 2), the precision of a FIXED DECIMAL variable should be ________ and the output format should be ________.

4.6 Examples of input/output

The following examples illustrate simple and complex input and output.

4.6.1 Calculations involving a right triangle

This program calculates the hypotenuse, area, perimeter, and acute angles of a right triangle, given the lengths of the legs. Notice that the ATAN function returns the angle measured in radians. The angles are being printed in both radians and degrees.

```
RTTRI: PROC OPTIONS(MAIN);
/*************************************************************/
/*                                                           */
/*  PROGRAM: RIGHT TRIANGLE                                  */
/*  AUTHOR:  C ZIEGLER                                       */
/*  VERSION: 07/27/84                                        */
/*                                                           */
/*  PROGRAM DESCRIPTION:                                     */
/*  ------------------------------------------------------  */
/*  THIS PROGRAM PRINTS INFORMATION ABOUT A RIGHT            */
/*  TRIANGLE                                                 */
/*                                                           */
/*  INPUT: THE LEGS (A & B) OF THE TRIANGLE                  */
/*                                                           */
/*  OUTPUT: LEGS (A & B), HYPOTENUSE, AREA, PERIMETER,       */
/*          ACUTE ANGLES                                     */
/*                                                           */
/*************************************************************/

DCL (A, B, C) FLOAT BIN,
    ANGLE_A   FLOAT BIN,
    ANGLE_B   FLOAT BIN;
DCL PI        FLOAT BIN  INIT (3.14159);

GET DATA (A,B);
C = SQRT (A*A + B*B);
PUT SKIP LIST ('HYPOTENUSE =',C);
PUT SKIP LIST ('AREA =',.5*A*B);
PUT SKIP LIST ('PERIMETER =',A+B+C);
ANGLE_A = ATAN(A/B);
ANGLE_B = PI/2 - ANGLE_A;
PUT SKIP LIST ('ACUTE ANGLES (RADIANS) =',ANGLE_A,ANGLE_B);
PUT SKIP LIST ('ACUTE ANGLES (DEGREES) =',180*ANGLE_A/PI,
                                          180*ANGLE_B/PI);
END RTTRI;
```

List-directed input and output are being used, with appropriate labels printed along with the data values.

4.6.2 Loan payment

This program separates a mortgage payment into payments of interest, escrow, and partial payment of the principal. The new balance owed is then calculated.

```
MORTG: PROC OPTIONS(MAIN);
/*************************************************************/
/*                                                           */
/*   PROGRAM: MORTGAGE PAYMENT                               */
/*   AUTHOR:  C ZIEGLER                                      */
/*   VERSION: 07/27/84                                       */
/*                                                           */
/*   PROGRAM DESCRIPTION:                                    */
/*   ------------------------------------------------------  */
/*   THIS PROGRAM PRINTS THE UPDATED MORGAGE INFORMATION     */
/*   AFTER A PAYMENT HAS BEEN MADE                           */
/*                                                           */
/*   INPUT: NAME OF MORTGAGE HOLDER, ACCOUNT NUMBER          */
/*          LOAN BALANCE, MONTHLY ESCROW AMOUNT, PAYMENT     */
/*                                                           */
/*   OUTPUT: NAME OF MORTGAGE HOLDER, ACCOUNT NUMBER         */
/*           OLD LOAN BALANCE, PAYMENT, MONTHLY ESCROW       */
/*           AMOUNT, INTEREST, NEW LOAN BALANCE              */
/*                                                           */
/*************************************************************

DCL NAME      CHAR(20),
    ACCT_NO   CHAR(5),
    OLD_BAL   FIXED DEC (8,2),
    ESCROW    FIXED DEC (6,2),
    PAYMENT   FIXED DEC (6,2);
DCL NEW_BAL   FIXED DEC (8,2),
    INTEREST  FIXED DEC (6,2);    /* PART OF PAYMENT */
DCL PRINC     FIXED DEC (6,2);    /* PART OF PAYMENT */
DCL RATE      FIXED DEC (3,2)  INIT (1.25);
DCL DATE      BUILTIN;

GET EDIT (NAME, ACCT_NO) (COL(1),A(20),A(5));
GET EDIT (OLD_BAL,ESCROW,PAYMENT)
         (COL(1),F(8,2),F(6,2),F(6,2));
INTEREST = RATE * OLD_BAL;
PRINC = PAYMENT - ESCROW - INTEREST;
NEW_BAL = OLD_BAL - PRINC;
PUT EDIT ('LOAN INFORMATION',DATE)
         (PAGE,COL(30),A,COL(50),A);
PUT SKIP;
PUT EDIT (NAME,ACCT_NO) (COL(30),A,COL(55),A);
PUT SKIP (3);
PUT EDIT ('OLD BALANCE','PAYMENT','ESCROW','INTEREST',
         'PRINCIPAL','NEW BALANCE')
         (COL(10),A,COL(24),A,COL(34),A,COL(44),A,
         COL(54),A,COL(64),A);
PUT SKIP(2);
PUT EDIT (OLD_BAL,PAYMENT,ESCROW,INTEREST,PRINC,NEW_BAL)
         (COL(10),(6)F(10,2));
END MORTG;
```

Simple edit-directed input and output are being used. Appropriate column headings are printed.

4.6.3 Temperature conversion table

If a list of corresponding Fahrenheit and centigrade temperatures is to be printed for temperatures from −20°F to 100°F, the list will not fit on a single page. If the columns of figures are to be labeled, the following executable code can be used.

```
TEMPCON: PROC OPTIONS(MAIN);
/*****************************************************************/
/*                                                               */
/*   PROGRAM: TEMPERATURE CONVERSION                             */
/*   AUTHOR:  R REDDY                                            */
/*   VERSION: 07/27/84                                           */
/*                                                               */
/*   PROGRAM DESCRIPTION:                                        */
/*   ----------------------------------------------------------- */
/*   THIS PROGRAM PRINTS A TABLE OF CORRESPONDING                */
/*   FAHRENHEIT AND CELSIUS TEMPERATURES.                        */
/*                                                               */
/*   INPUT: NONE                                                 */
/*                                                               */
/*   OUTPUT: FAHRENHEIT AND CELSIUS TEMPERATURES                 */
/*                                                               */
/*****************************************************************/
DCL (F,C) FLOAT BIN;

ON ENDPAGE (SYSPRINT)
  BEGIN;
    PUT PAGE EDIT ('PAGE',PAGENO(SYSPRINT)) (COL(18),A,A);
    PUT LINE(5) EDIT ('FAHRENHEIT CELSIUS') (A);
    PUT SKIP;
  END;

PUT PAGE EDIT ('TEMPERATURE TABLE') (COL(5),A);
PUT LINE(5) ('FAHRENHEIT CELSIUS') (A);

F = -20;
DO WHILE (F<=100);
  C = 5 * (F - 32)/9;
  PUT SKIP EDIT (F,C) (F(9,1),X(5),F(8,4));
  F = F + 1;
END;
END TEMPCON;
```

Automatic paging is being used. A printer file is set up for a standard number of lines per page. When there is an attempt to print beyond the last line, the

ENDPAGE condition is raised, the heading is printed on a new page, and the attempted output is completed.

This temperature procedure is straightforward, but not as efficient as it might be. The formula can be rewritten as

```
C = .5555555556*F - 17.777777778
```

It would be slightly more efficient to write the algorithm as

```
K = 5.0/9.0;            /* CELSIUS FOR   1 FAHRENHEIT */
C = -52.0*K;            /* CELSIUS FOR -20 FAHRENHEIT */
DO F = -20 TO 100;
  PUT SKIP LIST (F,C);
  C = C + K;
END;
```

The operations in the loop have been simplified, and the number of operations in the loop has been decreased.

4.6.4 Monthly sales

In the following report program the exception is raised at the beginning of the program for the first page, then afterward, whenever the month number changes. Thus all the data for January will be on the first page, for February on the second, and so forth.

```
SALES: PROC OPTIONS(MAIN);
/**********************************************************/
/*                                                        */
/*   PROGRAM: MONTHLY SALES                               */
/*   AUTHOR:  C ZIEGLER                                   */
/*   VERSION: 07/27/84                                    */
/*                                                        */
/*   PROGRAM DESCRIPTION:                                 */
/*   ---------------------------------------------------- */
/*   THIS PROGRAM PRINTS A REPORT OF MONTHLY SALES OF     */
/*   ACME CORP.                                           */
/*                                                        */
/*   INPUT: MONTH, DAY, CAST_IRON, STEEL, ALUMINUM,       */
/*          COPPER, ZINC                                  */
/*                                                        */
/*   OUTPUT: DATA ORGANIZED BY MONTHS                     */
/*                                                        */
/**********************************************************/
DCL MONTH      CHAR(2),
    DAY        CHAR(2),
    CAST_IRON  FIXED DEC (8),
    STEEL      FIXED DEC (8),
    ALUMINUM   FIXED DEC (8),
    COPPER     FIXED DEC (8),
    ZINC       FIXED DEC (8);
```

```
DCL OLD_MONTH   CHAR(2),
    MORE_DATA   BIT(1),
    TRUE        BIT(1)      INIT('1'B),
    FALSE       BIT(1)      INIT('0'B);

ON ENDFILE (SYSIN)
  MORE_DATA = FALSE;
ON ENDPAGE (SYSPRINT)
  BEGIN;
    PUT PAGE;
    IF OLD_MONTH = MONTH
      THEN
        DO;
          PUT EDIT ('ACME MATERIAL REPORT') (COL(57),A);
          PUT SKIP(0) EDIT ('____ ________ ______') (COL(57),A);
        END;
    PUT LINE(3) EDIT ('DATE','CASTIRON','STEEL','ALUMINUM','COPPER',
          'ZINC') (A,COL(10),(5)(X(12),A(8)));
  END;

MORE_DATA = '1'B;
GET EDIT (MONTH,DAY,CASTIRON,STEEL,ALUMINUM,COPPER,ZINC)
         (COL(1),A(2),X(1),A(2),(5)(X(5),F(8)));
IF MORE_DATA
  THEN
    OLD_MONTH = MONTH;
SIGNAL ENDPAGE (SYSPRINT);
DO WHILE (MORE_DATA);
  IF MONTH > OLD_MONTH
    THEN
      SIGNAL ENDPAGE(SYSPRINT);
  PUT EDIT (DAY, CASTIRON,STEEL,ALUMINUM, COPPER, ZINC)
        (COL(1),A(2),(5)(X(12),F(8)));
  OLD_MONTH = MONTH;
  GET EDIT (MONTH,DAY,CASTIRON,STEEL,ALUMINUM, COPPER, ZINC)
          (COL(1),A(2),X(1),A(2),(5)(X(5),F(8)));
END;
END SALES;
```

Notice that it is assumed that the data is grouped by months. If all the data for a single month fit on one page, the page break will come at the end of the month, activated by the SIGNAL instruction. If there are more data for a month than will fit on a single page, the automatic page break will occur at the end of the page and the column headings will be printed on the continuation page. Then, at the end of the month, the SIGNAL instruction will cause both the title and headings to be printed for the next month.

4.7 Summary

The two basic methods of organizing data are as a stream of characters or as a set of records. Stream input/output is controlled by the GET and PUT instructions. There are three types of stream I/O: data-directed, list-directed, and edit-directed. They can be categorized as follows:

1. Input
   a. Data-directed
      i. order controlled by data
      ii. free-format spacing
      iii. variables referenced are controlled by data
      iv. rarely used
   b. List-directed
      i. order controlled by program
      ii. free-format spacing
      iii. variables referenced are controlled by program
      iv. used with terminal or other variable-length input
   c. Edit-directed
      i. order controlled by program
      ii. format controlled by program
      iii. variables referenced are controlled by program
      iv. used with fixed-length, fixed-format input
2. OUTPUT
   a. Data-directed
      i. order controlled by program
      ii. standard format
      iii. variables referenced are controlled by program
      iv. only variables in output list
      v. used for debugging
   b. List-directed
      i. order controlled by program
      ii. standard format
      iii. values output controlled by program
      iv. constants, variables, or expressions in output list
      v. used primarily for "quick and dirty" output
   c. Edit-directed
      i. order controlled by program
      ii. format controlled by program
      iii. values output controlled by program
      iv. constants, variables, or expressions in output list
      v. used when output must be attractive

The edit-directed I/O is the most useful and important. The main format specifications are:

A(w)	For character values
B(w)	For bit values
C	For complex numbers
E(w,d)	For floating-point values
F(w,d)	For fixed-point values

P	For picture values
R(name)	For remote formats

The main specifications used for horizontal spacing are:

X(w)	For insertion of spaces
COL(n)	For tab positioning

The main specifications used for vertical spacing are:

PAGE	For page ejection
LINE(n)	For vertical positioning
SKIP(n)	For line feeds

Note that the PAGE and LINE options can be used only with printer files. They are associated with the internal counters PAGENO(printer) and LINENO(printer). The ENDPAGE option can be used to control paging.

4.8 Exercises

1. A set of data contains sales information as follows:

Cols.		
	1-20	Name of salesperson
	21-26	Total sales for Monday (with decimal point)
	27-32	" " " Tuesday
	33-38	" " " Wednesday
	39-44	" " " Thursday
	45-50	" " " Friday

Write a program that prints, for each salesperson, the data, the total weekly sales, and the commission of 15 percent of the total weekly sales. Print an appropriate heading and column headings.

2. Write a program that prints a table of square roots, cube roots, fourth roots, and fifth roots of numbers from 1 to 100. Print an appropriate title and column headings.

3. Payroll data is organized as follows:

Cols.		
	1-5	Employee ID
	6-25	Employee name
	26-28	Hours worked
	29-32	Hourly pay (with decimal point)

Write a program that prints, for each employee, the data, the gross pay, the federal tax withheld (15 percent of gross pay), the state tax withheld (8.2 percent of gross pay), retirement withheld (6.1 percent of gross pay), and net pay. Print an appropriate title and column headings.

4. The area between an arc and chord of a circle is given by the formula

$$A = \frac{\pi r^2 t}{360} - \frac{r^2 \sin(t)}{2}$$

Write a program that calculates *A* for all angles $1^0 < t \leq 180°$.

5
Control structures

OBJECTIVE: To handle a set of data selectively.

IN CHAPTER 2 WE discussed using the basic control structures to write structured programs. These basic structures can follow each other sequentially or can be nested, depending on the complexity of the algorithm. Their relationships depend on the analysis of the problem. Are several steps involved in the solution or are the parts made up of smaller components? The nesting of control structures is based on the hierarchy of functions needed in the program, as represented in a hierarchy chart.

In this chapter we look at the three basic control structures, sequence, selection, and repetition, as implemented in the PL/I language. We will use only those PL/I statements that do not violate the structured programming idea of entering each structure at the top and exiting it at the bottom. Indentation of subordinate structures and alignment of parallel structures will be used, "pretty printing" the PL/I code for easy reading.

5.1 Sequence structure

A sequence structure contains a group of statements that are executed one after the other as steps in carrying out some particular function. For example, the statements in figure 5–1 form a sequence that prints the average of four

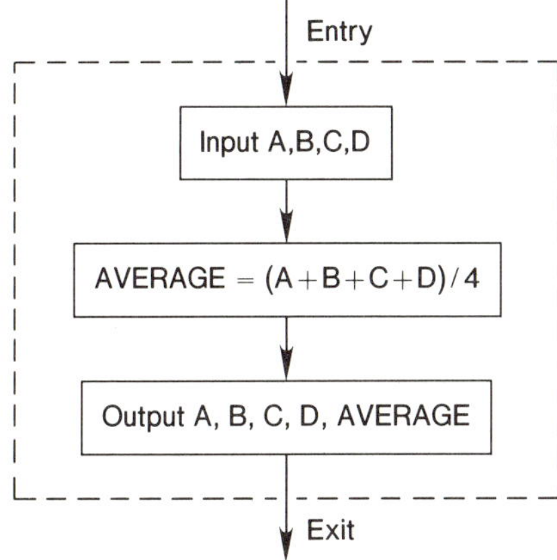

Figure 5–1

data values. The process boxes are labeled with a combination of English statements and mathematical formulas, not with PL/I statements. The corresponding PL/I code is

```
GET DATA (A,B,C,D);
AVERAGE =  (A+B+C+D)/4;
PUT DATA (A,B,C,D,AVERAGE);
```

If a sequence is nested inside another control structure it is written either as a *compound statement,* also known as a *DO group,*

```
DO;
  GET DATA (A,B,C,D);
  AVERAGE = (A+B+C+D)/4;
  PUT DATA (A,B,C,D,AVERAGE);
END;
```

or as a *block.*

```
BEGIN;
  GET DATA (A,B,C,D);
  AVERAGE = (A+B+C+D)/4;
  PUT DATA (A,B,C,D,AVERAGE);
END;
```

THE DO. . .END and BEGIN. . .END constructs are primarily grouping symbols, which usually occur in different contexts and are handled differently by the computer. DO. . .END is used for nesting sequences in the selection and repetition control structures. BEGIN. . .END nests the sequence of instructions that form an ON unit. It can be used in other contexts, but it is less efficient than a DO. . .END structure.

Review questions

1. Indicate whether each of the following statements is true or false.
  (a) In a sequence structure the statements are executed one after the other, in order.
  (b) A sequence structure has more than one statement in it.
  (c) When a sequence structure is nested inside another structure, it is written as a compound statement using a DO group.
  (d) DO groups and BEGIN . . . END blocks are used in different situations.
  (e) Other structures may be embedded in a sequence structure.
  (f) The executable statements of a procedure form a sequence structure

5.2 DOWHILE structure

The flowchart of the DOWHILE structure, which was introduced in chapter 2, is shown here as figure 5–2. The sequence of statements that makes up the

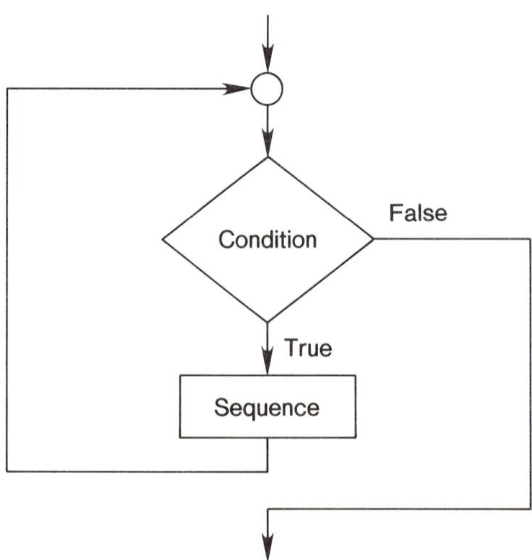

Figure 5–2

body of the loop is preceded by a conditional test. The statements within the body of the loop are executed repeatedly while the condition is true. When the condition is false the repetition terminates without executing the sequence, and control continues at the next statement after the end of the loop.

The PL/I control structure is written

```
DO WHILE (condition);
  sequence
END;
```

A DOWHILE loop can be used to handle many sets of input data, with the continuing condition that valid data be present. The termination condition of "no valid data present" can be detected by counting the data, recognizing the last valid data value, using a special trailer value after the data, or checking for an end-of-file. In any case, there must be an attempt to obtain the first data value ahead of the loop so that if no data is present, the repetition sequence will be omitted. In effect, the body of the loop processes one set of data, then obtains the next set, if there is one.

The DOWHILE structure is essentially written as a DO. . .END sequence with a repetition condition.

5.2.1 DOWHILE with counter control

If it is known how many data values are present, or if the data is being generated rather than input, a DOWHILE loop can be controlled by using a counter. The counter is initialized outside the loop and incremented inside the loop. The body of the loop is repeated until the counter reaches a predetermined point of termination.

PROGRAMMING HINT: EFFICIENCY Use FIXED BIN(15) variables for counters

GENERATING DATA VALUES

A simple example of a counter-controlled loop is the calculation of the product of numbers from one to twenty. The counter provides the numbers to be multiplied and the control. The body of the loop is repeated as long as the counter is less than twenty-one. The flowchart version of the algorithm for this example is given in figure 5–3.

The PL/I code for this example is

```
CNT = 2;
PROD = 1;
DO WHILE (CNT<=20);
                    /* REPEAT FOR CNT = 2,3,4,5,. . .20 */
  PROD = PROD * CNT;
  CNT = CNT + 1;
END;
PUT LIST (PROD);
```

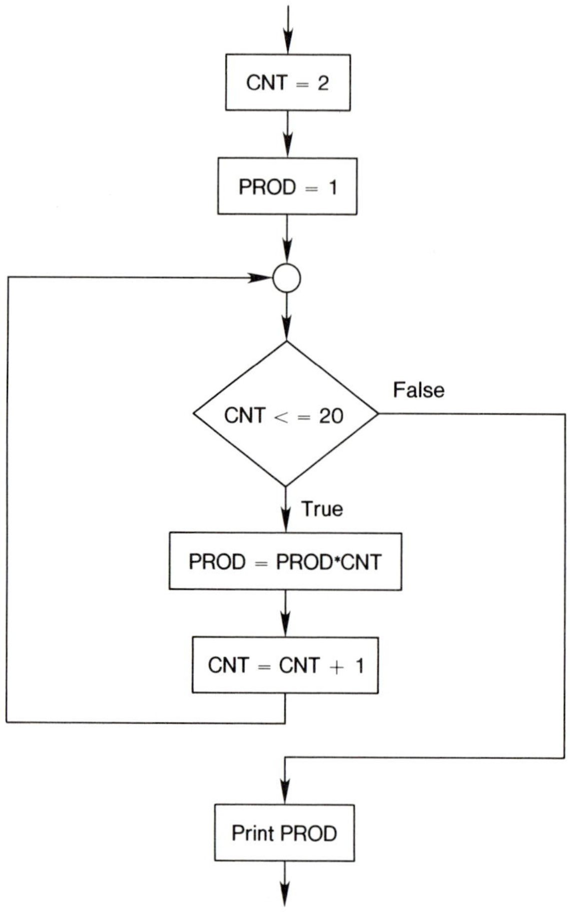

Figure 5–3

Notice that the statements of the nested sequence are indented to show the nesting. The repetition of the sequence continues as long as the condition CNT <= 20 is true. When CNT >20, control jumps over the sequence to the PUT LIST statement following the loop. The condition could also have been written as CNT < 21 or CNT ¬> 20. It is standard practice to assign the first value ahead of the loop, then change the value just before repeating the loop. The first value used for CNT was two rather than one because the product was initialized to one. Products are always initialized to one and sums are always initialized to zero.

PROGRAMMING HINT: LOGIC Initialize sums to zero, products to one.

GENERATING CONTROL VALUES

If the exact number of records in a file is known, the loop can be controlled by a counter. For example, assume that 100 names and addresses are to be read and printed. The flowchart for the algorithm is given in figure 5–4.

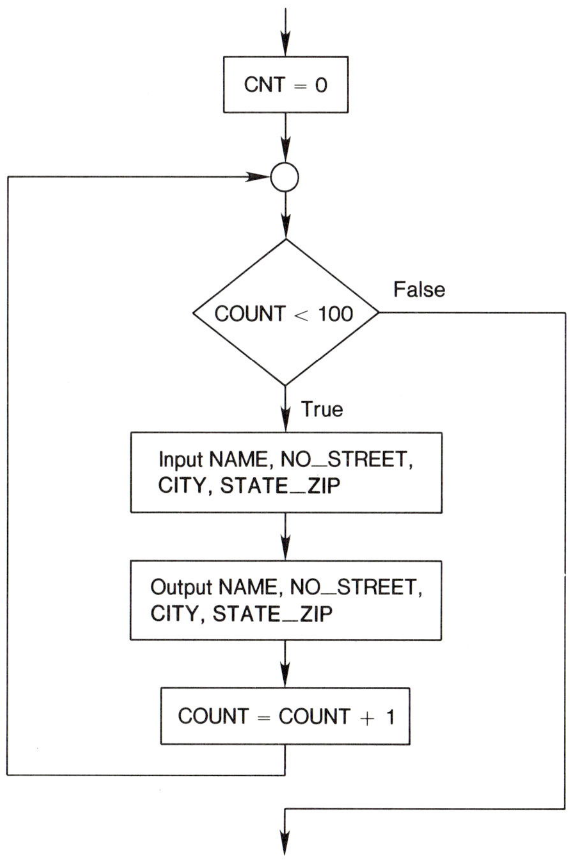

Figure 5–4

The count is initialized to zero so that each time the condition is checked, the count tells exactly how many sets of data have been read. The loop control variable is initialized just before the loop is entered, then updated at the bottom of the loop body, just before the condition is checked again. When the count is 99, the 100*th* record is read and printed, and the count is set to 100. This terminates the loop with a correct count of the number of records. If there is no data, the count is zero.

5.2.2 DOWHILE with trailer control

A *trailer* value is a special data value placed by the user at the end of the set of data to mark it. It functions as a user-supplied end-of-file value. With interactive input from a screen-formatted terminal, the user is asked to enter a particular value to indicate the end of the data. In the following example, which prints mailing labels, assume the user has been told to type Q for "quit" when there is no more data. The value of the name field can be checked to determine whether to repeat the loop or terminate it.

```
GET EDIT (NAME) (COL(1),A(20));
DO WHILE(NAME ¬= 'Q');
  GET EDIT (NO_STREET,CITY,ST_ZIP) (COL(21),(3)A(10));
  PUT EDIT (NAME,NO_STREET,CITY,ST_ZIP) ((4)(SKIP,A));
  GET EDIT (NAME) (COL(1),A(20));
END;
```

As long as there is data in the name field of the input, the body of the loop is executed. Data values other than the name are read inside the loop, as they are only present when there is a valid name.

A variation on this would be to read data from a noninteractive source that has a completely blank record after the last set of data values. In this case, all the fields would be present as part of the trailer data, but they would all contain blanks. The code for this variation is

```
GET EDIT (NAME,STREET,CITY,ST_ZIP) (COL(1),A(20),(3)A(10));
DO WHILE(NAME ¬= ' ');
  PUT EDIT (NAME,NO_STREET,CITY,ST_ZIP) ((4)(SKIP,A));
  GET EDIT (NAME,NO_STREET,CITY,ST_ZIP) (COL(1),A(20),(3)A(10));
END;
```

Only the NAME field needs to be checked for blanks. In both of these examples, the only initialization needed is the *priming read* of the data ahead of the loop, since the value of the data is itself being used as the control. However, if the trailer data is missing, a fatal error will occur.

PROGRAMMING HINT: CAUTION   Always use a priming read with DOWHILE.

5.2.3 DOWHILE with end-of-file check

If the system end-of-file is used to control the looping, a priming read must be used. Normal termination occurs when all the data has been read and processed. This situation is recognized when a special system-generated trailer value that follows the end of the data, called the *eof,* is read. Reading the eof causes the ENDFILE condition to be raised. The ENDFILE exception handler is used to set a flag to indicate that there is no more data. This flag, here named MORE_DATA, is tested by the DOWHILE, as in the following example.

```
DCL MORE_DATA   BIT(1);
 . . .
GET EDIT (NAME,STREET,CITY,ST_ZIP) (COL(1),A(20),(3)A(10));
DO WHILE(MORE_DATA);
  PUT EDIT (NAME,NO_STREET,CITY,ST_ZIP) ((4)(SKIP,A));
  GET EDIT (NAME,NO_STREET,CITY,ST_ZIP) (COL(1),A(20),(3)A(10));
END;
```

In the ON unit for end-of-file, a preinitialized flag is changed to show that the condition has occurred. The flag is set and reset as follows:

```
DCL MORE_DATA  BIT(1);
DCL TRUE       BIT(1)   INIT('1'B),
    FALSE      BIT(1)   INIT('0'B);
ON ENDFILE(SYSIN)
  MORE_DATA = FALSE;
MORE_DATA = TRUE;
 . . .
DO WHILE(MORE_DATA);
```

Used in a condition, a BIT(1) value of '1'B is interpreted as meaning true while '0'B is interpreted as false. It is not necessary to ask specifically whether the BIT variable is equal to some value. This improves the readability of the program.

PROGRAMMING HINT: STYLE Use BIT(1) variables as condition flags.

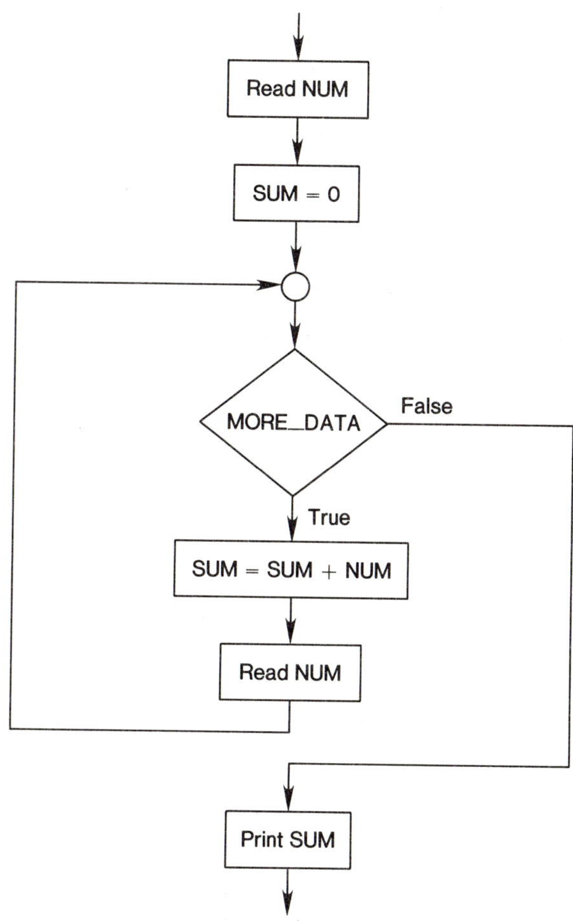

Figure 5–5

The following example calculates the sum of all data values in the system input file. The algorithm is shown first as the flowchart of figure 5–5.

The PL/I code for this is

```
DCL MORE_DATA  BIT(1);
DCL TRUE       BIT(1)    INIT('1'B),
    FALSE      BIT(1)    INIT('0'B);

ON ENDFILE(SYSIN)                       /*INDICATE NO DATA      */
  MORE_DATA = FALSE;

SUM = 0;
MORE_DATA = TRUE;                       /*ASSUME DATA PRESENT */
GET EDIT (NUM) (COL(1),F(6,2));         /*GET FIRST DATA       */
DO WHILE (MORE_DATA);
  SUM = SUM + NUM;
  GET EDIT (NUM) (COL(1),F(6,2)); /*GET NEXT DATA              */
END;
PUT SKIP LIST (SUM);
```

The ON unit is placed between the declarations and the executable statements. Unlike the declarations, it *is* an executable statement. However, when it is executed by stepping sequentially through the code, the only thing that happens is that the ENDFILE check is *established.* That is, the code of the ON unit is made available by enabling the condition and turning on the internal check for the condition. Establishing the ENDFILE check does not give MORE_DATA a value. MORE_DATA receives the value of zero only when the condition is raised during the processing of a GET statement, when the data item obtained is the eof. Since there are two GET statements in the example, the ON ENDFILE statement must be placed ahead of both. The condition can be raised by either.

This code segment works by turning on the end-of-file check, initializing the sum to zero (which clears the calculation area), initializing the control variable to true to show that data is expected, and then reading the first input value. The loop that sums the values is repeated until there is no more data and the eof is read. If the user has forgotten to provide any data, the loop is completely omitted and a sum of zero is printed. Control is transferred to the exception handler during the processing of whichever GET statement is unsuccessful. After MORE_DATA has been set to '0'B, control returns to the statement after the GET statement.

5.2.4 DOWHILE with multiple controls

The PL/I code for printing 100 names and addresses in the form of mailing labels can be written as follows:

```
COUNT = 0;
DO WHILE (COUNT< 100);
  GET LIST (NAME,NO_STREET,CITY,ST_ZIP);
  PUT EDIT (NAME,NO_STREET,CITY,ST_ZIP) ((4)(SKIP,A));
  PUT SKIP (3);
  COUNT = COUNT + 1;
END;
```

This code matches the flowchart of figure 5–4. Since the loop is controlled by a counter, the counter is initialized and there is no priming read. However, this can be dangerous. If there are more than 100 sets of data, only the first 100 are processed. If there are fewer than 100, a fatal ENDFILE condition is raised. If a trailer value is used instead of a counter, forgetting the trailer value will cause a fatal ENDFILE condition to be raised. Establishing an ON unit for the condition will not solve the problem, as the PUT statements will be executed even when the GET fails. But these problems can be avoided if the end-of-file check controls the looping, or if looping is dependent on both the end-of-file check and a counter or trailer value.

If at most 100 sets of names and addresses are to be printed from an input file, but there is a possibility of fewer than that in the file, the DOWHILE loop can be controlled by both a counter and a check for the end-of-file. The decision table for this is

More data	Y	Y	N	N
Count < 100	Y	N	Y	N
Print label	X			
Read data	X			
Repeat	X			
Exit		X	X	X

Since the body of the loop is executed and repeated only while there is more data and the count is still less than 100, the looping condition must be expressed as

```
DO WHILE(MORE_DATA & COUNT<100);
```

Remember that with a DOWHILE, the condition for continuing the processing is stated, not the termination condition.

The PL/I code for this is

```
DCL MORE_DATA   BIT(1);
DCL TRUE        BIT(1)    INIT('1'B),
    FALSE       BIT(1)    INIT('0'B);

ON ENDFILE(SYSIN)                         /* INDICATE NO DATA           */
  MORE_DATA = FALSE;

MORE_DATA = TRUE;                         /* ASSUME DATA PRESENT        */
COUNT = 0;                                /* 0 DATA VALUES AT START     */
GET EDIT (NAME,NO_STREET,CITY,ST_ZIP)
         (COL(1),A(20),(3)A(10));
DO WHILE (MORE_DATA & COUNT<100);
  PUT EDIT (NAME,NO_STREET,CITY,ST_ZIP) ((4)(SKIP,A));
  PUT SKIP(3);
  COUNT = COUNT + 1;                      /* COUNT VALUE JUST PROCESSED */
  GET EDIT (NAME,NO_STREET,CITY,ST_ZIP)
           (COL(1),A(20),(3)A(10));
END;
```

Notice that both of the control variables and the data values must be initialized. If there are fewer than 100 sets of data, the MORE_DATA condition stops the repetition with the COUNT accurately indicating the amount of data. If there are exactly 100 sets of data, the MORE_DATA condition and the variable COUNT stop the repetition. COUNT has the value 100. One drawback of this code is that if there are more than 100 sets of data, the 101*st* set is read, but not processed.

Review questions

1. Indicate whether each of the following statements is true or false.
   (a) In a DOWHILE loop the condition is tested at the end of the loop.
   (b) The body of a DOWHILE loop is executed when the condition is true.
   (c) A DOWHILE loop can be controlled by an ENDFILE condition.
   (d) A DOWHILE loop cannot be controlled by a data value.
   (e) A DOWHILE loop is terminated when the condition is true.

2. What values are printed by each of the following code segments?

```
(a) CNT = 1;
    DO WHILE (CNT <5);
       PUT LIST (CNT);
       CNT = CNT + 1;
    END;
(b) CNT = 1;
    DO WHILE (CNT <= 5);
       PUT LIST (CNT);
       CNT = CNT + 1;
    END;
(c) CNT = 0;
    DO WHILE (CNT < 5);
       PUT LIST (CNT);
       CNT = CNT + 1;
    END;
```

***3.** Which symbol on your terminal (or other input device) signifies an end-of-file?

4. Under what circumstances would each of the following conditions be used?

```
(a) DO WHILE (MORE_DATA);
(b) DO WHILE (X ¬= 0);
(c) DO WHILE (TALLY <= 100);
(d) DO WHILE (MORE_DATA & STR = ' ');
(e) DO WHILE (MORE DATA & CNT < 100);
(f) DO WHILE (CNT < 100 | NAME ¬= ' ');
(g) DO WHILE (MORE_DATA & CNT <=100 & NAME¬= ' ');
```

5. Complete the initialization of CNT so that five values of X will be printed.

(a)
```
GET LIST(X);
CNT=
DO WHILE (CNT < 5);
  PUT LIST(X);
  CNT=CNT+1;
  GET LIST(X);
END;
```
(b)
```
GET LIST(X);
CNT=
DO WHILE (CNT <= 5);
  PUT LIST(X);
  CNT=CNT+1;
  GET LIST(X);
END;
```
(c)
```
GET LIST(X);
CNT=
DO WHILE (CNT ¬= 5);
  PUT LIST(X);
  CNT=CNT+1;
  GET LIST(X);
END;
```

5.3 DOUNTIL structure (not in Subset G)

In chapter 2 the flowchart shown in figure 5–6 was given for the DOUNTIL structure. With this structure, the condition is tested after executing the statements in the loop. The sequence that forms the body of the loop is always executed at least once. The DOUNTIL loop terminates when the condition is true but continues when the condition is false. Even though the flowchart representation shows the condition at the bottom, the PL/I structure places it at the top (but executes it at the bottom).

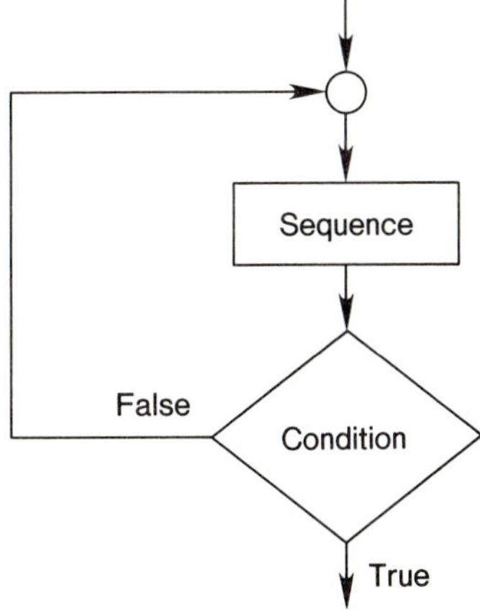

Figure 5–6

```
DO UNTIL (condition);
  sequence
END;
```

Like the DOWHILE, the DOUNTIL loop can be used with a controlling counter, trailer value, or end-of-file check. As before, the control variables should be initialized before entering the loop.

5.3.1 DOUNTIL with counter control

DOUNTIL can be used in the same situations as DOWHILE. In some other languages, DOUNTIL is the preferred structure; in PL/I, DOWHILE is preferred.

GENERATING VALUES

The code for calculating the product of the numbers one through twenty using a DOUNTIL loop is:

```
PROD = 1;
COUNT = 1;
DO UNTIL (COUNT = 20);
  COUNT = COUNT + 1;
  PROD = PROD * COUNT;
END;
PUT LIST (PROD);
```

The first time the DOUNTIL line is executed, the condition is not checked. After the COUNT has been incremented, the value of COUNT is used and then checked. When the value of twenty for COUNT is used in the multiplication, the loop terminates and the product is printed.

If twenty numbers are to be read and their sum printed, the code is:

```
SUM = 0;
CNT = 0;
DO UNTIL (CNT=20);
  GET EDIT (NUM) (COL(1),F(6,2));
  SUM = SUM + NUM;
  CNT = CNT + 1;
END;
PUT SKIP LIST (SUM);
```

Again, at the time the condition is evaluated, the count tells how many numbers have been read and processed. If there are fewer than twenty values in the input data, a fatal ENDFILE condition will be raised.

5.3.2 DOUNTIL with end-of-file check

When processing a file there is always the possibility of having no input data. In this situation, the DOUNTIL loop cannot be used with a priming read, because the body of the loop should not be executed even once. To avoid problems when there is no data, either DOUNTIL must be nested in an IFTHENELSE structure that prints an appropriate message, or an IFTHENELSE structure must be nested in DOUNTIL. These nested structures are outlined in the following examples.

```
DCL EOF   BIT(1);
DCL TRUE  BIT(1)  INIT('1'B),
    FALSE BIT(1)  INIT('0'B);

ON ENDFILE (SYSIN)                  /* INDICATE NO DATA      */
  EOF = TRUE;

EOF = FALSE;                        /* ASSUME DATA PRESENT */
GET EDIT (. . .) (. . .);           /* PRIMING READ          */
IF EOF
  THEN
    PUT LIST ('DATA MISSING');
  ELSE
    DO UNTIL (EOF);
      . . .                         /* PROCESS DATA          */
      GET EDIT (. . .) (. . .); /* GET NEXT DATA         */
    END;
```

```
DCL EOF    BIT(1);
DCL TRUE   BIT(1)  INIT('1'B),
    FALSE  BIT(1)  INIT('0'B);

ON ENDFILE (SYSIN)                  /* INDICATE NO DATA      */
  EOF = TRUE;

EOF = FALSE;                        /* ASSUME DATA PRESENT */
DO UNTIL (EOF);
  GET EDIT (. . .) (. . .);         /* GET DATA              */
  IF (¬EOF)
    THEN
      . . .                         /* PROCESS DATA          */
END;
```

The variable name EOF is more appropriate with DOUNTIL than the name MORE_DATA. With DOUNTIL, the control variable must be initialized to a false value. The repetition terminates when the variable becomes true. Therefore the exception handler for the end-of-file condition must make the variable true. The IF statement is necessary to avoid attempting to process data when none are present. The form of the first of the previous two examples is the more efficient, but using DOWHILE would be better. The form of the second example is appropriate when an exact number of values is to be read and processed. The following example shows this situation.

```
. . .
SUM = 0;
CNT = 0;                        /* 0 VALUES AT START      */
DO UNTIL (CNT=20 | EOF);        /* 20 VALUES AS EXPECTED  */
  GET EDIT (NUM) (COL(1),F(6,2));
  IF ¬EOF
    THEN
      DO;
        SUM = SUM + NUM;
        CNT = CNT + 1;          /* TALLY VALUE            */
      END;
END;
PUT SKIP LIST (SUM);
```

This program segment ends with the correct count in CNT.

PROGRAMMING HINT: CAUTION Use DOWHILE rather than DOUNTIL except when searching for a particular data value or reading only part of the data.

The other appropriate use of DOUNTIL is to search for a particular data value, as shown in the following example, which searches a list of names for the name 'JONES'.

```
. . .
DO UNTIL (NAME = 'JONES' | EOF);
  GET EDIT (NAME,NO_STREET,CITY,ST_ZIP)
           (COL(1),A(20),(3)A(10));
END;
IF EOF
  THEN
    PUT SKIP LIST ('JONES NOT FOUND');
```

Review questions

1. A DOUNTIL loop is executed ________________ times.

2. A DOUNTIL loop is repeated as long as the condition is ________________.

3. A DOUNTIL loop is terminated when the condition is ________________.

4. Indicate whether each of the following statements is true or false.

(a) A DOUNTIL loop is terminated as soon as the condition is true.
(b) In a DOUNTIL loop the condition is tested at the beginning of the loop.
(c) A DOUNTIL loop can be controlled by a counter.
(d) A DOUNTIL loop can be controlled by an ENDFILE condition.

5. How is DOUNTIL different from DOWHILE?

6. Why is DOWHILE better than DOUNTIL for reading an entire file?

7. In each of the following code segments, what fatal error condition can occur? How would you avoid it?

(a)
```
DO UNTIL (EOF);
   GET LIST (STR);
   PUT LIST (STR);
END;
```
(b)
```
GET LIST (STR);
DO UNTIL (EOF);
   PUT LIST (STR);
   GET LIST (STR);
END;
```
(c)
```
CNT = 1;
DO UNTIL (CNT = 10);
   GET LIST (STR);
   PUT LIST (STR);
END;
```

8. What does each of the following code segments print?

(a)
```
CNT = 1;
DO UNTIL (CNT = 5);
   PUT LIST (CNT);
   CNT = CNT + 1;
END;
```
(b)
```
CNT = 1;
DO UNTIL (CNT = 5);
   CNT = CNT + 1;
   PUT LIST (CNT);
END;
```
(c)
```
CNT = 1;
DO UNTIL (CNT < 5);
   PUT LIST (CNT);
   CNT = CNT + 1;
END;
```
(d)
```
CNT = 0;
DO UNTIL (CNT > 5);
   CNT = CNT + 1;
   PUT LIST (CNT);
END;
```

5.4 IFTHENELSE structure

The IFTHENELSE structure selects from two alternate control paths. PL/I provides several different ways of writing it. The general form of the structure is

```
IF condition
  THEN
    statement;
  ELSE
    statement;
```

or

```
IF condition
  THEN
    DO;
      sequence
    END;
  ELSE
    DO;
      sequence
    END;
```

When the condition is true, the statement or sequence in the THEN clause is executed and the statement or sequence in the ELSE clause is skipped. When the condition is false, the statement or sequence in the ELSE clause is executed, and in that case the statement or sequence in the THEN clause is skipped. The THEN clause is required, but the ELSE clause is optional. If an IFTHENELSE structure is used to select or omit a single alternative, rather than to choose between two alternatives, the condition can be worded so that just the THEN clause is used, or a null statement can be used in either the THEN or the ELSE part. A *null statement* consists of just a semicolon.

5.4.1 Simple IF structures

When the IFTHENELSE structure has single statements on both branches, as in the flowchart of figure 5–7, it is called a simple structure. The logic of

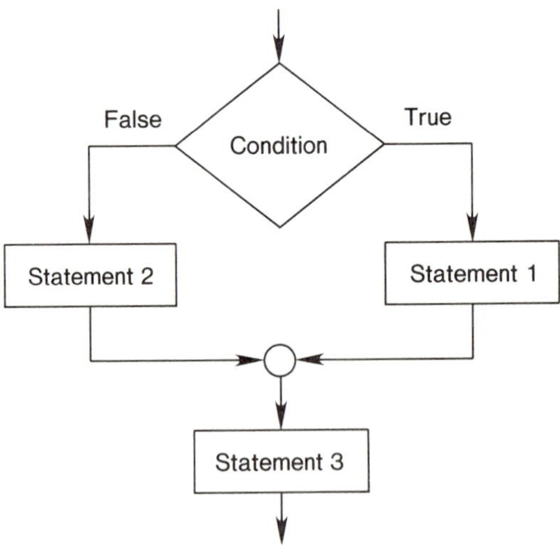

Figure 5–7

this structure is given by the following decision table:

Condition	Y	N
Statement 1	X	
Statement 2		X
Statement 3	X	X

This is coded as

```
IF condition              For example:  IF X = Y
  THEN                                    THEN
    statement 1;                            PUT SKIP LIST ('EQUAL');
  ELSE                                    ELSE
    statement 2;                            PUT SKIP LIST ('UNEQUAL');
statement 3;                            GET LIST (X,Y);
```

Notice that the indentation and the alignment of the parallel parts of the structure increases its clarity. Statement 3 is not part of the IFTHENELSE structure, so it is not indented, but it is aligned with the word IF. The semicolon after statement 1 closes the first branch of the structure, and the semicolon after statement 2 closes the second branch and the entire IF structure.

If the statement on one of the branches is missing, the structure can be written in one of the following forms:

```
IF condition              For example:  IF X > Y
  THEN                                       THEN
    statement 1;                               PUT SKIP LIST ('X LARGER');
statement 2;
                          or
                                        IF X > Y
                                             THEN
                                               PUT SKIP LIST ('X LARGER');
                                             ELSE;

IF ¬ condition            or            IF condition
  THEN                                       THEN;
    statement 1;                           ELSE
statement 2;                                 statement 1;
                                           statement 2;
```

For example:

```
IF ¬MORE_DATA             or           IF MORE_DATA
  THEN                                   THEN;
    PUT SKIP LIST ('THE END');           ELSE
                                           PUT SKIP LIST   ('THE END');
```

5.4.2 Complex IF structures

A nested sequence enclosed in DO . . . END, a DO group, is used if there is more than one statement on a true or false branch of an IFTHENELSE structure. The algorithm for this is shown in the flowchart of figure 5–8.

The logic of this structure is given by the following decision table:

Condition	Y	N
Statement 1	X	
Statement 2	X	
Statement 3		X
Statement 4		X
Statement 5	X	X

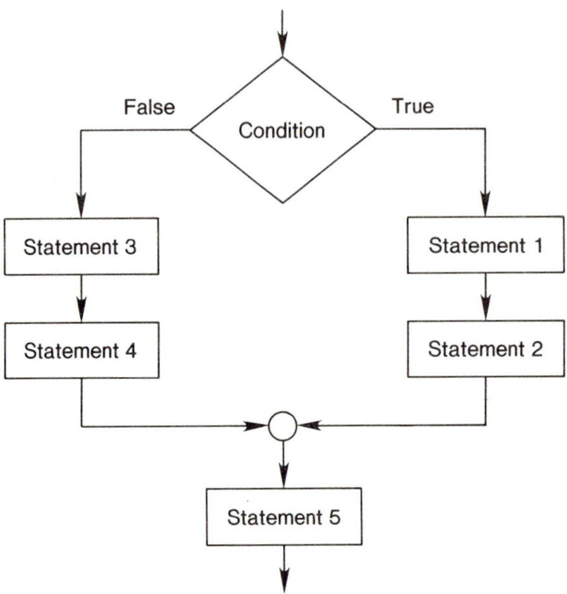

Figure 5–8

This is coded as:

```
IF condition                     For example:  IF X > Y
  THEN                                           THEN
    DO;                                            DO;
      statement 1;                                   PUT LIST ('LARGER=',X);
      statement 2;                                   PUT LIST ('SMALLER=',Y);
    END;                                           END;
  ELSE                                           ELSE
    DO;                                            DO;
      statement 3;                                   PUT LIST ('LARGER=',Y);
      statement 4;                                   PUT LIST ('SMALLER=',X);
    END;                                           END;
statement 5;
```

Either the THEN branch or the ELSE branch may be omitted, or one of them may have only a single statement on it. A branch with only a single statement does not need to be written as a DO group, and if it is not, it is aligned with the DO group of the other branch. Some of these variations are shown in the following examples:

```
IF condition                     For example:  IF A ¬= 0
  THEN                                           THEN
    DO;                                            DO;
      statement 1;                                   X = -B*Y/A;
      statement 2;                                   PUT SKIP DATA(X);
      statement 3;                                   PUT SKIP;
    END;                                           END;
statement 4;
```

```
IF condition              For example:  IF A = 0
  THEN;                                   THEN;
  ELSE                                    ELSE
    DO;                                     DO;
      statement 1;                            X = -B*Y/A;
      statement 2;                            PUT SKIP DATA (X);
      statement 3;                            PUT SKIP;
    END;                                    END;
statement 4;
```

```
IF condition              For example:  IF A ¬= 0
  THEN                                    THEN
    DO;                                     DO;
      statement 1;                            X = -B*Y/A;
      statement 2;                            PUT SKIP DATA (X);
    END;                                    END;
  ELSE                                    ELSE
    statement 3;                            PUT LIST ('NO SOLUTION');
statement 4;
```

5.4.3 Nested IF structures

Very often in practical situations, several conditions serve to distinguish a number of different cases. These are frequently implemented as nested IFTHENELSE structures. To avoid confusion when such structures are nested, none of the ELSE clauses should be omitted. Figures 5–9, 5–10, and 5–11 show some of the possible ways of nesting IF structures.

PROGRAMMING HINT: READABILITY When possible, use a SELECT statement instead of nested IF statements.

IF STRUCTURE INSIDE TRUE BRANCH OF ANOTHER IF STRUCTURE

The decision table for figure 5–9 is:

Condition 1	Y	Y	N
Condition 2	Y	N	—
Statement 1	X		
Statement 2		X	
Statement 3			X
Statement 4	X	X	X

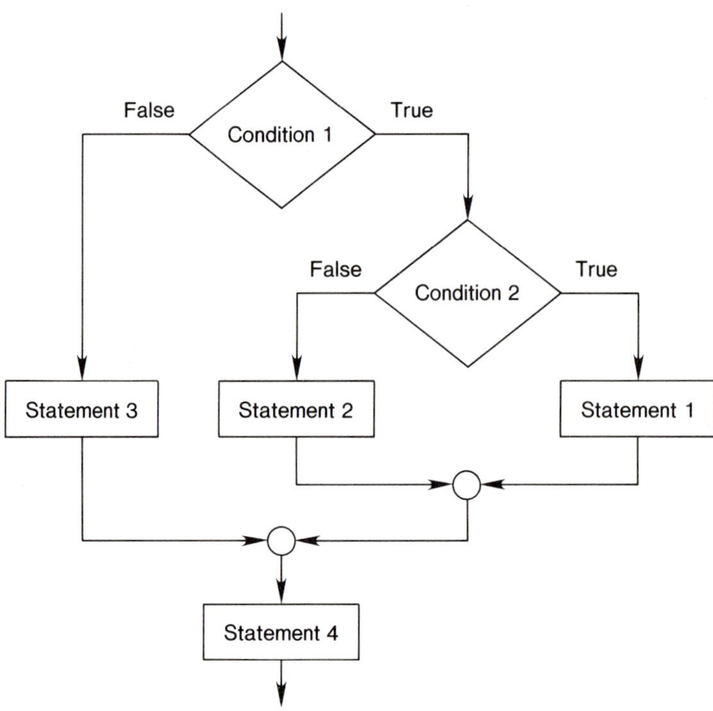

Figure 5–9

The code has the form:

```
IF condition 1
  THEN
    IF condition 2
      THEN
        statement 1;
      ELSE
        statement 2;
  ELSE
    statement 3;
statement 4;
```

Notice the alignment and indenting of the various parts of the structure.

IF STRUCTURE INSIDE FALSE BRANCH OF ANOTHER IF STRUCTURE

The decision table for figure 5–10 is:

Condition 1	Y	N	N
Condition 2	—	Y	N
Statement 1	X		
Statement 2		X	
Statement 3			X
Statement 4	X	X	X

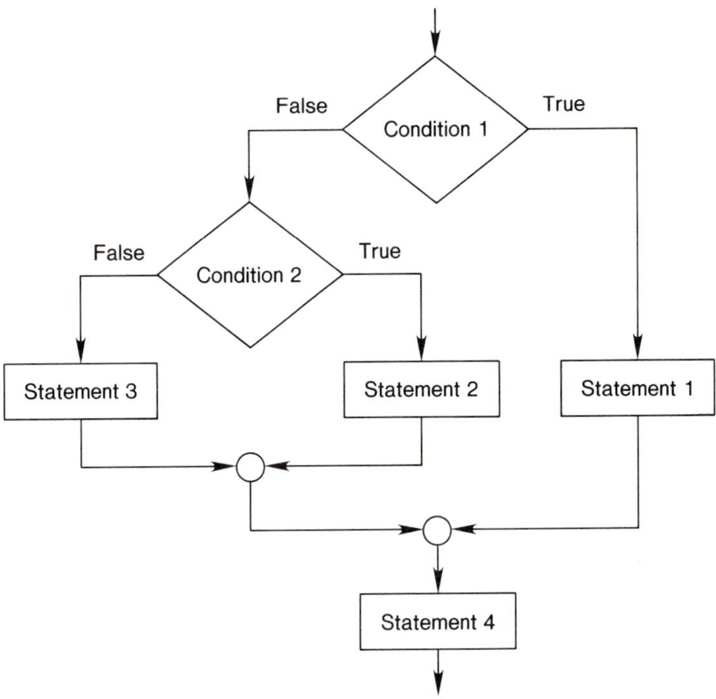

Figure 5–10

The code has the form:

```
IF condition 1
  THEN
    statement 1;
  ELSE
    IF condition 2
      THEN
        statement 2;
      ELSE
        statement 3;
statement 4;
```

BALANCED NESTED IF STRUCTURES

The decision table for figure 5–11 is:

Condition 1	Y	Y	N	N
Condition 2	Y	N	—	—
Condition 3	—	—	Y	N
Statement 1	X			
Statement 2		X		
Statement 3			X	
Statement 4				X
Statement 5	X	X	X	X

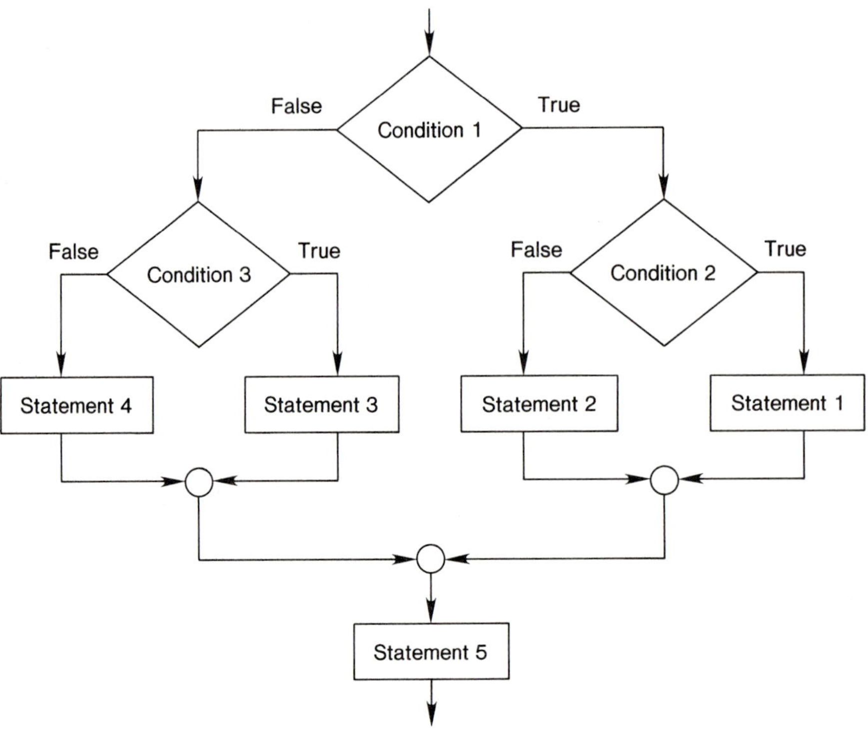

Figure 5-11

The code has the form:

```
IF condition 1
  THEN
    IF condition 2
      THEN
        statement 1;
      ELSE
        statement 2;
  ELSE
    IF condition 3
      THEN
        statement 3;
      ELSE
        statement 4;
statement 5;
```

When in doubt as to how the computer will interpret an IF structure, use a DO group. The general rule is that, starting with the innermost IF structure, each ELSE will belong with the nearest preceding IF.

PROGRAMMING HINT: CAUTION Nested IFTHENELSE structures must all have ELSE branches.

The computer cannot read the indentation used in the code. The indentation is only there to help the human reader. In both of the following sets of code,

```
IF condition 1
   THEN
     IF condition 2
       THEN
         statement 1;
       ELSE
         statement 2;
         statement 3;
```

```
IF condition 1
   THEN
     IF condition 2
       THEN
         statement 1;
   ELSE
     statement 2;
statement 3;
```

the computer understands the code as meaning:

Condition 1	Y	Y	N
Condition 2	Y	N	—
Statement 1	X		
Statement 2		X	
Statement 3	X	X	X

IFTHENELSE structures nested beyond two or three levels are awkward to set up and difficult to read. Programmers should avoid them whenever possible. Sometimes this can be done by using other types of structures, by breaking a procedure up into subprocedures, by reorganizing the algorithm, or by using compound conditions. Whenever structure nesting becomes complicated, proper indentation and alignment is essential.

Review questions

1. Indicate whether each of the following statements is true or false.
   (a) The IFTHENELSE statement may be used only for two-way branching.
   (b) The ELSE clause is required.
   (c) A null statement may be used in either a THEN or an ELSE clause.
   (d) A compound statement may be used in either a THEN or an ELSE clause.
   (e) The OTHERWISE clause is required in a SELECT statement.
   (f) When there are more than two choices, a SELECT statement is used instead of an IFTHENELSE statement.

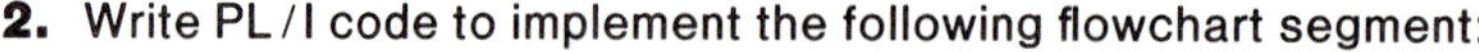

2. Write PL/I code to implement the following flowchart segment:

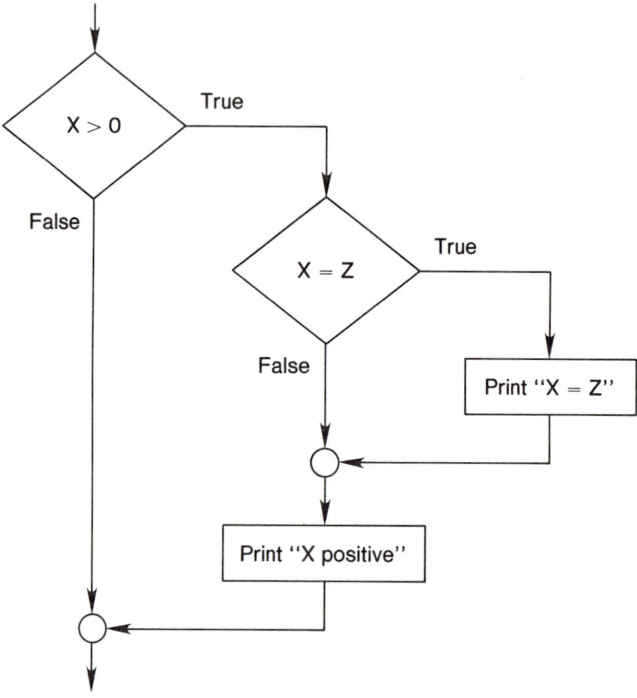

3. Write a segment of code that checks whether the values of X, Y, and Z are all equal, printing "equal" if they are.

4. Write a segment of code that validates data, setting STATUS to BAD if any of the fields NAME, ADDR, or TEL_NO are blank.

5. Write a segment of code that prints the character strings NAME_1, NAME_2, and NAME_3 in alphabetical order.

6. Write a segment of code that determines whether a triangle having sides of lengths *A*, *B*, and *C* is:
(a) An equilateral triangle (all sides are equal).
(b) An isosceles triangle (two sides are equal).
(c) A scalene triangle (no sides are equal).

5.5 Case structure

A case structure is used when there are more than two alternate types of data to be processed, or more than two ways of processing the data. Its most common use is in processing input records which have a code indicating the type of record. In PL/I the case structure may be implemented by nested IFTHENELSE structures or by the SELECT structure.

5.5.1 SELECT structure (not in a Subset G)

The two general forms of the SELECT structure are:

```
SELECT (expression);        Equivalent to  IF (expression = value 1)
  WHEN (value 1)                             THEN
    statement 1;                               statement 1;
  WHEN (value 2)                             ELSE
    statement 2;                               IF (expression = value 2)
   . . .                                         THEN;
  OTHERWISE                                        statement 2;
    statement n;                                 ELSE
END;                                               IF
                                                    . . .
                                                     ELSE
                                                       statement n;
```

```
SELECT;                     Equivalent to  IF (condition 1)
  WHEN (condition 1)                         THEN
    statement 1;                               statement 1;
  WHEN (condition 2)                         ELSE
    statement 2;                               IF (condition 2)
   . . .                                         THEN;
  OTHERWISE                                        statement 2;
    statement n;                                 ELSE
END;                                               IF
                                                    . . .
                                                     ELSE
                                                       statement n;
```

In the first form, the expression is expected to have one of the values specified in the WHEN clause. The statement following that WHEN will then be executed. The first WHEN clause that has the value of the expression will be selected if there is more than one. If there is none, the OTHERWISE clause will be selected. It is a fatal error if there is no clause to select; that is, if none of the values are correct and there is no OTHERWISE clause. Statements 1 through n may be simple statements or DO groups with nested control structures.

In the second form, the first true condition is selected. The OTHERWISE clause is selected if there is no true condition. Again, it is a fatal error if there is no clause to select. If there is more than one true condition, only the first one is selected.

As an example of the first form of SELECT structure, assume that the wages of employees of a company are calculated on an hourly, weekly, or monthly basis. The employee records have a field named WAGE_TYPE, which has the following values:

'H' Hourly basis for wage calculations
'W' Weekly basis
'M' Monthly basis

When a record is read, the type of calculation needed can be identified by looking at the WAGE_TYPE field. The following SELECT structure may be used.

```
SELECT (WAGE_TYPE);
  WHEN ('H')
    CALL HOURLY;
  WHEN ('W')
    CALL WEEKLY;
  WHEN ('M')
    CALL MONTHLY;
  OTHERWISE
    PUT SKIP LIST ('WAGE TYPE ERROR');
END;
```

In this example, HOURLY, WEEKLY, and MONTHLY are separate procedures that process the three types of wages. The OTHERWISE clause should be used for error processing or unforeseen alternatives.

The same situation could be processed using the second type of SELECT statement:

```
SELECT;
  WHEN (WAGE_TYPE = 'H')
    CALL HOURLY;
  WHEN (WAGE_TYPE = 'W')
    CALL WEEKLY;
  WHEN (WAGE_TYPE = 'M')
    CALL MONTHLY;
  OTHERWISE
    PUT SKIP LIST ('WAGE TYPE ERROR');
END;
```

5.5.2 Nested SELECT structure

Consider the problem of determining whether the sides of a triangle are all equal or all different. One way of doing this is to use the following SELECT structure, which contains a nested IFTHENELSE.

```
SELECT;
  WHEN (A = B)
    IF B = C
      THEN
        PUT SKIP LIST ('ALL EQUAL');
      ELSE
        PUT SKIP LIST ('TWO EQUAL');
```

```
  WHEN (A = C)
    PUT SKIP LIST ('TWO EQUAL');
  WHEN (B = C)
    PUT SKIP LIST ('TWO EQUAL');
  OTHERWISE
    PUT SKIP LIST ('ALL DIFFERENT');
END;
```

This example shows the use of separate conditions, one simple, one compound. It also shows the nesting of another structure inside a SELECT. It is possible for more than one condition to be true. However, only the first true condition is selected. If none of the conditions are true, the OTHERWISE clause is selected.

As an example of a SELECT nested inside a SELECT structure, consider the problem of finding the quadrant containing the point (X, Y).

```
SELECT;
  WHEN (X < 0)
    SELECT;
      WHEN (Y < 0)
        PUT SKIP LIST ('QUADRANT III');
      WHEN (Y = 0)
        PUT SKIP LIST ('NEGATIVE X AXIS');
      WHEN (Y > 0)
        PUT SKIP LIST ('QUADRANT II');
    END;
  WHEN (X = 0)
    SELECT;
      WHEN (Y < 0)
        PUT SKIP LIST ('NEGATIVE Y AXIS');
      WHEN (Y = 0)
        PUT SKIP LIST ('ORIGIN');
      WHEN (Y > 0)
        PUT SKIP LIST ('POSITIVE Y AXIS');
    END;
  WHEN (X > 0)
    SELECT;
      WHEN (Y < 0)
        PUT SKIP LIST ('QUADRANT IV');
      WHEN (Y = 0)
        PUT SKIP LIST ('POSITIVE X AXIS');
      WHEN (Y > 0)
        PUT SKIP LIST ('QUADRANT I');
    END;
END;
```

First the appropriate WHEN clause is selected, based on the value of X. Then the WHEN subclause that indicates the sign of Y is selected. There are no OTHERWISE clauses as all possible conditions have been explicitly included.

Review questions

1. Indicate whether each of the following statements is true or false.
   (a) When there are more than two possibilities, a SELECT statement must be used rather than an IFTHENELSE.
   (b) The OTHERWISE clause of the SELECT statement is required.
   (c) All true cases of a SELECT structure are executed.
   (d) A SELECT structure may have only one true case.
   (e) A SELECT structure must have at least one true case.
   (f) SELECT statements may not be nested.

2. Using a SELECT structure, write a segment of code that prints the character strings NAME_1, NAME_2, and NAME_3 in alphabetical order.

3. Using a SELECT structure, write a segment of code that determines whether a triangle having sides of lengths *A, B,* and *C* is:
   (a) An equilateral triangle (all sides are equal).
   (b) An isosceles triangle (two sides are equal).
   (c) A scalene triangle (no sides are equal).

4. Using a SELECT structure, write a segment of code that validates data, setting STATUS to BAD if any of the fields NAME, ADDR, or TEL_NO are blank.

5.6 Compound conditions

Nested IFTHENELSE structures often can be avoided by using compound conditions. A compound condition is composed of several simple conditions. The simple conditions use relational operators ("<", ">","=", "<=", ">=", "¬<", "¬>", "¬=") to compare data values. The result of each simple condition is a logical value of either true or false. The simple conditions are combined using logical operators. These operators take as their operands the logical values produced by the simple conditions.

PL/I has three basic logical operators, NOT, AND, and OR. These words are used in the 48-character set; in the 60-character set there are simple symbols.

5.6.1 Logical operators

The logical operators and their symbols are as follows:

<table>
<tr><th>Operation</th><th>60-character set</th><th>48-character set</th></tr>
<tr><td>Not</td><td>¬</td><td>NOT</td></tr>
<tr><td>And</td><td>&</td><td>AND</td></tr>
<tr><td>Or</td><td>|</td><td>OR</td></tr>
</table>

The operators are listed here in order of precedence. NOT has the highest precedence, followed by AND, then OR. NOT is a unary operator, which precedes its operand and has the effect of changing true to false and false to true. AND and OR are binary operators. They combine their two operands to produce a single logical value. The effect of these operators is given in the following tables, known as *truth tables:*

NOT operation

Relation	*¬ Relation*
A>B	¬(A>B) or A¬>B
True	False
False	True

The relation can be any relation such as A>B. If it is true, then the logical symbol ¬ produces false; if it is false, the result of the logical operation is true. The parentheses in ¬(A>B) are necessary because ¬ has higher precedence than >. Without the parentheses, the bit representation of A would be complemented rather than the value of the comparison negated.

AND operation

Relation 1	*Relation 2*	*Relation 1 & Relation 2*
A>B	C>D	A>B & C>D
True	True	True
True	False	False
False	True	False
False	False	False

The expression A>B & C>D is a compound condition made up of the simple condition A>B and the simple condition C>D. Each of the simple conditions is either true or false. There are four possible combinations of true and false for the simple conditions. The compound condition is true for only one of these. A>B & C>D is true only if A>B is true and C>D is also true.

OR operation

Relation 1	*Relation 2*	*Relation 1 | Relation 2*
A>B	C>D	A>B | C>D
True	True	True
True	False	True
False	True	True
False	False	False

The expression A>B | C>D is a compound condition made up of the simple condition A>B and the simple condition C>D. Again there are four possible combinations of true and false for the simple conditions. The compound condition is true for all but one of these. A>B | C>D is true if either A>B is true or C>D is true or both are true. It is false only if the simple conditions are both false.

The following examples show the relationship between the underlying variables, relational operators, and compound conditions:

Let A = 5; B = 3;
C = 7; D = 2;
E,F = 6;

then

$A>B$	is true
$C<D$	is false
$E = F$	is true

and

$A>B$ & $C<D$	is false
$A>B$ & $E=F$	is true
$C>D$ & $E=F$	is true
$A>B$ | $C<D$	is true
$C<D$ | $E=F$	is true
¬($A>B$) | $C<D$	is false

COMPOUND CONDITIONS

Compound conditions can be used in IF statements to avoid nesting IFTHENELSE structures. They also can be used to assign values to BIT(1) variables.

An IF statement of the form

```
IF relation 1 & relation 2
  THEN
    statement1;
  ELSE
    statement 2;
```

is equivalent to a nested structure of the form

```
IF relation 1
  THEN
    IF relation 2
      THEN
        statement 1;
      ELSE
        statement 2;
  ELSE
    statement 2;
```

Statement 1 is executed only when both the underlying relationships that form the simple conditions are true. In every other case, statement 2 is executed.

The compound IF statement

```
IF relation 1 | relation 2
  THEN
    statement 1;
  ELSE
    statement 2;
```

is equivalent to nested structures of the forms

```
IF relation 1
  THEN
    statement 1;
  ELSE
    IF relation 2
      THEN
        statement 1;
      ELSE
        statement 2;
```

and

```
SELECT;
  WHEN (relation 1)
    statement 1;
  WHEN (relation 2)
    statement 1;
  OTHERWISE
    statement 2;
END;
```

In this example, statement 1 is executed unless both the simple conditions of relation 1 and relation 2 are false. In that case, statement 2 is executed.

Let A = 5; B = 3;
C = 7; D = 2;
E,F = 6;

then

A>B	is true
C<D	is false
E = F	is true

In the statement

```
IF A>B & C<D                 Full condition is false
  THEN
    G=10;
  ELSE
    G=15;                    G has the value 15
```

In the statement

```
IF A>B & E=F                 Full condition is true
  THEN
    G=10;
  ELSE
    G=15;                    G has the value 10
```

In the statement

```
IF A>B | C<D                 Full condition is true
  THEN
    G=10;
  ELSE
    G=15;                    G has the value 10
```

In the statement

```
IF ¬A>B | C<D                Full condition is false
  THEN
    G=10;
  ELSE
    G=15;                    G has the value 15
```

The values of conditions may be stored in BIT(1) variables. If P, Q, R, and S are BIT(1) variables, then the following assignments can be made:

```
P = A>B & C<D;          P has the value '0'B
Q = A>B & E=F;          Q has the value '1'B
R = A>B | C<D;          R has the value '1'B
S = ¬(A>B) | C<D;       S has the value '0'B
```

An assignment of a condition to a BIT(1) variable stores the value '0'B for false and '1'B for true.

5.6.2 Order of logical operations

When relational operators, logical operators, and arithmetic operators are used in a logical expression without any parentheses, the operations are carried out from left to right in the following order:

1. The NOT operations are carried out from left to right.
2. All arithmetic is carried out.
3. All the relational expressions are evaluated as true or false.
4. The AND operations are carried out from left to right.
5. The OR operations are carried out from left to right.

The result is a single logical value.

```
Given              A = 3;  B = 5;  C = 6;  D = 1;

then                  A<B & A<C & A<D

is evaluated as       true &  true & false
                         true      & false
                                false
```

In a logical expression that has parentheses, the subexpression inside the parentheses is evaluated first. The order of evaluation inside the parentheses is the same as the order of evaluation given above.

```
Given              A1 = 3;  A2 = 7;   B = 5;
                    C = 7;  D1 = 2;  D2 = 4;
                    E = 6;  F1 = 2;  F2 = 1;

then               ¬(A1+A2>B) & C<D1+D2 | C=3*F1+F2

is evaluated as
                   ¬(10 >B) & C< 6 | C= 7          arithmetic
                      ¬true &  false | true        relations
                      false & false  | true        NOT
                           false     | true        AND
                                 true              OR
```

PROGRAMMING HINT: CLARITY Use parentheses in compound logical expressions.

Logical expressions assigned to logical variables are evaluated in the same way.

Given A = 1; B = 5; C = 2; D = 5;

then X = ¬(A>B) & C<D | C>B;

is evaluated as

```
X = ¬(false) & true | false
X = ¬ false  & true | false
X =   true   & true | false
X =          true   | false
X =                true
```

The value assigned to X is '1'B.

The truth tables can be rewritten for BIT(1) variables as

NOT

X	¬X
'1'B	'0'B
'0'B	'1'B

AND

X	Y	X&Y
'1'B	'1'B	'1'B
'1'B	'0'B	'0'B
'0'B	'1'B	'0'B
'0'B	'0'B	'0'B

OR

X	Y	X|Y
'1'B	'1'B	'1'B
'1'B	'0'B	'1'B
'0'B	'1'B	'1'B
'0'B	'0'B	'0'B

BIT(1) variables can be used anywhere a logical expression can be used. They may be used in assignment statements and in conditions. They may also be input and output.

5.6.3 Operations on bit strings

Applied to BIT strings of length greater than one, the logical operators operate on individual bits of the strings. The NOT operator changes all the '0'B bits to '1'B and all of the '1'B bits to '0'B. This is shown in the following example:

```
DCL B  BIT(4)  INIT('1001'B);

    value of B          value of ¬B
      '1001'B             '0110'B
```

The AND operator combines two BIT strings, giving the resultant string a '1'B where both of the operands were '1'B, otherwise '0'B, as in the following example:

```
DCL A  BIT(4)  INIT('1100'B),
    B  BIT(4)  INIT('1010'B);

    value of A      value of B      value of A & B
      '1100'B         '1010'B          '1000'B
```

The OR operator combines two BIT strings, giving the resultant string a '1'B where either of the operands were '1'B, otherwise '0'B, as in the following example:

```
DCL A  BIT(4)  INIT('1100'B),
    B  BIT(4)  INIT('1010'B);

    value of A      value of B      value of A | B
      '1100'B         '1010'B          '1110'B
```

Review questions

1. A compound condition with AND is true when ____________________.

2. A compound condition with OR is true when ____________________.

3. A BIT(1) variable represents true when it has the value ____________________.

4. A BIT(1) variable represents false when it has the value ____________________.

5. The ____________________ operator is used to reverse the zeros and ones in a bit string.

6. Given the variables X='0'B, Y='1'B, Z='1'B, and W='1'B, what is the value of each of the following expressions?
   (a) W | X & Z
   (b) X & W | Z
   (c) X & (W | Z)
   (d) ¬(Y | Z)
   (e) ¬Y | Z

7. Given the variables A=5, B=10, C=2, D=5, and E=3, what is the value of each of the following expressions?
   (a) A = B & C < D
   (b) A * C = B | E < C * D
   (c) A < D & A < C | A < B
   (d) ¬(A = B) & ¬(C = D)

5.7 Iterative DO structure

An iterative DO is a repetition statement designed for counting the number of times the loop body is repeated. The count is available in the body of the loop for use in calculations or output. Unlike the DOWHILE and the DOUNTIL, the loop termination condition is implicit rather than explicit. DOWHILE and DOUNTIL are preferred for most processing. The iterative DO is mainly used in processing tables and arrays, as discussed in chapter 7. The general form of this structure is:

```
DO variable = m1 TO m2;        or     DO variable = m1 TO m2 BY m3;
   . . .                                 . . .
END;                                  END;
```

where DO, TO, and BY are keywords. The variable, sometimes known as the *index variable,* is a counter. m1 is the value assigned to the variable at the time the loop processing begins. m2 is the test value, the limit beyond which the variable may not go. m3 is the *step size,* the amount by which the variable counts. When m3 is missing, the default step size of one is used. m1, m2, and m3 may be numeric constants, variables, or expressions. They are evaluated once, on entry to the loop. If m3 is positive, the variable is used to count up; if negative, to count down. If m3 is positive, the iterated DO structure is equivalent to

```
variable = m1
DO WHILE (variable <= m2);
   . . .
  variable = variable + m3;
END;
```

provided that neither m2 nor m3 is changed inside the loop. If m3 is negative, the iterated DO is equivalent to

```
variable = m1
DO WHILE (variable >= m2);
   . . .
  variable = variable + m3;
END;
```

provided that neither m2 nor m3 is changed inside the loop.

The condition is tested before the body of the loop is executed. If the test value is unreachable, control shifts to the statement immediately following the DO structure. Once the repetition has begun, it continues until the test value is passed.

There are two forms of iterative DO structures: simple DO and implied DO. Both can be nested. A simple iterative DO is an ordinary control structure, while an implied DO is used for control inside input and output instructions. The simple DO is a DO group with counter control. All the statements between DO and END form the body of the loop, as in other repetition structures. The implied iterative DO does not have a loop body or an END statement. Only a few examples of it will be given here. It will be discussed more fully in chapter 7 where it is used in the input and output of arrays.

5.7.1 Simple iterative DO structures

The following examples illustrate the effect of simple iterative DO structures. In

```
DO I = 1 TO 5;
  PUT LIST(I);              Prints  1   2   3   4   5
END;
```

the variable I takes on the values 1, 2, 3, 4 and 5, the body of the loop is executed five times, and the five values of I are printed. The repetition stops after using I = 5 in the execution of the body of the loop. No step size is given, so the default value of 1 is used for the increment. After the repetition has been completed, the index variable should not be used as its value is unreliable.

PROGRAMMING HINT: CAUTION Do not use a loop index outside the loop after a normal exit from the loop.

It is not necessary for the index variable to equal the limit value exactly.

```
DO I = 1 TO 8 BY 2;
  PUT SKIP LIST(I);         Prints  1   3   5   7
END;
```

In this example I is incremented by 2 and the values printed for I are 1, 3, 5, and 7. When I becomes 9 the repetition terminates.

When the values involved in the loop control are not integers, the limit must be specified carefully. In the following example,

```
DCL X FIXED DEC(4,3);

DO X = 0.0 TO 4.0 BY 2.0/3.0;
  PUT SKIP LIST(X);
END;
```

the values printed for X may be 0.000, 0.667, 1.334, 2.001, 2.668, and 3.335. The value 4.002 is too large and the repetition is terminated even though mathematically 6*(2/3) should be exactly 4.

PROGRAMMING HINT: ACCURACY Use integers for loop control.

In the following example the step size is negative and the index variable is decremented rather than incremented. The limit is therefore less than the initial value of the variable.

```
DO I = 5 TO 1 BY -1;
  PUT LIST(I);                 Prints  5   4   3   2   1
END;
```

The values printed for I are 5, 4, 3, 2, and 1, because the output statement is executed as long as I is greater than or equal to one.

```
DO I = 6 TO 1 BY -2;
  PUT LIST(I);                 Prints  6   4   2
END;
```

In this example the values printed are 6, 4, and 2. The variable never exactly equals the limiting value.

For efficiency, the index variable is usually declared to be FIXED BINARY. Usually FIXED BINARY(15) is sufficient.

Expressions and variables may be used in the loop control. Following are some of the possibilities:

Valid DO statements	*Invalid DO statements*
DO IND = 1 TO 10;	DO IND = 10 TO 1;
DO COUNT = 1 TO 50 BY 2;	DO COUNT = 1 TO 50 BY −2;
DO REAL = .1 TO 5.5 BY .2;	DO REAL = .1 TO −5.5 BY .2;
DO I = J+1 TO K-2 BY L;	
DO MAX = I-2 TO J BY N;	
DO S = 0 TO 100 BY 1/J;	
DO K = SQRT(X) TO SQRT(Y);	

Instead of giving a range of values for a DO index variable, an explicit list of values may be given.

`DO I = 1 TO 5;` is equivalent to `DO I = 1, 2, 3, 4, 5;`

An explicit list is useful when there are only a few values for the index, and there is no easy algorithm for calculating them. For example,

```
DO I = 1, 5, 6, 14, 17, 18;
  PUT LIST (I);                Prints  1   5   6   14   17   18
END;
```

causes the specified values to be printed. These two methods of specifying the values for the index variable may be used together, as in

```
DO K = 0, 2 TO 5, 10 TO 50 BY 10;
  PUT SKIP LIST(K);
END;
```

The values printed for K are 0, 2, 3, 4, 5, 10, 20, 30, 40, and 50. The body of the loop is executed with K equal to zero. Then K is set to 2 and the loop executed until K becomes 6. Then K is set to 10 and the loop is executed until K is greater than 50.

These examples of loop control have used a simple loop with only a single output statement in the body of the loop. In general there can be as many statements as necessary inside the DO loop. The execution of all the statements inside the loop is carried out until the value of the index variable exceeds the limit. Certain rules should be observed when using loops:

1. Control should not be transferred to a statement inside a loop from outside the loop. This would leave the index variable undefined, one reason for not using the GOTO statement.
2. Transfer of control from inside the loop to outside should take place either by satifying the loop condition or by using a LEAVE statement. In either case control transfers to the statement immediately following the loop.
3. The index variable should not be modified inside the loop, with one exception. The index can be set to the limit value when the loop is to be terminated early.
4. The index variable should not be used after transferring control from inside the loop to outside unless a LEAVE statement was used to exit the loop. If the loop was exited normally, the index variable may not have the expected value.

METHODS OF TERMINATION OF SIMPLE DO STRUCTURE

There are situations in which it is necessary to exit a loop without fulfilling the looping conditions. For example, if at most fifteen records are to be read and printed, but the processing should stop sooner if a record having 'LAST RECORD' on it is processed, then the index variable can be set to fifteen when the trailer record is found.

```
DO K=1 TO 15;
  GET EDIT (INFO) (A(80));
  IF INFO='LAST RECORD'
    THEN
      K=15;                     /* Stop repetition */
  PUT SKIP EDIT (INFO) (A);
END;
```

Setting K to fifteen stops the repetition after the output statement has been executed. K is tested, and control transfers to the statement following the end of the DO loop.

If at most fifteen records are to be read and listed using an iterated DO, there must be a way to exit the loop if the file contains fewer than fifteen values. There must be no attempt to process an eof as though it were an ordinary record. An IFTHENELSE is needed to separate the processing into the two cases of more data and no more data.

```
ON ENDFILE(SYSIN)
  MORE_DATA=FALSE;

MORE_DATA=TRUE;
DO K=1 TO 15;
  GET EDIT (INFO) (A(80));
```

```
  IF MORE_DATA
    THEN
      PUT SKIP EDIT (K,INFO) (F(5,0),X(2),A);
    ELSE
      K = 15;                        /* Stop repetition */
END;
```

Neither one of these examples uses a priming read because the loop would then terminate after the sixteenth record was read rather than after the fifteenth was processed.

LEAVE statement (not in Subset G) When the index variable is set to the limiting value, the repetition does not end at that point. The execution of the body of the loop is finished first. If the LEAVE statement is used, the repetition terminates immediately, as control transfers out of the loop from the point of the LEAVE statement to the statement immediately following the loop.

```
ON ENDFILE(SYSIN)
  MORE_DATA = FALSE;

MORE_DATA = TRUE;
DO K = 1 TO 15;
  GET EDIT (INFO) (A(80));
  IF ¬MORE_DATA
    THEN
      LEAVE;                        /* EXIT LOOP */
  PUT SKIP EDIT (K,INFO) (F(5,0),X(2),A);
END;
```

In this example the output statement is executed only if more data is available. The value of K after the loop is exited via the LEAVE statement is one higher than the number of lines printed. If the loop is exited normally, the value of K is unpredictable.

5.7.2 Nested DO structures

Iterative DO structures, like other structures, may be nested inside each other. When DO structures are nested, the index variables must be different, as shown in the following example:

```
DO I = 1 TO 3;
  DO J = 1 TO 4;
    PUT SKIP LIST (I,J);
  END;
END;
```

Indentation is used to show the nesting of the structures. This output statement is executed twelve times, four times with four different values of J for each of the three values of I. The values printed are:

I	*J*
1	1
1	2
1	3
1	4
2	1
2	2
2	3
2	4
3	1
3	2
3	3
3	4

The value of J, the index of the inner loop, changes more rapidly than the value of I. The value of I is initialized first, then J. I is 1, then J is 1, and the

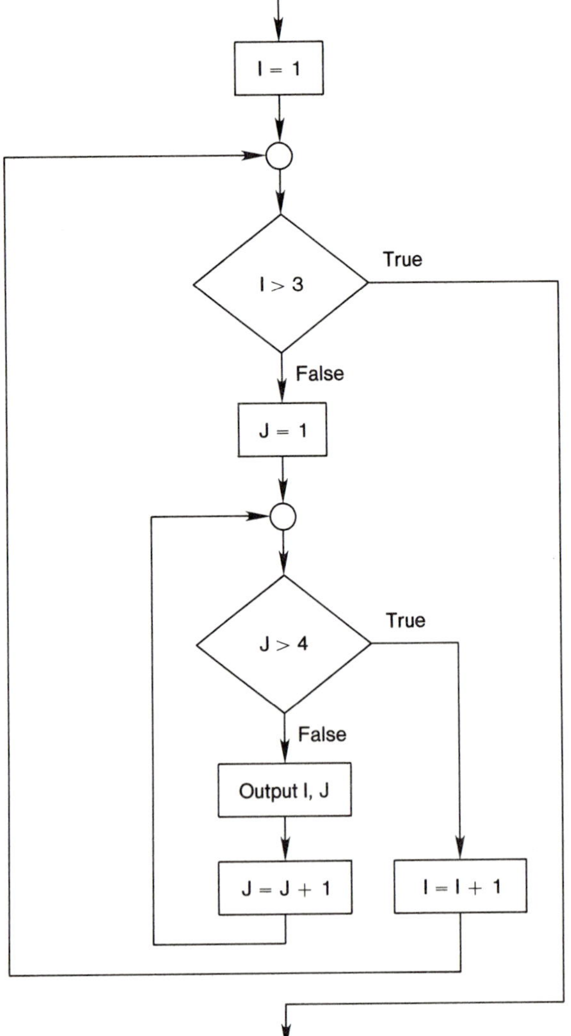

Figure 5–12

inner loop is executed until J has finished. The value of I is then incremented to 2 and J is reinitialized to 1. After I = 3 and J = 4 have been used, the inner loop is terminated, I is tested, and the outer loop is terminated. The flowchart of figure 5–12 shows the details of the loop control.

If three iterative DO structures are nested, as in

```
DO I = 1 TO 2;
  statement 1;
  DO J = 1 TO 3;
    statement 2;
    DO K = 1 TO 4;
      PUT SKIP LIST (I,J,K);
    END;
  END;
END;
```

then Statement 1 inside the DO loop with index I is executed two times. Statement 2 inside the DO loop with index J is executed six times, three times for each value of I. The output statement inside the DO loop with index K is executed four times for every combination of I and J, for a total of twenty-four times. The value of K changes most rapidly; that of I least rapidly. The values of J and K are not available at statement 1, and the value of K is not available at statement 2.

Index variables may be reused if the DO loops using them are do not overlap. The following example shows many ways of nesting DO loops.

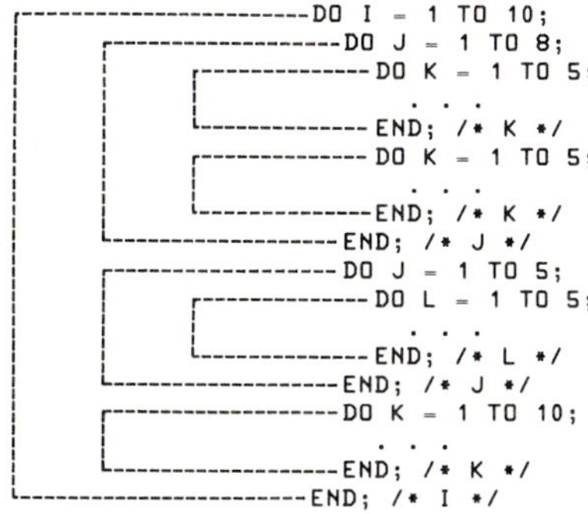

DO and END statements must be properly matched. Indentation and documentation can be used to emphasize the structure.

WHILE OPTION WITH ITERATIVE DO

The iterative DO and DOWHILE constructs can be combined to provide both counting and a continuation condition, as in the following example:

```
J = 0;
DO I = 1 TO 5 WHILE (J < 10);
  J = J + I;
  PUT SKIP LIST (I,J);
END;
```

The values printed are:

I	*J*
1	1
2	3
3	6
4	10

The WHILE condition should not refer to the index variable, since the order of processing of the iterative part and the WHILE part of the DO statement is implementation-dependent. The repetition in this example terminates when I = 5 has been used or when J reaches 10, whichever occurs first.

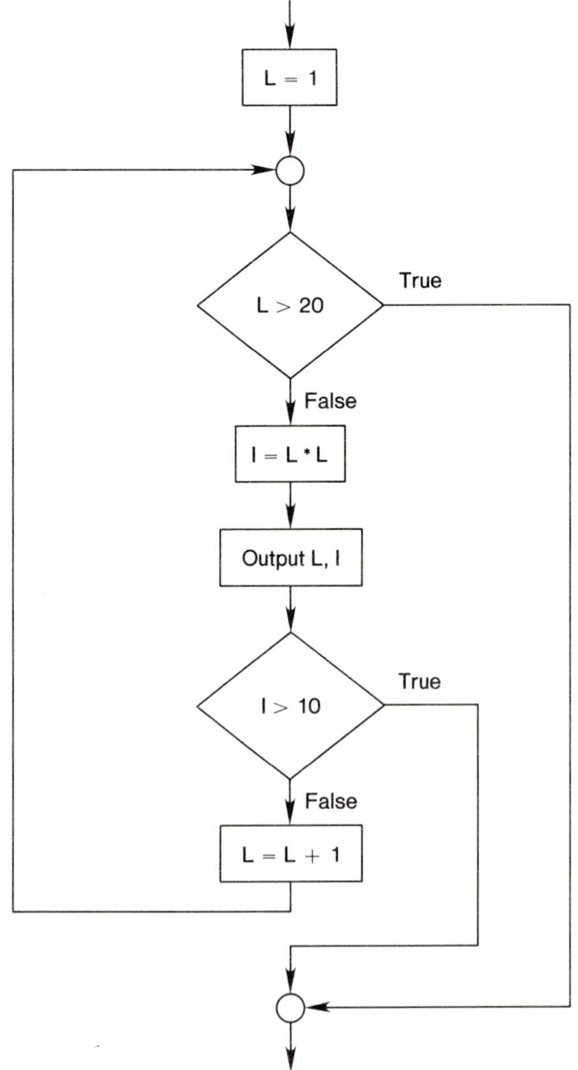

Figure 5–13

UNTIL OPTION WITH ITERATIVE DO

The DOUNTIL and iterative DO may be combined into a single structure.

```
DO L = 1 TO 20 UNTIL (I > 10);
  I = L * L;
  PUT SKIP LIST (L,I);
END;
```

This example prints the values

L	*I*
1	1
2	4
3	9
4	16

In this case, the comparison of the index variable with the limit provides an exit at the top of the loop, while the UNTIL condition provides an exit at the bottom of the loop. The flowchart is shown in figure 5–13.

5.7.3 Implied DO loop

The implied DO loop is an iterative DO used to control input or output. At this time only output examples will be given. The following statements

```
PUT EDIT ((120)'*') (A);
```

and

```
DO I = 1 TO 120;
  PUT EDIT ('*') (A(1));
END;
```

each print a line containing 120 asterisks. Using an implied DO, this would be written as

```
PUT EDIT (('*' DO I = 1 TO 120)) ((120)A(1));
```

The inner parentheses is the implied DO, ('*' DO I = 1 TO 120). It gives the character to be printed and counting control for repeatedly printing it.

Given the statements

```
DO K = 1 TO 5;
  PUT EDIT (K) (F(5,0));
END;
```

or

```
PUT SKIP EDIT ((K DO K = 1 TO 5)) (F(5,0));
```

the values one through five are printed on a single line. The effect of the implied DO is the same as using the simple iterative DO structure. The implied DO, (K DO K = 1 to 10), gives the variable being printed as K, then gives the counting control for obtaining the values of K.

Review questions

1. Indicate whether each of the following statements is true or false.

(a) An iterative DO statement is a "counting" statement.
(b) An iterative DO has an implied termination condition.
(c) The index variable of an iterative DO must not be used after terminating normally.
(d) The value of the index variable of an iterative DO should not be changed inside the loop.
(e) The index of an iterative DO can be used to count up or to count down.
(f) The LEAVE statement can be used to exit an iterative DO without affecting the index variable.
(g) An iterative DO cannot contain a WHILE or an UNTIL clause.
(h) Nested iterative DO statements may use the same index variable.

2. In the following iterative DO structure,

```
DO K = 1 TO 10 BY 2;
  . . .
END;
```

(a) The initial value assigned to K is ____________.
(b) The upper bound on the value of K is ____________.
(c) The index K takes on the values ____________.
(d) The repetition stops when ____________.

3. In the following iterative DO structure,

```
J = 1;
DO K = J TO 10 BY J-1;
  . . .
  J = J + 1;
END;
```

(a) The initial value assigned to K is ____________.
(b) The upper bound on the value of K is ____________.
(c) The index K takes on the values ____________.
(d) The repetition stops when ____________.

4. What values are assigned to the index in each of the following iterative DO statements?

```
(a) DO A = 1 TO 5;
(b) DO B = 1 TO 20 BY 4;
(c) DO C = 1.5 TO 2.8 BY .2;
(d) DO D = 2.8 TO .5 BY -1.0;
(e) DO E = SQRT(4.0) TO SQRT(E+12);
(f) DO F = 0,3,4,6;
(g) DO G = 1 TO 5, 10 TO 15 BY 2;
(h) DO H = 1 TO 5, 1 TO -5 BY -1;
(i) DO I = 1 TO 10 WHILE (I < 7);
(j) DO J = 1,3,7, 2 TO 10 UNTIL (J > 5);
(k) DO K = 1 TO 5 WHILE (K*K < 25),17,1 TO -5 UNTIL
    (K<0);
```

5. What values of J, K, and L would cause errors in the following loop control?

```
DO I = J TO K BY L;
```

6. Use an iterative DO to write a code segment that counts from 1 to 100 by 10 and prints the counts.

7. Use an implied DO to write a code segment that counts from 1 to 100 by 10 and prints the counts.

8. Use an iterative DO to write a code segment that counts backward from 100 to 1 and prints the counts.

9. Use an implied DO to write a code segment that counts backward from 100 to 1 and prints the counts.

10. What does each of the following code segments print?

```
(a) PUT LIST ((K DO K = 1 TO 10 BY 2));
(b) PUT LIST ((K*K DO K = 1 to 5));
(c) PUT LIST (((I+J DO J = 1 to 3) DO I = 1 TO 2));
(d) PUT LIST ((5 - K DO K = 4 TO 0 BY -1))
```

5.8 Block structure and exception handling

Events that occur occasionally during program execution, such as attempted division by zero, invalid input data, or no input available, are known as *exceptions*. These types of events may be expected to occur at rare intervals, but the exact time they will occur is unforeseeable. When they do occur, they usually cause program *interrupts*. That is, the hardware or operating system recognizes that processing cannot continue normally, and interrupts the program. The programmer, in turn, can handle these situations in one of two ways: ON units can be defined to provide special processing instructions, or the program can just be allowed to terminate abnormally. The default exception handlers that terminate the program treat the exception as an error and print diagnostic messages to help the programmer debug the program. If there is a program ON unit for the exception, the programmer may specify actions to aid in diagnosing the problem, or may take remedial action.

The general form of the ON statement that defines the exception handler when there is only a single statement to be executed is

```
On condition                For example:  ON ENDFILE(SYSIN)
  statement;                                 MORE_DATA = FALSE;
```

The ON statement is an executable statement. It has the effect of establishing a trap for the condition. More than one exception handler can be written for the same condition. Reestablishing an exception handler cancels the previous set of actions and puts into effect a new set. The statement in the exception handler that assigns FALSE to MORE_DATA is not executed with the ON statement. It is merely set up as a line of code, or more correctly, as a small unnamed procedure, to be used when the ENDFILE condition is raised by the system when the eof record is found.

At the time the exception is actually raised, the statement or statements in the exception handler are executed and control returns to the point in the program at which the exception was raised. With an ENDFILE condition, this is immediately after the input statement that failed to find data.

If there are two or more statements to be processed when an exception is raised, they must be enclosed in a BEGIN. . .END block.

5.8.1 BEGIN. . .END block

A segment of code written in a BEGIN. . .END block is like a small procedure that does not have a name. It is executed by control transferring to, or running into, the BEGIN statement. The general form of the BEGIN. . .END block is

```
BEGIN;
  statement_1;
  statement_2;
  statement_3;
  . . .
END;
```

The group of statements between the keyword BEGIN and the keyword END may include declarations as well as a sequence of executable statements. Any variables declared within the block can be used only within the block. They are *local* to it. BEGIN. . .END blocks can be used anyplace in a program where a sequence is needed; however, they are not as efficient as DO groups, so they are commonly used only in exception handlers and when local variables are desired. BEGIN. . .END blocks differ from DO groups in that DO groups may not be used in ON units, may not contain local declarations, and are not handled by the computer as though they were procedures.

The folowing example shows the use of a block in an exception handler.

```
ON ENDFILE (SYSIN)
  BEGIN;
    PUT LIST ('ALL THE RECORDS HAVE BEEN PROCESSED');
    MORE_DATA = FALSE;
  END;
```

This example shows an appropriate way to document the successful completion of the input processing while at the same time setting a flag to stop a repetitive loop.

5.8.2 Common ON conditions

An ON unit can be defined for each of the conditions to be handled by the program. Each ON statement specifies the particular exception it is handling. The ON statements must be placed in the program ahead of the statements likely to raise the exceptions. It is customary to place them immediately after the declarations.

The conditions can be categorized according to the type of statement that will raise them. Arithmetic operations can raise the following conditions:

CONVERSION	Value is not numeric
FIXEDOVERFLOW	Value has too many digits
OVERFLOW	Exponent is too large
UNDERFLOW	Exponent is too small
ZERODIVIDE	Divisor is zero
SIZE	Decimal value is too long

Each of these conditions can be considered to be an error in that either the arithmetic cannot be completed, or the answer will be inaccurate.

The conditions that can be raised during an input or output operation include the following:

ENDFILE	Attempt to read past end of data
ENDPAGE	Attempt to write beyond end of page
CONVERSION	Value is not the type expected
SIZE	Decimal value is too long
TRANSMIT	Transmission error
RECORD	Record is not size or type expected

Conditions that can be raised during manipulation of arrays and character strings include:

SUBSCRIPTRANGE	Attempt to access beyond end of array
STRINGRANGE	Attempt to access beyond end of string

The complete set of conditions can be found in the portion of any PL/I manual that lists runtime error messages.

Some of these conditions, such as ZERODIVIDE, are normally enabled even though there may not be an exception handler established for them. If the system did not detect them, the processing would come to a halt. Others, such as STRINGRANGE, are normally disabled as they do not prevent processing, and frequent checking makes a production program inefficient. When a program is being debugged, some of the condition interrupts which would not be used during a production run are enabled through the use of *compiler parameters,* instructions to the compiler on how to generate the code. This is done by prefacing the main procedure with a condition-enabling clause.

SIGNAL STATEMENT

Any interrupt that has been enabled will be raised automatically when the associated condition occurs. It is also possible for the program to raise a condition explicitly by using the SIGNAL instruction. For example, when a program is first tested, instead of using the complete set of input data, it may be appropriate to signal ENDFILE after only one or two sets of values have been processed. This would be done by the statement

```
SIGNAL ENDFILE (SYSIN);
```

After the exception handler has been executed, control returns to the statement immediately following the SIGNAL statement.

The various ON conditions are discussed in detail in Appendix C.

CONDITION STATUS DEFAULTS

Conditions differ in their default status. Some conditions are automatically enabled unless the programmer explicitly disables them. To protect the system, some conditions cannot be disabled. Other conditions are automatically disabled, because they make the processing inefficient. The programmer must explicitly enable them. The default statuses for the conditions that have been discussed in this chapter are:

Condition	*Default status*
CONVERSION	Enabled
FIXEDOVERFLOW	Enabled
OVERFLOW	Enabled
UNDERFLOW	Enabled
ZERODIVIDE	Enabled
SIZE	Disabled
ENDFILE	Enabled (cannot be disabled)
ENDPAGE	Enabled (cannot be disabled)

Those conditions that are normally disabled may be enabled for a single statement, a block, or an entire procedure. This is done by using a preface of the form

```
(condition):
```

Only those conditions that are enabled may have active exception handlers.

Those conditions that are normally enabled may be disabled for a single statement, a block, or an entire procedure by using a preface of the form

```
(NOcondition):
```

If an error occurs for which the condition has been disabled, the system will raise the ERROR condition. The ERROR condition cannot be disabled.

The following example shows the enabling and disabling of conditions.

```
DCL X       CHAR(5),
    Y       BIT(5),
    (N,M)   FIXED BIN(31),
    (A,B)   FIXED DEC(5);

X = '10A11';
(NOCONV): Y = X;                      ERROR condition is
                                      raised instead of
                                      CONVERSION
```

```
N = 1000000;
(NOFIXEDOVERFLOW): M = N * N;      ERROR condition is
                                   raised instead of
                                   FIXEDOVERFLOW

A = 12345;
(SIZE) : B = 10 * A;                SIZE condition is
                                   raised
```

The statements for which the CONVERSION and FIXEDOVERFLOW interrupts have been disabled will result in the ERROR condition being raised. Since the scope of the preface is only a single statement, the CONVERSION and FIXEDOVERFLOW conditions will still be raised in other places where the errors occur. The SIZE preface has the opposite effect. In the statement that follows it, the SIZE condition will be raised. At any other place in the program where the same error occurs, the ERROR condition will be raised instead.

If the programmer wants to specify the action to be taken for any type of error or to prevent an abnormal program termination, the condition should be enabled for the entire program and an ON unit established to handle it. ON units should also be established for any condition that cannot be disabled but which can be considered a part of normal processing. The SIZE condition is enabled for the entire program in the following example because it is prefaced to the main PROCEDURE statement.

```
(SIZE):
MPROG: PROC OPTIONS(MAIN);
  . . .
ON SIZE
   BEGIN;
     . . .
   END;
ON ENDFILE(SYSIN)
   BEGIN;
   . . .
   END;
  . . .
END MPROG;
```

When an exception handler has been defined for a condition, its definition remains in effect until another exception handler is defined for the same condition. An exception handler can be cancelled by defining another exception handler with a null action. In the following example, the page number is printed at the top of every page within the scope of the first ON unit for the ENDPAGE condition, but it is not printed within the scope of the second ON unit.

```
MPROG: PROC OPTIONS(MAIN);
  . . .
ON ENDPAGE(SYSPRINT)
   BEGIN;
      PAGENUM = PAGENUM + 1;
      PUT PAGE EDIT (PAGENUM) (COL(100),F(5,0));
   END;
```

```
  . . .
ON ENDPAGE(SYSPRINT);
  . . .
END MPROG;
```

Review questions

1. When an ON statement is executed, a ____________________ is set for the interrupt condition.

2. When an ON statement is executed, the exception handler is ____________________.

3. The ON unit is executed when the error condition or exception is ____________________.

4. The ENDFILE condition is raised when an input statement finds ____________________.

5. The ENDPAGE condition is raised when an output statement finds ____________________.

6. After an ON unit for an ENDFILE condition is executed, control continues ____________________.

7. After an ON unit for an ENDPAGE condition is executed, control continues ____________________.

8. The ____________________ can be used by the programmer to transfer control to an exception handler.

9. What is the effect of each of the following code segments?

```
(a) ON ENDFILE(SYSIN);
(b) ON ENDFILE(SYSIN)
      MORE = FALSE;
     . . .
    ON ENDFILE(SYSIN)
      EOF = TRUE;
(c) ON ENDFILE(SYSIN)
      BEGIN;
        MORE = FALSE;
        EOF = TRUE;
      END;
(d) ON ENDFILE(INFO)
      MORE_INFO = FALSE;
(e) ON ENDFILE(A)
      MORE_A = FALSE;
    ON ENDFILE(B)
      MORE_B = FALSE;
(f) ON ENDPAGE(SYSPRINT)
      PUT PAGE;
```

10. Each of the following ON statements is misleading or invalid. Why?

(a)
```
ON ENDFILE(SYSPRINT)
     MORE = FALSE;
```
(b)
```
ON ENDFILE(SYSIN)
     DO;
       MORE = FALSE;
     END;
```
(c)
```
ON ENDFILE(SYSIN)
     MORE = TRUE;
```

5.9 Examples using control structures

The following examples illustrate the use of the various control structures. In particular they show the nesting of control structures.

5.9.1 Rational numbers

This example prints all the rational numbers (fractions in lowest terms) that have denominators of less than 100.

```
FRACS: PROC OPTIONS (MAIN);
/**************************************************************/
/*                                                            */
/* PROGRAM: RATIONAL NUMBERS AS FRACTIONS                     */
/* AUTHOR: C ZIEGLER                                          */
/* VERSION: 07/17/84                                          */
/*                                                            */
/* PROGRAM DESCRIPTION                                        */
/* ---------------------------------------------------------- */
/* THIS PROGRAM PRINTS AS FRACTIONS ALL OF THE                */
/* RATIONAL NUMBERS OF THE FORM N/M WHICH ARE                 */
/* IRREDUCIBLE AND HAVE M < 100.                              */
/*                                                            */
/* INPUT: NONE                                                */
/*                                                            */
/* OUTPUT: FRACTIONS ARRANGED AS FOLLOWS                      */
/*          1/2                                               */
/*          1/3   2/3                                         */
/*          1/4   3/4                                         */
/*          1/5   2/5   3/5   4/5                             */
/*           . . .                                            */
/**************************************************************/

DCL (N,M)      FIXED BIN,      /* NUMERATOR & DENOMINATOR */
    (I,J,R)    FIXED BIN,
    K          FIXED BIN;
```

```
DO M = 2 TO 99;            /* FOR EACH DENOMINATOR                   */
  K = M - 1;
  PUT SKIP;
  DO N = 1 TO K;           /* FOR EACH POSSIBLE NUMERATOR            */
    I = N;
    J = M;
    DO UNTIL (I = 0);      /* CALCULATE GREATEST COMMON DIVISOR      */
      R = MOD(J,I);
      J = N;
      I = R;
    END;
    IF J = 1               /* IF GCD(M,N) IS 1, PRINT N/M            */
      THEN
        IF M < 10
          THEN
            PUT EDIT (N,'/',M) (F(4),A,F(1));/* M HAS 1 DIGIT   */
          ELSE
            PUT EDIT (N,'/',M) (F(3),A,F(2));/* M HAS 2 DIGITS */
  END;
END;
END FRACS;
```

The library routine MOD returns the remainder when J is divided by I and I and J are positive. This is used in the segment of code that calculates the greatest common divisor of M and N. If the greatest common divisor is one, then the numbers M and N are relatively prime and the fraction is in lowest terms. DOUNTIL is used for the innermost loop, as there is no need to check whether I is zero on entry to the repetition.

5.9.2 Wage calculation

This example uses a SELECT structure to calculate payroll information for different categories of employees. The logic is shown in the following decision table:

More data Wage_type	Y 'H'	Y 'W'	Y 'M'	Y Other	N *
Call HOURLY	X				
Call WEEKLY		X			
Call MONTHLY			X		
Print error message				X	
Input record	X	X	X	X	
Repeat	X	X	X	X	
Stop					X

The program assumes the existence of library procedures to process the different categories of wages. These procedures would be found in a user library.

```
WAGES: PROC OPTIONS (MAIN);
/************************************************************/
/*                                                          */
/* PROGRAM: WAGE CALCULATIONS                               */
/* AUTHOR: C ZIEGLER                                        */
/* VERSION: 07/17/84                                        */
/*                                                          */
/* PROGRAM DESCRIPTION                                      */
/*----------------------------------------------------------*/
/* THIS PROGRAM CALCULATES WAGES FOR HOURLY, WEEKLY         */
/* AND MONTHLY EMPLOYEES.                                   */
/*                                                          */
/* INPUT: WAGE CODE ('H','W','M')                           */
/*        EMPLOYEE INFORMATION                              */
/*                                                          */
/* OUTPUT: NONE                                             */
/*                                                          */
/* CALLS: HOURLY, WEEKLY, MONTHLY (PAYROLL LIBRARY)         */
/*                                                          */
/************************************************************/

DCL WAGE_TYPE   CHAR(1),
    EMP_INFO    CHAR(79);
DCL MORE_DATA   BIT(1),
    TRUE        BIT(1)  INIT('1'B),
    FALSE       BIT(1)  INIT('1'B);

ON ENDFILE (SYSIN)
  MORE_DATA = FALSE;

MORE_DATA = TRUE;
GET EDIT (WAGE_TYPE,EMP_INFO) (A(1),A(79));
DO WHILE (MORE_DATA);
  SELECT (WAGE_TYPE);
    WHEN ('H')
      CALL HOURLY;
    WHEN ('W')
      CALL WEEKLY;
    WHEN ('M')
      CALL MONTHLY;
    OTHERWISE
      PUT SKIP LIST ('WAGE TYPE ERROR', WAGE_TYPE,EMP_INFO);
  END;
  GET EDIT (WAGE_TYPE,EMP_INFO) (A(1),A(79));
END;
END WAGES;
```

When execution of the SELECT structure begins, the value of WAGE_TYPE is compared with the values in the WHEN clauses. Control transfers to the statement with the matching value. When the statement has been completed, control resumes with the GET EDIT statement after the SELECT structure.

5.9.3 Quadratic equations

This example illustrates the use of nested repetition and selection structures. It is based on an algorithm of chapter 2.

```
QUADEQ: PROC OPTIONS (MAIN);
/***************************************************************/
/*                                                             */
/* PROGRAM: QUADRATIC EQUATIONS                                */
/* AUTHOR: R REDDY                                             */
/* VERSION: 07/17/84                                           */
/*                                                             */
/* PROGRAM DESCRIPTION                                         */
/* ----------------------------------------------------------- */
/* THIS PROGRAM SOLVES QUADRATIC EQUATIONS                     */
/*                                                             */
/* INPUT: THE COEFFICIENTS OF THE EQUATIONS                    */
/*                  A, B, C                                    */
/*                                                             */
/*                  AX² + BX + C = 0                           */
/*                                                             */
/* OUTPUT: THE EQUATIONS, THE ROOTS                            */
/*                                                             */
/***************************************************************/


DCL (A,B,C)     FLOAT BINARY;
DCL (X,X1,X2)   FLOAT BINARY;
DCL (R,S)       FLOAT BINARY,
    MORE_DATA   BIT(1),
    TRUE        BIT(1)   INIT('1'B),
    FALSE       BIT(1)   INIT('0'B);

ON ENDFILE (SYSIN)
  MORE_DATA = FALSE;

MORE_DATA = TRUE;
GET LIST (A,B,C,);
DO WHILE (MORE_DATA);
  PUT SKIP EDIT (A,'XSQ+',B,'X+',C,'=0')
                (COL(1),F(5,2),A,F(5,2),A,F(5,2),A);
  IF A = 0
    THEN
      PUT SKIP LIST ('NOT QUADRATIC');
    ELSE
      DO;
        R = B*B - 4*A*C;
        SELECT;
          WHEN (R < 1)
            PUT SKIP LIST ('COMPLEX ROOTS');
```

```
          WHEN (R = 0)
            DO;
              X = -B/(2*A);
              PUT SKIP LIST ('DOUBLE ROOT',X);
            END;
          OTHERWISE
            DO;
              S = SQRT(R);
              X1 = (-B + S)/(2*A);
              X2 = (-B - S)/(2*A);
              PUT SKIP LIST ('ROOTS',X1,X2);
            END;
        END;
      END;
  PUT SKIP;
  GET LIST (A,B,C);
END;
END QUADEQ;
```

A small amount of optimization has been included in this code. The variables R and S have been introduced to avoid calculating B*B – 4*A*C more than once and to avoid calculating the square root of R more than once.

5.10 Summary

The basic control structures implemented by the PL/I DO ... END, DOWHILE, DOUNTIL, iterative DO, IFTHENELSE, and SELECT may be nested inside each other. DOWHILE, DOUNTIL, and iterative DO are used to control repetition based on a counter, a trailer value, or some other condition. The different types of loop control may be combined in the same statement. IFTHENELSE and SELECT statements provide a choice between alternatives. The control of DOWHILE, DOUNTIL, IFTHENELSE and one form of SELECT is provided by logical conditions. These may be simple BIT(1) variables or logical expressions built from simple comparison through the use of the logical operators &, | , and ¬.

ON units provide control when errors or other abnormal situations occur. The programmer has the option of ignoring the situation, printing an appropriate message, or taking remedial action.

5.11 Exercises

1. Write a program that generates and prints all of the Pythagorean triples found among the numbers 1 through 100. A Pythagorean triple is a set of numbers a, b, c such that $c^2 = a^2 + b^2$. The program should be efficient and not try all possible triples, but only those for which $a < b < c$.

2. Write a program that determines how to dispense change. The input to the program should be a price (dollars and cents) and a payment (dollar and

cents). The program should print the change as # of dollars, # of quarters, # of dimes, # of nickels, and # of pennies. For example, if an item with a price of $17.23 is paid for with a $50 bill, the change should be thirty-two dollars, three quarters, zero dimes, zero nickels, two pennies.

3. Write a program that calculates the square root of X using the Newton-Ralphson formula:

$$s_{k+1} = (s_k + x/s_k)/2$$

where $s_0 = x/2$ and $x > 0$.

4. Assume the data in a file has the following format:

Cols.	1-20	Student name
	21-23	Grade in PL/I (100 is maximum)
	24-26	Grade in FORTRAN ″
	27-29	Grade in PASCAL ″

If a student has not taken a course, the grade field is left blank. Write a program that will print the name of the best student in each course (assume there are no duplicate grades).

6
String data manipulation

OBJECTIVE: To handle text and other types of string data.

MANIPULATION OF CHARACTER STRINGS and bit strings is essential in almost all data processing, text processing, and software applications. String manipulation is the primary method of computing in word processing, text editing, and other forms of text processing. In data processing applications, character string manipulation is necessary to produce the titles, subtitles, and column headings of reports. It is also used in processing nonnumeric data such as lists of names and addresses and in validating numeric data.

Software applications involving data retrieval often use bit string manipulations. Bit strings are used for mapping and indexing the storage of data.

PL/I has a large number of built-in features used in string manipulation. The only string operators represented by symbols are concatenation (||), assignment (=), comparison (<, >, =), and the logical operators (¬, &, |). The other types of string manipulation are handled by library functions.

6.1 Character strings

Character string values are sequences of zero or more characters taken from the PL/I character set, introduced in section 2.2.1. The blank character is included. Character string literals are enclosed in quotation marks. Declarations of character variables were presented in section 3.3. The general form of the declaration is:

```
DCL var_name CHARACTER(n);
```

where n ≥ 0 specifies the number of characters to be stored for the variable. If n = 0, the value of the variable is the *null string*. Values may be assigned to character variables through initialization, explicit assignment, or input, as shown in the following example:

```
DECLARE STR    CHAR(5)   INIT('*&$%|'),    Initialization
        NAME   CHAR(10),
        ADDR   CHAR(20);

NAME = 'AL JOHNSON';                        Assignment
GET EDIT (ADDR) (A(20));                    Input
```

Character constants used in a program must be enclosed in quotation marks.

6.1.1 Character assignment

When an assignment statement is used to store data in a character variable, the data is copied into the variable storage area, character by character, starting at the left end. Each character occupies one byte of memory.

Character-to-character assignment

The following examples show assignment of values to character variables and the contents of the storage locations.

```
DECLARE STRN CHAR(8);
STRN = 'NEW YORK';

     STRN |N|E|W| |Y|O|R|K|       Exact fit

STRN = 'ROME';

     STRN |R|O|M|E| | | | |       Padded with blanks

STRN = 'CONSTANTINOPLE';

     STRN |C|O|N|S|T|A|N|T|       Truncated
```

If a value does not exactly fit the storage space available, it is stored left-justified and either truncated or padded with blanks on the right end. The following example shows the assignment of a variable to a longer variable.

```
DCL STRN1   CHARACTER(14) INIT ('ABCXMYNCLI4ROQ');
DCL STRN2   CHARACTER(12) INIT (' WXPRMKPLT');
```

STRN1	A	B	C	X	M	Y	N	C	L	I	4	R	O	Q	Exact fit
STRN2		W	X	P	R	M	K	P	L	T					Padded

```
STRN1 = STRN2;
```

STRN1		W	X	P	R	M	K	P	L	T					Padded
STRN2		W	X	P	R	M	K	P	L	T					Unchanged

The leading blank in the literal assigned to STRN2 is considered a character by the computer and so must be stored. When the value of STRN2 is assigned to STRN1, the entire character string is copied, including the leading blank. Since STRN1 has more storage space than is needed for the value, extra blanks are placed at the right end. The original value of STRN1 is lost. The value of STRN2 is unchanged.

The following example shows the assignment of a variable to a shorter variable.

```
DCL A_STR   CHAR(4) INIT ('SPQR'),
    B_STR   CHAR(10) INIT('ƀXYZWRSTƀƀ');
```

A_STR	S	P	Q	R							Exact fit
B_STR		X	Y	Z	W	R	S	T			Exact fit

```
A_STR = B_STR;
```

A_STR		X	Y	Z							Truncated
B_STR		X	Y	Z	W	R	S	T			Unchanged

The value of B_STR is copied to A_STR. The original contents of A_STR are lost. B_STR is unchanged. Since A_STR is shorter than B_STR, the extra characters are truncated.

NUMBER-TO-CHARACTER ASSIGNMENT

If the value being assigned to a character variable is not a character string, it is first converted to characters and then stored. For example:

```
DCL STR_A CHAR(8),
    STR_B CHAR(5);

STR_A = 3.5;                  Value is 'ƀƀƀ3.5ƀƀ'
STR_A = SQRT(X+27);           If X is 9, value is 'ƀƀƀƀƀ6ƀƀ'
STR_B = 3.5;                  Value is 'ƀƀƀ3.'
STR_B = SQRT(X+27);           If X is 9, value is 'ƀƀƀƀƀ'
```

The numbers are converted to characters, then the value is stored right-justified in a standard-size field, which is moved to the receiving variable and truncated or padded as needed. The standard field size is implementation-dependent.

6.1.2 Comparison of character data

Character data values may be compared for equality, inequality, or order, which results in a value of either true or false. The order of the values is determined by the *collating sequence,* the underlying order of the internal representation of the character set. The ordering of character data depends on the particular internal representation being used for the data. As long as the values contain only blanks and letters of the English alphabet, the collating sequence is the same as ordinary alphabetical order. When the values include special characters and digits, the collating sequence differs for ASCII, EBCDIC, BCD, and other internal codes. When the EBCDIC code is used, blanks precede special characters, which precede the letters A to Z, which precede the numeric digits. (See Appendix A.)

The comparison of two character strings is carried out character by character from left to right until the first nonidentical characters in corresponding positions are found. When once the differing characters have been identified, the logical value of the comparison is determined from the order of those characters in the collating sequence. The character which is earlier in the collating sequence is in the lesser of the two character strings. Comparison of the character strings depends on comparison of individual characters; it does not depend on the relative lengths of the character strings. This is shown in the following examples:

'AMKLRI' < 'AMKLRX'	True because 'I' < 'X'
'AMKLRI' < 'AMKLRB'	False because 'I' > 'B'
'AMKLRI' > 'AMKLRABC'	True because 'I' > 'A'
'AMKLRI' > 'AMKLRPAY'	False because 'I' < 'P'
'A3:7PX' < 'AK,6P4'	This depends on the particular code

Character string comparison may be used anywhere a condition is needed, as in the following program segments:

```
STR1 = 'AMKLRI';
STR2 = 'AMKLWX';
IF STR1 > STR2                          False
  THEN
    statement 1;
  ELSE
    statement 2;                        Statement 2 executed

STR1 = 'MOST';
STR2 = 'MOSTLY';
IF STR1 < STR2                          True
  THEN
    statement 1;                        Statement 1 executed
  ELSE
    statement 2;
```

If the character strings being compared are not the same length, the shorter string is padded with blanks on the right during the comparison process so that the comparison can proceed through all the characters of the longer string if necessary. This is necessary in the following examples:

'MXPQ54Z' = 'MXPQ54Zb̸'	True because 'b̸' = 'b̸'
'MXPQ54Z' = 'MXPQ54Z 7'	False because 'b̸' ¬= '7'
'JOHN' < 'JOHNSON'	True because 'b̸' < 'S'
'JOHNSON' < 'JOHNSON A B'	True because 'b̸' < 'A'

Comparison of character data is the basis of routines that sort data such as lists of names and addresses. Since the position of special characters in the collating sequence differs among the various internal representations used, all characters except letters of the alphabet and blanks must first be removed from the data. Otherwise a PL/I program that gave correct results on one computer would give incorrect results on another.

PROGRAMMING HINT: PORTABILITY Do not use special characters in character data.

6.1.3 Input/output of character data

Stream input and output of character data has been described in detail in chapter 4. Character data values obtained using data-directed and list-directed input must be written with quotation marks. The quotation marks are removed by the computer before the value is stored. Then the length of the data as it is stored is determined by both the data value and the declaration of the variable that receives it, as shown in the following example. Given the statements

```
DCL (STR1,STR2,STR3)  CHAR(5);        Fixed length
GET LIST (STR1,STR2,STR3);
```

and the data

```
 'ABC'      'STRING'    '12345'
```

the values are stored as

STR1	A	B	C		
STR2	S	T	R	I	N
STR3	1	2	3	4	5

Given the statements

```
DCL (STR1,STR2,STR3)  CHAR(5) VAR;    Varying length
GET LIST (STR1,STR2,STR3);
```

and the data

```
 'ABC'      'STRING'     '12345'
```

the values are stored as

STR1	A | B | C
STR2	S | T | R | I | N
STR3	1 | 2 | 3 | 4 | 5

If character data is obtained using edit-directed input, quotation marks must not be used unless they are intended to be part of the data. The length of the data as stored is determined by the declaration and the format, but independent of the characters found in the data. Given the statements

```
DCL STR CHAR(5);                          Fixed length
GET EDIT (STR) (COL(1),A(3));
```

and the data

```
 SPQR
```

the value is stored as

STR	S | P | Q | |

Given the statements

```
DCL STR  CHAR(5) VAR;                     Varying length
GET EDIT (STR) (COL(1),A(3));
```

and the data

```
 SPQR
```

the value is stored as

STR	S | P | Q

In this example, only the first three characters are read. They are stored in STR without padding.

INTERNAL I/O OF CHARACTER DATA

Sometimes a character string must be separated into parts; for example, separating the first name of an individual from the surname. Sometimes data must be combined; for example, placing a first name and a surname together in a new storage area. An assignment statement moves only a single data value to a new location. To move several values at once, or to separate a single value into parts, internal I/O can be used. The general forms of these statements are:

```
GET STRING(source_str) EDIT (input_list) (format);
```

and

```
PUT STRING(destination_str) EDIT (output_list) (format);
```

Internal input The STRING option of the GET statement allows a program to handle a character value as though it were an input stream. The positions of the character value are accessed under format control, and values are obtained for the variables of the input list.

In the following example, the character literal is separated into three parts, stored respectively in the variables FIRST, MIDDLE, and LAST.

```
DCL FIRST   CHAR(10) VARYING,
    MIDDLE  CHAR(3)  VARYING,
    LAST    CHAR(10) VARYING;

GET STRING('WILLIAM J. WILSON') EDIT (FIRST,MIDDLE,LAST)
                                     (A(8),A(3),A(6));
```

```
   FIRST    |W|I|L|L|I|A|M| |

   MIDDLE   |J|.| |

   LAST     |W|I|L|S|O|N|
```

The STRING option of the GET statement can be used to convert a character value to internal numeric form, provided that the character value can be interpreted as a valid numeric value. In the process, the editing characters are removed and the value is converted to the proper internal representation. The following examples show the conversion of a character string to two different numeric representations by direct assignment and with GET STRING input. All three of the examples produce the same results.

```
DCL BIN_NUM   FIXED BIN (15),
    DEC_NUM   FIXED DEC (7);

GET STRING(' -273 1254') EDIT (BIN_NUM,DEC_NUM) (F(5),F(5));
```

or

```
BIN_NUM = ' -273';
DEC_NUM = ' 1254';
```

or

```
BIN_NUM = -273;
DEC_NUM = 1254;
```

Notice that a GET statement can be used to convert appropriate character strings to numeric values in the same way that assignment of a character string to a numeric variable is used.

Internal output The STRING variation of the PUT statement has the opposite effect. The values of the variables of the output list are stored in the destination string as they would be in an output buffer. The following example puts the parts of the name in the previous example together in a more appropriate order for internal processing.

```
DCL NAME CHAR(18) VARYING;
PUT STRING(NAME) (LAST,' ',FIRST,MIDDLE) (A,A,A,A);
```

NAME	W	I	L	S	O	N		W	I	L	L	I	A	M		J	.	

Editing, such as inserting a blank between the last and first names, can be done as in other output.

The STRING option may also be used for conversion between numeric variables and character variables, as shown in the following example:

```
DCL PART_DATA       CHAR(80),
    PART_NO         FIXED BIN,
    QUANTITY        FIXED DEC(5),
    COST_PER_PART   FIXED DEC(4,2);
PART_NO = 5;
QUANTITY = 12;
COST_PER_PART = 7.50;
PUT STRING (PART_DATA) EDIT (PART_NO,QUANTITY*COST_PER_PART)
                            (F(5),F(8.2));
```

PART_DATA					5				9	0	.	0	0			. . .

The PART_NO is stored in the first five positions of PART_DATA. The result of multiplying QUANTITY by COST_PER_PART is converted to characters and stored in the next eight places. In the process, the product is edited and a decimal point and leading blanks inserted, just as it would be formatted for output. The rest of PART_DATA is filled with blanks. The character string PART_DATA plays the role of an output buffer.

6.1.4 Concatenation

The only operator defined just on string data is the concatenation operator. It is written as two vertical lines (||) or, on a keyboard that does not have vertical lines, as two exclamation points (! !). The concatenation operator takes two character strings and appends them, forming a single character string. For example,

```
STR1 = 'TEXT';
STR2 = 'BOOK';
STR  = STR1 || STR2;                Value is 'TEXTBOOK'
```

If a blank space is wanted between the words 'TEXT' and 'BOOK', as in 'TEXT BOOK', any of the following examples will provide it.

```
STR1 = 'TEXTb';
STR2 = 'BOOK';
STR  = STR1 || STR2;                Value is 'TEXT BOOK'
```

or

```
STR1 = 'TEXT';
STR2 = 'bBOOK';
STR  = STR1 || STR2;                     ''
```

or

```
STR1  = 'TEXT';
STR2  = 'BOOK';
SPACE = 'b̸';
STR   = STR1 || SPACE || STR2;            ''
```

or

```
STR1  = 'TEXT';
STR2  = 'BOOK';
STR   = STR1 || ' ' || STR2;              ''
```

Notice that both character literals and character variables can be used in concatenation. The values may include any characters of the character set, including blanks.

Concatenation can be used to space titles for list-directed input/output. Rather than assigning the title to a variable, it can be set up directly in the print buffer by using a character expression in the output list, not a simple variable.

The following example prints both a report title and column headings using list-directed I/O:

```
PUT SKIP LIST ((58)' '||'INVENTORY REPORT');
PUT SKIP LIST ((45)' '||'RECEIVED'||(25)' '||'ISSUED');
```

The repetition factors provide an easy way of introducing a sufficient number of blanks to center the headings.

6.1.5 Character library functions

Most character manipulation operations are too complicated to be written as simple operators in a programming language. Operations are needed to answer questions (such as "are all of the characters alphabetic?", "is a certain substring present?", "where in the string does a particular character appear?", "how long is the string?") and to edit strings by inserting, deleting, or replacing substrings. These answers and operations are provided by PL/I through built-in functions, the most common of which are presented in this section. There are also library functions that do not query or manipulate character strings, but return character strings as their values.

String query functions

LENGTH(str)	Returns the number of characters in the string
INDEX(str,substr)	Returns the starting position of the substring in the string
VERIFY(str,valid_chars)	Returns the first position in the string which does not contain one of the specified characters

String manipulation functions

TRANSLATE(str,chars,subs)	Replaces the characters in the string by their substitutes

String production functions

CHAR(num,leng)	Converts a number to type CHAR and truncates it to the length specified
REPEAT(str,n)	Concatenates n + 1 copies of the string
SUBSTR(str,pos,leng)	Returns the substring of the specified length starting at the specified position of the string
DATE( )	Returns the current date in the form YYMMDD
TIME( )	Returns the current time in the form HHMMSSmmm

The functions that query string data take one or more strings as arguments and return an answer, which may be numeric or character, depending on the function.

LENGTH FUNCTION

The LENGTH function returns the length of its argument as a fixed binary number. It may be used anywhere in the program that any other numeric value would be used. The argument may be a literal, a variable, or an expression.

The following example shows what is meant by length of a value.

```
DCL STR_F CHAR(10) INIT ('ABC'),
    STR_V CHAR(10) VARYING UNIT ('WXYZ');

LNG_F = LENGTH(STR_F);                     Value is 10
LNG_V = LENGTH(STR_V);                     Value is 4
L = LENGTH('P');                           Value is 1
L = LENGTH('');                            Value is 0
L = LENGTH('ABCDEƀƀ');                     Value is 7
L = LENGTH('TEXT'||'BOOK');                Value is 8
```

INDEX FUNCTION

The INDEX function returns the position of the first occurrence of a specified substring in a specified character string. If the substring does not occur, the function returns zero. The value is returned as a fixed binary number. The following example shows the use of the INDEX function to find the first occurrence of several different substrings.

```
DCL STR  CHAR(15) INIT('INSTITUTION'),
    M    FIXED BIN;

M = INDEX(STR,'T');                Value is 4
M = INDEX(STR,'TU');               Value is 6
M = INDEX(STR,'ƀ');                Value is 12
M = INDEX(STR,'X');                Value is 0
M = INDEX(STR,'TIN');              Value is 0
M = INDEX(STR,'TUTION');           Value is 6
M = INDEX(STR,'INSTITUTION');      Value is 1
```

Notice that the function returns the position of the first character of the substring if a match is found. If the substring occurs in more than one place, the position of the leftmost occurrence is returned.

The following example shows that the entire substring is to be matched, not individual characters.

```
M = INDEX('BEAD','ABED');                    Value is 0
```

The INDEX function may be used simply to determine whether a specified substring is present, as in the following example:

```
DCL STR   CHAR(10) INIT ('ROSEBUD'),
    M     FIXED BIN;
M = INDEX(STR,'BUD');               Look for substring
IF M>0                              Value is 5
  THEN
    PUT SKIP LIST ('SUBSTRING FOUND');
```

The INDEX function can also be used to convert a character code to a numeric code, provided the character code is a single character. At the same time, the value of the code can be validated. In the following example the variable SEX is expected to contain either 'M' or 'F'. The INDEX function returns one for 'M', two for 'F', and zero if the variable has an incorrect value.

```
DCL SEX  CHAR(1),
    CODE FIXED BIN;
GET EDIT (SEX) (A(1));
CODE = INDEX('MF',SEX);   Convert character code to numeric
IF CODE = 0
  THEN PUT SKIP LIST ('BAD CODE');
```

In a similar fashion, the letters of the alphabet can be converted to numbers.

```
DCL LETTER     CHAR(1),
    ALPHABET   CHAR(26) INIT('ABCDEFGHIJKLMNOPQRSTUVWXYZ'),
    VALUE      FIXED BIN;

VALUE = INDEX(ALPHABET,LETTER); Identify position in alphabet
IF VALUE = 0
  THEN PUT SKIP LIST ('NOT A LETTER');
```

In this example, 'A' will have the value one, 'B' will have the value two, and so forth.

The INDEX function can be used to validate data and find specific characters that need to be removed.

```
DCL NAME   CHAR(20) INIT ('JIM A. JOHNSON'),
    AMT    CHAR(8)  INIT ('$3562.50'),
    M      FIXED BIN;
```

```
M = INDEX(NAME,'.');                                    Locate'.'
IF M > 0                                                Value is 6
  THEN
    PUT SKIP LIST (NAME,'IN IMPROPER FORM');
M = INDEX(AMT,',$');                                    Locate '$'
IF M > 0                                                Value is 1
  THEN
    PUT SKIP LIST (AMT,'IN IMPROPER FORM');
```

PROGRAMMING HINT: Use INDEX to locate separators.

VERIFY FUNCTION

The VERIFY function is primarily used for data validation. This function checks for the presence of undesired characters or for the absence of specified characters rather than for their presence. It returns an integer indicating the leftmost position in the character string of a character that is not considered valid. If all the characters are among those listed as valid, it returns zero. It checks for individual characters, not a substring.

The following example shows its use to verify that a character string contains only digits:

```
DCL  STR_A  CHAR(5) INIT ('12X5'),
     STR_B  CHAR(5) INIT ('3750'),
     M      FIXED BIN;

M = VERIFY(STR_A,'0123456789');           Validate number
IF M > 0                                  M is 3
  THEN
    PUT SKIP LIST('BAD VALUE');
M = VERIFY(STR_B,'0123456789');           Validate number
 . . .                                    M is 0
```

PROGRAMMING HINT: Use VERIFY to validate data type.

TRANSLATE FUNCTION

The TRANSLATE function enciphers a character string by translating it from one set of characters to another, character by character. It returns a character string of the same length as its argument. The following example shows its use in editing data to remove unwanted characters:

```
DCL NAME  CHAR(20) INIT ('JIM A. JOHNSON'),
    AMT   CHAR(8)  INIT ('$3562.50'),
    M     FIXED BIN;

NAME = TRANSLATE(NAME,' ', '.');     Remove '.'
M = TRANSLATE(AMT,'0', '$');         Remove '$'
```

In this example, the period is replaced by a blank, leaving the value as JIMbAbbJOHNSON. The dollar sign is replaced by a zero, leaving the value as 03562.50. The positioning of the rest of the characters is not changed.

The TRANSLATE function replaces all occurrences of the individual characters specified. In the following example, all ones are replaced by As and all zeros are replaced by Xs.

```
DCL   STR_1   CHAR(7) INIT('1011000'),
      STR_2   CHAR(7);

STR_2 = TRANSLATE(STR_1,'AX', '10');      Value is 'AXAAXXX'
```

The following example replaces all the digits in a character string with Xs.

```
DCL STR  CHAR(10) INIT ('AB35KJ9J02');
STR = TRANSLATE(STR,'XXXXXXXXXX', '0123456789');
```

The resulting string is ABXXKJXJXX.

REPEAT FUNCTION (not in Subset G)

The REPEAT function takes a given string value and forms a new string consisting of the given value concatenated with itself a specified number of times. It returns a string consisting of n+1 copies of the original string, concatenated together. This is not equivalent to the use of n as a repetition factor. The following examples show the use of the REPEAT function:

```
STRNG = 'AXB';
STR1 = REPEAT(STRNG,2);              Value is 'AXBAXBAXB'

STRNG = '*';
STR1 = REPEAT(STRNG,5);              Value is '******'

N = 4;
BSTR = REPEAT('01'B,N);              Value is '0101010101'B

N = 0;
STR1 = REPEAT('ABC',N);              Value is 'ABC'
```

If the integer specified is zero or negative, the function returns the original string.

SUBSTR FUNCTION

The SUBSTR function copies a substring of specified length from a specified position of a string. This substring is returned as its value. The function can also be used as a pseudovariable, in which case it places a substring in a specified position of a string. The length is optional. If the length is not used, all characters from the specified position to the end of the source string are copied. The following example shows the use of SUBSTR as a function:

```
DCL STRN CHAR (14) INIT ('CONSTANTINOPLE');

STR_1 = SUBSTR(STRN,4,5);             Value is 'STANT'
STR_2 = SUBSTR(STRN,1,1);             Value is 'C'
STR_3 = SUBSTR(STRN,1,14);            Value is 'CONSTANTINOPLE'
STR_4 = SUBSTR(STRN,10);              Value is 'NOPLE'
```

In a loop, the SUBSTR function can be used to extract words from a sentence. This is shown in the following example:

```
DCL LINE   CHAR(32) VARYING
           INIT ('NOW IS THE TIME FOR ALL GOOD MEN'),
    WORD   CHAR(10) VARYING;

I = INDEX (LINE,' ');
DO WHILE (I > 1);
  WORD = SUBSTR(LINE,1,I-1);
  PUT SKIP LIST (WORD);
  LINE = SUBSTR(LINE,I+1);
  I = INDEX(LINE,' ');
END;
PUT SKIP LIST(LINE);
```

Notice that LINE is a CHARACTER VARYING variable. Every time a new value is assigned to it, it becomes shorter.

Used as a pseudovariable, SUBSTR replaces one substring with another. The one being replaced is identified as to position and possibly length. The following examples show this:

```
DCL STRN CHAR(14) INIT('CONSTANTINOPLE');
SUBSTR(STRN,4,5) = 'XXXXX';               Value is 'CONXXXXXINOPLE'

DCL STRN CHAR(14) INIT('CONSTANTINOPLE');
SUBSTR(STRN,10) = 'XXXXXXX';              Value is 'CONSTANTIXXXXX'

DCL STRN CHAR(14) INIT('CONSTANTINOPLE');
SUBSTR(STRN,1,4) = 'XXX';                 Value is 'XXX TANTINOPLE'

DCL STRN CHAR(14) INIT('CONSTANTINOPLE');
SUBSTR(STRN,1,10) = SUBSTR(STRN,5);       Value is 'TANTINOPLEOPLE'
```

Notice that the replacement string is padded or truncated as necessary.

The INDEX and SUBSTR functions can be used together to separate a string into two parts. This is shown in the following example:

```
DCL (NAME,FIRST,LAST) CHAR VARYING;

NAME = 'JOHN SMITH';
I = INDEX(NAME,' ');
IF I > 0
  THEN
    FIRST = SUBSTR(NAME,1,I-1);              Value is 'JOHN'
IF I < LENGTH(NAME)
  THEN
    LAST = SUBSTR(NAME,I+1);                 Value is 'SMITH'
```

Notice that the tests to determine whether I is greater than zero and less than the length of the name are necessary for data validation. Data validation is an important part of a program.

DATE FUNCTION

The DATE function accesses a system routine and obtains the current date, which is returned to the program as a string of six characters in the order

YYMMDD. YY is the last two digits of the year, MM is the month, and DD is the day. For example, on May 23, 1987, the instructions

```
DECLARE DATE  BUILTIN,
        TODAY CHAR(6);

TODAY = DATE;                             Get date '870523'

PUT SKIP EDIT(SUBSTR(TODAY,3,2),'/',SUBSTR(TODAY,5,2),'/',
              SUBSTR(TODAY,1,2)) ((5)A);
                                          Print '05/23/87'
```

store the date in a character variable, then take apart the year, month, and day, and print them in the form 05/23/87. Alternately, if the date is to be stored for printing on every page of output, it is more efficient to use the following method:

```
DCL DATE          BUILTIN,
    TODAY         CHAR(6),
    DAY           CHAR(8),
    (YY,MM,DD)    CHAR(2);

TODAY = DATE;                              Get date
YY = SUBSTR(TODAY,1,2);                    Extract year
MM = SUBSTR(TODAY,3,2);                    Extract month
DD = SUBSTR(TODAY,5,2);                    Extract day
DAY = MM || '/' || DD || '/' || YY;
PUT SKIP EDIT (DAY) (A);
```

The DATE function must be declared BUILTIN if it is used without an argument list, otherwise the computer will think it is a variable rather than a function. If it is used with an empty argument list,

```
TODAY = DATE();
```

then it does not have to be declared.

TIME FUNCTION

The TIME function accesses the system to return the time of day. Like the DATE function, it does not have any parameters, so it must either be shown with an empty argument list, or be declared as BUILTIN. The time of day is returned as a string of nine characters in the form HHMMSSmmm, where HH are hours, MM are minutes, SS are seconds, and mmm are milliseconds. System time is kept on a twenty-four-hour clock. Slightly after ten minutes past two in the afternoon is shown in the following example:

```
DCL NOW        CHAR(9),
    (HR,MIN)   CHAR(2),
    SEC        FIXED DEC(5,3);

NOW = TIME();                        Get time, e.g., '141006235'
HR = SUBSTR(NOW,1,2);                Extract hour
MIN = SUBSTR(NOW,3,2);               Extract minutes
SEC = SUBSTR(NOW,5)/1000;            Extract seconds
PUT SKIP EDIT (HR,MIN,SEC) (A(3),A(3),F(6.3));
                                     Would print '14 10 06.235'
```

6.1.6 Character conditions

STRINGSIZE CONDITION

The STRINGSIZE condition (abbreviated STRZ) is raised whenever a string value is too long for the string variable to which it is assigned. Normally this condition is not enabled and strings that are too long are truncated on the right when they are stored. If the program explicitly enables the STRINGSIZE condition, an ON unit can be established to allow programmer intervention or the printing of an error message. This is shown in the following example:

```
DCL STRNG CHAR(10) INIT('MANAGEMENT');
DCL TITLE CHAR(8);

ON STRINGSIZE
  PUT SKIP LIST('STRING OVERFLOW');

TITLE = STRNG;                    Condition is raised
                                  Value is 'MANAGEME'
```

STRINGSIZE is not a fatal condition. The processing continues after execution of the ON unit. In this example, the value is too long, so the condition is raised, the error message is printed, and the truncated value is stored in TITLE.

STRINGRANGE CONDITION

The STRINGRANGE condition (abbreviated STRG) is used with the SUBSTR function. Whenever the length parameter of the SUBSTR function is too long for the subject string, the condition is raised, signifying an attempt to access beyond the end of the string. It is also raised if the starting position is less than one. These situations are shown in the following example:

```
DECLARE STRNG  CHAR(15) INIT ('ELECTROMAGNETIC'),
        STR    CHAR(10);

ON STRINGRANGE
  PUT SKIP LIST('BOUNDARY ERROR ON ', STRNG);

K = 10;
(STRINGRANGE): STR = SUBSTR(STRNG,7,K);    Condition is raised
K = INDEX(STRNG,' ');
(STRINGRANGE): STR = SUBSTR(STRNG,K,3);    Condition is raised
```

Both of these assignment statements raise the condition. In the first one, there are only nine characters that can be copied, starting in position 7. In the second, there is no blank in the subject string of INDEX, so it returns zero, which is used as the position parameter of SUBSTR. STRINGRANGE is normally disabled. It can be enabled by using a condition preface before the statement where it may be raised, or before the procedure or block where it is wanted. It is a good condition to enable for program testing, but should be disabled for production runs as it is inefficient.

Review questions

1. Indicate whether each of the following statements is true or false.
   (a) Numbers cannot be assigned to CHARACTER variables.
   (b) It is possible for two character strings of different lengths to be equal.
   (c) The LENGTH of a character string is always greater than one.
   (d) No storage is allocated for a CHARACTER VARYING variable until a value is assigned to the variable.
   (e) The length of a character string includes the leading and trailing blanks.
   (f) Character string comparison is machine-independent.
   (g) The SIZE error is raised when a character value is assigned to a storage space that is too small.

2. Character values are ____________________-justified in storage.

3. The character used for padding when a value is too short is ____________________.

4. The result of the comparison of individual characters depends on the ____________________sequence.

5. What is printed by each of the following code segments?

```
(a) PUT LIST ('THE'||' IS'||' RED');
(b) DCL STR CHAR(6) INIT ('ABC');
    PUT LIST (LENGTH(STR));
    PUT LIST (STR);
(c) DCL STR CHAR(6) VAR INIT ('ABC');
    PUT LIST LENGTH(STR));
    PUT LIST (STR);
(d) DCL STR CHAR(6) VAR;
    GET EDIT (STR) (A(4));
    PUT LIST (LENGTH(STR));
```

6. What is the result of each of the following functions?

```
(a) INDEX('ABCDEFG','D')
(b) INDEX('ABCDEFG','BED')
(c) INDEX('ABCDEFG','ACE')
(d) VERIFY('ABCDEFG','D')
(e) VERIFY('ABCDEFG','BED')
(f) VERIFY('ABCDEFG','ACE')
(g) SUBSTR('ABCDEFG',3,2)
(h) SUBSTR('ABCDEFG',5)
```

7. Write a segment of code that puts a single-digit numeric value N into a character string LINE_NUM CHAR(5), left-justified.

8. Write a segment of code that puts a numeric value N of not more than five digits into a character string LINE_NUM CHAR(5), left-justified.

9. Write a segment of code that puts the first ten characters of NAME in LAST_NAME and the rest of NAME in FIRST_NAME.

10. Assume that NAME has some blanks in the middle. Write a segment of code that puts all the leading nonblank characters of NAME in LAST_NAME and the characters after the blanks in FIRST_NAME.

11. Assume that TEXT contains words separated by blanks, commas, and periods. Write a segment of code that prints a list of all the words in TEXT.

6.2 Bit strings

In the first five chapters, bit variables have been used mainly as flags and switches, in the form BIT(1). Like character strings, bit strings consisting of many bits may be used. Bit strings are used as flags, as logical variables, and for keeping track of set membership or memory layout.

VARYING ATTRIBUTE

Bit variables may be declared using the VARYING attribute. As with character strings, a maximum length must be declared. Bit values shorter than the maximum length only use part of the storage allocated. Their length is the length of the value rather than of the storage maximum, as seen in the following example:

```
DCL BSTR BIT(15) VARYING;
BSTR = '110100110'B;
PUT SKIP LIST (LENGTH(BSTR));                    Prints 9
```

In this example only the first nine bits of the storage area are used. The length as found by the LENGTH function is nine.

6.2.1 Bit assignment

When a bit string is declared without the VARYING attribute, an assignment statement may cause the value to be truncated on the right or to be padded on the right. If it is padded, the fill is bit zeros. If it is truncated, this can be detected by using the STRINGSIZE function.

```
DCL BST BIT(6);

(STRINGSIZE): BST = '1111'B;           Value is '111100'B
(STRINGSIZE): BST = '10101001'B;       Condition is raised
                                       Value is '101010'B
```

The results of bit expressions can also be assigned to bit variables.

6.2.2 Comparison of bit strings

Bit strings, like character strings, may be compared for equality or for order. Like character strings, if two bit strings to be compared are of different lengths, the shorter is padded on the right. With bit strings, a bit '0'B is used as the fill character. The comparison is carried out left to right, bit by bit. When unequal bits are found, the result of the comparison is known. The value with the '0'B bit is the lesser.

The following examples show the comparison of bit strings:

```
DCL (BST1,BST2) BIT(5);

BST1 = '11010'B;
BST2 = '11000'B;
IF BST1 > BST2                          True
  THEN
    statement 1;                        Statement 1 is executed
  ELSE
    statement 2;

DECLARE BSTR1 BIT(6),
        BSTR2 BIT(8);

BSTR1 = '110111'B;
BSTR2 = '11011101'B;
IF BSTR1 > BSTR2                        False
  THEN
    statement 1;
  ELSE
    statement 2;                        Statement 2 is executed
```

The result of bit string comparisons can be assigned to bit variables, as shown in the following examples:

```
DCL (A,B,C,D)  BIT(1),
    BSTR1    BIT(6) INIT ('001011'B),
    BSTR2    BIT(8) INIT ('00101100'B),
    BSTR3    BIT(8) INIT ('00011100'B);

A = BSTR1 < BSTR2;                            A is '0'B
B = BSTR1 = BSTR2;                            B is '1'B
C = BSTR1 > BSTR3;                            C is '1'B
D = BSTR2 < BSTR3;                            D is '0'B
```

Notice that when there are two equal signs, the left one is an assignment operator while the right one is a comparison.

6.2.3 Bit strings as flags

Bit strings of length greater than one can be used as conditional expressions, in the same way that those of length one are used. Where a BIT(1) variable is used as a flag to show that something has or has not taken place, or whether a comparison was true, bit strings of length greater than one give the result of many comparisons, or represent many flags, or are string values in their own right. When used in an IF statement, a bit value is taken to mean false if it contains only zero bits; otherwise it is true. This is shown in the following example:

```
DCL (A,B) BIT(3);

A = '010'B;
B = '000'B;
IF A                              True
  THEN
    statement 1;                  Statement 1 is executed
  ELSE
    statement 2;
IF B                              False
  THEN
    statement 3;
  ELSE
    statement 4;                  Statement 4 is executed
```

This leads to the strange situation that, given

```
DCL A BIT(3) INIT ('010'B);
```

both A and ¬A are true.

6.2.4 Input/output of bit strings

The input/output of bit strings was presented in chapter 4. In edit-directed I/O, the B specification is used.

6.2.5 Concatenation of bit strings

The concatenation operation used with bit strings is the same as that used with character strings. It appends one string to the end of another. This is shown in the following example:

```
DECLARE BST1 BIT(4) INIT('1011'B),
        BST2 BIT(6) INIT('100110'B),
        BST  BIT(10);

BST = BST1 || BST2;            Result is '1011100110'B
```

The repetition factor can be used with bit strings. This is shown in the following example:

```
DECLARE BSTR BIT(26);
BSTR = (2)'01'B || (3)'00'B || '1'B;

                Result is '01010000001'B
```

6.2.6 Logical operations on bit strings

The logical operators NOT, OR, and AND, which apply to the logical results of comparisons, can also be used with bit strings. The result of a comparison is a bit string of length one, with '1'B representing true and '0'B representing false. A bit string of length greater than one can be thought of as representing a string of "trues" and "falses."

NOT OPERATION ON STRINGS

The NOT operation on a bit string is applied individually to each bit that makes up the string. The result is a bit string the same length as the original, but with all the ones changed to zeros and all the zeros changed to ones, as shown in the following example:

```
DECLARE BSTR  BIT(6),
        B     BIT(6);

BSTR = '110100'B;
B = ¬BSTR;                    Result is '001011'B
```

Notice that since BSTR is a string of length greater than one, it is possible for both BSTR and ¬BSTR to be true.

AND OPERATION ON STRINGS

The AND operation requires two operands. When it is performed on two bit strings, it operates individually on pairs of bits from the two strings. When the bits of both operands are '1'B, the resulting bit is also a '1'B. When either or both bits are '0'B, the resulting bit is '0'B also. This is shown in the following example:

```
DCL BSTR1  BIT(10) INIT('1110101101'B),
    BSTR2  BIT(10) INIT('1011011010'B),
    BSTR3  BIT(10);

BSTR3 = BSTR1 & BSTR2;        Result is '1010001000'B
```

When BIT strings are used to keep track of many flags at once, the AND operation has several specific uses. Let us assume that in the bit string FLAGS the bits have the following meaning:

```
DCL FLAGS BIT(5);          Bit 1 means EOF
                           Bit 2 means I/O error
                           Bit 3 means record type A
                           Bit 4 means invalid record
                           Bit 5 means duplicate record
```

If the record is valid we want to make sure that bit 4 is turned off. This can be done by ANDing the string of FLAGS with a bit constant that has a zero in position 4 and ones in all other positions.

```
FLAGS = FLAGS & '11101'B;
```

If the original value of FLAGS was '10110'B, the operation

```
    '10110'B
&   '11101'B
    --------
    '10100'B
```

preserves all the original bits except the bit in position 4.

PROGRAMMING HINT: Use AND to selectively turn off a bit.

This same operation can be used to extract a specific bit for testing. If we wanted to know whether the record is of type A, the third bit can be extracted by ANDing the string with a constant that has a one in the third position and zeros in all other positions.

```
RTYPE = FLAGS & '00100'B
```

If the original value of FLAGS was '10110'B, the operation

```
  '10110'B
& '00100'B
  --------
  '00100'B
```

returns a value that can be tested, as in the following:

```
IF RTYPE                                      True
  THEN
    PUT SKIP LIST('TYPE ''A'' RECORD');
```

The AND operation can also be used to extract a section of a bit string. If we want to look at the left half of a sixteen-bit string, this can be done by ANDing the string with a constant that has ones in the eight high-order positions and zeros in the eight low-order positions.

```
B = '1011011101101101'B;
B1 = B & (8)'1'B;            Value is '1011011100000000'B

'1011011101101101'B      Operand
'1111111100000000'B      Mask
-------------------
'1011011100000000'B
```

This is known as a *masking operation.* It filters the operand through a mask which allows the left eight bits to pass, but blocks the right eight bits. Looked at another way, this could be thought of as an operation to clear the right eight bits without changing those on the left.

When an AND operation is performed on two bit strings of unequal length, the shorter string is extended to the length of the longer string by adding zero bits on the right. This extension is temporary, just for the duration of the operation. The following example shows this:

```
DECLARE B1  BIT(7)  INIT('1101011'B),
        B2  BIT(10) INIT('1110110110'B),
        B3  BIT(10);
B3 = B1 & B2;                    Result is '1100010000'B
```

In this example, neither the value nor the length of B1 have been changed.

PROGRAMMING HINT: Use AND to selectively extract a bit.

OR OPERATION ON STRINGS

Like AND and NOT, the logical OR operates on bit strings one bit at a time. If the corresponding bits of its two operands are both '0'B, the resulting bit is '0'B also. If either or both of the corresponding bits are '1'B, the resulting bit is '1'B. The following example shows this:

```
DECLARE BSTR1 BIT(5),
        BSTR2 BIT(5);

BSTR1 = '10110'B;
BSTR2 = '11010'B;
BSTR1 = BSTR1 | BSTR2;              Result is '11110'B
```

This has the effect of turning on all the bits in BSTR1 which were originally off except the last one. All the positions of BSTR1 which had zeros, except the last, corresponded to positions of BSTR2 which had ones.

The OR operation is used to set a bit within a bit string. For example, if the second position of FLAGS represents an I/O error, this position can be turned on when an error occurs by ORing the variable with a bit constant that has a one in this position and zeros in all other positions. For example, if FLAGS is '00010'B and the mask is '01000'B,

```
FLAGS = FLAGS | '01000'B;

          '00010'B
        | '01000'B
          --------
          '01010'B
```

the second highest bit is turned on. None of the other bits of FLAGS are affected.

PROGRAMMING HINT: Use OR to selectively turn on a bit.

6.2.7 BIT library functions

The most common of the BIT string library functions are presented in this section. Some of them are also character string functions, which can be used to query any type of string. Others apply only to bit strings.

String query functions

LENGTH(str)	Returns the number of bits in the string

String manipulation functions

BOOL(str1, str2, logicop)	Returns a bit string that is the result of applying the logical operation to the two strings

String production functions

SUBSTR(str, pos, leng)	Returns the substring of the specified length starting at the specified position of the string
UNSPEC(value)	Returns the bit string that is the internal representation of the value

LENGTH FUNCTION

The LENGTH function can be used whenever a bit variable is declared with the VARYING attribute. This function returns the number of bits stored in the variable, as shown in the following examples:

```
DCL BSTR      BIT(15) VARYING,
    (I,J,K)   FIXED BIN;

BSTR = '110110111'B;
I = LENGTH(BSTR);                              Value is 9
BSTR = '001'B;
J = LENGTH(BSTR);                              Value is 3
BSTR = '111111111'B || '000000001'B;
K = LENGTH(BSTR);                              Value is 15
```

The first two assignments to BSTR place values of fewer than fifteen bits in it. The length is exactly the length of the value in each case. The third assignment attempts to place a concatenated result containing eighteen bits in the variable. Since only the left fifteen will fit, the others are truncated and the length is fifteen.

SUBSTR FUNCTION

The SUBSTR function is used to copy substrings from bit strings or to replace substrings of bit strings. This is similar to its use with character strings. The uses of SUBSTR as a function and as a pseudovariable are shown in the following example:

```
DECLARE BSTR  BIT(15),
        B     BIT(8) VARYING;

BSTR = '110111101110101'B;
B = SUBSTR(BSTR,4,5);                  Value is '11110'B
B = SUBSTR(BSTR,1,6);                  Value is '110111'B
B = SUBSTR(BSTR,11);                   Value is '10101'B
```

As a pseudovariable, the function provides a way of replacing a substring of a bit value. This can be seen in the following example:

```
DECLARE BSTR  BIT(15),
        B     BIT(8);

BSTR = '110111101110101'B;
SUBSTR(BSTR,1,4) = '0011'B;      Result is '001111101110101'B
```

UNSPEC FUNCTION

The UNSPEC function returns a bit string that is the internal representation of a value. The function can also be used as a pseudovariable, in which case it stores a bit string in a variable that is not itself of the bit type. The argument may be of any type.

The function can be used to determine the type of a constant, as in

```
PUT SKIP LIST(2,UNSPEC(2));
```

which prints the value two followed by the internal bit string representation (which is implementation-dependent). This bit string is different depending on whether two is stored as a decimal number or a binary number. If the number is stored as fixed binary, the output is

```
2      '0000000000000010'B          Fixed binary
```

As FIXED DECIMAL (3) it might be

```
2      '0000000000101100'B          Fixed decimal
```

where the four rightmost bits ('1100') are the sign.

The output statement

```
PUT SKIP LIST ('A',UNSPEC('A'));
```

returns the internal code used for the letter 'A' whether it is ASCII, EBCDIC, or BCD. If the internal code is EBCDIC, the output is

```
'A'          '11000001'B
```

If a bit string is UNSPECed, the original string is returned, as in the following example:

```
DCL BSTR BIT(3);

BSTR = '101'B;
PUT SKIP LIST(BSTR,UNSPEC(BSTR));    Prints    '101'B '101'B
```

As a pseudovariable UNSPEC stores a bit string in a variable of another type. In the following example, the character variable CODE contains all ones, the representation of an unprintable character. This is a value at the top of the collating sequence, so it is useful in sorting, or in flagging a field as undefined.

```
DCL CODE  CHAR(1);
UNSPEC(CODE) = '11111111'B;
```

In the next example, the leftmost five bits of the numeric field ACCTNO are set to ones and the rest of the bits to zeros. This might be used to indicate that an account number is no longer in use. It would be used only internally. This is a printable fixed-binary value, but it is meaningless as an actual account number.

```
DECLARE ACCTNO  FIXED BIN;
UNSPEC(ACCTNO) = '11111'B;
```

The FIXED BIN variable is more than five bits long. When the bit constant is stored in it, the value is left-justified with zero fill on the right.

PROGRAMMING HINT: Use the pseudovariable UNSPEC to store code for unprintable characters.

BOOL FUNCTION

The BOOL function is actually sixteen functions in one. It provides all the mathematical Boolean functions on two variables. These include the AND, OR, and NOT functions already discussed. The more useful of the other functions are the exclusive OR ("P is true or Q is true but not both"), the equivalence ("P is equivalent to Q"), the NAND ("P and Q are not both true"), the NOR ("neither P nor Q is true"), and implication ("P implies Q"). The general form of the function is

```
BOOL(string1,string2,function_code)
```

where string1 and string2 are the bit string operands of the function and function_code specifies which of the sixteen functions is to be performed. This third argument must be a bit string of length 4. Four bits is sufficient to number the Boolean functions from zero through fifteen. The more common of these functions, their codes, and truth tables for BIT(1) operands are as follows. Note that the code is the same as the result column of the truth table for the function.

AND (code is '1000'B)

P	*Q*	*Result*
1	1	1
1	0	0
0	1	0
0	0	0

OR (code is '1110'B)

P	*Q*	*Result*
1	1	1
1	0	1
0	1	1
0	0	0

NOT (code is '0011'B)

P	*Result*
1	0
1	0
0	1
0	1

XOR (code is '0110'B)

P	*Q*	*Result*
1	1	0
1	0	1
0	1	1
0	0	0

EQUIV (code is '1001'B)

P	*Q*	*Result*
1	1	1
1	0	0
0	1	0
0	0	1

NAND (code is '0111'B)

P	*Q*	*Result*
1	1	0
1	0	1
0	1	1
0	0	1

NOR (code is '0001'B)

P	*Q*	*Result*
1	1	0
1	0	0
0	1	0
0	0	1

IMPL (code is '1011'B)

P	*Q*	*Result*
1	1	1
1	0	0
0	1	1
0	0	1

The following pairs of assignments are equivalent:

```
R = P & Q;
R = BOOL(P,Q,'1000'B);

R = P | Q;
R = BOOL(P,Q,'1110'B);

R = ¬P;
R = BOOL(P,Q,'0011'B);
```

Review questions

1. Indicate whether each of the following statements is true or false.
- **(a)** The VARYING attribute can be used with bit strings.
- **(b)** The padding character for bit strings is the blank.
- **(c)** It is possible for bit strings of different lengths to be equal.
- **(d)** Bit strings are compared as though they were binary values.
- **(e)** Inside the computer all types of data are represented as bit strings.
- **(f)** The logical operators only apply to bit strings of length 1.
- **(g)** Bit strings may have length 0.

2. What is the result of each of the following functions?

```
(a) SUBSTR('11000'B,2,3)
(b) SUBSTR('11000'B,3)
(c) LENGTH('10101'B)
(d) BOOL('10'B,'01'B,'0111'B)
(e) BOOL('10'B,'01'B,'0011'B)
```

3. Write a segment of code that turns the 5th bit of BSTR on.

4. Write a segment of code that turns the 5th bit of BSTR off.

5. Write a segment of code that prints ON if the 5th bit of BSTR is a '1' and OFF if it is a '0'.

6.3 Examples of string processing

The following examples show the use of character string manipulation for text processing and graphing.

6.3.1 Reading a sentence

This example assumes that input is taken from an input device of eighty characters, but that longer output strings are possible. The text is considered to be continuous from one input string to another. Input lines are collected until a period (.) is found, at which point a sentence is printed and the input starts all over again.

```
SENTNCE:PROC OPTIONS (MAIN):
/*********************************************************/
/*                                                       */
/* PROGRAM: READ AND PRINT SENTENCES                     */
/* AUTHOR: C ZIEGLER                                     */
/* VERSION: 07/17/84                                     */
/*                                                       */
/* PROGRAM DESCRIPTION                                   */
/* ----------------------------------------------------- */
/* THIS PROGRAM READS THE PIECES OF A SENTENCE, PUTS     */
/* THE SENTENCE TOGETHER, PRINTS IT, AND REPEATS UNTIL   */
/* ALL OF THE SENTENCES HAVE BEEN PRINTED.               */
/*                                                       */
/* INPUT: CHARACTER STRINGS OF 80 CHARACTERS             */
/*                                                       */
/* OUTPUT: SENTENCES OF FEWER THAN 4096 CHARACTERS       */
/*                                                       */
/*********************************************************/

DCL STR                  CHAR(80) VARYING,
    REST                 CHAR(80) VARYING;
DCL SENTENCE             CHAR(4096) VARYING;
DCL I                    FIXED BIN,
    MORE_DATA            BIT(1),
    END_OF_SENTENCE      BIT(1);
DCL TRUE                 BIT(1)  INIT('1'B),
    FALSE                BIT(1)  INIT('0'B);

ON ENDFILE (SYSIN)
  MORE_DATA = FALSE;

MORE_DATA = TRUE;
END_OF_SENTENCE = FALSE;
GET EDIT (STR) (COL(1),A(80));
SENTENCE = '';                      /*START WITH NULL STRING  */
DO WHILE (MORE_DATA);
  DO UNTIL (END_OF_SENTENCE);
    I = INDEX(STR,'.');             /*LOCATE '.'              */
    IF I > 0
      THEN
        DO;                         /*SEPARATE PARTS OF INPUT */
          STR = SUBSTR(STR,1,I);
          IF I < 80
            THEN
              REST = SUBSTR(STR,I+1);
            ELSE
              REST = '';
          END_OF_SENTENCE = TRUE;
        END;
    SENTENCE = SENTENCE || STR;     /*BUILD SENTENCE          */
    IF LENGTH(SENTENCE) = 4096
```

```
    THEN
      DO;
        PUT SKIP LIST ('SENTENCE TOO LONG');
        END_OF_SENTENCE = TRUE;
      END;
  GET EDIT (STR) (COL(1),A(80));
  END;
  PUT SKIP(2) LIST (SENTENCE);  /*PRINT SENTENCE          */
  END_OF_SENTENCE = FALSE;
  SENTENCE = REST;              /*START NEW SENTENCE      */
END;
END SENTNCE;
```

6.3.2 Creating an index

This program lists the major words in a text.

```
BLDINDX: PROC OPTIONS (MAIN);
/*********************************************************/
/*                                                       */
/* PROGRAM: BUILD AN INDEX OF A TEXT                     */
/* AUTHOR: R REDDY                                       */
/* VERSION: 07/17/84                                     */
/*                                                       */
/* PROGRAM DESCRIPTION                                   */
/* ----------------------------------------------------- */
/* THIS PROGRAM READS THE PIECES OF A TEXT AND PRINTS    */
/* A LIST OF ALL OF THE WORDS HAVING MORE THAN FOUR      */
/* LETTERS.                                              */
/*                                                       */
/* INPUT:CHARACTER STRINGS OF 80 CHARACTERS              */
/*                                                       */
/* OUTPUT: LIST OF WORDS                                 */
/*                                                       */
/*********************************************************/

DCL STR         CHAR(80);
DCL WORD        CHAR(80) VARYING;
DCL MORE_DATA   BIT(1),
    TRUE        BIT(1)  INIT('1'B),
    FALSE       BIT(1)  INIT('0'B);
    I           FIXED BIN,
    ALPHABET    CHAR(26) INIT ('ABCDEFGHIJKLMNOPQRSTUVWXYZ');

ONEND FILE (SYSIN)
  MORE_DATA = FALSE;

MORE_DATA = TRUE;
GET EDIT (STR) (A(80));
```

```
DO WHILE (MORE_DATA);
  DO UNTIL (STR = ' ');
    I = VERIFY(STR,1,ALPHABET);       /* FIND SEPARATORS     */
    IF I > 1
      THEN
        DO;
          WORD = SUBSTR(STR,1,I-1); /* COPY WORD FROM STR */
          IF LENGTH(WORD) > 4
            THEN
              PUT SKIP LIST (WORD);
        END;
    IF I < 80
      THEN
        STR = SUBSTR(STR,I+1);      /* REMOVE FROM STR     */
      ELSE
        STR = ' ';
  END;
  GET EDIT (STR) (A(80));
END;
END BLDINDX;
```

6.3.3 Graphing for the printer

The simplest way to draw the graph of a function on a computer when the output is to be printed is to draw the *X* axis longitudinally down the paper. As *X* varies, one row of the graph is printed for each *X*. The graph may be extended as far as desired in the positive *X* direction. In the following program, the minimum and maximum values of *X* may be changed and the equation for *Y* as a function of *X* may be changed to obtain a different graph.

```
GRAPH: PROC OPTIONS (MAIN);
/*********************************************************/
/*                                                       */
/* PROGRAM: GRAPHING (VERTICAL)                          */
/* AUTHOR:  C ZIEGLER                                    */
/* VERSION: 07/17/84                                     */
/*                                                       */
/* PROGRAM DESCRIPTION                                   */
/* ---------------------------------------------------- */
/* THIS PROGRAM GRAPHS THE FUNCTION                      */
/*                                                       */
/*             Y = 200*SIN(0.2*X)/X                      */
/*                        FOR X = 2 TO 100               */
/*                                                       */
/* INPUT: NONE                                           */
/*                                                       */
/* OUTPUT: GRAPH OF FUNCTION                             */
/*                                                       */
/*********************************************************/
```

```
DCL   LINE              CHAR(120);
DCL   X_MIN             FIXED BIN    INIT (2),
      X_MAX             FIXED BIN    INIT(100);
DCL   BLANK_LINE        CHAR(120)    INIT ((59)' ' || '!'),
      Y_AXIS            CHAR(120)    INIT ((59)'-' || '+'
            || (59)'-');
DCL   (X,Y)             FIXED BIN;

DO X = X_MIN TO X_MAX;
  IF X = 0                                /* SET UP BLANK LINE     */
    THEN
      LINE = Y-AXIS;
    ELSE
      LINE = BLANK_LINE;
  Y = 200*SIN(0.2*X)/X;
  IF Y > -60 & Y <= 60                    /* CHECK Y IN BOUNDS     */
    THEN
      SUBSTR(LINE,Y+60,1) = '*';          /* PUT PT (X,Y) ON LINE */
  PUT EDIT (LINE) (COL(1),A);
END;
END GRAPH;
```

6.3.4 Graphing for the monitor

If a graph is to be drawn for video display, the *Y* axis must be vertical, rather than the *X* axis. Both the horizontal and vertical size of the display are limited. In the following example it is assumed that there are eighty horizontal character positions and twenty-four vertical character positions. The graphing is done using characters. Standard PL/I does not interface with high-resolution graphics packages; however, the graphics obtained with such a package would be of better quality.

The entire 1920 display positions must be stored in a buffer. To save storage space, they are being stored as a bit string rather than a character string. As a bit string, they require 240 bytes of storage rather then 1920. Converting the bits to characters and replacing the zeros with blanks is less efficient in terms of processing time than storing the graph as characters. Often there is a trade-off in efficiency between space and time.

```
GRAPH   : PROC OPTIONS (MAIN);
/****************************************************************/
/*                                                              */
/* PROGRAM: GRAPHING (HORIZONTAL)                               */
/* AUTHOR:  C ZIEGLER                                           */
/* VERSION: 07/17/84                                            */
/*                                                              */
/* PROGRAM DESCRIPTION                                          */
/* ---------------------------------------------------------    */
```

```
/* THIS PROGRAM GRAPHS THE FUNCTION                          */
/*                                                           */
/*            Y = 50*SIN(3*X)/X                              */
/*                       FOR X = 2 TO 100                    */
/*                                                           */
/*            NO SCALING IS INCLUDED                         */
/*                                                           */
/* INPUT: NONE                                               */
/*                                                           */
/* OUTPUT: GRAPH OF FUNCTION                                 */
/*************************************************************/


DCL  LINE              BIT(1920);
DCL  PRT_LINE          CHAR(80);
DCL  X_MIN             FIXED BIN  INIT (2),
     X_MAX             FIXED BIN  INIT (100);
DCL  AXIS              CHAR(80)   INIT ((39)'-' || '+'
           || (40)'-');
DCL  (X,Y)              FIXED BIN,
     POS                FIXED BIN,    /* BIT POSITION OF PT */
     R                  FIXED BIN,    /* ROW POSITION OF PT */
     K                  FIXED BIN;

IF X_MIN < -39
  THEN
    X_MIN = -39;
IF X_MAX > 40
  THEN
     X_MAX = 40;
LINE = '0'B;
DO X = X_MIN TO X_MAX;
  Y = 50*SIN(0.2*X)/X;
  IF Y > -12 & Y <= 12                     /* CHECK Y BOUNDS    */
    THEN
      DO;
        POS = 80*(12-Y)+40+X;
        SUBSTR(LINE,POS,1) = '1'B;   /* PUT (X,Y) ON LINE */
      END;
END;
K = 1;
DO R = 1 TO 12;
  PRT_LINE = SUBSTR(LINE,K,80);
  PRT_LINE = TRANSLATE(PRT_LINE,' *','01');
  SUBSTR(PRT_LINE,40,1) = '|';
  K = K + 80;
  PUT EDIT (PRT_LINE) (COL(1),A);
END;
PUT EDIT (AXIS) (COL(1),A);
K = K + 80;
```

```
DO R = 13 TO 24;
  PRT_LINE = SUBSTR(LINE,K,80);
  PRT_LINE = TRANSLATE(PRT_LINE,' *','01');
  SUBSTR(PRT_LINE,40,1) = '|';
  K = K + 80;
  PUT EDIT (PRT_LINE) (COL(1),A);
END;
END GRAPH;
```

6.4 Summary

In many ways, character strings and bit strings are treated alike in PL/I. In both, values are stored left-justified, either padded or truncated on the right. Each character of a CHARACTER string occupies one byte of storage. Each bit of a bit string occupies one bit of storage. The operation of concatenation applies to both types of strings, as do the functions LENGTH and SUBSTR.

Character strings are used primarily for data validation, text processing, and setting up a print line. The main character string manipulation functions are:

VERIFY	Used to validate numeric or alphabetic data
INDEX	Used to locate substrings
SUBSTR	Used to extract or replace substrings

STRING I/O statements perform edit-directed I/O utilizing ordinary character strings as though they were I/O buffers.

Bit strings are used mainly as flags and as storage maps. The main bit string functions are:

UNSPEC	Used to inspect memory storage locations
BOOL	Used to switch individual bits on or off

The logical operations of AND, OR, and NOT can also be used with bit strings.

6.5 Exercises

1. Write a program that replaces all occurrences of the word PROGRAM in a text with the word PROCEDURE.
2. Write a program that reads text as character strings of length 80 and prints it as character strings of length 120.
3. Write a program that reads names in the order of

   ```
   first_name  middle_initial  last_name
   ```

separated by blanks, and prints them in the order

```
last_name, first_name middle_initial
```

with a comma after the last name and only single blanks.

4. Write a program that takes as input arithmetic expressions consisting of two numbers and a single operator, such as

25 − 17

4 + 298

. . .

and prints the expression and the answer.

5. Write a program that draws the graph of a pair of simultaneous linear equations of the form

$ax + by = c$

$dx + ey = f$

given input a, b, c, d, e, and f.

6. Write a program that reads data of the form

Cols.		
	1-5	ID number
	6-25	Name
	26-45	Address
	46-55	Telephone number

checks that each field has a value and that the ID number and telephone number are numeric, and edits the NAME field to be alphabetic. The data should be printed. If it is invalid, an appropriate error message should also be printed.

7
One-dimensional arrays

OBJECTIVE: To handle a homogeneous set of values.

AN ARRAY IS A data structure used to represent a collection of data, a group of data values all of which have the same form and represent the same thing. In business programming, one-dimensional arrays are used to store lists, such as names or prices, and two-dimensional arrays are used to store tables, such as tax rate tables. In scientific programming, one-dimensional arrays are used to store vectors, and two-dimensional arrays are used to store matrices, coefficients of simultaneous equations, or tables of values. Arrays can be used to represent seating arrangements in a theater, characters in a line of text, or points on a graph or picture. They provide an efficient way of storing, accessing, and manipulating a collection of values.

7.1 Concept of one-dimensional arrays

In mathematics and in formulas a subscripted variable is used to represent one of a collection of data. Thus V_t may mean velocity at time t. X_3 may mean the third value of X. This subscript notation can be extended to nonscientific areas: thus NAME_5 represents the fifth name on a list. It is assumed that there is either a natural order to the group of values, or that an order is imposed by writing them down. The subscript indicates where in the list a particular value occurs.

7.1.1 Subscripts

In general a subscripted variable written mathematically as

A_i where $i = 1, 2, 3, \ldots, 9, 10$

means that A is a collection of ten values which individually are referred to as

$A_1, A_2, A_3, A_4, A_5, A_6, A_7, A_8, A_9, A_{10}$

Notice that the subscripts do not have anything to do with the *values* of the various components of A, but only with their *order* in A.

In PL/I the notation must be modified so that all the symbols are printed on a single line. We can write the names of the items in a collection of ten values as A1, A2, A3, A4, A5, A6, A7, A8, A9, and A10. To a human reader these names appear to be related, but to a computer they are ten different variables, so they do not adequately represent the idea of a collection of values, which is part of the meaning of the mathematical notation. Unless a single name is used for the whole group, it cannot be manipulated as a group, only as single items.

In PL/I a variable is declared to be the name of an array. Individual elements in the array are indicated by writing the subscripts in parentheses. Thus V(T) represents velocity at time T, X(3) usually represents the third value of X, and NAME(5) is usually the fifth name on a list. The ten values of the array A are written as

```
A(1), A(2), A(3), A(4), A(5), A(6), A(7), A(8), A(9),
A(10)
```

The array identifier is A. The subscript within the parentheses following the name is not part of the name, but simply a means of distinguishing each element of the array if it is necessary to access individual elements. The subscript is also called an *index,* because it is often used as an index in iterative DO loops. Subscripts are always integers, but they may be constants, variables, or expressions. All of the following are valid references to array elements:

A(3)
LIST(K)
ARR(N-1)
PRICE(ITEM)

Arrays may be declared of any type, numeric or string (or some other types we have not yet discussed). All the operations that can be performed on single scalar variables of these types can also be performed on individual components of arrays. Individual components can be used in input/output operations. Elements of arrays can be accessed in any order by manipulating the subscripts.

Arrays may be accessed as a whole for input/output, for assignment, or for use in arithmetic operations. It is possible to access multidimensional arrays by using cross-sections; for instance, accessing an entire row or column of a table.

7.1.2 Declarations

Arrays must be explicitly declared. This is done by using a DECLARE statement similar to those used with scalar variables. In the declaration the name of the array is followed by information about its size and by the attributes of the type of element that makes up the array. Arrays must be *homogeneous;* that is, they must contain only one type of element.

The specification of the array in the declaration statement causes the computer to reserve storage for all the elements of the array. It also stores information about the array's size. The general form of the declaration of a one-dimensional array is:

```
DECLARE array_name(n:m) element_type;
```

where n is a constant giving the lowest possible value of the subscript, usually one, and m is a constant giving the highest possible value of the subscript. These are known as the *lower bound* and the *upper bound* of the array. They are separated by a colon. When the lower bound is one, it may be omitted and the declaration written as:

```
DECLARE array_name(m) element-type;
```

For example:

```
DECLARE A(10) FIXED DEC (5,2);
```

is equivalent to

```
DECLARE A(1:10) FIXED DEC (5,2);
```

Both of these declarations allocate space for ten fixed decimal values, which are to be accessed using the subscripts one through ten.

```
DCL X(10) FLOAT BIN;
```

is not equivalent to

```
DCL X(0:9) FLOAT BIN;
```

Both of these declarations allocate space for ten floating-point values, but the range of valid subscripts differs. The elements of the first array are accessed as X(1), X(2), . . . X(10). The elements of the second array are accessed as

X(0), X(1), . . . X(9). The subscript indicates the order of the elements, but not the position in the array unless the lowest subscript is one.

7.1.3 Storage organization

The storage allocated to an array A declared as FIXED DEC(5,2) consists of ten consecutive locations in memory, each containing enough space to store a fixed-decimal number of precision (5,2). It is not necessary to actually store ten values in the array. When the number of values is not known in advance, the declaration should anticipate a maximum number of values. The size of the array may be specified exactly or it may be overspecified, but it must not be underspecified, because the subscripts can be used only within the range given in the declaration. An attempt to access an element outside the declared size of the array will cause problems whether or not it raises an error condition.

The storage allocated to A may be thought of as a list of contiguous places, arranged as follows:

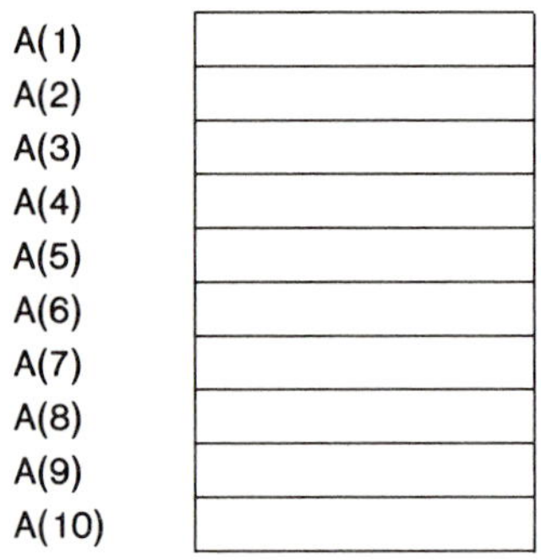

A(1)	
A(2)	
A(3)	
A(4)	
A(5)	
A(6)	
A(7)	
A(8)	
A(9)	
A(10)	

If an array is being used to store values from an experiment or for a graph, it might be appropriate to begin it with a zero subscript rather than a one. Storage for an array with zero-origin subscripting declared as

```
DECLARE X(0:5) FIXED BIN;
```

is as follows:

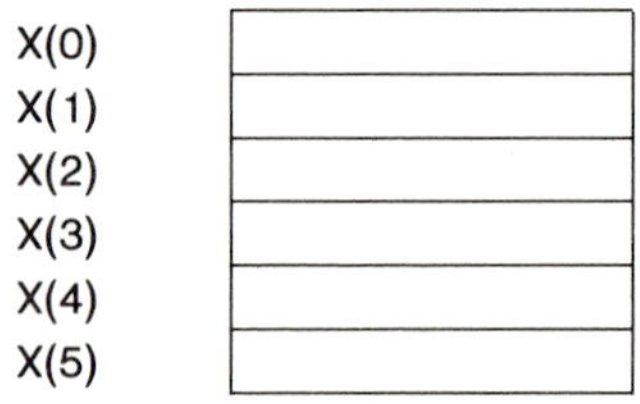

X(0)	
X(1)	
X(2)	
X(3)	
X(4)	
X(5)	

Notice that there are six elements in this array. To know the number of elements in an array and the position of each element, it is necessary to know the lower bound of the array.

Any integer values can be used as upper and lower bounds of an array provided that the upper bound is a larger value than the lower bound. For example,

```
DECLARE X(3:12) CHARACTER(5);
```

allocates space for ten character strings which will be accessed as X(3), X(4), X(5), X(6), X(7), X(8), X(9), X(10), X(11), and X(12). Each character string has room for five characters.

```
DECLARE X(-3:6) BIT(8);
```

allocates space for ten bit strings of eight bits each, accessed as X(−3), X(−2), X(−1), X(0), X(1), X(2), X(3), X(4), X(5), and X(6).

The following are additional examples of the declaration of one-dimensional arrays of various data types:

```
DCL  ACCT_NO(50) FIXED DEC (6,0);    For integer numbers
DCL  VALUE(80)   FIXED DEC (5,2);    For real numbers
DCL  MAP(10:50)  BIT(1);             For bit strings
DCL  BSTRN(20)   BIT(8) VARYING;     For bit strings
DCL  NAME(40)    CHAR(30);           For character strings
DCL  X(-10:10)   FLOAT BIN;          For real numbers
DCL  Y(-20:-1)   FIXED BIN;          For integer numbers
DCL  WORD(10)    CHAR(20) VARYING;   For character strings
```

With the exception of the BIT VARYING and CHAR VARYING arrays, all the elements of each array will have the same size. When the VARYING attribute is used, each element has the same maximum size, but the actual lengths may differ.

7.1.4 INITIAL attribute

NUMERIC ARRAYS

The INITIAL attribute may be used to assign values to the elements of an array provided values are assigned to all the elements. The declaration

```
DCL NUM(5) FIXED DEC(3,0) INIT(52,370,640,-138,9);
```

allocates storage and stores the initial values as shown:

NUM(1)	052
NUM(2)	370
NUM(3)	640
NUM(4)	−138
NUM(5)	009

Notice that the first number in the initialization list is stored in the first position of the array. The second number is in the second position, and so forth.

Through the use of an iteration factor all the elements of an array may be initialized to the same value. This is shown in the following example:

```
DCL NUM(0:5) FIXED DEC(4,0) INIT((6)837);     Iteration factor
```

NUM(0)	0837
NUM(1)	0837
NUM(2)	0837
NUM(3)	0837
NUM(4)	0837
NUM(5)	0837

The six preceding the number 837 is an *iteration factor*. It specifies the number of values to be stored. Then the fist of the six values is placed in the first position of the array regardless of the values used for subscripting. The following example clears an array by initializing it to zero:

```
DCL NUM(50)  FIXED BIN INIT((50)0);          50 zeros
```

Different parts of an array can be initialized to different values, as in the following example:

```
DCL NUM(6) FIXED DEC(4,0) INIT((2)6850,(3)27,9116);
```

NUM(1)	6850
NUM(2)	6850
NUM(3)	0027
NUM(4)	0027
NUM(5)	0027
NUM(6)	9116

Here the first two elements of the array contain 6850, the next three elements of the array contain 27, and the last element contains 9116. Altogether six values were specified, exactly the right number to fill the array.

If only part of the array is to be initialized, the exact number of values must still be specified. For the positions of the array that are to be left uninitialized, an asterisk is used in the initialization list, as follows:

```
DCL NUM(6)  FIXED DEC(4,0) INIT(7,8,*,15,28,916);
```

NUM(1)	0007
NUM(2)	0008
NUM(3)	\\\\\\\\\\
NUM(4)	0015
NUM(5)	0028
NUM(6)	0916

In general an asterisk is used in PL/I to indicate to the computer that it should use whatever is already available. In the case of initializing a variable or an array, an uninitialized one is not actually empty; it contains garbage left over from previous calculations, or a special bit pattern used as a general background fill.

PROGRAMMING HINT: CAUTION The INITIAL clause of an array declaration must specify values for all elements of the array.

STRING ARRAYS

Character and bit string arrays may be initialized. The following example shows the clearing of a character array; that is, filling it with blanks.

```
DCL NAME(25)   CHAR(30)   INIT((25)(30)' ');     25 blank values
```

A repetition factor is used to form a character string containing thirty blanks. Then an iteration factor of twenty-five is used to create a character string for each of the twenty-five elements of the array.

When string arrays are initialized using an iteration factor, there must be an explicit repetition factor, which is (1) in the following example:

```
DECLARE BST(4)  BIT(5) INIT((4)(1)'11011'B);    4 values of '11011'B
```

BST(1)	11011
BST(2)	11011
BST(3)	11011
BST(4)	11011
BST(5)	11011

In the following example, the number 3 is the repetition factor to form the bit string. The number 6 is the iteration factor to create the six strings needed.

```
DECLARE B(6)  BIT(6) INIT((6)(3)'10'B);  6 values of '101010'B
```

B(1)	101010
B(2)	101010
B(2)	101010
B(4)	101010
B(5)	101010
B(6)	101010

In the following example, the repetition factor of one is needed or a single character string of thirty characters would be created rather than six of five characters each.

```
DECLARE CHSTR(6)  CHAR(5) INIT((6)(1)'WWXXA');  6 values of 'WWXXA'
```

CHSTR(1)	WWXXA
CHSTR(2)	WWXXA
CHSTR(3)	WWXXA
CHSTR(4)	WWXXA
CHSTR(5)	WWXXA
CHSTR(6)	WWXXA

The following example stores the character string AXBAXB in each of the components of the array:

```
DECLARE CHSTRING(5) CHAR(6) INIT((5)(2)'AXB'); 5 values of 'AXBAXB'
```

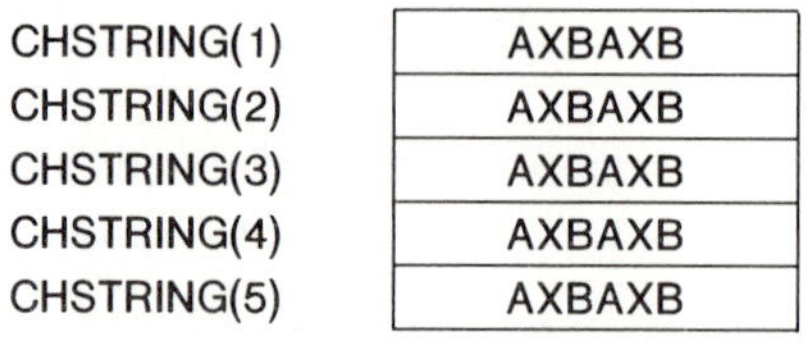

CHSTRING(1)	AXBAXB
CHSTRING(2)	AXBAXB
CHSTRING(3)	AXBAXB
CHSTRING(4)	AXBAXB
CHSTRING(5)	AXBAXB

Different parts of a string array can be initialized to different values, as in the following examples:

```
DECLARE CH(5)  CHAR(1) INIT(*,(3)(1)' ',*);
```

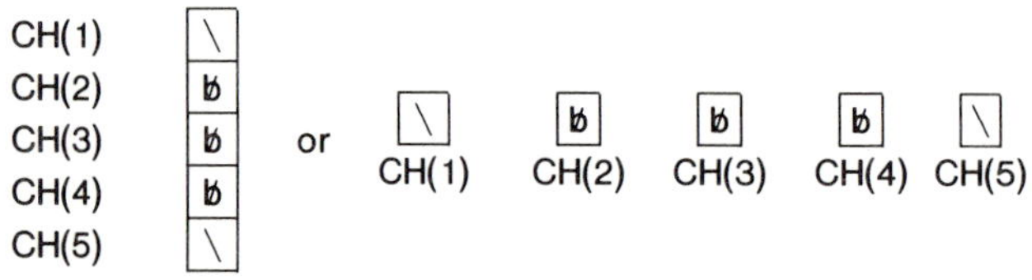

CH(1)	\
CH(2)	ƀ
CH(3)	ƀ
CH(4)	ƀ
CH(5)	\

or

\	ƀ	ƀ	ƀ	\
CH(1)	CH(2)	CH(3)	CH(4)	CH(5)

```
DECLARE B(5)  BIT(1) INIT((3)(1)'1'B,(2)(1)'0'B);
```

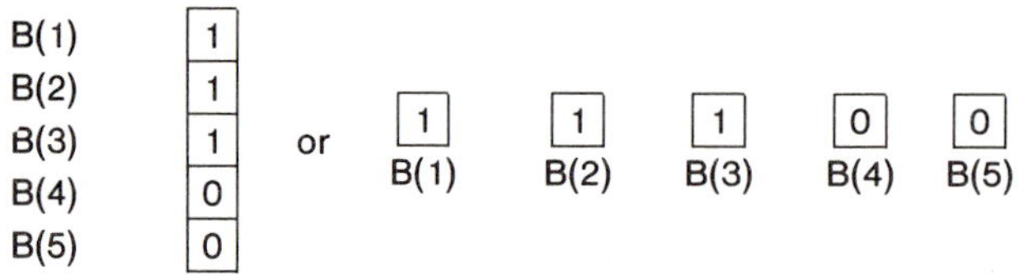

B(1)	1
B(2)	1
B(3)	1
B(4)	0
B(5)	0

or

1	1	1	0	0
B(1)	B(2)	B(3)	B(4)	B(5)

7.1.5 DEFINED option

The DEFINED clause of a declaration (abbreviated DEF) allows more than one name to be given to the same storage area. It can also be used to access a character or bit string as though it were an array. Used with the POSITION option, it allows a name to be given to part of a string storage area. The DEFINED clause cannot be used to change the type of the data being stored.

The following example shows a second name being given to a storage area:

```
DCL   WORD  CHAR(20),
      VERB  CHAR(20)  DEF(WORD);
```

The variable names WORD and VERB refer to the same twenty bytes of memory.

The following example shows a character string being redefined as an array:

```
DCL   WORD  CHAR(5) INIT('APPLE'),
      L(5)  CHAR(1) DEFINED(WORD);
```

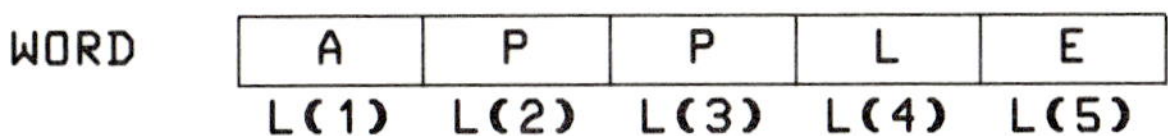

The letter 'A' can be extracted from the word by using the SUBSTR function, or by referring to L(1). The five elements of the array L are the five letters of WORD.

The DEFINED clause provides simple access to the parts of the date returned by the system routine as follows:

```
DCL  TODAY   CHAR(6),
     T(3)    CHAR(2) DEF(TODAY);
TODAY = DATE();
```

```
TODAY   | 87 | 06 | 29 |
          T(1) T(2) T(3)
```

T(1) is the year, T(2) is the month, and T(3) is the day. If only part of the date is wanted, the DEFINED option can be used to obtain the year, and the DEFINED option and POSITION (abbreviated POS) options together can be used to obtain the month or the day. This is shown in the following example:

```
DCL  TODAY   CHAR(6),
     YY      CHAR(2) DEF(TODAY),
     MM      CHAR(2) DEF(TODAY) POS(3),
     DD      CHAR(2) DEF(TODAY) POS(5);
TODAY = DATE();
```

```
TODAY   | 87 | 06 | 29 |
           YY   MM   DD
```

A variable used to redefine another variable may be either a scalar or an array, but it must not extend beyond the bounds of the base variable it redefines. The POSITION option specifies a starting point for the variable. If the base variable is a character string, the POSITION is understood as a character position. If the base variable is a bit string, it is a bit position.

PROGRAMMING HINT: Use DEFINED to access part of a character string.

Review questions

1. Indicate whether each of the following statements is true or false.
   (a) An array may be of any data type.
   (b) An array may have a mixture of data types.
   (c) A subscript indicates the position of an element in an array.
   (d) A subscript may be a numeric constant, variable, or expression.
   (e) The array declaration determines whether the elements of an array are stored in ascending or descending order.

(f) If an INITIAL clause is used in an array declaration, it must contain as many values as there are elements in the array.
(g) The lower bound of an array is always one.

2. How many elements are there in each of the following arrays?

```
(a) DCL A(8)       FIXED BIN;
(b) DCL B(0:14)    CHAR(10);
(c) DCL C(-7:-5)   BIT(8);
(d) DCL D(-1:20)   FLOAT BIN;
```

3. Which of the following are valid references to individual array elements, assuming the arrays have been declared?
(a) X(3)
(b) ARR(K)
(c) VECT(35-2*I)
(d) NAME(N(5))
(e) ARR_B
(f) Z(1.5)
(g) ADDR(0)
(h) A(A(K))
(i) N('10')

4. Show the storage arrangement for each of the following declarations:

```
(a) DCL X(6)       FIXED BIN      INIT(1,2,3,4,5,6);
(b) DCL C(3)       CHAR(4)        INIT((3)(2)'AB');
(c) DCL A(6)       FIXED DEC(3)   INIT((3)0,(3)1);
(d) DCL X(6)       CHAR(2)        INIT((6)(1)'X');
(e) DCL B(6)       BIT(2)         INIT((6)(1)'101'B);
(f) DCL N(-1:4)    FIXED BIN      INIT(-1,0,(4)*);
```

5. Write a segment of code that redefines a character string containing the value of TIME( ) so that the hour and minute parts can be accessed directly.

7.2 Input/output of one-dimensional arrays

There are two basic ways of performing input and output of arrays in PL/I. Referencing an entire array by name is very efficient because the components are accessed at a machine-language level, behind the scenes. Referencing an array through indexing is very flexible because it is program-controlled.

7.2.1 Input of arrays

The regular stream input statements can be used to obtain values for an array.

USING THE ARRAY NAME

If the input is obtained by name, the array name is specified as the data item in the input list. An example of this is:

```
DCL X(20) FIXED BIN;

GET LIST (X);                    List-directed input
```

The twenty values of the array are read from the input stream one by one until the array is full. In the input stream they must be separated by blanks or commas. If there are fewer than twenty values available, the ENDFILE condition is raised.

Edit-directed input may also be used. However, the format list must agree with the number of items in the array, and the data must be formatted in the input stream to match the list. This is shown in the following example:

```
DCL X(20) FIXED BIN;

GET EDIT (X) ((20)F(5,0));      Edit-directed input
```

In this example 100 characters are being read from the input stream in groups of five, each group being converted to a binary representation and stored in a single element of the array.

PROGRAMMING HINT: CAUTION Input an array by name only when there is enough data to fill the array.

USING INDEXING

More control can be obtained over the input process if iterative or implied DO loops are used and the elements of the array are obtained individually. This can be done by letting the index of the array be the index variable of a DO loop. The DOWHILE and DOUNTIL structures can be used also.

DO loops The following example uses an iterative DO loop to input an array:

```
DECLARE A(10) FIXED DEC(4),
        I     FIXED BIN;

DO I = 1 TO 10;
  GET LIST(A(I));
END;
```

The first time the body of the loop is executed, I is one and A(1) is obtained. The second time A(2) is obtained, then A(3), A(4), and so forth, through A(10). Fixed binary variables are used for indexing arrays, as they are the most efficient. By convention, they are often named I, J, or K, from ordinary mathematical usage.

PROGRAMMING HINT: EFFICIENCY Use fixed-binary variables for array indexing.

If edit-directed input is to be used, the values must be regularly spaced in the input stream. In the following example they are found on separate lines. The same format is used for each of the elements in the array.

```
DCL A(10) FIXED BIN,
    K     FIXED BIN;

DO K = 1 TO 10;
  GET EDIT (A(K)) (COL(1),F(4,0));
END;
```

Implied DO loop Implied loops provide a compromise between efficiency and flexibility. The loop is embedded in the input statement rather than being a regular control structure. An example is:

```
DCL ITEM(10) FIXED DEC(3,0),
    J        FIXED BIN;

GET EDIT ((ITEM(J) DO J = 1 TO 10)) (COL(1),(10)F(3,0));
```

The loop construct DO J = 1 TO 10 controls the repetition of everything immediately preceding it in the same set of parentheses in the input list. This is more efficient than the regular iteration structure as the repetition takes place within a single statement. The number of values read from each input record depends on the placement of the repetition factor in the format. In this example all ten values are read from a single record.

In the next example, five values are read from each of two records.

```
DCL ITEM(10) FIXED DEC(3,0),
    J        FIXED BIN;

GET EDIT ((ITEM(J) DO J = 1 TO 10)) ((2)(COL(1),(5)F(3,0)));
```

or

```
GET EDIT ((ITEM(J) DO J = 1 TO 10)) (COL(1),(5)F(3,0));
```

It is possible to input two or more arrays with a single input statement, as in the following example:

```
DCL ACCT(10)  FIXED DEC(5),
    NAME(10)  CHAR(20);

N = 10;
GET EDIT ((ACCT(I),NAME(I) DO I = 1 TO N))
         (COL(1),F(5),X(3),A(20));
```

The index variable I is used with both the account number and the name. Both are inside the same set of parentheses in the input list and the iteration applies to each. First I is set to one, then both ACCT(1) and NAME(1) are read. Then I is set to two and both ACCT(2) and NAME(2) are read. The input continues, obtaining pairs of values until I = 10 has been used. The repetition limit N may be any valid subscript value. Since the format does not have a repetition factor, the entire format is repeated after each ACCT-NAME has been read. The input stream can be thought of as having two columns, as shown:

```
11257   ADAMS JOHN
21543   ANDERSON JAMES
36620   LANE WILLIAM
43256   MAXWELL ANN
33522   NICHOLS SANDRA
36540   LOWELL MAX
77329   LEE MARY
34912   VALDEZ ART
92311   SANDERS JANE
06978   STEVENS CAROL
```

If the same data had been arranged as

```
11257  21543  36620  43256  33522  36540  77329  34912  92311  06978
ADAMS JOHN
ANDERSON JAMES
LANE . . .
```

both the input list and the format list would be as follows:

```
DCL ACCT(10)  FIXED DEC(5),
    NAME(10)  CHAR(20);

N = 10;
GET EDIT ((ACCT(I) DO I = 1 TO N),(NAME(I) DO I = 1 TO N))
         (COL(1),(N)(F(5),X(2)),(N)(COL(1),A(20)));
```

In this example the input list consists of two implied DO loops. The first reads ten account numbers; the second reads ten names. All the account numbers are read ahead of all the names. The input data and the format list match this. All the account numbers are found in a single record; each of the names occupies a separate record. The variable N, which is the upper limit of the implied DO loops, is also used as the repetition factor in the edit format.

PROGRAMMING HINT: CAUTION Use iterative or implied DO loops for array input only when the number of data values is known.

DOWHILE with counter One disadvantage of both the iterative DO and the implied DO is that when an ENDFILE condition is raised in the middle of the input, the computer will attempt to complete the input instruction. With an implied DO, this may raise a fatal error condition even when an ON unit is defined for the condition. Therefore the implied DO cannot be used to input data when the exact number of values is not known.

If values are to be counted as they are read, a DOWHILE or DOUNTIL loop can be used. The following example shows a DOWHILE loop controlled by a counter, which will input at most ten values, counting them.

```
DCL X(10)  FIXED BIN,
    ITEM   FIXED BIN,
    MORE   BIT(1),
    CNT    FIXED BIN;
DCL TRUE   BIT(1)      INIT('1'B),
    FALSE  BIT(1)      INIT('0'B);

ON ENDFILE(SYSIN)
  MORE = FALSE;

MORE = TRUE;
CNT = 0;
GET EDIT (ITEM) (COL(1),F(5));
DO WHILE (CNT < 10 & MORE);
  CNT = CNT + 1;
  X(CNT) = ITEM;
  GET EDIT (ITEM) (COL(1),F(5));
END;
```

Notice that the data is not being read directly into the array. If it were, reading an eleventh item at the bottom of the loop would cause an error. If the counter is initialized to zero, it will not have the correct value for subscripting the array in a priming read. If it is initialized to one, it will not give an accurate count of the data. Using a different variable for input gives the counter multiple uses, as in this example. It is used to control the loop, to count the data, and to subscript the array.

PROGRAMMING HINT: When the amount of data is not known, use DOWHILE to read data. Do not read it directly into an array.

DOUNTIL with counter A counter can also be used in a DOUNTIL loop to obtain data for an array. This is shown in the following example.

```
DCL X(10)  FIXED BIN,
    ITEM   FIXED BIN,
    EOF    BIT(1),
    CNT    FIXED BIN;
DCL TRUE   BIT(1)      INIT('1'B),
    FALSE  BIT(1)      INIT('0'B);

ON ENDFILE(SYSIN)
  EOF = TRUE;

EOF = FALSE;
CNT = 0;
DOUNTIL (CNT = 10 | EOF);
  CNT = CNT + 1;
  GET EDIT (X(CNT)) (COL(1),F(5));
END;
```

Notice that again the counter has multiple uses. It is used to subscript the array, to control the loop, and to count the number of items. Note that the count is not accurate if there are fewer than ten values.

7.2.2 Output of arrays

The stream output of arrays, like the input, has two forms: writing the array by name or writing the array using indexing. With indexing, repetition structures or an implied DO loop may be used.

USING THE ARRAY NAME

Any of the stream output statements may be used for printing an array by name. The simplest are the PUT LIST and PUT DATA statements, which use default spacing and standard formats to print the elements of the array in the order in which they are stored.

In the following example,

```
DCL ARR(6) FIXED BIN  INIT(10,20,30,40,50,60);
PUT SKIP LIST(ARR);
```

the output is:

```
 10           20           30           40           50
 60
```

The values are spread across the page, as many on a line as will fit.

In the following example,

```
DCL ARR(6) FIXED BIN  INIT(10,20,30,40,50,60);
PUT SKIP DATA(ARR);
```

the output is:

```
ARR(1)=  10     ARR(2)=  20     ARR(3)=  30     ARR(4)=  40
ARR(5)=  50     ARR(6)= 60;
```

The elements of the array are individually named and numbered. Again, default spacing is used.

In the following example,

```
DECLARE A(0:5) FIXED DEC(3,0) INIT(17,-23,169,0,34,8);
PUT SKIP DATA(A);
```

the output is:

```
A(0)=  17      A(1)=  -23     A(2)=  169     A(3)=   0
A(4)=  34      A(5)=    8;
```

The order of the output elements is dependent only on the order of the elements in storage.

Edit-directed output can be used to control the spacing so that the elements of the one-dimensional array are actually printed as a one-dimensional list, either vertically or horizontally. In the following example,

```
DCL ARR(6)  FIXED BIN  INIT(10,20,30,40,50,60);
PUT EDIT (ARR) (COL(1),(6)F(5,0));
```

the output is:

```
   10   20   30   40   50   60
```

The spacing arranges the six values on a single line.

In the following example,

```
DCL ARR(6)  FIXED BIN  INIT(10,20,30,40,50,60);
PUT EDIT (ARR) (COL(1),F(5,0));
```

the output is:

```
   10
   20
   30
   40
   50
   60
```

Each of the values is printed on a separate line.

USING INDEXING

Iterative DO loop The iterative DO loop used for array output has the advantage of allowing arrays that are not full to be printed. The following examples show simple printing using the loop:

```
DECLARE X(50)  FIXED DEC(3),
        (I,N)  FIXED BIN;
 . . .
DO I = 1 TO N;                       /* Assume N items in array */
  PUT SKIP LIST(X(I));
END;
```

In this example the N values in the array are printed in a vertical column. There is no control over horizontal spacing.

```
DECLARE X(50)  FIXED DEC(3),
        (I,N)  FIXED BIN;
 . . .
DO I = 1 TO N;                       /* Assume N items in array */
  PUT EDIT (X(I)) (COL(60),F(3,0));
END;
```

In this example the N values in the array are printed in a vertical column down the middle of the page.

With an iterative DO, the index variable is available inside the loop. This provides a simple way to number the lines of output.

```
DCL NAME(50)  CHAR(20),
    (I,N)     FIXED BIN;
 . . .
DO I = 1 TO N;                      /* Assume N items in array */
  PUT EDIT (I,NAME(I)) (COL(5),F(5,0),COL(20),A);
END;
```

In this example the output appears as:

```
   1         ADAMS JOHN
   2         SMITH JOE
   3         JOHNSON MARY
   4          . . .
```

The index variable is printed on each line, numbering the names in the list.

Implied DO loops If an iterative DO loop that prints an array is not used for anything else, the same output can be obtained more efficiently using an implied DO loop.

```
DCL NAME(50)  CHAR(20),
    (I,N)     FIXED BIN;
 . . .                               /* Assume N items in array */
PUT EDIT ((I,NAME(I) DO I = 1 TO N)
              (COL(5),F(5,0),COL(20),A);
```

This example prints the same set of names as the example above. Each name is on a separate line and the lines are numbered.

Review questions

1. Given the array A(10) FIXED BIN, and the input

```
125 42 767 -23 56 9 1027 927 888 -890
```

write a statement(s) to read the data into the array, using
(a) An iterative DO.
(b) An implied DO.
(c) The name of the array.

2. Given the array S(10) CHAR(6), write a statement(s) to read data into the array, using
(a) DOWHILE
(b) DOUNTIL

and the format (A(6)), assuming there may not be exactly sixty characters in the input.

3. Write a segment of code that uses DOWHILE to read data into an array X(10) FIXED BINARY in such a way that at most ten data items are actually read and a correct count is kept of the number of items in the array.

4. Write a segment of code that uses DOUNTIL to read data into an array X(10) FIXED BINARY in such a way that at most ten data items are actually read and a correct count is kept of the number of items in the array.

5. Given the array X(10) FIXED DEC(6,2), write a segment of code to print the values.
(a) Using the array name.
(b) Using an iterative DO.
(c) Using an implied DO.

6. Given the array X(10) FIXED DEC(6,2), write a statement(s) to print the values.
(a) On the same line.
(b) In a column.
(c) Two columns wide.

7.3 Array manipulation

As with input/output, assignment of arrays may be done by name or through the use of indexing. The values of one array may be assigned to another array, or a scalar value may be assigned to all elements of an array. Simple arithmetic may also be performed on arrays.

7.3.1 Array-to-array assignment

USING THE ARRAY NAME

If the elements of one array are assigned to another, they are copied one by one from the first array to the second. This can be done most efficiently by name.

```
DCL (A(10),B(10)) FIXED DEC(5,0);
 . . .
B = A;
```

The result of this code is that arrays A and B have the same values. For example:

B = A;				
	A(1)	010	B(1)	010
	A(2)	085	B(2)	085
	A(3)	164	B(3)	164
	A(4)	032	B(4)	032
	A(5)	559	B(5)	559
	A(6)	086	B(6)	086
	A(7)	012	B(7)	012
	A(8)	001	B(8)	001
	A(9)	−916	B(9)	−916
	A(10)	023	B(10)	023

Any original values of array B have been lost. In order to assign an array by name, the sizes of the source and destination arrays must be identical. In this example both A and B have ten elements. The upper and lower bounds, as well as the sizes, must be the same.

The array types may be different, as in the following example. As the array elements are copied, they are converted from the fixed-decimal source type to the fixed-binary destination type.

```
DECLARE A(6) FIXED DEC(3,0),                          (Best)
        B(6) FIXED BIN;
  . . .
B = A;
```

is equivalent to

```
DECLARE A(6) FIXED DEC(3,0),
        B(6) FIXED BIN,
        K    FIXED BIN;
  . . .
DO K = 1 TO 6;
  B(K) = A(K);
END;
```

USING INDEXING

The iterative DO should be used if only part of an array is to be copied or if the order of the elements is to be changed.

```
DECLARE A(6)   FIXED DEC(3,0),
        B(6)   FIXED DEC(3,0),
        (N,K)  FIXED BIN;
  . . .
DO K = 1 TO N;                         Copy N items
  B(K) = A(K);
END;
```

In this example, if the array A is not full, then the values cannot be assigned to B by name. An iterative DO is needed. If N is 3, the first half of the array B is changed, but the second half is left unchanged, as shown below:

Before				After			
A(1)	103	B(1)	1	A(1)	103	B(1)	103
A(2)	12	B(2)	5	A(2)	12	B(2)	12
A(3)	−7	B(3)	−10	A(3)	−7	B(3)	−7
A(4)	200	B(4)	2	A(4)	200	B(4)	2
A(5)	64	B(5)	−2	A(5)	64	B(5)	−2
A(6)	−42	B(6)	41	A(6)	−42	B(6)	41

In the following example the odd-numbered elements of B, that is, B(1), B(3), and B(5), obtain their values from A. The values of the even-numbered elements are unchanged.

```
DECLARE A(6) FIXED DEC(3,0),
        B(6) FIXED DEC(3,0),
        K    FIXED BIN;
  . . .
DO K = 1 TO 6 BY 2;
  B(K) = A(K);
END;
```

Before

A(1)	103	B(1)	1
A(2)	12	B(2)	5
A(3)	−7	B(3)	−10
A(4)	200	B(4)	2
A(5)	64	B(5)	−2
A(6)	−42	B(6)	41

After

A(1)	103	B(1)	103
A(2)	12	B(2)	5
A(3)	−7	B(3)	−7
A(4)	200	B(4)	2
A(5)	64	B(5)	64
A(6)	−42	B(6)	41

In the following example the elements of the array A are assigned to the array B in reverse order. B(6) has the same value as A(1), B(5) as A(2), and so forth.

```
DECLARE A(6)  FIXED DEC(3,0),
        B(6)  FIXED DEC(3,0),
        (J,K) FIXED BIN;
  . . .
J = 6;
DO K = 1 TO 6;
  B(J) = A(K);
  J = J - 1;
END;
```

Before

A(1)	103	B(1)	1
A(2)	12	B(2)	5
A(3)	−7	B(3)	−10
A(4)	200	B(4)	2
A(5)	64	B(5)	−2
A(6)	−42	B(6)	41

After

A(1)	103	B(1)	−42
A(2)	12	B(2)	64
A(3)	−7	B(3)	200
A(4)	200	B(4)	−7
A(5)	64	B(5)	12
A(6)	−42	B(6)	103

7.3.2 Scalar-to-array assignment

If a scalar value is assigned to an array, the value is assigned individually to each element of the array. This provides a convenient way to initialize an array. It is shown in the following example:

```
DECLARE NUM(10)   FIXED DEC(5,2),
        TEXT(20)  CHAR(100);
NUM = 0;
TEXT = ' ';
```

Each of the ten elements of the array NUM is given the value of zero. Each of the twenty elements of the array TEXT is filled with blanks. The character literal being used has only one blank, but it is stored left-justified with blank fill, so each element actually contains 100 blanks.

The scalar being used may be a variable or an expression. It may contain any value compatible with the attributes of the array.

```
DCL NUM(4)    FIXED DEC(5,2),
    X         FIXED DEC(3,0) INIT (425);
NUM = X;
```

In this example the value 425 is being stored in each element of the array. Since the precision of the scalar variable is different from that of the array, the value is being converted to the proper precision and the result is:

NUM(1)	425 00
NUM(2)	425 00
NUM(3)	425 00
NUM(4)	425 00

If only a few values of the array are to be given the value of a scalar, subscripts must be used.

```
DCL X(10) FIXED BIN,
    I     FIXED BIN;
  . . .
DO I = 1 TO 5;
  X(I) = 17;
END;
```

In this example, the value seventeen is being assigned only to the first five elements of the array X. The last five elements retain their previous values.

```
DCL X(10) FIXED BIN;
  . . .
X(2),X(3),X(8),X(9),X(10) = 329;
```

In this example, there is no simple formula for calculating the subscripts of the elements to be assigned the value. A multiple-assignment statement is better than using a loop.

PROGRAMMING HINT: MAINTAINABILITY Use an assignment statement to initialize an array.

7.3.3 Array arithmetic

All the arithmetic operators that can be used with scalar variables can also be used with arrays. The effect of using these operations with array names is as though the same operation were performed on all the numbers in the array at the same time. If the order in which the elements are manipulated is not important, by-name arithmetic is the most efficient.

The following three examples have the same result:

```
DCL A(5) FIXED BIN;
 . . .
A(1) = 12 * A(1);
A(2) = 12 * A(2);
A(3) = 12 * A(3);
A(4) = 12 * A(4);
A(5) = 12 * A(5);
```

```
DCL A(5) FIXED BIN,
         I    FIXED BIN;
 . . .
DO I = 1 TO 5;
  A(I) = 12 * A(I);
END;
```

```
DCL A(5) FIXED BIN;
 . . .
A = 12 * A;
```

The effect of this is:

	Before		After
A(1)	103	A(1)	1236
A(2)	12	A(2)	144
A(3)	−7	A(3)	−84
A(4)	200	A(4)	2400
A(5)	−42	A(5)	−504

Each individual element of the array is multiplied by the scalar.

With the addition statement

A = A + 23;

the effect is:

	Before		After
A(1)	103	A(1)	126
A(2)	12	A(2)	35
A(3)	−7	A(3)	16
A(4)	200	A(4)	223
A(5)	−42	A(5)	−19

Twenty-three is added individually to each element.

With the statements

X = 5;
A = A − X;

the effect is:

	Before		After
A(1)	103	A(1)	98
A(2)	12	A(2)	7
A(3)	−7	A(3)	−12
A(4)	200	A(4)	195
A(5)	−42	A(5)	−47

With the division statement

A = A / 3;

the effect is:

	Before		After
A(1)	103	A(1)	34
A(2)	12	A(2)	4
A(3)	−7	A(3)	−3
A(4)	200	A(4)	66
A(5)	−42	A(5)	−14

Note that the result of each division is converted to the FIXED BINARY type of the array A.

With the exponentiation

A = A ** 2;

the effect is:

	Before		After
A(1)	103	A(1)	10609
A(2)	12	A(2)	144
A(3)	−7	A(3)	49
A(4)	200	A(4)	40000
A(5)	−42	A(5)	1764

ARRAY-TO-ARRAY ARITHMETIC

When arithmetic operations are performed on two arrays, the operations are performed using the corresponding elements of the two arrays. The following three examples are equivalent.

```
DCL A(5) FIXED BIN,
    B(5) FIXED BIN;
 . . .
A(1) = A(1) * B(1);
A(2) = A(2) * B(2);
A(3) = A(3) * B(3);
A(4) = A(4) * B(4);
A(5) = A(5) * B(5);
```

```
DCL A(5) FIXED BIN,
    B(5) FIXED BIN,
    I    FIXED BIN;
 . . .
DO I = 1 TO 5;
  A(I) = A(I) * B(I);
END;
```

```
DCL A(5) FIXED BIN,
    B(5) FIXED BIN;
 . . .
A = A * B;
```

The effect is:

	Before				After		
A(1)	103	B(1)	1	A(1)	103	B(1)	1
A(2)	12	B(2)	5	A(2)	60	B(2)	5
A(3)	−7	B(3)	−10	A(3)	70	B(3)	−10
A(4)	200	B(4)	2	A(4)	400	B(4)	2
A(5)	−42	B(5)	41	A(5)	−1722	B(5)	41

Array B is not affected by the multiplication. The arrays must have exactly the same size and the same array bounds.

With the array addition statement

A = A + B;

the corresponding elements are added. The effect is:

Before				After			
A(1)	103	B(1)	1	A(1)	104	B(1)	1
A(2)	12	B(2)	5	A(2)	17	B(2)	5
A(3)	−7	B(3)	−10	A(3)	−17	B(3)	−10
A(4)	200	B(4)	2	A(4)	202	B(4)	2
A(5)	−42	B(5)	41	A(5)	−1	B(5)	41

With the array subtraction statement

A = A − B;

the corresponding elements are subtracted. The effect is:

Before				After			
A(1)	103	B(1)	1	A(1)	102	B(1)	1
A(2)	12	B(2)	5	A(2)	7	B(2)	5
A(3)	−7	B(3)	−10	A(3)	3	B(3)	−10
A(4)	200	B(4)	2	A(4)	198	B(4)	2
A(5)	−42	B(5)	41	A(5)	−83	B(5)	41

With the array division statement

A = A / B;

the corresponding elements are divided. The effect is:

Before				After			
A(1)	103	B(1)	1	A(1)	103	B(1)	1
A(2)	12	B(2)	5	A(2)	2	B(2)	5
A(3)	−7	B(3)	−10	A(3)	0	B(3)	−10
A(4)	200	B(4)	2	A(4)	100	B(4)	2
A(5)	−42	B(5)	41	A(5)	−1	B(5)	41

In all of these examples the result was stored in array A. It is also possible to store the result in a separate array, as in the following example:

```
DCL (A,B,C,D,E,F,G) (5) FIXED BIN;

C = A + B;
D = A - B;
E = A * B;
F = A / B;
G = A ** B;
```

All of these arrays contain five fixed binary numbers. Both array A and array B are unchanged by the arithmetic. The result of each individual operation is converted to the proper type for storage.

Review questions

1. Given the array A(5) FIXED BIN, show the result of each of the following assignment statements:
   (a) `A = 0;`
   (b)
   ```
   DCL B(5) FIXED BIN  INIT(1,2,3,4,5);
       A = B;
   ```
   (c)
   ```
   DCL B(5) FIXED BIN  INIT(1,2,3,4,5);
       A = B(3);
   ```
   (d)
   ```
   DCL B(5) FIXED BIN  INIT(1,2,3,4,5);
       A = 2;
       A = A + B;
   ```
   (e)
   ```
   DCL B(5) FIXED BIN  INIT(1,2,3,4,5);
       A = B;
       A = A - B(3);
   ```
   (f)
   ```
   A(1),A(3),A(5) = 1;
   A(2),A(4) = -1;
   ```

2. Given the array A(5) FIXED DEC(6) INIT(1,2,3,4,5), what is the result of each of the following statements?
   (a) A = A + 5;
   (b) A = A - 4;
   (c) A = 3 * A;
   (d) A = A / 3;
   (e) A = A ** 3;

3. Given the array A(5) FIXED DEC(4,2) INIT(1,2,3,4,5) and the array B(5) FIXED DEC(6) INIT(10,11,12,13,14), what is the result of each of the following statements?
   (a) A = A + B;
   (b) A = B - A;
   (c) A = B / A;
   (d) A = A - B;

*4. What is the result of executing the following segment of code on your computer? What does it say about the way arrays are referenced?

```
DCL A(5) FIXED BIN INIT(1,2,3,4,5);
A = A + A(2);
```

5. Write a segment of code that will add two to the first, third, fifth, . . . elements of array A(10) FIXED BIN.

6. Write a segment of code that will find the sum of the elements of an array A(10) FIXED BIN.

7. Write a segment of code that will reverse the order of the letters in a character string STR CHAR(20), redefining it as an array.

7.4 Array element access

Elements of an array can be accessed sequentially by indexing with iterative DO loops. They can also be accessed directly by explicitly specifying the subscripts. Sequential access is used when the entire array must be processed, particularly for such functions as finding the total, sorting the values, and searching for a particular value. Direct access is used primarily for looking up values in tables when their location is known.

7.4.1 Sequential access

We have already seen the use of sequential access in array input/output.

An array can be accessed sequentially in reverse order by counting down rather than up. This is shown in the following example:

```
DO K = CNT TO 1 BY -1;                    Print reversed
  PUT EDIT (AMT(K)) (COL(1),F(10,2));
END;
```

If only the second half of the array is wanted, the index may be started at midpoint, as in the following example:

```
DO K = (CNT+1)/2+1 TO CNT;                Print second half
  PUT EDIT (AMT(K)) (COL(1),F(10,2));
END;
```

If CNT is nine, this loop prints AMT(6), AMT(7), AMT(8), and AMT(9). If CNT is ten, it prints AMT(6), AMT(7), AMT(8), AMT(9), and AMT(10).

The following example prints the first half of the array in reverse order:

```
DO K = (CNT+1)/2 TO 1 BY -1;              Print first half
  PUT EDIT (AMT(K)) (COL(1),F(10,2));     reversed
END;
```

If CNT is nine or ten this prints AMT(5), AMT(4), AMT(3), AMT(2), and AMT(1).

7.4.2 Direct access

Array elements are accessed directly by specifiying the subscripts. Subscripts may be constants or scalar variables, and they may also be expressions that evaluate to an integer value within the range specified for the array. When the subscript is not a constant, it is evaluated first, the array bounds are checked, and then the array is accessed.

In the statements

```
X=3;
PUT SKIP LIST(ARR(FLOOR(SQRT(X))));
```

the computer accesses the array in the following steps:

1. Retrieve the value of X.
2. Find the square root of 3.
3. Convert 1.732 to an integer by truncating the fractional part.
4. Retrieve the value of ARR(1).

In the following example, a part number is used to look up the cost of the part:

```
DECLARE COST(1000) FIXED DEC(6,2),
        PART_NO    FIXED BIN;
 . . .
GET LIST (PART_NO);
PUT EDIT (COST(PART_NO)) (COL(1),F(8,2));
```

A data value can be used as a subscript provided that it is an appropriate value. Another example of this is the use of the month part of the date to obtain the name of the month in the following code segment:

```
DCL TODAY     CHAR(6),
    MM        FIXED BIN;
DCL MONTH(12) CHAR(8) VARYING
              INIT('JANUARY','FEBRUARY','MARCH',...
 . . .
TODAY = DATE();
MM = SUBSTR(TODAY,3,2,);
PUT EDIT (MONTH(MM)) (COL(1),A);
```

The following example uses parallel lists of names and addresses and scans the list of names for a specific name. The position of the name in the list is then used to look up the address. It is assumed that the name is in the list.

```
DCL NAME(100)     CHAR(20),
    ADDR(100)     CHAR(30);
DCL NAME_WANTED   CHAR(20);
 . . .
GET LIST (NAME_WANTED);
K = 1;
DO UNTIL (NAME(K) = NAME_WANTED);       Locate name
  K = K + 1;
END;
PUT SKIP LIST (NAME(K),ADDR(K));        Use address too
```

Review questions

1. Indicate whether each of the following statements is true or false.
   (a) An array may be accessed in any order.
   (b) When an array subscript is an expression, it is evaluated before the array is referenced.
   (c) Data values may not be used as subscripts.

2. Write a segment of code that stores the square roots of the numbers 1 to 100 in a one-dimensional array.

3. Write a segment of code that looks up a value of INCOME in a table and prints the corresponding tax rate. Use the tables

Income table	*Tax rate*
Income under 5000	0%
15000	16%
25000	28%
35000	38%
45000	46%
over 45000	52%

7.5 Array error condition

7.5.1 SUBSCRIPTRANGE condition

The SUBSCRIPTRANGE condition (abbreviated SUBRG) is used to check that all subscripts are within the bounds specified in the array declarations. Then if there is an attempt to access an element outside the specified bounds, the condition is raised. If the processing is not to terminate abnormally, an ON unit for the condition must be established. The SUBSCRIPTRANGE condition is normally disabled, but while a program is being tested, the condition should be enabled as a debugging aid.

PROGRAMMING HINT: TESTING Enable the SUBSCRIPTRANGE condition while a program is being tested.

After the testing is completed, the condition should be disabled for efficient production runs.

The establishment of an ON unit allows the programmer to print a message before termination. Without an ON unit, the system will print a standard error message, raise the SUBSCRIPTRANGE condition, and terminate the processing.

When a subscript is out of range, the system takes the following actions under the following conditions:

Condition	*ON unit*	*Action*
Disabled		Value is stored outside array
Enabled	Established	ON unit is executed
Enabled	Not established	SUBSCRIPTRANGE condition is raised

In the following example, the subscript is outside its declared range twice. The first time, the SUBSCRIPTRANGE condition has not been enabled.

No checking will be done; a value will be read from the input stream and stored according to a calculated offset from the beginning position of the array storage. The number will be stored outside the storage set aside for the array, which will probably inadvertently change the value of some other variable, which in turn may eventually cause abnormal termination. The second time, the computer will check the subscript value against the specified range and will terminate the processing abnormally, since an ON unit has not been established.

```
DECLARE X(9)  FIXED DEC(3,0),
        (I,J) FIXED BIN,
        XSUM  FIXED DEC(4,0);

GET EDIT((X(I) DO I = 1 TO 10)) (COL(1),(10)F(3,0));
SUM = 0.0;
DO J = 1 TO 10;
  (SUBSCRIPTRANGE): SUM = SUM + X(J);
END;
```

Notice that in both the implied and the iterative DO loops, the subscript of the array will become ten, although the array declaration specifies a maximum of nine. For debugging purposes it would be better to place the enabling preface at the beginning of the entire procedure, as in the following version of the same example:

```
(SUBSCRIPTRANGE):
MP: PROC OPTIONS (MAIN);
DECLARE X(9)  FIXED DEC(3,0),
        (I,J) FIXED BIN,
        XSUM  FIXED DEC(4,0);

ON SUBSCRIPTRANGE
  BEGIN;
    PUT EDIT ('ARRAY X OUT OF BOUNDS') (COL(1),A);
    PUT SKIP DATA (I,J);
  END;

I,J = 0;
GET EDIT((X(I) DO I = 1 TO 10)) (COL(1),(10)F(3,0));
XSUM = 0.0;
DO J = 1 TO 10;
  XSUM = XSUM + X(J);
END;
```

This version will not terminate abnormally, but will produce an unpredictable value for the XSUM. By printing an error message, some information about the problem is obtained. Notice that in order to obtain information as to which subscript caused the problem, it was necessary to print both subscripts. For this to be possible, J had to be initialized. Since subscript checking creates runtime overhead, it should be used only as a debugging tool, and should be removed from production programs. Adding and removing a condition preface can be done most easily if it is used as preface to a procedure rather than to individual statements.

Review questions

1. Given the array A(10), which of the following will raise the SUBSCRIPTRANGE condition?
   (a) A(10)
   (b) A(0)
   (c) A(1.5)
   (d) A('3')

2. Under what conditions should the SUBRG condition be
   (a) Enabled
   (b) Disabled
   (c) Raised
   (d) Used to establish an ON unit

7.6 Array library functions

Some of the standard operations on columns of numbers are available in PL/I as built-in array functions. Array library functions are of two types: functions that return information about arrays and functions that manipulate arrays.

Array specification functions	
DIM(array,1)	Returns number of elements in first dimension of array
LBOUND(array,1)	Returns lower bound of first subscript of array
HBOUND(array,1)	Returns upper bound of first subscript of array
Array manipulation functions	
SUM(array)	Returns sum of elements of array
PROD(array)	Returns product of elements of array (see Appendix B)
POLY(coef,var)	Returns value of polynomial

7.6.1 Array specification functions

The array specification functions query the array descriptor and return the information as integer values.

DIM FUNCTION

The DIM function returns the number of elements in a given dimension of an array. Its use with one-dimensional arrays is shown in the following example:

```
DCL A(5)     FIXED BIN,
    B(3:8)   FIXED DEC (6,0),
    C(0:15)  FLOAT BIN,
    N        FIXED BIN;
```

```
N = DIM(A,1);                         The value is 5
N = DIM(B,1);                         The value is 6
N = DIM(C,1);                         The value is 16
```

With one-dimensional arrays, the second argument is always one. With arrays of higher dimension, it indicates the dimension being queried.

HBOUND FUNCTION

The HBOUND function returns the maximum value of the subscript of a particular dimension of an array. The use of this function is shown in the following example:

```
DCL A(5)     FIXED BIN,
    B(3:8)   FIXED DEC (6,0),
    C(0:15)  FLOAT BIN,
    N        FIXED BIN;
```

```
N = HBOUND(A,1);                      The value is 5
N = HBOUND(B,1);                      The value is 8
N = HBOUND(C,1);                      The value is 15
```

With one-dimensional arrays, the second argument is always one. With higher-dimension arrays, it indicates the dimension being queried.

LBOUND FUNCTION

The LBOUND function returns the minimum value of the subscript of a particular dimension of an array. The use of this function is shown in the following example:

```
DCL A(5)     FIXED BIN,
    B(3:8)   FIXED DEC (6,0),
    C(0:15)  FLOAT BIN,
    N        FIXED BIN;
```

```
N = LBOUND(A,1);                      The value is 1
N = LBOUND(B,1);                      The value is 3
N = LBOUND(C,1);                      The value is 0
```

With one-dimensional arrays, the second argument is always one.

The primary use of these functions is to reduce the number of modifications of the program that would be needed if the size of the array is changed. In the following example, if a change must be made to the program because the array ARR is either too large or too small, the only line that needs to be changed is the array declaration.

```
DCL ARR(10) FLOAT BIN,
    (L,H)   FIXED BIN,
    I       FIXED BIN;
 . . .
L = LBOUND(ARR,1);
H = HBOUND(ARR,1);
DO I = L TO H;
  PUT SKIP LIST(ARR(I));
END;
```

When a declaration is used to allocate space for an array, an array descriptor is also stored. The values of LBOUND and HBOUND are obtained from the descriptor. By using the built-in functions to obtain the lower and upper bounds of the array, the iterative DO has been generalized so that it can be used with a one-dimensional array of any size.

7.6.2 Array manipulation functions

The array manipulation functions are SUM, PROD, and POLY. The PROD function is discussed in Appendix B.

SUM FUNCTION

The SUM function computes the sum of all the elements of a one-dimensional array and references the array by name. Its use is seen in the following example, which calculates the average of the five values in the array:

```
DCL X(5)  FLOAT BIN,
    XAVG  FLOAT BIN;

 . . .
XAVG = SUM(X) / 5.0;               /* CALCULATE AVERAGE */
```

The function call SUM(X) calculates and returns the value of X(1)+X(2)+X(3)+X(4)+X(5). This total is then divided by five. The function takes as argument an array of floating-point values. If it is used with numbers of some other type, they are automatically converted to floating point. The answer is returned as a floating-point value.

POLY FUNCTION

The POLY function is used to evaluate a polynomial. The function call

```
POLY (A,X)
```

means

$a_1 + a_2X + a_3X^2 + a_4X^3 + \ldots + a_{n+1}X^n$

The following example shows the use of this function:

```
DECLARE A(5) FIXED BIN INIT(2,5,3,-7,1),
        X    FIXED BIN,
        Y    FIXED BIN;

 . . .
Y = POLY(A,X);
```

This is equivalent to the assignment statement

```
Y = 2 + 5*X + 3*X**2 - 7*X**3 + 1*X**4;
```

If X is 2, the value −16 is assigned to Y. Using the POLY function is more efficient than using the assignment statement. However, the function returns a floating-point value, so it may be slightly inaccurate.

Review questions

1. What value is returned by the function for each of the following arrays?

(a)
```
DCL X(15) FIXED BIN;
M = DIM(X,1);
```
(b)
```
DCL Y(6:12) FIXED DEC(3);
N = DIM(Y,1);
```
(c)
```
DCL W(-5:5) FIXED BIN;
K = DIM(W,1);
```
(d)
```
DCL Z(-4:-1) FLOAT BIN;
J = DIM(Z,1);
```

2. What value is returned by the function for each of the following arrays?

(a)
```
DCL X(15) FIXED BIN;
M = HBOUND(X,1);
```
(b)
```
DCL Y(6:12) FIXED DEC(3);
N = HBOUND(Y,1);
```
(c)
```
DCL W(-5:5) FIXED BIN;
K = HBOUND(W,1);
```
(d)
```
DCL Z(-4:-1) FLOAT BIN;
J = HBOUND(Z,1);
```

3. What value is returned by the function for each of the following arrays?

(a)
```
DCL X(15) FIXED BIN;
M = LBOUND(X,1);
```
(b)
```
DCL Y(6:12) FIXED DEC(3);
N = LBOUND(Y,1);
```
(c)
```
DCL W(-5:5) FIXED BIN;
K = LBOUND(W,1);
```
(d)
```
DCL Z(-4:-1) FLOAT BIN;
J = LBOUND(Z,1);
```

4. Given the array A(5) FIXED BIN INIT(1,2,3,4,5), what is the value of each of the following functions?

(a) `SUM(A)`
(b) `POLY(A,-2)`

5. Write a segment of code that uses the POLY function to calculate the values of a polynomial

$y = a_0x^5 + a_1x^4 + \ldots + a_4x + a_5$

for all values of $x = 1, 2, 3, \ldots 10$.

7.7 Examples of one-dimensional arrays

The primary use of one-dimensional arrays is to store lists of data values. The order in which the values are stored is known as *key entry order.* If the input data is not in a useful order, it may be necessary to sort it. For example, if the list contains names and telephone numbers, it is simpler to have the computer sort the data than to do it by hand. If a particular telephone number is wanted, the list can be searched more easily if it is in alphabetical order than if it is in key entry order.

The following examples include sorting and searching lists, using lists of values in calculations, and using one-dimensional arrays in graphing and text processing.

7.7.1 Maximum and minimum values

This example shows an array being scanned to find the largest and smallest values. Both of them can be found with a single loop.

```
MINMAX: PROC OPTIONS(MAIN);
/*************************************************************/
/*                                                           */
/* PROGRAM: MINIMUM AND MAXIMUM ARRAY ELEMENTS               */
/* AUTHOR:   C ZIEGLER                                       */
/* VERSION: 7/17/84                                          */
/*                                                           */
/* PROGRAM DESCRIPTION                                       */
/* ------------------------------------------------------    */
/* THIS PROGRAM FINDS THE LARGEST AND SMALLEST ITEMS         */
/* IN AN ARRAY.                                              */
/*                                                           */
/* INPUT: ARRAY                                              */
/*                                                           */
/* OUTPUT: LARGEST AND SMALLEST VALUES                       */
/*                                                           */
/*************************************************************/

DCL A(20)         FIXED BIN,
    (AMAX,AMIN)   FIXED BIN,
    (K,N)         FIXED BIN;

GET LIST (A);
AMAX,AMIN = A(1);              /* START WITH FIRST VALUE */
DO K = 2 TO 20;
  IF A(K) < AMIN
    THEN
      AMIN = A(K);             /* SAVE ANY SMALLER VALUE */
    ELSE
      IF A(K) > AMAX
        THEN
          AMAX = A(K);         /* SAVE ANY LARGER VALUE  */
END;
PUT SKIP LIST(AMIN,AMAX);
END MINMAX;
```

Notice that AMAX and AMIN are initially assigned the first value in the array. The first value of AMAX must be the largest value at that point in the sequential scan; the first value of AMIN must be the smallest value at that point in the sequential scan. They must both be initialized to the value of A(1) rather than to zero because the array may contain just positive values, just negative values, or a mixture of both. Since A(1) is used in the initialization, the sequential access starts with A(2).

7.7.2 Billing

This example accumulates three totals while calculating the values for a new array. It takes the values for the number of items of each type ordered and the price of each type of item and calculates the cost for each part of the order. These values are obtained from two arrays of the same size by sequentially accessing them in parallel. At the same time, the total number of items ordered and the total cost are calculated.

```
BILLING: PROC OPTIONS(MAIN);
/****************************************************************/
/*                                                              */
/* PROGRAM: BILLING FOR SALE OF ITEMS                           */
/* AUTHOR:  C ZIEGLER                                           */
/* VERSION: 7/17/84                                             */
/*                                                              */
/* PROGRAM DESCRIPTION                                          */
/* ------------------------------------------------------------ */
/* THIS PROGRAM PRINTS THE TOTAL COST OF ITEMS                  */
/* ORDERED IN QUANTITY.                                         */
/*                                                              */
/* INPUT: ITEM NUMBERS AND PRICES, ORDER                        */
/*                                                              */
/* OUTPUT: BILLING FOR ORDER: ITEM NUMBERS, QUANTITY            */
/*         COST, TOTAL COST, TOTAL QUANTITY                     */
/*                                                              */
/****************************************************************/


DCL ITEM(10)        FIXED DEC(3,0),
    PRICE(10)       FIXED DEC(4,2),
    COST(10)        FIXED DEC(7,2),
    TOTAL_ITEM      FIXED DEC(5,0),
    TOTAL_COST      FIXED DEC(9,2),
    I               FIXED BIN;

GET LIST (ITEM,PRICE);
TOTAL_ITEM = 0.0;
TOTAL_COST = 0.0;
DO I = 1 TO 10;
  COST(I) = ITEM(I) * PRICE(I);
  TOTAL_ITEM = TOTAL_ITEM + ITEM(I);
  TOTAL_COST = TOTAL_COST + COST(I);
END;
```

```
DO I = 1 TO 10;
  PUT EDIT (I,ITEM(I),PRICE(I),COST(I)) (COL(1),F(2,0),
           COL(10),F(3,0),COL(20),F(6,2),COL(30),F(9,2));
END;
PUT EDIT (TOTAL_ITEM,TOTAL_COST)
         (COL(10),F(7,0),COL(30),F(10,2));
END BILLING;
```

Note that the iterative DO could be avoided by the use of array library functions and array arithmetic, as follows:

```
COST = ITEM * PRICE;
TOTAL_ITEM = SUM(ITEM);
TOTAL_COST = SUM(COST);
```

7.7.3 Sorting

PL/1 does not have a built-in function to sort a list of values. Instead, most computer systems have a utility program that sorts a data file. If there is a lot of data and it is stored in a file, the system sort utility is the most efficient way to sort the values. If a short list of values is to be sorted and the values can be stored in an array, the programmer can use computer resources most efficiently by writing a sort procedure.

Sorting algorithms fall into two categories: insertion sorts, where each data value is placed in its proper position in an array as it is read in; and exchange sorts, where all the data is read in, then the values are moved around until they are in the proper order. There are many different variations on these types, such as selection sort, bubble sort, shell sort, radix sort, quick sort, heap sort. Descriptions of these sorts can be found in books on data structures.

Sorts differ in the amount of storage required and the number of comparisons made. There is no one best sorting method. The method that is best for a particular application depends on the original order of the data and the amount of storage space available. Usually a trade-off must be made between space and time.

The following sections discuss two sorting techniques, a simple insertion sort and an exchange sort known as the bubble sort.

INSERTION SORT

The basic steps of the insertion sort, which are carried out for each input value, are:

1. Locate the position where the new value belongs.
2. Move the rest of the values down to make room for it.
3. Insert the new value.

This is shown in the flowchart of figure 7–1. The variable I is used to find the proper position in the array. J is used to move the rest of the array down. N keeps track of the number of elements in the array. The processing stops when the array has been filled or when the end-of-file has been found, whichever occurs first. The outer loop reads the data, placing the data items in the array one by one. The first inner loop finds the proper place in the array. The second inner loop moves the rest of the array elements down to create space for the new value. Then the insertion sort procedure follows, as shown in the insertion sort program.

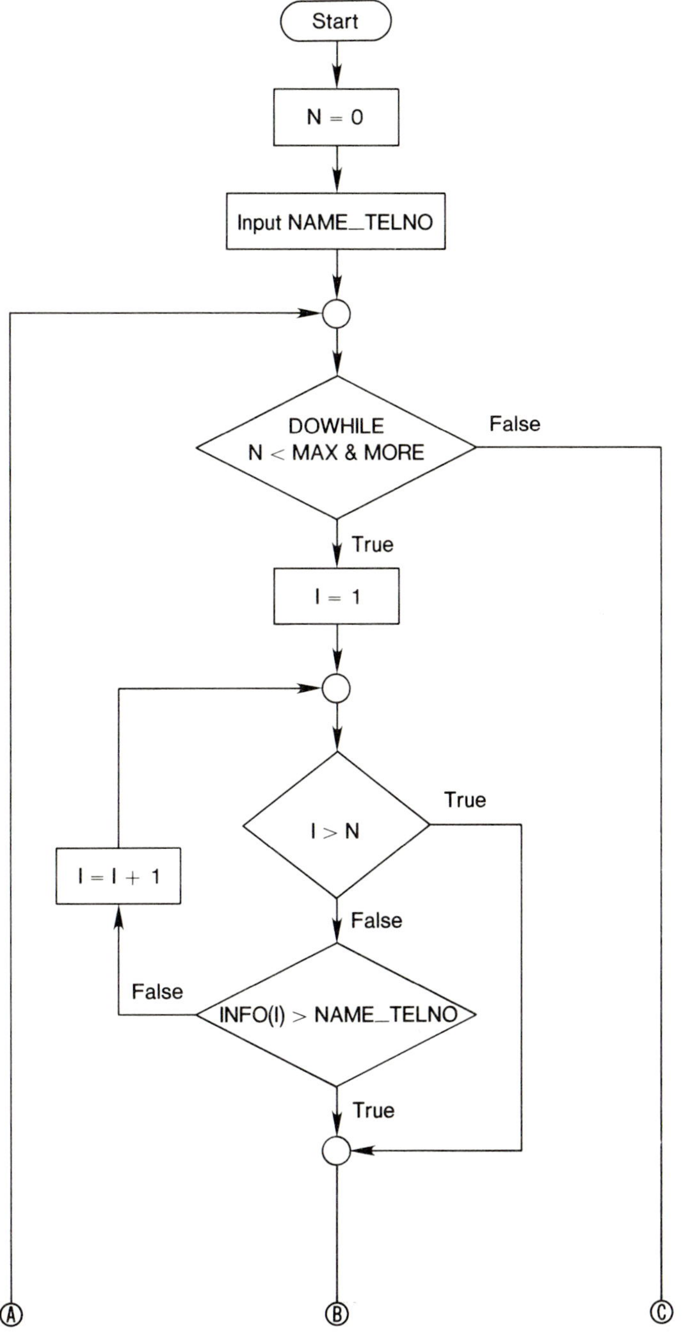

Figure 7–1

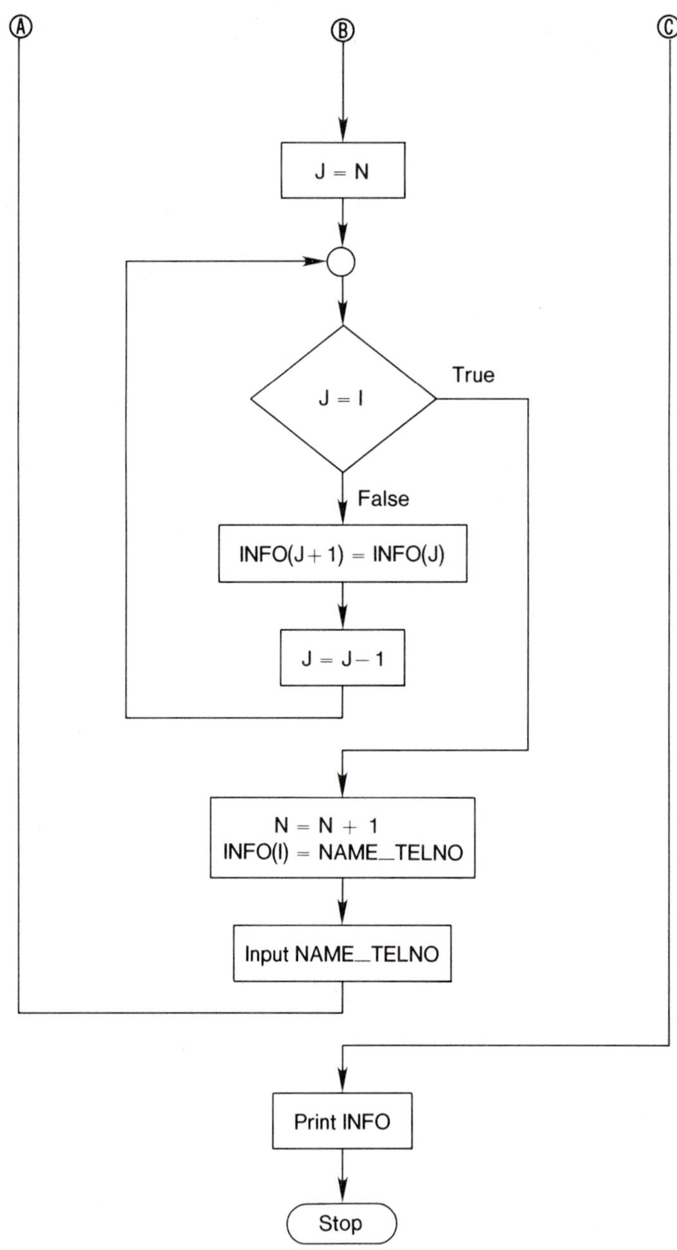

Figure 7–1 *continued*

```
SORT: PROC OPTIONS(MAIN);
/*****************************************************************/
/*                                                               */
/* PROGRAM: INSERTION SORT                                       */
/* AUTHOR: C ZIEGLER                                             */
/* VERSION: 7/17/84                                              */
/*                                                               */
/* PROGRAM DESCRIPTION                                           */
```

```
/* --------------------------------------------------------- */
/* THIS PROGRAM PERFORMS AN INSERTION SORT                   */
/*                                                           */
/* INPUT: CHARACTER DATA                                     */
/*                                                           */
/* OUTPUT: SORTED DATA                                       */
/*                                                           */
/*********************************************************** */

DCL INFO(100)   CHAR(30),
    NAME_TELNO  CHAR(30),
    (I,J,N)     FIXED BIN,
    MAX         FIXED BIN INIT(100),
    MORE        BIT(1);
DCL TRUE        BIT(1)    INIT('1'B),
    FALSE       BIT(1)    INIT('0'B);

ON ENDFILE(SYSIN)
  MORE = FALSE;

MORE = TRUE;
N = 0;
GET EDIT (NAME_TELNO) (COL(1),A(30));
DO WHILE (MORE & N < MAX);          /* FOR EACH INPUT VALUE    */
  I = 1;
  DO WHILE (INFO(I) <= NAME_TELNO & I <= N);
    I = I + 1;                      /* FIND POSITION IN LIST   */
  END;
  DO J = N TO I BY -1;              /* MOVE REST OF LIST DOWN */
    INFO(J+1) = INFO(J);
  END;
  INFO(I) = NAME_TELNO;             /* INSERT VALUE            */
  N = N + 1;
  GET EDIT (NAME_TELNO) (COL(1),A(30));
END;
PUT EDIT (INFO) (COL(1),A(30));
END SORT;
```

BUBBLE SORT

The bubble sort is a simple but somewhat inefficient exchange sort, used when the data are already in an array. The basic idea of the bubble sort is to make repeated passes through the array, letting each element "bubble up" to its proper place. This is done by starting at the bottom and comparing adjacent elements, exchanging them if they are in the wrong order. During the first pass, the smallest element works its way to the top. During the second pass, the second smallest element works its way to the second position, and so forth.

There are a number of small improvements that can be made in the basic bubble sort to increase its efficiency. The use of the flag in this example is one of them. The flag is used to indicate whether the elements of the list are already in order. This is the case if a pass through the list does not make any

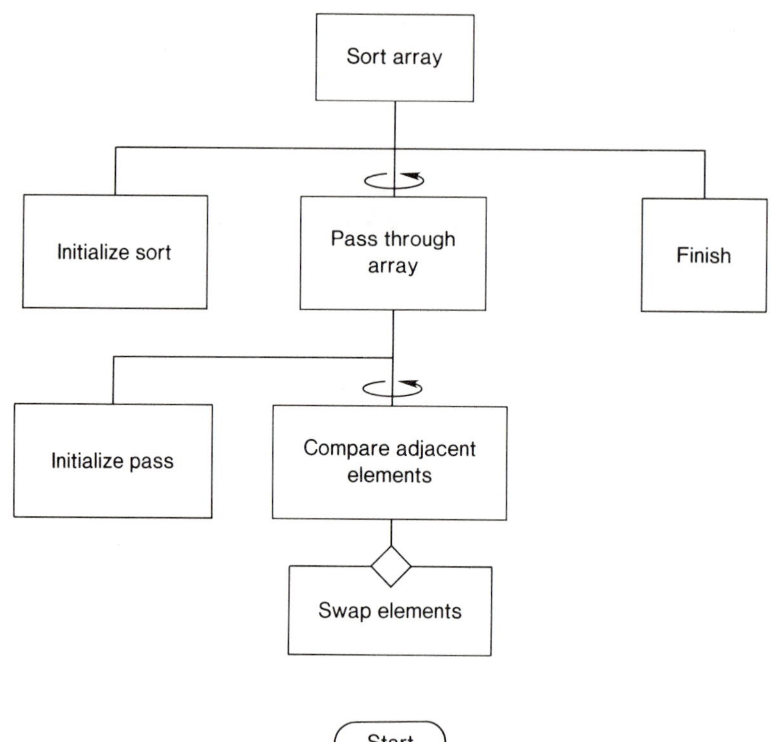

Figure 7–2

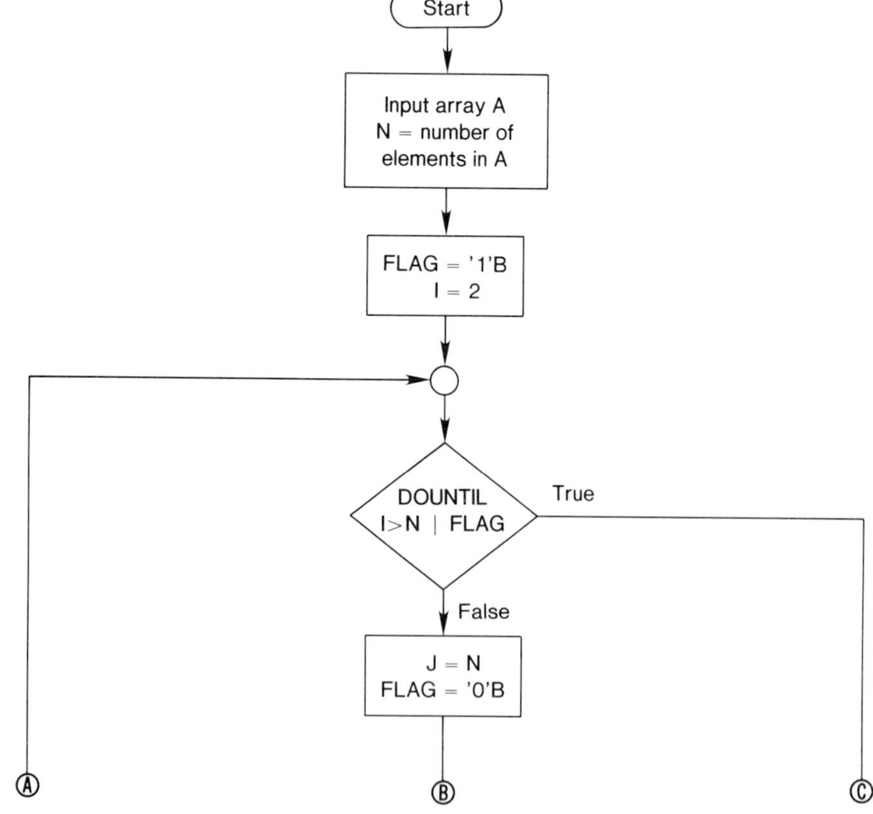

Figure 7–3

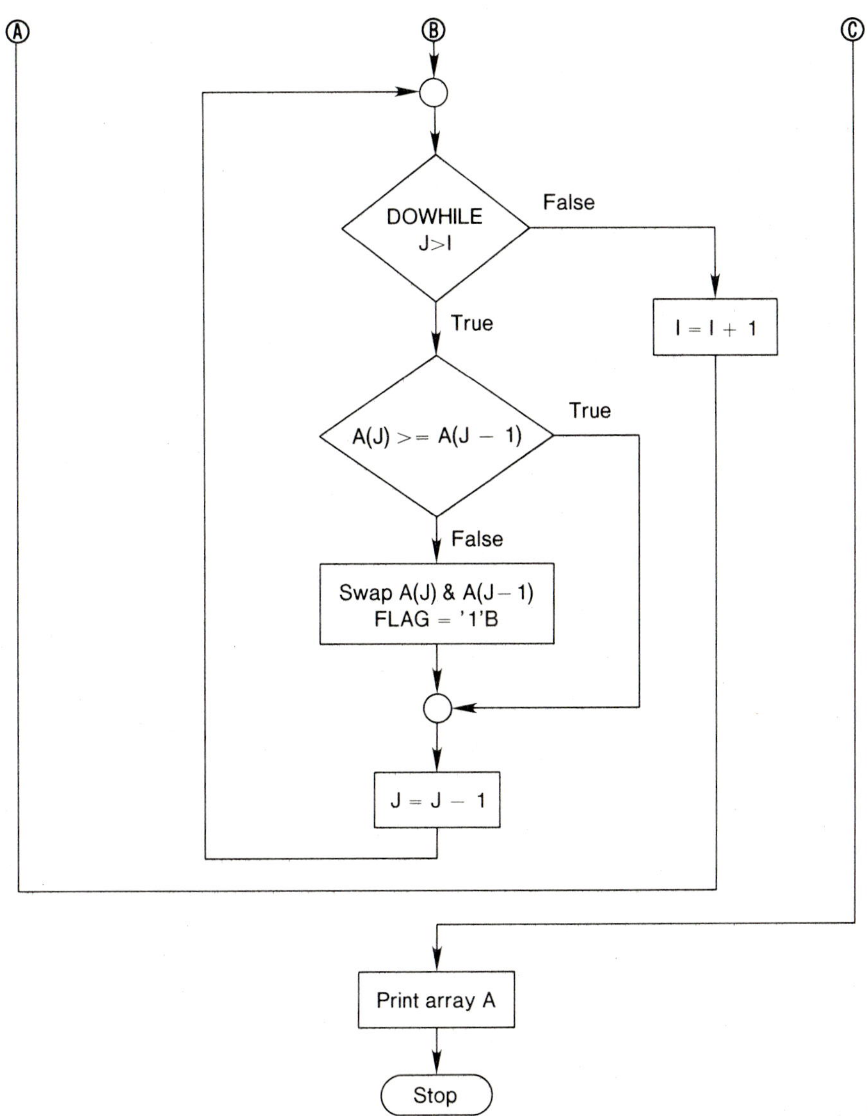

Figure 7–3 *continued*

exchanges. Another optimization is the increase in I every time a pass through the array is completed. Once an element of the array has reached its proper position, it does not need to be compared with other elements again.

A hierarchy chart for this is shown in figure 7–2. The flowchart of the bubble sort is shown in figure 7–3, and the procedure for this sort is shown in the bubble sort program.

```
BUBBLE: PROC OPTIONS(MAIN);
/*****************************************************/
/*                                                   */
/* PROGRAM: BUBBLE SORT                              */
/* AUTHOR: R REDDY                                   */
```

```
/* VERSION: 7/17/84                                                  */
/*                                                                   */
/* PROGRAM DESCRIPTION                                               */
/* ------------------------------------------------------------     */
/* THIS PROGRAM READS DATA THEN PERFORMS BUBBLE SORT                 */
/*                                                                   */
/* INPUT: ARRAY A                                                    */
/*                                                                   */
/* OUTPUT: SORTED DATA                                               */
/*                                                                   */
/*********************************************************************/

DCL A(100)          FIXED DEC(5,0),
    ATEMP           FIXED DEC(5,0),
    (I,J,N)         FIXED BIN,
    OUT OF ORDER    BIT(1);
DCL TRUE            BIT(1)    INIT('1'B),
    FALSE           BIT(1)    INIT('0'B);

 . . .
OUT_OF_ORDER = TRUE;                 /* REPEATEDLY SCAN LIST      */
DO I = 2 TO N WHILE(OUT_OF_ORDER);
  OUT_OF_ORDER = FALSE;
  DO J = N TO I BY -1;               /* FROM BOTTOM TO TOP        */
    IF A(J) < A(J-1)                 /* COMPARING ELEMENTS        */
      THEN
        DO;                          /* SWAP THOSE OUT OF ORDER */
          ATEMP = A(J);
          A(J) = A(J-1);
          A(J-1) = ATEMP;
          OUT_OF_ORDER = TRUE;
        END;
  END;
END;
PUT EDIT (A) (COL(1),F(5,0));
END BUBBLE;
```

7.7.4 Searching

When the location of an element in an array is not known, it can be found only by searching the array. If the element is not there and the array has not been sorted, the whole array must be searched. It is clear that it is more efficient to search if the array has already been sorted. Then it is only necessary to scan the array until the place where the element belongs has been found. The following examples of searching end by printing the position in the array where the item is found, or printing a message if it is not there.

LINEAR SEARCH

The flowchart of figure 7–4 shows a search of an unsorted array. The procedure for this is shown in the linear search program.

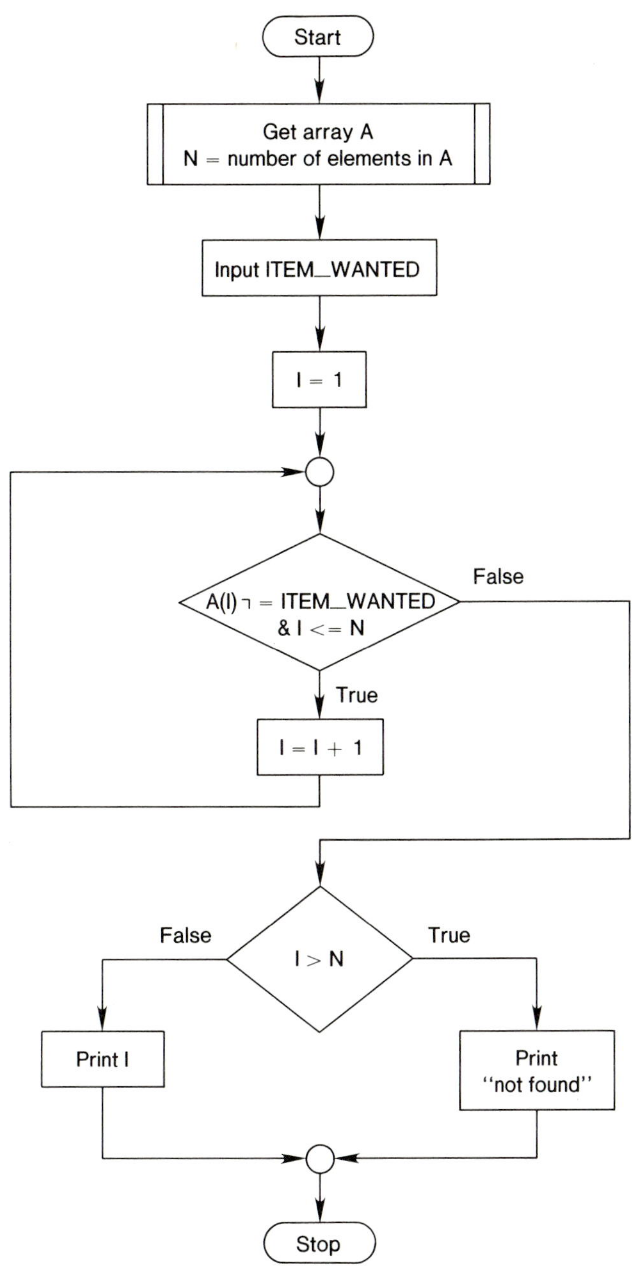

Figure 7-4

```
LINSRCH: PROC OPTIONS(MAIN);
/****************************************************************/
/*                                                              */
/* PROGRAM: LINEAR SEARCH                                       */
/* AUTHOR: C ZIEGLER                                            */
/* VERSION: 7/17/84                                             */
/*                                                              */
/* PROGRAM DESCRIPTION                                          */
```

```
/* ---------------------------------------------------------- */
/* THIS PROGRAM READS DATA THEN SEARCHS FOR IT IN A           */
/* TABLE USING A LINEAR SEARCH                                */
/*                                                            */
/* INPUT: ARRAY A                                             */
/*                                                            */
/* OUTPUT: POSITION OF DATA IN TABLE                          */
/*                                                            */
/**************************************************************/

DCL A(100)       FIXED BIN,
    (I,N)        FIXED BIN;
DCL ITEM_WANTED FIXED BIN;
 . . .
GET LIST (ITEM_WANTED);
I = 1;
DO WHILE (I <=N & A(I) ¬= ITEM_WANTED);
  I = I + 1;
END;
IF I > N
  THEN
    PUT SKIP LIST (ITEM_WANTED,'NOT FOUND');
  ELSE
    PUT SKIP LIST (ITEM_WANTED,'IS AT',I);
END LINSRCH;
```

Notice that an iterative DO was not used. When there are conditions depending on the value of the index variable, DOWHILE and iterative DO should not be combined, because the order of execution in the combination might not be strictly left to right.

A variation on this search is to leave one more position in the array than is needed and store the value wanted in that position before the search begins. This way, the search will always succeed. The location where the value is found can then be used to determine whether the value was already there. This procedure is shown as follows:

```
LINSRCH: PROC OPTIONS(MAIN);
CDL A(101)   FIXED BIN,
    (I,N)    FIXED BIN;
 . . .
GET LIST (ITEM_WANTED);
A(N+1) = ITEM_WANTED;
I = 1;
DO WHILE (A(I) ¬= ITEM_WANTED);
  I = I + 1;
END;
IF I > N
  THEN
    PUT SKIP LIST (ITEM_WANTED,'NOT FOUND');
  ELSE
    PUT SKIP LIST (ITEM_WANTED,'IS AT',I);
END LINSRCH;
```

BINARY SEARCH

When data has been sorted, a linear search can be used, which stops either when the value wanted is found or when the place where it belongs is found. However, this is not the most efficient type of search with sorted data; the binary search is better.

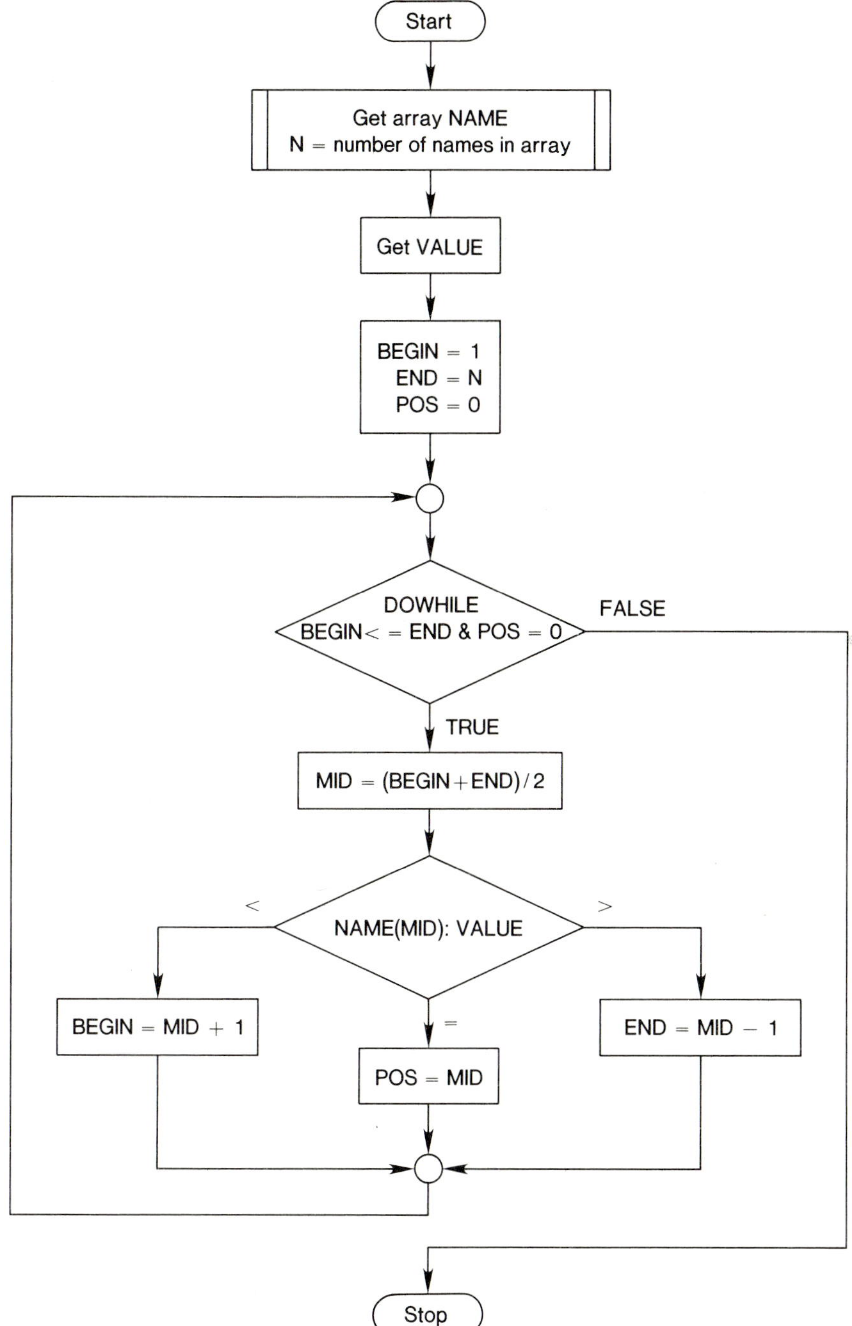

Figure 7–5

This search starts by probing the middle of the array to determine which half the item wanted belongs in; then the search is reduced to that half of the array. The middle of that half is probed to narrow the search to a quarter of the original array. Little by little the search homes in on the place where the value should be. This is similar to the way people look for a name in a telephone book.

The flowchart of figure 7–5 shows a binary search. The procedure is shown in the binary search program.

```
BINSRCH: PROC OPTIONS(MAIN);
/*****************************************************************/
/*                                                               */
/* PROGRAM: BINARY SEARCH                                        */
/* AUTHOR:  R REDDY                                              */
/* VERSION: 7/17/84                                              */
/*                                                               */
/* PROGRAM DESCRIPTION                                           */
/* ------------------------------------------------------------- */
/* THIS PROGRAM READS DATA THEN SEARCHS FOR IT IN A              */
/* TABLE USING A BINARY SEARCH.  THE DATA MUST BE IN             */
/* ALPHABETICAL ORDER.                                           */
/*                                                               */
/* INPUT:  . . .                                                 */
/*                                                               */
/* OUTPUT: POSITION OF DATA IN TABLE                             */
/*                                                               */
/*****************************************************************/

DCL NAME(100)        CHAR(20),
    VALUE            CHAR(20),
    (BEGIN,MID,END)  FIXED BIN,
    N                FIXED BIN,
    POS              FIXED BIN;

 . . .
BEGIN = 1;
END = N;
GET LIST (VALUE);
POS = 0;
DO WHILE(BEGIN <= END & POS = 0);
  MID = (BEGIN + END)/2;            /* FIND MIDDLE POSITION */
  SELECT;
    WHEN(NAME(MID) = VALUE)
      POS = MID;                    /* SAVE POSITION FOUND  */
    WHEN (NAME(MID) > VALUE)
      END = MID - 1;                /* SEARCH FIRST HALF    */
```

```
    OTHERWISE
      BEGIN = MID + 1;            /* SEARCH SECOND HALF    */
  END;
END;
IF POS > 0
  THEN
    PUT SKIP LIST VALUE,'AT',POS);
  ELSE
    PUT SKIP LIST (VALUE,'NOT FOUND');
END BINSRCH;
```

7.7.5 Graphing

The graphing program shown is similar to the example in section 6.3.4 of chapter 6. In that example, a two-dimensional graph was stored as a single bit string. This program is identical, except that the graph is stored as a one-dimensional array of character strings.

```
GRAPH: PROC OPTIONS (MAIN);
/*********************************************************************/
/*                                                                   */
/* PROGRAM: GRAPHING (HORIZONTAL)                                    */
/* AUTHOR: C ZIEGLER                                                 */
/* VERSION: 07/17/84                                                 */
/*                                                                   */
/* PROGRAM DESCRIPTION                                               */
/* --------------------------------------------------------------    */
/* THIS PROGRAM GRAPHS THE FUNCTION                                  */
/*                                                                   */
/*              Y = 100*SIN(0.2*X)/X                                 */
/*                          FOR X = 2 TO 100                         */
/*                                                                   */
/*              NO SCALING IS INCLUDED                               */
/*                                                                   */
/* INPUT: NONE                                                       */
/*                                                                   */
/* OUTPUT: GRAPH OF FUNCTION                                         */
/*                                                                   */
/*********************************************************************/


DCL  LINE(50)         CHAR(120);
DCL  X_MIN            FIXED BIN    INIT(2),
     X_MAX            FIXED BIN    INIT(100);
DCL  BLANK_LINE       CHAR(120)    INIT ((59)' ' || '|'),
     AXIS             CHAR(120)    INIT ((59)'-' || '+'
                                         || (59)'-');
DCL  (X,Y)            FIXED BIN,
     K                FIXED BIN;
```

```
IF X_MIN < -59          /* ADJUST BOUNDS TO FIT SCREEN     */
  THEN
    X_MIN = -59;
IF X_MAX > 60
  THEN
    X_MAX = 60;
LINE = BLANK_LINE;      /* SET UP SCREEN BUFFER            */
LINE(26) = AXIS;
DO X = X_MIN TO X_MAX;
  Y = 100*SIN(0.2*X)/X;               /* CALCULATE Y VALUE */
  IF Y > -25 & Y <= 25                /* CHECK  BOUNDS     */
    THEN
      SUBSTR(LINE(26-Y),60-X,1) = '*';    /* STORE POINT   */
END;
DO K = 1 TO 50;
  PUT EDIT (LINE(K)) (COL(1),A);
END;
END GRAPH;
```

7.7.6 Rate tables

In business applications, tables are commonly used to hold constants needed for computations. This program uses two such tables. The table containing the names of months is being used to print the date in a readable form, and the table containing numbers is being used to look up the price per item for purchase orders when quantity discounts are given. Direct access is used with the table of names; the other table is scanned serially. The program prints bills to be enclosed when the orders are shipped.

```
PRTBILL: PROC OPTIONS (MAIN);
/****************************************************************/
/*                                                              */
/* PROGRAM: PRINT BILL FOR PURCHASE                             */
/* AUTHOR: C ZIEGLER                                            */
/* VERSION: 07/17/84                                            */
/*                                                              */
/* PROGRAM DESCRIPTION                                          */
/* ------------------------------------------------------------ */
/* THIS PROGRAM PRINTS BILLS FOR PURCHASE ORDERS FOR            */
/* AN ITEM HAVING THE FOLLOWING PRICES                          */
/*                                                              */
/*            QUANTITY      PRICE PER ITEM                      */
/*              1-10            59.99                           */
/*             11-50            54.99                           */
/*             51-100           49.99                           */
/*           OVER 100           45.99                           */
/*                                                              */
/* INPUT: CUSTOMER NAME, ADDRESS, QUANTITY ORDERED              */
/*                                                              */
```

```
/* OUTPUT: BILL WITH CUSTOMER NAME, ADDRESS, QUANTITY              */
/*         PRICE PER ITEM, TOTAL PRICE                             */
/*                                                                 */
/*****************************************************************/

DCL  CUST_NAME       CHAR(20),
     CUST_ADDR       CHAR(20),
     CUST_ADDR       CHAR(20),
     QUANTITY        FIXED DEC (3);
DCL  PRICE           FIXED DEC (5,2),
     TOTAL_PRICE     FIXED DEC (7,2);
DCL  MONTH(12)       CHAR(4)   INIT (' JAN',' FEB',' MAR',
                                    ' APR',' MAY','JUNE'
                                    'JULY',' AUG','SEPT'
                                    ' OCT',' NOV',' DEC');
DCL  QUANT_TABLE(4) FIXED BIN INIT (0,10,50,100),
     PRICE_TABLE(4) FIXED DEC (5,2)
                              INIT(59.99,55.99,49.99,45.99);
DCL  MORE_DATA       BIT(1),
     TODAY           CHAR(6),
     YY              CHAR(2) DEF(TODAY),  /* PARTS OF DATE */
     MM              CHAR(2) DEF(TODAY) POS(3),
     DD              CHAR(2) DEF(TODAY) POS(5);
DCL  CURRENT_DATE    CHAR(13),
     K               FIXED BIN;
DCL  DATE            BUILTIN;
DCL  TRUE            BIT(1)    INIT('1'B),
     FALSE           BIT(1)    INIT('0'B);

ON ENDFILE (SYSIN)
  MORE_DATA = FALSE;

MORE_DATA = TRUE;
TODAY = DATE;
CURRENT_DATE = MONTH(MM)  || ' ' || DD || ', 19' || YY;
GET EDIT (CUST_NAME,CUST_ADDR,QUANTITY)
         (COL(1),A(20),A(20),F(3));
DO WHILE (MORE_DATA);
  K = 3;
  DO WHILE (QUANTITY <= QUANT_TABLE(K));
    K = K - 1;
  END;
  PRICE = PRICE_TABLE(K);
  TOTAL_PRICE = QUANTITY * PRICE;
  PUT PAGE;
  PUT EDIT ('HALLCRAFT COMPANY INC.',CURRENT_DATE)
        (LINE(5),COL(35),A,COL(55),A);
  PUT EDIT ('QUANTITY','PRICE PER ITEM','TOTAL PRICE')
        (LINE(7),COL(4),A,COL(15),A,COL(32),A);
  PUT EDIT (QUANTITY,PRICE,TOTAL_PRICE)
        (LINE(9),COL(5),F(5),COL(18),F(5,2),COL(35),F(7,2));
  PUT EDIT ('ORDERED BY',CUST_NAME,CUST_ADDR),
        (LINE(14),COL(40),A,COL(55),A,A);
```

```
     GET EDIT (CUST_NAME,CUST_ADDR,QUANTITY)
              (COL(1),A(20),A(20),F(3));
   END;
   END PRTBILL;
```

7.7.7 Data compression

This program compresses text by removing the trailing blanks from every input record.

```
CLEANUP: PROC OPTIONS (MAIN);
/*******************************************************************/
/*                                                                 */
/* PROGRAM: COMPRESS DATA BY REMOVING TRAILING BLANKS              */
/* AUTHOR: C ZIEGLER                                               */
/* VERSION: 07/17/84                                               */
/*                                                                 */
/* PROGRAM DESCRIPTION                                             */
/* --------------------------------------------------------------- */
/* THIS PROGRAM REMOVES TRAILING BLANKS                            */
/*                                                                 */
/* INPUT: 80 CHARACTER RECORDS                                     */
/*                                                                 */
/* OUTPUT: VARIABLE LENGTH RECORDS WITHOUT TRAILING                */
/*         BLANKS                                                  */
/*                                                                 */
/*******************************************************************/

DCL IN_TEXT   CHAR(80),
    OUT_TEXT  CHAR(80) VAR;
DCL CH(80)    CHAR(1)  DEF(IN_TEXT),
    K         FIXED BIN,
    MORE      BIT(1);
DCL TRUE      BIT(1)    INIT('1'B),
    FALSE     BIT(1)    INIT('0'B);

ON ENDFILE(SYSIN)
  MORE = FALSE;

MORE = TRUE;
GET EDIT (IN_TEXT) (COL(1),A(80));
DO WHILE (MORE);
  K = 80;
  DO UNTIL (CH(K) ¬= ' ');
    K = K - 1;
  END;
  OUT_TEXT = SUBSTR(IN_TEXT,1,K);
   . . .
  GET EDIT(IN_TEXT) (COL(1),A(80));
END;
END CLEANUP;
```

7.8 Summary

Information is kept in arrays when it cannot be processed one value at a time, but must be processed repeatedly. A one-dimensional array is a list of values of the same type. When the array is declared, the maximum possible size is established. If an array is not full, it is necessary to keep a count of the number of elements. An array may be referenced as a whole by using its name. Elements of an array may be referenced by using subscripts. It may be input and output either by name or by using indexing.

Arithmetic performed on numeric arrays is performed on each element of the array. The library functions DIM, LBOUND, and HBOUND return information about an array. The functions SUM, PROD, and POLY perform arithmetic on the elements of an array.

Character and bit arrays may be used to redefine strings so that individual characters or bits can be accessed easily.

7.9 Exercises

1. Write a program to compress text by replacing every embedded group of two or more blanks by a single blank and a count. For example, five blanks are replaced by 'b̸5'.

2. Write a program that reads numbers into an array that holds at most 100 numbers, and calculates the mean and standard deviation of the numbers using the following formulas:

$$\text{Mean } \bar{x} = \frac{1}{n}\sum_{k=1}^{n} x_k$$

$$\text{Standard deviation } s = \sqrt{\frac{\sum_{k=1}^{n} x_k - \bar{x}}{n-1}}$$

3. Write a program that improves the efficiency of the insertion sort discussed in section 7.7.3 by starting at the bottom of the list and moving the values down during the search for the correct position of the input value.

4. Write a program that uses a binary search to search a sorted list of names and prints the corresponding address(es). Assume that the names are not necessarily unique. The declarations are:

```
DCL NAME(100) CHAR(20),
    ADDR(100) CHAR(30);
```

5. Write a program that prints twenty lines of Pascal's triangle. The output should be as follows:

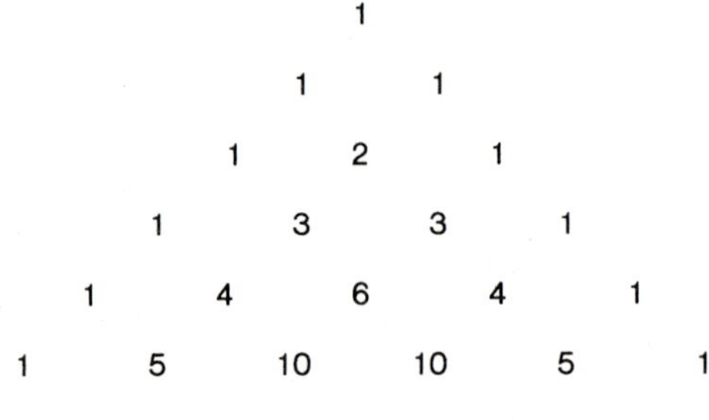

with n numbers being printed from the nth row $(1 < n \leq 20)$. The numbers are generated and stored in a one-dimensional array as follows:

Row 1: $X_1(1) = 1, X_1(K) = 0 \quad 1 < K \leq 20$
Row n: $X_n(1) = 1, X_n(K) = X_{n-1}(K-1) + X_{n-1}(K) \quad n < K \leq 20$

8
Multidimensional arrays

OBJECTIVE: To represent data having several independent variables.

MULTIDIMENSIONAL ARRAYS HAVE MORE than one subscript. They represent tables or other two or more dimensional arrangements of values and are used in many different types of applications. In business applications, for example, tables and charts are two-dimensional, theater seating plans are three-dimensional. In mathematics, arrays of more than one dimension represent matrices. In scientific and engineering applications, two-dimensional arrays are used to model data represented by two variables; three-dimensional arrays model data in three-dimensional space. The data may represent heat conduction, fluid flow, wave propagation through continuous media, vibration analysis, stress analysis in static and dynamic structures, and so forth. The data values can be thought of as arranged in rows and columns, and sheets or planes. Arrays of more than three dimensions represent data with more than three independent variables, or abstract vector spaces.

8.1 Concept of two-dimensional arrays

Two-dimensional arrays represent a two-dimensional arrangement of values, by rows and columns. To access an element requires two subscripts, one for the row and one for the column. In mathematical notation a value in an arrangement of three rows and five columns is referenced as:

A_{ij} where $i = 1, 2, 3$, and $j = 1, 2, 3, 4, 5$

The first subscript, i, indicates which row the value is in; the second subscript, j, indicates which column. The second subscript can also be thought of as indicating the position in the row. A is the name of the array. The elements of the array and their arrangement are as follows:

	Col 1	*Col 2*	*Col 3*	*Col 4*	*Col 5*
Row 1	$a_{1,1}$	$a_{1,2}$	$a_{1,3}$	$a_{1,4}$	$a_{1,5}$
Row 2	$a_{2,1}$	$a_{2,2}$	$a_{2,3}$	$a_{2,4}$	$a_{2,5}$
Row 3	$a_{3,1}$	$a_{3,2}$	$a_{3,3}$	$a_{3,4}$	$a_{3,5}$

Notice that the first subscript of all the elements of row 1 is 1, the first subscript of all the elements of row 2 is 2, and of row 3 is 3. The second subscript of all the elements of column 1 is 1, of column 2 is 2, and so forth. The element $a_{2,3}$ is found at the intersection of row 2 and column 3. It is the third element in row 2 and the second element in column 3. Also notice that as the elements in any single row are read, the first subscript remains constant and the second counts by one. As the elements in any single column are read, the second subscript remains constant and the first counts by one. In this particular example the subscripts represent the position of the element in the array as well as the order of the element with respect to other elements of the same row or column. In PL/I notation, subscripts represent the order of the elements rather than their actual storage location.

8.1.1 Subscripts

In PL/I the general form of reference to an element of a two-dimensional array is

```
A(row,col)
```

An array of three rows and five columns is represented as

A(1,1)	A(1,2)	A(1,3)	A(1,4)	A(1,5)
A(2,1)	A(2,2)	A(2,3)	A(2,4)	A(2,5)
A(3,1)	A(3,2)	A(3,3)	A(3,4)	A(3,5)

The name of the array is A. The array can be accessed either by name, or by accessing the individual elements. Subscripts indicated the element to be accessed.

8.1.2 Declarations

The only difference between declarations of arrays of more than one dimension and declarations of one-dimensional arrays is the number of subscripts. The computer uses the declaration statement to allocate storage for the elements of the array; to set up a descriptor for the array, which contains information about the number of dimensions and the upper and lower bound of each dimension; and to generate a formula used to find any requested element of the array. The general form of the array declaration is:

```
DECLARE array (l1:u1,l2:u2) type_attributes;
```

The array name is followed by the array bounds for each dimension, enclosed in parentheses, and by the type of elements in the array. l_1 and u_1 are the lower and upper bounds, respectively, of the first dimension of the array. l_2 and u_2 are the lower and upper bounds of the second dimension. The lower bounds are optional. If they are not explicitly declared, default lower bounds of 1 are used. If l_1 and l_2 are specified, u_1 must be greater than l_1, and u_2 must be greater than l_2.

8.1.3 Storage organization

Given the array declaration

```
DECLARE A(3,5) FIXED DEC (5);
```

the logical form of the array and the actual storage arrangement are as follows:

A(1,1) A(1,2) A(1,3) A(1,4) A(1,5)

A(2,1) A(2,2) A(2,3) A(2,4) A(2,5)

A(3,1) A(3,2) A(3,3) A(3,4) A(3,5)

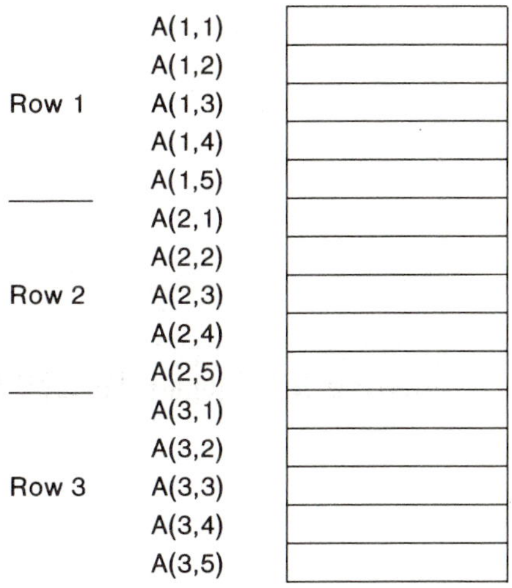

	A(1,1)	
	A(1,2)	
Row 1	A(1,3)	
	A(1,4)	
	A(1,5)	
	A(2,1)	
	A(2,2)	
Row 2	A(2,3)	
	A(2,4)	
	A(2,5)	
	A(3,1)	
	A(3,2)	
Row 3	A(3,3)	
	A(3,4)	
	A(3,5)	

Notice that the array is stored by rows. This is known as *row-major* order. It is the normal order for entering data into a computer or printing it out. The data is in sorted order by pairs of subscripts. Notice also that, reading down the list of subscripts, the second subscript changes most rapidly. It cycles through all its values before the first subscript changes.

The number of storage places needed for a two-dimensional array is a product of the number of elements in each row and the number of elements in each column. In this example, with three rows and five columns, there are fifteen elements.

As with one-dimensional arrays, the lower bound of a dimension does not have to be 1. The storage arrangement of the elements of an array declared as

```
DECLARE B(3:6,5:8) CHAR(10);
```

is as follows:

B(3,5) B(3,6) B(3,7) B(3,8)

B(4,5) B(4,6) B(4,7) B(4,8)

B(5,5) B(5,6) B(5,7) B(5,8)

B(6,5) B(6,6) B(6,7) B(6,8)

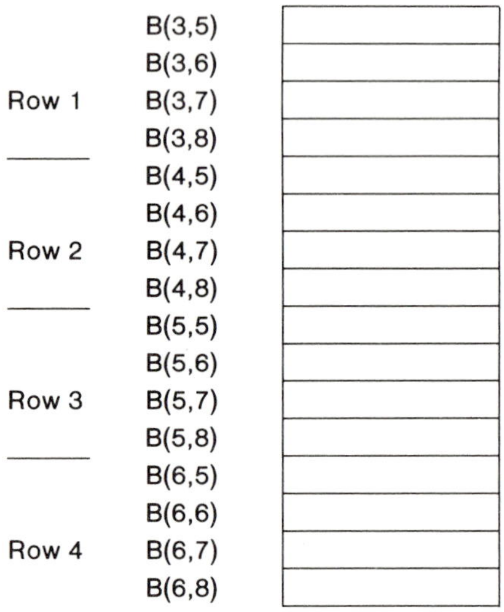

	B(3,5)	
	B(3,6)	
Row 1	B(3,7)	
	B(3,8)	
	B(4,5)	
	B(4,6)	
Row 2	B(4,7)	
	B(4,8)	
	B(5,5)	
	B(5,6)	
Row 3	B(5,7)	
	B(5,8)	
	B(6,5)	
	B(6,6)	
Row 4	B(6,7)	
	B(6,8)	

The first dimension is specified as 3:6 where 3 is the lower bound and 6 is the upper bound. The second dimension is specified as 5:8 where 5 is the lower bound and 8 is the upper bound. Altogether there are four rows, numbered 3 through 6, and four columns, numbered 5 through 8, for a total of sixteen storage places.

Notice that the row index starts at 3 and is incremented by one to 4, 5, and 6. The column index starts at 5 and has the values 5, 6, 7, and 8. The elements are still in order by rows and, within the rows, by columns, with the subscripts indicating that order, but not the locations of the elements.

The array declared as

```
DECLARE C(-2:3,4) FLOAT BIN;
```

is arranged by rows as

C(−2,1)	C(−2,2)	C(−2,3)	C(−2,4)
C(−1,1)	C(−1,2)	C(−1,3)	C(−1,4)
C(0,1)	C(0,2)	C(0,3)	C(0,4)
C(1,1)	C(1,2)	C(1,3)	C(1,4)
C(2,1)	C(2,2)	C(2,3)	C(2,4)
C(3,1)	C(3,2)	C(3,3)	C(3,4)

Data arranged this way can represent measurements taken at four different points from two seconds before some critical event occurred to three seconds afterwards. Negative subscripts should be used only if they represent a situation better than positive subscripts, since conceptually they are more difficult to work with, and therefore more error-prone.

When the exact amount of data is not known, the dimensions of an array can be overspecified and a count kept of the amount of data actually stored in it. However, large two-dimensional arrays use a large amount of memory. It is always advisable to calculate exactly how much space a large array will need.

8.1.4 INITIAL attribute

When the INITIAL attribute is used to initialize the elements of a two-dimensional array, the exact number of values needed must be given. The following declaration initializes an array that contains twelve values.

```
DCL X(3,4) FIXED DEC(5)
           INIT(3,12,-18,4,19,32,-45,17,62,-75,-8,13);
```

Although the values are actually stored in row-major order, conceptually they may be thought of arranged as follows:

	1	2	3	4
1	3	12	−18	4
2	19	32	−45	17
3	62	−75	−8	13

If a numeric array is to be cleared (that is, filled with zeros), an iteration factor can be used in the initialization, as in the following example:

```
DECLARE S(3,5) FIXED BIN INIT((15)0);
```

Since the array has fifteen elements, fifteen zeros are needed. Iteration factors can be used to store different values in different rows of an array, as in the following example:

```
DCL A(4,4) FIXED DEC(5,2)
           INIT((4)12.5,(4)18.3,(4)27.3,(4)65.9);
```

The initialization values are placed in order in the storage area for the array. Since the array is stored in row-major order, the first four values fill the first row. All the elements in the first row have an initial value of 12.5 in this example. The elements in the second row have an initial value of 18.3, the third row 27.3, and the last row 65.9.

If a string array is being initialized, a repetition factor must be used as well as an iteration factor. In the following example, all sixteen elements of the array initially contain 'XBCDƀ'.

```
DECLARE CHSTR(4,4) CHAR(5) INIT((16)(1)'XBCD');
```

The repetition factor of one indicates that only one copy of the quoted string is to be used in each value assigned. Since the character strings have space for five characters, the value is padded with a blank. The iteration factor of sixteen indicates that sixteen of these values are to be assigned to the array.

In the following example, the eight elements of the bit string array are all initialized to '10'B.

```
DECLARE BSTR(2,4) BIT(2) INIT((8)(1)'101'B);
```

Here the bit string is too long. The final '1'B is truncated to obtain the value to store.

In the following example each element receives the value 'ABCABCABC'.

```
DECLARE STR(3,4) CHAR(9) INIT((12)(3)'ABC');
```

The repetition factor is three, indicating that 'ABC' is used three times in each of the twelve values.

In the following example, each of the nine elements receives '10101010'B.

```
DECLARE BSTR(3,3) BIT(8) INIT((9)(4)'10'B);
```

As with single dimension arrays, the asterisk (*) can be used when one or more elements of an array are not to be initialized. The first and third rows of the following array are cleared. The middle row is not initialized.

```
DCL STR(3,10) CHAR(20) INIT((10)(1)' ',(10)*,(10)(1)' ');
```

An array should be initialized if it is being used to store semipermanent data, values that will not change during the execution of the program and will not change from one production run to another. If the values are being changed during execution, initializing an array is misleading to anyone reading or maintaining the program. It is better to explicitly assign the values to the array. If the values are constant within a production run, but change between runs, it is better to read them in as data and store them in the array.

8.1.5 DEFINED option

The same area of storage can be represented by either a one-dimensional array or a two-dimensional array. Occasionally, for ease in manipulating the data, it is desirable to have the same storage area interpreted both as a one-dimensional and as a two-dimensional array. For example, a one-dimensional array of words might be reinterpreted to be a two-dimensional array of letters. This is done through the DEFINED option of a declaration. Once storage has been allocated through a declaration, other declarations may refer to the same storage, as in the following example:

```
DECLARE WORD(10)        CHAR(20),
        LETTER(10,20)   CHAR(1) DEF (WORD);
```

The declaration of WORD causes storage to be allocated and a descriptor set up. The declaration of LETTER does not allocate any storage. Its only effect is to set up a second descriptor, which refers to the same 200 bytes of memory. Those bytes are grouped under the name WORD as ten elements of twenty bytes each. They are grouped under the name LETTER as ten rows of twenty elements, each of which is a single character, as follows:

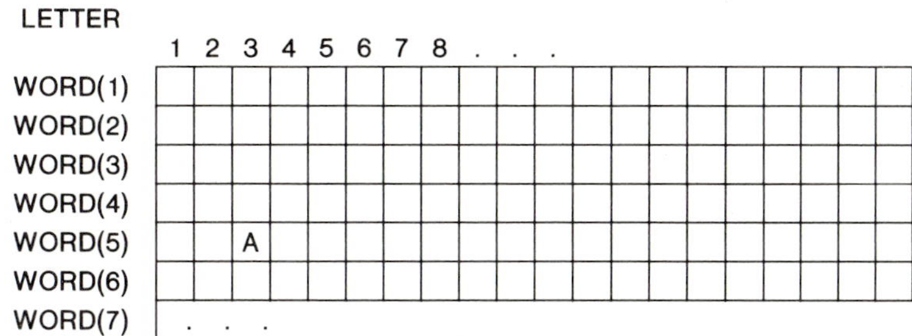

The letter A is the third letter of WORD(5). It is also LETTER(5,3).

When an array is redefined, the underlying element type cannot be changed. FIXED BINARY arrays can be redefined only as FIXED BINARY, CHARACTER as CHARACTER, and so forth. However, the number of dimensions and the bounds of the array may be changed. The following declarations all refer to the same values, in the same underlying order, having the same storage representation, but different logical arrangements:

```
DCL A(3,4)    FIXED DEC(3)
              INIT (1,2,3,4,5,6,7,8,9,10,11,12),
    B(12)     FIXED DEC(3) DEF (A),
    C(2,6)    FIXED DEC(3) DEF (A),
    D(6,2)    FIXED DEC(3) DEF (A),
    E(4,3)    FIXED DEC(3) DEF (A),
    F(1,12)   FIXED DEC(3) DEF (A);
```

These arrays represent the following arrangements:

```
       A              B              C                     D

 1   2   3   4        1     1  2  3   4   5   6         1   2
 5   6   7   8        2     7  6  9  10  11  12         3   4
 9  10  11  12        3                                 5   6
                      4              E                  7   8
                      5                                 9  10
                      6         1    2    3            11  12
                      7         4    5    6
                      8         7    8    9
                      9        10   11   12
                     10
                     11
                     12

                                F

         1  2  3  4  5  6  7  8  9  10  11  12
```

The underlying row-major storage order is the same for all. When an array is redefined, the values and storage are not changed in any way. Only the subscripting access method is changed.

Review questions

1. An element of a two-dimensional array is referenced using ____________ subscripts.

2. The first subscript is the ________________ number and the second subscript is the ________________ number.

3. A two-dimensional array is stored in ________________ order.

4. Show the storage arrangement of the elements of the array

```
DCL A(2,4) FIXED BIN INIT(1,2,3,4,5,6,7,8);
```

5. Fill in the table for the following arrays:
(a) `DCL A(3,4) FIXED DEC(3);`
(b) `DCL B(2:6,3:7) FIXED BIN(15);`
(c) `DCL C-2:4,6) FLOAT BIN;`
(d) `DCL D (-3:-1,-2:4) CHAR(1);`

	Lower bound		Upper bound		Number of elements
	First	Second	First	Second	
(a)					
(b)					
(c)					
(d)					

6. Write a declaration of an array having five rows and seven columns, which uses the INITIAL options to initialize row 1 to one, row 2 to two, and so forth.

7. Write a declaration of a 10 × 20 array of CHAR(20), initialized to blanks.

8.2 Input/output of two-dimensional arrays

With two-dimensional arrays, as with one-dimensional arrays, many different methods of input and output can be used. However, if the data is keyed into the computer in tabular form and the output is to be arranged as a table, edit-directed I/O is the most satisfactory method.

8.2.1 Input of arrays

An array can be input by name or by using indexing. If the input is by name, the values must be in row-major order. If the input uses indexing, value placement is controlled by the sequence of subscripts used. Either nested iterative loops or nested implied loops may be used, or a combination of both.

INPUT USING THE ARRAY NAME

If the data values for a two-dimensional array are arranged by rows in the input medium, input by name is most efficient. The incoming values are stored in consecutive locations in the array until it is full. This is shown in the following example. If the statements are

```
DCL VAL(3,4) FIXED BIN;
GET LIST(VAL);
```

and the data is

```
38 64 28 -35 26  172 14 0 -6 205 70 16
```

then the values are stored as

	VAL(1,1)	38
Row 1	VAL(1,2)	64
	VAL(1,3)	28
	VAL(1,4)	−35
	VAL(2,1)	26
Row 2	VAL(2,2)	172
	VAL(2,3)	14
	VAL(2,4)	0
	VAL(3,1)	−6
Row 3	VAL(3,2)	205
	VAL(3,3)	70
	VAL(3,4)	16

Notice that the computer does not have to use the subscripts to store the data, since it knows where the storage area begins and how many places there are. Input by name should not be used when the exact number of input values is not known, because of the chance of finding an end-of-file.

INPUT USING INDEXING

Since two-dimensional arrays have two subscripts, both of which count through the storage area, iterative DO loops can be used. Each of the following examples inputs the same data into the same storage area, in the same order, as in the example above.

```
DCL VAL(3,4) FIXED BIN,
    J        FIXED BIN;
DO J = 1 TO 4;
  GET LIST(VAL(1,J));
END;
DO J = 1 TO 4;
  GET LIST(VAL(2,J));
END;
DO J = 1 TO 4;
  GET LIST(VAL(3,J));
END;
```

```
DCL VAL(3,4) FIXED BIN,
    (I,J)    FIXED BIN;
DO I = 1 TO 3;
  DO J = 1 TO 4;
    GET LIST (VAL(I,J));
  END;
END;
```

The first of these examples is repetitious, using an iterative DO for each row of the array. The second example uses the variable I to count through the three rows, retaining the J indexing for each row. By nesting one DO loop inside the other, every combination of I and J is used. Since the J loop is inside, the J value varies faster than the I value, cycling through the numbers 1, 2, 3, and 4 for each value of I. This is the correct nesting for data in row-major order.

PROGRAMMING HINT: EFFICIENCY Process two-dimensional arrays in row-major order.

Occasionally it is more convenient to key in data in column-major order if it is already in tabular form. The same data as above, entered by columns, would appear as:

```
38 26 -6 64 172 205 28 14 70 -35 0 16
```

Since it is in column order, the first subscript must vary most rapidly, by being the index of the inner loop. The input statements are as follows:

```
DCL VAL(3,4) FIXED BIN,
    (I,J)    FIXED BIN;

DO J = 1 TO 4;
  DO I = 1 TO 3;
    GET LIST(VAL(I,J));
  END;
END;
```

In any of the above examples, edit-directed I/O statements could be used in place of the list-directed I/O statements. If the data is entered by rows as three separate records,

```
1    6    11   16   21
   38|  64|  28| -35|
   26| 172|  14|   0|
   -6| 205|  70|  16|
```

the PL/I code is

```
DCL VAL(3,4) FIXED BIN,
    (I,J)    FIXED BIN;

DO I = 1 TO 3;
  GET SKIP;
  DO J = 1 TO 4;
    GET EDIT (VAL(I,J)) (F(5));
  END;
END;
```

NESTING ITERATIVE AND IMPLIED LOOPS

The inner loop of the examples above can be written as an implied DO. This is shown in the following example:

```
DCL VAL(3,4) FIXED BIN,
    (I,J)    FIXED BIN;

DO I = 1 TO 3;
   GET EDIT ((VAL(I,J) DO J = 1 TO 4)) (COL(1),(4)F(5));
END;
```

Each time the GET EDIT statement is executed, the four values for a row of the array are read from a record.

NESTED IMPLIED DO LOOPS

The entire input can be handled with nested implied DO loops. Using the same data and placing it in the same array in the same order, the loop on the second subscript must be nested inside the loop on the first subscript, as in the following example:

```
DCL VAL(3,4) FIXED BIN,
    (I,J)    FIXED BIN;

GET EDIT(((VAL(I,J) DO J = 1 TO 4) DO I = 1 TO 3))
        (COL(1),(4)F(5));
```

8.2.2 Output of arrays

Two-dimensional arrays should be printed in table form. Edit-directed output should be used. If the array is full, it may be printed by name or by using indexing. The following examples all produce the same output.

```
DCL ARR(4,6) FIXED DEC(5,2);
 . . .
PUT EDIT (ARR)
        (COL(1),(6)F(7,2));
```

```
DCL ARR(4,6) FIXED DEC(5,2),
    (I,J)    FIXED BIN;
 . . .
DO I = 1 TO 4;
 PUT EDIT ((ARR(I,J) DO J = 1 TO 6))
          (COL(1),(6)F(7,2));
END;
```

```
DCL ARR(4,6) FIXED DEC(5,2),
    (I,J)    FIXED BIN;
 . . .
DO I = 1 TO 4;
  PUT SKIP;
  DO J = 1 TO 6;
    PUT EDIT (ARR(I,J))
          (F(7,2));
  END;
END;
```

```
DCL ARR(4,6) FIXED DEC(5,2),
    (I,J)    FIXED BIN;
 . . .
PUT EDIT (((ARR(I,J) DO J = 1 TO 6)
                     DO I = 1 TO 4))
         (COL(1),(6)F(7,2));
```

```
DCL ARR(4,6) FIXED DEC(5,2),
    I        FIXED BIN;
 . . .
DO I = 1 TO 4;
  PUT EDIT (ARR(I,*))
          (COL(1),(6)F(7,2));
END;
```

```
DCL ARR(4,6) FIXED DEC(5,2),
    I        FIXED BIN;
 . . .
PUT EDIT ((ARR(I,*) DO I = 1 TO 4))
         (COL(1),(6)F(7,2));
```

The output for these program segments has the form

```
ARR(1,1)  ARR(1,2)  ARR(1,3)  ARR(1,4)  ARR(1,5)  ARR(1,6)
ARR(2,1)  ARR(2,2)  ARR(2,3)  ARR(2,4)  ARR(2,5)  ARR(2,6)
ARR(3,1)  ARR(3,2)  ARR(3,3)  ARR(3,4)  ARR(3,5)  ARR(3,6)
ARR(4,1)  ARR(4,2)  ARR(4,3)  ARR(4,4)  ARR(4,5)  ARR(4,6)
```

The format statement used in these examples is set up to print one row at a time, except when nested iterative loops are used. In that case, only one element of the array can be printed at a time. The COL(1) format can be used only at the beginning of the row when an entire row is being printed. When one element at a time is being printed, the PUT SKIP instruction causes the carriage return and line feed.

The last two of the examples above use an asterisk (*) in place of the second subscript. ARR(I,*) refers to an entire row of the array at once. This is known as a *cross-section* or *slice* of the array. The asterisk indicates all values of the second subscript.

```
A(I,*)    is the same as    (A(I,J) DO J = 1 TO 6)
A(*,*)    is the same as    ((A(I,J) DO J = 1 TO 6) DO I = 1 TO 4)
A(*,*)    is also the same as   A   and as   (A(I,*) DO I = 1 TO 4)
A(*,J)    is the same as    (A(I,J) DO I = 1 TO 4)
```

When an asterisk is used in place of the second subscript, the I*th* row is being referenced. When an asterisk is used in place of the first subscript, the J*th* column is being referenced. When asterisks are used in place of both subscripts, the entire array is being referenced in row-major order.

Review questions

1. Write input statements that will read the data into an array

   ```
   DCL ARR(3,4) CHAR(4);
   ```

   for each of the following arrangements of data:
   (a) All the data on one line, row-major order.
   (b) One data value on each line, row-major order.
   (c) Four data values on each line, row-major order.
   (d) Three data values on each line, column-major order.

2. Show the arrangement of the output for the array

```
DCL X(5,3) FIXED BIN
           INIT(1,2,3,4,5,6,7,8,9,...15);
```

```
(a) PUT EDIT (X) (COL(1),F(3));
(b) PUT EDIT (X) (COL(1),(5)F(3));
(c) PUT EDIT (((X(I,J) DO I=1 TO 5) DO J=1 TO 3))
             (COL(1),(5)F(3));
(d) PUT EDIT ((X(K,K) DO K=1 TO 3)) (COL(1),F(3));
```

3. Write a segment of code that will read numbers into an array NUM(10,12) when the numbers are free-format and there may not be 120 of them.

4. How many times will the GET statement be executed in each of the following segments of code?

```
(a) DO I = 1 TO 10;
      DO J = 1 TO 8;
        GET LIST(X(I,J));
      END;
    END;
(b) I = 1;
    DO WHILE (I < 15);
      GET LIST((N(I,J) DO J = 1 TO 12));
      I = I + 1;
    END;
(c) DO I = 1 TO 20 BY 2;
      DO J = I TO 10;
        GET LIST(A(I,J));
      END;
    END;
```

5. How many data values are read into the array

```
DCL A(8,10)
```

by each of the following statements?

```
(a) GET LIST (A(8,*));
(b) GET LIST (A(*,10));
(c) GET LIST (A(*,*));
(d) GET LIST (A(8,10));
```

8.3 Array manipulation

The assignment of a scalar, a cross-section, or another array to a two-dimensional array takes place one element at a time. When one array is assigned to another, they must have the same size and the same upper and lower bounds for each dimension.

8.3.1 Scalar-to-array assignment

A two-dimensional array can be initialized using the array name in an assignment statement such as the following:

```
DECLARE TALLY(8,10) FIXED BIN;
```

```
TALLY = 0;
```

or

```
TALLY(*,*) = 0;
```

The zero is assigned individually to each element of the array TALLY. This can also be done using row or column cross-sections, as in the following examples:

```
DECLARE TALLY(8,10) FIXED BIN,
        I           FIXED BIN;
DO I = 1 TO 8;
  TALLY(I,*) = 0;
END;
```

```
DECLARE TALLY(8,10) FIXED BIN,
        J           FIXED BIN;
DO J = 1 TO 10;
  TALLY(*,J) = 0;
END;
```

Nested iterative DO loops can also be used.

```
DECLARE TALLY(10,10) FIXED BIN,
        (I,J)        FIXED BIN;
DO I = 1 TO 10;
  DO J = 1 TO 10;
    TALLY(I,J) = 0;
  END;
END;
```

8.3.2. Assignment of array cross-sections

In the example

```
DCL ARR_1(3,5)  FLOAT BIN,
    ARR_2(5)    FLOAT BIN,
    I           FIXED BIN;

DO I = 1 TO 3;
  ARR_1(I,*) = ARR_2;
END;
```

the values of ARR_2 can be assigned to each row of ARR_1 because there are as many elements in each row as there are in ARR_2. In the example

```
DCL ARR_A(3,5)  FIXED DEC(7),
    ARR_B(3)    FIXED BIN;
```

```
ARR_B = ARR_A(*,4);
```

the fourth column of ARR_A is assigned to ARR_B. In the process the numbers are converted from fixed decimal to fixed binary. ARR_B has the same number of elements as a single column of ARR_A.

8.3.3 Array-to-array assignment

If two arrays have exactly the same shape and size, one may be assigned to the other by name, or by using cross-sections, or element by element, as in the following examples:

```
DCL A(5,7) CHAR(1),
    B(5,7) CHAR(1);
 . . .
A = B;
```

```
DCL A(5,7) CHAR(1),
    B(5,7) CHAR(1),
    I      FIXED BIN;
 . . .
DO I = 1 TO 5;
  A(I,*) = B(I,*);
END;
```

```
DCL A(5,7) CHAR(1),
    B(5,7) CHAR(1),
    (I,J)  FIXED BIN;
 . . .
DO I = 1 TO 5;
  DO J = 1 TO 7;
    A(I,J) = B(I,J);
  END;
END;
```

Assignment using array name is the most efficient but provides the programmer with the least control. Element by element assignment is the least efficient but the most flexible. If an array is not full, element by element assignment is necessary.

8.3.4 Array arithmetic

All the arithmetic operators are defined for arrays of all dimensions as well as for scalars. The operations are performed element by element. If more than one array is involved, the arrays must have exactly the same shape and size.

A = A + 2;	Two is added to each element of A
A = A – 2;	Two is subtracted from each element of A
A = A* 2;	Each element of A is multiplied by two
A = A / 2;	Each element of A is divided by two
A = A ** 2;	Each element of A is squared

Each operation is the same whether A is a scalar, a one-dimensional array, or a multidimensional array.

If two arrays are added, subtracted, multiplied, or divided, or if one is raised to the power of the other, the effect is the same as if the operations were explicitly performed with corresponding pairs of elements from the two arrays. The following two examples are equivalent:

```
DCL (A,B) (3,5) FIXED DEC(5,2),
    (P,Q,R,S,T) (3,5) FLOAT BIN;
 . . .
P = A + B;
Q = A - B;
R = A * B;
S = A / B;
T = A ** B;
```

```
DCL (A,B) (3,5) FIXED DEC(5,2),
    (P,Q,R,S,T) (3,5) FLOAT BIN,
    (I,J)             FIXED BIN;
 . . .
DO I = 1 TO 3;
  DO J = 1 TO 5;
    P(I,J) = A(I,J) + B(I,J);
    Q(I,J) = A(I,J) - B(I,J);
    R(I,J) = A(I,J) * B(I,J);
    S(I,J) = A(I,J) / B(I,J);
    T(I,J) = A(I,J) ** B(I,J);
  END;
END;
```

Arithmetic may be done with array cross-sections as well as with individual elements. The following example forms the transpose of a matrix:

```
DECLARE MAT(3,5)   FLOAT BIN,
        T_MAT(5,3) FLOAT BIN,

 . . .
T_MAT(*,1) = MAT(1,*);
T_MAT(*,2) = MAT(2,*);
T_MAT(*,3) = MAT(3,*);
```

This has the following effect:

MAT

1	2	3	4	5
6	7	8	9	10
11	12	13	14	15

T_MAT

1	6	11
2	7	12
3	8	13
4	9	14
5	10	15

ROW/COLUMN MANIPULATIONS

Very often in business programs, and occasionally in scientific programs, row or column totals are needed. A technique known as *cross-footing* is used to validate the results of computations when totals are being calculated. Both the row totals and the column totals are calculated; then the sum of the row totals is compared with the sum of the column totals. If they are not the same, there is an error somewhere; for instance, an undetected overflow or underflow. The program in section 8.5.2 shows an example of cross-footing.

Review questions

1. Indicate whether each of the following statements is true or false.

(a) One array can be assigned to another if they have the same number and same type of elements.

(b) Any number of arrays may be added provided their declarations are identical, e.g.,

```
DCL (A,B,C)(5,6) FIXED BIN;
 . . .
A = A + B + C;
```

(c) A row of one array may be assigned to a column of another provided the row has the same number and type of elements as the column.

(d) Using indexing, values may be assigned to array elements in any order.

(e) Indexing must be used if an array is not full.

2. Given the array

```
DCL X(2,3) FIXED DEC(3) INIT (1,2,3,4,5,6);
```

show the results of each of the following assignment statements:

(a) X = X + 5;

(b) X = X − 4;

(c) X = X * 2;
(d) X = X / 2;
(e) X = X ** 2;

***3.** Given the array

```
DCL X(4,4) FIXED BIN INIT((4)(1,2,3,4));
```

does your computer give the same results for the following code segments? If they are not the same, can you explain the difference?

(a)
```
A = A(2,3) * A;
```
(b)
```
DO J = 1 TO 4;
   DO I = 1 TO 4;
      A(I,J) = A(2,3) * A(I,J);
   END;
END;
```

8.4 Multidimensional arrays

Although conceptually more difficult, arrays of dimensions higher than two are no more difficult for the computer to handle than one- or two-dimensional arrays. The allowable operations are the same, the manipulations are identical; only the input and output are different, as the data must be in a readable form, suggestive of the higher dimensions involved.

For example, a three-dimensional array can represent theater seats arranged in rows from front to back on different floors of a theater. It can represent numbers in a table that extends to several pages of a book; on each sheet the numbers are arranged in rows and columns. It can represent points in three-dimensional space.

A four-dimensional array might represent a table in an encyclopedia which extends to several volumes. Or it might represent seats in a number of different theaters housed in the same building.

Mathematically, an element in a three-dimensional array and one in a four-dimensional array are represented as:

$a_{i,j,k}$ and $a_{i,j,k,l}$

In PL/I notation these become:

```
A(I,J,K)     and     A(I,J,K,L)
```

If they represent a physical situation, the subscripts correspond to physical items of decreasing size. For example:

```
TICKET(FLOOR,ROW,SEAT)
NUMBER(SHEET,ROW,ITEM)
TICKET(THEATER,FLOOR,ROW,SEAT)
NUMBER(VOLUME,SHEET,ROW,ITEM)
```

8.4.1 Declarations

The PL/I array declaration

```
DECLARE A(2,3,4) FIXED BIN;
```

corresponds to the following arrangement of elements:

Sheet or plane 1

$$\begin{matrix} a_{1,1,1} & a_{1,1,2} & a_{1,1,3} & a_{1,1,4} \\ a_{1,2,1} & a_{1,2,2} & a_{1,2,3} & a_{1,2,4} \\ a_{1,3,1} & a_{1,3,2} & a_{1,3,3} & a_{1,3,4} \end{matrix}$$

Sheet or plane 2

$$\begin{matrix} a_{2,1,1} & a_{2,1,2} & a_{2,1,3} & a_{2,1,4} \\ a_{2,2,1} & a_{2,2,2} & a_{2,2,3} & a_{2,2,4} \\ a_{2,3,1} & a_{2,3,2} & a_{2,3,3} & a_{2,3,4} \end{matrix}$$

Notice that the first index is constant for a given sheet, the second index is constant for a given row, and the third represents the column. The row and column indices vary on each sheet, but they are the same from one sheet to another. Geometrically a three-dimensional array can be depicted as shown in figure 8–1.

The general form of the declaration of a multidimensional array is

```
DECLARE array(l₁:u₁,l₂:u₂,l₃:u₃, ... ) attributes;
```

where the l's are the lower bounds of each dimension and the u's are the upper bounds. Any lower bounds of 1 may be omitted. The declaration is used to allocate storage for the array and to set up a descriptor. Storage is allocated

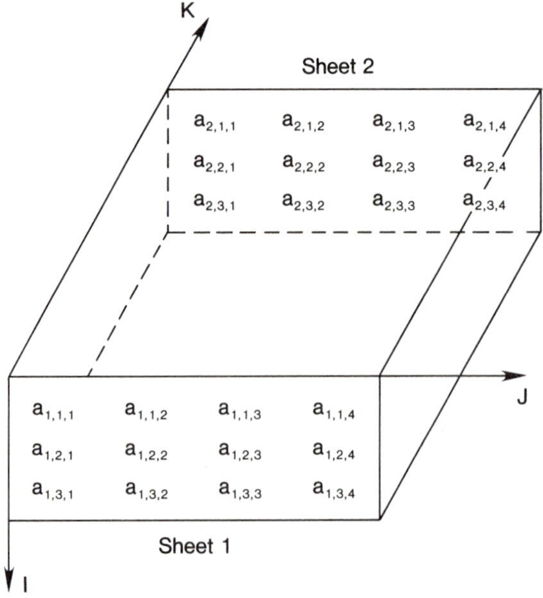

Figure 8–1

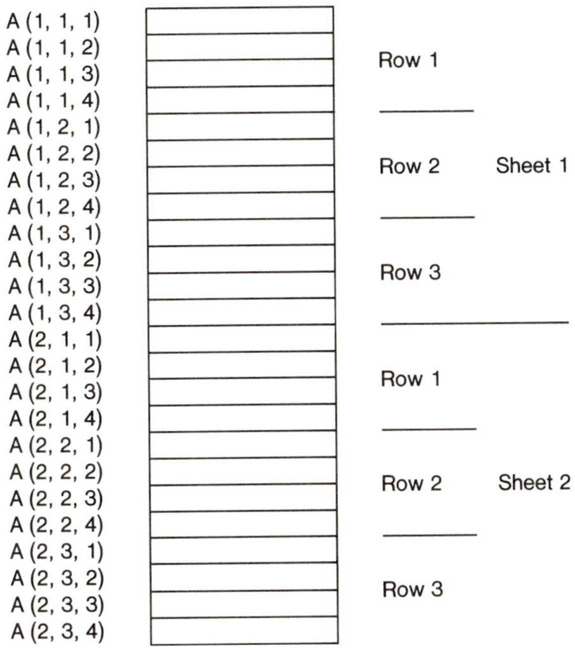

A (1, 1, 1)		
A (1, 1, 2)	Row 1	
A (1, 1, 3)		
A (1, 1, 4)		
A (1, 2, 1)		
A (1, 2, 2)	Row 2	Sheet 1
A (1, 2, 3)		
A (1, 2, 4)		
A (1, 3, 1)		
A (1, 3, 2)	Row 3	
A (1, 3, 3)		
A (1, 3, 4)		
A (2, 1, 1)		
A (2, 1, 2)	Row 1	
A (2, 1, 3)		
A (2, 1, 4)		
A (2, 2, 1)		
A (2, 2, 2)	Row 2	Sheet 2
A (2, 2, 3)		
A (2, 2, 4)		
A (2, 3, 1)		
A (2, 3, 2)	Row 3	
A (2, 3, 3)		
A (2, 3, 4)		

Figure 8–2

in such a way that the last subscript changes the most rapidly, and the first subscript changes the most slowly; that is, the elements are in ascending order of subscripts. This is seen in figure 8–2.

8.4.2 INITIAL attribute

Arrays of three or more dimensions can be initialized by means of an INIT clause. In the following example, each element of the array is given a different initial value.

```
DECLARE A(2,3,4)  FIXED BIN INIT (1,2,3,4,5,6,7,8,9,10,11,
                     12,13,14,15,16,17,18,19,20,21,22,23,24);
```

In the following example all elements are given the same initial value.

```
DECLARE A(2,3,4) FIXED DEC(5,2) INIT((24)0.0);
```

A 2 × 3 × 4 array has twenty-four elements to initialize. If an array is initialized, values must be specified for all elements of the array.

8.4.3 Input/output

As with one- and two-dimensional arrays, input and output may be by name or by using indexing. Using the array name, the order of transmission of the values is the order in which they are stored. Each of the following input examples stores the same values in the same array.

```
DCL ARR(3,5,4) FIXED DEC(5);
GET EDIT (ARR)
          (COL(1),(4)F(5));
```

```
DCL ARR(3,5,4) FIXED DEC(5),
      I          FIXED BIN;
DO I = 1 TO 3;
  GET EDIT (ARR(I,*,*))
           (COL(1),(4)F(5));
END;
```

```
DCL ARR(3,5,4) FIXED DEC(5),
    (I,J)      FIXED BIN;
DO I = 1 TO 3;
  DO J = 1 TO 5;
    GET EDIT (ARR(I,J,*))
             (COL(1),(4)F(5));
  END;
END;
```

```
DCL ARR(3,5,4) FIXED DEC(5),
    (I,J,K)    FIXED BIN;
DO I = 1 TO 3;
  DO J = 1 TO 5;
    DO K = 1 TO 4;
      GET EDIT (ARR(I,J,K))
               (COL(1),F(5));
    END;
  END;
END;
```

```
DCL ARR(3,5,4) FIXED DEC(5),
    (I,J,K)    FIXED BIN;
DO I = 1 TO 3;
  DO J = 1 TO 5;
    GET EDIT ((A(I,J,K)
               DO K = 1 TO 4))
             (COL(1),(4)F(5));
  END;
END;
```

```
DCL ARR(3,5,4) FIXED DEC(5),
    (I,J,K)    FIXED BIN;
DO I = 1 TO 3;
  GET EDIT (((A(I,J,K) DO K = 1 TO 4)
                       DO J = 1 TO 5))
           (COL(1),(4)F(5));
END;
```

```
DCL ARR(3,5,4)  FIXED DEC(5),
    (I,J,K)     FIXED BIN;
GET EDIT ((((A(I,J,K) DO K = 1 TO 4)
                      DO J = 1 TO 5)
                      DO I = 1 TO 3))
          (COL(1),(4)F(5));
```

Notice that the outermost loop controls the first subscript and the innermost loop controls the last subscript in both the iterative and implied DO loops.

Output of a three-dimensional array should include numbering the sheets. Each sheet should be separated from the preceding one by several blank lines. If the entire array will not fit on a single page, each sheet should be placed on a separate page, so that the output is in fact three-dimensional. This is shown in the following examples:

```
DCL P            FIXED BIN INIT ...
    Q            FIXED BIN INIT ...
    R            FIXED BIN INIT ...
BEGIN;
  VAL(P,Q,R) FLOAT BIN,
  (I,J,K)    FIXED BIN;
  . . .
```

```
DCL P            FIXED BIN INIT ...
    Q            FIXED BIN INIT ...
    R            FIXED BIN INIT ...
BEGIN;
  VAL(P,Q,R) FLOAT BIN,
  (I,J,K)    FIXED BIN;
  . . .
```

```
DO I = 1 TO P;
  PUT PAGE EDIT ('SHEET NO',I)
           (COL(1),A,F(3));
  PUT SKIP(2);
  DO J = 1 TO Q;
    PUT EDIT ((VAL(I,J,K)
             DO K = 1 TO R))
          (COL(1),(R)F(8,2));
  END;
 END;
END;
```

```
DO I = 1 TO P;
  PUT PAGE EDIT ('SHEET NO',I)
                 (COL(1),A,F(3));
  PUT SKIP(2);
  PUT EDIT (((VAL(I,J,K)
             DO K = 1 TO R)
               DO J = 1 TO Q))
           (COL(1),(R)F(8,2));
  END;
END;
```

Review questions

1. Select the answer that completes each of the following statements:

(a) The first subscript of a three-dimensional array represents a ________________ (column / plane / row).

(b) The second subscript of a three-dimensional array represents a ________________ (column / plane / row).

(c) The third subscript of a three-dimensional array represents a ________________ (column / plane / row).

(d) When a three-dimensional array is read or printed using the name, the elements of the array are transmitted in the order in which the ________________ (first / second / third) subscript changes most rapidly.

(e) When a three-dimensional array is read or printed using the name, the elements of the array are transmitted in the order in which the ________________ (first / second / third) subscript changes least rapidly.

2. How many elements are there in each of the following arrays?

```
(a) DCL A(2,3,5)           FIXED BIN;
(b) DCL B(-1:3,0:4,2:5) BIT(8);
(c) DCL C(2,3,4,5)         FIXED DEC(6,2);
(d) DCL D(2,2,2,2,2)       FLOAT BIN;
```

3. The array DCL SEAT(2,25,60) CHAR(1) is a map of seats at a theater. Write a segment of code that prints the seating chart with each of the two floors of the theater on a separate page and each of the twenty-five rows of seats on a separate line.

4. Write a segment of code that calculates coordinates of points on the surface $9X^2 + 4Y^2 + Z^2 = 144$ and stores them as the three-dimensional equivalent of a graph, in the array DCL V(12,12,12) BIT(1) where the order of the subscripts is understood as V(X,Y,Z).

8.5 Examples of multidimensional arrays

The following examples include standard mathematical matrix operations and various types of applications of arrays of two or more dimensions.

8.5.1 Matrix operations

Matrix operations as defined in mathematics are only partly the same as the arithmetic operations on arrays.

MATRIX ADDITION

This is the same as array addition.

```
DCL (MAT_A,MAT_B,MAT_C) (8,10) FLOAT BIN;
 . . .
MAT_C = MAT_A + MAT_B;
```

MATRIX SUBTRACTION

This is the same as array subtraction.

```
DCL (MAT_A,MAT_B,MAT_C) (8,10) FLOAT BIN;
 . . .
MAT_C = MAT_A - MAT_B;
```

MATRIX MULTIPLICATION

This is quite different from array multiplication. It involves the multiplication of the row vectors of the first array by the column vectors of the second array and finding the sum of each vector product. If A and B are 2 × 2 matrices,

$$A = \begin{pmatrix} a_{1,1} & a_{1,2} \\ a_{2,1} & a_{2,2} \end{pmatrix} \qquad B = \begin{pmatrix} b_{1,1} & b_{1,2} \\ b_{2,1} & b_{2,2} \end{pmatrix}$$

then their product C is:

$$C = \begin{pmatrix} c_{1,1} = a_{1,1} * b_{1,1} + a_{1,2} * b_{2,1} & c_{1,2} = a_{1,1} * b_{1,2} + a_{1,2} * b_{2,2} \\ c_{2,1} = a_{2,1} * b_{1,1} + a_{2,2} * b_{2,1} & c_{2,2} = a_{2,1} * b_{1,2} + a_{2,2} * b_{2,2} \end{pmatrix}$$

Two methods for doing this in PL/I are shown below. The first uses multiplication of cross-sections and the SUM function. The second shows the underlying calculations.

```
DCL MAT_A (8,10) FLOAT BIN,
    MAT_B (10,6) FLOAT BIN,
    MAT_C (8,6) FLOAT BIN;
 . . .
DO I = 1 TO 8;
  DO J = 1 TO 6;
    MAT_C(I,J) = SUM(MAT_A(I,*) * MAT_B(*,J));
  END;
END;
```

Notice that in this example, the matrices are not the same size. MAT_B must have the same number of rows as MAT_A has columns for the multiplication of the cross-sections to succeed. MAT_C must have the same number of rows at MAT_A and the same number of columns as MAT_B.

The details of this calculation are shown in the matrix multiplication program.

```
MATMULT: PROC OPTIONS (MAIN);
/*****************************************************************/
/*                                                               */
/* PROGRAM: MATRIX MULTIPLICATION                                */
/* AUTHOR: R REDDY                                               */
/* VERSION: 07/17/84                                             */
/*                                                               */
/* PROGRAM DESCRIPTION                                           */
/* ----------------------------------------------------------    */
/* THIS PROGRAM MULTIPLIES TWO MATRICES                          */
/*                                                               */
/* INPUT: MATRICES A AND B                                       */
/*                                                               */
/* OUTPUT: MATRICES A, B, AND C=A*B                              */
/*                                                               */
/*****************************************************************/

DCL MAT_A (8,10)  FLOAT BIN,
    MAT_B (10,6)  FLOAT BIN,
    MAT_C (8,6)   FLOAT BIN,
    SUM           FLOAT BIN,
    (I,J,K)       FIXED BIN;
GET SKIP LIST (MAT_A);
GET SKIP LIST (MAT_B);
DO I = 1 TO 8;
  DO J = 1 TO 6;
    SUM = 0.0;
    DO K = 1 TO 10;
      SUM = SUM + MAT_A(I,K) * MAT_B(K,J);
    END;
    MAT_C(I,J) = SUM;
  END;
END;
PUT SKIP(2) EDIT ('MATRIX A',MAT_A)
                 (COL(60),A,(8)(COL(1),((10)F(12.2))));
PUT SKIP(2) EDIT ('MATRIX B',MAT_B)
                 (COL(60),A(10)(COL(1),((6)F(12.2))));
PUT SKIP(2) EDIT ('MATRIX C',MAT_C)
                 (COL(60),A,(8)(COL(1),((6)F(12.2))));
END MATMULT;
```

Notice the use of the temporary variable SUM. The array element name C(I,J) could have been used instead of SUM, but referencing a scalar variable is more efficient than referencing an element of an array. Notice also that the single line of the program that performs a calculation is executed $8 \times 6 \times 10 = 480$ times. Multiplication of large matrices is inefficient.

Another common matrix operation is the calculation of the sum of the elements along the major diagonal (from upper left to lower right) of a square matrix, the calculation of the sum of the elements above that diagonal, and the sum of the elements below that diagonal. With the matrix

$$\begin{matrix} a_{1,1} & a_{1,2} & a_{1,3} & a_{1,4} \\ a_{2,1} & a_{2,2} & a_{2,3} & a_{2,4} \\ a_{3,1} & a_{3,2} & a_{3,3} & a_{3,4} \\ a_{4,1} & a_{4,2} & a_{4,3} & a_{4,4} \end{matrix}$$

the diagonal sum is

$$a_{1,1}+a_{2,2}+a_{3,3}+a_{4,4}$$

the upper sum is

$$a_{1,2}+a_{1,3}+a_{1,4}+a_{2,3}+a_{2,4}+a_{3,4}$$

and the lower sum is

$$a_{2,1}+a_{3,1}+a_{3,2}+a_{4,1}+a_{4,2}+a_{4,3}$$

The variation of subscripts within the terms of each sum is systematic. These properties of the subscripts may be utilized by indexes to calculate the diagonal, upper, and lower sums for a square matrix of any size, as shown in the following program:

```
DCL N          FIXED BIN   INIT ...
    MAT(N,N)   FLOAT BIN,
    (I,J)      FIXED BIN,
    DSUM       FLOAT BIN,     /* DIAGONAL SUM         */
    USUM       FLOAT BIN,     /* UPPER TRIANGULAR SUM */
    LSUM       FLOAT BIN;     /* LOWER TRIANGULAR SUM */

DSUM,USUM,LSUM=0.0;
DO I=1 TO N;
  DO J=1 TO N;
    SELECT;
      WHEN (I=J)
        DSUM=DSUM+MAT(I,J);
      WHEN (I>J)
        LSUM=LSUM+MAT(I,J);
      WHEN (I<J)
        USUM=USUM+MAT(I,J);
    END;
  END;
END;
```

8.5.2 Sales tax

An example of a three-dimensional table is the Optional State Sales Tax table in a federal income tax instruction booklet. For each of the fifty states, there is a two-dimensional table giving an amount of sales tax for each family size and each income bracket. If the table is stored in a computer, the tax figure could be accessed by using numeric codes for the state and the family size, and looking up the tax bracket. The sales tax lookup program shows a simplified version of this.

```
SALETAX: PROC OPTIONS (MAIN);
/****************************************************************/
/*                                                              */
/* PROGRAM: SALES TAX LOOKUP                                    */
/* AUTHOR:   C ZIEGLER                                          */
/* VERSION: 07/17/84                                            */
/*                                                              */
/* PROGRAM DESCRIPTION                                          */
/* ------------------------------------------------------------ */
/* THIS PROGRAM LOOKS UP THE ESTIMATED AMOUNT OF SALES          */
/* TAX IN THE TAX TABLES                                        */
/*                                                              */
/* INPUT: THE STATE CODE, INCOME, AND FAMILY SIZE               */
/*                                                              */
/* OUTPUT: THE ESTIMATED AMOUNT OF THE TAX                      */
/*                                                              */
/* EXTERNAL: SALES TAX TABLE, TABLE OF STATE ID'S               */
/*                                                              */
/****************************************************************/

DCL SALES_TAX(50,0:16,6) FIXED BIN  EXT,
    STATE_ID(51)         CHAR(2)    EXT;
DCL STATE                CHAR(2),          /* STATE        */
    INCOME               FIXED DEC(10,2),  /* GROSS INCOME */
    FAMILY               FIXED BIN;        /* FAMILY SIZE  */
DCL (I,F,S)              FIXED BIN;

GET LIST (STATE,INCOME,FAMILY);
S = 1;
STATE_ID(51) = STATE;
DO WHILE (STATE_ID(S) ¬= STATE);
  S=S+1;
END;
IF S>50
  THEN
    PUT SKIP LIST ('INVALID STATE CODE');
  ELSE
    DO;
      F=FAMILY;
      IF F>6
        THEN
          F=6;
      I=INCOME;
```

```
      IF I>40000
        THEN
          I=40000;
      I=(I - 8000)/2000;
      PUT SKIP LIST('ESTIMATED SALES TAX',SALES_TAX(S,I,F));
    END;
  END SALETAX;
```

The sales tax table is designed in such a way that the state, income, and family size values can be used to calculate the location of the proper array item. Since the tax figures change from year to year, they should not be built into the program, but read from some input medium. The number of states taxing sales, the size of the income brackets, and the family size considered are less likely to change, so they have been built in.

The entire tax table can be printed out in the familiar form

Optional State Sales Tax Tables

	AL						AK						AZ		
Income	1	2	3	4	5	6	1	2	3	4	5	6	1	2	·
8000	91	113	. . .												
10000															
12000			. . .												

five states to a line, by the following program:

```
DCL SALES_TAX(50,0:16,6) FIXED BIN,
    S_TAX(10,5,0:16,6)   FIXED BIN DEF(SALES_TAX),
    STATE_ID(51)         CHAR(2),
    S_ID(10,5)           CHAR(2), DEF(STATE_ID),
    (I,F,S1,S2)          FIXED BIN;
 . . .
PUT PAGE EDIT('OPTIONAL STATE SALES TAX TABLES') (A);
PUT SKIP(2);
DO S1=1 TO 10;
  PUT EDIT ((S_ID(S1,S2) DO S2=1 TO 5))(COL(10),(5)A(24));
  PUT SKIP(0) EDIT ((132)'_') (A);
  PUT EDIT ('INCOME',((F DO F=1 TO 6) S2=1 TO 5))
              (COL(1),A,COL(10),(30)F(4));
  PUT SKIP(0) EDIT((132)' ') (A);
  DO I=0 TO 16;
    PUT EDIT (2*I+8000,((S_TAX(S1,S2,I,*) DO S2=1 TO 5))
      (COL(1),F(6),COL(10),(30)F(4));
  END;
END;
```

This example includes the redefinition of the three-dimensional table to make it four-dimensional. This is done to simplify the indexing necessary to print the table, five elements per line. When the STATE_ID table is redefined, the alternate name has fewer elements. It is possible to redefine only part of an array, as in this example, but it is never possible to enlarge an array by redefining it.

8.5.3 Magic square

The row totals and column totals of a two-dimensional array can be stored in one-dimensional arrays. This is shown in the example of a magic square, which is a square array of numbers having the same sum for the numbers in each row, each column, and each of the two major diagonals. For example,

```
4   9   2
3   5   7
8   1   6
```

is a magic square of order three.

The magic square program checks whether an array is, in fact, a magic square. By changing the initial value of N, an array of any size can be analyzed.

```
MAGICSQ: PROC OPTIONS (MAIN);
/********************************************************************/
/*                                                                  */
/* PROGRAM: MAGIC SQUARE                                            */
/* AUTHOR:  C ZIEGLER                                               */
/* VERSION: 07/17/84                                                */
/*                                                                  */
/* PROGRAM DESCRIPTION                                              */
/* ------------------------------------------------------------     */
/* THIS PROGRAM CHECKS WHETHER A SQUARE ARRAY IS A MAGIC            */
/* SQUARE                                                           */
/*                                                                  */
/* INPUT: AN NxN SQUARE ARRAY (N=9)                                 */
/*                                                                  */
/* OUTPUT: THE ARRAY, ROW SUMS, COLUMN SUMS, SUMS OF THE            */
/*         MAIN DIAGONALS                                           */
/*                                                                  */
/********************************************************************/

DECLARE N                FIXED BIN   INIT(9);
BEGIN;
  DECLARE VAL(N,N)       FIXED DEC(5,2),
          RSUM(N)        FIXED DEC(6,2),
          CSUM(N)        FIXED DEC(6,2),
          RSUMTOT        FIXED DEC(7,2),
          CSUMTOT        FIXED DEC(7,2),
          DIAG_1         FIXED DEC(6,2),
          DIAG_2         FIXED DEC(6,2),
          (R,C)          FIXED BIN;

  DO R = 1 TO N;
    GET EDIT ((VAL(R,C) DO C = 1 TO N))(COL(1),(N)F(5,2));
  END;
  RSUM = 0;
  CSUM = 0;
```

```
      RSUMTOT = 0;
      CSUMTOT = 0;
      DIAG_1,DIAG_2 = 0;
      DO R = 1 TO N;                  /* FIND ROW AND COLUMN SUMS */
        DO C = 1 TO N;
          RSUM(R) = RSUM(R) + VAL(R,C);
          CSUM(C) = CSUM(C) + VAL(R,C);
        END;
        RSUMTOT = RSUMTOT + RSUM(R);
      END;
      DO C = 1 TO N;                  /* FIND DIAGONAL SUMS       */
        CSUMTOT = CSUMTOT + CSUM(C);
        DIAG_1 = DIAG_1 + VAL(C,C);
        DIAG_2 = DIAG_2 + VAL(10-C,C);
      END;
      IF RSUMTOT ¬= CSUMTOT
        THEN
          PUT SKIP LIST ('CALCULATION ERROR');
      DO R = 1 TO N;
        PUT SKIP EDIT (VAL(R,*),RSUM(R)) (COL(11),(N)F(10),F(10));
      END;
      PUT SKIP(2) EDIT (DIAG_2,CSUM,DIAG_1)
                       (COL(1),F(10),(N)F(10),F(10));
    END;
    END MAGICSQ;
```

Notice that the one-dimensional array RSUM has as many elements as there are rows in the two-dimensional array VAL. The one-dimensional array CSUM has as many elements as there are columns in VAL. The precisions of RSUM and CSUM must be large enough to hold the largest possible row sum and column sum.

8.5.4 Inventory control

Assume that a company owning a chain of ten stores has a centralized inventory control system. A total of 100 different items are sold in the stores. Some stores stock all the items, some only stock a few. Different stores may sell an item at different prices. For inventory purposes a printout is wanted that lists the number in stock and value of each item for each store, and the overall inventory value for each store. It should also list the overall number in stock and value of each item for the chain of stores and the overall inventory value for the chain.

```
INVTORY: PROC OPTIONS (MAIN);
/*********************************************************************/
/*                                                                   */
/* PROGRAM: PRINT CURRENT INVENTORY                                  */
/* AUTHOR:  C ZIEGLER                                                */
/* VERSION: 07/17/84                                                 */
/*                                                                   */
/* PROGRAM DESCRIPTION                                               */
/* -------------------------------------------------------------     */
```

```
/* THIS PROGRAM PRINTS THE CURRENT STATE OF THE INVENTORY FOR     */
/* EACH STORE IN THE CHAIN AND THE INVENTORY TOTALS FOR THE       */
/* CHAIN                                                          */
/*                                                                */
/* INPUT: THE QUANTITY ON HAND AND COST PER ITEM FOR EACH ITEM    */
/*        IN THE GENERAL INVENTORY.  THE INPUT MUST BE ARRANGED   */
/*        IN ORDER BY STORE NUMBER AND SECONDLY BY INVENTORY      */
/*        NUMBER                                                  */
/*                                                                */
/* OUTPUT: A TABLE OF ITEM NUMBER, QUANTITY ON HAND, ITEM COST,   */
/*         TOTAL COST PER ITEM, AND TOTAL VALUE OF INVENTORY FOR  */
/*         EACH STORE.  ALSO FOR EACH ITEM, THE TOTAL QUANTITY,   */
/*         TOTAL COST PER ITEM, AND TOTAL VALUE OF INVENTORY FOR  */
/*         THE CHAIN OF STORES.                                   */
/*                                                                */
/******************************************************************/

DCL M           FIXED BIN       INIT(100),
    N           FIXED BIN       INIT(10);
BEGIN;
  DCL ITEM(M,N)   FIXED DEC(3),
      PRICE(M,N)  FIXED DEC(5,2),
      VALUE(M,N)  FIXED DEC(8,2),
      RITEM(M)    FIXED DEC(4),
      CITEM(N)    FIXED DEC(5),
      TOT_RITEM   FIXED DEC(6),
      TOT_CITEM   FIXED DEC(6),
      RVALUE(M)   FIXED DEC(9,2),
      CVALUE(N)   FIXED DEC(10,2),
      TOT_RVALUE  FIXED DEC(11,2),
      TOT_CVALUE  FIXED DEC(11,2),
      (I,J)       FIXED BIN;

  DO J = 1 TO N;                              /**************************/
    GET EDIT ((ITEM(I,J),PRICE(I,J)           /* GET INVENTORY          */
              DO I = 1 TO M))                 /* INFORMATION            */
           (COL(1),F(3),F(5,2));              /* IN STORE ORDER         */
  END;                                        /**************************/
  RITEM,CITEM = 0;
  RVALUE,CVALUE = 0;
  TOT_RITEM = 0;
  TOT_CITEM = 0;
  TOT_RVALUE = 0;
  TOT_CVALUE = 0;
  VALUE = ITEM * PRICE;                   /* CALCULATE ITEM-PRICE */
  DO J = 1 TO N;
    PUT SKIP(3);                          /* PRINT STORE HEADINGS */
    PUT EDIT ('STORE',J)
           (COL(50),A,F(3));
    PUT SKIP(2);
    PUT EDIT ('ITEM',(I DO I = 1 TO M)) (COL(1),A,COL(6),(M)F(12));
    PUT EDIT ('QUANTITY',ITEM(*,J))
           (COL(1),A,COL(10),(M)F(12);
```

```
      PUT EDIT ('VALUE',VALUE(*,J))
               (COL(1),A,COL(10),(M)F(12,2));
      DO I = 1 TO M;                        /* CALCULATE STORE INVENTORY */
        CITEM(J) = CITEM(J) + ITEM(I,J);
        CVALUE(J) = CVALUE(J) + VALUE(I,J);
      END;
      PUT SKIP;
      PUT EDIT ('TOTAL ITEMS = ',CITEM(J),'TOTAL VALUE = ',CVALUE(J))
               (COL(1),A,F(5),X(5),A,F(11,2));
      RITEM = RITEM + ITEM(*,J);
      RVALUE = RVALUE + VALUE(*,J);
      TOT_CVALUE = TOT_CVALUE + CVALUE(J);/* CALCULATE STORE TOTALS*/
      TOT_CITEM = TOT_CITEM + CITEM(J);
    END;
    PUT PAGE;
    PUT EDIT ('INVENTORY TOTALS') (COL(5),A);
    PUT SKIP(2);
    PUT EDIT ('ITEM','QUANTITY','VALUE')
             (COL(2),A,COL(10),A,COL(22),A);
    DO I = 1 TO M;                          /* CALCULATE CHAIN TOTALS */
      PUT EDIT (I,RITEM(I),RVALUE(I))
               (COL(1),F(6),X(6),F(5),X(5),A,F(11,2));
      TOT_RVALUE = TOT_RVALUE + RVALUE(I);
      TOT_RITEM = TOT_RITEM + RITEM(I);
    END;
    PUT SKIP(5);
    IF TOT_RITEM = TOT_CITEM & TOT_RVALUE = TOT_CVALUE
      THEN
        PUT EDIT ('TOTAL ITEMS', TOT_RITEM,'TOTAL VALUE',TOT_RVALUE)
                 (COL(1),A,F(8),COL(1),A,F(13,2));
      ELSE
        PUT SKIP LIST ('CALCULATION ERROR IN TOTALS ');
  END;
  END INVTORY;
```

If a printout of the inventory tables is needed, the following code will print them.

```
PUT PAGE EDIT('QUANTITY ON HAND') (COL(30),A); /* PRINT ITEM TABLE*/
PUT EDIT ('ITEM',STORES','ITEM TOTAL')
         (COL(1),A,COL(30),A,COL(85),A);
DO I = 1 TO M;
  PUT EDIT (I,ITEM(I,*)),RITEM(I))
           (COL(1),F(5),COL(20),(N)F(8,0),COL(80),F(10,0));
END;
PUT SKIP(2);
PUT EDIT (CITEM,TOT_RITEM) (COL(20),(N)F(8,0),COL(80),F(10,0));

PUT PAGE EDIT('PRICE OF ITEMS') (COL(30),A); /* PRINT PRICE TABLE */
PUT EDIT ('ITEM','STORES') (COL(1),A,COL(30),A);
DO I = 1 TO M;
  PUT EDIT (I,PRICE(I,*)) (COL(1),F(5),COL(20),(N)F(8,0));
END;
```

```
PUT PAGE EDIT('VALUE ON HAND') (COL(30,A));   /* PRINT VALUE TABLE */
PUT EDIT ('ITEM','STORES','ITEM TOTAL')
         (COL(1),A,COL(30),A,COL(85),A);
DO I = 1 TO M;
  PUT EDIT (I,VALUE(I,*),RVALUE(I))
          (COL(1),F(5),COL(20),(N)F(8,0),COL(80),F(10,0));
END;
PUT SKIP(2);
PUT EDIT (CVALUE,TOT_CVALUE) (COL(20),(N)F(8,0),COL(80),F(10,0));
```

Notice that in this program, arrays have been initialized by name, the VALUE table has been calculated by name, and the RITEM and RVALUE arrays have been accumulated by cross-section. Where possible, the arrays have been printed by name or by cross-section. Also, the array bounds 100 and 10 have not been used in the program other than at the beginning of the declarations. If it is necessary to change the sizes of the tables, only the initial values of N and M need be changed. Arrays may be declared using variables for the bounds, provided that the variables have been initialized earlier in the declarations; in this case, in an enclosing block. With some systems the BEGIN...END block is not necessary. Using variable size arrays simplifies program maintenance, but it can be misleading. If the value of N or M is changed during execution of the program, the array bounds are *not* changed.

8.5.5 Saddle point

Assume that a two-dimensional array contains topographical measurements. The array is to be searched to find a "saddle point," a value that is the smallest in its column and largest in its row, or the smallest in its row and the largest in its column. Such a value might represent the location of a mountain pass. The search will stop when a single saddle point is found.

```
SADDLE: PROC OPTIONS (MAIN);
/***************************************************************/
/*                                                             */
/* PROGRAM: SADDLEPOINT                                        */
/* AUTHOR:  C ZIEGLER                                          */
/* VERSION: 07/17/84                                           */
/*                                                             */
/* PROGRAM DESCRIPTION                                         */
/* --------------------------------------------------------    */
/* THIS PROGRAM LOOKS FOR A SADDLE POINT IN AN ARRAY           */
/*                                                             */
/* INPUT: AN N x M ARRAY, N = 10, M = 12                       */
/*                                                             */
/* OUTPUT: THE LOCATION OF A SADDLE POINT IF THERE IS ONE      */
/*                                                             */
/***************************************************************/
```

```
DCL N            FIXED BIN INIT(10),
    M            FIXED BIN INIT(12),
BEGIN;
DCL MEAS(N,M)    FLOAT BIN,
    (I,J,K)      FIXED BIN,
    (MIN,MAX)    FLOAT BIN
    (IMIN,IMAX)  FIXED BIN,
    (JMIN,JMAX)  FIXED BIN;

GET LIST(MEAS);
/***********************************************************/
/* HUNT FOR ROW MIN - COL MAX                              */
/***********************************************************/
IMIN = 0;
IMAX = -1;
DO I = 1 TO N UNTIL (IMIN = IMAX); /* SCAN ARRAY BY ROWS */
  MAX = MEAS(I,1);
  JMAX = 1;
  DO J = 2 TO M;                   /*  FIND MAX OF COL I */
    IF MEAS(I,J) > MAX
      THEN
        DO;
          MAX = MEAS(I,J);
          JMAX = J;                /*  MAX AT (I,JMAX) */
        END;
  END;
  IMAX = I;
  IMIN = 0;
  MIN = MEAS (1,JMAX);
  DO K = 1 TO N;                   /*  FIND MIN OF ROW JMAX */
    IF MEAS(K,JMAX) < MIN
      THEN
        DO;
          MIN = MEAS(K,JMAX);
          IMIN = K;                /*   MIN AT (IMIN, JMAX) */
        END;
  END;
END;
IF IMIN = IMAX
  THEN
    PUT LIST ('SADDLE POINT AT',IMIN,JMAX);
  ELSE
    PUT LIST ('NO ROW MINIMUM - COLUMN MAXIMUM');
END SADDLE;
```

8.6 Summary

Multidimensional arrays can be declared in PL/I with as many as thirty-two subscripts. A two-dimensional array can be interpreted as a table, a seating plan, a representation of two-dimensional space, and so forth. A three-dimensional array can be interpreted as a table covering many pages, a seating plan for an auditorium with more than one floor, a representation of three-dimensional space, and so forth. Arrays of higher dimension cannot easily be given concrete interpretations. Nevertheless, they are useful in the study of data with many independent variables, or multidimensional spaces.

Multidimensional arrays may be of any type. Their manipulation follows the same rules as one-dimensional arrays. Arithmetic and input/output may use the array name or indexing. Arrays are stored and processed most efficiently with the last subscript varying most rapidly and the first subscript varying least rapidly.

Lower-dimensional arrays may be obtained or derived from higher-dimensional arrays as their cross-sections.

8.7 Exercises

1. Write a program to read the coefficients of a set of simultaneous equations having four variables in a two-dimensional array and the constant terms in a one-dimensional array. Print the equations. The output should resemble the following set of equations:

$$5X + 6Y + 7Z + \ \ 3W = 9$$

$$2X + 5Y - 9Z + \ \ 5W = 3$$

$$8X + 9Y + 3Z - 12W = 18$$

$$9X - 8Y + 1Z + \ \ 7W = 12$$

Assume the numbers have at most two digits each.

2. Write a program to read numbers into an array X(15,20) FIXED DEC(4,1). Sort the array so that the first column is in ascending order. Print the sorted array.

3. Write a program that reads data of the form

Cols.		
	1	Year in college (value 1-5)
	2	Sex (Value 'M' or 'F')
	3-22	Name

and counts the number of people who fall in each of the following categories:

		Year				
		1	2	3	4	5
Sex	'M'					
	'F'					

The program should print the tabulation, labeled. From the array, it should calculate the total number of students, the percentage of students of each sex and of each year, and the percentage of students falling in each of the categories. These values should be printed.

4. Write a program that uses an array DCL SEAT(40,6) CHAR(20) as a seating chart for an airplane. The input data is formatted as:

Cols.		
	1-2	Row number of seat wanted
	3	Seat number of seat wanted
	4-23	Name of passenger requesting seat

Process the input by storing the passenger name in the array if the seat requested is not taken, and confirming the reservation. If the seat is already taken, print an appropriate message. The output should include the seating chart of the airplane, showing which passengers have which seats.

5. The Boolean functions AND and OR can be defined as two-dimensional bit arrays, as follows:

AND	0	1
0	0	0
1	0	1

OR	0	1
0	0	1
1	1	1

There are sixteen such Boolean functions of two variables. Write a program that generates all sixteen functions, storing them in the array DCL BOOLEAN(16,2,2) BIT(1) and printing them in the form shown for AND and OR.

6. Write a program that finds a path through a maze. The maze consists of a 10 × 10 array of CHAR(1). The entrance position is MAZE(1,1) and the exit position is MAZE(10,10). As shown in the following sample data, the walls of the maze are Xs and the paths are blanks.

START			X	X				X	X	X	
	X			X	X		X				
	X	X		X			X	X	X		
						X					
		X		X	X	X	X		X	X	
		X		X		X			X		
		X		X				X	X		
		X				X			X		
				X		X	X				
	X	X	X				X		X		STOP

9 Procedures

OBJECTIVE: To build a library of reusable program modules.

THE MAIN CONTROL STRUCTURE in PL/I is the procedure. A *procedure* is a set of code that has a name, can be described functionally, and is written starting with a PROCEDURE (PROC) statement and ending with a matching END statement. It has the general form

```
proc-name: PROC [options];
procedure body consisting of
   declarations
   executable code
   definitions
END proc-name;
```

As we have seen in the previous chapters, a program is a procedure; moreover, it is a main procedure. In this chapter we will consider a variety of different types of secondary procedures: internal and external procedures, recursive procedures, subroutines, functions, and library functions. Besides the built-in library functions which are an integral part of PL/I, user libraries can be set up with procedures developed by programmers either for their own use or for sharing.

A *main procedure* is a procedure executed under the control of the operating system. It is identified by the OPTIONS clause of the PROCEDURE statement. A *subprocedure* is executed by a main procedure or another secondary procedure. Subprocedures can be classified as subroutines or functions.

A *subroutine* is invoked by a CALL statement. For example:

```
CALL SORT(LIST_OF_NAMES);
```

A *function* is invoked through the use of its name. For example, the square root function SQRT, in

```
Y = 2 * SQRT(27);
```

is accessed by using its name in an expression as though it were a variable.

Since subprocedures may be invoked by other subprocedures, it is possible for a procedure to invoke itself either directly or indirectly. Such a procedure is called *recursive*.

External procedures are procedures that are physically located outside the main procedure. The procedure SUB and the library function SQRT in figure 9–1 are external to the main procedure MP.

Internal procedures are procedures that are physically located inside other procedures. The procedure SUB in figure 9–2 is an internal procedure with respect to the main procedure MP.

A procedure should be designed so that it can be described *functionally*. That is, it performs a single specific function that may be described using a

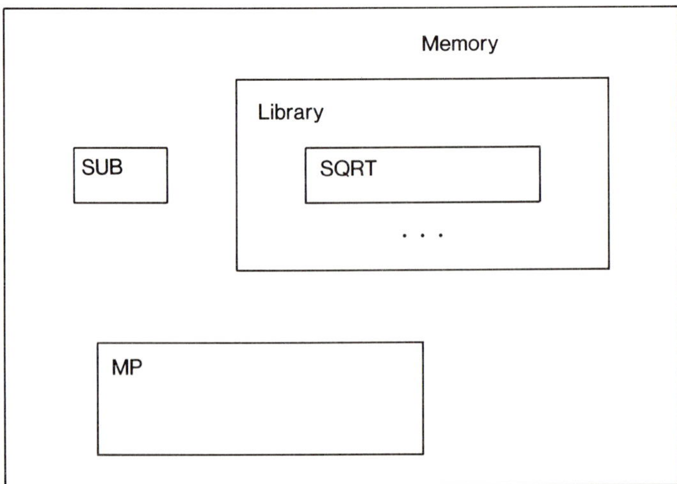

Figure 9–1

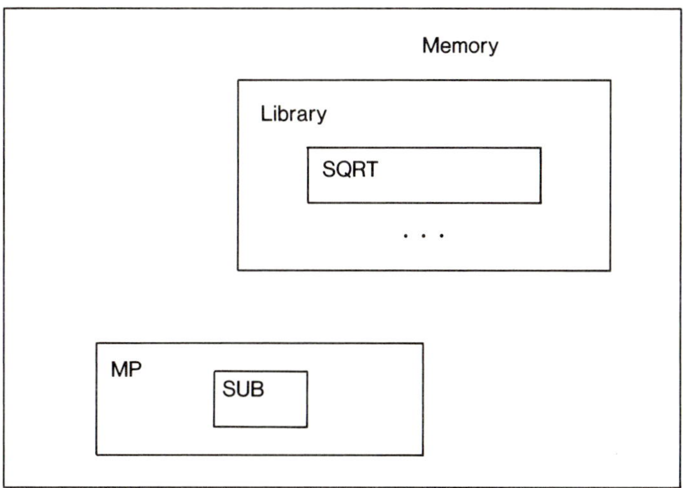

Figure 9–2

single verb. A main procedure is a set of PL/I code which obtains data, processes it, and produces output. These steps may be described as a single function, for example, calculation of the stresses in a bridge. The algorithm for doing this contains steps each of which can also be described functionally. These may be implemented as subprocedures. If a main procedure can be said to solve a complete problem, the subprocedures solve parts of the problem. Instead of writing one long program to solve the problem, it is better to write a procedure for each function to be performed. If a problem is complicated, the subfunctions can be implemented one at a time, with a different procedure being written and tested for each. The procedures, which are written and tested independently, can then be collected and a main procedure written which uses them to solve the problem. Each procedure should contain no more than one or two pages of code.

Defining subfunctions results in a modular program. Most production programs are very long and complex. If a program is developed in a modular fashion, a team of programmers can work on it. Modularity is an important aspect of programming style. Procedures implement program modules. They are the basic building blocks of a program.

PROGRAMMING HINT: MAINTAINABILITY Write modular programs.

If procedures are to be nested, the nesting should follow the lines of a hierarchy chart. Figure 9–3 shows a hierarchy chart implemented as one main procedure, MP, and three subprocedures. The subprocedures may be either internal or external. If the subprocedures are to be internal, they must be physically located in MP. In addition, SUBA may be nested in SUB1 because it performs a subfunction of SUB1. Either arrangement shown in figure 9–4 is correct.

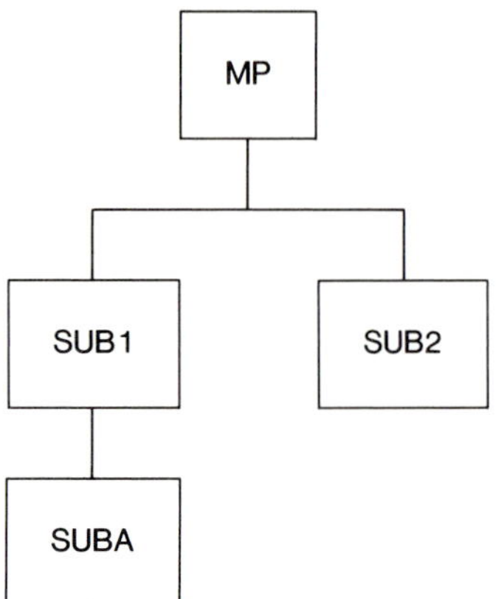

Figure 9–3

Program modules must be able to communicate with each other. They need to access some of the same data and send calculated values to each other. Communication can be accomplished through the environment, through variables available to both procedures, or explicitly by moving values back and forth. For example, the library function DATE used in

```
MP: PROC OPTIONS (MAIN);
  . . .
STR = DATE();
  . . .
END MP;
```

obtains the date from its general environment. It gets it from a location in memory and moves it to the program MP, where it is stored in STR. The movement of the date is shown in figure 9–5.

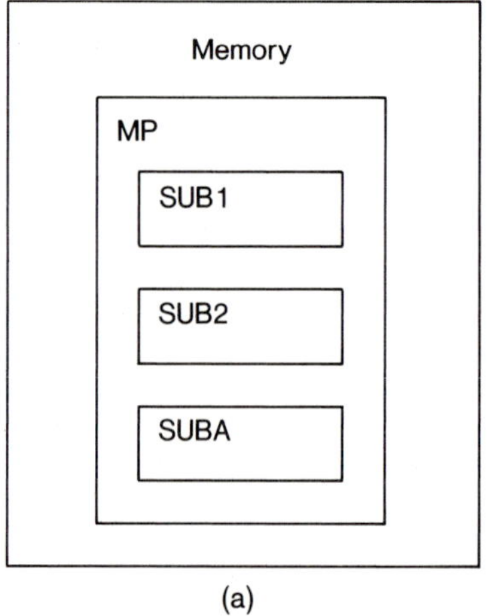

(a)

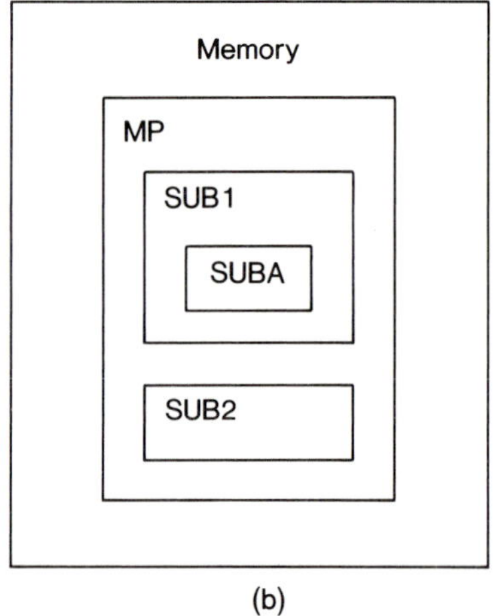

(b)

Figure 9–4

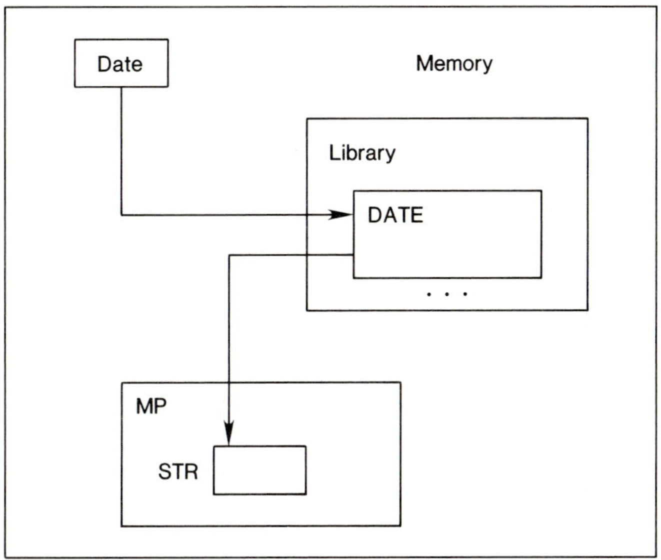

Figure 9–5

The library function SQRT used in

```
MP: PROC OPTIONS (MAIN);
  . . .
Y = 2 * SQRT(X);
  . . .
END MP;
```

obtains the value of X from the main procedure, then returns the value of the square root from the function to the main procedure. This is shown in figure 9–6.

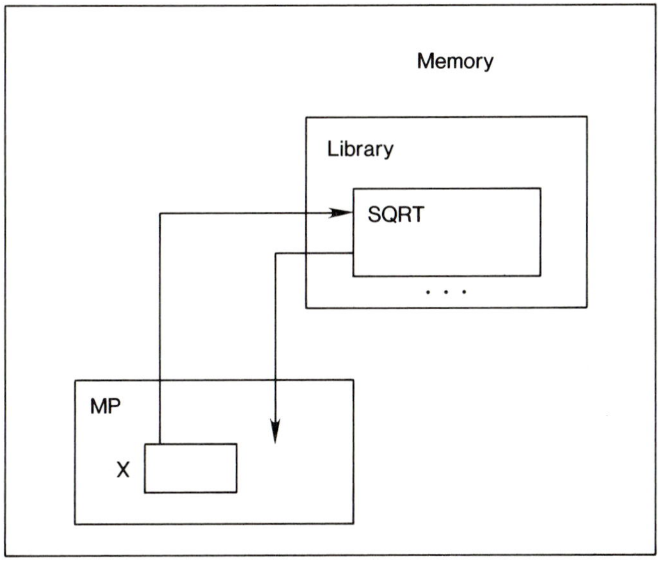

Figure 9–6

The value of the square root is returned into the middle of a calculation rather than to an explicit storage location.

9.1 Modularization

The hierarchy chart of figure 9–7 outlines the process of preparing bills from a rate table in which the unit charge depends on the quantity purchased. This models the way utility and other bills are figured. The rate table is a graduated table which may be generated or entered as data. There are two parts to the chart, building the rate table and preparing the bills.

The main purpose of the program shown in the chart is to prepare bills. Building the rate table is just part of the initialization, but it may be a complex part. Rather than including it in the main line of the processing, it can be made a separate procedure which is used as part of the initialization just as though it were in the library. The module GET_CHARGES appears in two different places in the chart. Since it would be inefficient to repeat the same code two places in the program, a separate procedure can be written which is then invoked in both places.

Each box of the chart contains a brief functional description of its purpose, so each box may appropriately be implemented as a separate procedure.

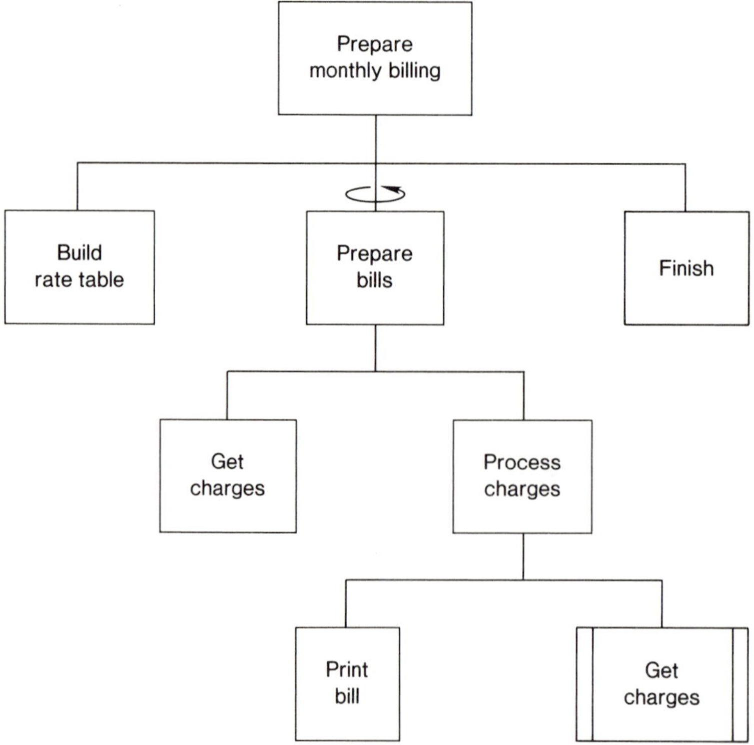

Figure 9–7

However, some inefficiency is involved in using procedures to implement program modules, so they must be used intelligently.

Most comprehensive computer languages support modular programming. It is the basis of most design strategies and implementation styles. Modularization is highly desirable when:

1. A function is needed that is not in the library.
2. There are complex but auxiliary functions to be performed in a program.
3. The same code is needed several places in a program.
4. Several programmers are working on a single program.
5. A program is too complex to be understood as a whole.
6. A program performs several independent functions.
7. Parts of the program can be used in other programs.

Writing a program as a group of procedures makes it easier to implement, debug, understand, and maintain. It is difficult to spread a program out on a desk if it is more than one or two pages long. If procedures are kept small, they can be spread out side by side for reading and debugging. If a program consists of many small procedures, they can be written and tested one at a time. It is far easier to debug several small procedures than one long one. If the procedures of a program are highly independent, changes made to one have a minimal effect on the others.

Review questions

1. A program is a ____________ procedure which may invoke ____________ procedures.

2. The two types of subprocedures in terms of the way they are invoked are ____________ and ____________.

3. The two types of subprocedures in terms of their placement in the program are ____________ and ____________.

4. Indicate whether each of the following statements is true or false.
   (a) The OPTIONS clause is used for a main procedure.
   (b) Every subprocedure must have a PROCEDURE statement.
   (c) A main procedure is always executed under direct control of the operating system.
   (d) A subprocedure is always executed under direct control of a main procedure.

5. Complete each of the following statements.
   (a) A ____________ (function/subroutine) is invoked using a CALL statement.
   (b) A ____________ (function/subroutine) is invoked by using its name in an expression, as though it were a variable.

(c) A procedure physically inside the main procedure is an ________________ (internal/external) procedure.
(d) A procedure physically outside the main procedure is an ________________ (internal/external) procedure.

6. Procedures communicate implicitly through the ________________.

7. Procedures communicate explicitly by ________________.

8. Each box of a hierarchy chart can be implemented as a ____________.

9.2 Subroutines

Procedures in PL/I can be classified based on the way they are invoked by a calling procedure. Function procedures are referenced by name in any context where an expression or variable is appropriate and return a single value to the calling program. Subroutines are referenced by a CALL statement. They may return one value, more than one value, or no values at all. Functions are usually used to calculate a single result. Subroutines are used in other situations. An algorithm can be implemented either as a function or a subroutine. However, sometimes a function procedure is more appropriate and other times a subroutine is more appropriate. The choice of a procedure type is a matter of style and convenience. In general, subroutines should be used when the purpose of the procedure is to perform input or output, calculate several values, rearrange data, or return an array or structure.

9.2.1 Subroutine structure

A subroutine is much like a main procedure. It has a header,

```
SUB: PROC;
```

which is followed by declarations and executable instructions. It ends with a matching END statement,

```
END SUB;
```

which repeats the name of the subprocedure. Unlike the names of main procedures, the names of internal procedures follow the rules for naming variables. It is customary to use meaningful names.

The general form of a subroutine is:

```
sub-name: PROC [(parameter-list)];
body of procedure consisting of
   [declarations]
   executable statements
   [definitions]
END sub-name;
```

A subroutine is invoked by a CALL statement, which has the general form

```
CALL sub-name [(argument-list)];
```

The subroutine is executed when it is called. Its execution terminates when the end of the subroutine is reached or an explicit RETURN is reached. The general form of a RETURN statement for a subroutine is just

```
RETURN;
```

The execution of a subprocedure is like the reading of a footnote or appendix. Attention is shifted to it for a while, then shifted back to the main subject. In the following program segment, a subprocedure is used to exchange the values of two variables.

```
MP: PROC OPTIONS(MAIN);
DCL (X,Y)    FIXED BIN;
 . . .
IF X > Y
  THEN
    CALL SWAP;
PUT SKIP LIST (X,Y);
 . . .
SWAP: PROC;                         /* EXCHANGE X & Y */
DCL TEMP   FIXED BIN;
TEMP = X;
X = Y;
Y = TEMP;
RETURN;
END SWAP;
```

After X and Y are compared, if X is greater than Y, the procedure SWAP is executed. Then the output statement in the main procedure is executed.

9.2.2 Internal subroutines (no arguments)

The code for internal subroutines is physically located between the main procedure header and the main procedure END statement, as in:

```
MP: PROC OPTIONS (MAIN);
 . . .                  /* BODY OF MAIN PROCEDURE */
SUB: PROC;
 . . .                  /* BODY OF SUBPROCEDURE   */
END SUB;
END MP;
```

Other internal procedures may be contained inside an internal subroutine. When this happens, the procedures are said to be nested. The following example shows three levels of nested procedures.

```
MP: PROC OPTIONS (MAIN);
 . . .
SUB1: PROC;              /* SUB1 IS IN MP */
 . . .
```

```
SUB2: PROC;                /* SUB2 IS IN SUB1 */
  . . .
END SUB2;
END SUB1;
END MP;
```

Although PL/I permits it, procedures generally are not nested more than three levels deep, because then the structure of the program becomes unclear and the execution rules become complicated.

Both nested and unnested internal procedures may be used in the same program. For instance:

```
MP: PROC OPTIONS (MAIN);
  . . .
SUB1: PROC;                    /* SUB1 IS IN MP   */
  . . .
SUBA: PROC;                    /* SUBA IS IN SUB1 */
  . . .
END SUBA;

SUBB: PROC;                    /* SUBB IS IN SUB1 */
  . . .
END SUBB;
END SUB1;

SUB2: PROC;                    /* SUB2 IS IN MP   */
  . . .
END SUB2;
END MP;
```

SUBA and SUBB are on the same level since both are nested in SUB1. SUB1 and SUB2 are on the same level since both are nested in the main procedure.

CALL AND RETURN STATEMENTS

A first-level subroutine is invoked by a CALL statement in the main procedure or in other subprocedures. For example:

```
MP: PROC OPTIONS (MAIN);
  . . .
CALL SUB1;
CALL SUB2;
  . . .
SUB1: PROC;                    /* SUB1 IS IN MP */
  . . .
CALL SUB2;
  . . .
END SUB1;
SUB2: PROC;                    /* SUB2 IS IN MP */
  . . .
END SUB2;
END MP;
```

The main procedure calls both SUB1 and SUB2. SUB1 also calls SUB2.

A second-level subroutine is invoked by a CALL statement in the first-level subprocedure enclosing it (and possibly in other subprocedures of the same first-level subprocedure). For example:

```
MP: PROC OPTIONS (MAIN);
 . . .
SUB1: PROC;                      /* SUB1 IS IN MP   */
 . . .
CALL SUBA;
 . . .
SUBA: PROC;                      /* SUBA IS IN SUB1 */
 . . .
CALL SUBB;
 . . .
END SUBA;
SUBB: PROC;                      /* SUBB IS IN SUB1 */
 . . .
END SUBB;
END SUB1;
END MP;
```

The first-level subroutine SUB1 calls the second-level subroutine SUBA, which is internal to SUB1. The second-level subroutine SUBA calls another second-level subroutine SUBB. Both are internal to SUB1.

The procedure in which the call statement appears is known as the *calling procedure.* The CALL statement has the effect of transferring control from the calling procedure to the called procedure. The execution of the calling procedure is suspended while the called procedure executes, then resumed when the called procedure terminates. While a procedure is executing, its *environment* consists of all the objects it can reference. When control shifts from one procedure to another, the execution environment changes.

When a subroutine is called, control is transferred to the first executable instruction of the subroutine. When control reaches the end of the subroutine or a RETURN statement is encountered, the calling program resumes control, starting at the first executable instruction after the CALL instruction. Figure 9–8 shows how the control passes back and forth between the procedures in the following example:

```
MP: PROC OPTIONS (MAIN);
CALL SUB1;
CALL SUB2;

  SUB1: PROC;
  CALL SUBA;
  CALL SUBB;
  CALL SUB2;

    SUBA: PROC;
    CALL SUBB;
    END SUBA;

    SUBB: PROC;
     . . .
    END SUBB;
```

```
    END SUB1;
    SUB2: PROC;
      . . .
    END SUB2;
END MP;
```

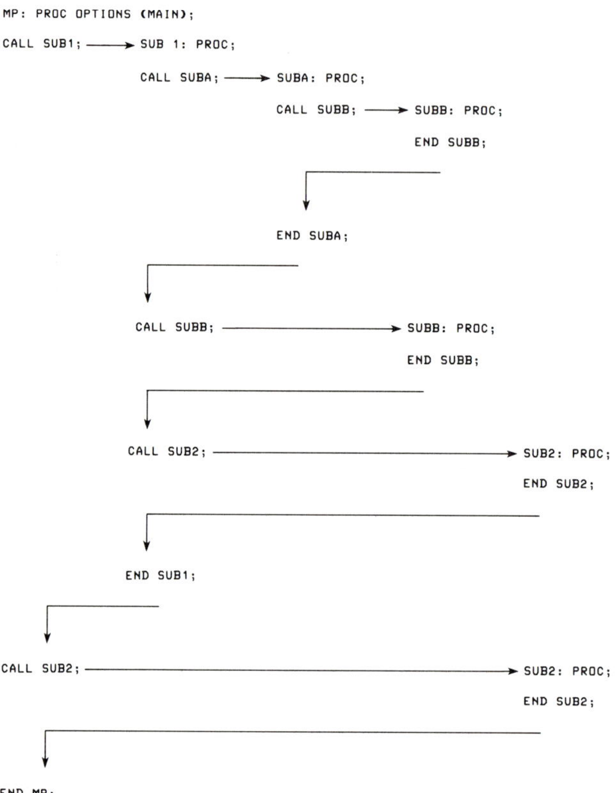
MP: PROC OPTIONS (MAIN);
CALL SUB1;
SUB 1: PROC;
CALL SUBA;
SUBA: PROC;
CALL SUBB;
SUBB: PROC;
END SUBB;
END SUBA;
CALL SUBB;
SUBB: PROC;
END SUBB;
CALL SUB2;
SUB2: PROC;
END SUB2;
END SUB1;
CALL SUB2;
SUB2: PROC;
END SUB2;
END MP;

Figure 9–8

LOCAL/GLOBAL NAMES

A subroutine can reference any variable or internal procedure name that can be referenced in the procedure in which it is nested. These names are called *global* because they belong to a larger environment. The variables declared in a main procedure are global to all the internal procedures. The names of the first-level subprocedures are also global, because they are actually labels in the main procedure. In figure 9–8, the names SUB1 and SUB2 are global; the names SUBA and SUBB are not. The main procedure can call only subroutines with global names. First-level subprocedures such as SUB1 and SUB2 can call any subprocedures with global names and any subprocedures nested immediately inside themselves. SUB1 can call itself, SUB2, SUBA, and SUBB. SUB2 can only call itself and SUB1. It cannot call SUBA and SUBB because they are inside SUB1.

Names immediately inside a procedure are *local* to it, rather than global. SUBA and SUBB are local to SUB1. A subprocedure may call another subprocedure whose name is global to it or whose name is local to it, but not a subprocedure that has a name which is neither local nor global. In the example above, the procedure names are available for calls, as shown in figure 9–9, where vertical lines indicate the accessibility of the procedures. The brackets to the left of the PL/I statements show the extent of the procedures. The lines to the right indicate the ranges of the possible locations of the CALL statements.

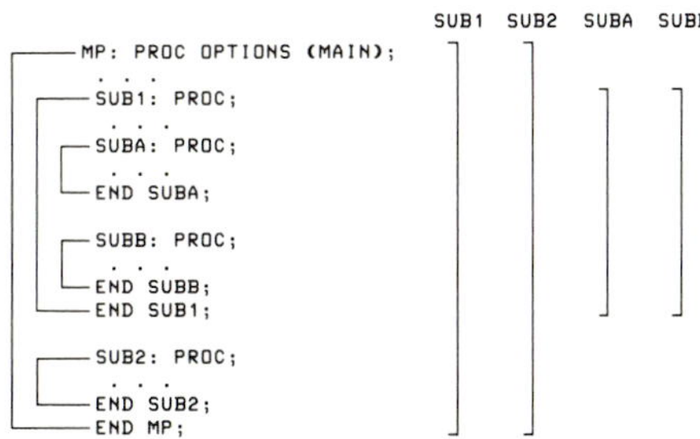

Figure 9–9

Static structure A hierarchy chart can be used to show the static structure of a program; that is, the physical placement of the procedures in the program. Figure 9–10 shows the structure of the example discussed above.

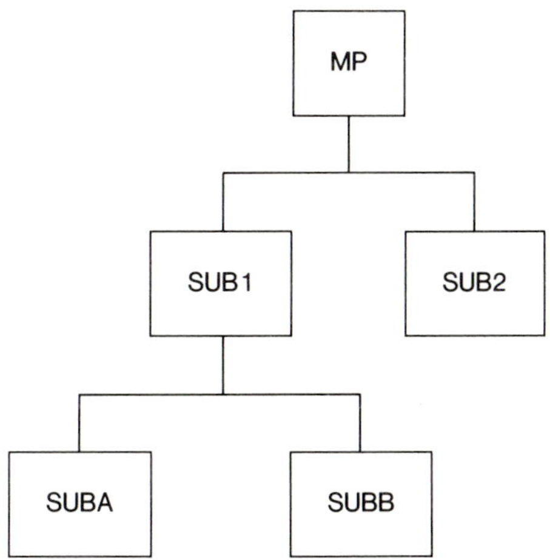

Figure 9–10

Each procedure knows the names of its "children" in the hierarchy chart. A procedure may call any procedure whose name is known to itself or its "ancestors" in the chart. Thus SUBA and SUBB may call SUB1, but SUB2 cannot call SUBA or SUBB.

A subroutine can also call any system procedure or any external procedure for which it has a declaration.

Dynamic structure The placement of CALL statements in a program defines the dynamic structure of the program. This is what is usually represented in hierarchy charts. For example, the program

```
MP: PROC OPTIONS (MAIN);
CALL SUB1;
CALL SUB2;

SUB1: PROC;
CALL SUBA;
CALL SUBB;
CALL SUB2;

SUBA: PROC;
CALL SUBB;
END SUBA;

SUBB: PROC;
END SUBB;
END SUB1;

SUB2: PROC;
END SUB2;
END MP;
```

has the dynamic structure shown in figure 9–11. The main procedure and SUB1 both call SUB2, which has a global name, defined in the main procedure. SUB1 and SUBA both call SUBB, which has a local name, defined in SUB1.

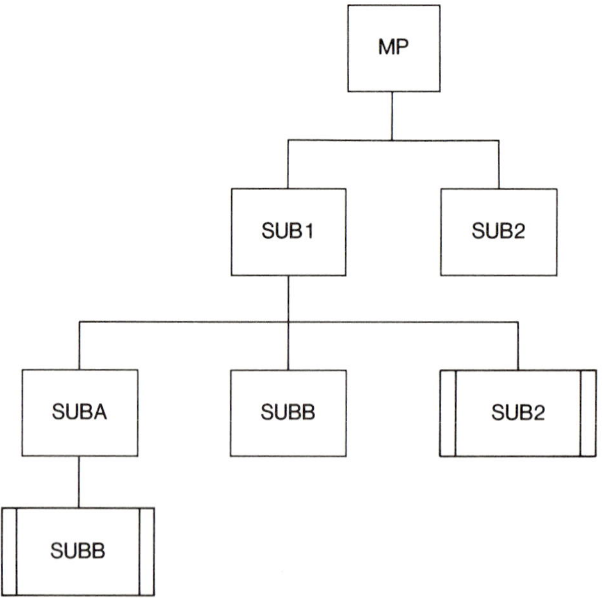

Figure 9–11

Global variables Variables declared in a main procedure are global and may be referenced by any internal subprocedure. For example:

```
MP: PROC OPTIONS (MAIN);
DCL X  FLOAT BIN;
 . . .
SUB: PROC;
 . . .
PUT SKIP LIST (X);               /* X IS GLOBAL */
 . . .
END SUB;
END MP;
```

Variables declared in a subprocedure are local. In this example,

```
MP: PROC OPTIONS (MAIN);
 . . .
SUB: PROC;
DCL (I,J)  FIXED BIN;
 . . .
PUT SKIP LIST (I,J);            /* I AND J ARE LOCAL */
 . . .
END SUB;
END MP;
```

I and J are local variables belonging to SUB and may only be referenced inside it.

The following program segment shows the basic steps in finding the largest value, smallest value, and average value in an array, using internal subroutines and global variables.

```
STAT: PROC OPTIONS (MAIN);
DCL X(20)    FIXED BIN,
    XMAX     FIXED BIN,
    XMIN     FIXED BIN,
    XAVG     FLOAT BIN;
DCL N        FIXED BIN,     /* NUMBER OF VALUES IN ARRAY */
    I        FIXED BIN;
 . . .                      /* GET ARRAY VALUES          */
CALL MAXMIN;
CALL GETAVG;
PUT SKIP LIST (XMAX,XMIN,XAVG);

MAXMIN: PROC;
XMIN = X(1);
XMAX = X(1);
DO I = 2 TO N;
  IF X(I) < XMIN            /* FIND MINIMUM VALUE        */
    THEN
      XMIN = X(I);
  IF X(I) > XMAX            /* FIND MAXIMUM VALUE        */
    THEN
      XMAX = X(I);
END MAXMIN;
```

```
GETAVG: PROC;
DCL XSUM   FIXED BIN;

XSUM = 0;
DO I = 1 TO N;                  /* CALCULATE SUM OF VALUES     */
  XSUM = XSUM + X(I);
END;
XAVG = XSUM/N;                  /* CALCULATE AVERAGE           */
END GETAVG;
END STAT;
```

It would be appropriate to write GETAVG as a function since it calculates a single value.

The two internal procedures MAXMIN and GETAVG are not nested because they are not related to each other in any meaningful way. They are both called by the main procedure. They process the same array X, which is global since it is declared in the main procedure. They share the variables I and N, which are also global. The results of the procedures are placed in the global variables XMAX, XMIN, and XAVG. XSUM is local. It does not need to be global since it is used only in the procedure GETAVG.

9.2.3 External subroutines

It would be useful to place procedures to find a maximum value, minimum value, and average value of an array in a library where they could be shared. In order to do this, the procedures would have to be written as external subroutines. External procedures are not nested in a main program. For example:

```
STAT: PROC OPTIONS (MAIN);
 . . .
END STAT;

MAXMIN: PROC . . .;
 . . .
END MAXMIN;

GETAVG: PROC . . .;
 . . .
END GETAVG;
```

External procedures are compiled separately and stored separately in the computer. On most systems they may be compiled in a single job, but they require separate job steps and are physically separated by JCL (job control) statements, as shown below.

```
      JCL to control compilation goes here
STAT: PROC OPTIONS (MAIN);
 . . .
END STAT;
      JCL to control compilation goes here
```

```
MAXMIN: PROC . . .;
 . . .
END MAXMIN;
       JCL to control compilation goes here
GETAVG: PROC . . .;
 . . .
END GETAVG;
       JCL to control execution goes here
```

The names of external subprocedures must follow the same rules as the names of main procedures. Since the names are external, they must be declared in any program that calls them. The general form of the declaration of the entry point of a subprocedure is:

```
DCL proc-name ENTRY (parameter-type-list);
```

For example:

```
DCL SQRT   ENTRY (FLOAT BIN);
DCL GETAVG ENTRY ((20)FIXED BIN, FLOAT BIN);
```

SUBPROCEDURE COMMUNICATION

Since MAXMIN and GETAVG are external to STAT, they cannot access any variables inside STAT; they can have only local variables. The values they need must be passed as arguments to them, as with system library routines. The array X and variable N provide the input values to both

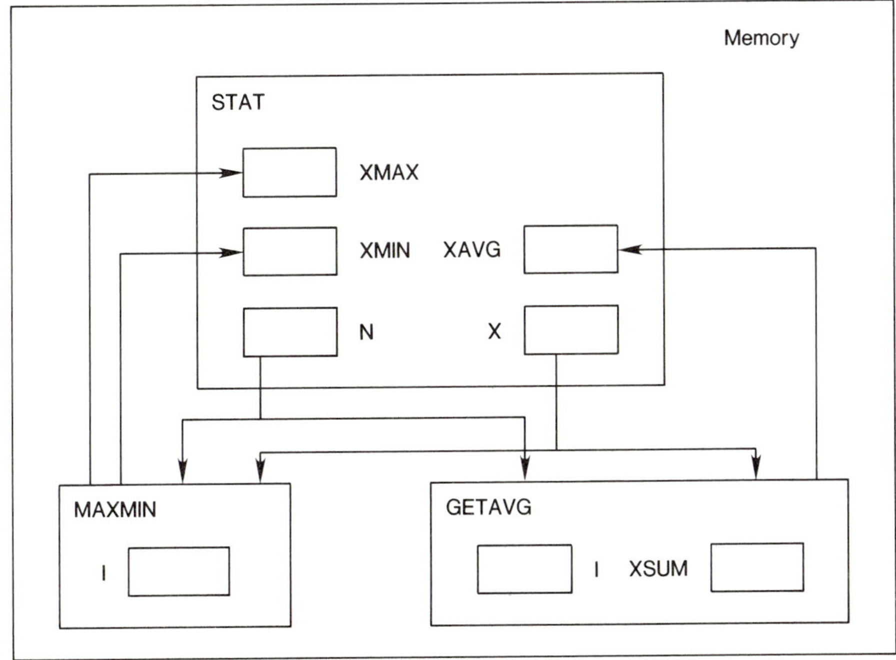

Figure 9–12

procedures. The scalar variables XMIN, XMAX, and XAVG store the output values. Both routines need variables for counting and partial results, but these values do not need to be shared. They can be local. Variable storage can be arranged as shown in Figure 9–12. Here, the values of N and X are passed to the subprocedures as they are needed, but they are not stored in the subprocedures. The values of XMAX, XMIN, and XAVG are passed back from the subprocedures.

The basic PL/I statements needed to pass the variables are the subprocedure headers, the subprocedure entry declarations in the calling procedure, and the CALL statements. These are shown in the following program segment:

```
STAT: PROC OPTIONS (MAIN);
DCL MAXMIN  ENTRY ((20)FIXED BIN, FIXED BIN, FIXED BIN,
                   FIXED BIN),
    GETAVG  ENTRY ((20)FIXED BIN, FIXED BIN, FLOAT BIN);
DCL X(20)   FIXED BIN,
    XMAX    FIXED BIN,
    XMIN    FIXED BIN,
    XAVG    FLOAT BIN;
DCL N       FIXED BIN;   /* NUMBER OF VALUES IN ARRAY */

 . . .                   /* GET ARRAY VALUES          */
CALL MAXMIN(X,N,XMAX,XMIN);
CALL GETAVG(X,N,XAVG);
 . . .
END STAT;

     JCL goes here

MAXMIN: PROC(X,N,XMAX,XMIN);
DCL X(20)   FIXED BIN,
    XMAX    FIXED BIN,
    XMIN    FIXED BIN,
    N       FIXED BIN;
DCL I       FIXED BIN;
 . . .                   /* FIND MAXIMUM AND MINIMUM  */
END MAXMIN;

     JCL goes here

GETAVG: PROC(X,N,XAVG);
DCL X(20)   FIXED BIN,
    XAVG    FLOAT BIN,
    N       FIXED BIN;
DCL I       FIXED BIN,
    XSUM    FIXED BIN;
 . . .                   /* CALCULATE AVERAGE         */
END GETAVG;
```

ARGUMENT/PARAMETER LISTS

The values are passed to a subroutine through an *argument list* in the CALL statement. A matching *parameter list* in the subroutine gives the variable names local to that subroutine. No storage is set aside in the subroutine for the variables named in the parameter list. Local storage is set aside for the other variables. Note that the two variables I are separate. There are actually two places in memory set aside for them, one in each subroutine. Although it is convenient to use the same names for variables in the calling program and the called program, it is not necessary. The routine GETAVG could have the parameter declarations

```
GETAVG: PROC(ARR,L,ARRAVG);
DCL ARR(20) FIXED BIN,
    ARRAVG  FLOAT BIN,
    L       FIXED BIN;
DCL I       FIXED BIN,
    XSUM    FIXED BIN;
 . . .                       /* CALCULATE AVERAGE */
END GETAVG;
```

The argument and parameter lists must match as to order and type of variable. When the types do not match, the computer converts the values when possible. ARR matches X, L matches N, and ARRAVG matches XAVG. The names are assigned as shown in Figure 9–13. Since the names are local to the subprocedure, the assignment is temporary, for the duration of the subprocedure execution only.

The inclusion of the argument types in the ENTRY declarations sets up type-checking routines, which compare the argument types with the parameter types when the subroutines are called. This is a helpful feature, because argument/parameter mismatches are a common type of error. The

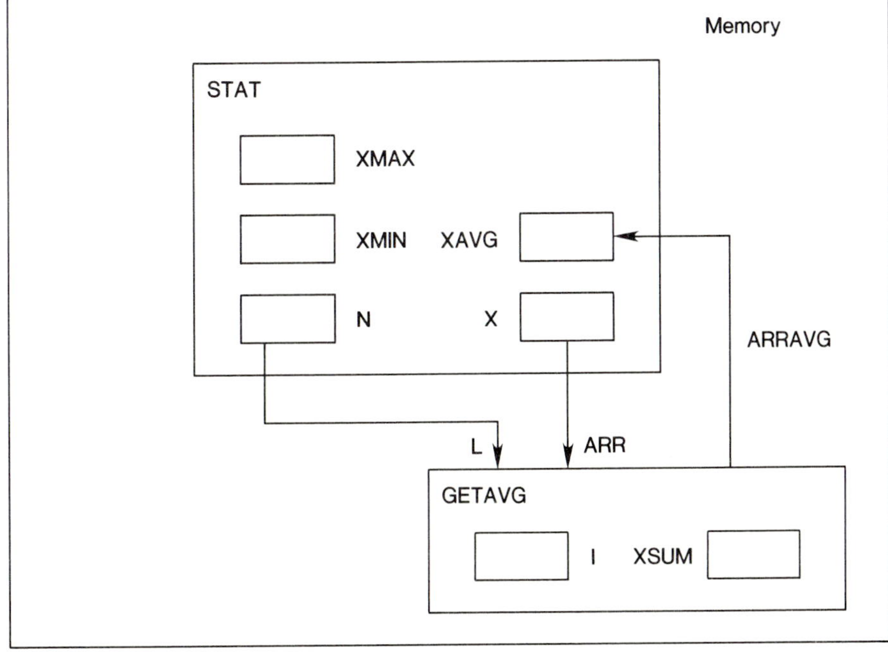

Figure 9–13

complete program to find the maximum, minimum, and average values in the array is given in section 9.8.2.

9.2.4 Internal subroutines (arguments)

Using local variables and parameters rather than global variables aids program maintenance. Since the declarations are close to the statements that use them and each procedure has declarations only for the variables it needs, the procedures are more readable.

PROGRAMMING HINT: MAINTAINABILITY Use local variables when possible.

Argument lists can be used with internal as well as external procedures. With internal procedures the basic steps needed to pass the parameters are the data declarations and argument/parameter lists. With internal subprocedures, the example of figure 9–13 is coded as follows:

```
STAT: PROC OPTIONS (MAIN);
DCL X(20)     FIXED BIN,
    XMAX      FIXED BIN,
    XMIN      FIXED BIN,
    XAVG      FLOAT BIN;
DCL N         FIXED BIN;       /* NUMBER OF VALUES IN ARRAY */

 . . .                         /* GET ARRAY VALUES          */
CALL MAXMIN(X,N,XMAX,XMIN);
CALL GETAVG(X,N,XAVG);
 . . .

MAXMIN: PROC(X,N,XMAX,XMIN);
DCL X(20)     FIXED BIN,
    XMAX      FIXED BIN,
    XMIN      FIXED BIN,
    N         FIXED BIN;
 . . .                         /* FIND MAXIMUM AND MINIMUM */
END MAXMIN;

GETAVG: PROC(X,N,XAVG);
DCL X(20)     FIXED BIN,
    XAVG      FLOAT BIN,
    N         FIXED BIN;
 . . .                         /* CALCULATE AVERAGE         */
END GETAVG;
END STAT;
```

The complete program is given in section 9.8.2. When parameter lists are used with internal procedures, the ENTRY declarations of the subroutine entry points are not used. Otherwise, the programs using internal and external subprocedures are identical except for the physical nesting of the subprocedures.

Review questions

1. Indicate whether each of the following statements is true or false.

(a) A function may return either a scalar value or an array.
(b) Every subprocedure must have a RETURN statement.
(c) A procedure may invoke only other procedures internal to it.
(d) The environment of a procedure consists of the objects that may be referenced within it.

2. Complete each of the following statements:

(a) A call to a subprocedure may include a list of ________________ (arguments / parameters).
(b) A subprocedure header may include a list of ________________ (arguments / parameters).
(c) A hierarchy chart shows the ________________ (dynamic / static) nesting of procedures.
(d) A source code listing shows the ________________ (dynamic / static) nesting of procedures.
(e) Variables declared in a procedure are ________________ (local / global) to it.
(f) Variables declared in the main procedure are ________________ (local / global) to other procedures.

3. Given the following code segment,

```
MP: PROC OPTIONS(MAIN);
A: PROC;
END A;
B: PROC;
DCL D ENTRY;
C: PROC;
END C;
END B;
END MP;
D: PROC;
END D;
```

what procedures can be called by each of the following;

(a) A
(b) B
(c) C
(d) D
(e) MP

4. Given the following code segment,

```
MP: PROC OPTIONS(MAIN);
DCL X;
A: PROC;
DCL Y;
END A;
B: PROC;
DCL Z;
```

```
DCL D ENTRY;
C: PROC;
DCL W;
END C;
END B;
END MP;
D: PROC;
DCL V;
END D;
```

what variables can be referenced by each of the following?
(a) A
(b) B
(c) C
(d) D
(e) MP

5. Write a subprocedure to read twenty floating-point values into an array X(20) and return them to the calling procedure.

6. Write a subprocedure to receive values of a maximum, minimum, and average FIXED BIN(10,2) number from a calling procedure and print them labeled.

9.3 Scope of variables

The three procedures, STAT, MAXMIN, and GETAVG are loaded into memory separately regardless of whether they are external or internal. Each procedure contains an executable code part and a data part. When the main procedure is executing, only the main procedure is in memory, as shown in figure 9–14a. Figure 9–14b shows the memory as it would be while the MAXMIN procedure is executing, and 9–14c shows the situation after

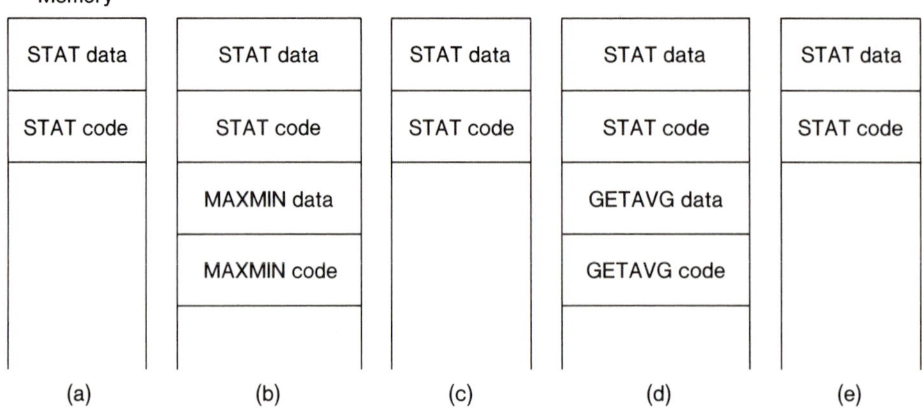

Figure 9–14

control returns to STAT. The MAXMIN routine is no longer in the memory. Figures 9–14d and 9–14e show the memory while GETAVG is executing, and after control again returns to STAT.

Before a procedure begins execution and after it finishes, its code and the data belonging to it are not in the memory. Global variables are available to a subprocedure because they are still in the memory, since execution of the main procedure has been suspended during subprocedure execution, but has not been finished. Variables local to a subprocedure are not available to the main procedure. They are not in the memory while the main procedure is executing, as the subprocedure execution has finished. Any values stored in local variables during subprogram execution are lost.

That part of a program where a variable may be referenced determines the *scope* of the variable. The local variables of subroutine MAXMIN are not available to GETAVG because the subroutines are not in memory at the same time. Similarly, the local variables of GETAVG are not accessible by MAXMIN. As figure 9–14 shows, different subprocedures may replace each other in memory.

The scope of a variable is based on the static nesting of the procedures. A variable is known in the procedure where it is declared and all procedures internal to the one where it is declared except where the variable name has been reused by redeclaring it.

Figure 9–15 shows the scope of the variables in a set of nested procedures. The vertical lines indicate the accessibility of the variables. Because of the duplicate variable names, each is shown subscripted by the name of the procedure where it is declared.

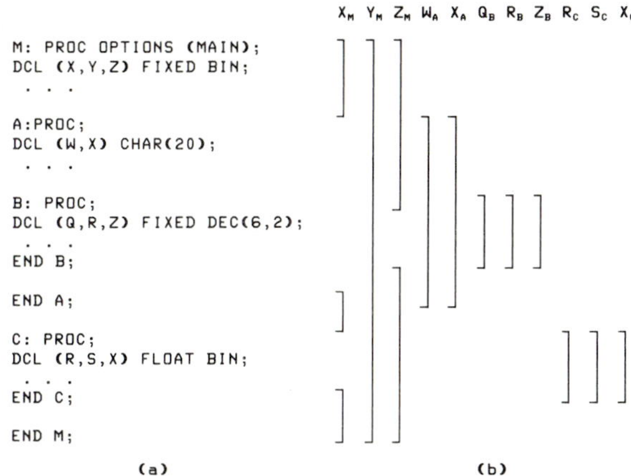
M: PROC OPTIONS (MAIN);
DCL (X,Y,Z) FIXED BIN;
. . .
A:PROC;
DCL (W,X) CHAR(20);
. . .
B: PROC;
DCL (Q,R,Z) FIXED DEC(6,2);
. . .
END B;
END A;
C: PROC;
DCL (R,S,X) FLOAT BIN;
. . .
END C;
END M;
(a)
X_M Y_M Z_M W_A X_A Q_B R_B Z_B R_C S_C X_C
(b)

Figure 9–15

The Y in the main procedure, called Y_M in the figure, is the only variable known to the entire program. The other variables of the main procedure, X_M and Z_M, are global, but become temporarily unavailable when the names X and Z are reused in new declarations. As there is a variable X in A and one in C, the X of the main procedure can be referenced only outside A and C. The X of A is local to A and is a different X from that of C. Altogether, at one time or another, three different memory locations are known as X. In the diagram they are called X_M, X_A, and X_C. The W of procedure A is known to B, which is inside A, but not to C, which is outside it. The Q and R of procedure B are not accessible anyplace outside B. The R of B and the R of C are different.

As shown in figure 9–15, variables come into existence on entry to the procedure where they are declared, go out of existence on exit from the procedure where they are declared, and may be temporarily suspended if their names are reused during their existence.

Since the scope of variables is complicated, particularly if names are reused, a good rule to follow is that an internal procedure should use only global names, or only local ones. The situation is further complicated in that undeclared variables default to global, so it is a good idea always to declare all variables explicitly.

PROGRAMMING HINT: MAINTAINABILITY Do not use both parameters and global variables in a subprocedure.

As seen in figure 9–15, two different variables of the same name do not have to be of the same type. However, it is good programming practice to avoid using the same variable name for two different objects as it avoids confusion.

Review questions

1. Complete each of the following statements.

(a) The scope of a variable depends on the ________________ (static/dynamic) nesting of the procedures.

(b) An undeclared variable is local to the ________________ (main procedure/subprocedure).

(c) The value of a local variable is ________________ (saved/lost) when control returns to the calling procedure.

(d) A variable may be referenced in the procedure in which it is declared and all procedures ________________ (nested in/called by) that procedure.

(e) When a local variable is given the same name as a global variable, the value of the global variable is ________________ (saved/lost) when the procedure with the local variable is invoked.

2. Given the following code segment,

```
MP: PROC OPTIONS(MAIN);
DCL X,Y;
A: PROC;
DCL U,V;
END A;
B: PROC;
DCL W,X;
DCL D ENTRY;
```

```
C: PROC;
DCL Y,Z;
END C;
END B;
END MP;
D: PROC;
DCL X,Z;
END D;
```

what variables can be referenced by each of the following?

(a) A
(b) B
(c) C
(d) D
(e) MP

9.4 Argument/parameter passing

When only local variables are used, the calling and the called program communicate through the parameters of the subroutine.

The following main procedure and subroutine share an array. The main procedure handles the input and output and the subroutine reverses the order of the elements of the array.

```
MP: PROC OPTIONS (MAIN);
DCL ARR(10)    FIXED BIN;
 . . .
CALL REVERSE(ARR);
 . . .
REVERSE: PROC (VECT);          /* REVERSE THE ELEMENTS OF */
                               /* THE ARRAY               */
DCL VECT(10)   FIXED BIN,
    TEMP       FIXED BIN,
    K          FIXED BIN;
DO K = 1 TO 5;
  TEMP = VECT(K);              /* SWAP TWO ELEMENTS       */
  VECT(K) = VECT(11-K);
  VECT(11-K) = TEMP;
END;
END REVERSE;
END MP;
```

The array ARR is passed to the subroutine through the matching of the array name in the call with the name VECT in the procedure heading. These two names apply to the same location in memory. The name VECT is associated with that location on entry to the subroutine, and the association between the name and the location is destroyed on exit from the subroutine. When the subroutine picks up the value of VECT(K), it is getting ARR(K). When it stores a value in VECT(K), it is storing it in ARR(K). The two names reference the same array variable, but have different scopes. The name ARR can be used for the variable anyplace in MP, but the name VECT can only be used inside REVERSE. The name ARR is global; the name VECT is local. Since the names refer to the same object, the declarations must be identical. Figure 9–16a shows the memory and variables before the call to REVERSE and figure 9–16b shows them during the execution of REVERSE. Both the name ARR and the name VECT are associated with the same array object while REVERSE is executing.

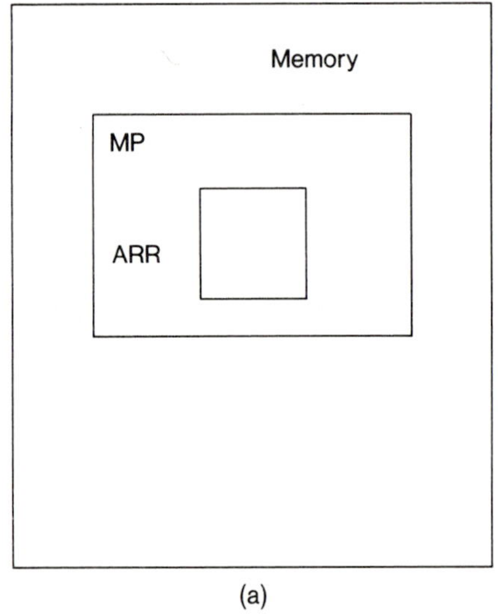

(a)

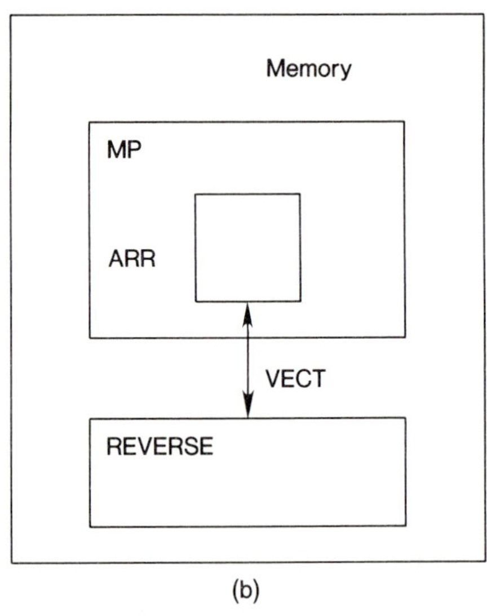

(b)

Figure 9–16

9.4.1 Argument/parameter matching

The argument list used in a call and the parameter list used in the subprocedure header must have the same number and types of variables, in the same order. This is seen in the following example:

```
MP: PROC OPTIONS(MAIN);
DCL ARR(10)    FIXED BIN,
    X          FLOAT BIN,
    STR        CHAR(20);
 . . .
CALL SUB(ARR,X,STR);
 . . .
SUB: PROC(Q,R,S);
DCL Q(10)      FIXED BIN,          /* Q MATCHES ARR */
    R          FLOAT BIN,          /* R MATCHES X   */
    S          CHAR(20);           /* S MATCHES STR */
 . . .
END SUB;
END MP;
```

The computer cannot tell by looking at the data what the type is. It is up to the programmer to make sure that argument and parameter lists agree as to number, order, and type of variables. Some PL/I compilers assist the programmer by checking the matching of the argument and parameter lists of calls to internal procedures and converting values as needed.

Through the use of parameters and local variables rather than global variables, the same subroutine can be used for two different sets of data in the main procedure. In the following example,

```
CALL SUB(X,Y);
 . . .
CALL SUB(A,X);
 . . .
SUB: PROC(J,K);
 . . .
```

during the first activation of SUB, J references the same location in memory as X, and K references the location Y. This is shown in figure 9–17a. During the second call, shown in 9–17b, K references X and J references A.

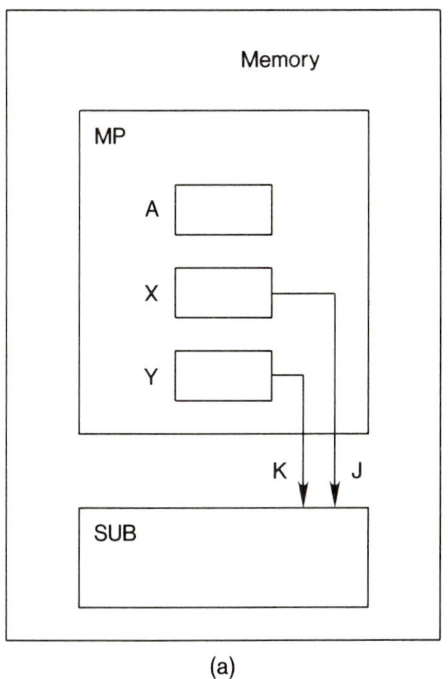

(a)

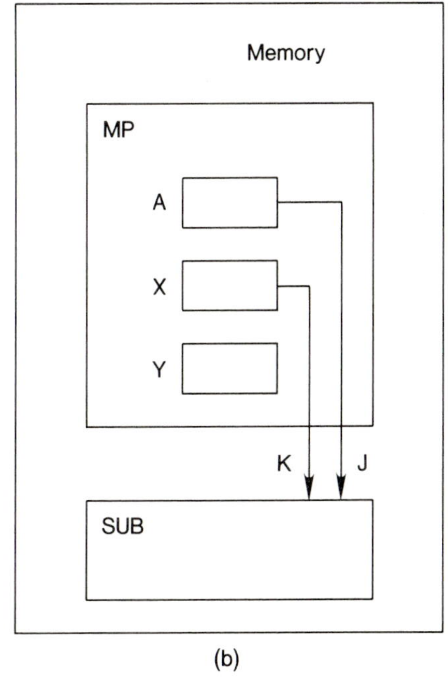

(b)

Figure 9–17

PROGRAMMING HINT: USEFULNESS Use parameters to generalize a routine.

9.4.2 Runtime description

When arrays and character strings are passed as parameters, their descriptors are also passed.

VARIABLE LENGTH STRINGS

If a generalized routine is to be used to process character strings of different sizes, an asterisk can be used in the declaration of the parameter, as in the following example:

```
DCL S_1  CHAR(10),
    S_2  CHAR(20);
 . . .
CALL SUB(S_1);
CALL SUB(S_2);
 . . .
SUB: PROC (STR);
DCL STR  CHAR(*);         /* THE STRING IS OF UNKNOWN LENGTH */
DCL LNG  FIXED BIN;
LNG = LENGTH(STR);        /* GET THE LENGTH OF THE STRING    */
```

Since the parameter of the subprocedure is declared to be fixed but of unknown length, the LENGTH function is used to obtain the length.

If character strings that have been declared CHAR(. . .) VARYING are passed as arguments, the matching parameters must also be CHAR(. . .) VARYING with the same maximum length. There are several ways of passing this information. In the following examples, STR can be of any length up to and including twenty characters. TEXT is the same length.

```
DCL STR      CHAR(20) VARYING;
. . .
CALL SUB(STR);

SUB: PROC (TEXT);
DCL TEXT     CHAR(20) VARYING;
```

The same maximum length has been used in both the calling procedure and the subprocedure. If a character string of a different length is stored in TEXT, it changes the length of STR since they refer to the same object in memory. For example,

```
TEXT = 'ABC';                /* BOTH STR AND TEXT HAVE LENGTH 3    */
                             /* AND REFER TO THE SAME STRING 'ABC' */
TEXT = 'NOW IS THE TIME';    /* BOTH HAVE LENGTH 15                */
```

In some implementations, character strings of different lengths may be passed to a fixed-length character string provided the lengths are passed as well and used in the parameter declaration, as in

```
DCL STR      CHAR(20) VARYING,
    LNG      FIXED BIN;
GET LIST (STR);
```

```
LNG = LENGTH(STR);
 . . .
CALL SUB(LNG,STR);

SUB: PROC (L,TEXT);
DCL L          FIXED BIN,
    TEXT       CHAR(L);
```

TEXT has fixed length, but its length is not known until SUB is called. Even though TEXT does not have the VARYING attribute, its length will be the same as that of STR at each call. However, in this situation SUB cannot change the length of TEXT or STR by storing a different character string in TEXT.

Also, in some implementations the parameter may have a fixed but unknown length, to be the same as the length of the value being passed. This is done by using an asterisk in the declaration.

```
DCL STR        CHAR(20) VARYING;
 . . .
CALL SUB(STR);

SUB: PROC(TEXT);
DCL TEXT       CHAR(*);
DCL LNG        FIXED BIN;
LNG = LENGTH(TEXT);
```

When the subroutine is called, the variable LNG picks up the length of STR. What is actually passed is not the value of the string variable, but a descriptor which gives the location and length of the string.

VARIABLE SIZE ARRAYS

Arrays of different sizes can be passed to a single subprocedure in much the same fashion as variable-length character strings of different lengths. The procedure SUB with the declarations

```
SUB: PROC(VECT);
DCL VECT(10)    FIXED BIN,
    TEMP        FIXED BIN;
 . . .
END SUB;
```

can only work with arrays of ten elements. The SUB procedure with either of the following sets of declarations can process any one-dimensional array of type FIXED BIN:

```
CALL SUB(ARR,N);

SUB: PROC (VECT,K);
DCL VECT(K)     FIXED BIN,
    K           FIXED BIN;
 . . .
END SUB;
```

```
CALL SUB(ARR);

SUB: PROC (VECT);
DCL VECT(*)     FIXED BIN;
 . . .
END SUB;
```

When the size of the array is explicitly passed, as in the first of these examples, the subscript range in the subprocedure is not necessarily the same as in the calling procedure. When the asterisk is used, the asterisk indicates any array not only of unknown size, but of unknown upper and lower bounds. The built-in functions HBOUND and LBOUND must be used to obtain the values of the upper and lower bounds, respectively, of the array VECT. This method is not available in some versions of PL/I.

With the declaration

```
DCL MATRIX(0:15,5:27). . . .
```

in a subprocedure when MATRIX is picked up as

```
CALL SUB(MATRIX);
  . . .
SUB: PROC(M);
DCL M(*,*) ...
```

then

```
LBOUND(M,1) is 0
HBOUND(M,1) is 15
LBOUND(M,2) is 5
HBOUND(M,2) is 27
```

There is no way to pass an array of an unknown number of dimensions. The function DIM returns the number of elements in a particular dimension of an array.

```
DIM(M,1) is 16
```

since there are sixteen rows in the matrix.

```
DIM(M,2) is 23
```

since there are twenty-three columns.

9.4.3 Use of parameters

The parameters of a subprocedure may be input parameters, output parameters, or both. The parameter of a subprocedure that reverses the elements of an array

```
CALL REVERSE(ARR);
```

is both an input and an output parameter. The subprocedure obtains values from ARR; it also stores values in ARR. The parameters X and N of MAXMIN and GETAVG were input parameters. Their values were used by the procedure, but not changed. The parameters XMAX, XMIN, and XAVG were output parameters. They were assigned values by the subprocedure. In the segment

```
CALL SUB(2*N,STR);
  . . .
SUB: PROC(A,B);
DCL A      FIXED BIN,
    B      CHAR(20);
```

the parameter A can only be an input parameter as 2*N is not a variable name. Although it has temporary storage attached to it, that storage is not accessible in the calling procedure. B is an input parameter if no values are assigned to it in SUB. It is an output or input/output parameter if a value is assigned to it. A is known as a *call-by-value* parameter since it only references temporary storage. B is a *call-by-reference* parameter since it refers to the same location as a variable in the calling procedure. Normally variables are passed by reference, but it is possible with nonoptimizing compilers to pass them by value, as in the following:

```
CALL SUB((I),J);
  . . .
SUB: PROC(A,B);
DCL A   FIXED BIN,
    B   CHAR(20);
```

Here A is a call-by-value parameter since the extra parentheses cause the corresponding argument to be treated as an expression rather than a simple variable.

There is a danger in using an expression rather than a variable as an argument, as seen in the above examples. The typing of expressions in PL/I follows complicated rules so it is easy to mismatch arguments and parameters. This can be avoided by declaring the entry points of internal procedures as well as external procedures. For example:

```
DCL SUB   ENTRY(FIXED BIN,CHAR(20));
  . . .
CALL SUB(3.14*X,SUBSTR(TEXT,K,L));
  . . .
SUB: PROC(N,STR);
DCL N      FIXED BIN,
    STR    CHAR(20);
```

The computer sets up the temporary storage for the arguments according to the types it is told that SUB requires. If there is a discrepancy between the declaration of the entry point and the real requirements of SUB, the wrong values will be picked up by SUB. Each routine has its own idea of the organization of the argument storage area and each accesses it according to its own understanding.

PROGRAMMING HINT: PORTABILITY   Match the types of arguments and parameters.

Any kind of expression, variable, constant, or literal may be passed as an argument. All of the following are valid:

```
CALL SUB(3);                  /* CALL BY REFERENCE */
CALL SUB(N);                  /* CALL BY REFERENCE */
CALL SUB((N));                /* CALL BY VALUE     */
CALL SUB(2*A-7);              /* CALL BY VALUE     */
CALL SUB(SIN(SQRT(X)));       /* CALL BY VALUE     */
```

The values will be picked up properly as long as the type assigned by the calling procedure to the argument matches the type expected by the subprocedure. An expression used as an argument is evaluated and assigned temporary storage before the subprocedure is called. Thus in CALL SUB (SIN(SQRT(X))); the square root is evaluated and assigned storage, which is passed to the sine function, which returns a value, which is stored and passed to SUB.

In CALL SUB((N)), provided an optimizing compiler is not being used, the value of N is picked up and assigned temporary storage. N is an input parameter only. Its value cannot be changed by the subprocedure.

There is a danger in using a constant rather than a variable as an argument, as in CALL SUB(3). If the default type of the constant is the same as the type expected by the subprocedure, it is possible for the subprocedure to change the internal value associated with the digit 3. Constants should not be used as call-by-reference arguments.

PROGRAMMING HINT: CAUTION Do not pass constants as arguments.

ENTRY ATTRIBUTE

The ENTRY attribute has several uses. It is used in a calling procedure if the subprocedure is external or if the calling procedure must be given some information about the parameters of the subprocedure. Its general form in a calling procedure is:

```
DCL entry-name ENTRY [(type-list)];
```

It is used in a subprocedure to indicate an alternate entry point. The general form is:

```
entry-name: ENTRY [(parameter-list)];
```

As an alternate entry point, it is used to assign a name to a place in the subprocedure and is included at that place.

A subprocedure may contain two or more entry points, as in the following example, where the INIT entry point is used to set up and initialize a matrix and the PRINT entry point is used to print the matrix.

```
MATRIX: PROC(MAT);
DCL MAT(20,20)  FIXED BIN,
    K           FIXED BIN;

INIT: ENTRY(MAT);
MAT = 0;
 . . .
RETURN;

PRINT: ENTRY(MAT);
PUT . . .;
 . . .
RETURN;
END MATRIX;
```

This use of multiple entry points is available in most versions of PL/I, but the form taken by the ENTRY statement is not standard. In some versions, all entry points must have the same parameters. Therefore the parameters need to be identified only in the procedure header. In other versions the parameter lists may differ; therefore each ENTRY statement must contain a parameter list.

The use of the RETURN statement in this example prevents control from reaching the PUT statement when entry is made at INIT. If it were not there, the freshly initialized matrix would be printed. Control would fall through the second ENTRY statement. An ENTRY statement is not executable; it simply associates a name with a location. The RETURN statement may be used wherever a return from a subprocedure is desired. It is usually used when there are multiple entry points. Placing a RETURN just ahead of the END statement does not affect the processing, but provides a parallel structure for the two parts of the procedure, which is aesthetically pleasing. The RETURN statement has the same effect on program control as reaching the end of a procedure.

Since this procedure has two entry points, which lead to code carrying out two different functions, it cannot be described functionally. This is an example of a communicational procedure, one that is built around a data structure and carries out several operations on the structure. The code segments belonging to the entry points "communicate" through the data structure.

Review questions

1. Complete each of the following statements.

(a) When values are passed to a subprocedure, the arguments and parameters must match as to ________________ (name/type).

(b) Normally variables are passed by ________________ (reference/value).

(c) Parameters whose values are used by the subprocedure are ________________ (input/output) parameters.

(d) Parameters whose values are changed by the subprocedure are ________________ (input/output) parameters.

(e) When an expression is used as an argument, for example in CALL SUBB(2*N−15); the expression is evaluated ________________ (before/after) the subprocedure is invoked.
(f) An entry point must be declared if the subprocedure is ________________ (internal/external).

2. In the statement CALL VALUE(MAX,2*N−K,SQRT(K)); which arguments are passed by references and which are passed by value?

3. Indicate whether each of the following statements is true or false.
(a) A communicational procedure has multiple entry points.
(b) The entry point of an external procedure must be declared in a procedure invoking it.
(c) The compiler uses an ENTRY declaration to determine what data types are to be passed.
(d) A RETURNS clause is used to return data.
(e) The length of a CHARACTER VARYING variable cannot be changed in a subprocedure.
(f) A procedure passes character strings and arrays by passing a descriptor.

4. Write the subroutine header and parameter declarations for each of the following:

(a)
```
DCL A(5)  FIXED BIN,
    B(10) FIXED BIN;
 . . .
CALL SUB(A);
CALL SUB(B);
```
(b)
```
DCL S  CHAR(5) VAR,
    T  CHAR(10) VAR;
 . . .
CALL SUB(S);
CALL SUB(T);
```
(c)
```
DCL S  CHAR(5),
    T  CHAR(10);
 . . .
CALL SUB(S);
CALL SUB(T);
```

9.5 Functions

A function differs from a subroutine in that a function always returns a single scalar value. It is called by using the function name and argument list wherever the value returned is to be used. Examples are the library functions, which may be used in such ways as:

```
Y = 3*SQRT(X);

PUT LIST(MAX(A,B,C));

STR = SUBSTR(STR,INDEX(STR,' '));
```

which embeds them in expressions, prints their values, or evaluates them to obtain parameters. In a function, the RETURN statement is utilized to return the value of the function rather than returning it through one of the parameters. A function should have only input parameters.

The general form of a function subprocedure is:

```
func-name: PROC (parameter-list) [RETURNS(result-type)];
body of function consisting of
   declarations
   executable code
   [definitions]
RETURN(expr);
END func-name;
```

If the RETURNS option is not present, the function name is used to establish a default type for the value being returned. If the function name begins with I–N, the type is FIXED BINARY; otherwise it is FLOAT BINARY.

9.5.1 Internal functions

Like subroutines, functions may be external or internal. The use of parameters, scope of variables, and access of subprocedures are the same for functions as for subroutines. The only differences lie in the way a function is invoked and the way its value is returned.

If a program often needs to calculate a cube root, it may be convenient to have a CBRT function, to be used in the same fashion as the SQRT function. The following example gives a procedure to calculate and return a cube root:

```
CBRT: PROC(X) RETURNS(FLOAT BIN);
DCL X FLOAT BIN;
RETURN(X**(1.0/3.0));
END CBRT;
```

There are more efficient and accurate ways of implementing a cube root procedure, but this is one of the simplest. By allowing the computer to calculate the value of 1.0/3.0, rather than using .333333, more accuracy can be obtained. If there is an entry declaration,

```
DCL CBRT ENTRY(FLOAT BIN) RETURNS(FLOAT BIN);
```

in the calling procedure, then the type passed as input to the procedure and the type returned from the procedure will be accurately passed. Any type conversion necessary will be automatic. This procedure can be used in any of the following ways:

```
Y = CBRT(27);
A = 2*CBRT(B-1.5);
N = SIN(CBRT(COS(1.25)));
PUT LIST (CBRT(X));
```

A user-defined function cannot be used as a pseudovariable on the left side of an assignment statement since user functions can only be set up to return values. The RETURNS statements in the entry declaration and in the procedure header establish the type returned. Neither statement is required, but if either is missing, the default type is assumed for that context. The RETURN statement controlling the exit from the procedure is necessary as it identifies the value being returned.

The library function ABS(X) may be implemented as follows:

```
ABS: PROC(X) RETURNS(FLOAT BIN);
DCL X    FLOAT BIN;

IF X >= 0
  THEN
    RETURN(X);
  ELSE
    RETURN(-X);
END ABS;
```

Here there are two RETURN statements for the two cases of positive and negative values of X. Even with the two RETURN statements, this is a functional procedure. It represents a single mathematical function. There is one entry point and, behind the scenes, only one exit—the internal housekeeping routine that releases the procedure and returns the value. Both RETURN statements return control to the same point in the calling procedure. It would not have been correct to have changed the sign of X if it was negative and then returned X. It is important to avoid changing the values of parameters when writing function procedures. The whole purpose of using a function procedure is to return a value that can be used immediately. There is no way of first checking the values of the arguments.

PROGRAMMING HINT: ACCURACY   Do not change the values of function parameters.

There is a problem with functions that can fail under certain circumstances. The SQRT function can fail if it is given a negative argument. If it fails, some value must still be returned, but it is important to indicate that the answer is not reliable. This can be done by printing an error message, as in the following simulation of the library SQRT routine, and by returning any convenient value.

```
SQRT: PROC(X) RETURNS(FLOAT BIN);
DCL X    FLOAT BIN;
DCL S    FLOAT BIN;

IF X < 0.0
  THEN
    DO;
      PUT SKIP LIST ('SQRT ERROR - NEGATIVE ARGUMENT');
      RETURN(X);
    END;
```

```
   ELSE
      DO;
         S = X/2;
         DO WHILE (ABS(S*S-X) < .00001*X);
            S = (S + X/S)/2;
         END;
         RETURN(S);
      END;
END SQRT;
```

User functions may return either character strings, bit strings, or numeric values. They may not return structures or arrays. A function is used when there is only a single scalar value to be returned to the calling program. A function that does something to its calling environment in addition to returning a value is said to be an *abnormal function* and to have *side effects.* In general, functions should not have side effects; that is, they should not do any input or output, change any global variables, or assign values to any of their parameters. An exception must be made for functions that can fail. On failure, they should print a relevant message and either return a harmless value or terminate the processing.

PROGRAMMING HINT: CAUTION Functions should not have side effects.

9.5.2 External functions

Functions as well as subroutines may be external. They are external if they are compiled separately from the calling procedure, in which case an entry point must be declared, as in the following example:

```
MP: PROC OPTIONS (MAIN);
DCL CBRT  ENTRY (FLOAT BIN) RETURNS (FLOAT BIN);
DCL X     FLOAT BIN;
GET LIST (X);
PUT SKIP LIST (X,CBRT(X));
END MP;

    JCL goes here

CBRT: PROC(X) RETURNS(FLOAT BIN);
DCL X FLOAT BIN;
RETURN(X**(1.0/3.0));
END CBRT;
```

The argument types and the type of the value returned should be included in the ENTRY declaration.

Review questions

1. Complete each of the following statements.
   (a) If function calls are nested, the ________________ (inside/outside) function is invoked first.

(b) The type returned by a function is determined by the ______________ (RETURN statement/RETURNS clause).

(c) The values of parameters should not be changed in ______________ (functions/subroutines).

(d) Explicit return statements must be used in ______________ (functions/subroutines).

(e) A function may not return a ______________ (string/array).

2. Write a function header and parameter declarations for each of the following functions called:

(a)
```
DCL (X,Y)  FLOAT BIN;
  . . .
Y = F(X);
```
(b)
```
DCL (I,J)  FIXED BIN,
    STR    CHAR(20);
  . . .
J = MANY(STR,I);
```
(c)
```
DCL ARR(2,3) FIXED DEC(6,2),
    COUNT    FIXED BIN;
  . . .
K = COUNT(ARR,ARR(1,1));
```
(d)
```
DCL (A,B)  CHAR(10) VARYING;
A = MERGE(A,B);
```

3. Write a function SIGN(K) to return the sign of a fixed binary number.

4. Write a function COUNT(STR,CH) to return the number of occurrences of the character which is its second parameter in the character string which is its first parameter.

5. Write a function SUMSQ(VECT) to return the sum of the squares of the FLOAT BIN elements of the one-dimensional array which is its parameter.

6. Write a function LOC(NAME_LIST,NAME) to return the position of a name in a list of names.

9.6 Recursive procedures

In PL/I there is no restriction on functions and subroutines calling themselves. Such a call is *recursive.* The classic example of a recursive function is n factorial, written $n!$. This is a mathematical function meaning the product of the integers from one through n. Five factorial is $1 \times 2 \times 3 \times 4 \times 5$. The general case $n!$ is defined mathematically as

$$n! = \begin{cases} 1 & \text{for } n = 0 \\ n(n-1)! & \text{for } n > 0 \end{cases}$$

This is a recursive definition as the factorial symbol (!), appears on the right side as well as the left side of the formula. Every recursive definition has at least two parts, one to define the function in terms of itself, and the other without the self-reference. This definition can be implemented in a straightforward manner as the recursive function procedure of the following example:

```
FACTL: PROC (N) RECURSIVE RETURNS(FIXED BIN);
DCL N  FIXED BIN;
IF N = 0
  THEN
    RETURN (1);
  ELSE
    RETURN (N*FACTL(N-1));
END FACTL;
```

The variable N counts down as the procedure is called repeatedly. Notice that the termination condition is checked ahead of the recursive call.

Recursive procedures are procedures that call themselves either directly or indirectly. Since in most implementations of PL/I recursive procedures are handled differently by the computer than nonrecursive ones, they must be declared to be RECURSIVE. As with other procedures, each time a

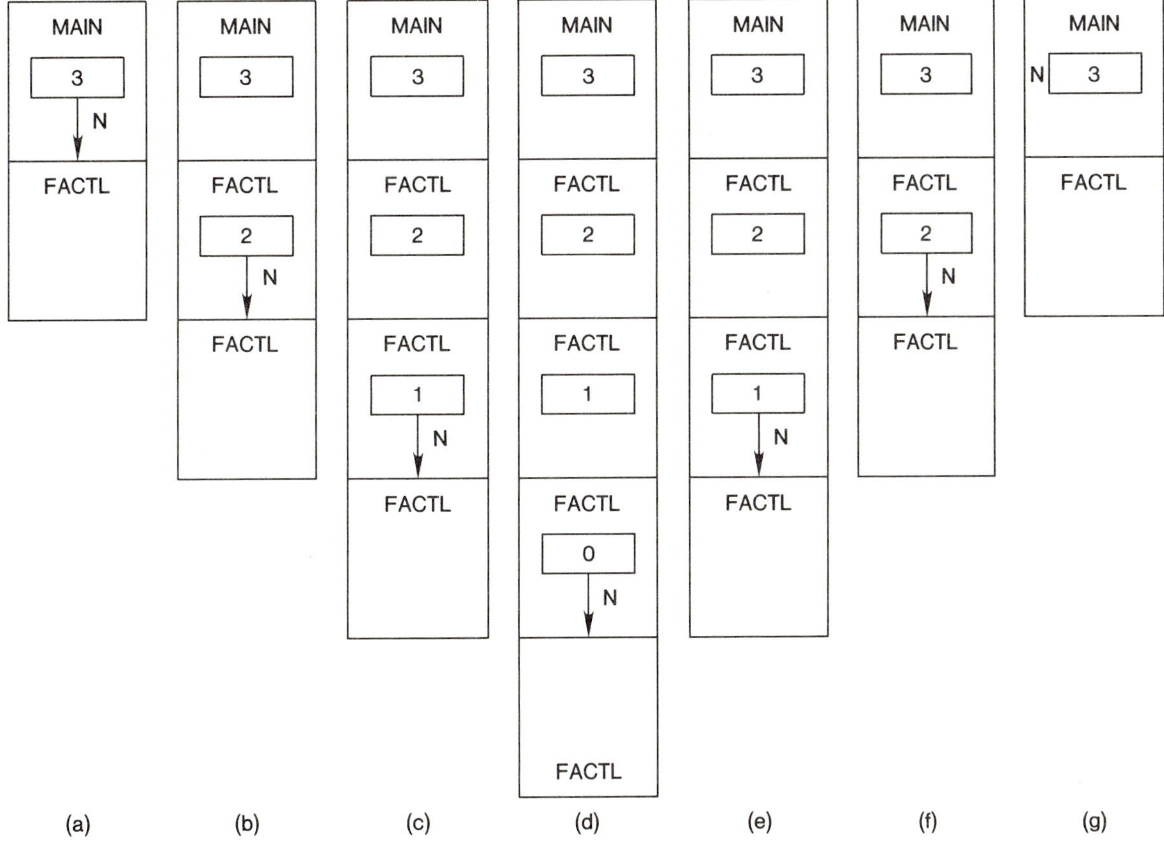

Figure 9–18

recursive procedure is called, a fresh copy is obtained and a local data area is set up. Figure 9–18 shows the memory for a main program call on FACTL passing the value 3.

Figure 9–18a shows the memory after the FACTL routine is called for the first time. The parameter N refers back to the value 3 in the main procedure. After the second call, shown in 9–18b, the parameter N refers to a value for N-1 in the first call of the procedure. At that time N was 3, so the new value of N is 2, but stored back in the calling procedure. The next call picks up a value of 1 for N. And in the last call, N is 0.

When N is 0, the function is exited returning the value 1. Control returns to the next operation after the function was invoked. Since the function was invoked in an expression, control returns to the multiplication, which could not be completed until the value of the factorial was known.

```
RETURN(N*FACTL(N-1));
```

had the value

```
RETURN(1*FACTL(0));
```

which on the return becomes

```
RETURN(1*1);
```

or

```
RETURN(1);
```

which in turn returns to the previous call where the multiplication is again completed. This continues until finally control returns to the main procedure, returning the value 6. The parameters are calculated on the recursive descent and the values are returned on the recursive ascent, as shown below:

	↓	*Main procedure*	↑	
N is 3		First call		Returns 3*2 = 6
N is 2		Second call		Returns 2*1 = 2
N is 1		Third call		Returns 1*1 = 1
N is 0		Fourth call		Returns 1

Any iterative procedure can be written recursively. The simple read/print loop of part a of the following example is written as a recursive procedure in part b.

```
READ_PRINT: PROC;
 . . .
GET EDIT (STR) (A(80));
DO WHILE(MORE);
  PUT SKIP EDIT (STR) (A);
  GET EDIT (STR) (A(80));
END;
END READ_PRINT;
```

(a)

```
READ_PRINT: PROC RECURSIVE;
 . . .
GET EDIT (STR) (A(80));
IF MORE
  THEN
    DO;
      PUT SKIP EDIT (STR) (A);
      CALL READ_PRINT;
    END;
END READ_PRINT;
```

(b)

The recursive call to READ_PRINT has the effect of sending control back to the top of the loop. In both routines, the repetition ends when the input statement detects the end of the file. The local variable STR in the recursive procedure has storage set aside for it each time the procedure is called. Thus there will be as many versions of STR in the memory as calls to the procedure, and as many calls as character strings in the input data. This example is given as an illustration of the use of recursion in the place of an iterative loop. It also illustrates the processing/printing of data on the *recursive descent.* If the statements composing the body of the loop were reversed,

```
CALL READ_PRINT;
PUT SKIP EDIT (STR) (A);
```

the data would be printed on the *recursive ascent* and its original order would be reversed.

Review questions

1. A ______________ procedure is a procedure that invokes itself either directly or indirectly.

2. Every recursive procedure must have a ______________ condition.

3. A recursive procedure may perform calculations and input/output either on the recursive ______________ or the recursive ______________.

4. Write a recursive function to implement the formula

$$C(n, k) = \begin{cases} 1 & k = 0 \\ \dfrac{(n - k + 1)\,C(n, k - 1)}{k} & 1 \le k \le n \end{cases}$$

5. Write a recursive function to implement the formula

$$C(n, k) = \begin{cases} 1 & k = 0 \\ C(n, k - 1) + C(n - 1, k - 1) & 1 \le k \le n \end{cases}$$

9.7 ON units

ON units function as unnamed, parameterless subprocedures that are explicitly set up and dynamically allocated space by the programmer. They may be called either explicitly or implicitly. The ON statement is the executable statement that establishes the ON unit. The scope of the ON unit starts with its establishment, but is otherwise the same as that of any other subprocedure defined at the same level. Figure 9–19 shows the scope of three different ON units.

The ENDFILE unit is defined in the main program. It is global beyond

```
                                ENDFILE  ENDPAGE  ZERODIVIDE
MP: PROC OPTIONS (MAIN);
 . . .
ON ENDFILE (...)
  BEGIN;
   . . .
  END;
 . . .
SUB1: PROC;
 . . .
ON ENDPAGE (...)
  BEGIN;
   . . .
  END;
 . . .
SUBA: PROC;
 . . .
END SUBA;
END SUB1;
ON ZERODIVIDE
  BEGIN;
   . . .
  END;
SUB2: PROC;
 . . .
END SUB2;
END MP;
```

Figure 9–19

the point at which it is defined. The ZERODIVIDE unit is also defined in the main program, but it is global only to SUB2. The ENDPAGE unit is defined in SUB1 and so is local to SUB1, beyond the point at which it is defined.

The environment of an ON unit is that in which it is established. In the following example,

```
MP: PROC OPTIONS(MAIN);
DCL X    FIXED BIN INIT(1);
ON ERROR                          /* ON UNIT IS IN MP */
  PUT SKIP LIST (X);
CALL SUB;
 . . .
SUB: PROC;                        /* SUB IS IN MP     */
DCL X    FIXED BIN INIT(2);
  SIGNAL ERROR;
 . . .
END SUB;
END MP;
```

the value 1 is printed. Since the ON unit is established in the main procedure, the X global to it is the X of the main procedure, not the X of the calling procedure. The SIGNAL statement functions as an explicit call. If the ON unit were executed because of an error, an implicit call, the result would be the same.

Review questions

1. Indicate whether each of the following statements is true or false.
   - (a) An ON unit is a form of subprocedure to the computer.
   - (b) The environment of an ON unit is static, the same as it would be if it were an ordinary subprocedure.
   - (c) The scope of an ON unit is the same as it would be if it were a subprocedure.
   - (d) Two ON units for the same condition can be established in the same procedure.

2. An ON condition is explicitly raised by the ______________ statement.

3. An ON condition is implicitly raised by ______________.

9.8 Examples of subprocedures

The following examples show the use of subroutine and function subprocedures.

9.8.1 Headings

Subroutines are commonly used to print page headings, column headings, and other lines that have an editing and documentation function. In this example, an internal subroutine is used to print a page heading. Figure 9–20 gives a hierarchy chart of the problem.

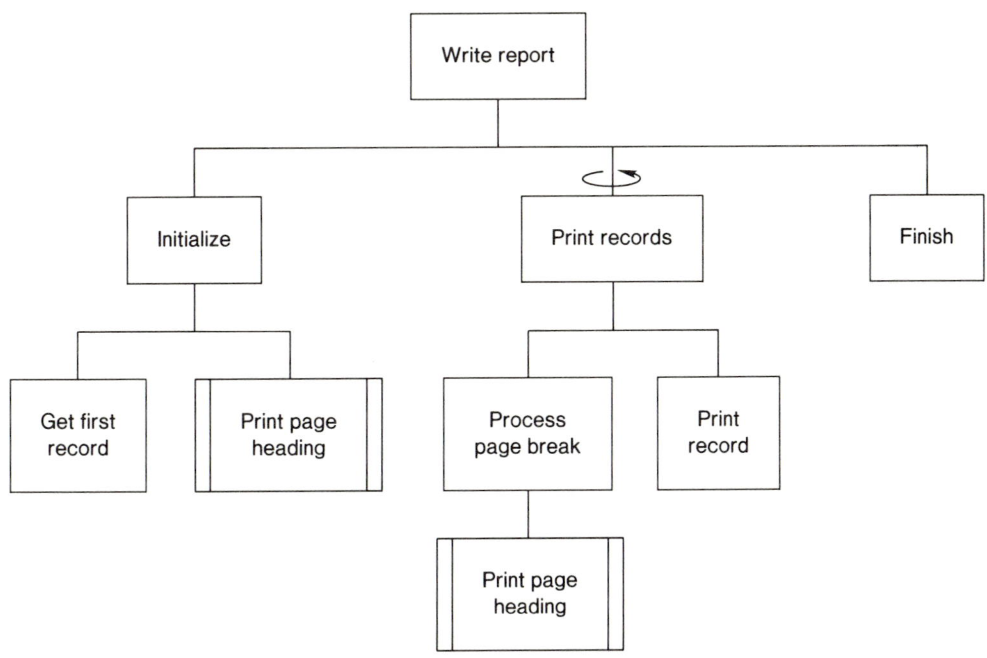

Figure 9–20

The subroutine is called at the beginning of the processing to print the heading on the first page. Thereafter it is called whenever fifty lines have been printed on a page. The line count is checked when the program is ready to print a fifty-first line on the page. If instead it were checked after the fiftieth line had been printed, there would be an extra page heading in the output if the last page contained exactly fifty records.

In this program, the subroutine starts a new page. Both local and global variables are used.

```
REPORT: PROC OPTIONS(MAIN);
/*************************************************************/
/*                                                           */
/* PROGRAM: WRITE REPORT                                     */
/* AUTHOR:  C ZIEGLER                                        */
/* VERSION: 07/17/84                                         */
/*                                                           */
/* PROGRAM DESCRIPTION                                       */
/* --------------------------------------------------------- */
/* THIS PROGRAM PRINTS RECORDS 50 TO A PAGE.                 */
/*                                                           */
/* INPUT: SYSIN - DETAIL RECORDS                             */
/*                                                           */
/* OUTPUT: SYSPRINT - LISTING OF RECORDS                     */
/*                                                           */
/*************************************************************/
DCL INFO      CHAR(80),
    LINE      FIXED BIN,
    MORE_DATA BIT(1);
DCL TRUE      BIT(1)    INIT('1'B),
    FALSE     BIT(1)    INIT('0'B);

ON ENDFILE (SYSIN)
  MORE_DATA = FALSE;

MORE DATA = TRUE;
GET EDIT (INFO) (A(80));
CALL HEADER;                  /* PRINT HEADING ON 1ST PAGE */
DO WHILE (MORE_DATA);
  IF LINE = 50
    THEN
      CALL HEADER;            /* PRINT HEADING ON NEXT PAGE */
  PUT EDIT (INFO) (A);
  LINE = LINE + 1;
  GET EDIT (INFO) (A(80));
END;


HEADER: PROC;
/*************************************************************/
/*                                                           */
/* SUBROUTINE: PRINT HEADING                                 */
/*                                                           */
/* THIS ROUTINE PRINTS A PAGE HEADING.                       */
/*                                                           */
/* OUTPUT VARIABLES: LINE                                    */
/*                                                           */
/*************************************************************/
DCL TITLE CHAR(12) INIT ('INFO LISTING');
```

```
PUT PAGE;
PUT EDIT (TITLE) (COL(40),A);
PUT SKIP(3);
LINE = 3;
END HEADER;

END REPORT;
```

The first call to the procedure HEADER returns control to the DOWHILE statement. After the second call, control returns to the PUT EDIT statement. The main procedure executes exactly as it would if the code of HEADER were placed in the main procedure everywhere there is a CALL statement. The variable LINE indicates how many lines have been printed at any given time. When fifty lines have been printed and there is another line to be printed, the HEADER procedure is called. Note that the subroutine reinitializes LINE.

9.8.2 Array statistics

This program is an example of the use of external procedures to find the maximum value, minimum value, and average value in an array.

```
DRIVER: PROC OPTIONS (MAIN);
/*****************************************************************/
/*                                                             */
/* PROGRAM: TESTING DRIVER FOR MAXMIN AND GETAVG               */
/* AUTHOR:  C ZIEGLER                                          */
/* VERSION: 07/17/84                                           */
/*                                                             */
/* PROGRAM DESCRIPTION                                         */
/* ----------------------------------------------------------- */
/* THIS PROGRAM TESTS THE EXTERNAL ROUTINES MAXMIN AND         */
/* GETAVG.                                                     */
/*                                                             */
/* INPUT: SYSIN - LIST OF 20 FIXED BINARY NUMBERS              */
/*                                                             */
/* OUTPUT: SYSPRINT - MAXIMUM, MINIMUM, AVERAGE VALUES         */
/*                                                             */
/*****************************************************************/
DCL MAXMIN    ENTRY(FIXED BIN, FIXED BIN, FIXED BIN,
                    FIXED BIN),
    GETAVG    ENTRY(FIXED BIN, FIXED BIN, FLOAT BIN);
DCL X(20)   FIXED BIN,
    XMAX    FIXED BIN,
    XMIN    FIXED BIN,
    XAVG    FLOAT BIN;
DCL I       FIXED BIN;

DO I = 1 TO 20;
  GET LIST (X(I));
END;
```

```
CALL MAXMIN(X,N,XMAX,XMIN);
CALL GETAVG(X,N,XAVG);
PUT SKIP LIST ('MAX =',XMAX,'MIN =',XMIN,'AVG =',XAVG);
END DRIVER;

      JCL goes here

MAXMIN: PROC(X,N,XMAX,XMIN);
/*************************************************************/
/*                                                           */
/* SUBROUTINE: FIND MAXIMUM AND MINIMUM VALUES IN ARRAY      */
/*                                                           */
/* OUTPUT PARAMETERS: XMAX, XMIN                             */
/*                                                           */
/*************************************************************/
DCL X(20)    FIXED BIN,
    N        FIXED BIN,
    XMAX     FIXED BIN,
    XMIN     FIXED BIN;
DCL I        FIXED BIN;

XMIN = X(1);
XMAX = X(1);
DO I = 2 TO N;
  IF X(I) < XMIN          /* FIND MINIMUM VALUE          */
    THEN
      XMIN = X(I);
  IF X(I) > XMAX;         /* FIND MAXIMUM VALUE          */
    THEN
      XMAX = X(I);
END MAXMIN;

      JCL goes here

GETAVG: PROC(X,N,XAVG);
/*************************************************************/
/*                                                           */
/* SUBROUTINE: CALCULATE AVERAGE VALUE IN ARRAY              */
/*                                                           */
/* OUTPUT PARAMETERS: XAVG                                   */
/*                                                           */
/*************************************************************/
DCL X(20)    FIXED BIN,
    N        FIXED BIN,
    XAVG     FLOAT BIN;
DCL I        FIXED BIN,
    XSUM     FIXED BIN;

XSUM = 0;
DO I = 1 TO N;            /* CALCULATE SUM OF VALUES     */
  XSUM = XSUM + X(I);
END;
XAVG = XSUM/N;            /* CALCULATE AVERAGE           */
END GETAVG;
```

A driver is a program written for the purpose of testing subprocedures. It calls them, provides data for them, and prints the values that are returned.

The same program can be written with internal procedures.

```
DRIVER: PROC OPTIONS (MAIN);
/*************************************************************/
/*                                                           */
/* PROGRAM: TESTING DRIVER FOR MAXMIN AND GETAVG             */
/* AUTHOR:  C ZIEGLER                                        */
/* VERSION: 07/17/84                                         */
/*                                                           */
/* PROGRAM DESCRIPTION                                       */
/* ------------------------------------------------------    */
/* THIS PROGRAM TESTS THE EXTERNAL ROUTINES MAXMIN AND       */
/* GETAVG.                                                   */
/*                                                           */
/* INPUT: SYSIN - LIST OF 20 FIXED BINARY NUMBERS            */
/*                                                           */
/* OUTPUT: SYSPRINT - MAXIMUM, MINIMUM, AVERAGE VALUES       */
/*************************************************************/
DCL X(20)   FIXED BIN,
    XMAX    FIXED BIN,
    XMIN    FIXED BIN,
    XAVG    FLOAT BIN;
DCL N       FIXED BIN;

DO I = 1 TO 20;
  GET LIST (X(I));
END;
CALL MAXMIN(X,N,XMAX,XMIN);
CALL GETAVG(X,N,XAVG);
PUT SKIP LIST ('MAX =',XMAX,'MIN =',XMIN,'AVG =',XAVG);

MAXMIN: PROC(X,N,XMAX,XMIN);
/*************************************************************/
/*                                                           */
/* SUBROUTINE: FIND MAXIMUM AND MINIMUM VALUES IN ARRAY      */
/*                                                           */
/* OUTPUT PARAMETERS: XMAX, XMIN                             */
/*                                                           */
/*************************************************************/
DCL X(20)   FIXED BIN,
    XMAX    FIXED BIN,
    XMIN    FIXED BIN;
DCL N       FIXED BIN;
DCL I       FIXED BIN;

XMIN = X(1);
XMAX = X(1);
DO I = 2 TO N;
  IF X(I) < XMIN            /* FIND MINIMUM VALUE          */
    THEN
      XMIN = X(I);
```

```
    IF X(I) > XMAX              /* FIND MAXIMUM VALUE          */
      THEN
        XMAX = X(I);
END MAXMIN:

GETAVG: PROC(X,N,XAVG);
/*************************************************************/
/*                                                           */
/* SUBROUTINE: CALCULATE AVERAGE VALUE IN ARRAY              */
/*                                                           */
/* OUTPUT PARAMETERS: XAVG                                   */
/*                                                           */
/*************************************************************/
DCL X(20)    FIXED BIN,
    XAVG     FLOAT BIN;
DCL N        FIXED BIN;
DCL I        FIXED BIN,
    XSUM     FIXED BIN;

XSUM = 0;
DO I = 1 TO N;                   /* CALCULATE SUM OF VALUES   */
  XSUM = XSUM  X(I);
END;
XAVG = XSUM/N;                   /* CALCULATE AVERAGE         */
END GETAVG;
END DRIVER;
```

The difference in coding between internal or external subprocedures is the need for the ENTRY declarations with external procedures.

9.8.3 Selection sort

This program shows the use of an external procedure to perform a selection sort. Note the use of the input parameters N and L in the declaration of the sort. This is a general character string sort that can be used with an array of any size made up of character strings of any length. As such, it would be a useful addition to a library.

```
SORT: PROC OPTIONS(MAIN);
/*************************************************************/
/*                                                           */
/* PROGRAM: SELECTION SORT                                   */
/* AUTHOR:  R REDDY                                          */
/* VERSION: 07/17/84                                         */
/*                                                           */
/* PROGRAM DESCRIPTION                                       */
/* ------------------------------------------------------    */
/* THIS PROGRAM TESTS AN EXTERNAL SUBROUTINE WHICH           */
/* PERFORMS GENERAL SELECTION SORTS OF CHARACTER STRINGS     */
/*                                                           */
```

```
/* INPUT: SYSIN - 30 CHARACTER RECORDS                              */
/*                                                                  */
/* OUTPUT: SYSPRINT - LISTING OF SORTED RECORDS                     */
/*                                                                  */
/******************************************************************/
DCL NAME(20)      CHAR(30),
    N             FIXED BIN(15);
DCL I             FIXED BIN(15),
    L             FIXED BIN (15)  INIT (30);
DCL SELSORT       ENTRY((20) CHAR(30),FIXED BIN(15),FIXED BIN(15));

GET EDIT (N) (COL(1),F(3));
DO I = 1 TO N;
  GET EDIT (NAME(I)) (COL(1),A(30));
END;
CALL SELSORT(NAME,N,L);
PUT EDIT (NAME) (COL(1),A);
END SORT;

           JCL goes here

SELSORT: PROC (INFO,N,L);
/******************************************************************/
/*                                                                */
/* SUBROUTINE: SORT AN ARRAY OF CHARACTER STRINGS USING           */
/* A BASIC SELECTION SORT.                                        */
/*                                                                */
/* PARAMETERS: INFO - INPUT/OUTPUT                                */
/*             N    - INPUT                                       */
/*             L    - INPUT                                       */
/*                                                                */
/******************************************************************/
DCL INFO(20)     CHAR(30),
    (N,L)        FIXED BIN(15);
DCL TEMP         CHAR(L),
    (I,J,M)      FIXED BIN(15);

M = N - 1;
DO I = 1 TO M;
  DO J = I + 1 TO N;          /* FIND SMALLEST VALUE REMAINING */
    IF INFO(J) < INFO(I)
      THEN
        DO;                   /* SWAP IT WITH VALUE AT I       */
          TEMP = INFO(I);
          INFO(I) = INFO(J);
          INFO(J) = TEMP;
        END;
  END;
END;
END SELSORT;
```

Since the array INFO is a parameter it does not require any storage. The sorting takes place in the original array in the calling program. INFO is both an input and output parameter since values are obtained from the array, compared, and replaced. This is an inefficient but straightforward type of sort. The first pass over the data moves the smallest value to the top position. The second pass moves the next smallest to the next to top position, and so forth.

9.8.4 Reverse an array

This subroutine reverses the order of numbers in a one-dimensional array. Since it uses only local variables, it could be either an internal or an external procedure.

```
REVERSE: PROC(VECT);
/*****************************************************************/
/*                                                               */
/* PROGRAM: REVERSE ARRAY                                        */
/* AUTHOR: R REDDY                                               */
/* VERSION: 07/17/84                                             */
/*                                                               */
/* PROGRAM DESCRIPTION                                           */
/* ----------------------------------------------------------    */
/* THIS SUBROUTINE REVERSES THE ORDER OF NUMBERS IN AN           */
/* ARRAY                                                         */
/*                                                               */
/* PARAMETERS: VECT - INPUT/OUTPUT                               */
/*                                                               */
/*****************************************************************/
DCL VECT(*)       FIXED BIN,
    TEMP          FIXED BIN,
    (H,K,L,M)     FIXED BIN;

L = LBOUND(VECT,1);         /* L IS LOWER BOUND OF VECT      */
H = HBOUND(VECT,1);         /* H IS UPPER BOUND OF VECT      */
M = (L+H)/2;                /* M IS MIDDLE POSITION OF VECT */
DO K = L TO M;              /* SWAP HALVES OF VECT           */
  TEMP = VECT(K);
  VECT(K)=VECT(H);
  VECT(H) = TEMP;
  H = H - 1;
END;
END REVERSE;
```

9.8.5 Reverse a character string

This function reverses the order of the characters in a string whose length is at most twenty. This can be implemented as a function because a character string is considered a scalar value, and it can be returned through a RETURN statement. Rather than altering the original character string, a new one is built, which is then returned. A second character string is used because functions should not alter any of their parameters.

```
REVERSTR: PROC(STR) RETURNS(CHAR(20) VARYING);
/***************************************************************/
/*                                                             */
/* PROGRAM: REVERSE CHARACTER STRING                           */
/* AUTHOR:  C ZIEGLER                                          */
/* VERSION: 07/17/84                                           */
/*                                                             */
/* PROGRAM DESCRIPTION                                         */
/* ----------------------------------------------------------- */
/* THIS SUBROUTINE REVERSES THE ORDER OF CHARACTERS IN A       */
/* CHARACTER STRING                                            */
/*                                                             */
/***************************************************************/
DCL STR                    CHAR(*);
DCL L                      FIXED BIN INIT(LENGTH(STR));
DCL RSTR                   CHAR(L),
    (I,J)                  FIXED BIN;

J = L;
DO I = 1 TO L;
  SUBSTR(RSTR,J,1) = SUBSTR(STR,I,1);
  J = J - 1;
END;
RETURN(RSTR);
END REVERSTR;
```

Note the way the LENGTH function is used in the initialization of L, and how L is then used in the declaration of RSTR. This could be done more efficiently as:

```
DCL STR                    CHAR(*);
DCL L                      FIXED BIN INIT(LENGTH(STR)),
    SCH(L)                 CHAR(1)    DEF(STR);
DCL RSTR                   CHAR(L),
    RCH(L)                 CHAR(1)    DEF(RSTR),
    (I,J)                  FIXED BIN;

J = L;
DO I = 1 TO L;
  RCH(J) = SCH(I);
  J = J - 1;
END;
```

Since any iterative algorithm can be implemented recursively, a second recursive version is given. Note that the string being returned is extended by one character at each level of recursion. The first character of the parameter string is appended to the end of the string being returned. This character is removed from the parameter before passing it down to the next level of recursion.

```
REVERSTR: PROC(STR) RECURSIVE RETURNS(CHAR(20) VARYING);
/**************************************************************/
/*                                                            */
/* PROGRAM: REVERSE CHARACTER STRING                          */
/* AUTHOR:  C ZIEGLER                                         */
/* VERSION: 07/17/84                                          */
/*                                                            */
/* PROGRAM DESCRIPTION                                        */
/* ---------------------------------------------------------- */
/* THIS SUBROUTINE REVERSES THE ORDER OF CHARACTERS IN A      */
/* CHARACTER STRING                                           */
/*                                                            */
/**************************************************************/
DCL STR                CHAR(20) VAR;
DCL L                  FIXED BIN;
DCL RSTR               CHAR(20) VAR,
    CH                 CH(1);

L = LENGTH(STR);
IF L = 1
  THEN
    RETURN (STR);                  /* RETURN LAST CHARACTER   */
  ELSE
    DO;
      CH = SUBSTR(STR,1,1);        /* OBTAIN FIRST CHARACTER */
      RSTR = SUBSTR(STR,2);        /* REMOVE FIRST CHARACTER */
      RETURN (REVRSTR(RSTR) || CH);
    END;
END REVERSTR;
```

9.8.6 Identity matrix

This is an example of a subroutine with several entry points. The INIT entry point is used to set up an identity matrix with ones along the major diagonal and zeros everywhere else. The PRINT entry point is used to print the matrix. The calling program first calls INIT, then alters the matrix, then calls PRINT. This is an example of a communicational procedure.

```
MATRIX: PROC(MAT,N);
/**************************************************************/
/*                                                            */
/* PROGRAM: IDENTITY MATRIX                                   */
/* AUTHOR:  C ZIEGLER                                         */
/* VERSION: 07/17/84                                          */
/*                                                            */
/* PROGRAM DESCRIPTION                                        */
/* ---------------------------------------------------------- */
/* THIS SUBROUTINE SETS UP AND PRINTS AN IDENTITY MATRIX      */
/*                                                            */
/* PARAMETERS: MAT - OUTPUT                                   */
/*             N   - INPUT                                    */
/*                                                            */
/**************************************************************/
```

```
DCL MAT(*,*)  FIXED BIN,
    N         FIXED BIN;
DCL K         FIXED BIN;

INIT: ENTRY(MAT,N);
MAT = 0;
DO K = 1 TO 20;
  MAT(K,K) = 1;
END;
RETURN;

PRINT: ENTRY(MAT,N);
PUT EDIT (MAT) (COL(5), (N)F(6,0));
RETURN;
END MATRIX;
```

Note that the name MATRIX is being used to "package" the INIT and PRINT routines, but does not ever need to be called. MATRIX and INIT refer to the same entry point.

9.8.7 Locate character

The string library function VERIFY returns the position of the first occurrence of a character not in its argument. We could define a similar useful function ANY which returns the position of the first occurrence of a character from its argument.

```
ANY: PROC(TEXT,STR) RETURNS(FIXED BIN);
/***************************************************************/
/*                                                             */
/* PROGRAM: LOCATE ANY OF SPECIFIED CHARACTERS                 */
/* AUTHOR:  R REDDY                                            */
/* VERSION: 07/17/84                                           */
/*                                                             */
/* PROGRAM DESCRIPTION                                         */
/* ----------------------------------------------------------- */
/* THIS FUNCTION RETURNS THE POSITION OF THE FIRST             */
/* OCCURRENCE OF A CHARACTER FROM STR IN TEXT                  */
/*                                                             */
/***************************************************************/
DCL TEXT    CHAR(*),
    STR     CHAR(*);
DCL (K,T)   FIXED BIN;

T = LENGTH(TEXT);
DO K = 1 to T;
  IF INDEX(STR,SUBSTR(TEXT,K,1)) > 0
    THEN
      RETURN(K);
END;
RETURN(0);
END ANY;
```

Note the use of zero as an error value to return if no matching character is found.

9.8.8 Recursive iteration

The following subroutine uses a DOWHILE loop to print data, the most efficient way to do this. However, as an illustration of the fact that any routine that can be written iteratively can be written recursively, two recursive versions are shown afterward.

```
READ_PRINT: PROC;
DCL STR     CHAR(80),
    MORE    BIT(1);
DCL TRUE    BIT(1)   INIT('1'B),
    FALSE   BIT(1)   INIT('0'B);

ON ENDFILE(SYSIN)
  MORE = FALSE;

MORE = TRUE;
GET EDIT (STR) (A(80));
DO WHILE(MORE);
  PUT SKIP EDIT (STR) (A);
  GET EDIT (STR) (A(80));
END;
END READ_PRINT;
```

The first recursive version reads and prints the data in exactly the same way as the iterative version. There is a priming read and the DOWHILE(MORE) is replaced by an IF MORE.

```
READ_PRINT: PROC RECURSIVE;
/*************************************************************/
/*                                                           */
/* PROGRAM: LIST RECORDS RECURSIVELY                         */
/* AUTHOR:  C ZIEGLER                                        */
/* VERSION: 07/17/84                                         */
/*                                                           */
/* PROGRAM DESCRIPTION                                       */
/* ------------------------------------------------------    */
/* THIS SUBROUTINE READS AND PRINTS RECORDS RECURSIVELY      */
/*                                                           */
/*************************************************************/
DCL STR  CHAR(80),
    MORE BIT(1);
ON ENDFILE(SYSIN)
  MORE = FALSE;

MORE = TRUE;
GET EDIT (STR) (A(80));
IF MORE
  THEN
    DO;
      PUT SKIP EDIT (STR) (A);
      CALL READ_PRINT;
    END;
END READ_PRINT;
```

Each time the procedure is called, it reads and prints one record. When finally the end-of-file is read, the recursion stops. The records are printed on the recursive descent. The output is in the same order as the input.

The second version prints the data on the recursive ascent. The difference between the two is merely the difference in the order of the output statement and the recursive call.

```
READ_PRINT: PROC RECURSIVE;
/****************************************************************/
/*                                                              */
/* PROGRAM: LIST RECORDS RECURSIVELY                            */
/* AUTHOR:  C ZIEGLER                                           */
/* VERSION: 07/17/84                                            */
/*                                                              */
/* PROGRAM DESCRIPTION                                          */
/* -----------------------------------------------------------  */
/* THIS SUBROUTINE READS AND PRINTS RECORDS RECURSIVELY         */
/*                                                              */
/****************************************************************/
DCL STR   CHAR(80),
    MORE  BIT(1);
DCL TRUE  BIT(1)  INIT('1'B),
    FALSE BIT(1)  INIT('0'B);

ON ENDFILE (SYSIN)
  MORE = FALSE;

MORE = TRUE;
GET EDIT (STR) (A(80));
IF MORE
  THEN
    DO;
      CALL READ PRINT;
      PUT SKIP EDIT (STR) (A);
    END;
END READ_PRINT;
```

The records are printed in reverse order than they were read in.

These routines could not handle a very large set of input data, as one record is stored in memory every time the procedure is called. Each activation of the procedure only knows about one of the STR variables. The printing doesn't start until the recursion stops and execution returns from the last activation. Thus the last record is printed first.

Placing the ON unit in the subprocedure is very inefficient because it establishes the ON unit every time the subprocedure is called. Each time, the local environment of the ON unit is saved. The functionality of the program is improved by having the ON unit defined in the same procedure that uses the input file. In the case of a nonrecursive subprocedure, this is the proper place for the ON unit. In the case of a recursive subprocedure, the placement of the ON unit depends on the environment desired for it.

9.9 Summary

Procedures may be classified as main procedures or subprocedures, depending on whether they are activated by the operating system or by a user procedure; as internal or external, depending on whether they are physically written inside a main procedure or outside it; as recursive or nonrecursive, depending on whether they invoke themselves or not; and as functions or subroutines, depending on the way they are invoked.

Functions and subroutines may be compared as follows:

Function	*Subroutine*
Invoked by using as a variable	Invoked by a CALL statement
Returns a value through a RETURN statement	Returns values through output parameters
Can only return scalar values	Can return any type of value
Must return exactly one value	Can return any number of values
Should not alter parameters	May alter parameters
May be recursive	May be recursive
Used to calculate value	Used to alter storage or do I/O

The environment of a procedure is the set of variables that may be referenced and procedures that may be invoked from inside the procedure. This consists of both global and local names. The local names are established by being declared in the procedure. The global names are established by being declared in procedures that statically contain the procedure.

The scope of procedure names determines which procedures may invoke which other procedures. The scope of variable names determines which procedures may reference which variables. The scope of ON units determines which ON units are in effect in each part of the program.

9.10 Exercises

1. This is a version of the "producer/consumer" problem. Write a program containing an array ARR(7) FIXED BINARY that calls a subroutine IN and a subroutine OUT to do the I/O. IN reads three numbers at a time and put them in the array. OUT prints five numbers at a time from the array. IN should be called whenever the array has room for three values. OUT should be called whenever the array contains five values. The array is used as a circular buffer. When a value is placed in the seventh position, the next value goes in the first position.

2. Records containing student grades have the following form:

Cols.	1-20	Student name
	21-23	Grade for week 1
	24-26	Grade for week 2
	. . .	
	63-65	Grade for week 15

Write a program that uses a function procedure to calculate the average grade for a student and a subroutine procedure to print the student's name, average grade, and letter grade (90-100 A, 80-89 B, 70-79 C, 60-69 D, below 60 F).

3. Write a program that reads three fixed binary numbers and calls a function TRIANG(A,B,C) which determines whether the numbers are acceptable as lengths of sides of a triangle (not too large or too small). If they are, it should call another function AREA(A,B,C) to obtain the area of the triangle, using the equations

$$S = (A+B+C)/2$$

$$AREA = \sqrt{S(S-A)(S-B)(S-C)}$$

4. Write a program that reads character strings of length 80 and calls a function that compresses the character strings, returning them with all the blanks removed.

5. Write a program that lets the computer solve a type of problem commonly found on intelligence tests. The data consists of sequences of six numbers. The computer is to determine the next number in the sequence. Use the following sets of data:

1	2	3	4	5	6
1	2	4	7	11	16
0	1	4	9	16	25
2	4	7	12	20	32

After reading a sequence of numbers into an array X, the main procedure should invoke a recursive function procedure F(X) which accepts a variable length array as a parameter and does the following: If all the X_i are the same, return the last X_i; otherwise set up an array Y such that $Y(K) = X(K+1)-X(K)$ and return the value of the last $X_i + F(Y)$.

6. Write a program that evaluates fully parenthesized arithmetic expressions. It should call a recursive function which, when there are nested parentheses, calls itself to evaluate the inner parentheses, and when there are no nested parentheses, returns the value of the inner expression. Use the following data:

((2 + 5) − (7 − (3 + 1)))
(8 − ((3 + 5) − 9))

***7.** The order of evaluation of each of the following expressions is implementation-dependent. Write a program having ON units or an abnormal function, whichever is appropriate, to determine the order of evaluation on your system.

(a)
```
N = 0;
K = '12X3';
X = 25/N + 1273/K;
PUT SKIP LIST(X);
```
(b)
```
P = F(X) > 7 | F(X) < 7;
PUT SKIP LIST(P);
```
(c)
```
DCL A(10) FIXED BIN INIT(1,2,3,4,5,6,7,8,9,10);
K = 1;
A(K) = 2*F(K) + 3*F(K);
PUT SKIP LIST(A);
A(K) = 2*F((K)) + 3*F(K);
PUT SKIP LIST(A);
A(K) = 2*F(K) + 3*F((K));
PUT SKIP LIST(A);
```

10
Data maintenance (stream files)

OBJECTIVE: To create, use, and keep up-to-date data.

STREAM FILES FOR INPUT and output of data were introduced in chapter 4. This chapter discusses their use in storing and processing large amounts of data. Up to this point we have assumed that data is processed only once. Some values are calculated or a report is printed, and that is the end of the need for the data. However, in most real-life situations, once data is collected, it is used many times and kept indefinitely. Different types of data are collected and used in different ways. Some, such as census data, is collected over a short period but reorganized and analyzed many times, being used for many kinds of population studies over a long period of time. Charge accounts and other billing records are accumulated slowly, updated periodically, and used on a regular basis at least once a month. Direct sales mailing lists are used repeatedly but rarely updated.

To be stored and accessed efficiently by a computer, data must be stored in a file on a magnetic tape or disk device. Files on these devices are machine-readable, hold large amounts of data, and can be accessed quickly. The choice of storage device depends on the use being made of the data. If data is kept up to date, it will outlast the computer that processes it.

10.1 File maintenance system

A group of programs that process a set of data, together with the files they use, is known as a *file maintenance system.* The center of the system is the data that is collected and maintained on one or more files, known as *master files.* Although the data changes with time, the storage form is semipermanent. The programs that process the data also change with time as needs are reassessed.

10.1.1 Master/transaction files

The basic steps in file maintenance are to create the file, update the file, and use the file. A master file is created from a source file which is often entered into the computer interactively. It differs from the original version of the master file in that the data in the source file has been visually inspected, but not validated. Also, it may need to be sorted and have duplicates eliminated. The file creation program must provide at least three sets of output: the first version of the master file, and progress and error reports.

To update data kept on a master file, other data containing the changes must be available from a second source at the same time the primary source, the master file, is available. An update data file is called a *transaction file.* A program must be written to combine the data from the two sources. So far we have been handling only one source of data, SYSIN, the standard system input file.

An update program must also provide at least two sets of output: the revised data, which is a new version of the master file, and reports on the progress of the update, including any data errors. So far, the only output file has been SYSPRINT, the standard system printer file. There is also a standard system output file, SYSOUT, which is used for devices such as disk, tape, or terminals where page control is not needed. When more files than these are needed, file declarations must be used.

Figure 10–1 shows the variety of different input and output files and programs needed to handle any set of permanent data. The output includes both machine-readable files being stored in the computer, reports concerning data entry, and answers to data queries.

Whether the processing is batch or interactive, it takes at least three programs to manage data. One program, which is only executed once, creates the original version of the master file. Another program updates and maintains the master file, and at least one other program writes reports from it or queries it. There may be additional programs to restructure the master

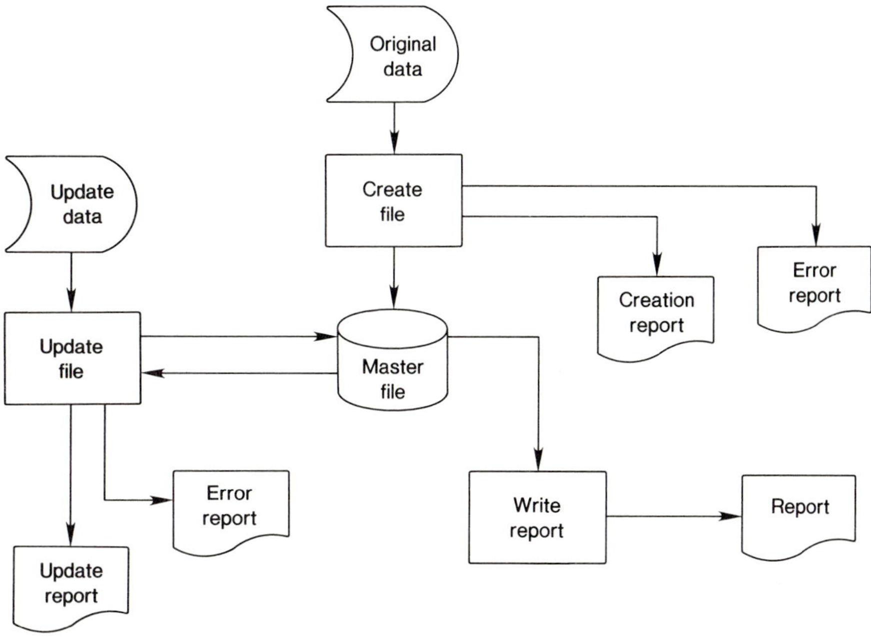

Figure 10–1

file or make backup copies of it. Many of these programs have more than one input file or more than one output file. A hierarchy chart showing the organization of the system is given in figure 10–2.

Figure 10–3 gives an HIPO (Hierarchy, Input, Processing, Output) chart of the system, which shows the input files, processing steps, and output files of one module of a hierarchy chart. This HIPO chart shows the top module, covering the complete system. It is equivalent to the diagram of figure 10–1. In the chart, step 1 is carried out once. Steps 2 and 3 may be carried out many times. The master file is used in all three steps. Where it appears on the output side, it is a new version of the file. The output master file of one step becomes the input master file of the next.

10.1.2 Work files

Besides ordinary input files and output files, and permanent data files, files may be set up to hold temporary results that will be needed again later in the

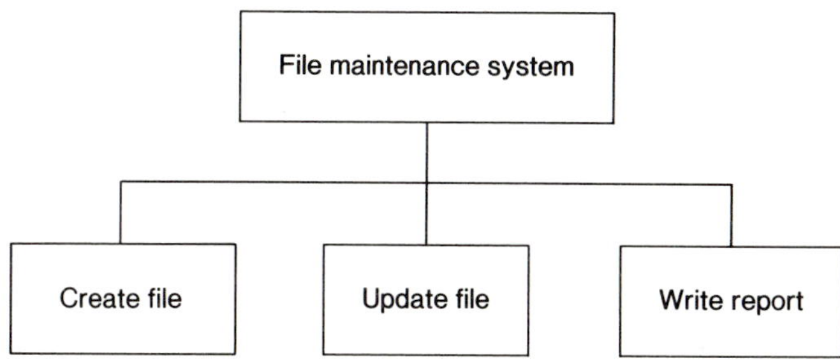

Figure 10–2

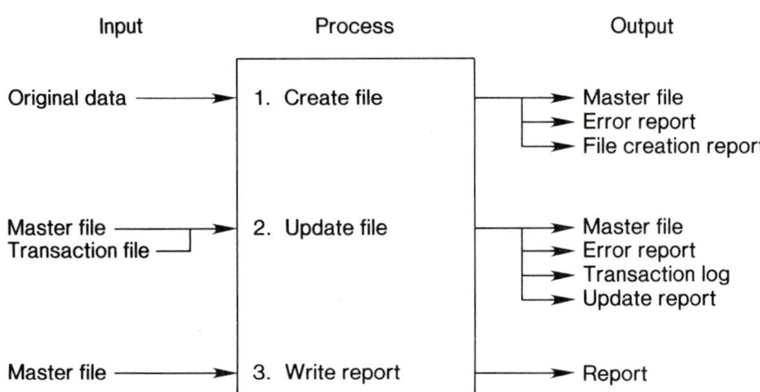

Figure 10–3

processing. Such temporary files are called *work files* or *scratch files.* They are built on mass storage devices. A work file is used first for output, then later for input in the same program. For example, if data is to be sorted, one or more work files will be needed.

Review questions

1. A file maintenance system requires the use of a ____________ file which has the original data, a ____________ file which is permanent and updated regularly, and a ____________ file which contains the updates.

2. The printed output from a file maintenance system consists of ____________ reports, ____________ reports, and ____________ reports.

3. The machine-readable version of a permanent file is usually stored on a ____________ or a ____________ device.

4. A file maintenance system requires a ____________, a ____________, and a ____________ program.

5. The three parts of an HIPO chart describe the ____________, the ____________, and the ____________ of a program.

6. Two kinds of files are used for both output and input: temporary ____________ files and permanent ____________ files.

7. The default system files are ____________, ____________, and ____________.

8. Files other than the default system files must be ____________.

10.2 CONSECUTIVE STREAM file declarations

Two access modes for files are available in PL/I: stream access and record access. The files of a file management system may be of either type, although record files are the most common. In this chapter we will discuss the declaration and use of stream files for data management. Record files will be discussed in chapters 15–17. The word "record" as used in this chapter refers to all the data from a single card reader card, terminal line, or printer line.

Those files provided automatically by the system, SYSIN, SYSOUT, and SYSPRINT, do not have to be declared and can be used without being referenced by name. They are convenient, but their names are not meaningful with respect to an application program. With a file maintenance system it is customary to declare all the files so that appropriate names can be used. When the programmer needs more than one input file, or more than one mass storage output or printer file, it is necessary to declare the extra files. If the programmer wants file attributes other than the default system attributes, file declarations are necessary.

The general form of a file declaration is:

```
DECLARE name FILE [mode] [use] [access] [ENV(organization)];
```

The mode may be SEQUENTIAL, DIRECT, or TRANSIENT.
The use may be INPUT, OUTPUT, PRINT, or UPDATE.
The access may be STREAM or RECORD.
The organization may be CONSECUTIVE, REGIONAL, INDEXED, or (on some systems) teleprocessing.
The file attributes may be specified in any order.

A file declaration is used by the system to set up a descriptor for the file. The descriptor contains information about the file status as well as the file attributes. It is used by the system in setting up a data path for the file and a buffer to hold records while they are being processed.

DEFAULT FILE ATTRIBUTES

The default system files SYSIN, SYSOUT, and SYSPRINT have the following implicit declarations:

```
DCL SYSIN    FILE SEQUENTIAL INPUT  STREAM ENV(CONSECUTIVE);
DCL SYSPRINT FILE SEQUENTIAL PRINT  STREAM ENV(CONSECUTIVE);
DCL SYSOUT   FILE SEQUENTIAL OUTPUT STREAM ENV(CONSECUTIVE);
```

If desired, they may be explicitly declared.

SYSIN file As the name indicates, SYSIN is an input file. Although it has been used up to this point as the source of all program data, it has only been mentioned by name in the context ENDFILE(SYSIN). It is sequential in that the data is read by the program in the same order in which it has been keyed in. It is stream; that is, the data is accessed as though it were one long character string. The input items are read from the input stream as it "passes" the device read/write head. And it is consecutive in that the data is not mixed in with other values.

SYSPRINT file SYSPRINT is the default output file for data that will eventually be sent to a printer, therefore its use is PRINT. It has only been mentioned by name in the context ENDPAGE(SYSPRINT).

SYSOUT file The default output file for data that is not in print format is SYSOUT. SYSOUT can be used for output to any of the peripheral devices. The data is placed in the file in the order and with the formatting indicated by the PUT statement used. The PAGE and LINE options are not available with SYSOUT.

User-named files The default values of the file attributes for user-named files are:

Mode	SEQUENTIAL (SEQL)
Use	INPUT
Access	STREAM
Organization	CONSECUTIVE

FILE NAMES

User file names are external, so they must follow the same rules as names for main procedures. In addition, the names should be appropriate for the organization, access, and use of the files. If a master file is to be read, appropriate file declarations might be:

```
DCL MASTER  FILE SEQL INPUT STREAM ENV(CONSECUTIVE);

DCL INVTORY FILE SEQL INPUT STREAM ENV(CONSECUTIVE);

DCL INVMAST FILE SEQL INPUT STREAM ENV(CONSECUTIVE);
```

Additional files needed for a file maintenance program might be declared as:

```
DCL TRANS  FILE SEQL INPUT STREAM ENV(CONSECUTIVE),
    ERROR  FILE SEQL PRINT STREAM ENV(CONSECUTIVE),
    REPORT FILE SEQL PRINT STREAM ENV(CONSECUTIVE);
```

With this choice of attributes, the master file could be a card, disk, or tape file, as could TRANS. ERROR and REPORT are both printer files, although they may be automatically spooled temporarily to some other medium.

PROGRAMMING HINT: CAUTION File names are subject to the rules for external names.

The optional parts of a file declaration may be omitted altogether and the default values of the attributes used, or they may be supplied by the OPEN statement. Using the default values, the MASTER, TRANS, ERROR, and REPORT files can be declared briefly as:

```
DCL MASTER FILE,
    TRANS  FILE,
    ERROR  PRINT FILE,
    REPORT PRINT FILE;
```

Declarations of work files follow the same form given above, except that the use attribute is not included in the declaration. Any attribute of a file that will be changed within a single program must be left out of the declaration. A temporary work file might be declared as:

```
DCL TEMP FILE SEQL STREAM ENV(CONSECUTIVE);
```

The default value of the mode of this file is INPUT, but the default may be overridden. The missing attribute can be provided at the time the file is opened. This permits the file to be opened for output when it is being created, and for input later when it is being read.

A temporary file that contains a table created using sequential access, to be used later with random access, would be declared as:

```
DCL TEMP FILE RECORD ENV(REGIONAL(1));
```

with both the processing mode and the use to be supplied at the time the file is opened.

The names MASTER, INVTORY, INVMAST, TRANS, ERROR, and REPORT refer to the data files as they are seen by the program. The actual files have permanent names, which are stored in a system catalog. JCL (job control) specifications are used to indicate to the computer how the program names are to be matched with the permanent names. Generally this is done by first assigning names for the system software to use in referencing the file. For example, the data to be accessed under the name MASTER may have the permanent name INV023Z. A temporary name F1 might be specified for the use of the operating system. The actual data is accessed by system software and passed to the program as it is needed, as shown in figure 10–4.

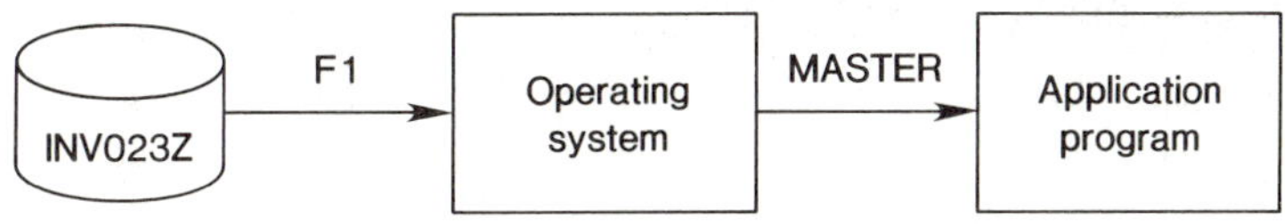

Figure 10–4

10.2.1 Processing mode

Files may be declared as either SEQUENTIAL (SEQL), DIRECT, or TRANSIENT. The default value for processing mode is SEQUENTIAL. The set of possible processing modes for a file is determined by the storage device and file organization.

SEQUENTIAL PROCESSING

With sequential processing the records are accessed in order, one after another in the same order they have on the storage medium. They are processed from first to last without jumping around or backing up. This kind of access is necessary when GET and PUT statements are being used, since the data in the file appears to be one long character string. Any boundaries of cards, lines, or other types of records are ignored. The files SYSIN, SYSPRINT, and SYSOUT can only be processed sequentially.

DIRECT PROCESSING

With direct processing, it is not necessary to start at the beginning of the file and access every record. They can be accessed in any order. Direct processing is used with REGIONAL and INDEXED files on random-access devices such as disks or drums.

TRANSIENT PROCESSING

Transient processing is the processing of records that have no permanent existence on a file but are obtained from or sent to an interactive terminal by a program set up to service many terminals. To call data on a keyboard or CRT a file is a convenient fiction that allows PL/I to handle it in the same way as other data. Transient processing is only available in versions of PL/I that support interactive programs.

10.2.2 File use

Files may be used for INPUT, OUTPUT, PRINT, or UPDATE. The default use is INPUT. These uses are attributes of the file name as declared in a program or part of a program, not attributes of the actual file as seen by the operating system or stored on the device. However, the set of possible uses is determined by the storage device, which grants permission for file access.

INPUT FILES

An input file has data to be used as input. Some input data is on devices such as a keyboard or card reader, and can only be used for input. Other input data is on permanent files that must not be changed. To protect the data and the device, the actual use of the file is restricted to "read only." Other input data is on permanent files that have other uses at other times. Trying to write to an INPUT file causes a system error. SYSIN is the system default INPUT file.

OUTPUT FILES

An output file has no data on it. It is available for data storage by the program. Any data that previously may have been present in the actual file is lost when an output file is opened. Attempting to read an output file causes a system error. SYSOUT is the system default output file.

PROGRAMMING HINT: CAUTION Opening a file for OUTPUT erases any previous contents of the file.

PRINT FILES

A print file is an output file destined for the printer. Print files may have carriage control characters used with them. LINE and PAGE options may be used in PUT statements when the PRINT attribute is used. These commands may not be used with OUTPUT files. Attempting to read a PRINT file causes a system error. SYSPRINT is the system default PRINT file.

PROGRAMMING HINT: The output page control options can only be used with PRINT files.

UPDATE FILES

UPDATE files are used when data in a file is being modified or deleted. Both reading and writing are needed to modify a file since data must be read before it can be changed. Data may always be read from UPDATE files. Under some circumstances new data can be inserted in UPDATE files without replacing existing data. This kind of file may be used only on devices such as the disk, which makes it possible to access a record twice. There is no system default UPDATE file.

10.2.3 File access

Data in a file may be accessed as a stream of characters or as a set of records. The default value for file access is STREAM. File access is independent of the storage device, but it is sometimes determined by the file organization.

STREAM ACCESS

A stream file appears to the program to be a single long character string. SYSIN, SYSPRINT, and SYSOUT are stream files. The transmission of stream file data is controlled by GET and PUT statements. The I/O statement controls the amount of information taken from or sent to the file, the selection of the information, and its location. The basic unit of information is the character even though more than one character is handled by an I/O statement. The data in a stream input file is converted from character to other types under control of the GET statement. For output files, the PUT statement converts other types of data to characters. A stream file is actually implemented using records, but record boundaries are ignored by the GET and PUT instructions unless alignment control commands such as SKIP and COL are used.

RECORD ACCESS

A record file is one on which file information comes in predetermined amounts called *records,* defined as being the amount of data handled by a single record I/O statement and transmitted in one operation. Records are accessed using READ and WRITE statements. The data is read and written as a whole, without formatting or type conversion. The size of a record is measured in bytes rather than characters, as it may contain data other than character data.

10.2.4 File organization

The ENVIRONMENT (abbreviated ENV) clause specifies the file's organization. There are many different options that may be used in this clause. These options are system-dependent, so it is necessary to consult a language reference manual for the particular computer being used, to determine which options are available. Depending on the system, the options may include specifying the print control code, record length, blocking factor, number of buffers, and other types of system information that may also be specified through the JCL. In general, it is better to provide this information with the JCL if the program code is not dependent on it. We will only use the file organization in the environment clause.

The default file organization is CONSECUTIVE. Alternate organizations are REGIONAL, INDEXED, and teleprocessing. These organizations vary slightly from system to system because they are software-dependent, but the concepts involved remain the same.

CONSECUTIVE ORGANIZATION

A consecutive file is one whose data is arranged in the order in which it is to be processed. The records are stored consecutively and can only be accessed using sequential processing. Records may be updated but there is no room to insert new records and no way to actually remove old records. In many systems, this is the only file organization that supports stream I/O.

Table 10–1 shows the file attributes compatible with CONSECUTIVE STREAM files on various devices.

Table 10–1

Device	*Mode*	*Use*	*Access*	*Organization*
Card reader	SEQUENTIAL	INPUT	STREAM	CONSECUTIVE
Line printer	SEQUENTIAL	OUTPUT PRINT	STREAM	CONSECUTIVE
Magnetic tape	SEQUENTIAL	INPUT OUTPUT PRINT	STREAM	CONSECUTIVE
Magnetic disk	SEQUENTIAL	INPUT OUTPUT PRINT	STREAM	CONSECUTIVE

REGIONAL AND INDEXED ORGANIZATIONS

Regional and indexed files are organized in such a way that individual records can be found directly, without reading the entire file. This is sometimes known as random access. With these file organizations both sequential and direct processing are supported. A record in a REGIONAL file is located by its position in the file. A record in an INDEXED file is located and identified by a data key looked up in an index. There are many varieties of regional and indexed files; some of these will be discussed in chapters 16 and 17. These file organizations can be used only with mass storage devices such as disk and drum.

TELEPROCESSING ORGANIZATION

Files organized for teleprocessing are available only in versions of PL/I that support interactive I/O. There is no standard way of declaring these files. The internal organization is that provided by the teleprocessing software of the installation. Teleprocessing files will be discussed in chapter 18.

Review questions

1. The PAGE and LINE options are available only on the system file ________ and files declared with the ________ attribute.

2. Complete each of the following statements:

(a) The GET and PUT statements are used with ________ (STREAM / RECORD) files.

(b) With both STREAM and RECORD files, data stored on the storage device is stored in a ________ (record / buffer).

(c) With both STREAM and RECORD files, data stored in the computer memory is stored in a ________ (record / buffer).

(d) When the information in a file is processed in the same order in which it resides in the file, the processing is ________ (SEQUENTIAL / DIRECT).

(e) When a file is being created, it is an ________ (INPUT / OUTPUT / UPDATE) file.

(f) When data is being used from a file that already exists, it is an ________ (INPUT / OUTPUT / UPDATE) file.

(g) When a master file is being updated, it is an ________ (INPUT / OUTPUT / UPDATE) file.

(h) When the information in a file is stored compactly with no wasted record positions, the file organization is ________ (CONSECUTIVE / REGIONAL / INDEXED).

(i) When the information in a file is stored for retrieval by position in the file, the file organization is ________ (CONSECUTIVE / REGIONAL / INDEXED).

(j) When the information in a file is stored for retrieval by a data key, the file organization is ________ (CONSECUTIVE / REGIONAL / INDEXED).

3. Indicate whether each of the following statements is true or false.

(a) When more than one input file is used in a program, the additional files must be declared.

(b) File attributes may be specified in any order.

(c) The default file attributes are SEQL, UPDATE, STREAM, and CONSECUTIVE.

(d) SYSOUT can be used for output to any output device.

(e) SYSPRINT can only be used for output to a printer.

(f) File names are limited to seven letters or digits and must start with a letter.

(g) The name of a file in a program must be the same as the actual name of the file in storage.

4. Write a full file declaration for each of the following files:

(a) SYSIN

(b) SYSOUT

(c) SYSPRINT

5. Write a full file declaration for each of the following situations:
  (a) A master file on magnetic tape which is being updated.
  (b) A transaction file being entered interactively from a single terminal.
  (c) A report being sent to a printer.
  (d) A temporary work file on the disk.

10.3 File availability

The terminology used with files is partly derived from the business office. Words such as "file," "record," "open," "close," "get," and "put" are used in programming languages in a way somewhat analogous to their everyday use. This makes a program more readable, just as using common mathematical notation and formulas makes a program more readable. In PL/I, before a file can be used it must be "opened." After it has been used it must be "closed." You "get" data from a file and "put" data into a file. In the file the data is stored in "records."

10.3.1 OPEN statement

Opening a file completes the file descriptor that was set up from the declaration, links the declared name with the external file, and checks the declared attributes against the actual file. It also positions the file at the beginning and sets up the data path. This makes the file available to the program. The OPEN statement must precede any input or output statements referring to a file. The general form of the OPEN statement is:

```
OPEN [mode] [use] [access] FILE (file_name) [TITLE (jcl_name)];
```

Examples of the simplest form of the OPEN statement are:

```
OPEN FILE (MASTER);
OPEN FILE (TRANS);
```

File attributes are not included in an OPEN statement if they are part of the file declaration.

FILE ATTRIBUTES

The mode, use, and access attributes of the file may be supplied in the OPEN statement if they are not part of the file declaration. The attributes should be included in the declaration if they remain the same throughout the program. For example, PRINT files cannot be used for anything except printing output. Their attributes should be included in the file declarations. The following example shows the declaration and OPEN statements for a work file used for both input and output.

```
DCL TEMP FILE SEQL STREAM ENV(CONSECUTIVE);
OPEN OUTPUT FILE (TEMP);
 . . .
OPEN INPUT FILE (TEMP);
```

Since a file is opened for a specific use, if it is to be accessed both for output (to build the file) and for input (to read the file) in a single program, it must be explicitly opened and closed. If it is first opened for output, it must be closed and opened again before it can be used for input.

PROGRAMMING HINT: CAUTION Opening a file positions the read/write head at the beginning of the file.

TITLE OPTION

If the title option is used, the programmer specifies in it the name that is to be used in the JCL. With the statements

```
OPEN FILE (ERROR)  TITLE ('P1'),
     FILE (REPORT) TITLE ('P2');
```

the JCL would have to identify P1 and P2 with specific files on particular devices. Files may be opened one at a time or, with some implementations of PL/I, several may be opened in a single instruction.

If the title option is not used, the file name used in the program must start with the same characters as the file name used in the JCL to identify the file to the operating system. Implementations differ as to the number of characters from the file name that can be used in the JCL.

DEFAULT STATUS

The files SYSIN, SYSOUT, and SYSPRINT are opened automatically at the beginning of program execution. If a user-named file is not explicitly opened and closed, the system will open it when it is first needed and close it at the end of the program. However, it is recommended that all user-named files be explicitly opened and closed. If files are open for as short a time as possible, there is less chance of spurious errors being introduced.

PROGRAMMING HINT: MAINTAINABILITY Open and close files explicitly.

10.3.2 CLOSE statement

The general form of the CLOSE statement is:

```
CLOSE FILE (file_name);
```

Files may be closed individually or, in some implementations of PL/I, several files may be closed in a single instruction. Some examples of the CLOSE statement are:

```
CLOSE FILE (MASTER);
CLOSE FILE (TRANS);
CLOSE FILE (ERROR),
      FILE (REPORT);
```

Closing a file makes it unavailable. In addition, if the file has been open for output, closing it causes an end-of-file mark to be written. If a temporary work file is to be created and then used as input in the same program, the declaration, OPEN, and CLOSE statements are as follows:

```
DCL TEMP FILE SEQL STREAM ENV(CONSECUTIVE);
 . . .
OPEN OUTPUT FILE(TEMP);
 . . .                              /* BUILD TEMP FILE         */
CLOSE FILE(TEMP);
OPEN INPUT FILE(TEMP);
 . . .                              /* USE TEMP FILE AS INPUT */
CLOSE FILE(TEMP);
```

The temporary file must be explicitly opened so that the use attribute can be specified. It must be explicitly closed before it can be reopened.

Rather than including the temporary file use in the OPEN statements, the file could be accessed under two different file names, both of which are associated by the TITLE option with the same JCL file name. This is shown in the following example:

```
DCL INTEMP FILE SEQL INPUT STREAM ENV(CONSECUTIVE),
    OUTEMP FILE SEQL OUTPUT STREAM ENV(CONSECUTIVE);
OPEN FILE(OUTEMP) TITLE ('TE');
 . . .                                 /* BUILD TEMP FILE         */
CLOSE FILE(OUTEMP);
OPEN FILE(INTEMP) TITLE ('TE');
 . . .                                 /* USE TEMP FILE AS INPUT */
CLOSE FILE(INTEMP);
```

It would be an error to have the files INTEMP and OUTEMP open at the same time.

When a file is opened for sequential access, it is positioned with its first record ready to be read or written. Opening a file a second time (after closing it first) positions it back at the beginning. Therefore a sequentially accessed file must not be closed until all processing is finished or the first record is needed again.

Review questions

1. Indicate whether each of the following statements is true or false.

(a) A file should be opened just before it is to be used.

(b) A file can be changed from OUTPUT to INPUT without closing it.

(c) An INPUT file can be closed and opened again without losing track of the reading position in it.

(d) Closing a sequential OUTPUT file causes an end-of-file to be written to it.

(e) A file cannot be used sometimes for INPUT and other times for OUTPUT.

(f) The OPEN statement can be used to change the attributes of a file.

2. When the statement OPEN INPUT FILE (TEMP) TITLE ('F1'); is executed,
   (a) ____________ will be checked for consistency.
   (b) ____________, ____________, and ____________ will be placed in the file descriptor for TEMP.
   (c) The file pointer will be positioned ____________.
   (d) ____________ will be obtained from the file.

3. Write an appropriate OPEN statement for stream processing of each of the following files:
   (a) DCL REPORT ENV(CONSECUTIVE);
   (b) DCL TRANSACTION ENV(CONSECUTIVE);

10.4 Stream access

Stream access is carried out through the use of the GET and PUT statements. Both treat the file as a single long character string, except that certain characters are used as end-of-record marks. Unless they are referred to by the editing formats, they are ignored by the input and output processing.

10.4.1 Input statements

The general forms of the input statements used with stream access are:

```
GET [FILE (file_name)] [SKIP(n)] LIST (input_list);
GET [FILE (file_name)] [SKIP(n)] DATA (input_list);
GET [FILE (file_name)] EDIT (input_list) (format_list);
```

The FILE clause is omitted when the system default files are used, but included for all user-named files. The GET operation is the same on all stream files on all devices. The only difference is that the underlying record length varies from one device to another and from one file to another.

10.4.2 Output statements

The general forms of the output statements used with stream access are:

```
PUT [FILE (file_name)] [alignment] LIST (output_list);
PUT [FILE (file_name)] [alignment] DATA (output_list);
PUT [FILE (file_name)] [alignment] EDIT (output_list) (format_list);
```

The FILE clause is omitted when the system default files are used, but included for all user-named files. The PUT operation is the same on all stream files except that the PAGE and LINE alignment options are only available on PRINT files, while the SKIP alignment option is available on all stream files. In addition, the underlying record length differs from one device to another and from one file to another.

Review questions

1. The FILE clause must be used in the GET statement for all INPUT files except ____________________.

2. The FILE clause must be used in the PUT statement for all OUTPUT files except ____________________ and ____________________.

10.5 File error conditions

10.5.1 ENDFILE condition

The ENDFILE condition is raised when there is an attempt to read beyond the end of the data in a file. The system recognizes the end of the file by a special end-of-file mark. The general form of the condition ON unit is:

```
ON ENDFILE(file_name) statement;
```

An ON unit should be established for each input file used.

10.5.2 ENDPAGE condition

The ENDPAGE condition is raised when there is an attempt to write beyond the end of the page in a PRINT file. The system recognizes the end of the page by an internal line counter. The general form of the condition ON unit is:

```
ON ENDPAGE(file_name) statement;
```

An ON unit should be established for each print file used.

10.5.3 ERROR condition

The ERROR condition is raised when any fatal error occurs for which no specific ON unit has been established. This includes but is not limited to errors in file processing. When a fatal error occurs, the system may not close the output files and save all the output data. If the output is wanted, an ON unit may be established for the ERROR condition. Its general form is:

```
ON ERROR statement;
```

The ON unit should be used to write an appropriate error message and close the files. For example,

```
ON ERROR
  BEGIN;
    PUT SKIP LIST ('EXECUTION ERROR');
    CLOSE FILE (SYSPRINT);
  END;
```

Review questions

1. The ENDFILE condition can be raised only by the system file ________________ and files declared with the ________________ attribute.

2. The ENDPAGE condition can be raised only by the system file ________________ and files declared with the ________________ attribute.

3. Write ON units to set appropriate end flags for the files SYSIN and SYSPRINT.

10.6 Examples of file maintenance

The basic file handling operations are creating a file, updating the file, and using the information from the file. With sequential access files, creating the file and using the file information are similar concepts. Both consist primarily of copying the information from one file to another.

10.6.1 Copying a file

A file is to be built from information on the system input file, and then is to be printed by the same program. No data validation is being carried out. Essentially the data on SYSIN is being copied to TEMP; then the data on TEMP is being copied to SYSPRINT. The files should be opened and closed as follows:

```
DCL TEMP FILE ENV(CONSECUTIVE);
/* OPEN FILE(SYSIN); */
OPEN OUTPUT FILE(TEMP);
   . . .                       /* LOOP COPYING SYSIN */
CLOSE FILE(TEMP);
/* CLOSE FILE(SYSIN); */

/* OPEN FILE(SYSPRINT); */
OPEN INPUT FILE(TEMP);
   . . .                       /* LOOP COPYING TEMP */
CLOSE FILE(TEMP);
/* CLOSE FILE(SYSPRINT); */
```

Opening and closing the system files is handled by the system. It is included here simply for purposes of illustration. When the temporary file is closed for the first time, the system puts an end-of-file mark on it. When it is used later as input, the ON ENDFILE condition is used to identify the end of the information in the file.

The following program stores information in a temporary file, then lists it.

```
COPY: PROC OPTION(MAIN);
/***********************************************************/
/*                                                         */
/* PROGRAM: BUILD A FILE AND LIST IT                       */
/* AUTHOR:  C ZIEGLER                                      */
/* VERSION: 07/17/84                                       */
/*                                                         */
/* PROGRAM DESCRIPTION                                     */
/* ------------------------------------------------------ */
/* THIS PROGRAM BUILDS A FILE THEN LISTS IT.               */
/*                                                         */
/* INPUT: SYSIN - 80 CHARACTER RECORDS                     */
/*                                                         */
/* OUTPUT: SYSPRINT - LISTING                              */
/*                                                         */
/* TEMPORARY FILE: TEMP - 80 CHARACTER RECORDS             */
/*                                                         */
/***********************************************************/
DCL TEMP   FILE ENV(CONSECUTIVE);
DCL INFO   CHAR(80),
    MORE   BIT(1);
DCL TRUE   BIT(1) INIT ('1'B),
    FALSE  BIT(1) INIT ('0'B);

/***********************************************************/
/*                                                         */
/* THIS SECTION BUILDS THE FILE                            */
/*                                                         */
/***********************************************************/
ON ENDFILE(SYSIN)
  MORE = FALSE;

MORE = TRUE;
OPEN OUTPUT FILE(TEMP);
GET EDIT (INFO) (COL(1),A(80));
DO WHILE(MORE);
  PUT SKIP FILE(TEMP) EDIT (INFO) (A);
  GET EDIT (INFO) (COL(1),A(80));
END;
CLOSE FILE(TEMP);

/***********************************************************/
/*                                                         */
/* THIS SECTION LISTS THE FILE                             */
/*                                                         */
/***********************************************************/
ON ENDFILE(TEMP)
  MORE = FALSE;

MORE = TRUE;
OPEN INPUT FILE(TEMP);
GET FILE(TEMP) EDIT (INFO) (COL(1),A(80));
```

```
DO WHILE(MORE);
  PUT SKIP EDIT (INFO) (A);
  GET FILE(TEMP) EDIT (INFO) (COL(1),A(80));
END;
CLOSE FILE(TEMP);
END COPY;
```

The part of the program that reads the temporary file is exactly parallel to the part that writes the temporary file. The only difference between using system files and a user-named file is that every reference to a named file must include the name. Thus the ON conditions for the system input file and the temporary file are:

```
ON ENDFILE(SYSIN) . . .
ON ENDFILE(TEMP) . . .
```

The output statements for the system printer file and the temporary file are:

```
PUT SKIP EDIT (INFO) (A);
PUT SKIP FILE(TEMP) EDIT (INFO) (A);
```

and the input statements for the system input file and the temporary file are:

```
GET EDIT (INFO) (A(80));
GET FILE(TEMP) EDIT (INFO) (A(80));
```

Also, files should be explicitly opened and closed.

10.6.2 Data validation

As an example of multiple output files, assume that input data is intended to be in ascending order by a key field, but that this needs to be checked. Data that is in order is written to one file, and data that is out of order, plus data with duplicate keys, is written to another file. The structure of the program is

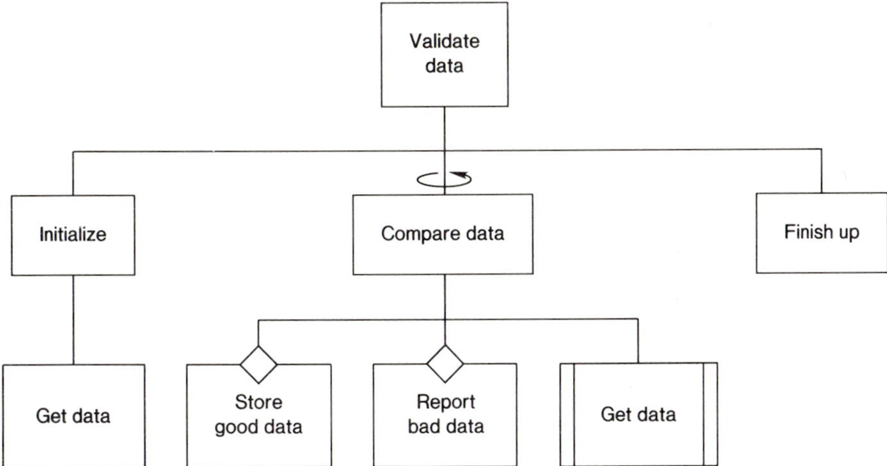

Figure 10–5

shown in figure 10–5. For this program, assume that the input is on SYSIN and there are two output files named GOOD and BAD.

```
CHKDATA: PROC OPTIONS(MAIN);
/*************************************************************/
/*                                                           */
/* PROGRAM: CHECK DATA FOR VALID KEY SEQUENCING              */
/* AUTHOR:  C ZIEGLER                                        */
/* VERSION: 07/17/84                                         */
/*                                                           */
/* PROGRAM DESCRIPTION                                       */
/* --------------------------------------------------------- */
/* THIS PROGRAM VALIDATES THE KEY SEQUENCING OF DATA,        */
/* WRITING THE SEQUENCED DATA TO ONE FILE, THE OUT OF        */
/* ORDER DATA TO ANOTHER.                                    */
/*                                                           */
/* INPUT: SYSIN - 80 CHARACTER RECORDS                       */
/*                COLS 1 -  8 KEY VALUE                      */
/*                     9 - 80 INFORMATION                    */
/*                                                           */
/* OUTPUT: GOOD - RECORDS IN KEY SEQUENCE                    */
/*         BAD  - RECORDS NOT ORIGINALLY IN KEY SEQUENCE     */
/*                                                           */
/*************************************************************/
DCL GOOD     FILE OUTPUT ENV(CONSECUTIVE);
DCL BAD      FILE OUTPUT ENV(CONSECUTIVE);
DCL INFO_KEY CHAR(8),
    INFO     CHAR(72),
    OLD_KEY  CHAR(8),
    MORE     BIT(1);
DCL TRUE     BIT(1)   INIT('1'B),
    FALSE    BIT(1)   INIT('0'B);

ON ENDFILE(SYSIN)
  MORE = FALSE;

MORE = TRUE;
OLD_KEY = LOW(8);
GET EDIT (INFO_KEY,INFO) (COL(1),A(8),A(72));
OPEN FILE(GOOD),
     FILE(BAD);
DO WHILE(MORE);
  IF OLD_KEY < INFO_KEY                /* CHECK DATA SEQUENCE */
    THEN
      DO;
        PUT SKIP FILE(GOOD) EDIT (INFO_KEY,INFO) (A,A);
        OLD_KEY = INFO_KEY;
      END;
    ELSE
      PUT SKIP FILE(BAD) EDIT (INFO_KEY,INFO) (A,A);
  GET EDIT (INFO_KEY,INFO) (COL(1),A(8),A(40));
END;
END CHKDATA;
```

The two files GOOD and BAD are open at the same time and are being written at more or less the same time. Nevertheless, the output does not come out all mixed up. The system sends the output data to two separate files. If the files were PRINT rather than OUTPUT files, the good and bad data would still be separated, but one file would be printed ahead of the other with each starting on a new page.

The variable OLD_KEY is initialized to a system-provided value by the library function LOW(length), which is lower in the collating sequence than any characters of the PL/I character set. This ensures that the first data key is considered to be a "good" key. There is a corresponding value HIGH(length) which is higher than any PL/I characters and can be used for comparison with data in descending order.

10.6.3 Sorting data

In section 10.6.2 above, the data in the BAD file can be processed if it is sorted first. An "in memory" sort routine cannot be used, as the amount of

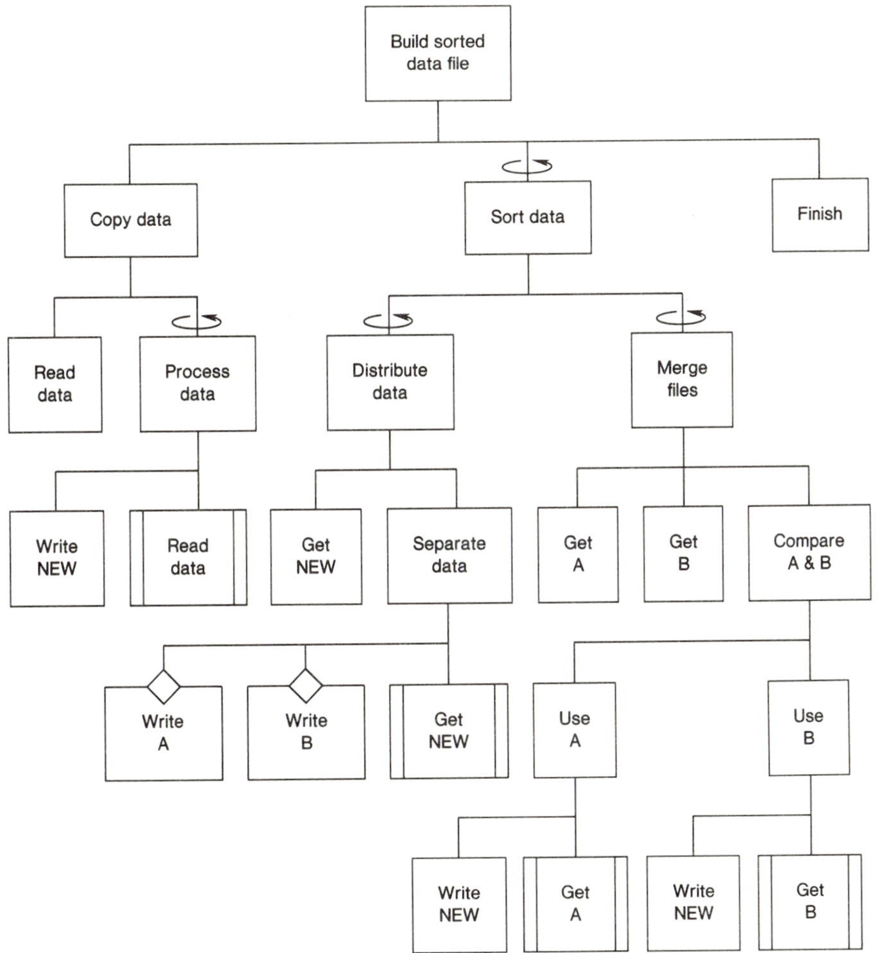

Figure 10–6

data is not known and there may be too much data to store in an array. Usually a system sort routine is available, which can be run as a separate program. If one is present, it should be used.

PROGRAMMING HINT: EFFICIENCY Use system sort utilities when possible.

If not, a merge sort similar to system utility sorts can be written. A merge sort requires several temporary work files. Figure 10–6 shows the structure of the sort.

Figure 10–7 gives the HIPO chart showing the use of the files. Steps 2 and 3 alternate until the data has been sorted.

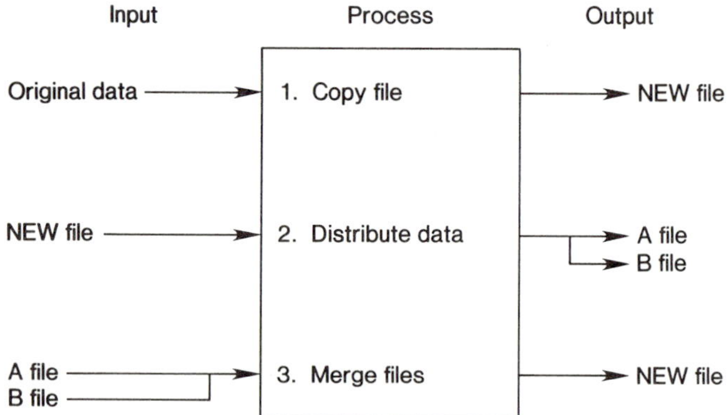

Figure 10–7

The following program shows the sort. A flag, SORTED, is used to indicate whether the records are in the correct order or not.

```
SORT: PROC OPTIONS(MAIN);
/*****************************************************************/
/*                                                               */
/* PROGRAM: MERGE SORT FOR FILES                                 */
/* AUTHOR:  C ZIEGLER                                            */
/* VERSION: 07/17/84                                             */
/*                                                               */
/* PROGRAM DESCRIPTION                                           */
/* ------------------------------------------------------------- */
/* THIS PROGRAM SORTS THE RECORDS IN A FILE.                     */
/*                                                               */
/* INPUT: OLD - 80 CHARACTER RECORDS, 8 CHARACTER KEY            */
/*                  COLS 1 -  8 KEY VALUE                        */
/*                       9 - 80 INFORMATION                      */
/*                                                               */
/* OUTPUT: NEW - SORTED VERSION OF INPUT                         */
/*                                                               */
/* TEMPORARY FILES: A AND B TO HOLD INTERMEDIATE DATA            */
/*                                                               */
/*****************************************************************/
```

```
DCL OLD     FILE SEQL STREAM ENV(CONSECUTIVE),
    NEW     FILE SEQL STREAM ENV(CONSECUTIVE),
    (A,B)   FILE SEQL STREAM ENV(CONSECUTIVE);
DCL INFO    CHAR(80);
DCL MORE    BIT(1),
    SORTED  BIT(1);
DCL KEY_LNG FIXED BIN INIT(8);
DCL TRUE    BIT(1)    INIT('1'B),
    FALSE   BIT(1)    INIT('0'B);

/**********************************************************/
/*                                                        */
/* THIS SECTION COPIES DATA FROM OLD FILE TO NEW FILE     */
/*                                                        */
/**********************************************************/
ON ENDFILE (OLD)
  MORE = FALSE;

MORE = TRUE;
OPEN INPUT FILE (OLD),
     OUTPUT FILE (NEW);
GET FILE (OLD) EDIT (INFO) (COL(1),A(80));
DO WHILE (MORE);
  PUT FILE (NEW) SKIP EDIT (INFO) (A(80));
  GET FILE (OLD) EDIT (INFO) (COL(1),A(80));
END;
CLOSE FILE (OLD),
      FILE (NEW);

/**********************************************************/
/*                                                        */
/* THIS SECTION SORTS THE DATA ON NEW FILE                */
/*                                                        */
/* PROCEDURES CALLED: DISTRIBUTE, MERGE                   */
/*                                                        */
/**********************************************************/
SORTED = FALSE;
DO WHILE (¬SORTED);
  CALL DISTRIBUTE;
  CALL MERGE;
END;

DISTRIBUTE: PROC;
/**********************************************************/
/*                                                        */
/* THIS PROCEDURE DISTRIBUTES THE DATA TO FILES A AND B   */
/*                                                        */
/**********************************************************/
DCL KEY     CHAR(KEY_LNG),
    OLD_KEY CHAR(KEY_LNG),
    INFO    CHAR(80-KEY_LNG),
    MORE    BIT(1),
    (I,K)   FIXED BIN;
```

```
DCL TRUE    BIT(1)     INIT('1'B),
    FALSE   BIT(1)     INIT('0'B);

ON ENDFILE(NEW)
  BEGIN;
    KEY = LOW(K);
    MORE = FALSE;
  END;

K = KEY_LNG;
I = 80 - K;
MORE = TRUE;
OPEN INPUT FILE (NEW);
OPEN OUTPUT FILE (A),
     OUTPUT FILE (B);
GET FILE (NEW) EDIT (KEY,INFO) (A(K),A(I));
DO WHILE (MORE);
  OLD_KEY = LOW(K);
  DO WHILE (OLD_KEY < KEY);                /* WRITE TO FILE A */
    PUT FILE (A) EDIT (KEY,INFO) (COL(1),A,A);
    OLD_KEY = KEY;
    GET FILE (NEW) EDIT (KEY,INFO) (A(K),A(I));
  END;
  OLD_KEY = LOW(K);
  DO WHILE (OLD_KEY < KEY);                /* WRITE TO FILE B */
    PUT FILE (B) EDIT (KEY,INFO) (COL(1),A,A);
    OLD_KEY = KEY;
    GET FILE (NEW) EDIT (KEY,INFO) (A(K),A(I));
  END;
END;
CLOSE FILE (NEW),
      FILE (A),
      FILE (B);
END DISTRIBUTE;

MERGE: PROC;
/************************************************************/
/*                                                          */
/* THIS SECTION MERGES THE DATA FROM A AND B ONTO NEW      */
/*                                                          */
/************************************************************/
DCL (A_KEY, B_KEY)     CHAR(KEY_LNG),
    (OLD_KEY,NEW_KEY) CHAR(KEY_LNG),
    (A_INFO, B_INFO)   CHAR(80-KEY_LNG),
    (MORE_A, MORE_B)   BIT(1),
    (K,I)              FIXED BIN;
DCL TRUE               BIT(1)     INIT('1'B),
    FALSE              BIT(1)     INIT('0'B);

ON ENDFILE (A)
  BEGIN;
    A_KEY = HIGH(K);
    MORE_A = FALSE;
  END;
```

```
ON ENDFILE (B)
  BEGIN;
    B_KEY = HIGH(K);
    MORE_B = FALSE;
  END;
K = KEY_LNG;
I = 80 - K;
SORTED = TRUE;
MORE_A = TRUE;
MORE_B = TRUE;
OLD_KEY = LOW(K);
OPEN OUTPUT FILE (NEW);
OPEN INPUT FILE(A),
     INPUT FILE(B);
GET FILE (A) EDIT (A_KEY,A_INFO) (A(K),A(I));
GET FILE (B) EDIT (B_KEY,B_INFO) (A(K),A(I));
DO WHILE (MORE_A | MORE_B);
  SELECT;
    WHEN (¬ MORE_B)
      CALL USE_A;
    WHEN (¬ MORE_A)
      CALL USE_B;
    WHEN (A_KEY < OLD_KEY & OLD_KEY <= B_KEY)
      CALL USE_B;
    WHEN (A_KEY <= B_KEY)
      CALL USE_A;
    WHEN (B_KEY < OLD_KEY & OLD_KEY <= A_KEY)
      CALL USE_A;
    WHEN (B_KEY <= A_KEY)
      CALL USE_B;
  END;
  IF NEW_KEY < OLD_KEY
    THEN
      SORTED = FALSE;
  OLD_KEY = NEW_KEY;
END;
CLOSE FILE (NEW),
      FILE (A),
      FILE (B);

USE_A: PROC;
PUT FILE (NEW) EDIT (A_KEY,A_INFO) (COL(1),A,A);
NEW_KEY = A_KEY;
GET FILE (A) EDIT (A_KEY,A_INFO) (COL(1),A(K),A(I));
END USE_A;

USE_B: PROC;
PUT FILE (NEW) EDIT (B_KEY,B_INFO) (COL(1),A,A);
NEW_KEY = B_KEY;
GET FILE (B) EDIT (B_KEY,B_INFO) (COL(1),A(K),A(I));
END USE B;
END MERGE;
END SORT;
```

This sort works by distributing the data from the input file into two other files according to runs in the data. As long as the data is in order it is written to the same file. When the order is broken, the output is switched to the other file. When all the data has been distributed, the two files are merged by comparing the first key from each and the old key, continuing the order if possible, otherwise writing the lower value to the output file, getting the next key, and working down through the files comparing keys. When the merged data is in order, the sort stops. If it is not in order, the distributing and merging phases are repeated. Sample data are shown in figure 10–8.

	Pass 1			Pass 2		
NEW	A	B	NEW	A	B	NEW
ADAMS	ADAMS					
CARTER	CARTER					
BROWN		BROWN				
JONES		JONES				
LEE		LEE				
LOPEZ		LOPEZ				
ARONS	ARONS					
JACKSON	JACKSON					
GRIFFIN		GRIFFIN				
MCDONALD		MCDONALD				
LUNA	LUNA					
			ADAMS	ADAMS		
			BROWN	BROWN		
			CARTER	CARTER		
			ARONS		ARONS	
			JACKSON		JACKSON	
			JONES		JONES	
			LEE		LEE	
			LOPEZ		LOPEZ	
			GRIFFIN	GRIFFIN		
			LUNA	LUNA		
			MCDONALD	MCDONALD		
						ADAMS
						ARONS
						BROWN
						CARTER
						GRIFFIN
						JACKSON
						JONES
						LEE
						LOPEZ
						LUNA
						MCDONALD

Figure 10–8

The data is copied to the NEW file so that the OLD file is not destroyed. This permits the OLD file to be assigned to a card reader instead of disk or tape. This type of sort is usually run with tape files. The data of the NEW file is distributed to files A and B according to the ascending runs shown. Files A and B are then merged and placed back on the NEW file. The data is again distributed to A and B and then merged for the last time to form the sorted file NEW.

Using the library function LOW in the key initialization of DISTRIBUTE ensures that the first data is put on file A. In the ON ENDFILE processing of the DISTRIBUTE procedure, if the last data is read and the end-of-file is found in the loop that puts the data on file A, the following loop will be omitted. The library function LOW(K) returns a character string of length K that has the lowest possible value in the collating sequence. Since this value is composed of unprintable characters, it is lower than any possible sort key.

```
LOW(K) < KEY
```

is always true.

The library function HIGH is used in the merge phase of the sort. It returns a character string composed of the highest possible value in the collating sequence, again an unprintable value. This ensures that in the key comparisons of the MERGE procedure, if either file is empty, the control will go through the part of the loop that only reads the other file.

```
HIGH(K) > A_KEY
```

and

```
HIGH(K) > B_KEY
```

are always true. The rules for merging the input files are:

A_KEY <= B_KEY	Use the A information unless OLD_KEY between A_KEY and B_KEY
A_KEY > B_KEY	Use the B information unless OLD_KEY between A_KEY and B_KEY
A file finished	Use the B information
B file finished	Use the A information
Both files finished	Return

To avoid having to check for the end-of-file on A and on B every time through the loop, those cases are converted into the key comparisons by setting the key high when a file is finished. When both files are finished, the comparison does not arise because the loop terminates. This is shown in the following decision table for the merge phase:

A eof	Y	–	N
B eof	Y	N	–
A key > B key	*	Y	N
A key <= B key	Y	N	Y
Write A info			X
Write B into		X	
Read A file			X
Read B file		X	
Repeat		X	X
Exit	X		

10.6.4 Master file/transaction file processing

With stream files, data must not be updated in place. Instead, a new master file must be built using a process very similar to the merge phase of the sort program in section 10.6.3. The update program matches the master records and the transaction records by keys. Although the files are merged, only the master record is written to the new file. It is not written until after all its matching transactions have been processed. Some master records may not have current transactions; some may have exactly one, and some may have more than one. Both the master file and the transaction file must already be in order by keys. Any transaction which has no matching master record is considered invalid.

Processing bank checks against a checking account is an example of master-transaction file processing. Some accounts may have no checks drawn on them; some may have more than one. If a check is found with no matching account, there is probably an error in the account number field of the check. Both the master file and the transaction file must be ordered in advance by account number. Then the two files are merged to form a new file, according to the following rules:

M_KEY < T_KEY	Use the master information
M_KEY = T_KEY	Use the transaction information to calculate the new balance
M_KEY > T_KEY	Use the transaction information to write an error message
M file finished	Use the transaction information to write an error message
T file finished	Use the master information
Both files finished	Done

As in the merge sort, when either file is finished, the key for that file is set high. When the master file key is high, any remaining transactions are invalid. When the transaction key is high, processing of the remaining master records, if any, continues. The decision table for this is:

T_eof	Y	–	N	N
M_eof	Y	N	N	–
M_KEY < T_KEY	–	Y	N	N
M_KEY = T_KEY	–	N	Y	N
M_KEY > T_KEY	–	N	N	Y
Update M data			X	
Invalid T data				X
Write M data		X		
Read M data		X		
Read T data			X	X
Repeat		X	X	X
Exit	X			

Whichever file is lagging behind in the comparison is the file that is read. The new master file is written only when all the transactions for a record have been processed.

The hierarchy chart for master file/transaction file processing is given in figure 10–9, and is shown in the following program.

```
ACCOUNT: PROC OPTIONS(MAIN);
/************************************************************/
/*                                                          */
/* PROGRAM: MASTER FILE UPDATE                              */
/* AUTHOR:  C ZIEGLER                                       */
/* VERSION: 07/17/84                                        */
/*                                                          */
/* PROGRAM DESCRIPTION                                      */
/* ------------------------------------------------------   */
```

```
/* THIS PROGRAM UPDATES THE RECORDS OF A MASTER FILE       */
/*                                                         */
/* INPUT: MASTER - ACCOUNT RECORDS                         */
/*                  COLS 1 -  8 KEY VALUE                  */
/*                       9 - 16 ACCOUNT BALANCE            */
/*         TRANS  - TRANSACTION RECORDS                    */
/*                  COLS 1 -  8 KEY VALUE                  */
/*                       9 - 16 TRANSACTION AMOUNT         */
/*                                                         */
/* OUTPUT: NEWMAST  - UPDATED MASTER FILE                  */
/*         SYSPRINT - ERROR LISTING                        */
/*                                                         */
/***********************************************************/
DCL MASTER   FILE INPUT  SEQL STREAM ENV(CONSECUTIVE),
    NEWMAST  FILE OUTPUT SEQL STREAM ENV(CONSECUTIVE),
    TRANS    FILE INPUT  SEQL STREAM ENV(CONSECUTIVE);
DCL 1 MAST_REC,
      5 M_KEY      CHAR(8),
      5 M_BAL      FIXED DEC(8,2),
    1 TRANS_REC,
      5 T_KEY      CHAR(8),
      5 T_AMT      FIXED DEC(8,2),
    MORE_M         BIT(1),
    MORE_T         BIT(1);
DCL TRUE           BIT(1)   INIT('1'B),
    FALSE          BIT(1)   INIT('0'B);

ON ENDFILE(MASTER)
  BEGIN;
    M_KEY = HIGH(8);
    MORE_M = FALSE;
  END;
ON ENDFILE(TRANS)
  BEGIN;
    T_KEY = HIGH(8);
    MORE_T = FALSE;
  END;

MORE_M = TRUE;
MORE_T = TRUE;
OPEN FILE (MASTER),
     FILE (TRANS),
     FILE (NEWMAST);
GET FILE (MASTER) EDIT (MAST_REC) (A(8),F(8,2));
GET FILE (TRANS) EDIT (TRANS_REC) (A(8),F(8,2));
DO WHILE (MORE_M | MORE_T);
  SELECT;
    WHEN (M_KEY < T_KEY)         /*FINISHED WITH MASTER RECORD */
      DO;
        PUT FILE (NEWMAST) EDIT (M_KEY,M_BAL) (A,F(8,2));
        GET FILE (MASTER) EDIT (MAST_REC) (A(8),F(8,2));
      END;
```

```
      WHEN (M_KEY = T_KEY)         /* MASTER RECORD FOUND          */
        DO;
          M_BAL = M_BAL - T_AMT;
          GET FILE (TRANS) EDIT (TRANS_REC) (A(8),F(8,2));
        END;
      WHEN (M_KEY > T_KEY)         /* MASTER RECORD MISSING        */
        DO;
          PUT SKIP LIST ('INVALID KEY - ', T_KEY);
          GET FILE (TRANS) EDIT (TRANS_REC) (A(8),F(8,2));
        END;
    END,
  END;
  CLOSE FILE(MASTER),
        FILE(TRANS),
        FILE(NEWMAST);
  END ACCOUNT;
```

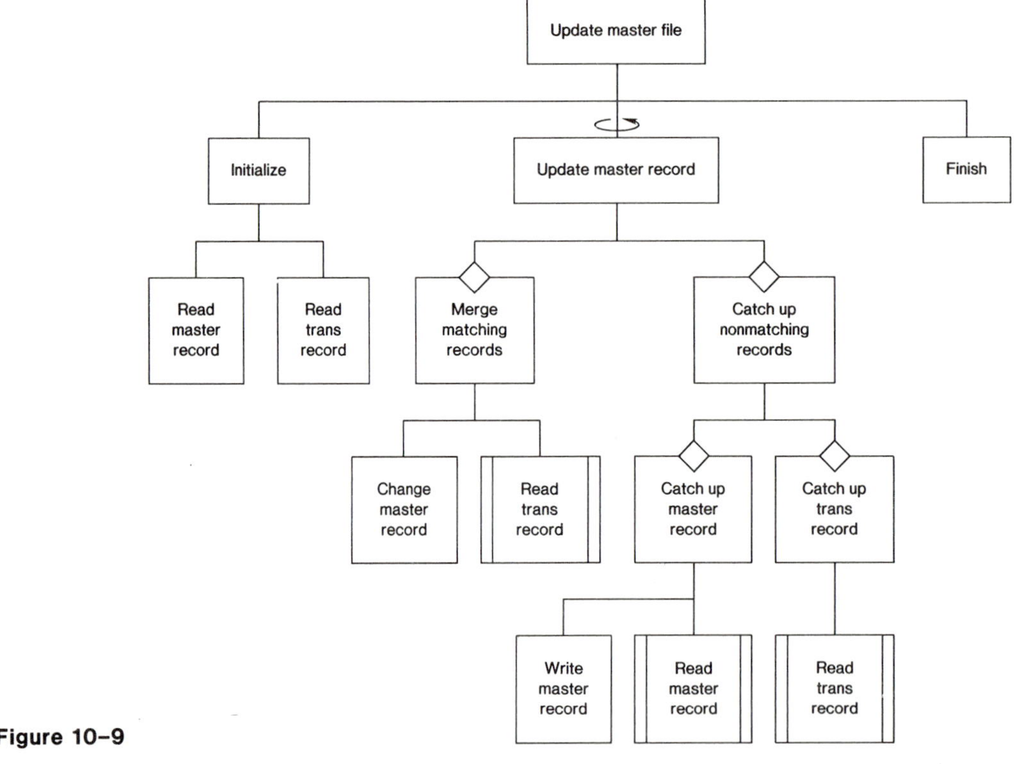

Figure 10–9

10.7 Summary

The various options of a file declaration are as follows:

```
                                   INPUT
                 (SEQUENTIAL)     (OUTPUT)    (STREAM   ENV(CONSECUTIVE);  )
DCL name FILE   {DIRECT     }     {      }    {         ENV(REGIONAL);     }
                 (TRANSIENT )     (PRINT )    (RECORD   ENV(INDEXED);      )
                                  (UPDATE)              ENV(teleprocessing);
```

Any of the attributes that are not included in the declaration may be included in the OPEN statement for the file. A file should be explicitly opened just before its first use and explicitly closed just after its last use. If a file is to be reused in the same program, it must be closed and opened again. The OPEN statement has the side effect of positioning the file at the beginning. The CLOSE statement has the side effect of writing an end-of-file record if the file has been open for output.

The GET and PUT statements are used for stream input/output. These statements may be used with the system default files SYSIN, SYSPRINT, and SYSOUT without declaring them. They may be used with any other files that are declared.

A few of the most common functions to be performed on stream files are:

1. Copying a file.
2. Merging two files.
3. Updating a file by making a revised version of it.
4. Sorting a file.

10.8 Exercises

1. Write a program that prints names of the titles of all projects funded by XYZ Corp., from a file that has the form:

Cols.		
	1- 4	Project number
	5-10	Date of grant
	11-20	Source of grant
	21-40	Name of primary researcher
	41-50	Title of project

2. Write a program that reads a file having the form:

Cols.		
	1-20	Name
	21-40	Address
	41-49	Social Security number
	50-60	Job title
	61-65	Office location
	66-72	Telephone
	73-80	Salary (xxxxx.xx)

which is sorted by Social Security number. The program should write the information to a file MASTER. Assume that there may be duplicate records and write records with any duplicate Social Security numbers to a file DUPL.

3. Write a program that looks up all the dates in file INFILE, which has the form:

Cols. 1-6 Date (YYMMDD)

in a master file RIVFILE, which has the form:

Cols.		
	1- 6	Date of measurements (YYMMDD)
	7-10	Height of river in feet (xx.xx)
	11-15	Rate of flow in cu. ft/sec.
	16-20	Location
	21-24	Time

Assume the dates are in the same order in each file. For each date in INFILE for which there is information in RIVFILE, print the date and the information.

4. Adapt the sort program in section 10.6.3 to sort a file having the form:

Cols.		
	1- 5	Account number
	6-25	Name
	26-31	Date entered (YYMMDD)
	32-80	Information

in ascending order by date and within each date, in ascending order by account number.

5. Write a program based on the master file update program in section 10.6.4 which updates a file by removing all records which do not have current transactions. Assume there is at most one transaction for each master record with the transaction having the form:

Cols. 1-8 T_key

A revised master file should be created, as well as a file containing all of the inactive accounts.

11 Structures

OBJECTIVE: To handle input, processing, and output of heterogeneous data.

IN THE PRECEDING CHAPTERS values have been stored both individually and grouped in arrays. Data for business applications usually takes a different form. Business records contain many values, some of them alphabetic, some of them numeric. The data in a typical business record are heterogeneous in that the items are of different types and sizes, yet they belong together, since they usually are information about a single customer, single employee, or single subsidiary. Business records in a single file, such as a customer file, usually all have the same structure. They all contain the same type of information, organized in the same way. For instance, each record may contain the name, address, telephone number, credit rating, and purchase history of a single customer. Such a record is described in PL/I as a structure.

A *structure* is a data aggregate which has an overall name and whose parts are referenced by their names rather than by position. The structure definition describes the types, order, and grouping of the underlying parts. For instance, figure 11–1a pictorially describes a form to be filled in, which is shown in 11–1b after it has been completed. This type of form may be displayed on a CRT screen for interactive data entry or retrieval.

CUSTOMER DATA
NAME
ADDRESS
TELEPHONE
ACCOUNT BALANCE

(a)

CUSTOMER DATA
NAME John Smith
ADDRESS 1423 Center St Las Playas CA 91723
TELEPHONE (213) 579-3120
ACCOUNT BALANCE $153.79

(b)

Figure 11–1

The character strings and numbers that have been filled in are the values for the fields of the structure defined by the form. The PL/I equivalent of this form might be the following structure:

```
1 CUSTOMER_DATA,
  5  NAME              CHAR(20),
  5  ADDRESS,
     10 STREET_ADDR    CHAR(30),
     10 CITY_ADDR      CHAR(20),
  5  TELEPHONE         CHAR(10),
  5  ACCT_BALANCE      FIXED DEC(9,2);
```

CUSTOMER_DATA and ADDRESS are both structures. CUSTOMER_DATA is the major structure and ADDRESS is a minor structure. NAME, STREET_ADDR, CITY_ADDR, TELEPHONE, and ACCT_BALANCE are all elementary items. An *elementary item* is an element of a structure which is not itself a structure.

11.1 Structure declaration

Structures may be used to hold a collection of related data, or they may be used to break a character string into parts. When a structure is declared, its fields are separated by commas. A semicolon may be used at the end of the structure.

11.1.1 Record description

CUSTOMER_DATA describes a collection of related data about a single customer, which needs to be stored and processed together. Such a collection is usually stored as a record. Since the ADDRESS field of CUSTOMER_DATA consists of two subfields, a street address and a city address, it is itself a structure. Data may be broken into substructures and subfields to any extent desired. Both of the following are valid declarations for the address shown:

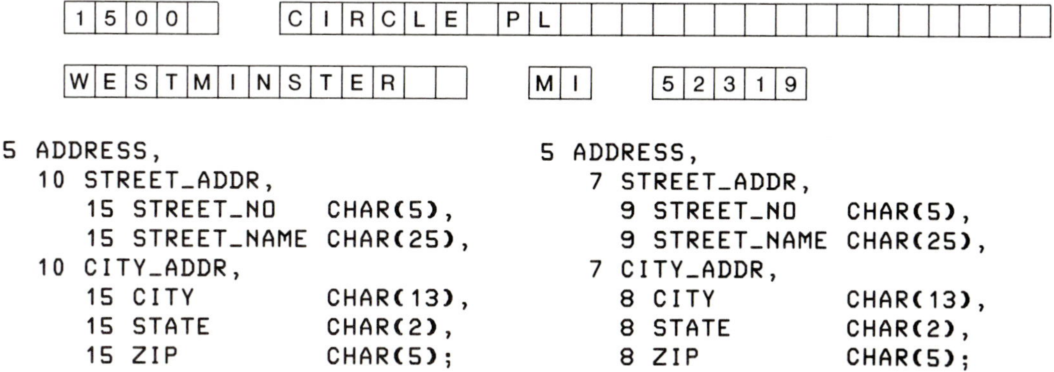


```
5 ADDRESS,
   10 STREET_ADDR,
      15 STREET_NO    CHAR(5),
      15 STREET_NAME  CHAR(25),
   10 CITY_ADDR,
      15 CITY         CHAR(13),
      15 STATE        CHAR(2),
      15 ZIP          CHAR(5);
```

```
5 ADDRESS,
   7 STREET_ADDR,
      9 STREET_NO    CHAR(5),
      9 STREET_NAME  CHAR(25),
   7 CITY_ADDR,
      8 CITY         CHAR(13),
      8 STATE        CHAR(2),
      8 ZIP          CHAR(5);
```

LEVEL NUMBERS

The name of the major structure is assigned level number 1. The parts of the structure are assigned a higher number and are named in the order they are to have in storage. Parts of subparts have even higher numbers. Parts of a structure must be declared immediately after the structure.

NAME, ADDRESS, TELEPHONE, and ACCT_BALANCE are the parts of CUSTOMER_DATA, therefore they must have the same level number. STREET_ADDR and CITY_ADDR are the parts of ADDRESS, so they must have the same level number, higher than that of ADDRESS. The parts of STREET_ADDR do not have to have the same level number as the parts of CITY_ADDR. However, the parts of STREET_ADDR must share the same level number and the parts of CITY_ADDR must share the same level number. If the name ADDRESS refers to a collection of five elementary items all of which are scalar variables, then it must not be thought of as referring to a string of fifty characters. The type of the identifier ADDRESS is structure, not character. ADDRESS is like a box that contains two other boxes, which contain objects. Objects may be taken out of and put into the boxes, but the boxes cannot be moved. Their only purpose is to group the objects inside.

CUSTOMER_DATA is a *logical structure* in that it represents the arrangement of data as seen by the programmer. The actual physical arrangement of the data may be slightly different.

STRUCTURE TYPE

Type declarations are only used with elementary items. Most structures are heterogeneous in that the elementary items do not all have the same type. Arrays and scalar values have types such as CHAR and FIXED BIN. Structures do not. A structure defines its own type. It is only compatible with structures with a similar organization.

```
1 A,                          1 B,                        1 C,
   5 A1     CHAR(10),            3 B1     CHAR(6),           5 C1   CHAR(10),
   5 A2,                         3 B2,                       5 C2   FIXED BIN,
     7 A21 FIXED BIN,              5 B21  FIXED DEC(2),      5 C3   CHAR(2);
     7 A22 CHAR(2);                5 B22  BIT(16);
```

Structures A and B are compatible while structure C is different. It is the "structure" that determines compatibility, not the types of the elementary elements. When data is moved from one structure to another, by referencing the structure name, individual elements can be converted from one type to another, truncated, padded, and so forth, as needed. They cannot be rearranged or grouped differently.

STRUCTURE NAMES

A major structure may be referenced as a whole. Its minor structures and elementary items may also be referenced. The following references are examples of those that may be used for the structure above:

CUSTOMER_DATA	Refers to the entire structure
NAME	Refers to the first 20 characters stored
ADDRESS	Refers to a minor structure of 50 characters
TELEPHONE	Refers to the next 10 characters stored
ACCT_BALANCE	Refers to the last 5 bytes of storage
STREET_ADDR	Refers to a minor structure storing 30 characters
STREET_NO	Refers to the first 5 characters stored in STREET_ADDR

Overloading of names If more than one structure is needed with the same configuration, to hold data of the same general nature, only one of the structures needs to be fully declared. If duplication of names is appropriate, the other structures can be declared to be LIKE the first. For example:

```
DCL 1 TODAY,
      5 YEAR      CHAR(2),
      5 MONTH     CHAR(2),
      5 DAY       CHAR(2);
DCL 1 DAY_OF_BIRTH  LIKE TODAY;
```

is equivalent to:

```
DCL 1 TODAY,
      5 YEAR      CHAR(2),
      5 MONTH     CHAR(2),
      5 DAY       CHAR(2);
DCL 1 DAY_OF_BIRTH,
      5 YEAR      CHAR(2),
      5 MONTH     CHAR(2),
      5 DAY       CHAR(2);
```

Both of these are stored as:

	TODAY		DAY_OF_BIRTH
YEAR	86	YEAR	54
MONTH	12	MONTH	03
DAY	17	DAY	21

When a name such as DAY has more than one meaning, that is, refers to more than one storage location, the name is said to be *overloaded*.

Qualification of names Any reference to YEAR, MONTH, or DAY in the structures TODAY or DAY_OF_BIRTH is rejected by the compiler as ambiguous because these names apply to elements of both structures. The name of the element must be *qualified* by using the form:

```
structurename.elementname
```

as in

```
DAY_OF_BIRTH.YEAR = 62;
PUT LIST (TODAY.DAY);
```

11.1.2 Subdivision of character strings

The DEFINED attribute was used in chapter 7 to redefine a date as an array. Redefining a date as a structure provides more appropriate data names. Both are shown in the following example:

```
DCL TODAYS_DATE  CHAR(6);
DCL NOW(3)       CHAR(2)  DEF (TODAYS_DATE);
DCL 1 TODAY               DEF (TODAYS_DATE),
      2 YEAR     CHAR(2),
      2 MONTH    CHAR(2),
      2 DAY      CHAR(2);

TODAYS_DATE = DATE();
```

The structure TODAY and the array NOW do not have any allocated storage. They provide additional names and internal structure for the character string TODAYS_DATE, as shown below:

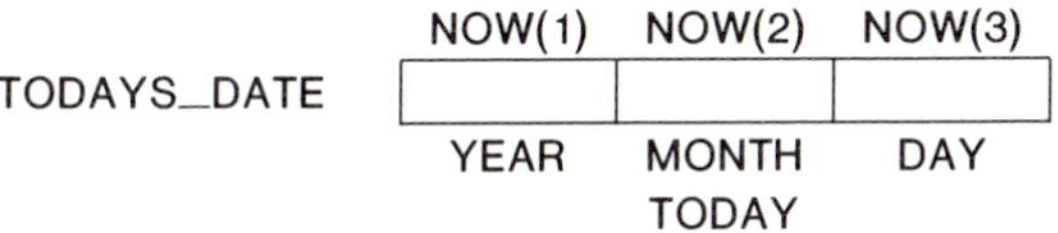

Because the DATE function returns a character string, the base type which the structure and array redefine must be a character string.

PROGRAMMING HINT: Use a structure to access parts of a character string.

The DEFINED attribute can be used anytime it is necessary to reconfigure a string storage location. The contents of the location are not altered by it, only the grouping into parts. Thus a character string can be reconfigured as a structure or an array.

```
DCL NAME          CHAR(20);
DCL 1 STRUCT              DEF (NAME),
      5 LAST      CHAR(10),
      5 FIRST     CHAR(9),
      5 INITIAL   CHAR(1);
DCL LETTER(20)    CHAR(1) DEF (NAME);
```

In this example, the character string NAME is reconfigured as consisting of a last name, first name, and initial. It is also reconfigured as an array of twenty individual letters.

11.1.3 Subdivision of arrays

A numeric array can be reconfigured as a numeric array of a different shape.

```
DCL ARRAY(2,10)    FIXED BIN,
    1 VALUES                 DEF (ARRAY),
      5 ROW_1(10)  FIXED BIN,
      5 ROW_2(10)  FIXED BIN,
    BRRAY(10,2)    FIXED BIN DEF (ARRAY),
    NUMBERS(20)    FIXED BIN DEF (ARRAY);
```

In this example, the array ARRAY is configured as a structure in order to provide names for the rows of the array, as an array of a different shape just to show that it can be done, and as a one-dimensional array for convenience in handling it.

In each example, the underlying data type remains unchanged. The type and value of a data item cannot be changed by redefining it; only the shape and size can be changed. The value of a data object is not affected in any way by having more than one name attached to it.

PROGRAMMING HINT: CAUTION Redefining data does not change the internal contents of storage, only the way it is accessed.

11.1.4 Classification of items

Structures provide an appropriate way to separate data into parts, to reconfigure data, and to show integral relationships between separate data items. They may be used to group similar data elements as a way of systematizing the declarative part of a procedure, and streamlining code. In the following example, the declarations of input values and totals have been grouped for clarity.

```
DCL DATA_IN             CHAR(32),
    1 AMTS_IN           DEF (DATA_IN),
      5 INTEREST        CHAR(8),
      5 PRINCIPAL       CHAR(8),
```

```
        5 INSURANCE          CHAR(8),
        5 TAXES              CHAR(8);
DCL  1 TOTALS,
        5 TOT_INT            FIXED DEC(8,2),
        5 TOT_PRINC          FIXED DEC(8,2),
        5 TOT_INS            FIXED DEC(8,2),
        5 TOT_TAX            FIXED DEC(8,2);
```

The input can be read as a single character string DATA_IN. Since AMTS_IN redefines DATA_IN, the variables grouped under AMTS_IN access four different substrings of DATA_IN. The first eight characters are the INTEREST, the next eight are PRINCIPAL, and so forth.

The totals are grouped only for documentation and convenience. For readability, the totals have been arranged in the same order as the input values.

PROGRAMMING HINT: STYLE Group similar items into structures.

11.1.5 Complex structures

Some of the examples of structures have shown more than one level of grouping; that is, have shown structures with other structures as elements. Arrays may also be nested in structures, as shown in the following example:

```
DCL  1 INDEX_ENTRY,
        5 TOPIC     CHAR(20),
        5 PAGE(10) FIXED BIN;
```

This structure holds up to ten page numbers for a topic. The fifth page number can be referenced as:

```
PAGE(5)
```

or

```
INDEX_ENTRY.PAGE(5)
```

The following example shows a structure nested inside an array:

```
DCL  1 ADDRESS_LIST(100),
        5 NAME   CHAR(20),
        5 ADDR   CHAR(30);
```

This list consists of 100 name-address pairs. The fifth name and address can be referenced as:

```
NAME(5)          ADDR(5)
```

or

```
ADDRESS_LIST(5)
```

Although neither NAME nor ADDR is an array, their inclusion in an array makes them ambiguous data names. They must be used with subscripts.

The storage arrangement for an array nested in a structure is shown in the following example:

```
DCL 1 STRUCT,
      5 X(3)  FIXED BIN,
      5 Y(5)  FIXED BIN;
```

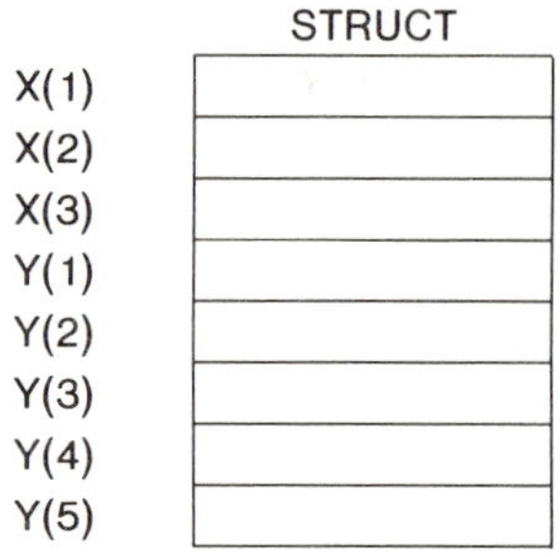

	STRUCT
X(1)	
X(2)	
X(3)	
Y(1)	
Y(2)	
Y(3)	
Y(4)	
Y(5)	

One element of the structure entirely precedes the next element. In the following example, where the structure is inside the array, each array element contains both structure elements.

```
DCL 1 ARR(3),
      5 X  FIXED BIN,
      5 Y  FIXED BIN;
```

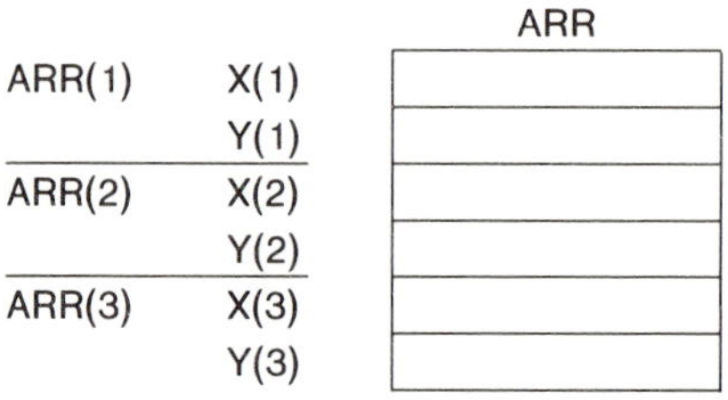

		ARR
ARR(1)	X(1)	
	Y(1)	
ARR(2)	X(2)	
	Y(2)	
ARR(3)	X(3)	
	Y(3)	

Arrays and structures may be nested as needed. For example:

```
DCL 1 INDEX(25),
      5 TOPIC    CHAR(20),
      5 PAGE(10) FIXED BIN;
```

In this example, INDEX(10) references the tenth topic and its pages; TOPIC(10) references the tenth topic; and PAGE(10,8) references the eighth page number of the tenth topic.

Review questions

1. Indicate whether each of the following statements is true or false.
   (a) A structure may contain homogeneous or heterogeneous data.
   (b) A structure name refers to the collection of elementary items in the structure.

(c) A structure declaration shows the grouping but not the storage order of the elementary items.
(d) A structured declaration shows the storage order but not the spacing of the elementary items.
(e) A name can be used in several separate structures.
(f) The name of a major structure must have level number 1.
(g) Elements at the same level must have the same level number even when they are in different substructures.

2. When the same data name belongs to two objects in the same procedure, the name must be ________________ to distinguish them.

3. Two structures have the same type if they have the same ________________ of elementary items.

4. Type attributes apply only to the ________________ of structures.

5. The ________________ option is used to declare the elements of two structures identical.

6. The ________________ option is used to apply a second description to the same storage area.

7. Write a structure declaration that describes the following input line:

Cols.	1-20	Name
	21-23	Age
	24-30	Income (dollars and cents)
	31-80	Educational history

8. Redefine the following structure so that no array is used.

```
DCL 1 FAMILY,
      5 FATHER   CHAR(20),
      5 MOTHER   CHAR(20),
      5 CHILD(3) CHAR(20);
```

9. Redefine the following character string as a structure.

```
DCL NOW  CHAR(9);  stores time as HHMMSSmmm
```

11.2 Structure operations

Like scalar values and arrays, structures may be initialized, used in assignment statements, and used in arithmetic expressions when appropriate. A structure may be used in these ways only if the individual elementary items of the structure all are of the appropriate type. For a structure to be used in arithmetic, the elementary items all must be numeric. For a structure to be initialized, an appropriate value must be provided for each of the underlying items.

11.2.1 INITIAL attribute

The INITIAL attribute cannot be used on a structure as a whole, only on the elementary parts. This permits heterogeneous structures to be initialized, as in the following example:

```
DCL 1  ACCT_INFO,
       5  NAME      CHAR(20)    INIT (' '),
       5  ACCT_NO   CHAR(5)     INIT (' '),
       5  BALANCE   FIXED DEC   INIT (0);
```

11.2.2 Structure assignment (not in Subset G)

A structure may be assigned a value of a scalar, or of another structure if it is compatible.

CONTROLLED BY ORDER

When the name of a structure is used in an assignment statement and the value being assigned is a scalar, the scalar value is assigned individually to each elementary item of the structure.

```
DCL VALUES,
   5  A      FIXED BIN,
   5  B      FIXED DEC (5,2);

VALUES = 3;
```

is equivalent to

```
        A = 3;
        B = 3;
```


Since the structure name is an abbreviated way of referring to all the individual elements of the structure, it can be used whenever the same operation is to be performed on all the elements. Thus independent totals collected in a structure can be initialized by a simple assignment statement.

```
DCL 1 TOTALS,
      5 TOT_INT             FIXED DEC(8,2),
      5 TOT_PRINC           FIXED DEC(8,2),
      5 TOT_INS             FIXED DEC(8,2),
      5 TOT_TAX             FIXED DEC(8,2);

TOTALS = 0;
```

is equivalent to:

```
TOT_INT, TOT_PRINC, TOT_INS, TOT_TAX = 0;
```

If the value being assigned is another structure, the elementary items are matched on a one-to-one basis, according to their order, and the individual values are copied. The structures must be compatible.

```
DCL 1   VALUES,
        5  A           FIXED BIN,
        5  B           FIXED DEC (5,2);
DCL 1   OLD_VALUES,
        5  B          FIXED BIN INIT (17),
        5  C          FIXED BIN INIT (-5);

VALUES = OLD_VALUES;             /* A OF VALUES IS 17    */
                                 /* B OF VALUES IS -5.00 */
```

is equivalent to:

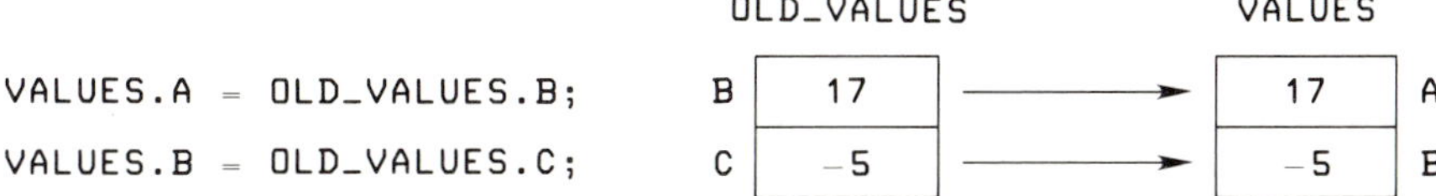

B of OLD_VALUES is copied to A of VALUES. C of OLD_VALUES is copied to B of VALUES. The execution of the assignment statement takes into consideration the types of the source and receiving fields, but ignores their names. Using the name B twice in this example does not cause a problem.

CONTROLLED BY NAME

If identical names in two different structures are intended to identify corresponding elementary items, assignments of just those fields may be made by basing the assignment on the item names rather than their order. This is done by using the BY NAME option. Values are copied to fields of the same name.

```
DCL 1   VALUES,
        5  A       FIXED BIN          INIT (9),
        5  B       FIXED DEC (5,0)    INIT (3);
DCL 1   OLD_VALUES,
        5  B       FIXED BIN          INIT (17),
        5  C       FIXED BIN          INIT (-5);

VALUES = OLD_VALUES, BY NAME;    /* A OF VALUES IS  9    */
                                 /* B OF VALUES IS 17    */
```

is equivalent to:

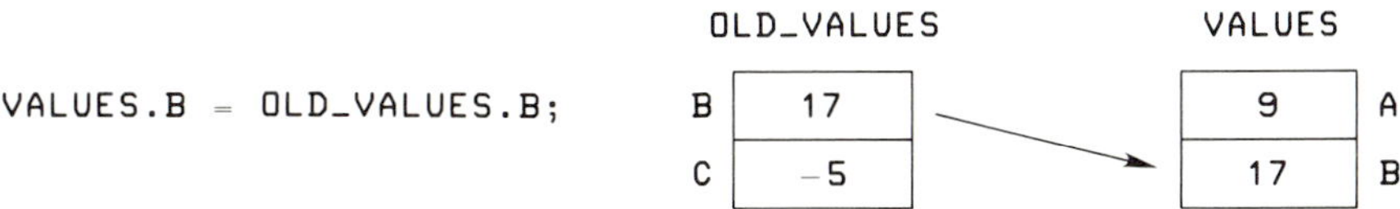

The only elementary name that appears in both structures is B. The values are matched by name. There is no field in VALUES with the name C, so the value of OLD_VALUES.C is not assigned to anything. There is no field in

OLD_VALUES with the name A, so the value of VALUES.A is not changed.

The use of duplicate names provides a simple way of rearranging elements of a structure. If two structures are declared with the same item names occurring in both, but in a different order and spaced differently, as in the following example,

```
DCL 1 TODAY,
      5 YEAR    CHAR(2),
      5 MONTH   CHAR(2),
      5 DAY     CHAR(2);
DCL 1 DAY_OUT,
      5 MONTH   CHAR(2),
      5 FILL_1  CHAR(1)    INIT('/'),
      5 DAY     CHAR(2),
      5 FILL_2  CHAR(1)    INIT('/'),
      5 YEAR    CHAR(2);
```

then the values of the elements of one structure may be assigned to the other structure BY NAME. If TODAY contains 860712 and the assignment

```
DAY_OUT = TODAY, BY NAME;
```

then DAY_OUT contains 07/12/86.

	TODAY
YEAR	86
MONTH	07
DAY	12

	DAY_OUT
MONTH	07
FILL_1	/
DAY	12
FILL_2	/
YEAR	86

The elements of the structures are matched by their names rather than by their order.

11.2.3 Structure arithmetic

Structures may be used in the arithmetic operations of addition, subtraction, multiplication, division, and exponentiation.

STRUCTURE/SCALAR ARITHMETIC

When one operand is a scalar and the other a structure, the scalar is applied to each elementary item of the structure.

```
DCL 1   VALUES,
        5  A       FIXED BIN,
        5  B       FIXED DEC (5,2);
DCL 1   OLD_VALUES,
        5  B       FIXED BIN        INIT (17),
        5  C       FIXED BIN        INIT (-5);

VALUES = 2* OLD_VALUES;       /* A OF VALUES IS  34     */
                              /* B OF VALUES IS -10.00 */
```

STRUCTURE/STRUCTURE ARITHMETIC (not in Subset G)

When both operands are structures, the arithmetic is carried out by matching the elementary items, which must be grouped the same way in both structures.

Controlled by order The elementary items are used in the order in which they are declared. The two first elements are matched, then the second elements, and so forth. In the following example, A of STRUCT_1 is matched with C of STRUCT_2. B of STRUCT_1 is matched with B of STRUCT_2. And C of STRUCT_1 is matched with D of STRUCT_2.

```
DCL 1   STRUCT_1,
          5  A      FIXED BIN           INIT (3),
          5  REST,
             10  B  FIXED BIN           INIT (-1),
             10  C  FIXED DEC (5,2)     INIT (10.50);

DCL 1   STRUCT_2,
          3  C      FIXED BIN           INIT (17),
          3  PART_2,
             5  B   FIXED BIN           INIT (-5),
             5  D   FIXED BIN           INIT (21);

STRUCT_1 = STRUCT_1 + STRUCT_2;          /* STRUCT_1.A IS 20    */
                                         /* STRUCT_1.B IS -6    */
                                         /* STRUCT_1.C IS 31.50 */
```

This has the following effect:

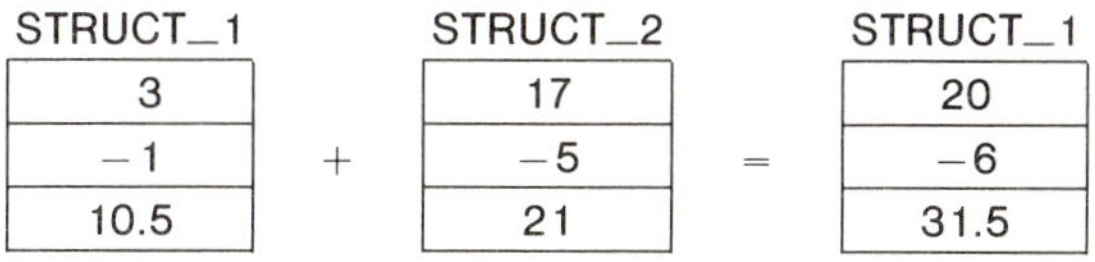

STRUCT_1		STRUCT_2		STRUCT_1
3		17		20
−1	+	−5	=	−6
10.5		21		31.5

The single arithmetic statement

```
STRUCT_1 = STRUCT_1 + STRUCT_2
```

is equivalent to the three statements

```
STRUCT_1.A = STRUCT_1.A + STRUCT_2.C;
STRUCT_1.REST.B = STRUCT_1.REST.B + STRUCT_2.PART_2.B;
STRUCT_1.REST.C = STRUCT_1.REST.C + STRUCT_2.PART_2.D;
```

or the three statements

```
A = A + STRUCT_2.C
REST.B = REST.B + PART_2.B;
REST.C = REST.C + D;
```

The identifiers do not need to be qualified completely, only enough to avoid ambiguity. Arithmetic of structures can only be performed when the structures are compatible.

Controlled BY NAME When arithmetic is controlled BY NAME, the matching of the elementary items is based on their names rather than on their order. In the following example, field B of STRUCT_1 is matched with field B of STRUCT_2. Field C of STRUCT_1 is matched with field C of STRUCT_2. There is no A in STRUCT_2 and no D in STRUCT_1 so the A field of STRUCT_1 and the D field of STRUCT_2 do not participate in the arithmetic. The A field is unchanged.

```
DCL 1  STRUCT_1,
       5  A        FIXED BIN         INIT (3),
       5  REST,
          10  B    FIXED BIN         INIT (-1),
          10  C    FIXED DEC (5,2)  INIT (10.50);
DCL 1  STRUCT_2,
       3  C        FIXED BIN         INIT (17),
       3  PART_2,
          5  B     FIXED BIN         INIT (-5),
          5  D     FIXED BIN         INIT (21);

STRUCT_1 = STRUCT_1 + STRUCT_2, BY NAME;    /* STRUCT_1.A IS 3     */
                                            /* STRUCT_1.B IS -6    */
                                            /* STRUCT_1.C IS 27.50 */
```

This is the equivalent of:

```
REST.B = REST.B + PART_2.B;
REST.C = REST.C + STRUCT_2.C;
```

The A value of STRUCT_1 is not changed. The D value of STRUCT_2 is not used.

Review questions

1. Indicate whether each of the following statements is true or false.
   (a) Structures are compatible when they group the same number of elementary items in the same way.
   (b) Structures are compatible when their elementary items match as to number and type.
   (c) When a scalar value is assigned to a structure, it is assigned to each elementary element of the structure.
   (d) When one structure is assigned to another, the structures must be identical.

2. Given the structures

```
DCL 1 A,
      5 B  FIXED BIN,
      5 C,
        9 D  FIXED DEC(3),
        9 E  FLOAT BIN;
DCL 1 X,
      3 Y  CHAR(3),
      3 Z  CHAR(5),
```

what is the result of each of the following assignment statements?
(a) A = 17;
(b) X = 'ABCDE';
(c) C = 0;
(d) A = '123';

3. Given the structures

```
DCL 1 A,
      2 E,
        3 C FIXED BIN(15),
      2 D   FIXED DEC(5,2);
DCL 1 B,
      5 E,
        9 D FIXED BIN(15)     INIT (-81),
      5 C   FIXED DEC(5,2)    INIT (14.3);
```

what is the result of each of the following assignment statements?
(a) A = B;
(b) A = B, BY NAME;
(c) A = B + B;
(d) A = 2 * B, BY NAME;

11.3 Structure library functions

11.3.1 STRING function

The STRING function converts string values to structure elements and converts structure values to string. It provides a convenient way of combining elements of structures or separating strings into parts for assignment or input/output. The general form of the function is:

```
STRING(structure)
```

Given the statements

```
DCL STR          CHAR(22);
DCL 1 NAME,
      5 LAST    CHAR (10)   INIT ('SIGURDSON'),
      5 FIRST   CHAR (10)   INIT ('HAROLD'),
      5 MID     CHAR (2)    INIT ('V');

STR = STRING(NAME);
```

the assignment concatenates the elements of NAME and stores the result in STR.

NAME

LAST	S	I	G	U	R	D	S	O	N	
FIRST	H	A	R	O	L	D				
MID	V									

becomes:

STR

S	I	G	U	R	D	S	O	N		H	A	R	O	L	D					V	

Used in an output statement, STRING simplifies the editing format. Given the statements

```
DCL STR          CHAR(22);
DCL 1 NAME,
      5 LAST     CHAR (10)   INIT (SIGURDSON),
      5 FIRST    CHAR (10)   INIT (HAROLD),
      5 MID      CHAR (2)    INIT (V);

PUT EDIT (STRING(NAME)) (COL(1),A);
```

the output is printed as:

```
SIGURDSONbHAROLDbbbbV
```

Only one A format specification is needed because the value returned by STRING is a single character string.

Used as a pseudovariable, STRING breaks a character string into pieces.

```
STRING(NAME) = 'MACMILLAN REGINALD  P'
```

stores the value as:

NAME

LAST	M	A	C	M	I	L	L	A	N	
FIRST	R	E	G	I	N	A	L	D		
MID	P									

In this form, the function can be used for input into structures. Given the statement

```
GET EDIT (STRING(NAME)) (A(22));
```

and the data

```
EDWARDSbbbALONZObbbbJb
```

```
LAST    has the value 'EDWARDSbbb'
FIRST   has the value 'ALONZObbbb'
MID     has the value 'Jb'
```

only one A format specification is needed as one character string is being obtained from the input. STRING stores the character string in the parts of the structure, placing the first ten characters in LAST, the next ten in FIRST, and the last two in MID.

Review questions

1. Given the structure

```
DCL 1 TODAY,
        5 YY   CHAR(2),
        5 MM   CHAR(2),
        5 DD   CHAR(2);
```

use the STRING and DATE functions to store the date in the structure.

2. Given the structures

```
DCL 1 ADDR,
      5 STREET_ADDR CHAR(20) INIT('APT  12 384 MAIN ST'),
      5 CITY_ADDR   CHAR(20) INIT('CENTERVILLE WI 49216');
DCL 1 LOC,
      5 APT         CHAR(7),
      5 STREET      CHAR(13),
      5 CITY        CHAR(12),
      5 STATE       CHAR(3),
      5 ZIP         CHAR(5);
```

use the STRING function to move the information from ADDR to LOC.

11.4 Structure input/output

Since a structure name is an abbreviated way of referring to a collection of variables, the input and output of a structure is the same as the input and output of the collection of variables that make up the structure.

11.4.1 Input of structures

Structures can be input element by element using either the structure name or a list of elementary item names. In either case, there must be a format specification for each elementary item, as shown in the following example:

```
DCL 1 NAME,
      5 LAST     CHAR(20),
      5 FIRST    CHAR(10),
      5 MIDDLE   CHAR(10);

GET EDIT (NAME) (A(20),A(10),A(10));
```

or

```
GET EDIT (LAST,FIRST,MIDDLE) (A(20),A(10),A(10));
```

Structures of mixed types may be input the same way. The format specification for each elementary item causes it to be converted to the proper internal form. For example,

```
DCL 1 MEASUREMENTS,
      5 ID       CHAR(5),
      5 HEIGHT   FIXED BIN,
      5 WEIGHT   FLOAT BIN;

GET EDIT (MEASUREMENTS) (A(5),F(8),F(5,3));
```

or

```
GET EDIT (ID,HEIGHT,WEIGHT) (A(5),F(8),F(5,3));
```

If a structure contains only character fields, the data can also be read as a single character string and redefined. Or the STRING function can be used. Both redefinition and the STRING function take a single character string and divide it into parts. For example,

```
DCL ENTIRE_NAME CHAR(40);
DCL 1 NAME                DEF(ENTIRE_NAME),
      5 LAST     CHAR(20),
      5 FIRST    CHAR(10),
      5 MIDDLE   CHAR(10);

GET EDIT (STRING(NAME)) (A(40));
```

or

```
GET EDIT (ENTIRE_NAME) (A(40));
```

Both of these input statements take the same forty characters from the input stream and store them in the name.

11.4.2 Output of structures

Stream output of structures is usually element-by-element output. Whether the name of the structure is used, or a list of elementary items, there must be one format specification for each item. This is shown in the following example:

```
DCL 1 MEASUREMENTS,
      5 ID       CHAR(5),
      5 HEIGHT   FIXED BIN,
      5 WEIGHT   FLOAT BIN;

PUT EDIT (MEASUREMENTS) (COL(5),A(5),X(7),F(8),X(3),E(10,3));
```

or

```
PUT EDIT (ID,HEIGHT,WEIGHT)
         (COL(5),A(5),X(7),F(8),X(3),E(10,3));
```

If all the elementary items are character strings, the output may be treated as a single character string by using the DEFINED clause or the STRING function.

```
DCL ENTIRE_NAME CHAR(40);
DCL 1 NAME                  DEF(ENTIRE_NAME),
      5 LAST     CHAR(20),
      5 FIRST    CHAR(10),
      5 MIDDLE   CHAR(10);

PUT EDIT (STRING(NAME)) (A(40));
```

or

```
PUT EDIT (ENTIRE_NAME) (A(40));
```

OUTPUT EDITING

Output structures are often used to show, in a readable fashion, exactly how the output line is to look. Given the structure

```
DCL 1 DAY_OUT,
    5 MONTH  CHAR(2),
    5 FILL_1 CHAR(1)   INIT('/'),
    5 DAY    CHAR(2),
    5 FILL_2 CHAR(1)   INIT('/'),
    5 YEAR   CHAR(2);
```

and the statement

```
PUT SKIP EDIT (DAY_OUT) ((5)A);
```

then the output for December 17, 1986 is:

```
12/17/86
```

The spacing and punctuation are included in the structure. Each elementary item of the structure, including the slashes, is included in the format. The same edit form of output could be obtained from the simpler structure

```
DCL 1 TODAY,
      5 MONTH  CHAR(2),
      5 DAY    CHAR(2),
      5 YEAR   CHAR(2);
```

by using

```
PUT SKIP EDIT (TODAY.MONTH,'/',TODAY.DAY,'/',TODAY.YEAR) ((5)A);
```

However, this is less readable than including the editing characters in the structure as fillers.

A third editing method is available if the data structure is configured as a single character string. Given the structure

```
DCL  CURRENT_DATE  CHAR(6),
     1  THIS_DAY            DEF (CURRENT_DATE),
        5  MONTH   CHAR(2),
        5  DAY     CHAR(2),
        5  YEAR    CHAR(2);
```

and the statement

```
PUT SKIP EDIT (CURRENT_DATE) (P'XX/XX/XX');
```

or

```
PUT SKIP EDIT (MONTH || DAY || YEAR) (P'XX/XX/XX');
```

the output for December 17, 1986 is:

```
12/17/86
```

When the editing characters are not part of the structure, the structure may be converted to a single character string and the editing characters may be inserted by using a P format. Descriptions of the P format for output of data follow.

P FORMAT

A P format is a picture or template of the form of the value. There is one character in the format for each position of the output field. The particular format character indicates what type of character will be printed. Some format characters are themselves printed; others indicate the type of data values that can be printed. Any format character can be repeated by using a repetition factor. The format characters fall into the following categories:

Position-holding character
Insertion character
Zero-suppression character
Floating character
Alignment character

Position-holding characters

The position-holder format characters are replaced by the value stored in the output variable.

Position holder	*Meaning*
X	Holds a position for one output character
A	Holds a position for an alphabetic character
9	Holds a position for a digit

The choice of the format depends on the type of value to be output.

All three format characters, X, A, and 9, may be used in printing a single character string. With X and A formats, the data must be CHARACTER. With the 9 format, the data may be either numeric or CHARACTER. The output line is set up using the P format symbols, which are then replaced with the values being output. Given the output statement

```
PUT EDIT ('5','A9$','DECEMBER',25) (P'9',P'XXX',P'(8)A',P'99');
```

the output line is set up as:

```
9XXXAAAAAAAA99
```

which is replaced by the values, giving

```
5A9$DECEMBER25
```

With CHARACTER values, the value is placed left-justified in the X, A, and 9 positions of the format. The particular character falling in an A position must be alphabetic. The particular character falling in a 9 position must be a digit. Any character of the collating sequence can be used in an X position. A and 9 formats are used with character strings when data validation is wanted. If the value is the wrong kind, the CONVERSION condition is raised.

The 9 format is the only position holder for numeric values. BINARY and DECIMAL numbers placed in 9 format positions are aligned right-justified unless the alignment is explicitly indicated.

Examples of the A, X, and 9 formats are given in table 11–1.

Value	*Format*	*Output*	*Comment*
'A6%'	P'XXX'	A6%	
'A6%'	P'XX'	A6	Truncates on right
'A6%'	P'XXXX'	A6%ƀ	Blank fills on right
'ABC'	P'AAA'	ABC	
'ABC'	P'AA'	AB	Truncates on right
'ABC'	P'AAAA'	ABCƀ	Blank fills on right
'ABC'	P'(5)A'	ABCƀƀ	Repetition factor of 5
'A6%'	P'AAA'		Error—value not alphabetic
'A @'	P'AAA'	A @	Blank, $, @, and # are considered alphabetic
125	P'999'	125	
125	P'(5)9'	00125	Repetition factor, zero fill on left
12.5	P'999'	012	Point aligned at right, zero fill on left
.125	P'999'	000	Point aligned at right, zero fill on left
125	P'99'		Error—high-order digits truncated
–125	P'999'	125	Digits only
'A6%'	P'A9X'	A6%	Picture format characters can be mixed

Table 11–1

Given the statement

```
PUT EDIT ('ABC',125,'1.25') (P'AAAAA',P'9999',P'XXXXX');
```

the output is printed as:

```
ABCƀƀƀ1251.25ƀ
```

Insertion characters The insertion characters are used in formats to edit output. They are not part of the stored value but are printed to increase readability. They are placed in the formats in the positions where they are to be printed, as shown in the following table:

Insertion character	*Use*
/	Printed in the position where it occurs
B	Left blank
$	Printed in the position where it occurs (must be at one end of a number)
,	Printed in the position where it occurs
.	Printed in the position where it occurs
+	Printed in the position where it occurs if the number is positive, otherwise left blank (must be at one end of a number)
-	Printed in the position where it occurs if the number is negative, otherwise left blank (must be at one end of a number)
S	Sign of the number is printed in the position where it occurs
CR	Printed in the position where it occurs if the number is negative, otherwise left blank (must be at the right end of a number)
DB	Printed in the position where it occurs if the number is negative, otherwise left blank (must be at the right end of a number)
E	Printed in the position where it occurs (is the E for exponential numbers)

Note in the table both CR (for "credit") and DB (for "debit") are used to indicate a negative number. With financial programs, positive numbers are used for the ordinary state of an account. With a checking account, the ordinary condition is one of credit, so DB is an appropriate way to indicate a negative number. With a charge account, the ordinary condition is one of debit, so CR is an appropriate way to indicate a negative number.

Examples of the use of insertion characters are given in table 11–2.

Table 11–2

Value	*Format*	*Output*	*Comment*
101236	P'99/99/99'	10/12/36	
5693120	P'999B9999'	569 3120	
125	P'$999'	$125	
1.25	P'$999'	$001	Point aligned at right, zero fill on left
125	P'9,999'	0,125	Zero fill on left
125	P'999.'	125.	
125	P'99.9'	12.5	Inserted point is not meaningful in terms of value
325784	P'$9,999,999'	$0,325,784	
125	P'999+'	125+	
-125	P'999+'	125ƀ	
125	P'999-'	125ƀ	
-125	P'999-'	125-	
125	P'S999'	+125	
125	P'S(5)9'	+00125	
-125	P'S999'	-125	
125	P'999CR'	125ƀƀ	
-125	P'999CR'	125CR	

Table 11–2 *continued*

Value	*Format*	*Output*	*Comment*
125	P'999DB'	125ƀƀ	
-125	P'999DB'	125DB	
12.5	P'99E99'	12E00	Truncated

Given the statement

```
PUT EDIT (021786,1475,-2910)
        (P'99/99/99',X(5),P'$999.99',X(5),P'99.99DB');
```

the output is printed as:

```
02/17/86ƀƀƀƀƀ$014.75ƀƀƀƀƀ29.10DB
```

Zero-suppression characters Readability of numbers is improved if leading zeros are not printed. The zero-suppression characters have this effect. They cause leading zeros to be replaced with a blank or an asterisk.

Zero-suppression character	*Effect*
Z	Replaces leading zeros with blank spaces in the positions where it occurs
*	Printed instead of leading zeros in the positions where it occurs

The asterisk (*) is used for protection when printing checks. When leading zeros are suppressed, any insertion characters among the leading zeros are also suppressed. Examples of zero-suppression characters are given in table 11–3.

Table 11–3

Value	*Format*	*Output*	*Comment*
125	P'ZZZ99'	ƀƀ125	Zero fill on left is suppressed
0203	P'ZZZ9'	ƀ203	Only leading zeros are suppressed
0000	P'ZZZ9'	ƀƀƀ0	
0000	P'ZZZZ'	ƀƀƀƀ	
2137	P'Z,Z99'	2,137	
125	P'Z,Z99'	ƀƀ125	Comma is suppressed
0	P'ZZ.'	ƀƀƀ	Decimal point is suppressed
125	P'*,***'	**125	
125	P'(5)*'	**125	

Given the statement

```
PUT EDIT (123456,1326) (P'Z,ZZZ,ZZZ',X(5),P'(6)*9');
```

the output is printed as:

```
ƀƀ123,456ƀƀƀƀƀ***1326
```

Floating characters Floating characters combine the insertion and zero-suppression features. The floating character itself replaces the rightmost leading zero and causes the rest of the leading zeros to be replaced with blanks. If there is no leading zero, the floating character replaces the leftmost digit of the value.

Floating character	Effect
$	Precedes value
+	Precedes value when the number is positive, otherwise blank
-	Precedes value when the number is negative, otherwise blank
S	Sign precedes value

Table 11–4 gives examples of the use of floating characters. Only one floating character can be used in a format. It is shown to be floating by appearing more than once in a leading editing string.

Table 11–4

Value	Format	Output	Comment
125	P'$$$9'	$125	
125	P'$$9999'	b$0125	
125	P'$$9'	$25	May be fatal
125	P'$$,$99'	bb$125	Comma suppressed
-125	P'$$$$9'	b$125	May be fatal
125	P'++++9'	b+125	
-125	P'++++9'	bb125	Number negative
-125	P'----9'	b-125	
125	P'----9'	bb125	Number positive
-125	P'SSSS9'	b-125	
-125	P'SS9'	125	May be fatal
125	P'SSS9'	+125	

Given the statement

```
PUT EDIT (-27,148,3685) (P'----9',P'$$$$9',P'(5)S9');
```

the output is printed as:

```
bb-27b$148b+3685
```

Alignment character The character V is used as an alignment character. It does not represent a position in the printed output, but indicates where the internal decimal point of the value is to be aligned with respect to the format. The integral part of the value is right-justified in the part of the format to the left of the V and the fractional part of the value is left-justified in the part of the format to the right of the V. If there is no alignment character in the format, the decimal point is aligned with the right end. Since the alignment character does not insert a printable decimal point, the decimal point insertion character is needed as well. Leading zeros to the right of the alignment character cannot be suppressed. This is shown in table 11–5.

Given the statement

```
PUT EDIT (12.5,0.147,123456) ((3)P'Z,ZZZ,ZZZV.99');
```

the output is printed as:

```
bbbbbbb12.50bbbbbbbbbb.14bb123,456.00
```

Value	Format	Output	Comment
12.5	P'99V.9'	12.5	
.35	P'9V99'	035	No space taken by alignment character
.35	P'9V9'	03	Truncation on right
.35	P'V999'	350	Zero fill on right
.35	P'9V.99'	0.35	
.35	P'9.V99'	0.35	
.07	P'ZV.99'	b.07	
.07	P'ZV.Z9'		Error—no suppression allowed after v
.35	P'Z.V99'	bb35	Insertion character suppressed
.35	P'ZV.99'	b.35	
.35	P'V99.9'	35.0	Alignment and printed point are independent

Table 11–5

Review questions

1. Given the structure

```
DCL 1 HEADING,
      5 TITLE     CHAR(30),
      5 PAGENUM   CHAR(3);
```

write a segment of code that
(a) Reads data into HEADING element by element.
(b) Reads data into HEADING as a whole using STRING.
(c) Reads data into HEADING as a whole using DEFINED.

2. Given the structure

```
DCL 1 INVENTORY,
      5 PART_NO    CHAR(5),
      5 SUPPLIER   CHAR(20),
      5 COST       FIXED DEC(6,2),
      5 ON_HAND    FIXED BIN;
```

write a segment of code that
(a) Reads data into INVENTORY using the structure name.
(b) Reads data into INVENTORY using the elementary item names.

3. Using the structure of question 1 above, write a segment of code that
(a) Prints data from HEADING element by element.
(b) Prints data from HEADING as a whole using STRING.
(c) Prints data from HEADING as a whole using DEFINED.

4. Using the structure of question 2 above, write a segment of code that
(a) Prints data from INVENTORY using the structure name.
(b) Prints data from INVENTORY using the elementary item names.

5. Rewrite the INVENTORY structure in a form that can be used with the following input/output statements:

```
GET EDIT (INVENTORY) (A(5),A(20),A(6),A(8));
PUT EDIT (INVENTORY) (COL(1),A,(3)(X(5),A));
```

6. For each of the following values and P formats, what does the output look like?

Value	*Format*	*Output*
35.98	999V99	
35.98	ZZZ.99	
35.98	$$9V.99	
−27.50	S,S99V.99	
−27.50	Z,Z99V.99CR	
−27.50	$,$99V.99DB	
987	$$,$99V.99CR	
2471.6	9,999BB99S	
−51.333	9,999BB99S	
987	$$,$99V.99CR	

7. For each of the following values and P formats, what does the output look like?

Value	*Format*	*Output*
'XYZ'	AAA	
'XYZ'	AA	
'XYZ'	ABABA	

8. Write a program segment that prints the system TIME in the form HH:MM:SS.mmm.

11.5 Picture variables

The P format is used with stream output. Later on we shall see that stream output is less efficient than record output. Since record declarations often use PICTURE (abbreviated PIC) variables, and picture variables are very similar to P format, this is an appropriate place to introduce I/O records even though record output will not be discussed until chapter 15.

PROGRAMMING HINT: EFFICIENCY Use P format with stream I/O, PICTURE variables with record I/O.

11.5.1 PICTURE variable declarations

Inside a program, records are represented as structures. A record can be thought of as a structure used for input or output. If the structure describes input from a card reader or output to a printer, only character and picture variables are permitted. The PICTURE variable descriptions are exactly the same as P formats but their use is different. A distinction is made between variables used for input and variables used for output. Input data must not have editing characters. For example:

```
DCL 1 IN_DATA,              /* UNEDITED INPUT DATA */
      5 NAME         CHAR(20),        [or PIC'(20)A']
      5 ADDR         CHAR(20),        [or PIC'(20)X']
      5 ACCT_NO      CHAR(6),         [or PIC'(6)X']
      5 NO_ORDERED   PIC'9999',
      5 COST         PIC'9999V99';
DCL 1 PRINT_DATA,           /* EDITED OUTPUT DATA */
      5 NAME         CHAR(20),        [or PIC'(20)A']
      5 ADDR         CHAR(20),        [or PIC'(20)X']
      5 ACCT_NO      CHAR(6),         [or PIC'(6)X']
      5 NO_ORDERED   PIC'ZZZ9',
      5 COST         PIC'(5)$9V.99';
```

The values of PICTURE variables are stored as character strings.

11.5.2 Picture variable input/output

Picture variables may be used for both input and output.

INPUT PICTURE VARIABLES

Only A, X, 9, T, and V format characters may be used in input variables. They represent the computer's understanding about the value stored in the variable. The value is actually stored in a character form exactly as it was found in the input stream. No place in storage is occupied by T or V. T indicates the position where the sign of a number is to be found as an "overpunched" or "overstruck" character. V indicates the understood position of the decimal point. Neither a decimal point nor a leading sign may be used in the data value. The value being input is not validated at the time of the input, although it must be of the proper type if it is to be used successfully. The effect of input picture variables is shown in the following example:

```
ABC |123 |5*Q |715 |45K |816 |XYZ |561 |PQR |987 |    |
```

```
DCL 1  DATA_IN,
       5  STR_1     PIC'AAA',
       5  NUM_1     PIC'999',
       5  STR_2     PIC'XXX',
       5  NUM_2     PIC'T999',
       5  STR_3     PIC'AAA',
       5  NUM_3     PIC'99V9',
       5  STR_4     PIC'XXXX',
       5  NUM_4     PIC'9999',
       5  STR_5     PIC'XX',
       5  NUM_5     PIC'99';

GET EDIT (DATA_IN) ((10)A(3));
```

The result is:

STR_1	A B C	NUM_1	1 2 3	
STR_2	5 * Q	NUM_2	7 1 5	Sign overstrike
STR_3	4 5 K	NUM_3	8 1 6	
STR_4	X Y Z	NUM_4	5 6 1	Blank fill
STR_5	P Q	NUM_5	9 8	Truncation

Although they contain characters incompatible with the picture given, STR_3 and NUM_4 are not recognized as invalid at the time of input. However, if either is assigned to another variable or otherwise accessed, the conversion condition will be raised. Note that both digital and alphabetic data are stored in bytes as characters, left-justified, with adjustments to the storage size made at the right end.

OUTPUT PICTURE VARIABLES

Any of the picture format characters may be used in output variables. The pictures describe the way the data would look if it were to be printed using an A format. The difference between PIC variables and P format lies in the time when the editing takes place. With P formats, the items in an output list are edited one by one as they are sent to the print buffer. With picture variables used for output, the values are edited when they are assigned to the variables. The edited form of the value is actually stored in the variable as characters, one byte per printable format character. This is shown in the following examples:

Value assigned	*Picture*	*Storage*	*Value stored*
'ABC'	PIC'XXX'	A B C	'ABC'
'ABC'	PIC'XXXX'	A B C	'ABCb'
'ABC'	PIC'XX'	A B	'AB'
'ABC'	PIC'XBXBX'	A B C	'AbBbC'
'125'	PIC'9999'	1 2 5	'125b'
125	PIC'9999'	0 1 2 5	'0125'
125	PIC'Z999V9'	1 2 5 0	'b1250'
3714.95	PIC'$9,999V.99'	$ 3 , 7 1 4 . 9 5	'$3,714.95'
−29	PIC'ZZZ.99CR'	2 9 . 0 0 C R	'b29,00CR'

All the format characters reserve a storage position except V.

With the use of records, three data descriptions usually are necessary: one for the input data, one for an efficient computational form of the data, and one for the edited output data. When both input and output records are described for several media, as in the following example,

```
DCL 1 IN_DATA,
      5 NAME          CHAR(20),
      5 ADDR          CHAR(20),
      5 ACCT_NO       CHAR(6),
      5 NO_ORDERED    PIC'9999',
      5 COST          PIC'9999V99';
DCL 1 DISK_DATA,
      5 NAME          CHAR(20),
      5 ADDR          CHAR(20),
      5 ACCT_NO       CHAR(6),
      5 NO_ORDERED    FIXED BIN,
      5 COST          FIXED DEC(6,2);
DCL 1 PRINT_DATA,
      5 NAME          CHAR(20),
      5 ADDR          CHAR(20),
      5 ACCT_NO       CHAR(6),
      5 NO_ORDERED    PIC'ZZZ9',
      5 COST          PIC'(5)$9V.99';
```

the input and output statements might be:

```
GET SKIP EDIT (IN_DATA) (A(20),A(20),A(6),A(4),A(6));
PUT EDIT (PRINT_DATA)
     (COL(1),A(20),COL(30),A(20),COL(60),A(6),
         COL(5),A(4),COL(15),A(10));
```

Notice that only A format specifications are used in the output statements. The field widths for input and output do not include any space for the V format character, but do include space for all other editing characters of the picture formats because those characters are part of the value in storage.

The DISK_DATA structure can be written to the disk using stream I/O, but it involves automatic conversion of the numeric data to character in the output process. This is unnecessary and inefficient for a storage medium that is accessible only by the computer. Record I/O as described in chapter 15 should be used.

In the input record, the account number remains in character form because it is not involved in any arithmetic. Declaring it as type CHAR is the same as declaring it as picture X. If picture 9 were used, automatic type validation of the data value would take place every time the data value is accessed.

With the declarations above, the assignments

```
DISK_DATA = IN_DATA;
PRINT_DATA = DISK_DATA;
```

not only move the data values from structure to structure, but cause the values of NO_ORDERED and COST to be converted from character to fixed binary and fixed decimal, respectively. Then those values are converted back to character according to the output editing pictures.

Picture data of a numeric type may be used in arithmetic, but doing so is inefficient. Both binary and decimal arithmetic are usually implemented at the hardware level, but character arithmetic is generally not available on a machine. Numeric picture variables, like CHAR variables, are converted to fixed decimal internally before any arithmetic is performed, and converted back to picture afterwards. For this conversion to be possible at all, the numeric pictures must not contain any format characters that would appear on a print line, except for a leading sign. Once a number has been edited for output, it can no longer be used in arithmetic.

PROGRAMMING HINT: CAUTION Numbers edited with * $, CR DB may not be used in arithmetic.

Picture variables may be classified according to the types of format characters used in the picture.

Classification	*Format symbols*	*Examples*	*Use*
Alphabetic	A	PIC'(6)A'	Input
Alphabetic edited	A B	PIC'AAAB(8)A'	Output
Alphanumeric	X	PIC'(15)X'	Input
Alphanumeric edited	X B /	PIC'XXBX/X'	Output
Numeric	9 V T	PIC'T9V99'	Input
Numeric edited	9 V $, . CR DB + − S	PIC'$$$,$$9V.99'	Output

The edited categories of picture variables are used for output and the unedited ones for input.

RECORD VARIANTS

Sometimes a file contains data organized in more than one type of record. A very general record may be defined for use in the actual input statement. It can then be reconfigured as record variants, as in the following example:

```
DCL IN_DATA              CHAR(80);
DCL 1 ID_DATA                       DEF (IN_DATA),
      5 NAME             CHAR(20),
      5 ADDR             CHAR(20),
      5 OCCUPATION       CHAR(40);
DCL 1 ACCT_DATA                     DEF (IN_DATA),
      5 ACCT_NO          CHAR(8),
      5 AMT(10)          PIC'9999V99';

GET EDIT (IN_DATA) (A(80));
```

The description used in the input statement must correspond to the size and arrangement of data in the file. It cannot be a redefinition of another data object. The variant record descriptions must not be longer than the description they redefine, but they may be shorter. Picture and character types may be mixed as desired, as both describe characters.

Review questions

1. Indicate whether each of the following statements is true or false.
   (a) When P formats are used for output, the values are edited at the same time that they are moved to the output buffer.
   (b) When PIC variables are used for input, the values are not edited.
   (c) When PIC variables are used in an assignment statement, the values being moved to them unedited.
   (d) When PIC variables are used for output, the values are not edited until they are moved to the output buffer.
   (e) A number that has been edited for output cannot be used in arithmetic.
   (f) A storage position is allocated for each character except 'V,' in a PICTURE specification.
   (g) P format and PIC specification may only be used with structures.
   (h) Once a numeric value has been edited, it may not be edited again.

2. For each of the following declarations, what is actually contained in storage?

   (a) DCL A PIC'999V99' INIT(14.9);
   (b) DCL B PIC'ZZZ.99' INIT(20.144);
   (c) DCL C PIC'$$9V.99' INIT(31);
   (d) DCL D PIC'SSSS.V99' INIT(.05);
   (e) DCL E PIC'(5)A' INIT('HAT');
   (f) DCL F PIC'(5)A' INIT('MANHATTAN');

3. Write a structure declaration for use with data in the form

Cols.		
	1-5	Sample number
	6-10	Location code
	11-15	Depth in inches
	16-19	Acidity
	20-22	Grain size

   where each measurement is recorded to three decimal places and the input statement is:

```
GET EDIT (STRING(SOIL_SAMPLE)) (A(22));
```

4. Write an output structure declaration that can be used with the output statement

```
PUT EDIT (STRING(SALES)) (A);
```

   to print information from the following structure, in a readable form:

```
DCL 1 SALES_INFO,
      5 ITEM_NO          CHAR(5),
      5 INFO,
        9 QUANTITY       FIXED BIN,
        9 ITEM_COST      FIXED DEC(6,2),
        9 TAX            FIXED DEC(4,2),
        9 TOTAL_COST     FIXED DEC(8,2);
```

11.6 Structure storage

The word length on most modern computers is four bytes. For efficient input and output, structures describing records should be set up in such a way that the total amount of storage space allocated for the structure is a multiple of four bytes. For example, in the records IN_DATA, DISK_DATA, and PRINT_DATA,

```
DCL 1 IN_DATA,
      5 NAME        CHAR(20),        [or PIC'(20)A']
      5 ADDR        CHAR(20),        [or PIC'(20)X']
      5 ACCT_NO     CHAR(6),         [or PIC'(6)X']
      5 NO_ORDERED  PIC'9999',
      5 COST        PIC'9999V99';
DCL 1 DISK_DATA,
      5 NAME        CHAR(20),
      5 ADDR        CHAR(20),
      5 ACCT_NO     CHAR(6),
      5 NO_ORDERED  FIXED BIN,
      5 COST        FIXED DEC(6,2);
DCL 1 PRINT_DATA,
      5 NAME        CHAR(20),        [or PIC'(20)A']
      5 ADDR        CHAR(20),        [or PIC'(20)X']
      5 ACCT_NO     CHAR(6),         [or PIC'(6)X']
      5 NO_ORDERED  PIC'ZZZ9',
      5 COST        PIC'(5)$9V.99';
```

the sizes of the variables are:

Variable	*Size*
NAME	20 bytes
ADDR	20 bytes
ACCT_NO	6 bytes
NO_ORDERED	4 bytes in IN_DATA
	2 bytes in DISK_DATA
	4 bytes in PRINT_DATA
COST	6 bytes in IN_DATA
	4 bytes in DISK_DATA
	10 bytes in PRINT_DATA (including the editing symbols)

11.6.1 Scalar storage

Storage requirements are to some extent implementation-dependent. The ones given here are typical.

FIXED-BINARY STORAGE

On a machine with a 32-bit word length, all fixed-binary declarations of fifteen bits or fewer require two bytes of memory for storage. One additional bit is used for the sign. Fixed-binary variables with sixteen through thirty-one bits require four bytes of memory. The default size on most machines is two bytes.

Declaration	*Space allocated*
FIXED BIN	2 bytes
FIXED BIN(7)	2 bytes
FIXED BIN(15)	2 bytes
FIXED BIN(16)	4 bytes
FIXED BIN(31)	4 bytes

Fixed-binary numbers are aligned on either half-word or full-word boundaries, depending on the amount of space needed. Thus the structure

```
DCL 1   STRUCT_A,
        3  X          FIXED BIN(15),
        3  Y          FIXED BIN(15),
        3  Z          FIXED BIN(15);
```

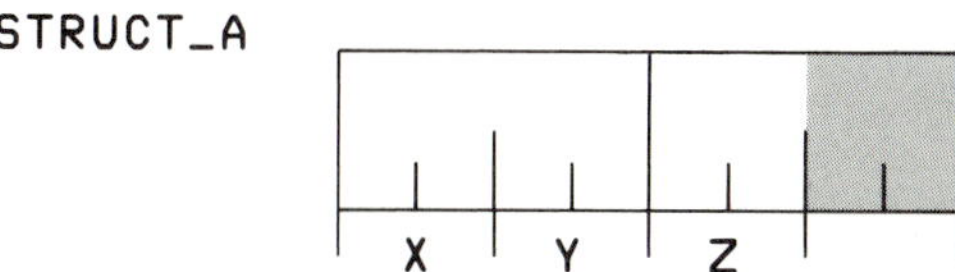

has three adjacent half-words of storage allocated for it. The variables are stored contiguously in memory. But the structure

```
DCL 1   STRUCT_B,
        3  X          FIXED BIN(31),
        3  Y          FIXED BIN(15),
        3  Z          FIXED BIN(31);
```

requires six half-words of storage, as both X and Z are aligned on full-word boundaries and Y requires a half-word of storage, which must be between the storage allocated for X and that allocated for Z. The extra half-word of storage is wasted.

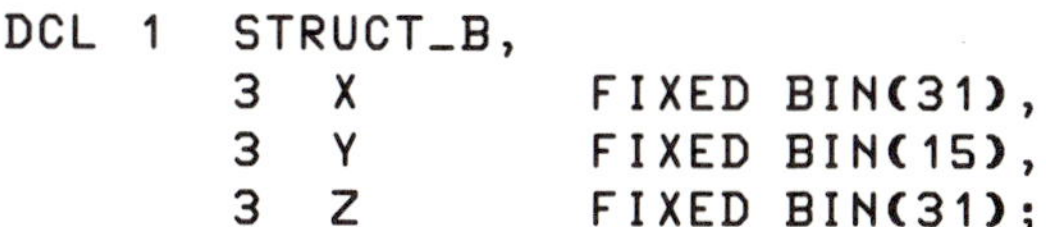
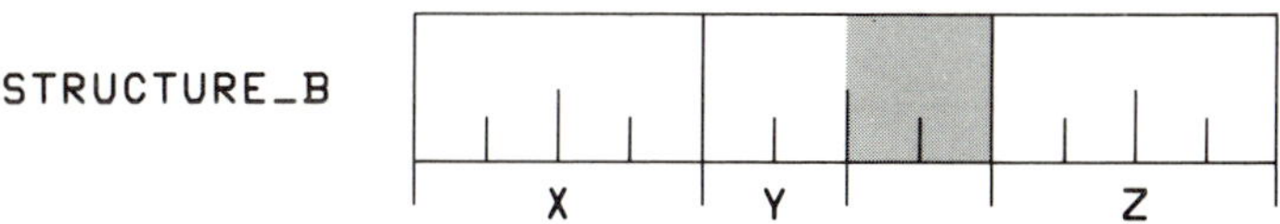

If a structure is used as a record, the total size of the structure, including the slack bytes, must be known.

FLOAT-BINARY STORAGE

Depending on the machine and the operating system, there may be three underlying sizes of float-binary storage. The default precision is twenty-one, which, with both exponent and mantissa, requires four bytes of storage and is aligned on a full-word boundary. If the precision is greater than twenty-one but not greater than fifty-three, eight bytes are needed and the storage is aligned on a double-word boundary. If greater precision is available, it requires twelve or more bytes of storage.

FIXED-DECIMAL STORAGE

When storing a fixed-decimal value, two digits are placed in each byte. An additional half-byte is needed for the sign. The decimal point is not stored with the number. If N = number of digits, then CEIL((N+1)/2) bytes storage is needed.

Storage can only be allocated in bytes, so some space is wasted when decimal variables are declared to have an even number of digits. Fixed-decimal storage is aligned on byte boundaries.

Declaration	*Space allocated*	
FIXED DEC(5,2)	3 bytes	Exact fit
FIXED DEC(6,2)	4 bytes	Zero fill
FIXED DEC(6,0)	4 bytes	Zero fill
FIXED DEC(7,2)	4 bytes	Exact fit

Any unneeded half-bytes (called nibbles) are filled with zeros. The structure

```
DCL 1  STRUCT,
       3  X        FIXED DEC(5,2)   INIT (123.45),
       3  Y        FIXED DEC(6)     INIT (-123456),
       3  Z        FIXED DEC(7,2)   INIT (12345.67);
```

is stored as:

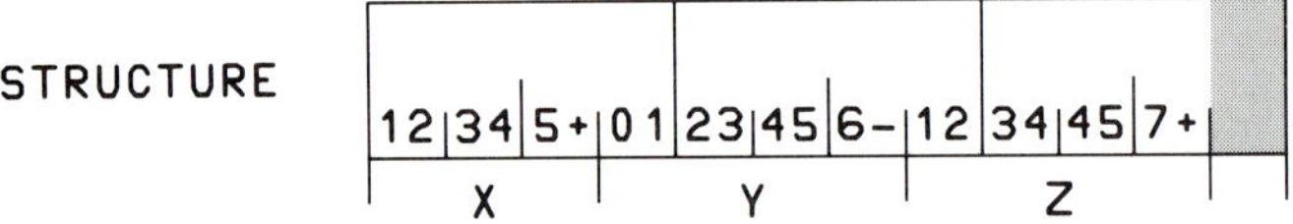

FLOAT-DECIMAL STORAGE

Float-decimal data is stored in the same form as float-binary data. If the precision is six or smaller, four bytes of storage are needed, aligned on a full-word boundary. If it is greater than six, but not greater than sixteen, eight bytes of storage are needed, aligned on a double-word boundary. The wide varieties of numeric data types available in PL/I are supported by a much smaller number of machine data types. Using default precision avoids the waste of storage and decreases the chance of error.

CHARACTER STRING STORAGE

Character data is stored one character per byte and is aligned on a byte boundary.

BIT STRING STORAGE

For efficiency, most compilers pack bit strings. Up to eight BIT(1) flags can be placed in a single byte. Bit strings in a structure can be packed only if they are adjacent. In

```
DCL 1 STRUCT_1,
      5 X       BIT(1),
      5 Y       BIT(1),
      5 Z       FIXED BIN(15);
```

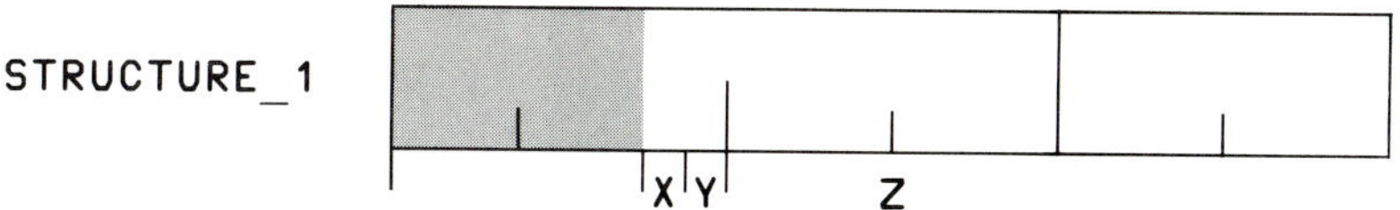

the bit strings are stored together in a single byte so that only three bytes of the full word are being used. But in

```
DCL 1 STRUCT_2,
      5 X       BIT(1),
      5 Z       FIXED BIN,
      5 Y       BIT(1);
```

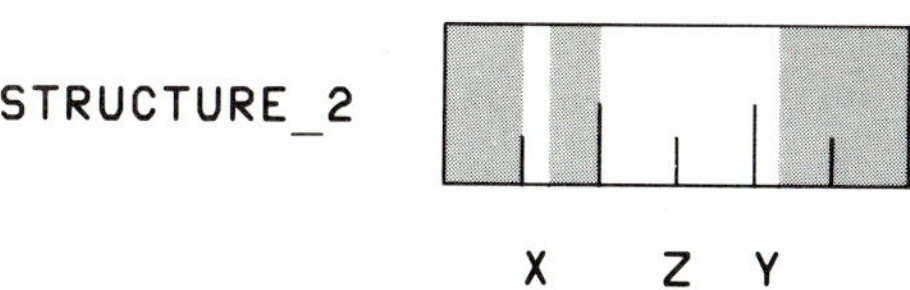

the bit strings each require an entire byte, so that three bytes of one full word and one byte of another are used. In a byte-oriented computer, STRUCT_1 requires three bytes of storage, while STRUCT_2 requires four. In a word-oriented computer, STRUCT_1 requires one full word of storage, while STRUCT_2 requires two.

11.6.2 Structure storage

Structures may be stored either ALIGNED or UNALIGNED. The default value is ALIGNED. If UNALIGNED storage is used, word and half-word boundaries are ignored. This saves space since both numeric and character data start on byte boundaries. However, it can cause errors as the operands of arithmetic instructions must be aligned on half-word or full-word boundaries.

If ALIGNED storage is used, determining the amount of storage allocated for a structure involves knowing the number of bytes needed for each element and the required alignment of the element. The computer memory is divided into bits, bytes, half-words, words, and double words. Because of the underlying hardware, different types of data must have storage allocated on particular types of memory boundaries.

Alignment	*Data type*
Double-word boundary	FLOAT BIN(22)—FLOAT BIN(53) FLOAT BIN (default) FLOAT DEC(7)—FLOAT DEC(16)
Word boundary	FLOAT BIN(1)—FLOAT BIN(21) FLOAT DEC(1)—FLOAT DEC(6) FLOAT DEC (default) FIXED BIN(16)—FIXED BIN(31)
Half-word boundary	FIXED BIN(1)—FIXED BIN(15) FIXED BIN (default)
Byte boundary	FIXED DEC (all) CHAR (all) PIC (all)

When setting up the storage space, the compiler carefully plans the placement of structures so as to minimize wasted storage. The following diagram shows storage allocation for a structure of mixed types:

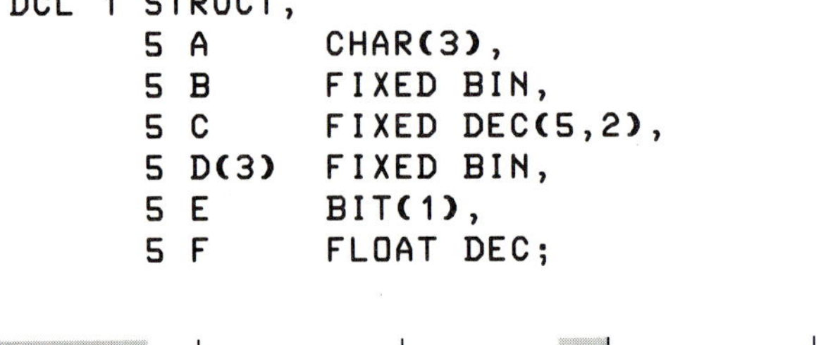

```
DCL 1 STRUCT,
      5 A     CHAR(3),
      5 B     FIXED BIN,
      5 C     FIXED DEC(5,2),
      5 D(3)  FIXED BIN,
      5 E     BIT(1),
      5 F     FLOAT DEC;
```

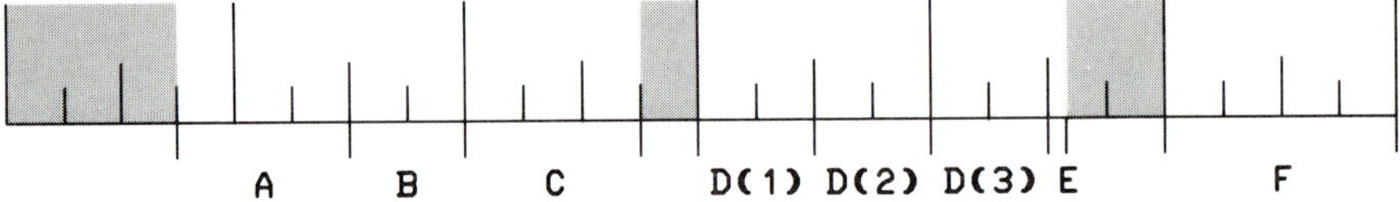

The structure must itself be aligned on a full-word boundary if it is to be used for input and output. Since the most compact arrangement of the fields does not begin on a full-word boundary, three extra bytes may be used at the beginning. The overall length of the structure is six full words or twenty-four bytes, even though the values do not occupy that much space. The actual alignment of a structure is implementation-dependent.

The most compact ALIGNED storage for STRUCT is that shown above. As indicated by the shading, two bytes are wasted, also part of another. A starts on a byte boundary which is neither a half-word or a full-word boundary. B starts on a half-word boundary. C starts on a full-word boundary. E uses only one of eight bits in its byte. The variable F requires four bytes of storage starting on a full-word boundary. Each element of the array D and the variable B require a half-word of storage. The other variables may be placed on any byte boundary.

For most applications other than record I/O, the programmer does not need to be concerned with the actual storage arrangements. The computer keeps track of the locations and sizes of the variables.

Review questions

1. For efficient use of disk storage, it is recommended that storage be allocated for structures in multiples of ________________ bytes.

2. Fixed-binary numbers are aligned on ________________ or ________________ boundaries depending on their precision.

3. Fixed-decimal numbers are stored ________________ to a byte.

4. In determining the amount of storage allocated for a structure, it is necessary to know the ________________ and ________________ of each elementary item.

11.7 Examples of structures

This program is an example of the use of variant records to store several different types of information. It also shows the difference between input and output structures.

11.7.1 Charge account

The input data consists of customer records, which are arranged so that personal information about a customer (account number, name, and address) is followed by a number of records of purchases. The first character in each record indicates which type it is. The records are being listed with spacing between the customers. The output is edited for readability.

```
CHARGE: PROC OPTIONS(MAIN);
/*****************************************************************/
/*                                                               */
/* PROGRAM: LIST A FILE OF CHARGE ACCOUNT RECORDS                */
/* AUTHOR:  C ZIEGLER                                            */
/* VERSION: 07/17/84                                             */
/*                                                               */
/* PROGRAM DESCRIPTION                                           */
/* ----------------------------------------------------------    */
/* THIS PROGRAM LISTS A FILE OF CURRENT CHARGE ACCOUNT           */
/* ACTIVITY.                                                     */
/*                                                               */
/* INPUT: CUSTF — TWO TYPES OF RECORDS                           */
/*                 COLS      1 RECORD TYPE                       */
/*                               'A' FOR CUSTOMER                */
/*                               'B' FOR CHARGE                  */
/*                       2 -  6 ACCOUNT NUMBER                   */
/*               TYPE A                                          */
/*                       7 -  9 ACCOUNT TYPE                     */
/*                      10 - 29 NAME                             */
/*                      30 - 59 ADDRESS                          */
/*                      60 - 66 TELEPHONE                        */
```

```
/*              TYPE B                                          */
/*                      7 - 12 DATE                             */
/*                     13 - 20 ITEM CODE                        */
/*                     20 - 21 DEPARTMENT NUMBER                */
/*                     22 - 23 STORE NUMBER                     */
/*                     24 - 34 PRICE                            */
/*                                                              */
/* OUTPUT: SYSPRINT - THREE TYPES OF RECORDS                    */
/*              TYPE A & AND TYPE B FROM THE INPUT              */
/*              TYPE C WITH TOTAL PRICE FOR THE ACCOUNT         */
/*                                                              */
/****************************************************************/
DCL CUSTF FILE SEQL INPUT STREAM ENV(CONSECUTIVE);
DCL 1 CUST_REC,
      5 ACCT_TYPE     CHAR(3),
      5 NAME          CHAR(20),
      5 ADDR          CHAR(30),
      5 TELNO         CHAR(7);
DCL 1 CHG_REC,
      5 CHG_DATE      CHAR(6),
      5 ITEMNO        CHAR(8),
      5 DEPTNO        CHAR(2),
      5 STORENO       CHAR(2),
      5 PRICE         PIC '(10)9V99';
DCL 1 CHG_INFO,
      5 FILL_1        CHAR(10)        INIT (' '),
      5 CHG_DATE      PIC '99/99/99',
      5 FILL_2        CHAR(10)        INIT (' '),
      5 ITEMNO        CHAR(15),
      5 PRICE         PIC '(6)ZV.99';
DCL REC_TYPE          CHAR(1),
    ACCTNO            CHAR(5),
    TOT_PRICE         FIXED DEC(8,2);
DCL MORE_DATA         BIT(1),
    TRUE              BIT(1)    INIT('1'B),
    FALSE             BIT(1)    INIT('0'B);

ON ENDFILE(CUSTF)
  MORE_DATA = FALSE;

MORE_DATA = TRUE;
OPEN FILE (CUSTF);
GET FILE (CUSTF) EDIT (REC_TYPE,ACCTNO) (A(1),A(5));
REC_TYPE = '1';
TOT_PRICE = 0;
DO WHILE (MORE_DATA);
  SELECT(REC_TYPE);
    WHEN ('1')                  /* PROCESS FIRST CUSTOMER   */
      DO;
        GET FILE (CUSTF) EDIT (STRING(CUST_REC)) (A(60));
        PUT PAGE;
        PUT SKIP LIST (CUST_REC);
      END;
```

```
      WHEN ('A')                          /* PROCESS NEXT CUSTOMER   */
        DO;
          PUT EDIT ((42)'-') (COL(42),A);
          PUT EDIT (TOT_PRICE) (COL(42),P'$$$,$$$V.99');
          GET FILE (CUSTF) EDIT (STRING(CUST_REC)) (A(60));
          PUT PAGE;
          PUT SKIP LIST (CUST_REC);
          TOT_PRICE = 0;
        END;
      WHEN ('B')                          /* PROCESS CHARGE RECORD   */
        DO;
          GET FILE (CUSTF) EDIT (STRING(CHG_REC)) (A(24));
          CHG_INFO = CHG_REC, BY NAME;
          PUT EDIT (STRING(CHG_INFO)) (A);
          TOT_PRICE = TOT_PRICE + CHG_REC.PRICE;
        END;
      OTHERWISE
        PUT SKIP LIST ('INVALID RECORD TYPE',REC_TYPE,ACCTNO);
    END;
    GET FILE (CUSTF) EDIT (REC_TYPE,ACCTNO) (COL(1),A(1),A(5));
  END;
  PUT EDIT ((42)'-') (COL(42),A);
  PUT EDIT (TOT_PRICE) (COL(42),P'$$$,$$$V.99');
  END CHARGE;
```

Note the use of STRING for both input and output. Also note the A format specifications for PIC variables and P format for a numeric variable. A special record type is being used for the first customer record so that the TOT_PRICE field is not printed at that time. In the arithmetic statement, qualification is used because the data name, PRICE, is ambiguous. The priming read obtains enough of the data to be sure that there is data present and to determine which record variant to use.

11.8 Summary

Structures are used to subdivide character strings, group related heterogeneous data, group unrelated objects of similar use, and describe records. They can be input and output. In some implementations of PL/I they can be used in arithmetic and assignment statements.

When structures are used to describe input and output lines, PICTURE variables are often used. These provide a way of formatting a line separately from the actual I/O. The same type of formatting can be done in edit-directed I/O using the P format. It is particularly useful with business applications. PICTURE variables and P format provide an easier way to edit numbers than is possible otherwise.

11.9 Exercises

1. Write a program that reads data of the form

Cols.		
	1-20	Student name
	21-23	Grade on exam 1 (max is 100)
	24-26	Grade on exam 2 (max is 100)
	...	
	33-35	Grade on exam 5 (max is 100)

Any or all of the grades may be missing (blank field). Your program should calculate the average numeric grade for each student and print the student's name, five exam grades, and average grade on a single line. Use structures for input and output and a nested array for the grades.

2. Write a program that reads data of the form

Cols.		
	1-20	Name
	21-25	Account number
	26-30	Transaction number
	31-40	Transaction amount (dollars and cents, no decimal point)

Assume that the records have been sorted by account number and that there are at most twenty records for each account. Processing one account at a time, read the records into an array of structures, sort them on the transaction number, and print them.

***3.** Write a program to determine how each of the following items is stored on your computer:

```
(a) FIXED BIN(15)  INIT(25);
(b) FIXED BIN(31)  INIT(67);
(c) FIXED DEC(6,1) INIT(3.5);
(d) CHAR(5)        INIT('ABC');
(e) CHAR(5) VAR    INIT('XYZ');
(f) BIT(3)         INIT('111'B);
(g) BIT(5)  VAR    INIT('1101'B);
```

***4.** The following program prints the internal bit representation of the structure. Run it on your computer and locate each of the elementary items in the output. How are the items aligned? Are any descriptors included in the output? What fill is used for slack bits and bytes?

```
TRY: PROC OPTIONS(MAIN);
DCL 1 STRUCT,
      5 A     BIT(3)         INIT('111'B),
      5 B     FIXED BIN(31)  INIT(67),
      5 C     CHAR(5)        INIT('ABC'),
      5 D     FIXED BIN(15)  INIT(25),
```

```
        5 E     CHAR(5) VAR    INIT('XYZ'),
        5 F(9)  FIXED DEC(1)   INIT(1,2,3,4,5,6,7,8,9);
DCL P           POINTER,
    STR         CHAR(30)       BASED(P);
P = ADDR(STRUCT);
PUT SKIP LIST(UNSPEC(STR));
END TRY;
```

12
Report design

OBJECTIVE: To structure output to be readable.

MOST PRINTED COMPUTER OUTPUT, including that from the assignments of previous chapters, takes a form we can call a report. In this chapter we will discuss methods of structuring reports.

12.1 Report structure

A *report* consists of a heading, information that is grouped according to the value of a particular field (the topic of the group), and some sort of conclusion, summary, or footing. The groups themselves may be structured, having headings, detailed lines of information, and footings. There may be several levels of groupings. In addition, there may be page headings and page footings. This book is in the form of a report in that there is an introduction and a table of contents at the beginning, appendices and an index at the end, and information grouped into chapters. Each chapter itself has a heading, a footing in the form of exercises, and information grouped into sections. The structure of this book should be drawn as shown in figure 12–1.

This hierarchy chart differs from an outline of the book in that it represents the structure, not the contents. In a report, groups similar to the

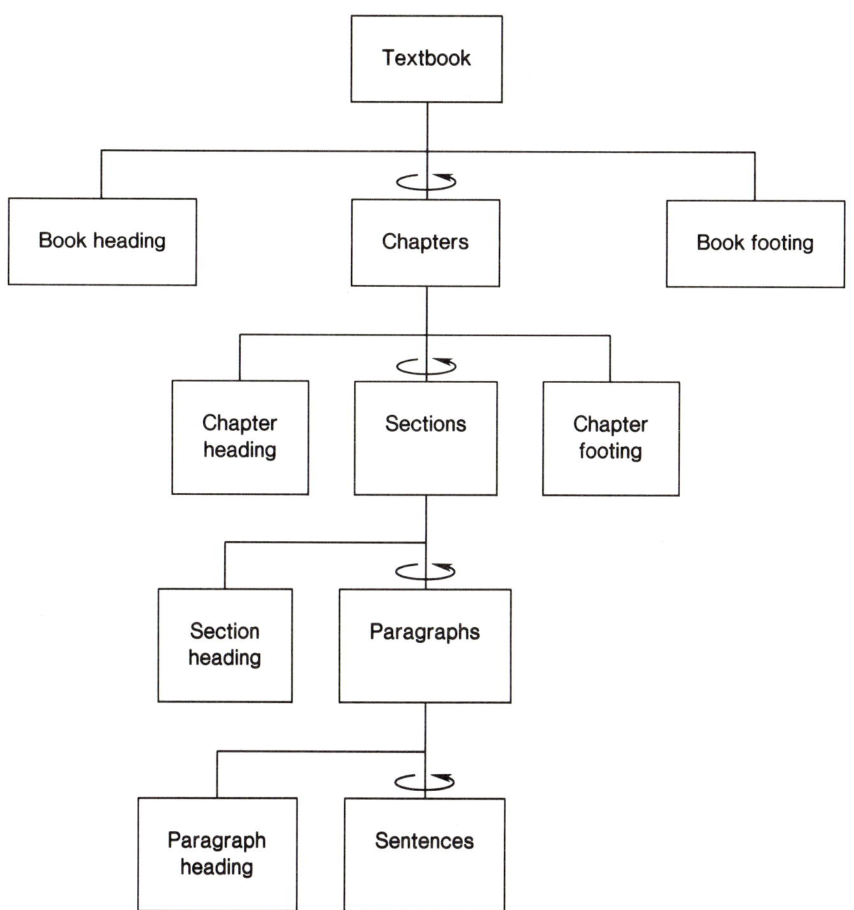

Figure 12–1

chapters, sections, and paragraphs of this book are known as *control groups*. The lowest level control group is made up of records, in this example the sentences in the paragraphs. Note that figure 12–1 does not represent a program. It is a hierarchy chart of data—output data. Note also that there are no section and paragraph footings in the chart. When a group is partitioned into smaller groups, headings and footings are optional.

Input data generally has a similar structure. The data that makes up the white pages of a telephone book has the input structure shown in figure 12–2.

The first letter of the name is significant in terms of the processing, so it appears separately in the chart. It is an integral part of the name for sorting and, along with the other information, can be thought of as forming a single record. This letter is a *control field*. A change in its value controls the division of the telephone book into sections. This change in value is called a *control break*.

A telephone book also has a physical structure consisting of sections with section headings and pages with page headings. Part of the problem of

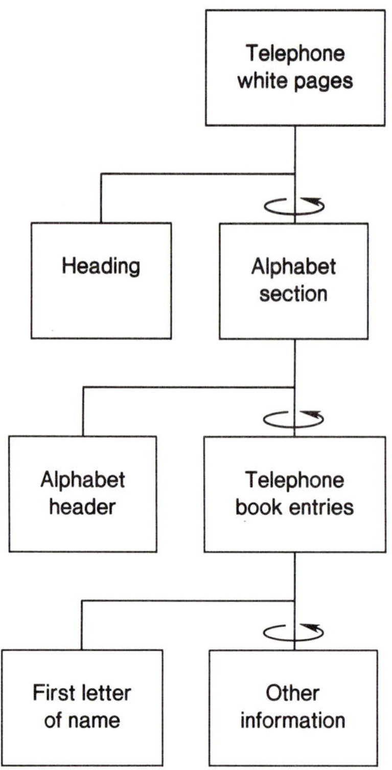

Figure 12–2

designing a report is to synchronize the physical structure and logical structures of the output data.

The general form of data stored in a computer, with two levels of grouping, is shown in the hierarchy chart of figure 12–3. The corresponding general form of a report-writing program is shown in figure 12–4, where there is a correspondence between the input and output structures of the data and the structure of the program.

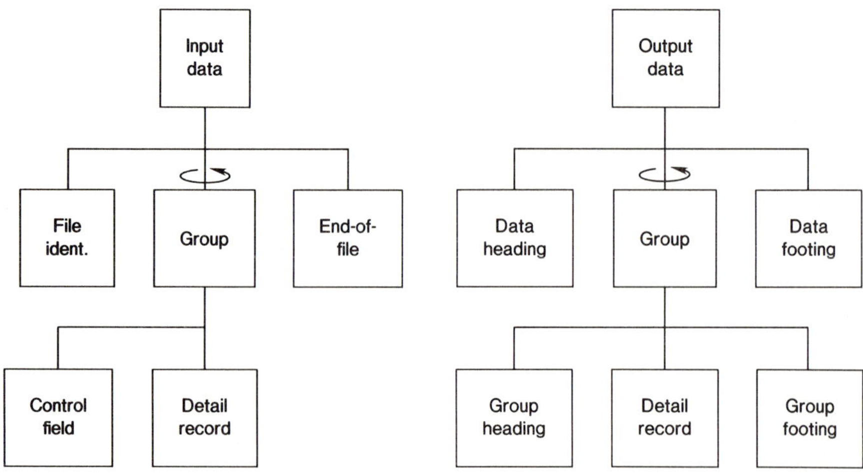

Figure 12–3

12.1.1 Headings and footings

In the program hierarchy chart of figure 12–4 the report organization consists of two levels, the entire report, and the control group. A heading and a footing is being printed for each. This reflects the most general situation. If the groups are further subdivided, similar additional levels are added to the charts.

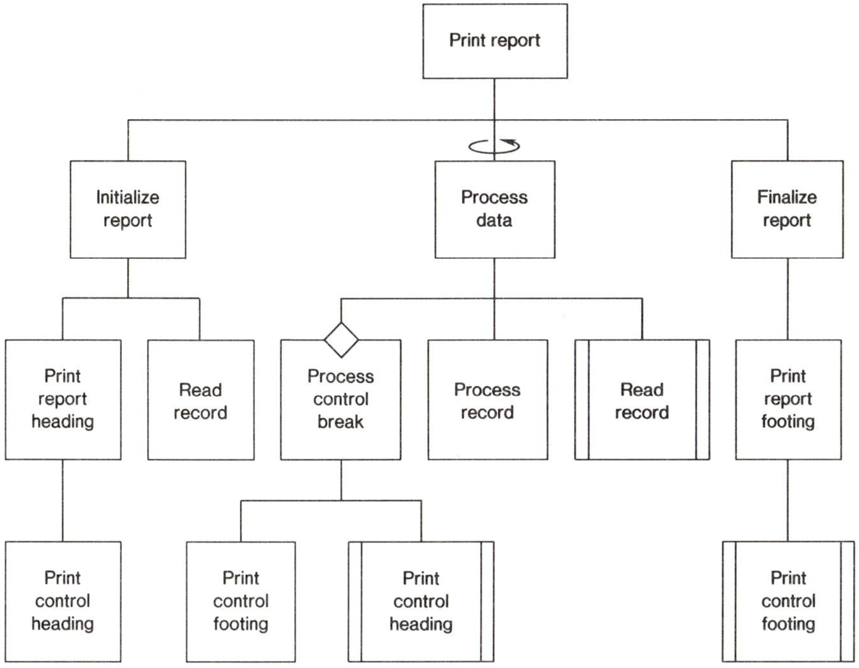

Figure 12–4

There may be a report heading containing such information as:

The title of the report
The date
Corporate or institutional identification
Some type of introduction

A report footing might consist of:

A report summary
Report totals

If the control group is a physical group such as a page, there may be:

A page heading containing a page number
Report identification
A date
Column titles

A page footing might contain:

Page totals
A page summary
A page number

If the control group is a logical group, the control heading would contain:

Group identification
Column titles

The control footing might contain:

A group summary
Group totals

Headings and footings are the editing lines of the report. Although they may contain small amounts of data, the major part of the data lies in between, in the detail lines of the control group. If we compare figures 12–3 and 12–4, attempting to match corresponding parts of the hierarchies, we obtain the correspondences of figure 12–5.

The system is data-driven in the sense that the program modules in the second column are triggered by the arrival of the data in the first column. There may or may not be actual file identification data on the file read by

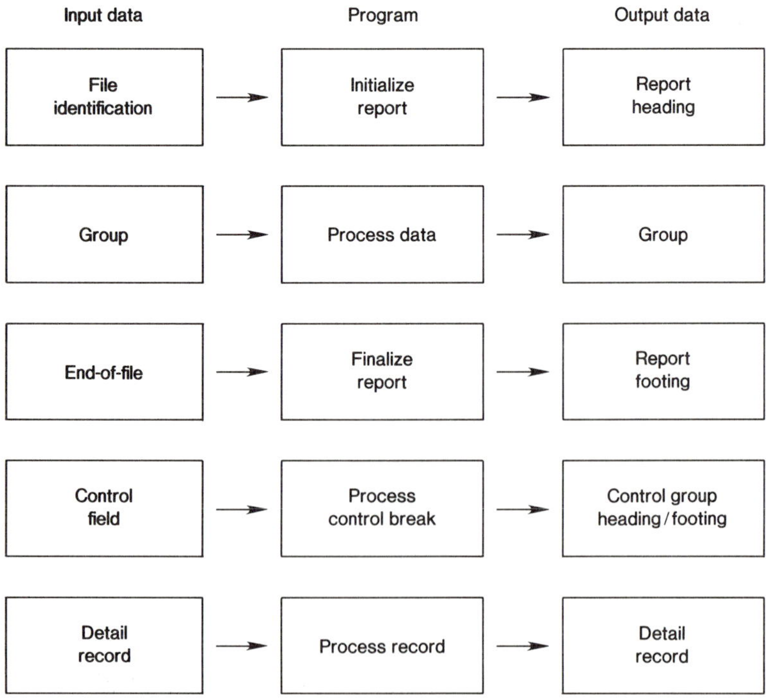

Figure 12–5

the program. (There is always file identification information that is read by the system.) In any case, the presence of the beginning of the data file makes the report possible. If there is no data, in most cases there is no report. The recognition of the end of the file is the trigger for finishing the report. The data and its processing is in the middle. The change of value of a control field causes a control break. Processing the control break includes ending the old control group and starting the new one. Note that in addition to the priming read, the program initialization includes a priming write of the report and group headings.

Most of the input and output boxes are shown more than once in the hierarchy chart. If their implementation requires more than a few lines of code, they may appropriately be implemented as internal procedures. This has the effect of moving the input and output out of the main line of processing so that the main line contains only the actual processing of the data. A skeleton program for printing a two-level report would look like this:

```
DCL IN_DATA     CHAR(. . .),
    1 DETAIL_LINE      DEF (IN_DATA),
      5 CONTROL_VALUE  CHAR(. . .),
      5 OTHER_DATA     CHAR(. . .);
DCL MORE_DATA          BIT(1),
    OLD_VALUE          CHAR(1);
DCL TRUE               BIT(1)      INIT('1'B),
    FALSE              BIT(1)      INIT('0'B);

ON ENDFILE(SYSIN)
  MORE_DATA = FALSE;

MORE_DATA = TRUE;
GET EDIT (IN_DATA) (A(. . .));
IF MORE_DATA
  THEN
    DO;
      OLD_VALUE = CONTROL_VALUE;
      CALL REPORT_HEADING;
      CALL CONTROL_HEADING;
    END;
DO WHILE (MORE_DATA);
  IF OLD_VALUE ¬= CONTROL_VALUE
    THEN
      DO;
        CALL CONTROL_FOOTING;
        OLD_VALUE = CONTROL_VALUE;
        CALL CONTROL_HEADING;
      END;
  CALL PROCESS_DETAIL_RECORD;
  GET EDIT (IN_DATA) (A(. . .));
END;
CALL CONTROL_FOOTING;
CALL REPORT_FOOTING;
```

All the processing at the beginning of the report is carried out before entering the DOWHILE loop, including printing the complete initial set of headings and initializing the control variable. All the final processing is carried out after terminating the DOWHILE loop, including printing the complete final set of footings. Usually the priming read provides the initial value for the control variable and control heading. The initial value must be the same as the first control field value being processed on the first time through the loop. Inside the DOWHILE loop the individual records are processed, being checked first for a change in the value of the control field. The occurrence of a control break triggers the printing of both the footing that finishes one group and the heading that starts another group.

Control footings commonly contain counts and totals of the records in the control group. These fields are initialized in the control headings and printed in the control footings. Assume that an enrollment report is to be printed for a university which is divided into colleges, which in turn are divided into departments. Counting the individual students in a department is part of the processing of the details. Counting the students in a college is part of the processing of the departments. The following example shows the placement of the initialization of each counter, the placement of the counting statements, and the printing of the totals:

```
ROSTER: PROC OPTIONS (MAIN);
 . . .
COLLEGE_HEADING: PROC;
 . . .
COLLEGE_CNT = 0;
END COLLEGE_HEADING;

DEPT_HEADING: PROC;
 . . .
DEPT_CNT = 0;
END DEPT_HEADING;

PROCESS_STUDENT: PROC;
 . . .
DEPT_CNT = DEPT_CNT + 1;
END PROCESS_STUDENT;

DEPT_FOOTING: PROC;
 . . .
PUT EDIT (DEPT_CNT) (COL(25),F(4));
COLLEGE_CNT = COLLEGE_CNT + DEPT_CNT;
END DEPT_FOOTING;

COLLEGE_FOOTING: PROC;
 . . .
PUT EDIT (COLLEGE_CNT) (COL(25),F(6));
END COLLEGE_FOOTING;
END ROSTER;
```

12.1.2 Detail lines

Each detail line of a report represents one input record. The values for an output detail line may include calculations from that record and values being accumulated, such as record counts and running totals. A detail line differs from a footing in that the footing does not depend on any single record, but summarizes the entire group.

Review questions

1. Report information can be grouped into main sections, subsections, and so forth. Such groupings are called ________________.

2. In a report, a field whose value identifies a group of the report is known as a ________________ field.

3. Footings and headings are printed when a ________________ takes place.

4. Each input record corresponds to a ________________ line of a report.

5. Indicate whether each of the following statements is true or false.
   - **(a)** According to the methodology of Chapter 12, the design of a report-generating program should involve matching the structure of the input and the structure of the output.
   - **(b)** When printing a report, there is a priming write as well as a priming read.
   - **(c)** The final control break takes place when the last data record is read.
   - **(d)** Every group of a report may have a heading and a footing.

12.2 Control-break processing

In the logical structure of the data, a control break is recognized by comparing an old value of the control field with the new value of the control field. In the physical structure of the data, a control break is recognized by the occurrence of an interrupt. The end-of-file is such a control break. If the output control groups are the pages of the reports, then the end-of-page is a control break.

Control breaks can also occur based on program variables. If a new page is begun or a summary is printed every time a counter or a total reaches a predetermined value, the counter or total is a control field even though it is not part of an input record.

PROGRAMMING HINT: Check for control break before processing data.

12.2.1 Nested control groups

Many reports have more than one level of control group. Reports prepared for a university which is divided into colleges might have the structure shown below.

```
Report heading
  Heading College 1
    Heading Department A
      . . .
    Footing Department A
    Heading Department AA
      . . .
    Footing Department AA
      . . .
  Footing College 1
  Heading College 2
    Heading Department B
      . . .
    Footing Department B
    . . .
  Footing College 2
  . . .
Report footing
```

In the figure, the department headings and footings are properly nested inside the college headings and footings. The structure would have more levels if, for instance, the university had several campuses, or if the information being processed for each department consisted of groups of records such as enrollment in programs or classes. When data consist of nested control groups, each identified by a control field, checking for control breaks proceeds from the smallest, innermost group to the largest, outermost group, as in the following example:

```
IF DEPT_ID ¬= OLD_DEPT_ID
  THEN
    DO;
      CALL DEPT_FOOTING;
      OLD_DEPT_ID = DEPT_ID;
      IF COLLEGE_ID ¬= OLD_COLLEGE_ID
        THEN
          DO;
            CALL COLLEGE_FOOTING;
            OLD_COLLEGE_ID = COLLEGE_ID;
            CALL COLLEGE_HEADING;
          END;
      CALL DEPT_HEADING;
    END;
```

Here the nesting of the control-break checking and processing is the opposite of the nesting of the control groups.

A second way of handling this in a program is to have the college heading routine call the department heading routine and the college footing routine call the department footing routine, as in the following program segment:

```
IF COLLEGE_ID ¬= OLD_COLLEGE_ID
  THEN
    DO;
      CALL COLLEGE_FOOTING;
      OLD_COLLEGE_ID = COLLEGE_ID;
      CALL COLLEGE_HEADING;
    END;
  ELSE
    IF DEPT_ID ¬= OLD_DEPT_ID
      THEN
        DO;
          CALL DEPT_FOOTING;
          OLD_DEPT_ID = DEPT_ID;
          CALL DEPT_HEADING;
        END;

COLLEGE_HEADING: PROC;
  . . .
CALL DEPT_HEADING;
END COLLEGE_HEADING;

COLLEGE_FOOTING: PROC;
CALL DEPT_FOOTING;
  . . .
END COLLEGE_FOOTING;
```

The call to DEPT_HEADING is the last executable statement of COLLEGE_HEADING and the call to DEPT_FOOTING is the first executable statement of COLLEGE_FOOTING.

12.2.2 Overlapping control groups

Generally output from control groups does not exactly fit the pages of the report. If the physical structure of a report affects the output, that is, if the pages are to have headings and possibly footings, a *structure clash* may occur. The synchronization problems are compounded if, for readability, the output is to be arranged so that no control heading comes at the bottom of a page, a control footing is not broken between two pages, and so forth. Using the ENDPAGE condition is not enough to solve these problems, since some of the situations to be avoided depend on knowing that a page is almost full, not that it is completely full.

PROGRAMMING HINT: Check for end-of-page immediately before printing.

The page situation should be checked immediately before printing every time output is attempted. The following decision table shows the checks for adequate spacing so that each college starts on a new page. Page breaks occur otherwise when a page is full, when a footing will not fit on the page, or when a heading will not fit on the page or will be the last item on a page. Note that printing of headings is followed by the printing of a detail line, since the space check for a heading includes room for at least one detail line. However, when a footing is printed, the space must be checked again before the next footing is printed. Note also that when a heading is due to be printed, a detail record is always present, but that this is not the case with footings.

College heading	Y	N	N	N	N	N	N	N	N
Department heading	Y	Y	Y	N	N	N	N	N	N
Data record	Y	Y	Y	Y	Y	—	—	—	—
Department footing	N	N	N	N	N	Y	Y	N	N
College footing	N	N	N	N	N	N	N	Y	Y
Room for dept heading	—	Y	N	—	—	—	—	—	—
End-of-page	—	—	—	Y	N	—	—	—	—
Room for dept footing	—	—	—	—	—	Y	N	—	—
Room for coll footing	—	—	—	—	—	—	—	Y	N
Print page footing	X		X	X			X		X
Start new page	X		X	X			X		X
Print page heading	X		X	X			X		X
Print dept footing						X	X		
Print coll footing								X	X
Print coll heading	X								
Print dept heading	X	X	X						
Print detail line	X	X	X	X	X				

When a page footing is being used, enough space must be left at the end of the page to print the footing before advancing to the next page. In order to use the automatic ENDPAGE condition, the default value used for the number of lines per page may have to be changed. This can be done using the PAGESIZE option of the OPEN statement. The default value is commonly set at sixty lines per page, which, depending on the alignment of the paper, leaves little or no space at the bottom of the page. The following example shows the PAGESIZE option being used to leave five lines at the bottom, which are then used to print the page number.

```
ON ENDPAGE(PRINTER)
  BEGIN;
    PUT FILE (PRINTER) EDIT (PAGEND(PRINTER))
                            (LINE(58),COL(60),F(3));
    PUT FILE (PRINTER) PAGE;
    PUT FILE (PRINTER) EDIT (PAGE_TITLE)
                            (LINE(3),COL(30),A);
    PUT FILE (PRINTER) SKIP(2);
  END;

OPEN FILE (PRINTER) PAGESIZE(55);
  . . .
PUT EDIT (DETAIL_LINE) (. . .);
```

Setting the page size at fifty-five causes the ENDPAGE condition to be raised when there is an attempt to print on the fifty-sixth line of a page. Executing the ON unit prints the page number on line 58 of the full page, prints a page heading on the third line of the next page, and returns to the output statement. The output is then printed starting on line 6 of the new page.

The SIGNAL statement can be used to activate the ON unit when a new page is needed even if the current page is not full. If the department heading requires five print lines, must not be split between pages, and must be followed by at least one detail line, it must be started earlier than line 51 of the page. Whenever the control break processing indicates that the department heading is needed, before printing it, the value of LINENO can be checked and ENDPAGE signaled if necessary, as in the following example:

```
IF DEPT_ID ¬= OLD_DEPT_ID
  THEN
    DO;
      IF LINENO(PRINTER) > 50
        THEN
          SIGNAL ENDPAGE (PRINTER);
      CALL DEPT_HEADING;
    END;
```

This could also be structured as:

```
IF DEPT_ID ¬= OLD_DEPT_ID
  THEN
    CALL DEPT_HEADING;
 . . .
DEPT_HEADING: PROC;
IF LINENO(PRINTER) > 50
  THEN
    SIGNAL ENDPAGE (PRINTER);
 . . .
END DEPT_HEADING;
```

PROGRAMMING HINT: Adapt paging to accommodate headings and footings.

Review questions

1. Complete each of the following statements.

(a) Logical control breaks are recognized by ________________ (change of value of a control field / an interrupt).

(b) Physical control breaks are recognized by ________________ (change of value of a control field / an interrupt).

(c) A physical input control break is handled by an ________________ (ENDFILE / ENDPAGE) exception handler.

(d) A physical output control break is handled by an ________________ (ENDFILE/ENDPAGE) exception handler.
(e) A check must be made for an input control break before ________________ (processing/printing) the data.
(f) A check must be made for an output control break before ________________ (processing/printing) the data.
(g) If there are several levels of control groups, the control field of the ________________ (smallest/largest) must be checked first.
(h) A page of a report should not start with a ________________ (heading/footing).
(i) A page of a report should not end with a ________________ (heading/footing).

12.3 Program documentation

Throughout this book, a single standard of documentation has been used for all the sample programs. This standard is similar to those in use in commercial programming shops. Program documentation consists of:

1. Design documentation: hierarchy charts, flowcharts, decision tables.
2. Implementation documentation: program specification, revision and maintenance history, record of testing/verification.
3. Code documentation: procedure prefaces, pretty printing, interlineal comments.
4. Standardization: structures, names, algorithms, documentation.

12.3.1 Procedure prefaces

Each external procedure should be prefaced with a box containing as much information as is needed, identifying the following:

The program
The programmer
The program version
The program function
The input form
The range of input values
The output form
The range of output values
Any internal codes or tables
Any time-sensitive information
Any work files
Any other external procedures needed
Any special equipment needed
Any special handling needed

This information is designed to help the user determine whether the procedure suits the needs of the organization, and to assist in using it properly. It is basic introductory information giving an outside view of the procedure. To assist in program maintenance, if the procedure declarations are not completely self-documenting, the preface should include a box containing a glossary of the variables.

In this book, internal procedures have been prefaced with a box describing their function. If an internal procedure has any degree of complexity, it should be more thoroughly documented. The preface of an internal procedure should be designed to introduce the procedure, indicate its position in the module hierarchy, and explain the interfaces. It should include identification of the following:

The procedure
The procedure function
The calling procedures
The explicit and implicit parameters
Any called procedures
Any external relationships

Implicit parameters are those global variables being used or modified by the procedure. Parameter documentation should include any assumptions being made about their types or values on entry and any changes being made. They should also be identified as input, output, or input/output parameters. External relationships are identification and descriptions of files, system codes, system routines needed, and so forth.

PROGRAMMING HINT: USABILITY AND MAINTAINABILITY Document thoroughly.

12.3.2 Pretty printing

Pretty printing improves the appearance of a program, makes it more readable, and makes it easier to maintain. In the examples in this book, the following rules have been observed:

1. The parts of the program are grouped in this order:
   Declarations
   ON units
   Executable code
   Remote formats
   Internal procedures
2. Declarations are grouped according to their use as:
   Parameters
   Files
   Records
   Internal variables
   Constants
3. Subordinate clauses are indented two spaces.

4. Parallel clauses are aligned.
5. Blank lines are used to visually separate
   Declarations and executable code
   Procedures and ON units
6. Interlineal comments, in boxes, are used only at the beginnings of program sections.
7. Offset comments are used whenever they clarify the code.

12.3.3 Interlineal comments

Interlineal comments have been used sparingly. Well-written code is highly self-documenting. Mixing comments in with the code can make a program more difficult to read. Comments should be used to help the reader locate important parts of the code, or to explain code that needs clarifying.

Comments that identify sections of the code are placed in boxes similar to procedure preface boxes. They interrupt the visual flow of the code and serve as section headings. Simpler identification can be placed out of line to the right.

Comments that clarify obscure code are placed in boxes to the right of the code. There they are out of the way, and do not interfere with the reading of the code. They can be ignored when they are not needed.

12.3.4 Standardization

Using standard control structures such as DOWHILE and DOUNTIL helps make a program readable. The more programs are standardized with respect to documentation, pretty printing, selection of programmer-determined names, control structures, and algorithms, the easier they are to write, read, and maintain.

Review questions

1. Some of the types of diagrams used in design documentation are ____________________ and ____________________.

2. Some of the types of code documentation are ____________________ and ____________________.

3. Some of the types of implementation documentation are ____________________ and ____________________.

4. Indicate whether each of the following statements is true or false.
   (a) The diagrams used in design documentation provide a view of program logic, control flow, and data flow that is independent of the programming language.
   (b) Implementation documentation gives the history of the program implementation.

(c) Code documentation is designed primarily for the maintenance programmer.
(d) A program can never contain too many comments.
(e) Interlineal comment boxes and offset comments may be used interchangeably.

5. Each of the following segments of code is legitimate PL/I. What does each one print? What could be done to improve each one?

(a)
```
A = 5;     B = 3;
IF A > B THEN PUT SKIP LIST (A); PUT SKIP
LIST(B);
```
(b)
```
DO = 1;
TO = 10;
WHILE = 20;
DO DO = TO TO WHILE WHILE (DO < 2 *TO);
  PUT LIST(DO);
END;
```
(c)
```
AREA = 5;
PI = 7;
RADIUS = PI * AREA * AREA;
PUT SKIP LIST(RADIUS);
```
(d)
```
            X = 1;
LINE_1: IF X > 10
           THEN
              GO TO LINE_2;
        PUT SKIP LIST(X);
        X = X + 1;
        GO TO LINE_1;
LINE_2: . . .
```
(e)
```
L /* LENGTH */ = 5 /* FEET */;
W /* WIDTH */ = 7 /* INCHES */;
A /* AREA */ = 12 * W * L /* CONVERT FEET TO INCHES */
PUT SKIP LIST(A);
```

12.4 Example of a report

Let us assume that the university report being printed is simply a list of the students majoring in each department. A utility sort is available to sort the student records by college, within each college by department, and to alphabetize the names within each department. The result is a file containing the names of the students, grouped by department and college, along with department and college identification. There are no special heading or footing records in the file, so the department and college identification fields must be used as control fields. The following program will print the list of majors, organized so that each college starts on a separate page (so that the list may be easily separated into sections to be sent to the various college deans).

```
MAJORS: PROC OPTIONS (MAIN);
/**********************************************************/
/*                                                        */
/* PROGRAM: DEPARTMENT_MAJORS                             */
/* AUTHOR:  C ZIEGLER                                     */
/* VERSION: 07/17/84                                      */
/*                                                        */
/* PROGRAM DESCRIPTION:                                   */
/* ----------------------------------------------------- */
/*   THIS PROGRAM PRINTS AN ALPHABETIZED LIST OF          */
/* STUDENTS MAJORING IN EACH DEPARTMENT.                  */
/*                                                        */
/* INPUT: SEQUENTIAL FILE OF STUDENT INFORMATION SORTED  */
/* BY DEPARTMENT AND COLLEGE, AND ALPHABETIZED WITHIN    */
/* EACH DEPARTMENT.                                       */
/*                 COLS 1 - 20 STUDENT NAME               */
/*                     21 - 26 STUDENT NUMBER             */
/*                     27 - 29 DEPARTMENT ID              */
/*                     30 - 32 COLLEGE ID                 */
/*                                                        */
/*                                                        */
/* OUTPUT: REPORT - COLLEGE REPORTS SHOWING THE STUDENT  */
/* MAJORS, GROUPED BY MAJOR DEPARTMENTS.  THE NAME AND   */
/* STUDENT NUMBER OF EACH MAJOR ARE PRINTED.  THE        */
/* NUMBER OF MAJORS IS PRINTED FOR EACH DEPARTMENT,      */
/* EACH COLLEGE, AND THE ENTIRE UNIVERSITY.              */
/*                                                        */
/**********************************************************/

DCL STUDENT   FILE INPUT ENV(CONSECUTIVE),
    REPORT    FILE PRINT ENV(CONSECUTIVE);
DCL 1  STU_INFO,                          /* INPUT RECORD */
       5  STU_NAME     CHAR(20),
       5  STU_ID       CHAR(5),
       5  DEPT_ID      CHAR(3),
       5  COLL_ID      PIC'999';
DCL 1  MAJOR_INFO,                        /* OUTPUT RECORD */
       5  FILLER_1     CHAR(20) INIT (' '),
       5  STU_ID       CHAR(5),
       5  FILLER_2     CHAR(3)  INIT (' '),
       5  STU_NAME     CHAR(20);
DCL 1  COUNTS,
       5  DEPT_CNT     FIXED BIN,
       5  COLL_CNT     FIXED BIN,
       5  UNIV_CNT     FIXED BIN;
DCL 1  CONTROL_FIELDS,
       5  OLD_DEPT_ID  CHAR(3),
       5  OLD_COLL_ID  PIC'999';
DCL COLL_NAME(5)       CHAR(10)  INIT('ARTS',
                                      'BUSINESS',
                                      'SCIENCE',
                                      'EDUCATION',
                                      'ENGINEERING');
```

```
DCL CURRENT_DATE        CHAR(6),
    1  CURR_DATE                 DEF (CURRENT_DATE),
       5  YEAR          CHAR(2),
       5  MONTH         CHAR(2),
       5  DAY           CHAR(2),
    TODAYS_DATE         CHAR(6),
    1  TODAY                      DEF (TODAYS_DATE),
       5  DAY           CHAR(2),
       5  MONTH         CHAR(2),
       5  YEAR          CHAR(2);
DCL MORE_DATA           BIT(1),
    TRUE                BIT(1)    INIT('1'B),
    FALSE               BIT(1)    INIT('0'B);

ON ENDFILE (STUDENT)
  MORE_DATA = FALSE;
ON ENDPAGE (REPORT)
  BEGIN;
    PUT FILE (REPORT) EDIT (PAGENO(REPORT))
            (LINE(53),COL(60),F(3));
    CALL PAGE_HEADING;
  END;

MORE_DATA = TRUE;
CURRENT_DATE = DATE();
TODAY = CURR_DATE, BY NAME;
OPEN FILE (STUDENT),
     FILE (REPORT) PAGESIZE(55);
GET FILE (STUDENT) EDIT (STU_INFO) (R(STU_FILE_FORMAT));
IF MORE_DATA
  THEN
    DO;
      OLD_COLL_ID = COLL_ID;
      OLD_DEPT_ID = DEPT_ID;
      CALL UNIV_HEADING;
      CALL COLL_HEADING;
      CALL DEPT_HEADING;
    END;
DO WHILE (MORE_DATA);
  IF DEPT_ID¬= OLD_DEPT_ID
    THEN
      DO;
        CALL DEPT_FOOTING;
        IF COLLEGE_ID¬= OLD_COLLEGE_ID
          THEN
            DO;
              CALL COLL_FOOTING;
              CALL COLL_HEADING;
            END;
        CALL DEPT_HEADING;
      END;
  MAJOR_INFO = STU_INFO, BY NAME;
  PUT FILE (REPORT) EDIT (MAJOR_INFO) (COL(1),A,A,A,A);
```

```
    DEPT_CNT = DEPT_CNT + 1;
    GET FILE (STUDENT) EDIT (STU_INFO) (R(STU_FILE_FORMAT));
  END;
  CALL DEPT_FOOTING;
  CALL COLL_FOOTING;
  CALL UNIV_FOOTING;
  CLOSE FILE (STUDENT),
        FILE (REPORT);

/************************************************************/
/*  REMOTE PRINT FORMATS                                    */
/************************************************************/
STU_FILE_FORMAT: FORMAT(COL(1),A(20),A(5),A(3),A(3));
CNT_FORMAT: FORMAT(SKIP(3),COL(40),A,F(6));

UNIV_HEADING: PROC;
/************************************************************/
/*  PROCEDURE TO PRINT HEADING FOR ENTIRE REPORT            */
/************************************************************/
PUT FILE (REPORT) EDIT ('CADRON UNIVERSITY',
                         'LIST OF MAJORS',
                            TODAYS_DATE)
        (LINE(30),COL(50),A,COL(52),A,COL(55),P'99/99/99');
UNIV_CNT = 0;
END UNIV_HEADING;

COLL_HEADING: PROC;
/************************************************************/
/*  PROCEDURE TO PRINT HEADING FOR COLLEGE CONTROL GROUP */
/************************************************************/
SIGNAL ENDPAGE (REPORT);
PUT FILE (REPORT) EDIT ('COLLEGE OF ',COLL_NAME(COLL_ID))
        (LINE(4),COL(50),A,A);
COLL_CNT = 0;
END COLL_HEADING;

DEPT_HEADING:PROC;
/************************************************************/
/*  PROCEDURE TO PRINT HEADING FOR DEPT CONTROL GROUP      */
/************************************************************/
IF LINENO(REPORT) > 50
  THEN
    SIGNAL ENDPAGE (REPORT);
PUT FILE (REPORT) EDIT ('DEPARTMENT',DEPT_ID,
        'STUDENT ID','STUDENT NAME')
        (SKIP(3),COL(50),A,F(5),SKIP(2),COL(20),A,X(20),A);
DEPT_CNT = 0;
END DEPT_HEADING;

PAGE_HEADING: PROC;
/************************************************************/
/*  PROCEDURE TO PRINT PAGE HEADING                         */
/************************************************************/
```

```
PUT FILE (REPORT) EDIT ('MAJOR REPORT',TODAYS_DATE,
                        COLL_NAME(COLL_ID))
         (PAGE,LINE(2),COL(80),A,X(4),P'XX/XX/XX',
                      COL(80),A,X(2),A);
END PAGE_HEADING;

PAGE_FOOTING: PROC;
/**************************************************************/
/* PROCEDURE TO PRINT PAGE FOOTING                            */
/**************************************************************/
PUT FILE (REPORT) EDIT ('PAGE',PAGENO(REPORT))
         (LINE(58),COL(55),A,F(5));
END PAGE_FOOTING;

DEPT_FOOTING: PROC;
/**************************************************************/
/*  PROCEDURE TO PRINT FOOTING FOR DEPT CONTROL GROUP         */
/**************************************************************/
IF LINENO(REPORT) > 50
  THEN
    SIGNAL ENDPAGE (REPORT);
PUT FILE (REPORT) EDIT
         ('TOTAL NUMBER OF MAJORS IN THE DEPARTMENT',
           DEPT_CNT)(R(CNT_FORMAT));
OLD_DEPT_ID = DEPT_ID;
COLL_CNT = COLL_CNT + DEPT_CNT;
END DEPT FOOTING;

COLL_FOOTING: PROC;
/**************************************************************/
/*  PROCEDURE TO PRINT FOOTING FOR COLLEGE CONTROL GROUP */
/**************************************************************/
PUT FILE (REPORT) SKIP(3);
IF LINENO(REPORT) > 50
  THEN
    SIGNAL ENDPAGE (REPORT);
PUT FILE (REPORT) EDIT
         ('TOTAL NUMBER OF MAJORS IN THE COLLEGE',
           COLL_CNT)(R(CNT_FORMAT));
OLD_COLL_ID = COLL_ID;
UNIV_CNT = UNIV_CNT + COLL_CNT;
END COLL_FOOTING;

UNIV_FOOTING: PROC;
/**************************************************************/
/*  PROCEDURE TO PRINT FOOTING FOR ENTIRE REPORT              */
/**************************************************************/
PUT FILE (REPORT) SKIP(3);
IF LINENO(REPORT) > 50
  THEN
    SIGNAL ENDPAGE (REPORT);
```

```
PUT FILE (REPORT) EDIT
          ('TOTAL NUMBER OF MAJORS IN THE UNIVERSITY',
           UNIV_CNT)(R(CNT_FORMAT));
END_UNIV_FOOTING;

END MAJORS;
```

Note that each heading and footing routine checks for its own space requirements. The output formatting of this example is simpler than would be true of a real production program.

12.5 Summary

A large number of business applications of computers involve the production of reports. Scientific output takes the form of a report if it consists of many pages of output each of which must be dated, titled, and otherwise formatted for readability. The algorithms used in both types of applications are the same. Control breaks, based on data values or line counters, identify the need to advance to a new page with new headings. Hierarchical groupings of data provide multiple levels of control breaks.

To be useful, programs should not only produce attractive and accurate output, but they should themselves be attractive and be described accurately. Any type of program expected to have an extended life and be used by more than one person should be documented and pretty-printed to simplify program maintenance. In a programming shop there are standards for documentation, appearance, and implementation of programs.

12.6 Exercises

1. Write a program that prints a trigonometric table for angles from .00 radians to 6.28 radians by .01. The table should have columns giving the angle, sine, cosine, tangent, cosecant, secant, and cotangent. Each page should have a page number, title, and column headings.

2. Write a program that prints a report on the condition of roads in counties of your state. The input has the form:

Cols.		
	1-20	County name
	21-25	Road ID
	26-28	Road length
	29	Road condition ('P' for paved, 'G' for gravel, 'U' for other)

   The data is grouped by counties. The report should print the data by countries, using headings such as PULASKI CO, ROAD, PAVED, GRAVEL, OTHER. There may be more than one input record for a road which, for example, is partly paved and partly gravel. Print each county name only once. Print one detail line for each road in the county, giving its length in the appropriate column(s). Also, print column totals for each county and for the state as a whole.

3. Write a program that reads text from lines at most 80 characters long and prints the text in lines 120 characters long. Each page of the output should be numbered, dated and titled. Each output line should end at a break between words. No page should either start or finish with a single line of a paragraph.

13
Storage management

OBJECTIVE: To save or discard program values and allocate storage when needed.

IN CHAPTER 9, THE lifespans of global and local variables were discussed. In general, global variables exist for the duration of program execution while local variables exist for the duration of subprocedure execution. Default rules control the existence and the nonexistence of variables. At times the programmer needs to explicitly control the existence of variables.

Variables can be categorized as INTERNAL or EXTERNAL, static or dynamic. INTERNAL and EXTERNAL refer to the scope of the name, while static and dynamic refer to the location of the storage associated with the name. All names except file names default to INTERNAL; all storage defaults to dynamic.

In PL/I, all user-named objects belong to one of four storage classes: STATIC, AUTOMATIC, BASED, or CONTROLLED. STATIC storage is allocated at the time the main procedure is loaded. AUTOMATIC,

BASED, and CONTROLLED are dynamic storage classes. Storage for an AUTOMATIC object is allocated when the procedure containing its declaration is loaded. Storage for BASED and CONTROLLED objects is allocated during program execution. Some types of variables default to static, others to dynamic. It is possible for the programmer to override the default storage class of a variable through declaration attributes. The default types are:

Internal procedure entry point	AUTOMATIC, INTERNAL
External procedure entry point	Static, EXTERNAL
File	Static, EXTERNAL
Global variable (in main procedure)	AUTOMATIC, INTERNAL
Local variable (in subprocedure)	AUTOMATIC, INTERNAL
External variable	Static, EXTERNAL

The following example shows declarations of the different types of storage as they might be explicitly given in a procedure:

```
SUB:PROC;                    /*AUTOMATIC STORAGE OF SUB          */
DCL A  CHAR(20) STATIC,      /*INTERNAL STATIC STORAGE           */
    B  CHAR(2),              /*AUTOMATIC STORAGE                 */
    C  CHAR(20) EXT,         /*EXTERNAL STATIC STORAGE           */
    D  CHAR(20) BASED (P),   /*USER-ALLOCATED DYNAMIC STORAGE    */
    E  CHAR(20) CTL;         /*USER-ALLOCATED DYNAMIC STORAGE    */
```

The storage for the code of procedure SUB is automatic whether it is a main procedure or a subprocedure. Space for the procedure is allocated when the procedure is invoked and must be loaded into memory for execution. When the procedure is exited, the space is reclaimed. Every time the procedure is invoked, space is allocated and it is loaded anew. The variables A and C, which are static, are allocated storage space for the duration of the execution of the main procedure. The variable B belongs to the default storage class for local variables. It is not necessary to declare it AUTOMATIC. The space for B is allocated and freed every time SUB is invoked. Space for D and E must be explicitly allocated and freed by the programmer. P is a pointer variable. If it is not declared, it defaults to global and is stored in the main procedure's data area.

Figure 13–1 assumes that SUB is a subroutine and shows its placement and that of its variables in the memory immediately after the subroutine is invoked. Descriptors for D and E are shown in the diagram, but not storage for D and E, as it has not yet been allocated.

For a character string variable, the descriptor contains information about the length and location of the variable. When the character string variable belongs to the BASED or CONTROLLED storage class, the descriptor does not contain location information until storage has been explicitly allocated. Storage allocated by the programmer is in the static area.

After space is explicitly allocated for D and E, the storage appears as shown in figure 13–2.

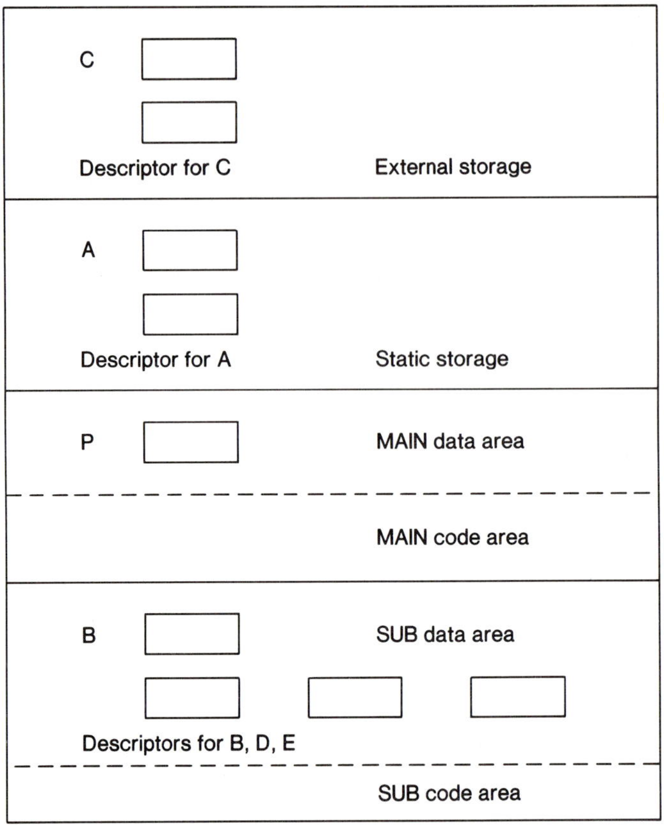

C

Descriptor for C

External storage

A

Descriptor for A

Static storage

P

MAIN data area

MAIN code area

B

SUB data area

Descriptors for B, D, E

SUB code area

Figure 13–1

Static storage means that once storage has been allocated for a variable, it is permanent. *Dynamic storage* means that the variable will not always be found in the same place in memory and sometimes will not be there at all. When a dynamic variable is moved from one location to another, the old value is lost and the variable becomes "undefined." The programmer must be aware of circumstances that cause the relocation of procedures and variables.

13.1 Procedure storage

The main procedure of any program is in the automatic storage class, although it must be in the computer during the entire execution of the program. It is treated by the operating system as though it were an operating system subprocedure. Procedure storage is automatic because space for the code is allocated when it is loaded for execution. The variables of a procedure are global to all internal procedures. The code and data storage areas of a procedure are retained until the procedure is exited because the variables must be available to internal procedures. Any undeclared variables default to

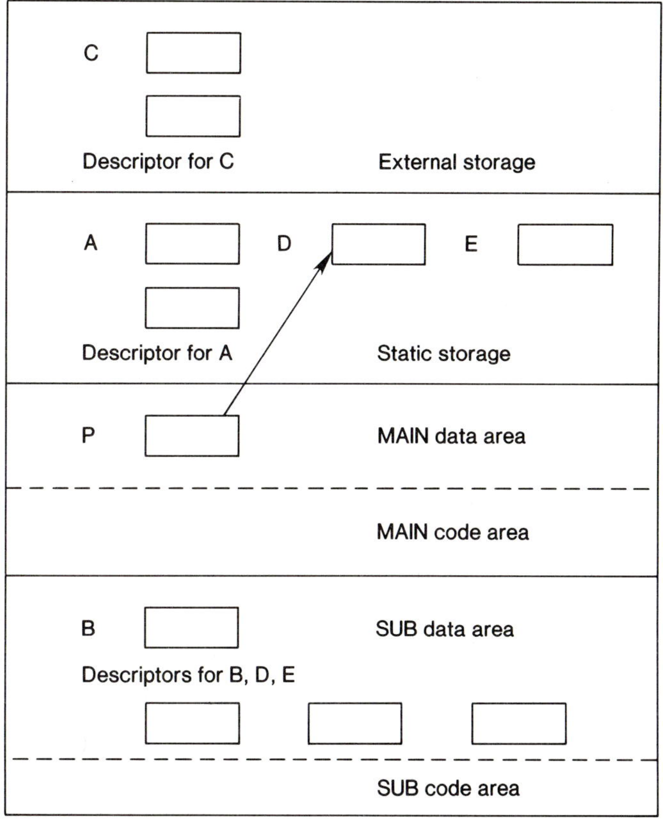

Figure 13–2

global and therefore are placed within the main procedure, as shown in the following example:

```
MP: PROC OPTIONS (MAIN);
KNT = 0;                               /* KNT IS GLOBAL */
DO K = 1 to 10;                        /* K IS GLOBAL   */
  CALL SUB;
END;

SUB: PROC;
KNT = KNT + 1;
GET LIST (NUMBER);                      /* NUMBER IS GLOBAL *
PUT SKIP LIST (KNT,NUMBER);
END SUB;
END MP;
```

Space for KNT is allocated with the main procedure, making it possible to initialize KNT there and have it shared with the subprocedure. Storage for NUMBER is also allocated within the main procedure even though it is not referenced there.

Any procedure called within another procedure where its name is not known is presumed to be external. The names of all library procedures are

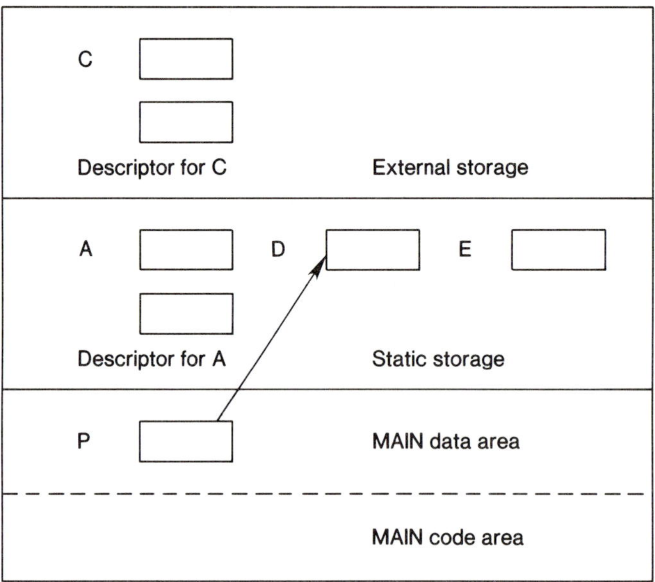

Figure 13–3

external. In some systems, an external procedure cannot be invoked unless its name is declared as ENTRY or BUILTIN.

The code for each subprocedure begins with an unseen *prologue,* which sets up the automatic storage, locates the values of the parameters, and locates any external objects. It ends with an unseen *epilogue,* which releases the automatic storage. Any descriptors in the automatic storage area of a procedure are lost when the procedure is exited. Therefore, after the return from SUB shown in figure 13–2, the storage areas for D and E remain but the descriptors are lost, as shown in figure 13–3.

In the figure, the storage area for E has become completely inaccessible. That for D is still accessible through P (which is global), but there is no way of knowing whether the data it contains is numeric or string, or how many bytes were allocated for it. Even the name has been lost. A reinvocation of SUB would restore the D descriptor, but the code and data areas of SUB might not be in the same place in memory as before. The old value of E would remain lost and its memory space could not be reclaimed. The new E would have a new location. Inaccessible storage locations such as the old E are known as *garbage.* They occupy space that could be reused if all space that is explicitly allocated were to be explicitly freed.

If space for D is explicitly allocated a second time, it is not the same space. Two values of D become available, accessed through different pointers.

Review questions

1. The scope of a name is ________________ or ________________.

2. The PL/I storage classes are ________________, ________________, ________________, and ________________.

3. Procedures have ______________________ storage.

4. Variables default to ______________________ storage.

5. File names have ______________________ scope.

6. Main procedure names have ______________________ scope.

7. A (an) ______________________ name is only available in the procedure where it is declared and procedures internal to it.

8. A (an) ______________________ name is available in any procedure where it is declared and procedures internal to them.

9. Complete each of the following statements:
   (a) ______________________ (static / automatic) storage is allocated when a procedure is loaded.
   (b) ______________________ (static / dynamic) storage is allocated before execution of the main procedure begins.
   (c) An ______________________ (Internal / automatic) refers to the environment where the name can be used.
   (d) ______________________ (Internal / automatic) refers to the location where the value can be found.
   (e) An undeclared variable is ______________________ (local / global).
   (f) When a variable is static, its ______________________ (description / location) is in the procedure where it is declared.

10. What is the storage class of each user name in the following code segment?

```
A: PROC OPTIONS(MAIN);
DCL B FILE;
DCL C ENTRY;
CALL C;
CALL D;
D: PROC;
E= 3;
 . . .
END D;
END A;
```

   (a) A
   (b) B
   (c) C
   (d) D
   (e) E

13.2 Static storage

Although procedures have storage reallocated automatically every time they are invoked, it is possible to declare variables in them which have continuity from one invocation of a procedure to another. Variables may be retained by declaring them either STATIC or EXTERNAL. An EXTERNAL variable is available in any procedure where it has been declared EXTERNAL (abbreviated EXT), while a STATIC variable is only available within a single procedure.

13.2.1 EXTERNAL variables

Unlike local names, which define new data objects when they are redeclared, external names denote the same data object everywhere they are declared, as shown in the following example:

```
SUB1: PROC;
DCL A    FIXED BIN,      /*DEFAULT IS INT, VARIABLE IS LOCAL       */
    B    FIXED BIN EXT; /*VARIABLE IS AVAILABLE TO ALL PROCEDURES */
  . . .
END SUB1;

SUB2: PROC;
DCL A    FIXED BIN,       /* THIS IS A DIFFERENT VARIABLE A        */
    B    FIXED BIN EXT;   /* THIS IS THE SAME VARIABLE B           */
  . . .
END SUB2;
```

Since the storage for external variables already exists, the INITIAL option may not be used in their declarations.

The EXT attribute allows data to be shared between routines that are not in a direct line of call. If procedures C and D of figure 13–4 share an array that is unknown to any other modules, the array can be declared EXT and placed in static storage. It can be accessed by any routine in the program. Such an array is *common* rather than global, as it must be declared EXT in every routine using it. The name of the variable provides the connection between routines. However, with the exception of file information, using common rather than global variables is not advised. Their use makes programs harder to understand and maintain.

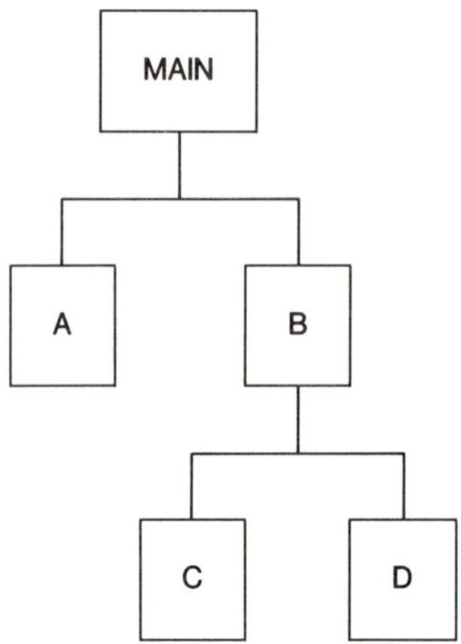

Figure 13–4

PROGRAMMING HINT: MAINTAINABILITY Avoid using EXTERNAL variables.

If modifications must be made, there is no easy way to locate all procedures that share the common data, short of searching the entire program. Instead, variables which must be shared by routines not in a direct line of call should be declared in the lowest level procedure that has a direct line of call to all the procedures using the variables.

In Figure 13–4, any variables shared by procedures C and D should be declared in procedure B. Any variables shared by procedures A and C should be declared in the main procedure. If this is done and the variables passed as arguments, locating all the references to the variables is fairly straightforward, as only the calling modules need to be checked.

13.2.2 STATIC variables

Space for internal procedures is dynamically allocated every time they are invoked. Therefore, any local variables may possibly be relocated when an internal procedure is invoked a second time. If the values of local variables must be retained from one invocation to the next, the variables must be declared STATIC. STATIC variables are placed in a reserved data area, which remains in the memory during execution along with the main procedure.

```
SUB: PROC;
DCL A FIXED BIN STATIC INIT(0), /* STATIC, INITIALIZED ONLY ONCE */
    B FIXED BIN INIT(0);        /* AUTOMATIC, INITIALIZED IN EVERY
                                   CALL */
```

The variables in this static area are not global. They cannot be referenced from any procedure except the one in which they are declared, or procedures nested in it. Their locations are available throughout the job step but their access names are not. And where they are unnamed, they are inaccessible. They are handled by the computer in the same way as automatically allocated variables, except that space for them is allocated at the time the program is loaded.

Static variables make it possible for a subprocedure to keep track of its own history—to know whether it has been called before or how many times it has been called. If KNT in the following program segment were not declared STATIC, it would be reinitialized to zero every time SUB is called and would be one on every return from SUB. Since it is STATIC, the previous value is available on each new call to SUB. It starts at zero and counts the number of calls to SUB.

```
MP: PROC OPTIONS (MAIN);
 . . .
CALL SUB;
```

```
SUB: PROC;
DCL KNT FIXED BIN STATIC INIT(0);
KNT = KNT + 1;
 . . .
END SUB;
END MP;
```

STATIC variables are used to initialize counters and totals known only to a subprocedure. Stylistically, their use violates the rule against initializing nonconstants in the declarations. However, if it were not done here, the variable KNT would have to be placed in the calling procedure, initialized there, and passed to SUB even though the calling procedure does not need to know about it. It is desirable to limit the knowledge of variables to as few procedures as possible, in order to improve the readability and maintainability of the program by increasing the independence of the procedures.

PROGRAMMING HINT: MAINTAINABILITY Place variable declarations in such a way that the names have minimal scope.

Review questions

1. What values are printed by the following code segment?

```
MP: PROC OPTIONS(MAIN);
 . . .
CALL SUB;
CALL SUB;
SUB: PROC;
DCL X  FIXED BIN  INIT(2),
    Y  FIXED BIN  INIT(3) STATIC;
X = X + Y;
Y = X + Y;
PUT SKIP LIST(X,Y);
END SUB;
END MP;
```

2. Write a code segment that counts the number of times a subroutine is invoked. Show the initialization of the counter in the following situations:
(a) Passing the counter as an argument.
(b) Using an EXTERNAL counter.
(c) Using a STATIC counter.

13.3 Dynamic storage

Storage of a program object is dynamic when its location may change during the course of program execution. This change in location may occur either automatically or at the programmer's direction.

13.3.1 Automatic storage

The storage of internal procedures and their local variables (those not declared STATIC) is *dynamic*. Storage is allocated whenever a procedure is invoked. The original version of the procedure and its data area are loaded into memory every time. When control returns to the calling procedure, the space occupied by the called procedure is reclaimed by the system. As shown in figure 13–5, an internal procedure need not reside in the same place in memory when it is called a second time.

Procedure B is called for the first time in procedure A. Thus MP, A, and B are all in the memory, as shown in 13–5b. After control returns from B to A and from A to MP, procedure B is called again and the memory contains MP and B, as shown in 13–5c. The variables in B have different memory locations on the second call. If a variable is declared with an initial value, that value initializes each invocation, since all calls activate identical copies of the procedure. If there is no initial value, the value from the previous call is no longer there.

```
MP: PROC OPTIONS (MAIN);
CALL A;
CALL B;

A: PROC;
CALL B;
END A;

B: PROC;
END B;
END MP;
```

(a)

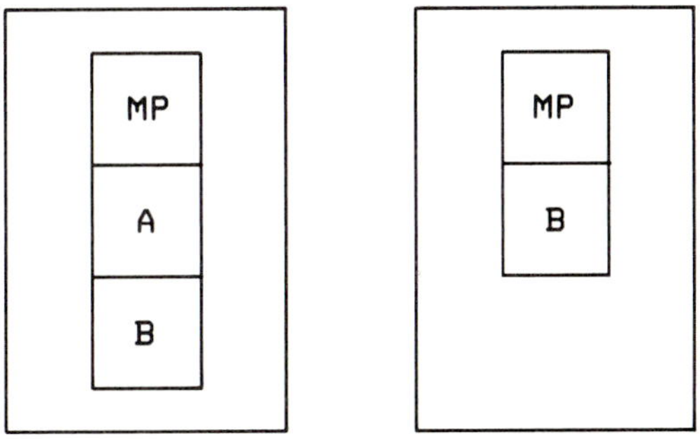

(b)

(c)

Figure 13–5

13.3.2 ALLOCATE and FREE statements

As seen in figure 13–3, a static portion of the memory is set aside for the programmer's allocation of based and controlled variables. This storage is manipulated through the ALLOCATE and FREE instructions. Declarations of based and controlled variables cause variable descriptors to be set up, but no storage is set aside for values.

The ALLOCATE instruction assigns an unused part of static memory to the variable, superimposing the description on that part of memory, and attaching the variable name to it. The general form of the ALLOCATE statement is:

```
ALLOCATE variable [SET pointer];
```

The SET option is used with some BASED variables.

The FREE instruction detaches the name from the storage location, making the name available for reuse, and making the space available for reallocation. The general form of the FREE instruction is:

```
FREE variable;
```

The computer treatment of any variable contains the following behind-the-scenes operations:

Allocating storage
Attaching a name (which activates an access path)
Referencing (to assign or retrieve a value)
Detaching the name (deactivating the access path)
Reattaching a name (reactivating an access path)
Deallocating storage
Destroying an access path

With different classes of variables these actions take place at different times. At the time a procedure and the automatic variables declared in it are loaded, storage is allocated, the name is attached, and access is activated. When the procedure terminates, the names and access paths are deactivated and storage is deallocated. With objects of other storage classes, these operations are separate. Table 13–1 shows the times at which the operations are performed for the different classes of variables.

Table 13–1

Variable type	*Storage allocated*	*Name attached*	*Name detached*	*Storage deallocated*
STATIC	At load time	On invocation	On exit	At end
EXT	At load time	At load time	At end	At end
AUTO	On invocation	On invocation	On exit	On exit
CTL	On request	On request	On request	On request
BASED	On request	On request	On request	On request
Parameter	—	On invocation	On exit	—

STATIC variables have storage allocated at the time the main procedure is loaded, but the name and access path are activated only when the procedure in which the names are declared is loaded, and name and access are deactivated when the procedure containing the declarations is exited. A second loading of the subprocedure results in a reactivation of the same access path.

Names used as dummy parameters are activated and access set up by the prologue of the called procedure. The names themselves are automatic and internal, but the storage need not be. The names are deactivated by the epilogue. The names of based and controlled variables, however, are activated when the procedure is entered and deactivated when it is left.

13.3.3 CONTROLLED variables

Controlled variables have user-allocated storage. They must be declared with the attribute CONTROLLED (abbreviated CTL). At compile time the name and the type are bound and a description of the variable is created from the declaration. The name of the variable is local or global depending on the placement of the declaration, but the variable cannot be referenced until the program explicitly allocates storage. The general form of the declaration is:

```
DCL variable type CONTROLLED;
```

An area of static storage is available for such variables. Space is allocated by use of an ALLOCATE instruction, where the variable is a controlled variable such as:

```
DCL INFO CHAR(80) CTL;
ALLOCATE INFO;
```

Once storage has been allocated, like STATIC storage it may be accessed as long as the name of the variable is available. However, unlike STATIC storage space may be allocated more than once. If a second ALLOCATE statement is executed, the original space is made inaccessible as long as the name is attached to the second location. The effect of the statements

```
DCL INFO CHAR(80) CTL;
 . . .
ALLOCATE INFO;
INFO = 'ABC';
ALLOCATE INFO;
INFO = 'XYZ';
FREE INFO;
```

is shown in figure 13–6.

Figure 13–6a shows the static storage area after the first assignment statement has been executed. Allocating space for a controlled variable does not assign a value to it; an explicit assignment statement is needed. Figure 13–6b shows the area after the second assignment statement has been executed. The name INFO is attached to the second space allocated, but there is an internal link to the earlier storage so that it is not lost. Figure 13–6c shows the storage after the execution of the FREE statement. The space where 'XYZ' was stored has been detached and can be reclaimed by the system for reuse.

Controlled variables provide a way of retaining more than one version of data, only the most current being accessible. When processing of the current data has finished, the storage space may be deallocated by the FREE instruction, which has the side effect of detaching the name and description from the current version and reattaching them to the previous version.

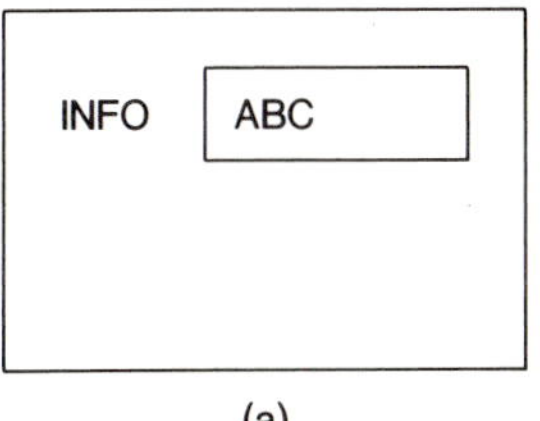

(a)

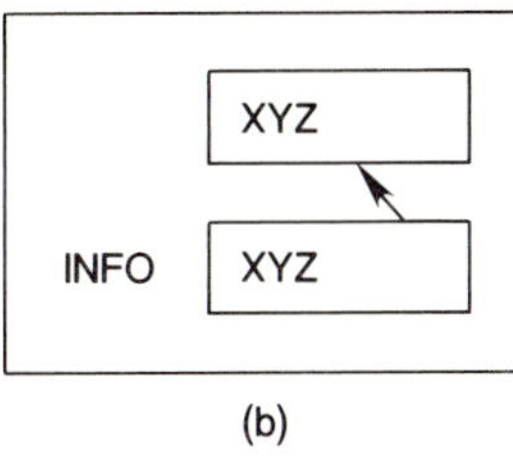

(b)

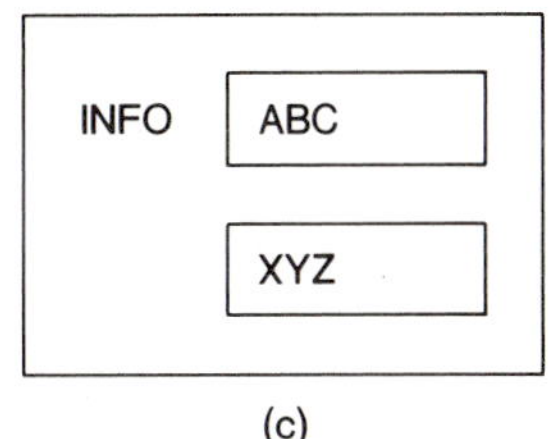

(c)

Figure 13–6

Using a controlled variable in a loop stores many versions of the variable. The following program segment stores the counter as shown in the diagram.

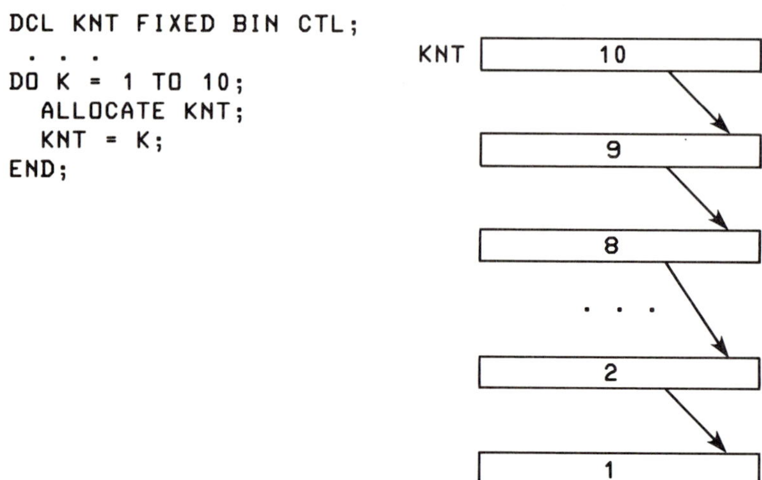

The last number to be stored is the one referenced by the variable name. If this allocation loop is followed by the code segment

```
DO K = 1 TO 10;
  PUT LIST (KNT);
  FREE KNT;
END;
```

then the numbers are listed in the order

```
10 9 8 7 6 5 4 3 2 1
```

With each ALLOCATE an additional value is stored until ten have been stored. Then with each FREE a value is removed from storage, starting with the last one. The built-in function ALLOCATION(var) returns zero when no storage is currently occupied by values of the controlled variable. Otherwise, depending on the implementation, it returns one or the number of current versions of the variable. This function can be used to print the numbers, as follows:

```
DO WHILE (ALLOCATION(KNT) > 0);
  PUT LIST (KNT);
  FREE KNT;
END;
```

The combined loops for allocating and freeing KNT have the effect shown in figure 13–7. Every time the body of the first loop is executed, another location is allocated for KNT until there are ten versions of the variable. Every time the body of the second loop is executed, one of these locations is released until there are no versions of KNT left.

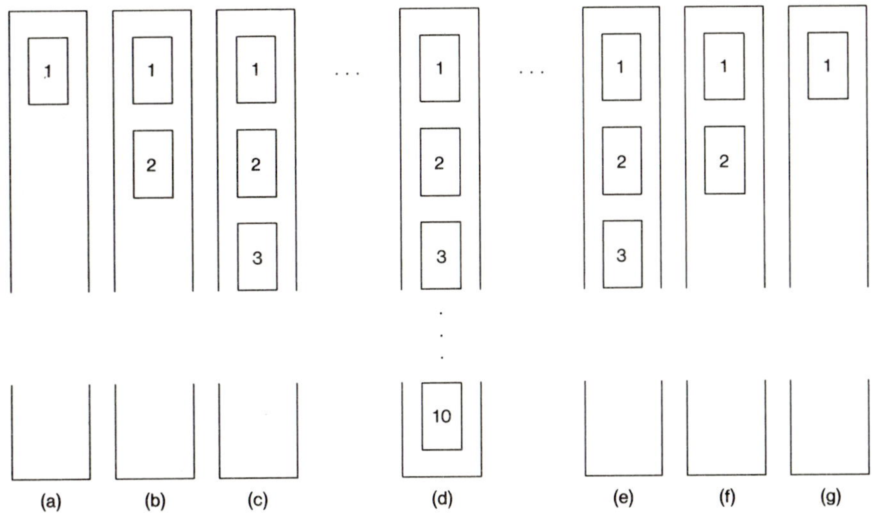

Figure 13–7

13.3.4 BASED variables

The declaration of a BASED variable does not set aside any storage space. Instead, it provides a pattern or description that can be applied to different areas of memory. With based variables, the programmer can select the area of memory to be accessed. Based variables may be declared either with an explicit pointer, using the general form

```
DCL variable type BASED (pointer);
```

or without an explicit pointer,

```
DCL variable type BASED;
```

In either case, storage is allocated and access is activated by an ALLOCATE statement. If a pointer is explicitly associated with the based variable, the ALLOCATE statement uses it to activate an access path to the storage. In the following example,

```
DCL STR   CHAR(20) BASED (P);
DCL P     POINTER;
  . . .
ALLOCATE STR;
```

P

STR

P is a pointer variable pointing to the storage allocated for STR. The based variable is referenced as P –> STR or just as STR.

In the following example,

```
DCL STR   CHAR(20) BASED;
DCL P     POINTER:
  . . .
ALLOCATE STR SET (P);
```

the declaration does not associate a pointer with the based variable. Since a based variable cannot be referenced without a pointer, the pointer is explicitly set when storage is allocated. The name STR is not associated with the storage by the ALLOCATE statement. It serves simply to indicate the amount of storage needed. The lack of association between P and STR in a declaration means that the string cannot be referred to as STR, but only as P -> STR.

It is possible to have two pointers to the same based variable, as follows:

```
DCL STR CHAR(20) BASED (P);
DCL (P,Q) POINTER;
  . . .
ALLOCATE STR SET (Q);
```

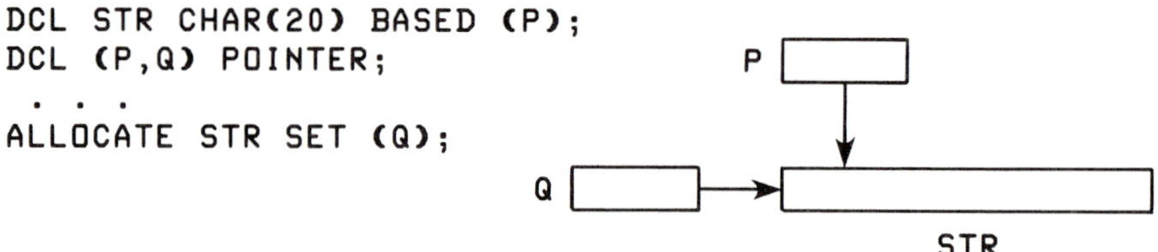

Here the ALLOCATE statement explicitly sets Q to point to the based storage and implicitly sets P to point to it. The storage location can be referenced as STR, as P -> STR, or as Q -> STR. The next example,

```
DCL STR CHAR(20) BASED (P);
ALLOCATE STR;
Q = P;
```

sets up two access paths to the based variable with the same result. Again storage can be accessed as either STR, P -> STR, or Q -> STR.

It is possible to have more than one description used with the same storage space. In the example

```
DCL STR_A   CHAR(20) BASED (P),
    STR_B   CHAR(20) BASED (P);
ALLOCATE STR_A;
```

the same storage space is accessed as STR_A, STR_B, P -> STR_A, or P -> STR_B.

With the code

```
DCL STR_A   CHAR(20) BASED (P),
    STR_B   CHAR(20) BASED (Q);
ALLOCATE STR_A;
Q = P;
```

the same storage space is accessed as STR_A, STR_B, P -> STR_A, Q -> STR_B, P -> STR_B, or Q -> STR_A. Any pointer can be used with any BASED description.

When the based variable is a structure, as in:

```
DCL 1 IDENT   BASED (P),
      5 NAME  CHAR(20),
      5 ADDR  CHAR(30);
```

the pointer variable P can be used to access any level of the structure. For instance:

```
P -> IDENT
P -> NAME
P -> ADDR
```

Unlike CONTROLLED variables, several versions of a BASED variable may be accessible at the same time. In the following example,

```
DCL STR CHAR(20) BASED (P);
DCL (P,Q) POINTER;
 . . .
ALLOCATE STR SET (P);
ALLOCATE STR SET (Q);
```

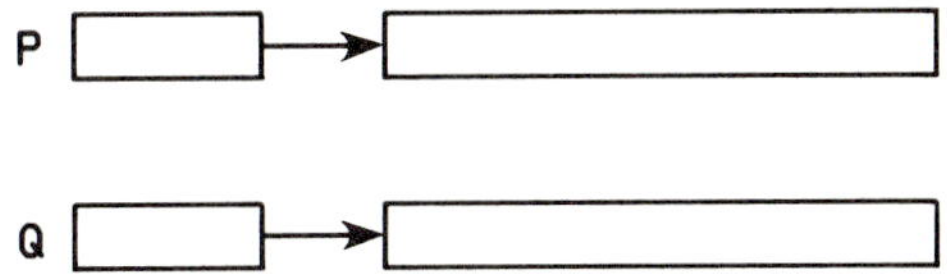

P

Q

two storage locations are set up, pointed to by P and Q, respectively. They can be accessed by

```
P -> STR
```

and

```
Q -> STR
```

Storage allocated for based variables becomes inaccessible when there is no longer any pointer to it, and it cannot be recovered. Former values are preserved only if the programmer saves an access path to them. In figure 13–8, the storage area where 'ABC' is stored has been lost. If it is intended

```
DCL STR CHAR(20) BASED;
DCL (P,Q) POINTER;
 . . .
ALLOCATE STR SET (P);
P->STR = 'ABC';
ALLOCATE STR SET (Q);
Q->STR = 'XYZ';
P = Q;
```

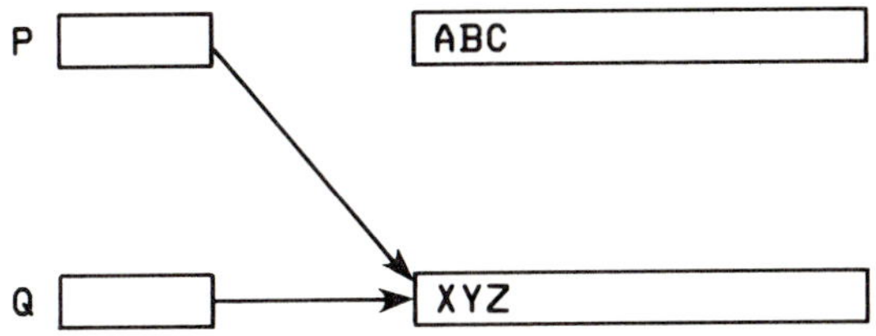

P

ABC

Q

XYZ

Figure 13–8

that storage be deallocated, the variable should be explicitly freed, as in:

```
FREE P -> STR;
P = Q;
```

PASSING BASED VARIABLES

Like that for CONTROLLED variables, storage for BASED variables is located in the static area. This makes it possible to allocate storage in one procedure and reference it in another, simply by passing the pointer between them. This is shown in the following example:

```
MP: PROC OPTIONS (MAIN);
DCL P     POINTER;
 . . .
CALL SUBA(P);
CALL SUBB(P);

SUBA: PROC(Q);
DCL Q     POINTER,
    STR   CHAR(20) BASED (Q);
ALLOCATE STR;
END SUBA;

SUBB: PROC(R);
DCL R     POINTER,
    TXT   CHAR(20) BASED (R);
TXT = 'NOW IS THE TIME';
END SUBB;
END MP;
```

In SUBA based storage is allocated in the static storage area. The variable P, also known locally as Q and R, is implicitly set to point to it. In SUBB a value is assigned to that storage. The pointer, storage place, and value are available in the main procedure as well as in SUBB and are available in any procedure to which P is passed. SUBA and SUBB have separate descriptions of the character string. Since these descriptions are local, the computer does not check whether they are compatible.

REDEFINITION OF DATA

BASED variables may be used for the redefinition of data when differences in the underlying data types do not permit the DEFINED clause to be used. In the following example,

```
DCL NUMBER FIXED DEC (7,2) BASED (P);
DCL NBITS  BIT (32)        BASED (P);
ALLOCATE NUMBER;
```

the numeric variable is being redefined as a bit string. Both NUMBER and NBITS can be used to access the same four bytes of memory, permitting manipulation of bits within the number or display of the internal coding and structure of the number.

It is not even necessary for based variables accessing the same memory location to have the same length. In

```
DCL STR    CHAR(20) BASED (P),
    FRONT  CHAR(10) BASED (P);
ALLOCATE STR;
```

twenty character positions have been allocated. STR refers to all of these but FRONT only refers to the first ten positions.

RUNTIME DIMENSIONING OF ARRAYS

Based variables may be used to change the actual dimensioning of arrays. The following program segment shows the basic steps in the runtime allocation of an array. If the value of N is five, exactly enough space for a five-item list is allocated. If the value is ten, exactly enough space for a ten-item list is allocated.

```
MP: PROC OPTIONS (MAIN);
DCL P       POINTER,
    ARR(N)  FIXED BIN BASED (P),
    N       FIXED BIN;
GET LIST(N);
ALLOCATE ARR;
. . .
FREE ARR;
END MP;
```

Review questions

1. Storage for ____________________ variables is allocated when a procedure is loaded.

2. Storage for ____________________ variables must be explicitly allocated by the program.

3. ____________________ variables may be explicitly allocated storage or may reference already existing storage.

4. Storage for based and controlled variables is made available by the ____________________ statement.

5. Storage for based and controlled variables is made unavailable by the ____________________ statement.

6. Indicate whether each of the following statements is true or false.
   (a) Automatic variables may have their names detached and reused.
   (b) Only one controlled variable can be used in a program.
   (c) Old versions of controlled variables are retained.
   (d) Based variables of the same name are distinguished by the use of pointers.

(e) Only one based variable can be used to describe a given storage area.
(f) Several based variables may use the same pointer.
(g) Several pointers may be used with the same based variable.

7. What is printed by the following code segment?

```
DCL VALUE CTL;
DO I = 5 TO 8;
  ALLOCATE VALUE;
  VALUE = I;
END;
DO I = 1 TO 4;
  PUT LIST (VALUE);
  FREE VALUE;
END;
```

8. Write a segment of code using a based variable that places blanks in all the bytes of the following structure:

```
DCL 1 PERSON    BASED,
      5 NAME    CHAR(20),
      5 AGE     FIXED BIN(31),
      5 HEIGHT  FIXED DEC(3,1),
      5 WEIGHT  FIXED DEC(5,2);
```

9. Write declarations using based variables that describe a record having either the sixty characters of a title, or ten fields of five-digit integers.

10. Write a declaration for a node of a trinary (three-branched) tree. Use a based structure.

13.4 POINTER variables

A POINTER variable (abbreviated PTR) is a variable that takes a memory addresses as its values. When a pointer variable is not pointing to a location, rather than being zero or blank, it should be given the value NULL by using the built-in function. NULL, like DATE and TIME, does not have any arguments. It may be declared BUILTIN. If NULL is not declared, it must be used with an empty argument list to identify it as a function.

```
DCL P    POINTER;
DCL NULL BUILTIN;
P = NULL;
```

or

```
DCL P   POINTER;
P = NULL();
```

Because of the nature of pointer variables, it would be meaningless to obtain values for them through input or to try to output them. However, one pointer variable may be assigned to another. Assignments may also be made by SETting a pointer variable; that is, by allocating space to a based variable based on the pointer variable, or implicitly, by using the pointer variable in a reference to a based variable. Given the following declarations,

```
DCL INFO       CHAR(80) BASED (P);
DCL (P,Q,R,S) PTR;
```

then each of the following statements assigns a value to a pointer variable.

```
ALLOCATE INFO;
ALLOCATE INFO SET (Q);
R = P;
S = NULL();
```

The first statement assigns the address of the allocated storage to P, the variable associated with INFO. The second explicitly assigns a different address to Q. The statement "R = P" assigns the same address to R that is stored in P, and the last statement assigns an address of null to S, an address that is understood as not referring to any actual memory location. There is also a library function ADDR, which assigns the locations of automatically allocated variables to pointers.

```
P = ADDR(ARRAY);
```

Any based-variable description may be applied to any pointer variable whether there is a pointer associated with the based variable or not, and whether the location pointed to stores an appropriate value or not. In the following code segment,

```
DCL ARRAY(2,5) PIC '(5)9V99';
DCL 1 STRUCT   BASED,
      5 ROW_1  CHAR(35),
      5 ROW_2  CHAR(35);
 . . .
P = ADDR(ARRAY);
 ... P->STRUCT ...
```

STRUCT refers to the array as a structure containing two character strings.

Since pointer variables can be used to access any part of the program's work area, they must be used carefully.

ERROR SITUATIONS

Two types of errors are commonly made with based variables. First, pointers are reassigned leaving *garbage,* as in the following statements:

```
DCL STR  CHAR(20) BASED (P);
ALLOCATE STR;
STR = 'ABC';
P = . . .
```

The value 'ABC' and the storage that contains it can no longer be accessed because of the new assignment to P. In addition, the storage cannot be reclaimed and reused because it was not explicitly freed.

Second, as seen in the following example, Q is a *dangling reference*:

```
DCL STR   CHAR(20) BASED (P),
    (P,Q) POINTER;
ALLOCATE STR;
Q = P;
FREE STR;
```

The pointer P has a null value because the allocated storage associated with it has been freed. However, the pointer variable Q has not been given a new value and contains the address of a portion of memory that has been released. If the memory location is reused for some other value, Q will point to the wrong thing. The value of Q should have been explicitly set to null with

```
Q = NULL();
```

Review questions

1. Indicate whether each of the following statements is true or false.
 (a) A pointer variable may take as its value the address of another variable.
 (b) Any based variable may use any pointer variable to access memory.
 (c) The values of pointer variables may be printed.
 (d) The values of pointer variables may be assigned to other pointer variables.
 (e) A null pointer variable is one that does not have anything stored in it.
 (f) When a based variable is freed, the associated pointer variable automatically becomes null.
 (g) A pointer variable may point to another pointer variable.

13.5 AREA and OFFSET variables (not in Subset G)

As discussed above, storage for based and controlled variables is allocated within a static data area. If the space is needed only for the duration of an internal procedure, a named data AREA can be declared, which is local to the procedure and used for its storage.

```
DCL A      AREA (1000),         /* STORAGE FOR BASED VARIABLES */
    P      OFFSET(A),           /* POINTER IN STORAGE AREA     */
    STR    CHAR(20) BASED;
ALLOCATE STR IN (A) SET (P);
```

The size of the area is declared in bytes, but variables of all types may be allocated within it by using the name in the ALLOCATE statement. Variables pointing into such an area are called OFFSET rather than POINTER. They are associated with the AREA through their declarations. AREA variables cannot be compared, but they may be assigned or transmitted to or from mass storage. This provides a way of saving dynamically allocated storage.

If an assignment of an area is made, as in:

```
DCL (A,B)       AREA,
    P           OFFSET (A),
    Q           OFFSET (B),
    STR         CHAR(20) BASED;
ALLOCATE STR IN (A) SET (P);              /* STORAGE SET UP IN A       */
STR= 'ABCDE';                             /* 'ABCDE' STORED IN A       */
B = A;                                    /* DUPLICATE IS IN B         */
Q = POINTER(B,P);                         /* Q POINTS TO 'ABCDE' IN B */
```

then the same character string is stored in both areas. It is accessible in A through P–>STR and accessible in B using the built-in function POINTER(B,P)–>STR. In order to access variables after area assignment, the OFFSET attribute causes the pointer variable to contain a location value relative to the beginning of the area. After A is copied into B, the new copy of STR is in the same position relative to the beginning of the new area as the original STR is in the old area. P–>STR and Q–>STR are used for access in areas A and B, respectively. The POINTER function takes as its arguments an AREA and an OFFSET defined on a different area. In some implementations P may be assigned directly to Q. The OFFSET equivalent of a NULL value is NULLO. Areas are initialized with the built-in function EMPTY.

```
DCL A   AREA;
DCL P   OFFSET(A);
A = EMPTY();
P = NULLO();
```

Review questions

1. Complete each of the following statements:
   (a) Storage for based variables accessed by pointer variables is in a (an) ____________________ (named/unnamed) static data area.
   (b) Storage for based variables accessed by offset variables is in a (an) ____________________ (named/unnamed) static data area.
   (c) Input and output of based structures can only be implemented using ____________________.

13.6 Examples of user storage control

The examples in this section show how various types of abstract data structures can be implemented using BASED and CONTROLLED variables.

13.6.1 Stack implementation

Controlled variables are designed to implement stacks. A data stack, like a stack of books or dishes, is built from the bottom up and items are removed from the top. Sometimes this is known as LIFO (last in, first out) storage. The most recently stored value is the first retrieved and removed from the stack. At any one time, only the top item can be accessed.

In the following program, the input data is listed in reverse order, starting with the last record.

```
STACK: PROC OPTIONS (MAIN);
/*************************************************************/
/* PROGRAM: EXAMPLE OF A STACK                               */
/* AUTHOR:  C ZIEGLER                                        */
/* VERSION: 07/17/84                                         */
/*                                                           */
/* PROGRAM DESCRIPTION                                       */
/* --------------------------------------------------------- */
/* THIS PROGRAM STORES DATA IN A STACK THEN LISTS IT.        */
/* A CONTROLLED VARIABLE IS USED FOR THE STACK.              */
/*                                                           */
/* INPUT: SYSIN - 80 CHARACTER RECORDS                       */
/*                                                           */
/* OUTPUT: SYSPRINT - LISTING                                */
/*                                                           */
/*************************************************************/
DCL ITEM      CHAR(80) CTL;
DCL IN_ITEM   CHAR(80),
    MORE_DATA BIT(1);
DCL TRUE      BIT(1)   INIT('1'B),
    FALSE     BIT(1)   INIT('0'B);

ON ENDFILE (SYSIN)
  MORE_DATA = FALSE;

MORE_DATA = TRUE;
GET EDIT (IN_ITEM) (COL(1),A(80));
DO WHILE (MORE_DATA);                      /* BUILD STACK */
  ALLOCATE ITEM;
  ITEM = IN_ITEM;
  GET EDIT (IN_ITEM) (COL(1),A(80));
END;
DO WHILE (ALLOCATION(ITEM) > 0);            /* LIST STACK  */
  PUT SKIP LIST (ITEM);
  FREE ITEM;
END;
END STACK;
```

The input variable IN_ITEM is used to avoid allocating storage when the end-of-file is read. Note that this method of handling input uses a large amount of storage and would only work with a small amount of data, because all the input items are actually stored in the static memory area even though only one item is accessible at any one time. The FREE statement releases one item from the stack every time it is executed and makes the previous item available.

13.6.2 Simulation of recursion

Controlled variables are used to hide, then uncover past values in the same way a recursive procedure hides local variables, by pushing them on a stack so that only the top one is available. A value must be placed in the variable by an input or assignment statement. This can only be done after the space has been allocated, as in the following example:

```
SAVE_1: PROC RECURSIVE;
DCL NUM          FIXED BIN;
GET LIST (NUM);
IF ¬EOF
  THEN
    DO;
      PUT LIST(NUM);
      CALL SAVE_1;
      PUT LIST (NUM);
    END;
RETURN;
END SAVE_1;
```

```
SAVE_2: PROC;
DCL N          FIXED BIN,
    NUM        FIXED BIN CTL;
GET LIST (N);
DO WHILE (¬EOF);
  PUT LIST (N);
  ALLOCATE NUM;
  NUM = N;
  GET LIST (N);
END;
DO WHILE (ALLOCATION(NUM)>0);
  PUT LIST (NUM);
  FREE NUM;
END;
END SAVE_2;
```

Procedure SAVE_1 is a recursive function to print a list of numbers both forward and backward. Procedure SAVE_2 simulates the recursion, printing the numbers in order in a loop that saves them, then printing them in reverse order in a loop that retrieves them. With each ALLOCATE an additional value is stored until the last one has been stored. Then with each FREE a value is removed from storage, starting with the last one.

13.6.3 Dynamic array simulation (linked lists)

Based variables may be used for storing any kind of data that contains a small but not initially known number of values. If the number of values is known

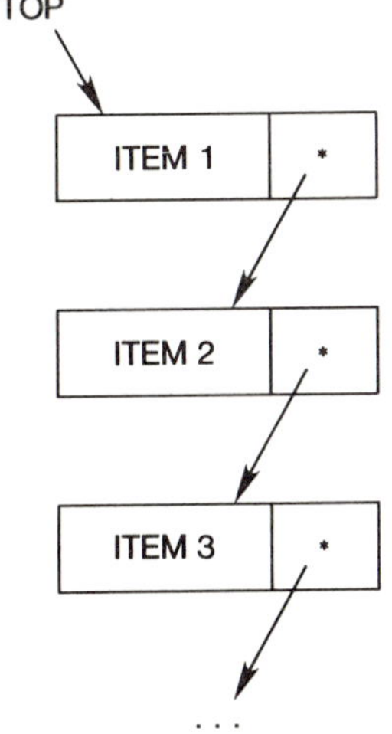

Figure 13–9

before the data is obtained, runtime dimensioning of an array can be used as described in section 13.3.4. If the amount of data is not known, to use an array would waste space, because a maximum size would have to be anticipated. Instead, an array can be simulated by a linked list. Figure 13–9 illustrates a linked list.

The following program forms the linked list shown in figure 13–9, then lists it. The output is in the same order as the input.

```
MP: PROC OPTIONS (MAIN);
/***************************************************************/
/*                                                             */
/* PROGRAM: EXAMPLE OF A FIFO LINKED LIST                      */
/* AUTHOR:  C ZIEGLER                                          */
/* VERSION: 07/17/84                                           */
/*                                                             */
/* PROGRAM DESCRIPTION                                         */
/* ----------------------------------------------------------- */
/* THIS PROGRAM STORES DATA IN A FIRST-IN FIRST-OUT            */
/* LINKED LIST THEN LISTS IT.                                  */
/*                                                             */
/* INPUT: SYSIN - 80 CHARACTER RECORDS                         */
/*                                                             */
/* OUTPUT: SYSPRINT - LISTING                                  */
/*                                                             */
/***************************************************************/
DCL TOP   POINTER;

CALL BUILD(TOP);
CALL LIST(TOP);


BUILD: PROC(TOP);
/***************************************************************/
/*                                                             */
/* THIS PROCEDURE BUILDS THE LIST                              */
/*                                                             */
/***************************************************************/
DCL TOP            PTR;
DCL (P,PREV)       PTR,
    MORE           BIT(1),
    TRUE           BIT(1)  INIT('1'B),
    FALSE          BIT(1)  INIT('0'B),
    NULL           BUILTIN;
DCL IN_DATA        CHAR(80);
DCL 1 NODE         BASED(P),
      5 INFO       CHAR(80),
      5 LINK       POINTER;

ON ENDFILE(SYSIN)
  MORE = FALSE;

MORE = TRUE;
```

```
TOP = NULL;
GET EDIT (IN_DATA) (A(80));
DO WHILE (MORE);
  ALLOCATE NODE;
  INFO = IN_DATA;
  IF TOP = NULL
    THEN
      TOP = P;
    ELSE
      PREV->LINK = P;
  LINK = NULL;
  PREV = P;
  GET EDIT (IN_DATA) (A(80));
END;
END BUILD;

LIST: PROC(TOP);
/****************************************************************/
/*                                                              */
/* THIS PROCEDURE PRINTS THE LIST                               */
/*                                                              */
/****************************************************************/
DCL (TOP,P)    PTR,
    NULL       BUILTIN;
DCL 1 NODE     BASED(P),
      5 INFO   CHAR(80),
      5 LINK   PTR;

P = TOP;
DO WHILE (P¬=NULL);
  PUT SKIP LIST (INFO);
  P = LINK;
END;
END LIST;
END MP;
```

Each node of the linked list consists of the information being stored and a pointer to the next node. The last node in the chain has a null pointer. The first node in the chain is pointed to by the variable TOP. This simulates an array or queue since the first value stored is at the beginning of the chain, ready to be accessed first (FIFO: first in, first out). The character strings cannot be accessed directly—there is nothing corresponding to subscripts—but the array can be printed by a list-processing procedure. Unlike CONTROLLED variables, past values of BASED variables may be recovered without destroying them if they have been chained together.

13.6.4 Stack simulation (linked lists)

A LIFO linked structure can be used to simulate a stack. Figure 13–10 shows storage allocation for a stack. Many linked structures using pointer variables,

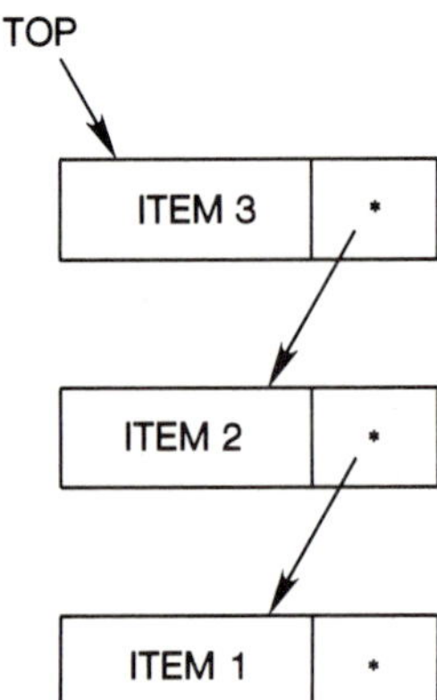

Figure 13–10

including the stack, can be handled more easily through the use of recursive procedures. All or part of the linked structure can be passed, just by passing a pointer to the part wanted.

The following recursive procedures build the linked list from the bottom up, then list it in top-down order. Each element of the stack consists of two values, the value placed on the stack and the pointer to the next value.

```
MP: PROC OPTIONS(MAIN);
/**************************************************************/
/*                                                            */
/* PROGRAM: EXAMPLE OF A LIFO LINKED LIST                     */
/* AUTHOR:  C ZIEGLER                                         */
/* VERSION: 07/17/84                                          */
/*                                                            */
/* PROGRAM DESCRIPTION                                        */
/* ---------------------------------------------------------- */
/* THIS PROGRAM STORES DATA IN A LAST-IN FIRST-OUT            */
/* LINKED LIST THEN LISTS IT. RECURSION IS USED.              */
/*                                                            */
/* INPUT: SYSIN - 80 CHARACTER RECORDS                        */
/*                                                            */
/* OUTPUT: SYSPRINT - LISTING                                 */
/*                                                            */
/**************************************************************/
DCL TOP        POINTER,
    MORE       BIT(1),
    TRUE       BIT(1)    INIT('1'B),
    FALSE      BIT(1)    INIT('0'B),
    NULL       BUILTIN;

ON ENDFILE (SYSIN)
  MORE = FALSE;

MORE = TRUE;
TOP = NULL;
CALL BUILD(TOP);
CALL LIST(TOP);
```

```
BUILD: PROC (P) RECURSIVE;
/*************************************************************/
/*                                                           */
/* THIS PROCEDURE BUILDS THE LIST RECURSIVELY                */
/*                                                           */
/*************************************************************/
DCL P         POINTER,
    Q         POINTER,
    STR       CHAR(80);
DCL 1 NODE    BASED(Q),
      5 INFO  CHAR(80),
      5 LINK  POINTER;

GET EDIT (STR) (A(80));
IF MORE
  THEN
    DO;
      ALLOCATE NODE;
      INFO = STR;
      LINK = P;
      P = Q;
      CALL BUILD(P);
    END;
  ELSE
    P = NULL;
END BUILD;

LIST: PROC (P) RECURSIVE;
/*************************************************************/
/*                                                           */
/* THIS PROCEDURE PRINTS THE LIST RECURSIVELY                */
/*                                                           */
/*************************************************************/
DCL P         POINTER;
DCL 1 NODE    BASED(P),
      5 INFO  CHAR(80),
      5 LINK  POINTER;

IF P ¬= NULL
  THEN
    DO;
      PUT SKIP EDIT (INFO) (A);
      CALL LIST(LINK);
    END;
END LIST;

END MP;
```

The LIST procedure prints the node information on the recursive descent, that is, from the top down. If the information were to be printed in reverse order, all that is needed is to change the order of the PUT and CALL statements to

```
CALL LIST(LINK);
PUT SKIP EDIT (INFO) (A);
```

so that the information is printed on the recursive ascent. Unlike the definition of a true stack, these nodes are not being removed as they are printed.

These routines work because the allocated nodes are all in static storage. Thus the pointers are all located in static storage and point to other places in static storage. When the subroutines are exited, the structure still exists and is still accessible. The pointer TOP is passed (by reference) to the routine BUILD on the first call. When BUILD allocates space for the NODE structure, the address of the structure is assigned to P, which is a local name for a storage location back in the main procedure. When BUILD is called a second time, the ALLOCATE instruction assigns an address to the LINK field of the previously allocated structure. Only when there is no more data is the list completed by assigning NULL to the last link field. The first P (call it P_1) is the same as TOP. P_2 is the same as P_1 ->LINK, P_3 is the same as P_2 ->LINK, and so forth.

Figure 13–11 shows the storage layout.

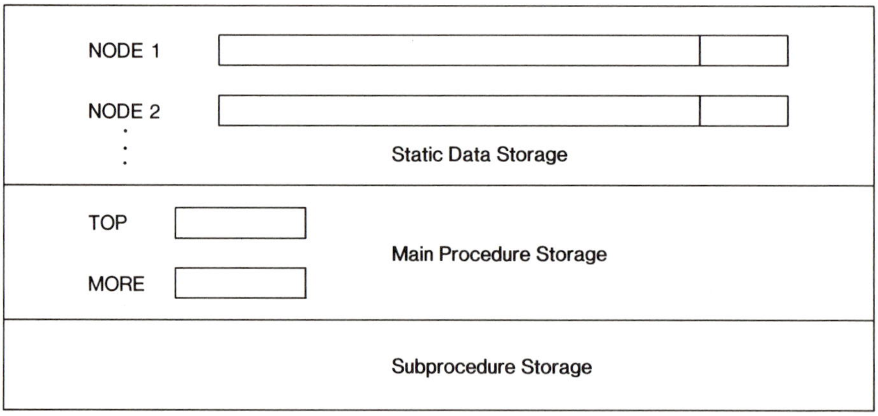

Figure 13–11

13.6.5 Tree structure

Diagrams such as organization charts, hierarchy charts, and family trees can be implemented using based variables and pointers. Linked tree structures can be used to implement diagrams or to sort data, using what is in one sense the reverse of a binary search. The next example builds the binary tree of figure 13–12, then lists it. Many different outputs are possible, depending on the order of the statements in the LIST procedure.

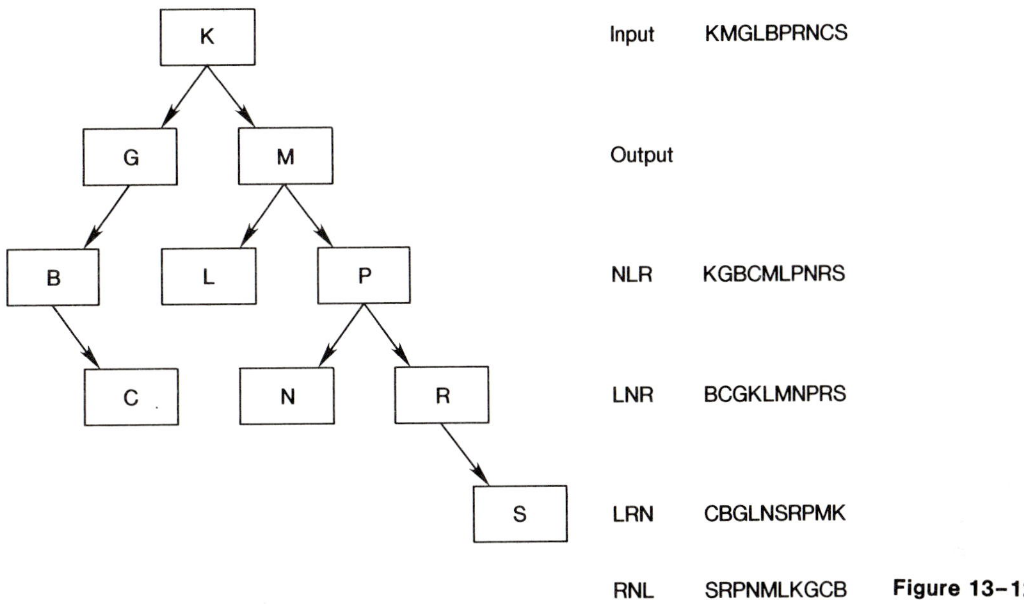

Figure 13–12

Notice that the nodes of the tree are in alphabetical order from left to right. This is an example of a binary tree being used to alphabetize information not originally in order.

```
TREE: PROC OPTIONS(MAIN);
/*****************************************************************/
/*                                                               */
/* PROGRAM: EXAMPLE OF LINKED TREE                               */
/* AUTHOR:   C ZIEGLER                                           */
/* VERSION: 07/17/84                                             */
/*                                                               */
/* PROGRAM DESCRIPTION                                           */
/* ------------------------------------------------------------ */
/* THIS PROGRAM STORES DATA IN A ALPHABETICALLY ORDERED         */
/* LINKED TREE THEN LISTS IT. RECURSION IS USED.                 */
/*                                                               */
/* INPUT: SYSIN - 80 CHARACTER RECORDS                           */
/*                                                               */
/* OUTPUT: SYSPRINT - LISTING                                    */
/*                                                               */
/*****************************************************************/
DCL ROOT      POINTER,
    LETTER    CHAR(1),
    MORE      BIT(1);
DCL TRUE      BIT(1)    INIT('1'B),
    FALSE     BIT(1)    INIT('0'B);

ON ENDFILE (SYSIN)
  MORE = FALSE;
```

```
MORE = TRUE;
ROOT = NULL();
GET EDIT (LETTER) (A(1));
DO WHILE (MORE);
  CALL BUILD(ROOT,LETTER);
END;
CALL LIST(ROOT);

BUILD: PROC (P,CH) RECURSIVE;
/*****************************************************************/
/*                                                               */
/* THIS PROCEDURE BUILDS THE TREE RECURSIVELY                    */
/*                                                               */
/*****************************************************************/
DCL P           POINTER,
    CH          CHAR(1);
DCL 1 NODE      BASED(P),
      5 INFO    CHAR(1),
      5 LEFT    POINTER,
      5 RIGHT   POINTER;

IF P = NULL()
  THEN
    DO;
      ALLOCATE NODE;
      INFO = CH;
      LEFT = NULL();
      RIGHT = NULL();
    END;
  ELSE
    SELECT;
      WHEN (CH < INFO)
        CALL BUILD(LEFT,CH);
      WHEN (CH > INFO)
        CALL BUILD(RIGHT,CH);
      OTHERWISE
        PUT SKIP LIST ('DUPLICATE');
    END;
END BUILD;

LIST: PROC (P) RECURSIVE;
/*****************************************************************/
/*                                                               */
/* THIS PROCEDURE PRINTS THE TREE RECURSIVELY                    */
/*                                                               */
/*****************************************************************/
DCL P           POINTER;
DCL 1 NODE      BASED(P),
      5 INFO    CHAR(1),
      5 LEFT    POINTER,
      5 RIGHT   POINTER;
```

```
IF P ¬= NULL()
  THEN
    DO;
      CALL LIST(LEFT);
      PUT EDIT (INFO) (A);
      CALL LIST(RIGHT);
    END;
END LIST;
END TREE;
```

The program lists the information in left-node-right (LNR) order (alphabetical) because of the order of the statements

```
CALL LIST(LEFT);
PUT SKIP LIST (INFO);
CALL LIST(RIGHT);
```

To list the information in node-left-right (NLR) order, the order of the statements would have to be:

```
PUT SKIP LIST (INFO);
CALL LIST(LEFT);
CALL LIST(RIGHT);
```

To list it in left-right-node (LRN) order, the statements would be:

```
CALL LIST(LEFT);
CALL LIST(RIGHT);
PUT SKIP LIST (INFO);
```

13.6.6 Information hiding

If based variables are used to simulate an abstract data structure such as a stack or queue, there may be more than one routine handling the same structure. Putting all such routines together, localizing the structure to one part of the program, makes it easier to maintain the program. It is often advisable to include all the routines that process a single data structure in the same procedure when implementing a modularized program. This can be done by using multiple entry points. The procedure itself serves as a package containing a declaration of the data structure and of the operations available on it. The procedure is no longer functional in nature, but rather *communicational* as it controls all communication between the larger program and the data structure.

This is known as *information hiding.* It is used with abstract data structures such as stacks, queues, and trees, which can be implemented in more than one way. By combining all the routines manipulating the data structure, any changes to the implementation can be made transparent to the rest of the program. For example, a stack package might be implemented, as in the following example:

```
STACK: PROC RECURSIVE;
/*************************************************************/
/*                                                           */
/* THIS PROCEDURE IMPLEMENTS A STACK PACKAGE USING           */
/* A LINKED LIST.                                            */
/*                                                           */
/*************************************************************/
DCL (P,Q)     POINTER,
    1 NODE    BASED,
      5 INFO  CHAR(80) VAR,
      5 LINK  POINTER;
DCL STR       CHAR(80) VAR,
    TEMP      CHAR(80) VAR;

INIT_STACK: ENTRY(P);
/*************************************************************/
/*                                                           */
/* THIS PART INITIALIZES THE STACK.                          */
/* IT RETURNS A POINTER TO AN EMPTY STACK.                   */
/*                                                           */
/*************************************************************/
P = NULL();
RETURN;

EMPTY: ENTRY(P) RETURNS(BIT(1));
/*************************************************************/
/*                                                           */
/* THIS PART TESTS WHETHER THE STACK IS EMPTY.               */
/* IT RETURNS TRUE OR FALSE.                                 */
/*                                                           */
/*************************************************************/
IF P = NULL(1)
  THEN
    RETURN ('1'B);
  ELSE
    RETURN ('0'B);

PUSH: ENTRY (STR,P);
/*************************************************************/
/*                                                           */
/* THIS PART PUSHES A STRING ON THE STACK                    */
/*                                                           */
/*************************************************************/
ALLOCATE NODE SET (Q);
Q-> INFO = STR;
Q-> LINK = P;
P = Q;
RETURN;
```

```
POP: ENTRY(P) RETURNS(CHAR(20) VAR);
/****************************************************************/
/*                                                              */
/* THIS PART POPS A STRING OFF THE STACK.                       */
/* IT RETURNS THE STRING.                                       */
/* IF THE STACK WAS EMPTY, IT PRINTS AN ERROR                   */
/* MESSAGE AND RETURNS A BLANK STRING.                          */
/*                                                              */
/****************************************************************/
IF P = NULL()
  THEN
    DO;
      PUT SKIP LIST ('ERROR - EMPTY');
      TEMP = ' ';
      RETURN (TEMP);
    END;
  ELSE
    DO;
      TEMP = P-> INFO;
      Q = P->LINK;
      FREE P->NODE;
      P = Q;
      RETURN(TEMP);
    END;

END STACK;
```

By calling INIT_STACK with different arguments, more than one stack can be implemented.

The same stack package can be implemented using CONTROLLED variables, as follows:

```
STACK: PROC RECURSIVE;
/****************************************************************/
/*                                                              */
/* THIS PROCEDURE IMPLEMENTS A STACK PACKAGE USING              */
/* CONTROLLED VARIABLES.                                        */
/*                                                              */
/****************************************************************/
DCL STR      CHAR(80) VAR,
    INFO     CHAR(80) VAR CTL,
    TEMP     CHAR(80) VAR,
    TRUE     BIT(1)   INIT('1'B),
    FALSE    BIT(1)   INIT('0'B);

EMPTY: ENTRY RETURNS(BIT(1));
/****************************************************************/
/*                                                              */
/* THIS PART TESTS WHETHER THE STACK IS EMPTY.                  */
/* IT RETURNS TRUE OR FALSE.                                    */
/*                                                              */
/****************************************************************/
```

```
IF ALLOCATION(INFO) = 0
  THEN
    RETURN (TRUE);
  ELSE
    RETURN (FALSE);


PUSH: ENTRY(STR);
/*************************************************************/
/*                                                           */
/* THIS PART PUSHES A STRING ON THE STACK                    */
/*                                                           */
/*************************************************************/
ALLOCATE INFO;
INFO = STR;
RETURN;


POP: ENTRY(P) RETURNS(CHAR(20) VAR);
/*************************************************************/
/*                                                           */
/* THIS PART POPS A STRING OFF THE STACK.                    */
/* IT RETURNS THE STRING.                                    */
/* IF THE STACK WAS EMPTY, IT PRINTS AN ERROR                */
/* MESSAGE AND RETURNS A BLANK STRING.                       */
/*                                                           */
/*************************************************************/
IF EMPTY()
  THEN
    DO;
      PUT SKIP LIST ('ERROR - EMPTY');
      TEMP = ' ';
    END;
  ELSE
    DO;
      TEMP = INFO;
      FREE INFO;
    END;
RETURN(TEMP);
END STACK;
```

Unlike the package using linked lists to implement a stack, this package can be used only to set up a single stack.

13.6.7 Database prototyping

Some types of databases consist of many sets of information with similar structures. The structures consist of various types of nodes, which are linked together and accessed through the names of the links. A database of family histories would contain tree structures, one instance of which is shown in figure 13–13.

There would be one structure somewhat like this for each individual in the database. Since some people know more about their ancestors than others,

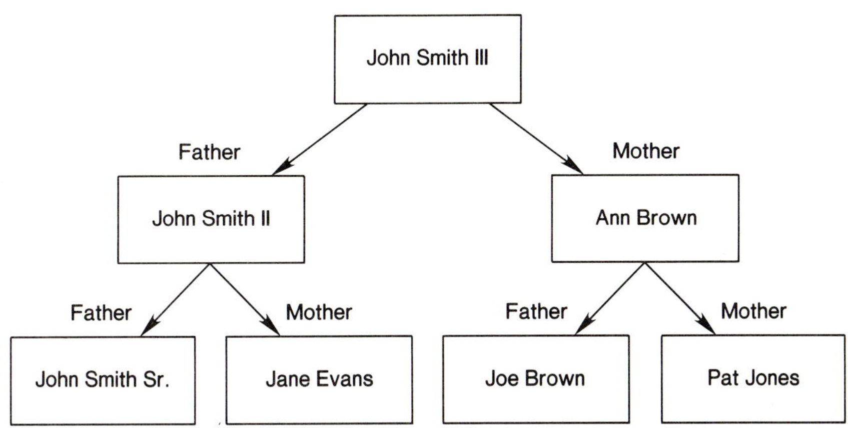

Figure 13-13

some of the family trees would have more levels than others, and some would be missing nodes on various levels. Each is a binary tree, but since they contain varying amounts of information, a linked structure is more appropriate than an array.

If each family tree is to be stored in a file, AREA variables must be used.

Assume that the input consists of the name of an individual followed by the names of the individual's ancestors arranged in such a way that the name of each person in the family precedes his/her parents' names. Each name is preceded by a code stating the person's relationship to the individual whose family tree is being constructed. Possible input would be as follows:

```
'JOHN SMITH III'
F 'JOHN SMITH II'
F F 'JOHN SMITH SR'
M 'ANN BROWN'
F M 'JANE EVANS'
M M 'PAT JONES'
M F 'JOE BROWN'
```

A database program to build a file of family trees follows.

```
HISTORY: PROC OPTIONS(MAIN);
/*************************************************************/
/* PROGRAM: DATABASE OF FAMILY TREES                         */
/* AUTHOR:  C ZIEGLER                                        */
/* VERSION: 07/17/84                                         */
/*                                                           */
/* PROGRAM DESCRIPTION                                       */
/* ------------------------------------------------------    */
/* THIS PROGRAM STORES NAMES OF FAMILY MEMBERS IN A          */
/* BINARY TREE THEN WRITES EACH TREE TO A FILE.              */
/*                                                           */
/* INPUT: SYSIN - CODES AND NAMES                            */
/*                                                           */
/* OUTPUT: ANCESTOR - FILE OF FAMILY TREES                   */
/*                                                           */
/*************************************************************/
```

```
DCL ROOT      OFFSET(FAMILY),
    FAMILY    AREA(2000),
    RECORD    CHAR(2000) DEF(FAMILY),
    STR       CHAR(20) VAR,
    MORE      BIT(1);
DCL TRUE      BIT(1)      INIT('1'B),
    FALSE     BIT(1)      INIT('0'B);

ON ENDFILE (SYSIN)
  MORE = FALSE;

MORE = TRUE;
ROOT = NULL();
GET LIST (STR);
DO WHILE (MORE);
  CALL BUILD(ROOT);
  PUT FILE(ANCESTOR) LIST(RECORD);
END;


BUILD: PROC (P) RECURSIVE;
/*************************************************************/
/*                                                           */
/* THIS PROCEDURE BUILDS THE TREE RECURSIVELY                */
/*                                                           */
/*************************************************************/
DCL P            OFFSET(FAMILY);
DCL 1 PERSON     BASED(P),
      5 NAME     CHAR(20),
      5 FATHER   OFFSET(FAMILY),
      5 MOTHER   OFFSET(FAMILY);

SELECT;
  WHEN (STR = 'F')
    DO;
      GET LIST (STR);
      CALL BUILD(FATHER);
    END;
  WHEN (STR = 'M')
    DO;
      GET LIST (STR);
      CALL BUILD(MOTHER);
    END;
  OTHERWISE
    IF P = NULLO()
      THEN
        DO;
          ALLOCATE PERSON IN (FAMILY);
          NAME = STR;
          FATHER = NULLO();
          MOTHER = NULLO();
        END;
```

```
      ELSE
        PUT SKIP LIST ('ERROR');
END;
END BUILD;
END HISTORY;
```

Input and output using files will be discussed in the next chapters.

13.7 Summary

The scope of names is INTERNAL or EXTERNAL. These attributes have the following uses:

INTERNAL: Names may be shared only by nested procedures.
EXTERNAL: Names may be shared by any procedures.

The storage classes of STATIC, AUTOMATIC, BASED, and CONTROLLED have the following uses:

STATIC: Value is retained from one invocation to the next.
AUTOMATIC: Value is reinitialized at every invocation.
BASED: Description may be applied to any place in storage.
CONTROLLED: Maintains a stack of values.

The last three are dynamic storage classes. In particular, BASED storage and POINTER variables provide a natural way to implement diagrams that contain arrows.

13.8 Exercises

1. Write and test a package that implements a queue (a FIFO list) using based variables. Do not use recursion.
2. Write and test a package that implements a queue (a FIFO list) using based variables and recursion.
3. Adapt the linked-stack package to be an external procedure, implementing a stack that can store heterogeneous data. Use the structure

```
DCL 1 NODE          BASED,
      5 LINK        POINTER,
      5 DATATYPE    FIXED BIN,
      5 INFO        CHAR(80);
```

   Call it to store information structured in several different ways, including noncharacter data. Note that any parameter being stored as INFO must have a length of not greater than eighty bytes.
4. Write a program that builds a family tree for a person and all of his or her descendants. The input data has the form:

Cols.		
	1-20	Name
	21-22	Number of children
	23-42	Name of first child
	43-62	Name of second child
	. . .	

Nodes of this tree do not have the same number of immediate descendants. Use a based structure of the following form:

```
DCL 1 PERSON       BASED,
      5 NAME       CHAR(20),
      5 #_CHILD    FIXED BIN,
      5 CHILD(N)   PTR;
```

where N and #_CHILD have the same value. Print the names from the tree in node-left-right order, indenting each generation five spaces from the parent generation.

5. Write a program that sets up a small database for computer science classes. Use the following structures:

```
DCL 1 DEPT,
      5 DEPT_ID      CHAR(4),
      5 #_COURSES    FIXED BIN,
      5 COURSES      PTR;
DCL 1 COURSE(N)      BASED,   /* N = #_COURSES */
      5 COURSE_ID    CHAR(4),
      5 TITLE        CHAR(20),
      5 #_SECTIONS   FIXED BIN,
      5 SECTIONS     PTR;
DCL 1 SECTION(K)     BASED,   /* K = #_SECTIONS */
      5 SECTION_ID   CHAR(4),
      5 TIME         CHAR(8),
      5 PLACE        CHAR(6),
      5 INSTR        CHAR(10);
```

Read a file QUERY which has records of the form:

Cols.		
	1-4	Department ID
	5-8	Course ID

and print all the section information for all sections of each course in the QUERY file.

14
File characteristics

OBJECTIVE: To store data in an efficient, machine-readable form.

ALTHOUGH PERIPHERAL DEVICES VARY widely in their physical characteristics, the operating system treats the data from each device as though it were stored on a file. A *file* is simply a collection of records, which are stored together logically on a peripheral device and contain related data. A special physical record indicates the beginning of the data area containing the file and another indicates the end of the file space. The file has a name, which is known to the device. The details of the record organization in the file, of the variations between records, and of the access methods are device-dependent.

Except on the smallest computers, the CPU and operating system do not directly control the peripheral devices and the transmission of data. The difference in speeds is too great. The CPU operates at electronic speed, while most of the peripheral devices have both electronic and mechanical components. The speed of card readers is dependent on the speed with which the cards can be moved from the feed bin through the read stations to the stacker bin. The speed of printers is dependent on the rate at which the paper can be moved through, pausing long enough for each line to be printed. And the speed of magnetic tape devices is controlled by the rate at which the tape can be wound. Magnetic disks rotate and the read/write heads move in and out.

Interfacing the CPU with the peripheral devices are small, specialized computers known as I/O processors or channels and device controllers. The channels handle I/O from many devices while the device control units (CU) are usually integrated with the devices, as shown in figure 14–1.

The CPU and I/O processors run independently of each other. They communicate through memory locations which are accessible to both. The channel leaves flags for the CPU indicating whether the channel is available or busy. Other flags indicate whether or not there is information in a file buffer.

When a program is loaded for execution, buffer space is set aside in main memory for all the data files needed by the program. During execution of a program, when an I/O request is received from the program, the CPU places information in the locations of the memory reserved for communication with the channel, telling the channel what I/O is needed.

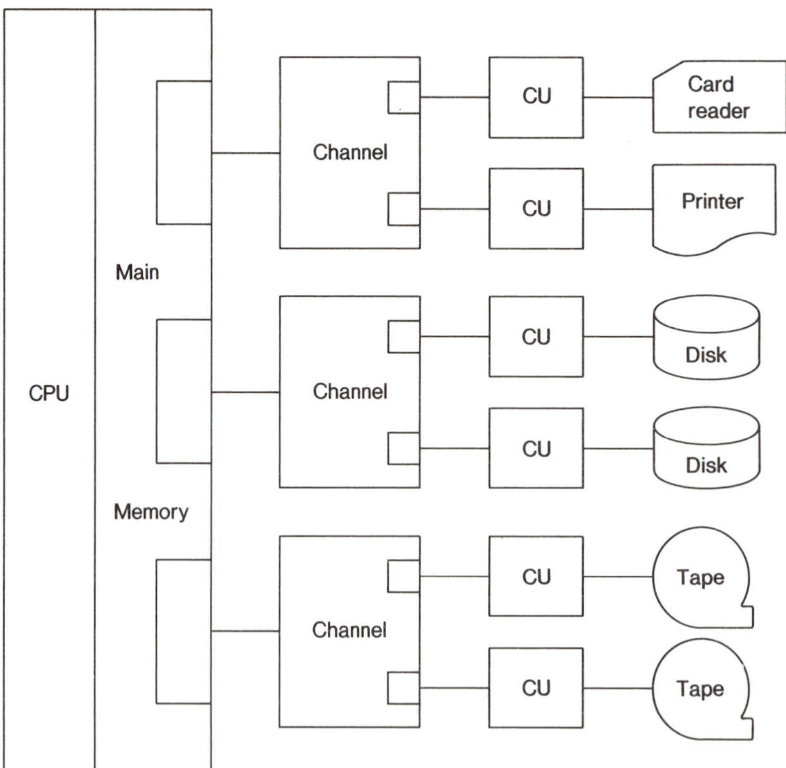

Figure 14–1

The channel obtains input records from a device and places them in the memory buffer, or it obtains output records from the memory buffer and transmits them to a device. While the channel is directing the input and output, the CPU is free to work on another program. Program execution must wait for the I/O to be completed. The device control unit (CU) turns the device on or off, locates the file, and reads and writes the records. It communicates with the channel through reserved locations in the channel's memory.

Many nonscientific programs are *I/O bound,* that is, they spend most of their execution time waiting for data to be transmitted. With some devices it is possible to reduce the delay by blocking the records; with others, such as the unit record devices, it is not.

14.1 Unit record devices

The card reader and line printer are *unit record devices.* Their physical characteristics impose a predetermined size on the records. The most common size card has eighty columns; a maximum of eighty characters can be punched on it. Printers commonly come with line lengths of 80, 120, or 132 characters. A *physical record* is the amount of data actually read or written in a single operation. This is the amount of space allocated in memory for the buffer. With a card reader a physical record is a single card; with a line printer it is one line. A *logical record* is the amount of data requested by an input statement or referenced by an output statement using RECORD I/O. With STREAM I/O, the use of the SKIP and COL specifications is related to logical record size. With unit record devices, logical records correspond to physical records.

14.1.1 Card reader

The card reader is a slow device. Its transmission speed is measured in cards per minute whereas other devices are measured in bytes per second or per millisecond. The card reader senses the positions of the holes in a card, column by column, as the card moves past a read station. The holes in each column represent one character. *Hollerith* is the most common character representation used in punching cards. Intermediate devices convert the Hollerith character code to the native character code of the computer and store the result in a buffer in main memory. The program may not need all the columns of the card, but they are stored in the buffer whether or not they are used. The following program segment illustrates the process of obtaining data from the card reader.

```
DCL STR  CHAR(60);
GET EDIT (STR) (A(60));
. . .
/* THE COMPUTER WAITS WHILE THE FIRST CARD IS READ INTO THE  */
/* BUFFER. THEN THE FIRST SIXTY CHARACTERS OF THE CARD ARE   */
/* MOVED TO THE SPACE ALLOCATED FOR STR.                     */
```

```
. . .
GET EDIT (STR) (A(60));
. . .
/* THE REMAINING TWENTY CHARACTERS IN THE BUFFER ARE MOVED    */
/* TO THE SPACE ALLOCATED FOR STR. THE COMPUTER WAITS WHILE   */
/* THE SECOND CARD IS READ INTO THE BUFFER. THEN THE FIRST    */
/* FORTY CHARACTERS ARE MOVED TO THE SPACE ALLOCATED FOR      */
/* STR, PLACED AFTER THE TWENTY ALREADY THERE.                */
. . .
GET EDIT (STR) (A(60));
. . .
/* THE REMAINING FORTY CHARACTERS IN THE BUFFER ARE MOVED     */
/* TO THE SPACE ALLOCATED FOR STR. THE COMPUTER WAITS         */
/* WHILE THE THIRD CARD IS READ INTO THE BUFFER. THEN THE     */
/* FIRST TWENTY CHARACTERS ARE MOVED TO THE SPACE             */
/* ALLOCATED FOR STR.                                         */
```

At any point, if the record being read is the end-of-file record, the ENDFILE exception is raised.

Each set of cards placed in the card reader must be followed by an end-of-file card or the computer will wait indefinitely for more data.

A card file can be characterized as follows:

1. File capacity: no limit.
2. Physical record size: 80 characters.
3. Logical record size: maximum of 80 characters.
4. Record type: character (some card readers also accept binary).
5. File organization: consecutive (the card reader does not skip cards).
6. File structure: header and end-of-file cards are system-dependent.
7. Access mode: sequential (cards move through the card reader in the order in which they are stacked).
8. Typical access speed: 800 bytes per second (usually given as 600 cards/minute).
9. Use: input only.
10. Blocking: none.
11. Buffering: usually several buffers are set up so that the computer can anticipate the need for data and read ahead.

On large machines, card reader input does not go directly to the program requesting it. It is spooled to a disk file by a utility program and saved until the application program is executed. The disk file is configured to simulate the characteristics of a card file (except for speed). Spooling the data evens out the work load and reduces execution delays.

A card reader file is declared as:

```
DCL file_name FILE [SEQL] [INPUT] [access] [ENV(CONSECUTIVE)];
```

The access may be STREAM or RECORD.

In the past, the card reader was the primary input device for the computer. Now it is used mainly to enter large amounts of raw data quickly.

14.1.2 Line printer

Line printers come in many sizes, speeds, and qualities of print. The one described here is typical of many installations. Line printers are relatively slow devices, although they seem fast compared to small desktop printers. A line printer operates by printing an entire line at once. The paper moves through the printer at the same speed whether lines are being skipped or data is being printed. The printer speed is independent of the amount of data being printed. If a line is skipped or a blank line is being printed, the operation of the printer is exactly the same.

Since paper of different widths may be used, the record size would appear to be controllable. However, the physical record size, the size of the buffer, is the maximum width of paper that may be used.

As with card readers, data is usually spooled to a disk file. That way program execution does not have to wait for the printer to be available. The disk file is given the characteristics of the printer (except for access speed). The following are typical characteristics:

1. File capacity: no limit.
2. Physical record size: 133 characters.
3. Logical record size: maximum of 133 characters (132 for data).
4. Record type: character.
5. File organization: consecutive (the printer does not actually skip lines, it just advances the paper).
6. File structure: no header line, no end-of-file line.
7. Access mode: sequential (lines are printed from top to bottom on the page).
8. Typical access speed: 6400 bytes per second (usually given as 1200 lines/minute).
9. Use: output only.
10. Blocking: none.
11. Buffering: usually several buffers are set up so that the computer can fill one buffer while another is being printed.

The advancement of the paper in a line printer is controlled by the first character in the print buffer. This character is not printed. The standard system file SYSPRINT has the PRINT attribute. This means that data placed in the buffer starts in the second position. The page format control words PAGE, SKIP, and LINE direct the computer to place certain printer-control characters in the first position. If none of these directives are used, the control character for single spacing is placed in the first position. The paper is advanced before printing takes place, rather than afterward.

In some versions of PL/I more than one set of printer-control characters is available. The ENVIRONMENT clause of a file declaration is used to indicate which set is wanted. If any printer-control characters are being used, the file must be declared with the PRINT attribute. If the OUTPUT attribute is used, the printer-control characters are not recognized, but treated as part of the data.

The following program segment illustrates the handling of printer files.

```
DCL STR  CHAR(60) INIT ('ABCDEFGHIJKLMNOPQRSTUVWXYZ');
PUT EDIT (STR) (PAGE,A(26));
/* THE PRINT BUFFER IS FILLED WITH BLANKS. THE PAGE-EJECT    */
/* CONTROL CHARACTER IS PLACED IN POSITION 1. THEN STR IS    */
/* COPIED INTO POSITIONS 2 THROUGH 27 OF THE PRINT BUFFER,   */
/* WHICH ARE DATA POSITIONS 1 THROUGH 26.                    */

PUT EDIT (STR,STR) (A(26),COL(120),A(26));

/* STR IS COPIED INTO POSITIONS 28 THROUGH 53 OF THE PRINT   */
/* BUFFER. THE SECOND REFERENCE TO STR CAUSES THE            */
/* CHARACTER STRING 'ABCDEFGHIJKLM' TO BE COPIED INTO        */
/* POSITIONS 121 THROUGH 133 (120-132 OF THE DATA). IF       */
/* THERE IS ONLY ONE BUFFER, THE PROCESSING STOPS WHILE      */
/* THE BUFFER IS TRANSMITTED TO THE PRINTER. THEN THE        */
/* BUFFER IS REINITIALIZED, THE CONTROL CHARACTER FOR        */
/* SINGLE SPACING IS PLACED IN POSITION 1 OF THE BUFFER,     */
/* AND THE CHARACTER STRING 'NOPQRSTUVWXYZ' IS PLACED IN     */
/* DATA POSITIONS 1 THROUGH 13.                              */

END PRINTER;

/* AS PART OF THE TERMINATION OF THE PROGRAM, THE BUFFER     */
/* IS TRANSMITTED TO THE PRINTER.                            */
```

If the processing terminates abnormally, the final contents of the print buffer may not be transmitted to the printer.

A printer file is declared as

```
DCL file_name FILE [SEQL] PRINT [STREAM] [ENV(CONSECUTIVE)];
```

if printer-control formats are to be used, or as

```
DCL file_name FILE [SEQL] OUTPUT [access] [ENV(CONSECUTIVE)];
```

if they are not.

The access is STREAM or RECORD if the vertical spacing is not being controlled.

On some systems additional information about the printer-control character set is placed in the environment clause.

Review questions

1. The ____________________ is a small computer that handles I/O processing for one or more peripheral devices.

2. The ____________________ is a small computer that handles I/O processing for a single device.

3. The ____________________ and the ____________________ communicate through memory locations in the CPU.

4. The ____________________ and the ____________________ communicate through memory locations in the channel.

5. For a unit record device, the ____________________ size and ____________________ size are the same.

6. The most common unit record devices are the ____________________ and the ____________________.

7. The speed of a card reader is measured in ____________________.

8. The speed of a line printer is measured in ____________________.

9. Indicate whether each of the following statements is true or false.
   (a) I/O is carried out by the I/O processors without interrupting the CPU until the I/O is completed.
   (b) Device control units turn the devices on and off, locate the file, read and write the records.
   (c) Channels and device control units are used because of the difference in the amount of data in the memory and in the peripheral storage.
   (d) On large computers, input is spooled to a disk because the CPU is too slow.
   (e) On some systems, output data is spooled to a disk file until the printer is available.
   (f) The physical characteristics of a unit record device limit the use of the device and the size of the records.
   (g) Multiple buffers are used to save space.
   (h) In a PRINT file, the first character of each physical record is not available for data storage.

10. How long would it take for the card reader described in section 14.1.1 to read 10,000 cards?

11. How long would it take for the line printer described in section 14.1.2 to print 10,000 lines?

14.2 Blocked record devices

The unit record approach to file organization is inefficient with small records. Storage media such as magnetic tape and magnetic disk are designed so that records can be *blocked*. Each physical record is a *block*. That is, each physical record contains many logical records. The *blocking factor* is the number of logical records in each block. If the blocking factor is three, each physical record contains three logical records, as shown in figure 14–2.

Physical record

Record 1	Record 2	Record 3	Gap	Record 1	. . .

Figure 14–2

Between physical records there are gaps, blank spaces on the medium where no data is recorded, known as interblock gaps. The computer is able to recognize the beginning and ending of a physical record so that only the data is read. Blocking allows a magnetic tape or disk to be accessed efficiently. There are no predetermined sizes for the physical records, but some sizes are more efficient than others. The amount of buffer space set aside for each file depends on the size of the physical records (the maximum size if they are not all the same), as each buffer contains one physical record.

A large blocking factor decreases data access time but increases the computer memory requirements of a program. Since a block is the amount of data transmitted between memory and a peripheral device in one device access, if the blocking factor is large, more logical records are transmitted each time the device is accessed and fewer device accesses are needed to access an entire file. Time is wasted with every device access because the record position must be physically located before it can be read or written. The type of device and the amount of memory available for buffers impose limits on the size of the physical record.

A small blocking factor saves memory at the expense of data access time. The buffer size is small, but many device accesses are needed to access the entire file.

14.2.1 Magnetic tape

Magnetic tape files can be thought of as containing the equivalent of card records, fastened end to end. In substance, computer tapes are similar to high-quality audio tapes, having a ferrous oxide recording coating on one side. Like audio tapes they are read/recorded starting at one end. They may be rewound and reused. With some tape drives they may be read/recorded backward as well as forward.

The data is stored on a tape, both across and along the length of the tape. Each byte of data is placed across the tape, using all but one of the positions on what are known as tracks. Consecutive bytes of data are placed one after another along the tape. This is shown in figure 14–3.

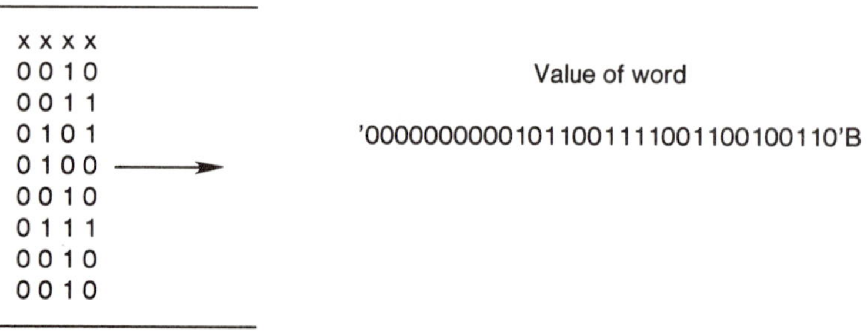

Figure 14–3

The four bytes of a 32-bit word are written in four columns across the tape. The eight bits of each byte are written in one column, on eight longitudinal lines known as tracks. An extra track contains a parity bit used for error checking. Most tapes have either seven or nine tracks, depending on the word size of the machine and the internal character code used.

Following is a description of a typical magnetic tape unit:

1. Tape density: 1600 bpi (bits per inch).
2. Tape length: 2400 feet (28,800 inches).
3. Tape capacity: 46,080,000 bytes (theoretical).
4. Physical record size: minimum of 4 bytes, maximum of approximately 46,000,000 bytes (theoretical).
5. Interblock gap: .6 inch (960 bytes).
6. Logical record size: limited by physical record size.
7. Record type: character or binary, fixed length or variable length.
8. File organization: consecutive (the tape device cannot physically skip sections of the tape).
9. File structure: header record, physical records followed by an end-of-file record, gaps between physical records.
10. Access mode: sequential forward (some tape drives can process the tape backward as well).
11. Typical read/write speed: 100 inches per second (160,000 bytes per second, 160 bytes per millisecond—theoretical).
12. Start/stop time: 1 millisecond.
13. Use: input and output (a tape is updated by writing a new version).
14. Blocking: on request.
15. Buffering: automatic.

Usually the system sets up several buffers so that the computer can anticipate the need for data and read ahead, or fill one buffer while another is being written.

A file written using STREAM I/O is a *character file*. It contains data written in ASCII, EBCDIC, BCD, or some other character code. These codes are shown in Appendix A. A file written using RECORD I/O is a *binary file* regardless of the type of data stored in the records.

The header record, which functions as a label record, contains information that identifies the file and describes the record type, length, and blocking factor. The label record is usually set up automatically by the system. In some programming languages the programmer has the option of constructing the label record, but this cannot be done in PL/I. When a file is created using one programming language and processed using another language, it is important to know the structure of the label.

The physical records on a tape are separated by interblock gaps. The tape drive does not run continuously: it starts when data is to be transmitted and stops afterward. A certain amount of tape passes under the read/write head during the starting and stopping processes, forming the interblock gap. On a system where this is .6 inch, a physical record size of less than 960 bytes is inefficient, wasting more than half the tape.

A magnetic tape file is declared as:

```
DCL file_name FILE [SEQL] [use] [access] [ENV(CONSECUTIVE)];
```

The use is INPUT or OUTPUT. The access is STREAM or RECORD.

On many systems additional information about the file is placed in the environment clause, but doing so makes the program less flexible. Instead it is recommended that all possible file and record parameters be placed in the JCL.

PROGRAMMING HINT: EFFICIENCY Block records for magnetic tape storage.

14.2.2 Magnetic disk

A *magnetic disk* is a platter coated with a ferrous oxide recording surface on one or both sides. Disks come in all sizes, from the tiny three-and-a-half-inch disks used in some portable computers to disks several feet in diameter. Disks for mainframe computers generally come in removable disk packs, each of which contains a stack of two-sided platters. The platters are permanently positioned with room for a recording arm between each pair. Figure 14–4 shows this arrangement.

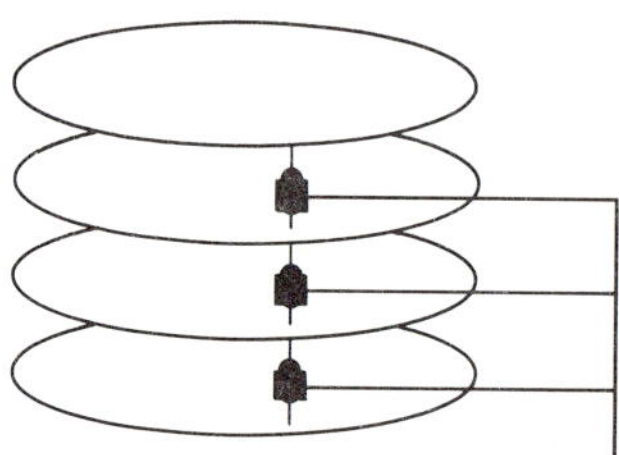

Figure 14–4

Two read/write heads are positioned between each pair of platters, one for the surface above and one for the surface below. The recording on the surfaces is in concentric circles, called *tracks*. The arms with the read/write heads move in and out together, finding the particular track needed. Since all the read/write heads move together, all the tracks directly above and below the track needed are available at the same time. The tracks positioned vertically above each other, which can be read or written without further head movement, together form a *cylinder*. When file space is allocated, tracks are selected from the same cylinder to minimize head motion.

Two types of mechanical motion are involved in selecting a record from a disk file. The heads must be moved to the correct track and the disk must rotate until the record needed is directly under the read/write head. The disks rotate continuously, but there is a delay averaging half a rotation involved in finding a record. The head motion is the slower of the two motions.

PROGRAMMING HINT: EFFICIENCY Allocate disk file space by cylinders.

A disk pack is divided into cylinders, a cylinder is divided into tracks, tracks are divided various ways into physical records, and physical records are divided into logical records. Figure 14–5 shows a schematic drawing of a disk platter.

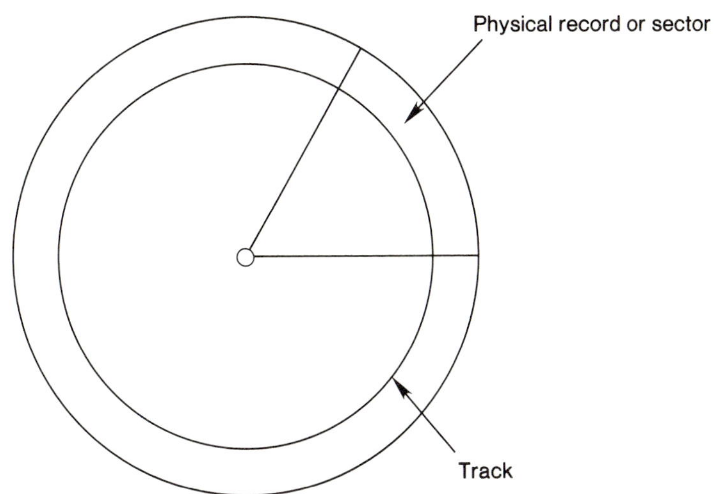

Figure 14–5

A typical disk might have the following characteristics (figures given are for the IBM 3380 disk):

1. Disk pack capacity: 1770 cylinders.
2. Cylinder capacity: 15 tracks.
3. Track capacity: 47,968 bytes.
4. Total capacity: 1,260,000,000 bytes (theoretical).
5. Physical record size: minimum of 4 bytes, maximum of approximately 47,000 bytes (theoretical).
6. Interblock gap: 480 bytes (known as overhead).
7. Logical record size: limited by physical record size.
8. Record type: character or binary, fixed length or variable length.
9. File organization: consecutive, regional, or indexed.
10. File structure: header record, physical records followed by an end-of-file record.
11. Access mode: sequential or direct.
12. Typical access speed: average head motion 16 milliseconds, average rotational delay 8.4 milliseconds, transmission speed 3,000,000 bytes per millisecond (theoretical).
13. Use: input, output, and update (may rewrite or delete records).
14. Blocking: automatic and on request.
15. Buffering: automatic.

A magnetic disk file is declared as:

```
DCL file_name FILE [SEQL] [use] [access] [ENV(CONSECUTIVE)];
```

or

```
DCL file_name FILE [mode] [use] [access] ENV(REGIONAL);
```

or

```
DCL file_name FILE [mode] [use] [access] ENV(INDEXED);
```

The mode is SEQUENTIAL or DIRECT. The use is INPUT, OUTPUT, or UPDATE. The access is STREAM or RECORD.

Additional information about the file, such as number of buffers, block size, or record length can be placed in the environment clause. However, this makes the program less flexible. Instead it is recommended that all possible file and record parameters be placed in the JCL.

The logical record positions of disk files are numbered. This makes it possible to access records in more than one way. Records can be read or written sequentially, disregarding the numbers. A record can be read from or written into a specific position identified by number. Or a record can be read from or written into a specific position identified by a key other than the record number (usually a name or ID number), which can be looked up in an index to obtain the record number.

On many systems there are three or more types of REGIONAL files and two or more types of INDEXED files. We will consider only one type of each here.

Review questions

1. Complete each of the following statements.

(a) The amount of data transmitted between the CPU and a peripheral device is a ________________ (physical/logical) record.

(b) The amount of data that fits into a memory buffer is a ________________ (physical/logical) record.

(c) A magnetic tape used for EBCDIC characters must have ________________ (seven/nine) tracks.

(d) A file that is written using STREAM I/O is a ________________ (character/binary) file.

(e) A file that is written using RECORD I/O is a ________________ (character/binary) file.

(f) A large blocking factor ________________ (increases/decreases) average file access time.

(g) A large blocking factor ________________ (increases/decreases) file capacity.

(h) A large blocking factor ________________ (increases/decreases) memory requirements.

2. The unused space between physical records is called the ________________.

3. The number of logical records that fit into a physical record is known as the ________________.

4. How many records of eighty bytes each can be stored on the magnetic tape described in section 14.2.1 when:
(a) They are unblocked.
(b) The blocking factor is 100.

5. How many records of eighty bytes each can be stored on the magnetic disk described in section 14.2.2 when:
(a) They are unblocked and records may not be split between tracks.
(b) The blocking factor is 100 and blocks may not be split between tracks.

6. How long would it take to read a file containing 100,000 records of eighty bytes each from the magnetic tape described in section 14.2.1 when:
(a) They are unblocked.
(b) The blocking factor is 100.

7. How long would it take to read a file containing 100,000 records of eighty bytes each from the magnetic disk described in section 14.2.2 when:
(a) They are unblocked and records are not split between tracks.
(b) The blocking factor is 100 and blocks are not split between tracks.

8. How many records of eighty bytes each can be stored on a single track of the magnetic disk described in section 14.2.2 when:
(a) They are unblocked and records may not be split between tracks.
(b) The blocking factor is 100 and blocks may not be split between tracks.

14.3 Dynamic record devices

Both unit record and blocked record devices handle files stored in a semipermanent form. Other I/O devices such as teletype terminals and CRT (cathode ray tube) or VDT (video display tube) terminals handle records that exist only for the very short time they reside in the device buffer or are displayed on the screen. These devices can be called *dynamic record devices.* Terminals can be used to prepare data for batch processing and then display the results. They can be used to imitate on-line files, or for true interactive processing.

The keyboard and display of a terminal are two separate I/O devices. Since the characters typed on the keyboard are generally echoed on the display, many of their characteristics are the same. Since some terminals can be used in either a block mode, a line mode, or a character mode, there is no one unit of data. The basic input or display line, terminated with a carriage return, is a *record* or *segment.* The amount of data displayed by a screen in block mode is a *message,* followed by an end-of-message character. A group of messages makes up a *transaction.* Each transaction carries extra information besides the data. The transaction descriptor identifies the terminal. In addition the transaction may have an ID number and time stamp to show when it entered the system. Depending on the language implementation, the part of the operating system that handles the transmission of data between terminals and the program is known as a transaction or message processor.

Transactions entering or leaving the system are stored in queues. There is one input queue and one output queue for each terminal referenced by a program. These queues are "dynamic files" in the sense that new data may be placed in them at any time. When data is removed from them to be read by the program or displayed on the terminal display, the data no longer exists in the file. The oldest records are removed first.

The following are typical characteristics of a dynamic record device:

1. File capacity: no limit.
2. Physical record size: 80 characters.
3. Logical record size: at most 80 characters.
4. File organization: teleprocessing (dynamic sequential).
5. File structure: queue of transactions, messages, records with overhead.
6. Access mode: sequential or transient.
7. Typical access speed: 1200 baud, 133 bytes per second (1200 bits per second including overhead).
8. Use: input and output.
9. Blocking: on request (the message is the block as it is one or more records).
10. Buffering: the queue takes the place of a buffer.

Two different types of files may be declared for dynamic record devices. When a program running in batch mode is addressing a terminal as an ordinary consecutive file, the access mode is sequential. Only one terminal may be handled through a file of this type. In this situation, the file is declared as:

```
DCL file_name FILE SEQL [use] RECORD ENV(teleprocessing);
```

The use is INPUT or OUTPUT.

With true interactive programming a file may be used to communicate with many terminals. In this situation the access mode is transient and the file is declared as:

```
DCL file_name FILE KEYED TRANSIENT [use] RECORD
              ENV(teleprocessing);
```

The use is INPUT or OUTPUT.

With sequential processing the file is not keyed, as the only terminal being addressed is identified with the file by the JCL. With transient processing, the file is used to communicate with many terminals. A key is used to identify the terminal for each transaction.

Review questions

1. Indicate whether each of the following statements is true or false.
   (a) A dynamic record device is one in which records are stored for a short duration of time.
   (b) Dynamic record devices cannot be used for batch processing.
   (c) A CRT terminal can be accessed in either character, line, or block mode.
   (d) A CRT terminal is a random-access device.
   (e) With TRANSIENT files, keys are used to identify terminals.
   (f) A separate queue is maintained for each TRANSIENT file.

2. How long would it take to display a file of 100,000 records of 80 bytes each on the terminal described in section 14.3?

14.4 File organization

Depending on the device, four different basic file organizations are available. These organizations affect the use of the file. The most widely used of these are CONSECUTIVE, INDEXED, and REGIONAL.

14.4.1 CONSECUTIVE files

A file organized consecutively can only be accessed sequentially, even when it is on a random-access device such as a disk. The records must be read or written in order. A consecutive disk file is used in exactly the same way as a magnetic tape file, except that records can be updated in place. The file can be modified without being recopied if no new records are to be inserted. A program to copy a consecutive disk file is identical to one that copies a consecutive tape file.

The basic file operations are to insert records, modify records, and delete records. With consecutive disk files, records can be inserted only if the file is copied. Records can be modified in place provided the record size is not changed. They can be deleted simply by marking them "deleted" and rewriting them. They cannot be physically removed unless the file is copied, omitting them.

14.4.2 INDEXED files

A disk file that has indexed organization can be accessed either sequentially or randomly. A logical or symbolic key is used to access each record. This key may be part of the logical record or some other value associated with the record. When the file is accessed sequentially, all the records may be accessed, or the key can be used to skip unwanted records. When the file is accessed randomly, the key is used to go directly to the record wanted. The operating system looks up the key in an index to obtain the file position of the record.

Some indexed files are maintained in key order, others are maintained in entry order. The records of files maintained in key order are stored in ascending order according to the values of the key field. Any records added to the file are inserted in the proper position in the file. Files maintained in entry order have new records added at the end.

When direct access is used with indexed files, some of the record positions are intentionally left vacant so that more records can be added when the file is updated. With indexed files, records can be inserted if space is available. Records can be modified in place provided the record size is not changed, or they can be deleted completely. Some systems do not allow the programmer to block indexed files.

Some types of indexed files maintain indexes on more than one key field. One of these, designated as the *primary key,* controls the actual record storage.

14.4.3 REGIONAL files

A disk file with regional organization can be accessed either sequentially or randomly. In the most common form of REGIONAL file, the *relative record number,* which is the record's position in the file, is used as the *storage key.* When the file is accessed sequentially, all the records may be accessed, or the record number can be used to skip unwanted records. When the file is accessed randomly, the storage key is used to go directly to the record wanted. The operating system can use the storage key to calculate the physical position of the record on the disk.

The storage key is usually calculated from the logical or symbolic record key. When records are blocked, the storage key is used to locate the block. The symbolic key is then needed to identify the record. Records are usually in order by storage key, not by symbolic key.

PROGRAMMING HINT: EFFICIENCY Use SEQL access rather than DIRECT access when possible.

When direct access is used with regional files, some of the record positions are intentionally left vacant so that more records can be added when the file is updated. With regional files, records can be inserted or appended if space is available. Records can be modified in place provided the record size is not changed. They can be deleted by marking them "deleted." Some systems do not allow the programmer to block regional files.

Review questions

1. The basic file operations are __________, __________, and __________ records.

2. In a CONSECUTIVE file, records can be inserted only if __________.

3. In a CONSECUTIVE file, records can be logically but not physically ____________.

4. In a CONSECUTIVE file, records can only be accessed ____________.

5. In an INDEXED file, records can be accessed ____________ or ____________.

6. In a REGIONAL file, records can be accessed ____________ or ____________.

7. In a (an) ____________ file, records are located by a physical key and identified by a logical or symbolic key.

8. In a (an) ____________ file, records are both located and identified by a logical or symbolic key.

9. In a (an) ____________ file, records are located by scanning the file, but identified by a logical or symbolic key.

10. Records can be inserted or deleted in a (an) ____________ or ____________ file.

14.5 File error processing

Certain error conditions can be raised during file access.

14.5.1 UNDEFINEDFILE condition

This condition is raised during the processing of the OPEN statement for a file. It happens if the program file name cannot be associated with an actual file, either because of a JCL error or a mismatch of file attributes between the program, the JCL, and the actual file.

14.5.2 TRANSMIT condition (not in Subset G)

This condition is raised if there is a hardware I/O error. Establishing an ON unit for this condition is useful only if the situation is such that the operation can be attempted again.

14.5.3 RECORD condition (not in Subset G)

This condition is raised if the size of the record in the file is not the same as the size declared in the program. If an ON unit is established for this condition, the I/O will be completed and the record padded or truncated as needed. If no ON unit is established, the condition is fatal.

14.5.4 ENDFILE condition

This condition is raised by sequential processing when there is an attempt to read beyond the end of the data and the end-of-file record is obtained. This record is physically the last record in each type of file except teleprocessing files. Since a teleprocessing file is potentially endless, the ENDFILE condition does not apply to it. The ENDFILE condition was discussed in detail in chapter 10.

14.5.5 ENDPAGE condition

This condition is raised by a PRINT file when there is an attempt to write beyond the end of the page. The condition is not available with any other types of file, as it is enabled by the PAGE output specification. The ENDPAGE condition was discussed in detail in chapter 10.

14.5.6 KEY condition

This condition is raised by either sequential or direct processing when an invalid key is used with a REGIONAL or INDEXED file. The key may be invalid for the operation being performed or it may have a value that cannot be used at all as a key for the file. The KEY condition is discussed in detail in chapters 16 and 17.

Review questions

1. If a file is declared as:

```
DCL F1 FILE INPUT RECORD SEQL ENV(CONSECUTIVE);
```

an ON unit is needed for the ____________ condition.

2. If a file is declared as:

```
DCL F2 FILE PRINT ENV(CONSECUTIVE);
```

an ON unit is needed for the ____________ condition.

3. If a file is declared as:

```
DCL F3 FILE INPUT RECORD KEYED SEQL ENV(INDEXED);
```

ON units are needed for the ____________ and ____________ conditions.

4. If a file is declared as:

```
DCL F4 FILE OUTPUT RECORD KEYED DIRECT
ENV(INDEXED);
```

an ON unit is needed for the ____________ condition.

5. If a file is declared as:

```
DCL F5 FILE UPDATE RECORD KEYED SEQL
ENV(REGIONAL);
```

ON units are needed for the ________________ and ________________ conditions.

6. If a file is declared as:

```
DCL F6 FILE RECORD KEYED DIRECT ENV(REGIONAL);
```

an ON unit is needed for the ________________ condition.

14.6 Selection of file type

Different types of devices are used for different applications. Table 14–1 shows some of the situations in which these devices should be used.

Device	*Frequency of use*	*Order of data*	*Type of use*
Magnetic tape	Infrequent	Sorted	Backup, logs input, output
Magnetic disk	Continuous	Sorted/unsorted	Database
Terminal	On request	Unsorted	Transactions

Table 14–1

Magnetic tape provides medium-speed, high-volume storage. Tapes are compact; they can be removed from the computer, stored in vaults, or shipped through the mail. They are used primarily to store large amounts of data that are needed only periodically. In addition they are used to back up the on-line data files, provide a duplicate copy of critical information, and store outdated information that cannot be discarded.

Magnetic disks provide high-speed, high-volume storage. Since they are rarely removed from the computer, they are used to store large amounts of data that need to be constantly accessible. They are also used for temporary files. On-line systems, such as business database systems, are stored on disks. The operating system files, compilers, and file management programs are stored on disks.

Different types of disk files are used for different applications. When data are *volatile,* that is, records are being added and deleted frequently, REGIONAL or INDEXED files are needed. When transactions have been sorted, SEQL updating is usually the most efficient. Table 14–2 shows some of the situations in which these files should be used.

Data	*Environment*	*Mode*	*Position*	*Organization*
Volatile	Batch	SEQL	KEYED	REGIONAL
Volatile	On-line	DIRECT	KEYED	REGIONAL
Stable	Batch	SEQL	Unkeyed	CONSECUTIVE
Stable	On-line	DIRECT	KEYED	INDEXED

Table 14–2

Data to be accessed in both a batch-processing environment and an on-line environment should have INDEXED organization.

Review questions

1. Random-access files are only available on a (an) ________________ device.

2. When fast data access is most important, a (an) ________________ device should be used.

3. When physical portability of data is most important, a (an) ________________ device should be used.

4. When frequency of access is high, a (an) ________________ device should be used.

5. Complete each of the following statements:
   (a) When only a few transactions are being processed, ________________ (DIRECT/SEQL) access should be used.
   (b) When transactions are not in order, ________________ (DIRECT/SEQL) access should be used.
   (c) When transactions include insertions and deletions, ________________ (CONSECUTIVE/REGIONAL/INDEXED) organization is the least efficient.
   (d) When transactions are not in order, ________________ (CONSECUTIVE/REGIONAL/INDEXED) organization is the least efficient.
   (e) When master records are to be processed in symbolic key order, ________________ (CONSECUTIVE/REGIONAL/INDEXED) organization is the least efficient.

14.7 Examples of file use

Within the limitations in record size and file access imposed by the various devices, programs handling files are device-independent.

14.7.1 Copy tape file

A magnetic tape file can be copied even though the record structure is not known. When copying a tape there is no need to look at the details of the record; only the size is important. It is assumed that the records are 1200 bytes long. Both STREAM and RECORD processing can be used with the same file. RECORD processing is the more efficient, but this example uses STREAM processing. RECORD processing will be discussed in chapter 15.

```
COPY: PROC OPTIONS (MAIN);
/****************************************************************/
/* PROGRAM: COPY A FILE                                         */
/* AUTHOR:  C ZIEGLER                                           */
/* VERSION: 07/17/84                                            */
/*                                                              */
/* PROGRAM DESCRIPTION                                          */
/* ------------------------------------------------------------ */
/* THIS PROGRAM COPIES A CHARACTER FILE                         */
/*               FILE IS CONSECUTIVE                            */
/*               RECORD LENGTH IS 1200                          */
/*                                                              */
/* INPUT: OLD_FILE TITLE 'F1'                                   */
/*              RECORD HAS 1200 CHARACTERS                      */
/*                                                              */
/* OUTPUT: NEW_FILE TITLE 'F2'                                  */
/*                                                              */
/****************************************************************/

DCL OLD_FILE   FILE SEQL INPUT  STREAM ENV(CONSECUTIVE),
    NEW_FILE   FILE SEQL OUTPUT STREAM ENV(CONSECUTIVE);
DCL FILE_REC   CHAR(1200);
DCL MORE_DATA  BIT(1),
    TRUE       BIT(1)    INIT('1'B),
    FALSE      BIT(1)    INIT('0'B);
ON ENDFILE (OLD_FILE)
  MORE_DATA = FALSE;

MORE_DATA = TRUE;
OPEN FILE (OLD_FILE) TITLE ('F1'),
     FILE (NEW_FILE) TITLE ('F2');
GET FILE (OLD_FILE) EDIT (FILE_REC) (COL(1),A(1200));
DO WHILE (MORE_DATA);
  PUT FILE (NEW_FILE) EDIT (FILE_REC) (COL(1), A(1200));
  GET FILE (OLD_FILE) EDIT (FILE_REC) (COL(1), A(1200));
END;
CLOSE FILE (OLD_FILE),
      FILE (NEW_FILE);
END COPY;
```

This program would work with CONSECUTIVE files of the same record size on any other appropriate input and output devices. The actual devices used are determined by the JCL.

14.7.2 Copy tape file to disk

Some disk systems limit the size of records that can be stored. This program assumes that the input tape of section 14.7.1 is being copied to a disk file which will not handle records larger than 512 bytes. For convenience, the tape record is broken into three equal parts of 400 bytes each. Disk and tape are known as *mass storage* devices.

```
COPY: PROC OPTIONS (MAIN);
/*************************************************************/
/* PROGRAM: COPY A FILE                                      */
/* AUTHOR:  C ZIEGLER                                        */
/* VERSION: 07/17/84                                         */
/*                                                           */
/* PROGRAM DESCRIPTION                                       */
/* ------------------------------------------------------- */
/* THIS PROGRAM COPIES A CHARACTER FILE                      */
/*               FILE IS CONSECUTIVE                         */
/*                                                           */
/* INPUT: OLD_FILE TITLE 'F1'                                */
/*                 RECORD LENGTH IS 1200 BYTES               */
/*                                                           */
/* OUTPUT: NEW_FILE TITLE 'F2'                               */
/*               RECORD LENGTH IS 400 BYTES                  */
/*                                                           */
/*************************************************************/

DCL OLD_FILE   FILE SEQL INPUT  STREAM ENV(CONSECUTIVE),
    NEW_FILE   FILE SEQL OUTPUT STREAM ENV(CONSECUTIVE);
DCL IN_REC     CHAR(1200),
    REC(3)     CHAR(400) DEF(IN_REC);
DCL MORE_DATA  BIT(1),
    TRUE       BIT(1)    INIT('1'B),
    FALSE      BIT(1)    INIT('0'B);

ON ENDFILE (OLD_FILE)
  MORE_DATA = FALSE;

MORE_DATA = TRUE;
OPEN FILE (OLD_FILE) TITLE ('F1'),
     FILE (NEW_FILE) TITLE ('F2');
GET FILE (OLD_FILE) EDIT (FILE_REC) (COL(1), A(1200));
DO WHILE (MORE_DATA);
  PUT FILE (NEW_FILE) EDIT (REC(1)) (COL(1), A(400));
  PUT FILE (NEW_FILE) EDIT (REC(2)) (COL(1), A(400));
  PUT FILE (NEW_FILE) EDIT (REC(3)) (COL(1), A(400));
  GET FILE (OLD_FILE) EDIT (FILE_REC) (COL(1), A(1200));
END;
CLOSE FILE (OLD_FILE,
      FILE (NEW_FILE);
END COPY;
```

14.8 Summary

Selecting storage devices and file attributes is strongly influenced by a file's anticipated use. Each storage device has its own physical characteristics, which limit the choice of file attributes. In practice, many computer installations do not have the full range of common storage devices.

Line printers and CRT terminals are the most common types of user output devices. Card readers and terminals are the most common types of user input devices. Magnetic tapes and disk are used for machine-readable, semipermanent storage.

In declaring a file, the organization, processing, use, and mode are specified. Organization has to do with the physical arrangement of the records in the file. The processing attribute indicates the way the record positions are being located in the file. The use attribute specifies the direction of transmission between the memory buffer and the file, and the mode attribute indicates how the file buffer is being accessed by the program.

14.9 Exercises

1. Write a program that accepts, as input from the terminal, a record size for a mass storage input file and a record size for a mass storage output file, then copies the input file to the output file, combining and breaking the records as necessary to reformat the data.

***2.** Look up the limitations on record sizes on your computer using different I/O devices.

***3.** Determine how many I/O buffers your system automatically sets up for different devices.

***4.** Determine whether records can be blocked on your computer using the following,
(a) CONSECUTIVE files
(b) REGIONAL files
(c) INDEXED files
and what the default blocking is.

5. Write a program that creates a CONSECUTIVE disk file of 10,000 records of 400 bytes each. Compare the number of tracks needed on the disk and the amount of processing time used for the following:
(a) Unblocked records.
(b) A blocking factor of ten.
(c) A blocking factor of twenty.

15
Data maintenance (record files)

OBJECTIVE: To keep data up to date efficiently.

THE MOST COMMON FILE organization for data maintenance uses consecutive records and sequential processing. As we saw in chapter 14, this is the only organization possible with unit record devices such as the card reader and line printer, and the only efficient organization with magnetic tapes. Only two-dimensional media such as disk, drum, and CRT screen can have anything other than sequential access. Even with randomly organized files on random-access devices, sequential access is possible.

Sequential access means accessing the data in the order in which it is made available by the peripheral device when it reads a file from beginning to end. With a card reader, this is the order in which the cards are stacked; with magnetic tape, this is the order of the records on the tape. In this chapter we will discuss only those record files that not only have sequential access but, from the programmer's point of view, have *consecutive organization* of records. That is, records are stored next to each other without room for other information between them.

15.1 CONSECUTIVE RECORD file declarations

CONSECUTIVE files can be used for either STREAM or RECORD I/O. In chapter 10 they were used only for stream access, but in this chapter they will be used only for RECORD access. Both types of access may be used in the same program, but not for the same file at the same time. STREAM files are organized as records behind the scenes. Therefore the same actual data files may be accessed both ways. RECORD access is used with CONSECUTIVE files for I/O efficiency. With RECORD I/O, the data is transmitted without any editing.

The general form of a declaration for use with a consecutive record file is:

```
DCL file_name FILE [SEQL] [use] RECORD ENV(CONSECUTIVE);
```

The use is INPUT, OUTPUT, or UPDATE. Table 15–1 shows the file use attributes that are compatible with various devices.

Device	*Mode*	*Use*	*Access*	*Organization*
Card reader	SEQUENTIAL	INPUT	RECORD	CONSECUTIVE
Line printer	SEQUENTIAL	OUTPUT	RECORD	CONSECUTIVE
Magnetic tape	SEQUENTIAL	INPUT OUTPUT	RECORD	CONSECUTIVE
Magnetic disk	SEQUENTIAL	INPUT OUTPUT UPDATE	RECORD	CONSECUTIVE

Table 15-1

UPDATE of sequential files is possible only on a truly random-access device such as a disk. This file use is not available on the other devices shown in the table as there is no efficient way to physically relocate the read/write head back to the beginning of the current record so that an updated version may replace the old version.

The PRINT option is not available with RECORD files since it implies the use of column, line, and page editing formats in the I/O statements and no editing or formatting is carried out during record I/O.

Review questions

1. The most common file organization is ________________ with ________________ processing.

2. Indicate whether each of the following statements is true or false.
   (a) Sequential access is possible with both unit record and blocked record devices.
   (b) STREAM files are actually organized as records on the storage device.
   (c) With RECORD I/O, data is edited as it is transmitted.
   (d) RECORD files can be used with both PRINT and OUTPUT.
   (e) CONSECUTIVE files can be used with both STREAM and RECORD I/O.

(f) Records in a CONSECUTIVE file are stored next to each other in order.
(g) The same CONSECUTIVE file may be used at one time for STREAM access and at another time for RECORD access.

3. Files may be updated in place on ________________ devices.

15.2 File availability

Both record and stream files are made accessible by opening them and made inaccessible by closing them.

15.2.1 OPEN statement

The general form of the OPEN statement is:

```
OPEN FILE (file_name) [mode] [use] [access] [TITLE (title)];
```

The mode, use, and access options of the OPEN statement are used when the file declaration does not contain the necessary information. This allows a file to be used in a program, more than once, with different attributes. A temporary RECORD file is opened for creation, then closed and reopened for listing by the following:

```
OPEN FILE (TEMP) OUTPUT TITLE ('T1');
 . . .
OPEN FILE (TEMP) INPUT TITLE ('T1');
```

The title option is used to associate the file name used in the program with a file name known to the operating system. Opening a file for sequential processing positions it at the beginning of the first record.

15.2.2 CLOSE statement

The general form of the CLOSE statement is:

```
CLOSE FILE (file_name);
```

Closing a consecutive record file that has been open for sequential OUTPUT causes an end-of-file record to be written.

PROGRAMMING HINT: CLARITY When a file is used more than once in a program, put the changing file attributes in the OPEN statements.

Review questions

1. Given a file declaration,

```
DCL F FILE RECORD ENV(CONSECUTIVE);
```

write a statement that:
(a) Opens it for reading.
(b) Opens it for writing.
(c) Opens it for update.
(d) Closes it.

2. Opening a file positions the read/write head ________________.

3. Closing an OUTPUT file causes a(an) ________________ to be written.

4. The TITLE option is used when the file name used in the program is not known to the ________________.

15.3 Record access

With RECORD files the basic input and output statements are READ and WRITE.

15.3.1 Input statements

With sequential access files the READ statement has three possible forms:

```
READ FILE (file_name) INTO (variable);
READ FILE (file_name) SET (pointer_name);
READ FILE (file_name) IGNORE (expression);
```

These statements may be used to access either an INPUT or an UPDATE file. The execution of any of them has the effect of obtaining a record from the peripheral device and storing it in the file buffer if it is not already there. If the records are not blocked, every time a READ statement is executed, the peripheral device is accessed. If the records are blocked, the device is accessed only when the record wanted is not already in the buffer. In either case, when the record is found in the buffer, it is made available to the program.

The three processing options of the READ statement are known as *move mode* (INTO), *locate mode* (SET), and *skip sequential mode* (IGNORE). They make a record available to the program by setting up an access path.

MOVE-MODE PROCESSING

In move-mode processing, the record is copied from the buffer into a character string variable or a structure. The following examples show some of the possibilities:

```
DCL NAME CHAR(80);
 . . .
READ FILE (NAMEF) INTO (NAME);
```

In the first example, a record is moved into the string NAME. In some systems, if the record is not eighty bytes long, the RECORD condition is raised. With others, the record is stored left-justified and padded or truncated as necessary.

```
DCL 1 EMP_INFO,
      5 NAME    CHAR(20),
      5 ADDR    CHAR(30),
      5 TEL_NO  CHAR(10);
 . . .
READ FILE (EMPFILE) INTO (EMP_INFO);
```

In this example, a record is moved into the structure EMP_INFO as though EMP_INFO were a character string sixty bytes long. The first twenty bytes of the record are stored in NAME, the next thirty bytes are stored in ADDR, and the last ten bytes are stored in TEL_NO. If the record does not have exactly sixty bytes, it may be stored left-justified and padded or truncated to fit, or the RECORD condition may be raised.

In the following example,

```
DCL 1 ACCT_INFO,
      5  ACCT_NO     CHAR(5),
      5  ACCT_TYPE   PIC'9',
      5  ACCT_BAL    FIXED DEC(7,2),
      5  ACCT_HIST   CHAR(70);
 . . .
READ FILE (ACCTF) INTO (ACCT_INFO);
```

a record is moved into the structure ACCT_INFO. Even though this is a structure of mixed types, the record is moved as though ACCT_INFO were a character string eighty bytes long. The first five bytes of the record are stored in ACCT_NO, the next byte in ACCT_TYPE, four bytes in ACCT_BAL, and the remainder in ACCT_HIST. The bit pattern placed in ACCT_BAL is later interpreted as a fixed-decimal number. It must have been stored on the peripheral device in the same form, not as character digits but as the internal representation appropriate for a fixed-decimal number. No conversion or type checking takes place when a record is read.

The following program segment shows the basic steps in reading a file and printing the records using move-mode processing:

```
DCL INFILE FILE SEQL INPUT RECORD ENV(CONSECUTIVE);
 . . .
READ FILE (INFILE) INTO (IN_REC);
DO WHILE (MORE_INPUT);
  PUT SKIP LIST (IN_REC);
  READ FILE (INFILE) INTO (IN_REC);
END;
```

LOCATE-MODE PROCESSING

With locate-mode processing the record is not copied from the buffer; instead, it is processed in the buffer. A system pointer always indicates the current position in the buffer. With locate-mode processing, a named pointer is used as well. Once the pointer has been set, a based variable can be superimposed on the buffer to give names to the record and its fields. This is shown in the following examples:

```
DCL STR   CHAR(80) BASED (P);
DCL P     POINTER;
  . . .
READ FILE (CUST_FILE) SET (P);
```

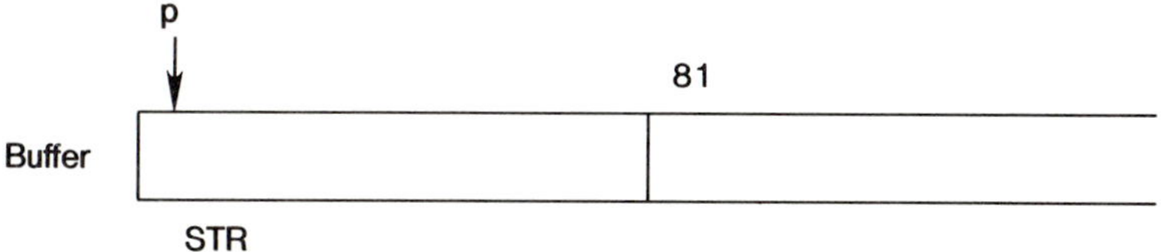

The process of setting P to point to the record in the buffer associates the name STR with eighty bytes of storage in the buffer. The pointer indicates the beginning of the eighty bytes. STR may be shorter than the actual record, but it should not be longer.

In the following example,

```
DCL 1 EMP_INFO                BASED (EMP_PTR),
      5 NAME     CHAR(20),
      5 ADDR     CHAR(30),
      5 TEL_NO   CHAR(10);
DCL EMP_PTR      POINTER;
  . . .
READ FILE (EMPFILE) SET (EMP_PTR);
```

the pointer variable EMP_PTR indicates the sixty bytes of buffer that are to be referenced by the name EMP_INFO. The first twenty of these are known as NAME, the next thirty as ADDR, and the last ten as TEL_NO, as follows:

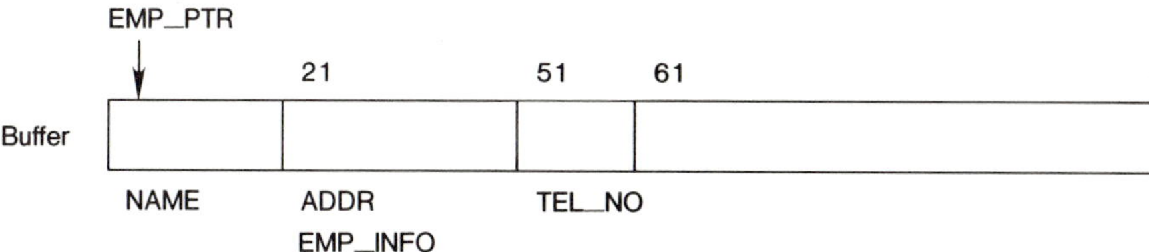

The buffer can be thought of as similar to an array. It can be scanned by moving the pointer along it. This is done by means of the READ statement. After a second read, the pointer indicates the second record, and the names are associated with it as follows:

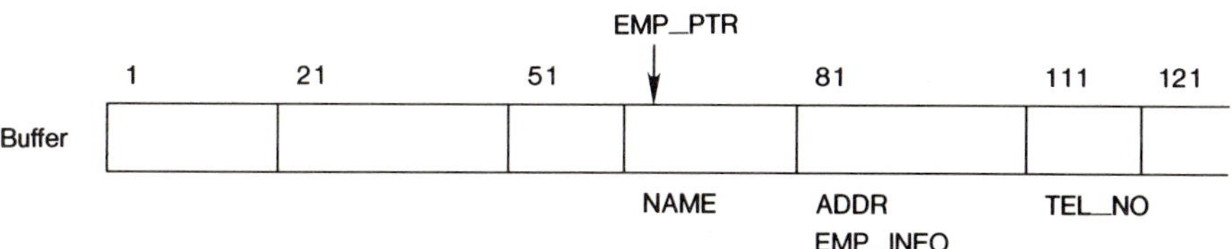

When the pointer has been moved to the last record in the buffer, the next READ statement causes the buffer to be refilled and the pointer relocated to the beginning.

As with move-mode processing, the data elements may be of any type. It is up to the programmer to describe the record in a way that is consistent with the data actually stored in the buffer.

In this example,

```
DCL 1   MEAS_INFO              BASED,
        5  MEAS_DATE   CHAR(6),
        5  MEAS_TIME   CHAR(6),
        5  MEAS_ID     CHAR(4),
        5  MEAS(6)     FIXED BIN;
DCL P                  POINTER;
 . . .
READ FILE (MEASURE) SET (P);
```

the structure is not based on any specific pointer variable. It is associated with the file buffer only through references to the structure which make specific use of the pointer, such as:

```
P-> MEAS_INFO
```

or

```
P-> MEAS(4)
```

The following program segment shows the basic steps in reading a file and printing the records using locate-mode processing:

```
READ FILE (DATAF) SET (P);
DO WHILE (MORE_DATA);
  PUT SKIP LIST (P-> DATA_REC);
  READ FILE (DATAF) SET (P);
END;
```

Since the file buffer is essentially one long string of data, record variants may be handled by superimposing different structures on the same part of the buffer. The record descriptions used in the following program segment,

```
DCL 1   CUST_DATA                                 BASED (C),
        5  REC_TYPE          CHAR(1),
        5  ACCTNO            CHAR(5),
        5  NAME              CHAR(20),
        5  ADDR              CHAR(30);
DCL 1   ACCT_DATA                                 BASED (A),
        5  REC_TYPE          CHAR(1),
        5  NEW_BAL           PIC '(5)9V99',
        5  CHARGE(5),
           9  CHG_AMT        PIC '9999V99',
           9  CHG_DATE       CHAR(6);
DCL (A,C)                    POINTER;
 . . .
READ FILE (CHGFILE) SET (C);
A = C;
```

superimpose both records on the same portion of the buffer, as follows:

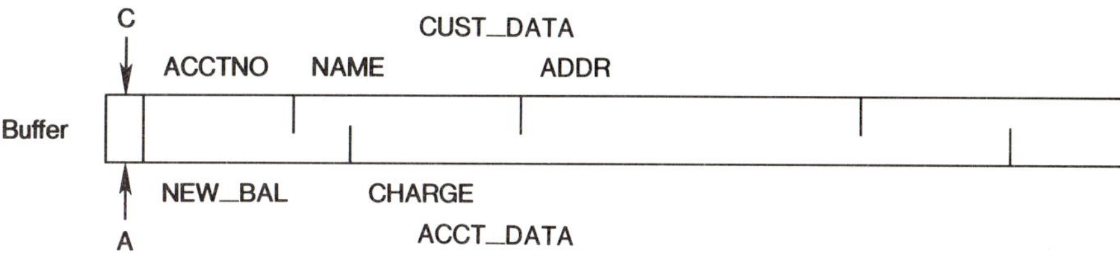

By reading the REC_TYPE from either record description,

```
IF CUST_DATA.REC_TYPE = 'C'
```

or

```
IF ACCT_DATA.REC_TYPE = 'A'
```

the type code can be checked and the correct record description used. Notice that the record descriptions do not have the same length and that the fields do not match in either size, type, or placement. Most consecutive file implementations support variable-length records.

PROGRAMMING HINT: EFFICIENCY Use locate-mode input to save memory space.

SKIP-SEQUENTIAL PROCESSING (not in Subset G)

The third form of the READ statement, with the IGNORE option, is used when the computer is to pass over a certain number of records before retrieving one for processing. This form of the statement must be followed by an additional READ statement which actually retrieves the record. This is shown in the following examples:

```
DCL STR CHAR(320);
 . . .
READ FILE (DATFILE) IGNORE (9);
READ FILE (DATFILE) INTO (STR);
```

In this first example, the tenth record is retrieved and copied into STR. Since the file is organized consecutively and is open for sequential access, the device controller reads the first nine records before retrieving the tenth. This can be done very efficiently in a single rotation of the disk (for a disk file) if the records are all on one track or cylinder. The nine records being skipped are not transmitted to the buffer. Only the block containing the wanted record is transmitted. If all records being skipped are already in the buffer, no disk access is necessary.

```
DCL STR  CHAR(80) BASED (P),
    P    POINTER;
 . . .
X = 14;
READ FILE (DATFILE) IGNORE (5*X-1);
READ FILE (DATFILE) SET (P);
```

Here the number of records to be ignored is calculated. Then a block of records is obtained so that the record wanted can be processed either in the program data area or, in this case, in the buffer.

The following program segment shows the basic steps in reading a file and printing every tenth record using skip-sequential processing:

```
READ FILE (DATAF) IGNORE (9);
IF MORE_DATA
  THEN
    READ FILE (DATAF) INTO (DATA_REC);
DO WHILE (MORE_DATA);
  PUT SKIP LIST (DATA_REC);
  READ FILE (DATAF) IGNORE (9);
  IF MORE_DATA
    THEN
      READ FILE (DATAF) INTO (DATA_REC);
END;
```

It is important not to attempt to read the tenth record unless you know that the end of the file has not been reached.

15.3.2 Output statements

There are three output statements for sequential-access record files. The general forms of the statements are:

```
WRITE FILE (file_name) FROM (variable);
LOCATE based_variable FILE (file_name) [SET (pointer)];
REWRITE FILE (file_name) FROM (variable);
```

The first two of these are used with OUTPUT files, and the third is used with UPDATE files. The first and third place data in the output buffer, the second one does not. The three forms of output processing are known respectively as *move mode, locate mode,* and *update mode.*

MOVE-MODE PROCESSING

The WRITE statement can only be used with a CONSECUTIVE file when the file is being created. Since this is the statement that stores a new record in a file, files can be extended only by creating new copies of them. The WRITE statement has the effect of causing a record to be placed in the output buffer. When the buffer is full, its contents are transmitted to the peripheral device.

The following program segment shows the basic steps in creating a file using move-mode processing:

```
GET EDIT (STR) (COL(1),A(80));
DO WHILE (MORE_DATA);
  WRITE FILE (DATAF) FROM (STR);
  GET EDIT (STR) (COL(1),A(80));
END;
```

LOCATE-MODE PROCESSING (not in Subset G)

The LOCATE statement is used to find the next available space in the output buffer. Its only effect is to move the buffer pointer to just past the current record position and reserve enough space for the output data. If the based variable does not have an associated pointer, the SET option must be used. The LOCATE statement is followed by an assignment statement that stores the record in the buffer. This is shown in the following examples:

```
DCL STR   CHAR(80)   BASED (P),
    P     POINTER;
  . . .
LOCATE STR FILE (TXTFILE);
STR = 'NOW IS THE TIME';
```

In the first example, the SET option is not used because STR has an associated pointer. Note that the pointer is never explicitly used.

```
DCL STR   CHAR(80)   BASED,
    P     POINTER;
  . . .
LOCATE STR FILE (TXTFILE) SET (P);
P->STR = 'NOW IS THE TIME';
```

In this example, STR does not have an associated pointer. The LOCATE instruction assigns the address of a buffer record position to the pointer P, which is then explicitly used to store the character constant.

If one file is to be copied to another and the records are large, using locate mode is more efficient in both space and time than using move mode. The following program segment shows the basic steps in copying a file using locate-mode input and output:

```
DCL DATA_REC   CHAR(80)   BASED;
  . . .
READ FILE (INFILE) SET (IN_PTR);
DO WHILE (MORE_DATA);
  LOCATE DATA_REC FILE (OUTFILE) SET (OUT_PTR);
  OUT_PTR->DATA_REC = IN_PTR->DATA_REC;
  READ FILE (INFILE) SET (IN_PTR);
END;
```

The declaration of DATA_REC sets up a descriptor but does not allocate storage. No storage is used other than the buffers and storage for the pointers. The name DATA_REC can be used twice in the assignment statement because its only effect is to specify the amount of data to be moved from the input buffer to the output buffer. Its use in the LOCATE statement does not assign the name to the output buffer, but specifies the amount of space needed in the buffer.

UPDATE-MODE PROCESSING

The general form of the updating statement is:

```
REWRITE FILE (file_name) FROM (variable);
```

This statement can only be used with disk files. The system software maintains a pointer to the current file position of each file in use. The REWRITE statement causes the file pointer to back up to the beginning of the most recently read record. The output record is written in the same record position, replacing the most recently read record.

The following example shows a file being searched until a specific record is found, which is then replaced. The record being sought must have some kind of key field by which it can be identified. Do not assume that the records are in any particular order.

```
DO UNTIL (FILE_KEY = KEY_WANTED | EOF);
  READ FILE (INFOF) INTO (FILE_REC);
END;
IF ¬EOF
  THEN
    REWRITE FILE(INFOF) FROM (NEW_REC);
```

The file is read until the record is found. If it is missing, the entire file is read and the EOF flag is set. If the record was found, the REWRITE statement causes the file to be repositioned to the beginning of the record and the data from NEW_REC replaces it. The data originally in the record is no longer there, but a copy is in the structure FILE_REC. The new record must be the same size as the one it replaces.

The following example shows a record being modified by changing the value of a field. To do this, the entire record must be read and rewritten.

```
DO UNTIL (FILE_KEY = KEY_WANTED | EOF);
  READ FILE (INFOF) INTO (FILE_REC);
END;
IF ¬EOF
  THEN
    DO;
      FILE_REC.MEAS = 0;
      REWRITE FILE(INFOF) FROM (FILE_REC);
    END;
```

Review questions

1. The basic input and output statements for record files are ____________ and ____________.

2. The ____________ statement is used to replace a record.

3. The three forms of the input statement are used for ____________, ____________, and ____________ mode processing.

4. The three forms of the output statement are used for ____________, ____________, and ____________ mode processing.

5. Complete each of the following statements:

(a) The record is processed in the area allocated to the record description in ____________ (move-mode / locate-mode) processing.

(b) The record is processed in the file buffer in ________________ (move-mode / locate-mode) processing.
(c) An explicit pointer is used in ________________ (locate-mode / skip-sequential) processing.
(d) A number is used in ________________ (locate-mode / skip-sequential) processing.
(e) With ________________ (locate-mode / update-mode) processing, a REWRITE statement causes a record to be placed in the file buffer.
(f) With ________________ (locate-mode / update-mode) processing, an assignment statement causes a record to be placed in the file buffer.

15.4 File error conditions

A number of error conditions can be raised during file access. These were discussed in section 14.5 of chapter 14. Any ON units that are established must be identified with particular files. It is possible to establish different ON units for the same condition for different files. It is also possible to establish ON units for different conditions for a single file. For example,

```
ON ENDFILE (TRANS)
  MORE_T = FALSE;
ON ENDFILE (MASTER)
  MORE_M = FALSE;
ON UNDEFINEDFILE (TRANS)
  PUT SKIP LIST ('TRANSACTION FILE MISSING');
```

If a second ON unit for the same condition is established for the same file, it replaces the previous exception handler. For example,

```
ON ENDFILE (INFILE)
  MORE_DATA = FALSE;
 . . .                    /* PART 1 */
ON ENDFILE (INFILE)
  MORE_INPUT = FALSE;
 . . .                    /* PART 2 */
```

In the first part of this example, the variable MORE_DATA is used to indicate the status of the file. In the second part, a different variable, MORE_INPUT, is used instead. The scope of an ON unit is dynamic rather than static. Once the ON unit has been established, it remains in effect until the procedure that contains it is exited, unless a second ON unit is established for the same condition (as in this example) or its effect is explicitly cancelled by a REVERT statement.

The ENDFILE condition is the most useful one for sequential file processing. This condition is raised when there is an attempt to read beyond the end of the data and the end-of-file record is obtained.

Review questions

1. Indicate whether each of the following statements is true or false.
 (a) THE ENDFILE condition is raised when there is no data record to read.
 (b) Only one ENDFILE unit at a time may be established for each file.
 (c) It does not matter where the ENDFILE exception handler is placed in a procedure.
 (d) More than one ON unit can be established for a file.

15.5 File maintenance

When a file has been declared a RECORD file, the GET and PUT statements cannot be used for input and output. The I/O statements for use with CONSECUTIVE RECORD disk files are READ, WRITE, LOCATE, and REWRITE. Table 15–2 shows the conditions under which they may be used.

Table 15–2

File attributes	*Valid operations*
SEQL INPUT	READ ... INTO ... READ ... SET ... READ ... IGNORE ...
SEQL OUTPUT	WRITE ... FROM ... LOCATE ... SET ...
SEQL UPDATE	READ ... INTO ... READ ... SET ... READ ... IGNORE ... REWRITE ... FROM ...

Unlike magnetic tape files or STREAM files, a CONSECUTIVE RECORD disk file may be updated without being copied as long as no new records are to be added. Updating a file involves reading the file until the desired record is found, then replacing that record with a new or revised version of it. This is done with the REWRITE statement.

If a record is to be deleted, it cannot actually be removed from a consecutive file without making a new version of the entire file. It can, however, be blanked out or given a special mark to show that it is no longer active. Often the first word of a record is used as identification, whether of the file, the record type, or the activity status of the record. To delete a record, a special bit pattern such as '(8)1'B can be placed in the first byte of the record. The following example finds a record, then deletes it by marking it.

```
DCL 1  FILE_REC,
       5 REC_TYPE  BIT(8),
       5 REC_INFO  CHAR(79);
DCL INACTIVE       BIT(8)   INIT('(8)1'B);
```

```
 . . .
DO UNTIL (FILE_KEY >= KEY_WANTED);
  READ FILE (INFOF) INTO (FILE_REC);
END;
IF FILE_KEY = KEY_WANTED
  THEN
    DO;
      REC_TYPE = INACTIVE;
      REWRITE FILE(INFOF) FROM (FILE_REC);
    END;
```

Here the record contains an extra byte being used as a flag to indicate whether or not the record has been deleted.

PROGRAMMING HINT: STYLE Reserve the first byte of a record for a file ID or status flag.

The DOUNTIL loop finds the record wanted. It is assumed that the records are in order by key fields. If the record is not found, the search stops as soon as the computer has read past the place where it should be. On the average, half the records must be read either to find a particular record or to determine that it is not there. If the record is found, the INACTIVE flag is set and the same record is rewritten to its original position in the file.

If records are being marked as deleted, programs which access the file should include a check for deleted records in the validation process. This is done in the following program segment, which prints the active records from a file.

```
DCL INACTIVE  BIT(8)  INIT ('(8)1'B);
 . . .
READ FILE (INFILE) INTO (FILE_REC);
DO WHILE (MORE_DATA);
  IF REC_TYPE ¬= INACTIVE
    THEN
      PUT SKIP LIST (FILE_REC);
  READ FILE (INFILE) INTO (FILE_REC);
END;
```

The algorithm for copying a file and inserting new records is the same for CONSECUTIVE RECORD files as the algorithm for merging files used in section 10.6.3 of chapter 10.

Review questions

1. Consecutive files on a magnetic ________________ can be updated in place, provided there are no insertions.

2. Consecutive files on a magnetic ________________ can only be updated by copying.

3. If a file contains 10,000 records, the average search length for a particular record is ____________ records.

4. If a file is to be searched, it must be possible to identify each record by a ____________ field.

5. An extra byte should be reserved at the beginning of each record for ____________.

6. A record is deleted from a CONSECUTIVE file without copying the file by ____________.

7. The REWRITE statement is used to ____________ a record or ____________ a record.

15.6 Examples using RECORD files

The following examples illustrate the major types of file maintenance for CONSECUTIVE RECORD files. These include examples of revising files by omitting invalid or inactive records, copying a file, and updating a file in place.

15.6.1 Record validation

Because no data conversion takes place during record input, the programmer can validate data values before they are used and so avoid raising the CONVERSION exception. The following program checks for valid numeric values, writes the valid records to a disk file, and prints the invalid records. Then the valid file is listed.

The input is obtained from a transaction file. This type of validation is needed when data are being entered into the computer for the first time.

```
VALID: PROC OPTIONS (MAIN);
**************************************************************/
/*                                                           */
/* PROGRAM: VALIDATE INPUT DATA                              */
/* AUTHOR:  C ZIEGLER                                        */
/* VERSION: 07/17/84                                         */
/*                                                           */
/* PROGRAM DESCRIPTION                                       */
/*----------------------------------------------------------*/
/* THIS PROGRAM VALIDATES DATA FROM A TRANSACTION           */
/* FILE, WRITING THE VALID RECORDS TO A NEW FILE AND        */
/* PRINTING THE INVALID RECORDS                              */
/*                                                           */
/* INPUT: OLDFILE - TRANSACTIONS                             */
/*                  COLS 1 -  5 ACCOUNT NUMBER               */
/*                       6 - 25 NAME                         */
/*                      26 - 32 AMOUNT                       */
```

```
/*                                                          */
/* OUTPUT: NEWFILE - VALID TRANSACTIONS                     */
/*         SYSPRINT - INVALID TRANSACTIONS                  */
/*                                                          */
/************************************************************/
DCL OLDFILE    FILE SEQL RECORD ENV (CONSECUTIVE),
    NEWFILE    FILE SEQL RECORD ENV (CONSECUTIVE);
DCL 1  TRANS_REC,
       5  ACCT_NO    CHAR(5),
       5  NAME       CHAR(20),
       5  CH_AMT     CHAR(7),
          AMOUNT     PIC '99999V99'  DEF (CH_AMT);
DCL VALID_REC        CHAR(32);
DCL MORE_DATA        BIT(1),
    TRUE             BIT(1)          INIT('1'B),
    FALSE            BIT(1)          INIT('0'B);
DCL DIGITS           CHAR(10)        INIT('0123456789');

/************************************************************/
/*                                                          */
/* THIS SECTION CREATES A FILE OF VALID RECORDS.            */
/*                                                          */
/************************************************************/
ON ENDFILE (OLDFILE)
  MORE_DATA = FALSE;

MORE_DATA = TRUE;
OPEN INPUT  FILE (OLDFILE) TITLE('T1'),
     OUTPUT FILE (NEWFILE) TITLE('T2');
PUT LIST ('INVALID DATA');
READ FILE (OLDFILE) INTO (TRANS_REC);
DO WHILE (MORE_DATA);
  IF VERIFY(ACCT_NO,DIGITS) = 0 & VERIFY(CH_AMT,DIGITS) = 0
    THEN
      WRITE FILE (NEWFILE) FROM (TRANS_REC);
    ELSE
      PUT SKIP LIST (TRANS_REC);
  READ FILE (OLDFILE) INTO (TRANS_REC);
END;
CLOSE FILE (OLDFILE),
      FILE (NEWFILE);

/************************************************************/
/*                                                          */
/* THIS SECTION LISTS THE FILE OF VALID RECORDS.            */
/*                                                          */
/************************************************************/
ON ENDFILE (NEWFILE)
  MORE_DATA = FALSE;

MORE_DATA = TRUE;
PUT PAGE LIST ('VALID DATA');
OPEN INPUT FILE (NEWFILE);
```

```
READ FILE (NEWFILE) INTO (VALID_REC);
DO WHILE (MORE_DATA);
  PUT SKIP LIST (VALID_REC);
  READ FILE (NEWFILE) INTO (VALID_REC);
END;
CLOSE FILE (NEWFILE);
END VALID;
```

The VERIFY function can only be used with string data. By redefining the AMOUNT field of the record, the value can be accessed as a character string for validation and as a numeric value, with a decimal point position, for use in arithmetic. The field can be redefined because the underlying representation is the same for CHARACTER digits and PICTURE digits.

Each file is opened before it is used and closed as soon as its processing for that use has been completed. In the first section the records are read into a storage location, which is then either printed or written to another file. Stream output is the easiest way to send output to the printer.

15.6.2 Locate-mode file handling

The following example shows the copying of a file using locate-mode processing for both input and output. This is the most efficient way to copy a file.

```
COPY: PROC OPTIONS (MAIN);
/**************************************************************/
/*                                                            */
/* PROGRAM: COPY A SEQUENTIAL FILE                            */
/* AUTHOR:  C ZIEGLER                                         */
/* VERSION: 07/17/84                                          */
/*                                                            */
/* PROGRAM DESCRIPTION                                        */
/* -------------------------------------------------------- */
/* THIS PROGRAM COPIES A FILE HAVING RECORDS OF 5000          */
/* CHARACTERS                                                 */
/*                                                            */
/* INPUT: OLDFILE - 5000 CHARACTER RECORDS                    */
/*                                                            */
/* OUTPUT: NEWFILE - SAME RECORDS                             */
/*                                                            */
/**************************************************************/
DCL OLDFILE   FILE SEQL INPUT  RECORD ENV (CONSECUTIVE),
    NEWFILE   FILE SEQL OUTPUT RECORD ENV (CONSECUTIVE);
DCL DATA_REC  CHAR(5000)       BASED;
DCL IN_PTR    POINTER,
    OUT_PTR   POINTER,
    MORE_DATA BIT(1);
DCL TRUE      BIT(1)      INIT('1'B),
    FALSE     BIT(1)      INIT('0'B);
```

```
ON ENDFILE (OLDFILE)
  MORE_DATA = FALSE;

MORE_DATA = TRUE;
OPEN FILE (OLDFILE),
     FILE (NEWFILE);
READ FILE (OLDFILE) SET (IN_PTR);
DO WHILE (MORE_DATA);
  LOCATE DATA_REC FILE (NEWFILE) SET (OUT_PTR);
  OUT_PTR->DATA_REC = IN_PTR->DATA_REC;
  READ FILE (OLDFILE) SET (IN_PTR);
END;
CLOSE FILE (OLDFILE),
      FILE (NEWFILE);
END COPY;
```

If move-mode processing were used, a data storage area of 5000 bytes would be used, besides the two buffers of 5000 or more bytes each. With locate-mode processing, only the two buffers are needed.

15.6.3 Revising a file

The following example creates a new file from a file that contains inactive records, leaving them out. The records to be deleted can be identified by the value '(8)1'B in the first byte.

```
REVISE: PROC OPTIONS (MAIN);
/**************************************************************/
/*                                                            */
/* PROGRAM: CREATE A NEW VERSION OF A FILE                    */
/* AUTHOR:  C ZIEGLER                                         */
/* VERSION: 07/17/84                                          */
/*                                                            */
/* PROGRAM DESCRIPTION                                        */
/* ---------------------------------------------------------- */
/* THIS PROGRAM COPIES A CONSECUTIVE FILE, REMOVING           */
/* RECORDS THAT HAVE BEEN MARKED AS INACTIVE                  */
/*                                                            */
/* INPUT: OLDFILE - MASTER FILE                               */
/*                  COL      1 RECORD TYPE                    */
/*                       2 - 80 INFORMATION                   */
/*                                                            */
/* OUTPUT: NEWFILE - NEW VERSION OF MASTER FILE               */
/*                                                            */
/**************************************************************/
DCL OLDFILE  FILE SEQL INPUT  RECORD ENV (CONSECUTIVE),
    NEWFILE  FILE SEQL OUTPUT RECORD ENV (CONSECUTIVE);
DCL 1 FILE_REC,
      5 REC_TYPE  BIT(8),
      5 REC_INFO  CHAR (79);
```

```
DCL INACTIVE       BIT(8)      INIT ('(8)1'B);
DCL MORE_DATA      BIT(1),
    TRUE           BIT(1)      INIT('1'B),
    FALSE          BIT(1)      INIT('0'B);

ON ENDFILE (OLDFILE)
  MORE_DATA = FALSE;

MORE_DATA = TRUE;
OPEN FILE (OLDFILE),
     FILE (NEWFILE);
READ FILE (OLDFILE) INTO (FILE_REC);
DO WHILE (MORE_DATA);
  IF REC_TYPE ¬= INACTIVE
    THEN
      WRITE FILE (NEWFILE) FROM (FILE_REC);
  READ FILE (OLDFILE) INTO (FILE_REC);
END;
CLOSE FILE (OLDFILE),
      FILE (NEWFILE);
END REVISE;
```

15.6.4 Master file update (record modification)

Sequential-access disk files can be updated in place, unlike other sequential-access files. Updating is similar to file merging. However, the RECORD update algorithm differs from the STREAM update algorithm of section 10.6.4 (chapter 10), which created a new file, in that only those master records that have been modified need to be rewritten. A flag is used to indicate whether the record has been changed. Also, when the transaction file ends, there is no reason to process the rest of the master file.

Since the master file is being updated in place, it is opened for UPDATE. For simplification, only record modifications are included in this decision table and program. It is assumed that there are no "inactive" or "deleted" records in the file. The program updates the master record by subtracting an amount from the balance in the master record for each transaction.

T_key = HIGH	Y	Y	N	N	N	N
M_key = HIGH	—	—	N	N	N	—
M_key < T_key	—	—	Y	Y	N	N
M_key = T_key	—	—	N	N	Y	N
M_key > T_key	N	N	N	N	N	Y
Record changed	Y	N	Y	N	—	N
"Record not found"						X
Modify record					X	
Rewrite master file	X		X			
Change flag = true					X	
Change flag = false			X			
Read master file			X	X		
Read transaction file					X	X
Repeat			X	X	X	X
Exit	X	X				

This decision table differs from that of section 10.6.4 only in that the repetition is controlled by the transaction file and those master records not changed are not rewritten. All the transactions must be processed. If the master file ends first, an error message must be written for any remaining transactions. If the transaction file ends first, the remaining master records do not need to be processed since the file is not being copied.

The hierarchy chart of figure 15–1 differs from that of figure 10–9 only in that the writing of the master record is conditional. The writing takes place only if the master record has been changed.

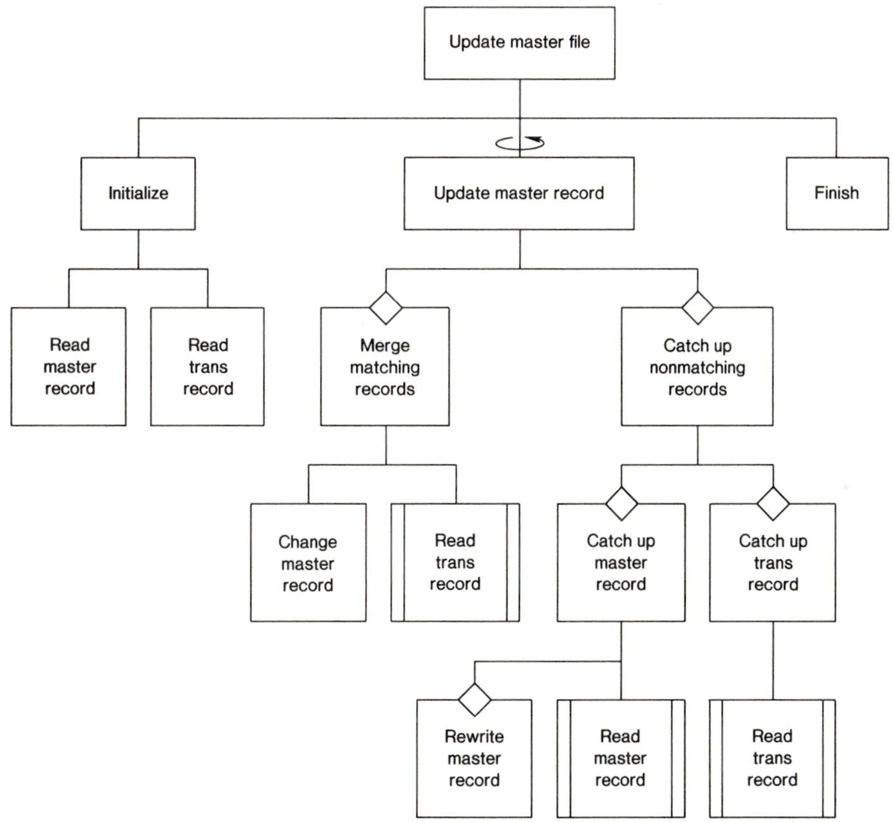

Figure 15–1

```
UPDATE: PROC OPTIONS (MAIN);
/****************************************************************/
/*                                                              */
/* PROGRAM: UPDATE A SEQUENTIAL FILE                            */
/* AUTHOR:  C ZIEGLER                                           */
/* VERSION: 07/17/84                                            */
/*                                                              */
/* PROGRAM DESCRIPTION                                          */
/* -----------------------------------------------------------  */
```

```
/* THIS PROGRAM UPDATES A SEQUENTIAL DISK FILE. IT       */
/* IS ASSUMED BOTH INPUT FILES ARE IN THE SAME ORDER,    */
/* SORTED ON THE KEY FIELD. THE BALANCED LINE ALGOR-     */
/* ITHM IS USED.                                         */
/*                                                       */
/* INPUT: MAST - MASTER FILE                             */
/*                 COLS 1 -  8 KEY VALUE                 */
/*                      9 - 20 ACCOUNT BALANCE           */
/*        TRANS - TRANSACTION FILE                       */
/*                 COLS 1 -  8 KEY VALUE                 */
/*                      9 - 16 AMOUNT                    */
/*                                                       */
/* OUTPUT: MAST - UPDATED MASTER FILE                    */
/*         SYSPRINT - ERROR LISTING                      */
/*                                                       */
/*******************************************************/
DCL MAST           FILE SEQL UPDATE RECORD ENV (CONSECUTIVE),
    TRANS          FILE SEQL INPUT  RECORD ENV (CONSECUTIVE);
DCL 1  M_REC,
       5  M_KEY    CHAR(8),
       5  M_BAL    PIC 'S(10)9V99';
DCL 1  T_REC,
       5 T_KEY     CHAR(8),
       5 T_AMT     PIC '(6)9V99';
DCL CHANGED        BIT(1),
    MORE_T         BIT(1),
    MORE_M         BIT(1),
    TRUE           BIT(1)    INIT('1'B),
    FALSE          BIT(1)    INIT('0'B);


ON ENDFILE (MAST)
  BEGIN;
    MORE_M = FALSE;
    M_KEY = HIGH(8);
  END;
ON ENDFILE (TRANS)
  BEGIN;
    MORE_T = FALSE;
    T_KEY = HIGH(8);
  END;
MORE_M = TRUE;
MORE_T = TRUE;
CHANGED = FALSE;
OPEN FILE (MAST),
     FILE (TRANS);
READ FILE (MAST) INTO (M_REC);
READ FILE (TRANS) INTO (T_REC);
DO WHILE (MORE_T);                /* PROCESS ALL TRANSACTIONS */
  SELECT;
    WHEN (M_KEY < T_KEY)          /* MASTER FILE LAGS BEHIND  */
      DO;
```

```
        IF CHANGED
          THEN
            DO;
              REWRITE FILE (MAST) FROM (M_REC);
              CHANGED = FALSE;
            END;
        READ FILE (MAST) INTO (M_REC);
      END;
    WHEN (M_KEY = T_KEY)        /* FILES MATCH                    */
      DO;
        M_BAL = M_BAL - T_AMT; /* PROCESS MODIFICATIONS          */
        CHANGED = TRUE;
        READ FILE (TRANS) INTO (T_REC);
      END;
    WHEN (M_KEY > T_KEY)        /* TRANSACTION FILE LAGS BEHIND */
      DO;
        PUT SKIP LIST ('INVALID KEY - ', T_KEY);
        READ FILE (TRANS) INTO (T_REC);
      END;
  END;
END;
IF CHANGED
  THEN
    REWRITE FILE (MAST) FROM (M_REC);
CLOSE FILE (MAST),
      FILE (TRANS);
END UPDATE;
```

15.6.5 Master file update (record insertion, modification, and deletion)

The following decision table is an adaptation of the decision table of section 15.6.4, modified to include a transaction code in each transaction record and all three types of file updates: record insertion, record modification, and record deletion. It updates master records by subtracting an amount from a

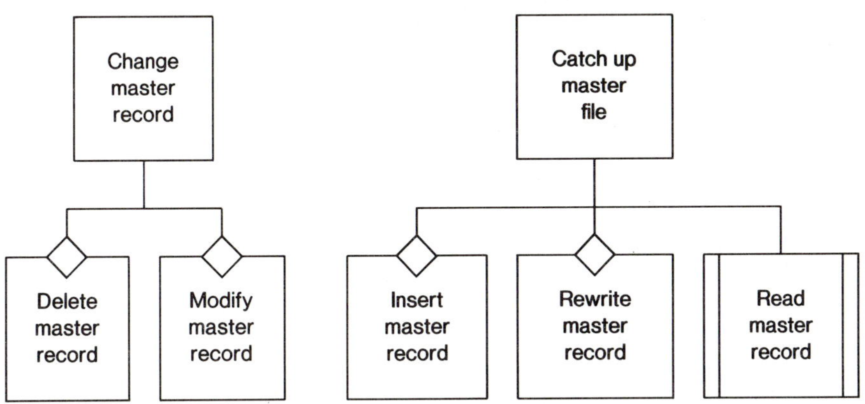

Figure 15–2

balance in the master record for each transaction that modifies the record. It deletes a record by placing '(8)1'B in the record type field.

T_key = HIGH	Y	Y	N	N	N	N	N	N	N	N	N	N
M_key = HIGH	—	—	N	N	N	N	N	N	N	—	—	—
M_key < T_key	—	—	Y	Y	N	N	N	N	N	N	N	—
M_key = T_key	—	—	N	N	Y	Y	Y	Y	Y	N	N	—
M_key > T_key	N	N	N	N	N	N	N	N	N	Y	Y	—
Code = insertion	*	*	—	—	Y	Y	N	N	N	Y	N	N
Code = modification	*	*	—	—	N	N	—	Y	N	N	—	N
Code = deletion	*	*	—	—	N	N	—	N	Y	N	—	N
Record "inactive"	—	—	—	—	Y	N	Y	N	N	—	—	—
Record changed	Y	N	Y	N	—	—	—	—	—	N	N	—
"Invalid code"												X
"Record missing"							X				X	
"Duplicate record"						X						
Modify record					X			X				
Mark "inactive"									X			
Write insertion file										X		
Change flag = true					X			X	X			
Change flag = false			X									
Rewrite Master_file	X		X									
Read master file			X	X								
Read transaction file					X	X	X	X	X	X	X	X
Repeat			X	X	X	X	X	X	X	X	X	X
Exit	X	X										

Two flags are used, one for a deleted or inactive record, the other for a changed record. The inactive flag is the first byte of the record itself. The change flag is not part of the record but indicates any change to the record that must be rewritten to the file. This includes freshly deleted records as well as modified records.

The program handles the insertions by writing them to a new transaction file, which can be merged with the master file at a later time, unless there already was an inactive record with the same key. In that case the new record replaces the inactive record.

For this problem, the lower levels of the hierarchy chart of figure 15–1 should be expanded, as in figure 15–2. Since records are being deleted, when a transaction matches a record already in memory, it is necessary to check whether it is an active record. In the following program, notice the redefinition of the last field of the transaction record to provide for two different record structures.

```
UPDATE: PROC OPTIONS (MAIN);
/*************************************************************/
/*                                                           */
/* PROGRAM: UPDATE A SEQUENTIAL FILE                         */
/* AUTHOR:  C ZIEGLER                                        */
/* VERSION: 07/17/84                                         */
/*                                                           */
/* PROGRAM DESCRIPTION                                       */
/* --------------------------------------------------------- */
/* THIS PROGRAM UPDATES A SEQUENTIAL DISK FILE.              */
/* IT MODIFIES RECORDS AND MARKS RECORDS AS DELETED.         */
```

```
/* INSERTIONS ARE NOT PROCESSED, BUT ARE WRITTEN TO     */
/* A SEPARATE FILE. IT IS ASSUMED BOTH INPUT FILES      */
/* ARE IN THE SAME ORDER, SORTED ON THE KEY FIELDS.     */
/*                                                      */
/* ALGORITHM: BALANCED LINE                             */
/*                                                      */
/* INPUT: MAST - MASTER FILE                            */
/*                COLS      1  RECORD TYPE              */
/*                     2 -  9 KEY VALUE                 */
/*                    10 - 20 ACCOUNT BALANCE           */
/*        TRANS - TRANSACTION FILE                      */
/*                COLS      1  RECORD TYPE              */
/*                              'I' FOR INSERTION       */
/*                              'D' FOR DELETION        */
/*                              'M' FOR MODIFICATION    */
/*                     2 -  9 KEY VALUE                 */
/*                    10 - 20 ACCOUNT BALANCE ('I')     */
/*                    10 - 16 AMOUNT ('M')              */
/*                                                      */
/* OUTPUT: MAST - UPDATED MASTER FILE                   */
/*         INSERT - INSERTION FILE                      */
/*         SYSPRINT - ERROR LISTING                     */
/*                                                      */
/********************************************************/
DCL MAST           FILE SEQL UPDATE RECORD ENV (CONSECUTIVE),
    TRANS          FILE SEQL INPUT  RECORD ENV (CONSECUTIVE),
    INSERT         FILE SEQL OUTPUT RECORD ENV (CONSECUTIVE);
DCL 1  M_REC,
       5  M_TYPE   BIT(8),
       5  M_KEY    CHAR(8),
       5  M_BAL    PIC '(9)SV99';
DCL 1  T_REC,
       5  T_TYPE   CHAR(1),
       5  T_KEY    CHAR(8),
       5  T_BAL    PIC '(9)SV99',
          T_AMT    PIC '(5)9V99'  DEF (T_BAL);
DCL CHANGED        BIT(1),
    MORE_T         BIT(1),
    MORE_M         BIT(1),
    TRUE           BIT(1)         INIT('1'B),
    FALSE          BIT(1)         INIT('0'B);
DCL INACTIVE       BIT(8)         INIT ('(8)1'B);

ON ENDFILE (MAST)
  BEGIN;
    MORE_M = FALSE;
    M_KEY = HIGH(8);
  END;
ON ENDFILE (TRANS)
  BEGIN;
    MORE_T = FALSE;
    T_KEY = HIGH(8);
  END;
```

```
MORE_M = TRUE;
MORE_T = TRUE;
CHANGED = FALSE;
OPEN FILE (MAST),
     FILE (TRANS),
     FILE (INSERT);
READ FILE (MAST) INTO (M_REC);
READ FILE (TRANS) INTO (T_REC);
DO WHILE (MORE_T);               /* PROCESS ALL TRANSACTIONS   */
  SELECT;
    WHEN (M_KEY < T_KEY)         /* MASTER FILE LAGS BEHIND    */
      DO;
        IF CHANGED
          THEN
            DO;
              REWRITE FILE (MAST) FROM (M_REC);
              CHANGED = FALSE;
            END;
        READ FILE (MAST) INTO (M_REC);
      END;
    WHEN (M_KEY = T_KEY)         /* FILES MATCH               */
      DO;
        SELECT;
          WHEN (T_TYPE = 'I')    /* PROCESS REPLACEMENT       */
            IF M_TYPE = INACTIVE
              THEN
                DO;
                  M_REC = T_REC;
                  CHANGED = TRUE;
                END;
              ELSE
                PUT SKIP LIST ('DUPLICATE RECORD - ',T_KEY);
          WHEN (T_TYPE = 'M')    /* PROCESS MODIFICATION       */
            IF M_TYPE = INACTIVE
              THEN
                PUT SKIP LIST ('RECORD MISSING - ',T_KEY);
              ELSE
                DO;
                  M_BAL = M_BAL - T_AMT;
                  CHANGED = TRUE;
                END;
          WHEN (T_TYPE = 'D')    /* PROCESS DELETION           */
            IF M_TYPE = INACTIVE
              THEN
                PUT SKIP LIST ('RECORD MISSING - ',T_KEY);
              ELSE
                DO;
                  M_TYPE = INACTIVE;
                  CHANGED = TRUE;
                END;
          OTHERWISE
            PUT SKIP LIST ('INVALID TRANS CODE - ',T_KEY);
        END;
```

```
          READ FILE (TRANS) INTO (T_REC);
        END;
      WHEN (M_KEY > T_KEY)          /* TRANSACTION FILE LAGS BEHIND */
        DO;
          IF T_TYPE = 'I'           /* PROCESS INSERTION            */
            THEN
              WRITE FILE (INSERT) FROM (T_REC);
            ELSE
              PUT SKIP LIST ('RECORD MISSING - ',T_KEY);
          READ FILE (TRANS) INTO (T_REC);
        END;
    END;
  END;
IF CHANGED
  REWRITE FILE (MAST) FROM (M_REC);
CLOSE FILE (MAST),
      FILE (TRANS),
      FILE (INSERT);
END UPDATE;
```

15.7 Summary

CONSECUTIVE files are used for data that does not need to be processed randomly. This includes temporary data such as transaction files and semipermanent data such as nonvolatile master files, which can be updated in place or are used primarily for writing reports. While CONSECUTIVE is a file organization and SEQUENTIAL is a mode of processing that can be used with various file organizations, programs written for CONSECUTIVE files can be transferred with few changes to other types of files.

CONSECUTIVE files provide the most efficient way to organize the disk if space is at a premium. SEQUENTIAL processing is the most efficient way to process a disk file if time is at a premium and the file or files are in the desired order.

The basic file maintenance operations are to insert, modify, and delete records. With CONSECUTIVE RECORD files, records may be modified and deleted without creating a new version of the file. This is not possible with STREAM files. RECORD processing provides efficiency. Since STREAM processing, depending on the implementation, cannot be used with other types of files, programs using RECORD processing are more adaptable.

The standard file-merging algorithm used in the sort program of section 10.6.3 is the basis for the file-update algorithm of section 15.6.5. The sort of that section can be used with RECORD files as well as STREAM files. The balanced line-update algorithm used in section 15.6.5 is the basis for all sequential updating algorithms.

15.8 Exercises

1. Write a program that uses a driver to call external procedures. One procedure should create a CONSECUTIVE RECORD file of fixed length

records from a STREAM file having information of the form:

n_1 $X(1)$ $X(2)$ . . . $X(n_1)$

n_2 $x(1)$ $X(2)$ . . . $X(n_2)$

. . . $n_1, n_2, \ldots < 20$

The other procedure should list the file.

2. Adapt the sort program of section 10.6.3 to RECORD files.

3. Write a program that merges two RECORD files, MASTER and NEW, which have records of the form:

Cols.		
	1-5	Student ID
	6-80	Student information

Both files have been sorted in ascending order on the ID field. Create a new master RECORD file NEWMAST. Neither file contains duplicates, but there may be some IDs that occur in both files. If so, put the record from MASTER in NEWMAST and write the duplicate to a printer file DUPL.

4. Write a program that prints a report from two RECORD files, BOOK, which has the form:

Cols.		
	1-10	ISBN
	11-20	Library of Congress number
	21-40	Author
	41-60	Title
	61-64	Edition

and CIRCUL, which has the form:

Cols.		
	1-10	Library of Congress number
	11-12	Copy
	13-32	Borrower
	33	Status ('C' checked out, 'O' overdue, 'L' lost, 'B' bindery, 'S' shelved, 'X' unknown)

Assume that the files are both in ascending order by Library of Congress number. Assume that the file BOOK is correct and does not contain duplicates. The file CIRCUL may contain duplicate key values. The report should list each BOOK record for which there are CIRCUL records, along with the CIRCUL records. If the status field does not contain a valid code, give it the code 'X'. The output should be readable.

5. Write a program that reads records from a file TEXT and replaces every occurrence of the word "computer" with the word "processor." The records are of varying length, with a maximum size of eighty characters. The program should rewrite the records in the file, moving words from one record to the next, if necessary, to make them fit.

6. Adapt the program of section 15.6.5 for a transaction file that includes many insertions and only a few deletions and modifications. Instead of modifying the file and writing the insertions to a separate file, create a new version of the master file, inserting the new records and deleting those that are to be deleted. At the same time, print a list of all the records being deleted.

16
Indexed files

OBJECTIVE: To access data efficiently both sequentially and randomly.

INDEXED FILES ARE THE simplest type of direct-access file to use. Basically they are files that contain records having unique keys which can be used to store and retrieve the records. An index of the keys is automatically built when the file is created, and updated when records are inserted or deleted. When a record is accessed using direct access, the index is searched for the key, the address of the record found, and the record retrieved. This is all done automatically. Since indexed files are designed for direct access, they must be placed on mass storage devices such as the disk.

There are many variations on the index idea; consideration of these variations is beyond the scope of this book. The file organization introduced in this chapter deals with data that is accessed either by means of the index, or sequentially.

16.1 File organization

The logical organization of an indexed file is shown in figure 16–1. Each block of data contains many records. In the figure there are three data blocks each of which can hold five records. Each of the three data blocks has one or more empty record positions. The index, a single block, is full. The records are arranged in alphabetical order. In this example, the record keys are shown as single letters, with one index entry for each block. The highest key in the block and a pointer to the block are stored in each index entry. The extra space in the blocks is used when new records are inserted. With an insertion or deletion, the records are moved around so that the new record is placed in the correct position to maintain the sorted order.

The index is used in direct access and skip-sequential access but ignored in straight-sequential access.

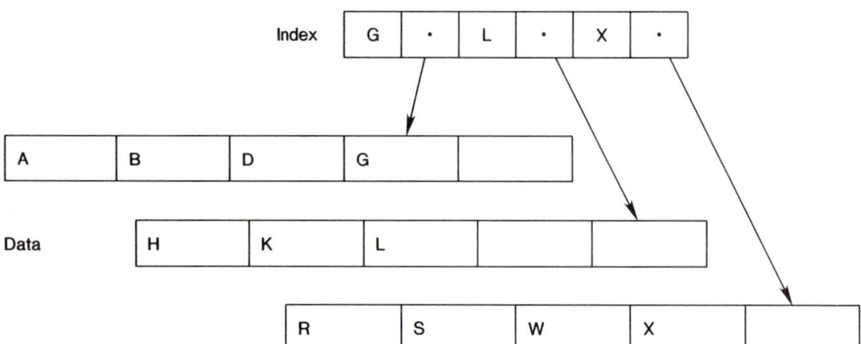

Figure 16–1

16.1.1 Storage

Physically the file is divided into three parts: the index, the data area, and an overflow area. When a data block is full, any extra data is stored in the overflow area, as shown in figure 16–2. Overflow data decreases the efficiency of the file, because accessing data in the overflow area requires more disk accesses than data in the regular data area.

In figure 16–2 the file of figure 16–1 is shown after records M, O, P, Z, Y, and Q have been added. Two of the blocks are full and the extra records that would not fit have been placed in the overflow area. The data blocks are chained to the overflow area. The records in the overflow area are chained so that any record can be found by following the correct pointer from the index, scanning the block, and if necessary, scanning the overflow chain. Overflow records are not blocked. Note that the records shown in a data block and the attached overflow chain are in alphabetical order.

When space is allocated for an indexed file and the file is first created, it

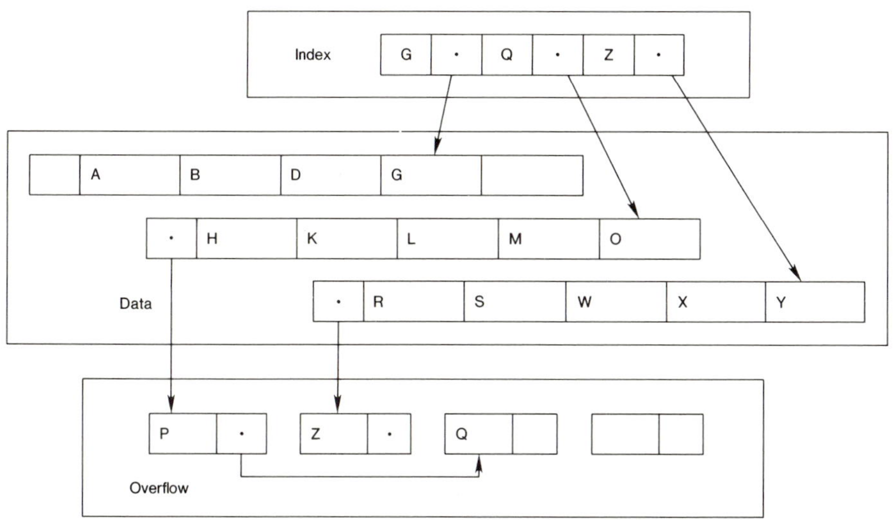

Figure 16–2

should be set up so that the keys are representative of the final range of keys and sufficient space has been left unused. This decreases the need for overflow storage.

16.1.2 Keys

With indexed files, the keys must be unique character values. They may have digits, letters, or any characters of the PL/I character set. However, special characters are not usually used since their position in the collating sequence differs from one character code to another. Since names are not always unique, IDs are usually assigned for use as keys. Automobile license numbers, Social Security numbers, and account numbers are examples of typical keys.

Keyed data may be stored on a file either in entry order or in key order. *Entry order* is the order in which the data is written to the file; *key order* is the collating sequence order applied to the record keys. Indexed files are created in entry order and listed in key order. So that the order is correct for sequential processing, key order and entry order must be the same with indexed sequential files. That is, a file must be originally created from records that have been sorted in key order. For other types of indexed files, key order and entry order may be different.

With some implementations, keys must be embedded in the records as part of the record data. With other file management system software they are stored separately.

Review questions

1. One common type of indexed file is divided physically into three areas, for ____________________, ____________________, and ____________________.

2. Records may be retrieved from indexed files using either ________ or ________ access.

3. When an indexed sequential file is created, the records must be in key order because ________.

4. An efficient indexed file has very few records in the ________ area.

5. When an indexed file is created, extra space must be available for ________ of records.

16.2 INDEXED file declarations

In most implementations, indexed sequential files can be used only for RECORD processing. They may be accessed using either sequential or direct access, and unlike consecutive files, records may actually be inserted and deleted. The general form of the file declaration is:

```
DCL file_name FILE [KEYED] [mode] [use] RECORD ENV(INDEXED);
```

The mode may be SEQUENTIAL or DIRECT. The use may be INPUT, OUTPUT, or UPDATE. The KEYED attribute is not used for ordinary sequential processing. A file is declared as KEYED only when the keys are being used in the access. Keys must be used when the file is first created so that the index can be set up. The keys must also be used for direct access and one form of skip-sequential access.

16.2.1 SEQUENTIAL processing

Indexed files may be used for sequential processing in exactly the same way consecutive disk files are used.

UNKEYED

Following are examples of declarations of unkeyed sequential-indexed files:

```
DCL INFILE  FILE SEQL INPUT  RECORD ENV(INDEXED);
DCL OUTFILE FILE SEQL OUTPUT RECORD ENV(INDEXED);
DCL MASTERF FILE SEQL UPDATE RECORD ENV(INDEXED);
```

These files are indistinguishable from CONSECUTIVE RECORD files. They can be processed with the algorithms of section 15.6 but cannot be processed using direct access or using keys. Even if the files were previously created using the KEYED attribute, the keys and index are ignored with these declarations.

KEYED

Following are examples of the declaration of indexed files for sequential access using the KEYED option:

```
DCL INFILE  FILE KEYED SEQL INPUT  RECORD ENV(INDEXED);
DCL OUTFILE FILE KEYED SEQL OUTPUT RECORD ENV(INDEXED);
DCL MASTERF FILE KEYED SEQL UPDATE RECORD ENV(INDEXED);
```

Sequential access of a KEYED file means that the records must be accessed in order, but that some of the records may be skipped. With each READ or WRITE statement a key is provided to indicate which record is wanted. Intervening records are ignored. This is a variation of skip-sequential processing with the records identified by key rather than by counting. Both types of skip-sequential processing may be used with indexed files.

Keyed skip-sequential processing may be used to list all the records from a section of the indexed file. On some systems, the key must be embedded in the information being stored in the file; on others, it may be separate. With embedded keys, the KEYTO option is unnecessary.

An indexed sequential file must be created using the KEYED option so that the index may be set up.

16.2.2 DIRECT processing

Direct processing is used primarily for on-line query systems and on-line updating. When a file is declared as DIRECT, the KEYED option must be specified. The following declarations show the possibilities:

```
DCL IN_FILE   KEYED DIRECT INPUT  RECORD ENV(INDEXED);
DCL OUT_FILE  KEYED DIRECT OUTPUT RECORD ENV(INDEXED);
DCL MAST_FILE KEYED DIRECT UPDATE RECORD ENV(INDEXED);
```

With direct access, all input/output statements must include a key. The keys may be processed in any order. When the keys have been sorted, keyed sequential processing should be used for efficiency. When they have not been sorted or only a few scattered master records are needed, direct processing should be used.

Review questions

1. If an INDEXED file is declared without the KEYED attribute, it is processed in the same way as a (an) ____________ file.

2. A KEYED INDEXED file must be keyed for sequential OUTPUT when ____________.

3. Write a declaration for the indexed file IN_F, sections of which are to be read.

4. Write a declaration for the indexed file OUT_F, which is to have records inserted on-line.

5. Write a declaration for the indexed file INFO, which is to be queried on-line.

6. When records are read sequentially from an INDEXED file which does not use embedded keys, the ____________________ option should be used.

16.3 File availability

An indexed file is made accessible by opening it and inaccessible by closing it.

16.3.1 OPEN statement

The general form of the OPEN statement is:

```
OPEN FILE (file_name) [mode] [use] [TITLE (title)];
```

The mode and use options of the OPEN statement are specified when the file declaration does not contain the necessary information. There is no access option, as the file must have RECORD access. The title option is used to associate the file name with a name known to the operating system.

16.3.2 CLOSE statement

The general form of the CLOSE statement is:

```
CLOSE FILE (file_name);
```

Closing an indexed file that has been open for sequential OUTPUT causes an end-of-file record to be written.

Review questions

1. Indicate whether each of the following statements is true or false.
   (a) The OPEN statement makes an INDEXED file accessible.
   (b) The TITLE option of the OPEN statement is required.
   (c) The CLOSE statement always causes an end-of-file to be written.
   (d) An INDEXED file may be OPENed with the PRINT option.
   (e) An INDEXED file may be OPENed as a STREAM file.

2. Write OPEN statements for an INDEXED file that is to be created and listed in the same program.

3. Write OPEN statements for an INDEXED file that is to be queried on-line and updated on-line in the same program.

16.4 Record access

The input/output statements used with indexed files are READ, WRITE, LOCATE, REWRITE, and DELETE.

16.4.1 Input statements

Sequential input may be keyed or unkeyed. It may be in move mode, locate mode, or skip-sequential mode. The READ statement for indexed files has five possible forms:

```
READ FILE (file_name) INTO (variable) [KEY (expression)];
READ FILE (file_name) INTO (variable) [KEYTO (variable)];
READ FILE (file_name) SET (pointer) [KEY (expression)];
READ FILE (file_name) SET (pointer) [KEYTO (variable)];
READ FILE (file_name) IGNORE (expression);
```

The use of these statements without the key clause is similar to their use with CONSECUTIVE files.

The KEY clause of the READ statement indicates to the computer the record wanted from the file. The KEYTO clause is used to retrieve a record key from the file along with the key when sequential processing is used.

Only one type of READ statement, move mode, is available for direct input. The record key must be provided.

MOVE-MODE PROCESSING

The READ . . . INTO forms of the input statement are used for move-mode processing. The statement

```
READ FILE (MASTER) INTO (MAST_REC);
```

obtains the next record in sequence from the buffer and stores it in MAST_REC. The ENDFILE condition is raised when the end-of-file record is read.

The following program segment shows the basic steps in reading and listing an indexed file sequentially without using keys.

```
READ FILE (MASTER) INTO (MAST_REC);
DO WHILE (MORE_DATA);
  PUT SKIP LIST (MAST_REC);
  READ FILE (MASTER) INTO (MAST_REC);
END;
```

This same program segment can be used with CONSECUTIVE files.

The statement

```
READ FILE (MASTER) INTO (MAST_REC) KEY (M_KEY);
```

obtains the record having its key equal to the value of M_KEY and stores it in MAST_REC. M_KEY must have a valid character value at the time this statement is executed. If it does not, the KEY condition is raised. The KEY condition is also raised if the record is not found.

The following example shows the basic steps in using the key to selectively read and list the file.

```
GET EDIT (M_KEY) (COL(1),A(8));
DO WHILE (MORE_KEYS);
  READ FILE (MASTER) INTO (MAST_REC) KEY (M_KEY);
  PUT SKIP LIST (MAST_REC);
  GET EDIT (M_KEY) (COL(1),A(8));
END;
```

A key value is obtained from an input stream for each record to be read from the indexed file. With sequential processing, these key values must be in the same order as the records in the file, otherwise the KEY condition is raised. With direct processing, the keys may be in any order. The KEY condition is also raised if there is a key for which no record can be found.

The statement

```
READ FILE (MASTER) INTO (MAST_REC) KEYTO (M_KEY);
```

is used with sequential processing to obtain the next record in sequence from the buffer and store it in MAST_REC. The computer stores the record key in M_KEY. The ENDFILE condition is raised when the end-of-file record is read.

The following example shows the basic steps in listing the records between two specific keys where the first key must actually be that of a record in the file, but the last key may be anything higher in the collating sequence.

```
GET EDIT (FIRST_KEY,LAST_KEY) (A(8),A(8));
M_KEY = FIRST_KEY;
READ FILE (INXFILE) INTO (DATA_REC) KEY (M_KEY);
DO WHILE (M_KEY <= LAST_KEY & MORE_DATA);
  PUT SKIP LIST (DATA_REC);
  READ FILE (MASTER) INTO (MAST_REC) KEYTO (M_KEY);
END;
```

If the keys were names, the first key could be 'Esterhazy, Philip' and the last one might be 'M '. Then, starting with the record for Philip Esterhazy, all the records in the file through the Ls would be printed.

In this example, the READ statement with the KEY option provides a key to the file software and requests the matching record. The READ statement with the KEYTO option requests the next record in sequence and its key. The record is retrieved and placed in MAST_REC and the key is placed in M_KEY. If LAST_KEY is higher than any key in the file, the loop terminates with the ENDFILE condition.

All three forms of the move-mode READ statement are used with sequential processing. With direct processing the KEY clause must be used.

LOCATE-MODE PROCESSING

The READ. . .SET forms of the input statement provide locate-mode processing. The statement

```
READ FILE (MASTER) SET (P);
```

moves the file pointer down the buffer to the next record position and stores the memory address of that position in P. P must be a pointer variable. If there is a based variable associated with P, this statement superimposes the based variable on the record position in the buffer. The use of this statement for sequential processing of indexed files is the same as its use with CONSECUTIVE files.

The statement

```
READ FILE (MASTER) SET (P) KEY (M_KEY);
```

moves the file pointer to the position of the record having its key equal to the value of M_KEY and stores the memory address of that position in P. The KEY condition is raised if there is no record with that key. This form of the statement may be used for skip-sequential processing or direct processing.

The statement

```
READ FILE (MASTER) SET(P) KEYTO (M_KEY);
```

moves the file pointer to the next record position, stores the memory address of that position in P, and stores the key of the record in that position in M_KEY. This form of the statement is used only with sequential processing when the record keys are not embedded.

UNKEYED SKIP-SEQUENTIAL PROCESSING (not in Subset G)

When skip-sequential processing is available with an indexed file, it takes two forms. A key may be used to locate the starting position for the processing, or a number may be used as with a CONSECUTIVE file. The READ. . .IGNORE form of the input statement, as in

```
READ FILE (MASTER) IGNORE (9);
```

moves the file pointer ahead nine record positions without transmitting any data to the program. It is then ready to read the tenth record. The ENDFILE condition is raised when the end-of-file record is read.

16.4.2 Output statements

The general forms of the output statements are:

```
WRITE FILE (file_name) FROM (var) KEYFROM (expr);
LOCATE based_var FILE (file_name) [KEYFROM (expr)]
                      [SET (pointer)];
REWRITE FILE (file_name) [FROM (var)] [KEY (expr)];
DELETE FILE (file_name) [KEY (expr)];
```

These statements are used for move-mode, locate-mode, and update-mode processing.

MOVE-MODE PROCESSING

The WRITE. . .FROM form of output provides move-mode processing. The statement

```
WRITE FILE (MASTER) FROM (MAST_REC) KEYFROM (M_KEY);
```

causes the value of the record MAST_REC to be written to the file using the key value M_KEY. It is placed in a position such that the order of the keys is preserved. The KEY condition is raised if there already is a record with that key in the file. The KEYFROM clause is needed with indexed files as a record cannot be stored properly unless its key is known.

The WRITE statement is used both in creating an indexed file and in adding records to an already existing file. The basic steps in creating a file are shown in the following program segment:

```
GET EDIT (M_KEY,MAST_REC) (A(8),A(72));
DO WHILE (MORE_DATA);
  WRITE FILE (MASTER) FROM (MAST_REC) KEYFROM (M_KEY);
  GET EDIT (M_KEY,MAST_REC) (A(8),A(72));
END;
```

This program segment may be used with files declared as KEYED SEQL OUTPUT, KEYED SEQL UPDATE, or KEYED DIRECT UPDATE.

LOCATE-MODE PROCESSING (not in Subset G)

The LOCATE form of output, for example,

```
DCL PTR_REC CHAR(40) BASED (P);
LOCATE PTR_REC FILE (MASTER);
```

causes the file pointer to move to the next record position in the output buffer. The memory address of that position is stored in the pointer P. It sets aside the space required for the record description PTR_REC in the buffer, but does not store any data in the buffer. Notice that PTR_REC must be a based variable with an associated pointer.

The statement

```
LOCATE PTR_REC FILE (MASTER) SET (Q);
```

moves the file pointer to the next record position in the output buffer, sets aside the space required for the record description PTR_REC at that position, and stores the memory address of the position in Q. It does not store any data in the buffer.

When a key is used, the locate-mode statement takes the form

```
LOCATE PTR_REC FILE (MASTER) KEYFROM (M_KEY);
```

or

```
LOCATE PTR_REC FILE (MASTER) KEYFROM (M_KEY) SET (P);
```

UPDATE-MODE PROCESSING

The update statements REWRITE and DELETE can be used only on devices that support random access, such as the disk.

REWRITE statement The REWRITE statement takes three forms:

```
REWRITE FILE (MASTER);
REWRITE FILE (MASTER) FROM (MAST_REC);
REWRITE FILE (MASTER) FROM (MAST_REC) KEY (M_KEY);
```

Without the FROM clause, the REWRITE statement causes the most recently read record to be written back to its previous position in the file. If the record has been changed, the new version replaces the old version.

The unkeyed form of the REWRITE. . .FROM statement causes the most recently read record to be replaced in the file by the record MAST_REC. The keyed form of the REWRITE. . .FROM statement replaces the record in the file with key value M_KEY with the record MAST_REC. The KEY condition is raised if there is no record in the file with that key.

Without the KEY clause, the REWRITE statement can be used only for processing of SEQL UPDATE files. With the KEY clause, the statement is used either for processing of SEQL UPDATE files or processing of DIRECT UPDATE files.

DELETE statement Both forms of the DELETE statement effectively remove a record from the file.

```
DELETE FILE (MASTER);
DELETE FILE (MASTER) KEY (M_KEY);
```

Without the KEY CLAUSE, the DELETE statement deletes the most recently read record of the file. With the KEY clause, it deletes the record from the file specified by M_KEY. If there is no record with that key in the file, the KEY condition is raised.

Review questions

1. No KEY clause is used on a REWRITE or DELETE statement for sequential I/O because ____________________.
2. DIRECT OUTPUT files are not possible because ____________________.
3. The same KEY clause is used for READ, REWRITE, and DELETE because they all ____________________.
4. The two forms of skip sequential processing use a (an) ____________________ clause and a (an) ____________________ clause on the READ statement.
5. The KEY condition is raised with an OUTPUT INDEXED file when ____________________.
6. The KEY condition is raised with an INPUT INDEXED file when ____________________.

16.5 File error conditions

File error conditions were discussed in detail in section 14.5. The ENDFILE and KEY conditions are the most useful conditions for indexed files.

All file processing error condition ON units must be identified with particular files. ON units for the same condition can be established for different files, and different ON units can be established for a single file.

ENDFILE CONDITION

The ENDFILE condition is raised by sequential processing when there is an attempt to read beyond the end of the data. The use of the condition is the same with all types of files. With indexed files it can be raised only by a READ statement for a file declared to be SEQUENTIAL INPUT.

KEY CONDITION

The KEY condition is raised by sequential processing when keys are not used in order, when a record cannot be found, or when a key does not have a valid character value. With direct processing, the order of the keys is not important. This is summarized in table 16–1.

Table 16–1

Statement	*Meaning of key condition*
READ . . . KEY . . .	Invalid key or record missing
REWRITE . . . KEY . . .	"
DELETE . . . KEY . . .	"
READ . . . KEYTO . . .	Key conversion error
WRITE . . . KEYFROM . . .	Invalid key, duplicate key, [key out of order]
LOCATE . . . KEYFROM . . .	"

The meaning of the KEY exception depends on the operation being attempted. Note in table 16–1 that the keyword used in the key option indicates the error category.

The library function ONKEY may be used to print the value of an invalid key. This is shown in the following example:

```
ON KEY (DATA_FILE)
  BEGIN;
    PUT SKIP LIST ('INVALID KEY - ',ONKEY);
    KEY_ERROR = TRUE;
  END;
```

The different meanings of the KEY condition can be distinguished by looking at the value returned by the library function ONCODE. This is shown in the following example:

```
ON KEY (DATA_FILE)
  BEGIN;
    PUT SKIP LIST ('KEY ERROR - ',ONCODE);
    KEY_ERROR = TRUE;
  END;
```

The set of error codes is implementation-dependent and can be found in a reference manual for the particular version of PL/I used.

PROGRAMMING HINT: An ON unit for the KEY condition is needed for each KEYED file.

Review questions

1. The ENDFILE condition can be raised only if the INDEXED file has the ____________________ and ____________________ attributes.

2. The KEY condition can be raised only if the INDEXED file has the ____________________ attribute.

3. The library function ONKEY, used with the KEY condition, contains the value of ____________________.

4. The library function ONCODE, used with the KEY condition, indicates ____________________.

5. If the KEY condition is raised by a READ statement it usually means that ____________________.

6. If the KEY condition is raised by a WRITE statement it usually means that ____________________.

7. If the KEY condition is raised by a REWRITE statement it usually means that ____________________.

8. If the KEY condition is raised by a DELETE statement it usually means that ____________________.

16.6 File maintenance

Indexed files which are to be used for direct access must be created using keyed-sequential access with the records in key order. A file may then be updated using either sequential processing or direct processing.

To insert a new record, the WRITE statement is used. If there already is a record in the file with the same key, the KEY condition is raised. It is not necessary to check for the presence of a record with that key before writing the new one. The basic steps used to insert a record in an indexed file are:

1. Get the new record.
2. Write it to the file.

An example of this is:

```
GET LIST (KEY_VALUE,DATA_REC);
WRITE FILE (MASTER) FROM (DATA_REC) KEYFROM (KEY_VALUE);
```

To delete a record, the DELETE statement is used. If sequential processing is being used, the basic steps are:

1. Get the key of the record being deleted.
2. Check whether the record is in the file.
3. Delete it.

An example of this is:

```
ON KEY (MASTER)
  RECORD_FOUND = FALSE;
RECORD_FOUND = TRUE;
GET LIST (KEY_VALUE);
READ FILE (MASTER) INTO (DATA_REC) KEY (KEY_VALUE);
IF RECORD_FOUND
  THEN
    DELETE FILE (MASTER);
```

The record must be read before it is deleted as no key clause is used in the DELETE statement. The KEY condition is raised by the READ statement if the file does not contain a record with that key.

The READ statement is not needed when a record is being deleted using direct access. Then the basic steps are simply:

1. Get the key.
2. Delete the record.

For example,

```
GET LIST (KEY_VALUE);
DELETE FILE (MASTER) KEY (KEY_VALUE);
```

When a record is to be modified using sequential processing, it must be read first. Assume the field ADDR of a record is being changed. Then the basic steps are:

1. Get the changes.
2. Get the record to be changed.
3. Make the modification.
4. Rewrite the record.

For example,

```
ON KEY (MASTER)
  RECORD_FOUND = FALSE;
RECORD_FOUND = TRUE;
GET LIST (KEY_VALUE,NEW_ADDR);
READ FILE (MASTER) INTO (DATA_REC) KEY (KEY_VALUE);
IF RECORD_FOUND
  THEN
    DO;
      ADDR = NEW_ADDR;
      REWRITE FILE (MASTER) FROM (DATA_REC);
    END;
```

The REWRITE statement does not use a key, because the record is to replace the record that was read most recently. The KEY condition is raised if the READ statement requests a record that is not in the file.

When a record is being modified using direct processing, the REWRITE statement must be preceded by a READ statement if only part of the record is being changed. The basic steps are the same as for sequential processing except that the key clause is needed. This is shown in the following program segment:

```
ON KEY (MASTER)
  RECORD_FOUND = '0'B;
RECORD_FOUND = '1'B;
GET LIST (KEY_VALUE,NEW_ADDR);
READ FILE (MASTER) INTO (DATA_REC) KEY (KEY_VALUE);
IF RECORD_FOUND
  THEN
    DO;
      ADDR = NEW_ADDR;
      REWRITE FILE (MASTER) FROM (DATA_REC) KEY (KEY_VALUE);
    END;
```

If the entire record is being replaced, the REWRITE statement can be used without the preceding READ statement, as in the following program segment:

```
GET LIST (KEY_VALUE,NEW_DATA);
REWRITE FILE (MASTER) FROM (NEW_DATA) KEY (KEY_VALUE);
```

The KEY condition is raised if there is no record in the file with that key.

PROGRAMMING HINT: WARNING The key field of a record must not be changed when a record is modified.

When the file is open for sequential update, the READ, REWRITE, and DELETE statements may be used. Records cannot be inserted, but they may be modified using REWRITE or deleted using DELETE. Neither REWRITE nor DELETE uses a KEY clause with sequential processing. The record being rewritten or deleted is the last one previously read. The REWRITE statement replaces the record; the DELETE statement marks it as deleted. With indexed files, when a record has been deleted it can no longer be retrieved. The system automatically checks records for the deletion mark and ignores them.

With direct update, records may be read and then rewritten or deleted, or they may be rewritten or deleted without previous reading. The key clause is required. Also, new records may be written to the file.

Review questions

1. The ____________________ statement is used to insert a new record.

2. The ____________________ statement is used to replace a record.

3. The ____________________ and ____________________ statements are used to modify a record.

4. With sequential access, the ____________________ and ____________________ statements are both needed to delete a record.

5. With direct access, the ____________________ statement is used to delete a record.

6. Write a segment of code to delete a record that has key '12345' from file INFO.
   (a) Use sequential access.
   (b) Use direct access.

16.7 Examples using indexed files

The examples in this section provide a representative sample of creating, updating, and processing indexed files using sequential and direct access, move-mode, locate-mode, and skip-sequential processing.

16.7.1 Listing a file (sequential)

The following example shows the listing of an indexed file using sequential access.

```
LIST: PROC OPTIONS (MAIN);
/**********************************************************/
/*                                                        */
/* PROGRAM: LIST AN INDEXED FILE                          */
/* AUTHOR:  C ZIEGLER                                     */
/* VERSION: 07/17/84                                      */
/*                                                        */
/* PROGRAM DESCRIPTION                                    */
/* -----------------------------------------------------  */
/* THIS PROGRAM LISTS AN INDEXED FILE                     */
/*                                                        */
/* INPUT: DATAF - 80 CHARACTER RECORDS                    */
/*                                                        */
/* OUTPUT: SYSPRINT - LISTING OF THE RECORDS              */
/*                                                        */
/**********************************************************/
DCL DATAF           FILE SEQL  INPUT RECORD ENV(INDEXED);
DCL STR             CHAR(80);
DCL MORE_DATA       BIT(1),
    TRUE            BIT(1)     INIT('1'B),
    FALSE           BIT(1)     INIT('0'B);

ON ENDFILE (DATAF)
  MORE_DATA = FALSE;

MORE_DATA = TRUE;
OPEN FILE (DATAF);
READ FILE (DATAF) INTO (STR);
```

```
DO WHILE (MORE_DATA);
  PUT SKIP LIST (STR);
  READ FILE (DATAF) INTO (STR);
END;
CLOSE FILE (DATAF);
END LIST;
```

The only difference between this program and a program to list a CONSECUTIVE file is the declared file organization. The file is not declared as KEYED because all the records are being read in the order in which they are stored. They are in key-sequence order, but the key is not needed to retrieve them. As with other types of files, when sequential processing is used, the ENDFILE condition is raised when the end-of-file has been read.

16.7.2 Listing a file (skip sequential)

If the file is to be listed using the KEYED option, keys must be provided from another file. This type of skip-sequential processing is shown in the following program.

```
LIST: PROC OPTIONS (MAIN);
/**********************************************************/
/*                                                        */
/* PROGRAM: SELECTIVELY LISTS AN INDEXED FILE             */
/* AUTHOR:  C ZIEGLER                                     */
/* VERSION: 07/17/84                                      */
/*                                                        */
/* PROGRAM DESCRIPTION                                    */
/* ------------------------------------------------------ */
/* THIS PROGRAM LISTS SELECTED RECORDS FROM AN            */
/* INDEXED FILE.                                          */
/*                                                        */
/* INPUT: SYSIN - COLS 1 -  8 KEY VALUE                   */
/*              SORTED BY ASCENDING KEY VALUE             */
/*        DATAF - INDEXED FILE                            */
/*                COLS 1 -  8 KEY VALUE                   */
/*                     9 - 80 RECORD INFORMATION          */
/*                                                        */
/* OUTPUT: SYSPRINT - RECORDS MATCHING KEYS               */
/*                                                        */
/**********************************************************/
DCL DATAF      FILE KEYED SEQL INPUT RECORD ENV(INDEXED);
DCL DATA_REC        CHAR(80),
    KEY_WANTED      CHAR(8);
DCL MORE_DATA       BIT(1),
    RECORD_FOUND    BIT(1),
    TRUE            BIT(1)     INIT('1'B),
    FALSE           BIT(1)     INIT('0'B);

ON ENDFILE (SYSIN)
  MORE_DATA = FALSE;
```

```
ON KEY(DATAF)
  BEGIN;
    PUT SKIP LIST ('RECORD NOT FOUND -',KEY_WANTED);
    RECORD_FOUND = FALSE;
  END;

MORE_DATA = TRUE;
RECORD_FOUND = TRUE;
OPEN FILE (DATAF);
GET EDIT (KEY_WANTED) (COL(1),A(8));
DO WHILE (MORE_DATA);
  READ FILE (DATAF) INTO (DATA_REC) KEY (KEY_WANTED);
  IF RECORD_FOUND
    THEN
      PUT SKIP LIST (DATA_REC);
    ELSE
      RECORD_FOUND = TRUE;
  GET EDIT (KEY_WANTED) (COL(1),A(8));
END;
CLOSE FILE (DATAF);
END LIST;
```

The KEY condition is raised if the record requested is not present or if the key is invalid, that is, not character, or out of order.

The two types of sequential input may be combined to read just part of a file. In the following example, the keys of the first and last records wanted are read from SYSIN. Those records and all records between them are listed from the data file.

```
LIST: PROC OPTIONS (MAIN);
/************************************************************/
/*                                                          */
/* PROGRAM: LISTS PART OF AN INDEXED FILE                   */
/* AUTHOR:  C ZIEGLER                                       */
/* VERSION: 07/17/84                                        */
/*                                                          */
/* PROGRAM DESCRIPTION                                      */
/* ------------------------------------------------------- */
/* THIS PROGRAM LISTS RECORDS STARTING WITH A GIVEN         */
/* KEY, FROM AN INDEXED FILE.                               */
/*                                                          */
/* INPUT: SYSIN - COLS 1 -  8 FIRST KEY VALUE               */
/*                     9 - 16 LAST KEY VALUE                */
/*        DATAF - INDEXED FILE                              */
/*                COLS 1 -  8 FIRST KEY VALUE               */
/*                     9 - 80 RECORD INFORMATION            */
/*                                                          */
/* OUTPUT: SYSPRINT - LISTING OF RECORDS FROM FIRST         */
/*          THROUGH LAST KEY VALUE, INCLUSIVE               */
/*                                                          */
/************************************************************/
```

```
DCL DATAF      FILE  KEYED SEQL INPUT RECORD ENV(INDEXED);
DCL DATA_REC         CHAR(80),
    FIRST_KEY        CHAR(8),
    LAST_KEY         CHAR(8);
DCL RECORD_FOUND     BIT(1),
    MORE_DATA        BIT(1),
    REC_KEY          CHAR(8);
DCL TRUE             BIT(1)      INIT('1'B),
    FALSE            BIT(1)      INIT('0'B);

ON ENDFILE (DATAF)
  MORE_DATA = FALSE;
ON KEY(DATAF)
  BEGIN;
    PUT SKIP LIST ('RECORD NOT FOUND -',FIRST_KEY);
    RECORD_FOUND = FALSE;
  END;
MORE_DATA = TRUE;
RECORD_FOUND = TRUE;
OPEN FILE (DATAF);
GET EDIT (FIRST_KEY,LAST_KEY) (COL(1),A(8),A(8));
READ FILE (DATAF) INTO (DATA_REC) KEY (FIRST_KEY);
REC_KEY = FIRST_KEY;
IF RECORD_FOUND
  THEN
    DO WHILE (MORE_DATA & REC_KEY <= LAST_KEY);
      PUT SKIP LIST (DATA_REC);
      READ FILE (DATAF) INTO (DATA_REC) KEYTO (REC_KEY);
    END;
CLOSE FILE (DATAF);
END LIST;
```

ON units are established for both the KEY and ENDFILE conditions for DATAF. If the key for the starting record for the listing is invalid, the KEY condition is activated. The ENDFILE condition is raised when the end-of-file record has been read.

16.7.3 Listing a file (direct)

This program lists selected records from an indexed file, using DIRECT access.

```
LIST: PROC OPTIONS (MAIN);
/*************************************************************/
/*                                                           */
/* PROGRAM: SELECTIVELY LISTS AN INDEXED FILE                */
/* AUTHOR:  C ZIEGLER                                        */
/* VERSION: 07/17/84                                         */
/*                                                           */
/* PROGRAM DESCRIPTION                                       */
/* ------------------------------------------------------    */
```

```
/* THIS PROGRAM LISTS SELECTED RECORDS FROM AN              */
/* INDEXED FILE.                                            */
/*                                                          */
/* INPUT: SYSIN - COLS 1 -  8 KEY VALUE                     */
/*                SORTED BY KEY VALUE                       */
/*        DATAF - INDEXED FILE                              */
/*                COLS 1 -  8 KEY VALUE                     */
/*                     9 - 80 RECORD INFORMATION            */
/*                                                          */
/* OUTPUT: SYSPRINT - RECORDS MATCHING KEYS                 */
/*                                                          */
/************************************************************/
DCL DATAF        FILE KEYED DIRECT INPUT RECORD ENV(INDEXED);
DCL DATA_REC     CHAR(80),
    KEY_WANTED   CHAR(8);
DCL MORE_DATA    BIT(1),
    RECORD_FOUND BIT(1),
    TRUE         BIT(1)     INIT('1'B),
    FALSE        BIT(1)     INIT('0'B);

ON ENDFILE (SYSIN)
  MORE_DATA = FALSE;
ON KEY (DATAF)
  BEGIN;
    PUT SKIP LIST ('RECORD NOT FOUND -',KEY_WANTED);
    RECORD_FOUND = FALSE;
  END;

MORE_DATA = TRUE;
RECORD_FOUND = TRUE;
OPEN FILE (DATAF);
GET EDIT (KEY_WANTED) (COL(1),A(8));
DO WHILE (MORE_DATA);
  READ FILE (DATAF) INTO (DATA_REC) KEY (KEY_WANTED);
  IF RECORD_FOUND
    THEN
      PUT SKIP LIST (DATA_REC);
    ELSE
      RECORD_FOUND = TRUE;
  GET EDIT (KEY_WANTED) (COL(1),A(8));
END;
CLOSE FILE (DATAF);
END LIST;
```

By changing the processing mode to SEQL, this program could be used for skip-sequential processing. With skip-sequential processing the keys to the records wanted must be in order; the KEY condition is raised if they are out of order. With DIRECT processing they may be in any order. With both types of processing, the KEY condition is raised if the record is missing.

16.7.4 Creating a file

An indexed sequential file must be created using the KEYED option. The following example shows the file being created using SEQL OUTPUT.

```
CREATE: PROC OPTIONS (MAIN);
/************************************************************/
/*                                                          */
/* PROGRAM: CREATE AN INDEXED FILE                          */
/* AUTHOR:   C ZIEGLER                                      */
/* VERSION: 07/17/84                                        */
/*                                                          */
/* PROGRAM DESCRIPTION                                      */
/* -------------------------------------------------------- */
/* THIS PROGRAM CREATES AN INDEXED FILE                     */
/*                                                          */
/* INPUT: SYSIN - COLS 1 THRU 8  KEY VALUE                  */
/*                     9 THRU 80 DATA                       */
/*          RECORDS IN ASCENDING ORDER BY KEY VALUE         */
/* OUTPUT: DATAF - INDEXED FILE                             */
/*                                                          */
/************************************************************/
DCL DATAF      FILE   KEYED SEQL OUTPUT RECORD ENV(INDEXED);
DCL 1 DATA_REC,
      5 DATA_KEY      CHAR(8),
      5 DATA_INFO     CHAR(72);
DCL MORE_DATA         BIT(1),
    TRUE              BIT(1)      INIT('1'B),
    FALSE             BIT(1)      INIT('0'B);

ON ENDFILE (SYSIN)
  MORE_DATA = FALSE;
ON KEY (DATAF)
  PUT SKIP LIST ('SEQUENCE ERROR - ',DATA_KEY);

MORE_DATA = TRUE;
OPEN FILE (DATAF);
GET EDIT (DATA_REC) (COL(1),A(80));
DO WHILE (MORE_DATA);
  WRITE FILE (DATAF) FROM (DATA_REC) KEYFROM (DATA_KEY);
  GET EDIT (DATA_REC) (COL(1),A(80));
END;
CLOSE FILE (DATAF);
END CREATE;
```

This program differs from a consecutive file creation program in that the file is declared as KEYED and the key is referenced in the WRITE statement. The keys are used to check the order of the records and to build the index. The KEY condition is raised if a record is out of order, if a duplicate key is found, or if the key is invalid.

Some file management software requires space to be set aside for an

INDEXED file in advance of the initial data being loaded in the file. If this is the case, the file should be declared as UPDATE rather than OUTPUT in the file creation program.

16.7.5 Master file update (record modification, skip-sequential processing)

If the records in an indexed file are blocked and there are transactions to be processed for a large fraction of the records, sequential updating is the most efficient. If there are few transactions, direct processing is the most efficient. In the following decision table it is assumed that the transaction records have been sorted and that there may be master records with no transactions and others with one or more transactions.

This algorithm assumes that there are priming reads of both files and that the old key is initialized to the key value from the priming transaction. The only type of updating included is the modification of records.

T-eof	Y	N	N	N
Record found	—	Y	*	N
Old key = new key	*	Y	N	Y
"Record not found"				X
Modify record		X		
Rewrite record	X		X	
Old key = new key			X	
Read T_file		X		X
Read M_file			X	
Repeat		X	X	X
Exit	X			

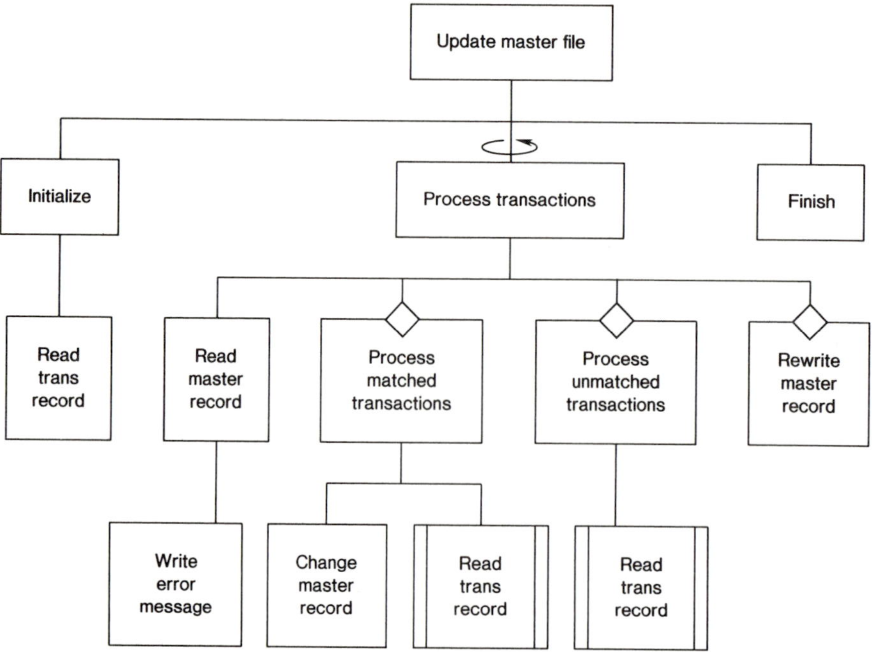

Figure 16–3

"Record found" means that the record matching the current transaction is already in the memory. "Old key ¬= new key" means that a new master record is needed.

The hierarchy chart of figure 16–3 differs from the chart of figure 15–1 because only master records for which there are transactions are read.

```
UPDATE: PROC OPTIONS (MAIN);
/**********************************************************/
/*                                                        */
/* PROGRAM: UPDATES AN INDEXED FILE                       */
/* AUTHOR:   C ZIEGLER                                    */
/* VERSION: 07/17/84                                      */
/*                                                        */
/* PROGRAM DESCRIPTION                                    */
/* ---------------------------------------------------    */
/* THIS PROGRAM MODIFIES RECORDS OF AN INDEXED FILE       */
/* USING SKIP SEQUENTIAL PROCESSING.                      */
/*                                                        */
/* INPUT: TRANSF - COLS 1 -  8 KEY VALUE                  */
/*                       9 - 20 ACCOUNT BALANCE           */
/*        MASTERF - COLS 1 -  8 KEY VALUE                 */
/*                        9 - 16 TRANSACTION AMOUNT       */
/*                                                        */
/* OUTPUT: UPDATED MASTER FILE                            */
/*                                                        */
/**********************************************************/
DCL MASTERF       FILE KEYED SEQL   UPDATE RECORD ENV(INDEXED),
    TRANSF        FILE SEQL  INPUT  RECORD ENV(CONSECUTIVE);
DCL 1 M_REC,
      5 M_KEY     CHAR(8),
      5 M_BAL     PIC 'S(10)9V99';
DCL 1 T_REC,
      5 T_KEY     CHAR(8),
      5 T_AMT     PIC '(6)9V99';
DCL RECORD_FOUND BIT(1),
      MORE_T      BIT(1),
      OLD_KEY     CHAR(8);
DCL   TRUE        BIT(1)       INIT('1'B),
      FALSE       BIT(1)       INIT('0'B);

ON KEY (MASTERF)
  BEGIN;
    PUT SKIP LIST ('RECORD NOT FOUND - ',T_KEY);
    RECORD_FOUND = FALSE;
  END;
ON ENDFILE (MASTERF)
  BEGIN;
    PUT SKIP LIST ('RECORD NOT FOUND - ',T_KEY);
    RECORD_FOUND = FALSE;
  END;
```

```
 ON ENDFILE (TRANSF)
   BEGIN;
     MORE_T = FALSE;
     T_KEY = HIGH(8);
   END;

MORE-T = TRUE;
RECORD_FOUND = TRUE;
OPEN FILE (MASTERF),
     FILE (TRANSF);
READ FILE (TRANSF) INTO (T_REC);
OLD_KEY = T_KEY;
DO WHILE (MORE_T);                        /* PROCESS ALL TRANSACTIONS */
  READ FILE(MASTERF) INTO(M_REC) KEY (T_KEY); /* GET MASTER RECORD    */
  IF RECORD_FOUND
    THEN
      DO;
        DO WHILE(OLD_KEY = T_KEY); /* PROCESS TRANSACTIONS FOR MASTER */
          M_BAL = M_BAL - T_AMT;
          READ FILE (TRANSF) INTO (T_REC);
        END;
        REWRITE FILE (MASTERF) FROM (M_REC);
      END;
    ELSE
      DO;
        DO WHILE (OLD_KEY = T_KEY); /* SKIP TRANSACTIONS FOR MISSING*/
          READ FILE (TRANSF) INTO (T_REC); /* MASTER RECORD           */
        END;
        RECORD_FOUND = TRUE;
      END;
   OLD_KEY = T_KEY;
END;
CLOSE FILE (MASTERF),
      FILE (TRANSF);
END UPDATE;
```

This program could be used for direct processing by changing the master file access mode to DIRECT and omitting the ON ENDFILE(MASTERF) exception handler.

16.7.6 Master file update (record modification, direct access)

If only a few transactions are to be processed against a master file, direct processing is the most efficient. In the following decision table it is assumed that the transaction records have not been sorted. Because of this, no provision is made for processing more than one transaction per master record.

T-eof	Y	N	N
Record found	*	Y	N
"Record not found"			X
Modify record		X	
Rewrite record		X	
Read T_file		X	X
Read M_file		X	X
Repeat		X	X
Exit	X		

Since direct access is being used and the transactions are not sorted, the master file is read every time the transaction file is read. The hierarchy chart of figure 16–4 differs from that of figure 16–3 in this respect.

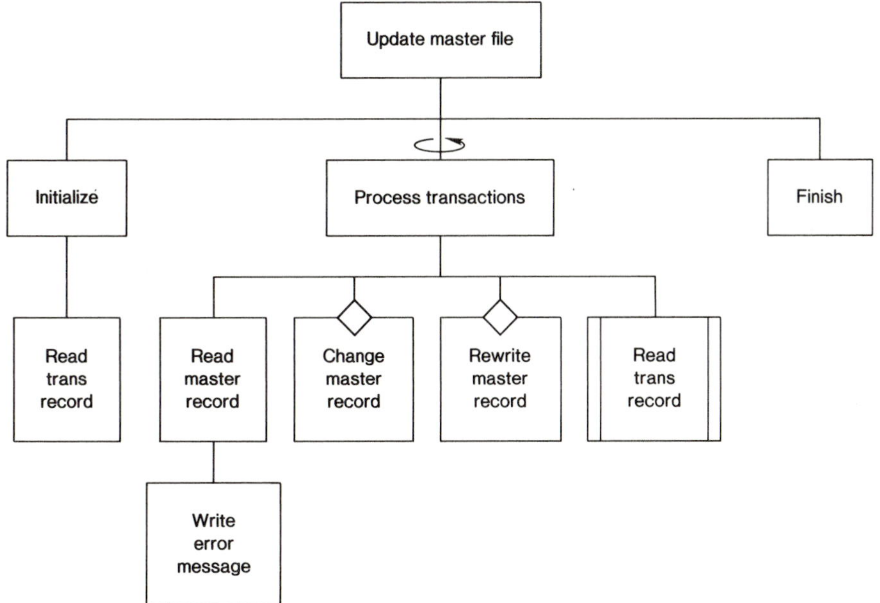

Figure 16–4

With DIRECT access, no key comparisons are necessary; the computer retrieves only the records wanted. The master records are updated by subtracting an amount from the balance for each transaction. It is assumed that this is the only type of transaction. The program is as follows:

```
UPDATE: PROC OPTIONS (MAIN);
/*****************************************************************/
/*                                                               */
/* PROGRAM: UPDATES AN INDEXED FILE                              */
/* AUTHOR:  C ZIEGLER                                            */
/* VERSION: 07/17/84                                             */
/*                                                               */
/* PROGRAM DESCRIPTION                                           */
/* ---------------------------------------------------------     */
```

```
/* THIS PROGRAM MODIFIES RECORDS OF AN INDEXED FILE    */
/* USING DIRECT ACCESS.                                */
/*                                                     */
/* INPUT: TRANSF - COLS 1 -  8 KEY VALUE               */
/*                      9 - 20 ACCOUNT BALANCE         */
/*       MASTER F - COLS 1 -  8 KEY VALUE              */
/*                        9 - 16 TRANSACTION AMOUNT    */
/*                                                     */
/* OUTPUT: UPDATED MASTER FILE                         */
/*                                                     */
/*******************************************************/
DCL MASTERF       FILE KEYED DIRECT UPDATE RECORD ENV(INDEXED),
    TRANSF        FILE SEQL   INPUT  RECORD ENV(CONSECUTIVE);
DCL 1  M_REC,
       5 M_KEY    CHAR(8),
       5 M_BAL    PIC '(10)S9V99';
DCL 1  T_REC,
       5 T_KEY    CHAR(8),
       5 T_AMT    PIC '(6)9V99';
DCL RECORD_FOUND BIT(1),
       MORE_T     BIT(1),
       TRUE       BIT(1),       INIT('1'B),
       FALSE      BIT(1),       INIT('0'B);


ON KEY (MASTERF)
  BEGIN;
    RECORD_FOUND = FALSE;
    PUT SKIP LIST ('RECORD NOT FOUND - ',T_KEY);
  END;
ON ENDFILE (TRANSF)
      MORE_T = FALSE;


MORE-T = TRUE;
RECORD_FOUND = TRUE;
OPEN FILE (MASTERF),
     FILE (TRANSF);
READ FILE (TRANSF) INTO (T_REC);
DO WHILE (MORE_T);                  /* PROCESS ALL TRANSACTIONS */
  RECORD_FOUND = TRUE;
  READ FILE (MASTERF) INTO (M_REC) KEY (T_KEY);
  IF RECORD_FOUND
    THEN
      DO;
        M_BAL = M_BAL - T_AMT;        /* MODIFY MASTER RECORD     */
        REWRITE FILE (MASTERF) FROM (M_REC) KEY (T_KEY);
      END;
    ELSE
      RECORD_FOUND = TRUE;
  READ FILE (TRANSF) INTO (T_REC);
END;
```

```
CLOSE FILE (MASTERF),
      FILE (TRANSF);
END UPDATE;
```

16.7.7 Master File Update (record insertion, modification, deletion)

The following decision table shows the complete master file update for indexed files using direct processing. It is assumed that the transaction file has not been sorted. The transaction code indicates whether a record is to be inserted, modified, or deleted.

The program updates the master record by subtracting an amount from a balance in the master record for each transaction. Insertions and deletions are possible with direct processing. It is not necessary to check first for the presence of the record before an insertion or deletion is carried out. The hierarchy chart of figure 16–5 is similar to that of figure 16–4, with the addition of the extra file operations.

The decision table does not show the error processing, which is based on the results of attempting to insert, modify, or delete records.

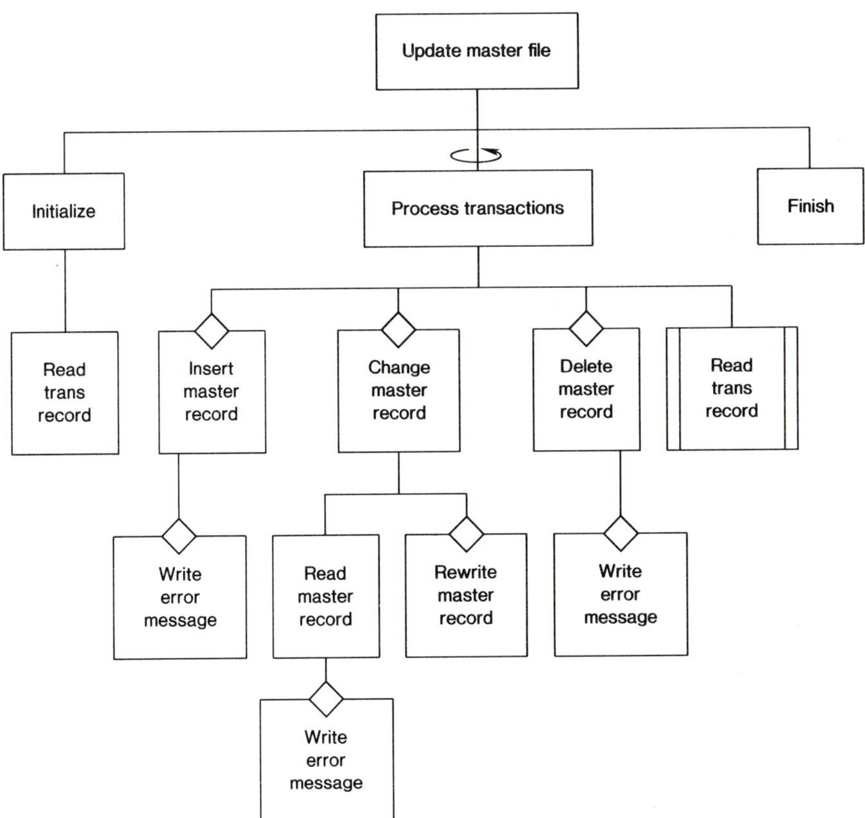

Figure 16–5

T_eof	Y	N	N	N	N
Code = insertion	*	Y	N	N	N
Code = modification	*	N	Y	N	N
Code = deletion	*	N	N	Y	N
"Invalid code"					X
Modify record			X		
Insert T_rec		X			
Delete M_rec				X	
Read T_file		X	X	X	X
Repeat		X	X	X	X
Exit	X				

This algorithm would be used for on-line updating of the file, as shown in the following program.

```
UPDATE: PROC OPTIONS(MAIN);
/************************************************************/
/*                                                          */
/* PROGRAM: UPDATE AN INDEXED FILE                          */
/* AUTHOR:  C ZIEGLER                                       */
/* VERSION: 07/17/84                                        */
/*                                                          */
/* PROGRAM DESCRIPTION                                      */
/* -------------------------------------------------------- */
/* THIS PROGRAM UPDATES AN INDEXED DISK FILE.  IT           */
/* INSERTS RECORDS, MODIFIES RECORDS, AND DELETES           */
/* RECORDS USING DIRECT PROCESSING.                         */
/*                                                          */
/* INPUT: MASTERF - AN INDEXED MASTER FILE                  */
/*            COL      1  RECORD CODE                       */
/*                 2 - 9  KEY VALUE                         */
/*                10 - 20 ACCOUNT BALANCE                   */
/*        TRANSF -  THE TRANSACTION FILE                    */
/*            COL      1  TRANSACTION CODE                  */
/*                          'I' FOR INSERTION               */
/*                          'D' FOR DELETION                */
/*                          'M' FOR MODIFICATION            */
/*                 2 - 9  KEY VALUE                         */
/*                10 - 16 AMOUNT                            */
/*                                                          */
/* OUTPUT: UPDATED MASTER FILE                              */
/*                                                          */
/************************************************************/
DCL MASTERF FILE KEYED DIRECT UPDATE RECORD ENV(INDEXED),
    TRANSF  FILE SEQL   INPUT  RECORD ENV(CONSECUTIVE);
DCL 1  M_REC,
       5  M_CODE   CHAR(1),
       5  M_KEY    CHAR(8),
       5  M_BAL    PIC '(9)S9V99';
DCL 1  T_REC,
       5  T_CODE   CHAR(1),
       5  T_KEY    CHAR(8),
       5  T_AMT    PIC '(9)S9V99';
```

```
DCL MORE_T          BIT(1),
    KEY_ERROR       BIT(1),
    TRUE            BIT(1)     INIT('1'B),
    FALSE           BIT(1)     INIT('0'B);

ON KEY (MASTERF)
  KEY_ERROR = TRUE;
ON ENDFILE (TRANSF)
  MORE_DATA = FALSE;

MORE_T = TRUE;
OPEN FILE (MASTERF),
     FILE (TRANSF);
READ FILE (TRANSF) INTO (T_REC);
DO WHILE (MORE_T);                 /* PROCESS ALL TRANSACTIONS */
  SELECT;
    WHEN (T_CODE = 'I')            /* PROCESS INSERTION        */
      DO;
        WRITE FILE (MASTERF) FROM (T_REC) KEYFROM (T_KEY);
        IF KEY_ERROR
          THEN
            DO;
              PUT SKIP LIST ('DUPLICATE RECORD - ',T_KEY);
              KEY_ERROR = FALSE;
            END;
      END;
    WHEN (T_CODE = 'M')            /* PROCESS MODIFICATION     */
      DO;
        READ FILE (MASTERF) INTO (M_REC) KEY (T_KEY);
        IF KEY_ERROR
          THEN
            DO;
              PUT SKIP LIST ('RECORD NOT FOUND - ',T_KEY);
              KEY_ERROR = FALSE;
            END;
          ELSE
            DO;
              M_BAL = M_BAL - T_AMT;  /* MODIFY MASTER RECORD */
              REWRITE FILE (MASTERF) FROM (M_REC) KEY (T_KEY);
            END;
      END;
    WHEN  (T_CODE = 'D')                    /* PROCESS DELETION */
      DO;
        DELETE FILE (MASTERF) KEY (T_KEY);
        IF KEY_ERROR
          THEN
            DO;
              PUT SKIP LIST ('RECORD NOT FOUND - ',T_KEY);
              KEY_ERROR = FALSE;
            END;
      END;
    OTHERWISE
      PUT SKIP LIST ('INVALID TRANS CODE - ',T_KEY);
  END;
```

```
  READ FILE (TRANSF) INTO (T_REC);
END;
CLOSE FILE (TRANSF),
      FILE (MASTERF);
END UPDATE;
```

With direct access, the record can be written or deleted without being read first. For each type of file operation, the KEY exception means the operation was not successful.

16.8 Summary

An INDEXED file is used when both sequential and direct access are needed. The file must be created using the KEYED attribute so that the system can set up the index (or indexes) needed for direct access. After that, sequential access is used when some or all of the records are needed, in key order. If only a few records are needed, direct access is the best. If many of the records are needed, but the transaction file or other accessing list is not in order, it is best to sort it first, then access the INDEXED file sequentially. The three file operations of record insertion, modification, and deletion can be carried out under either sequential or direct access.

The KEYED attribute must be used for direct access. It may be used for sequential access, and should be used if only part of the file is being processed. With the KEYED attribute, the index is used. Otherwise the file is scanned sequentially from the beginning.

The uses of the various file types are:

SEQL INPUT	To write a report from a file.
SEQL OUTPUT	To create a file.
SEQL UPDATE	To update a file when there are many transactions and no insertions. The transactions must be in key order.
DIRECT INPUT	To write a report from selected records.
DIRECT UPDATE	To update a file when there are not very many transactions or there are insertions.

Table 16–2 shows the different possible combinations of file attributes and the input/output statements that may be used with each one. Note that there is no DIRECT OUTPUT.

File attributes	*Valid operations*
SEQUENTIAL INPUT [KEYED]	READ ... INTO ... [KEY ...] READ ... INTO ... [KEYTO ...] READ ... SET ... [KEY ...] READ ... SET ... [KEYTO ...] READ ... IGNORE ...
SEQUENTIAL OUTPUT [KEYED] (not available on some systems)	WRITE ... FROM ... [KEYFROM ...] LOCATE ... [KEYFROM ...] [SET ...]

Table 16–2

File attributes	*Valid operations*
SEQUENTIAL UPDATE [KEYED]	READ ... INTO ... [KEY ...] READ ... INTO ... [KEYTO ...] READ ... SET ... [KEY ...] READ ... SET ... [KEYTO ...] READ ... IGNORE ... REWRITE ... FROM ...] DELETE ...
DIRECT INPUT KEYED	READ ... INTO ... KEY ...
DIRECT UPDATE KEYED	READ ... INTO ... KEY WRITE ... FROM ... KEYFROM ... REWRITE ... FROM ... KEY ... DELETE ... KEY ...

Table 16–2
continued

16.9 Exercises

1. Write a program that merges two RECORD files, MASTER and NEW, which have records of the form:

Cols.	1-5	Student ID
	6-80	Student information

MASTER is an INDEXED file with ID as the key field. NEW is a CONSECUTIVE file which has been sorted in ascending order on the ID field. Insert the records from NEW in MASTER, using skip-sequential processing. Neither file contains duplicates, but there may be some IDs that occur in both files. If so, write the record in NEW to a printer file DUPL. Check on the accuracy of your program by printing the original and the updated master files.

2. Write a program that prints a report from an INDEXED file, BOOK, which has the form:

Cols.	1-10	ISBN
	11-20	Library of Congress number
	21-40	Author
	41-60	Title
	61-64	Edition

which uses the ISBN as the key field, and a CONSECUTIVE file CIRCUL, which has the form:

Cols.	1-10	ISBN
	11-20	Library of Congress number
	21-22	Copy
	23-42	Borrower
	43	Status ('C' checked out, 'O' overdue, 'L' lost, 'B' at bindery, 'S' shelved, 'X' unknown)

and is in ascending order by Library of Congress number. Assume that the file BOOK is correct and does not contain duplicates. The file CIRCUL may contain duplicate key values. The report should list each BOOK record for which there are CIRCUL records, along with the CIRCUL records. If the status field does not contain a valid code, give it the code 'X'. The output should be readable. Use DIRECT access.

3. Write a driver routine and external procedures to create, update, and list an INDEXED file. The original data is on a CONSECUTIVE file SOURCE which has records of the form:

Cols.	1-5	Farm name
	6-12	Location
	13-15	Soil type
	16-20	Plant number
	21-30	Hybrid parentage
	31-80	Experimental information

The records are in ascending order by plant number. One external subroutine should build an INDEXED file HYBRID using the plant number as the key. Another external subroutine should read plant numbers from the unsorted CONSECUTIVE file PLANT, which has records of the form:

Cols.	1-5	Plant number
	6-55	Experimental information

Replace the experimental information stored in the corresponding HYBRID record with the new information. Use DIRECT access. Another external subroutine should list the INDEXED file. Print both the original file and the updated file.

17
Regional files

OBJECTIVE: To randomly access data efficiently.

REGIONAL FILES GIVE THE programmer more control over the positioning of information on the disk than do other file organizations. They are the most efficient file organizations for direct access, but are not usually suitable for sequential access.

There are many different types of REGIONAL files. All use the position of the record in the file as the key for accessing the record, but the details of the different types differ from one implementation of PL/I to another. The only type of regional file we will consider here is the type sometimes known as REGIONAL(1) or relative.

17.1 File organization

A relative file consists of a predetermined number of consecutive record positions. Each record has a relative position in the file, which is used as the key for accessing it; for example, the fifth record can be obtained by writing KEY(5). The position of a record in a file is its *relative record number.* Record numbering starts with zero on some computers and one on others. When there is a record number zero, it is usually used for general information about the file rather than for part of the data.

17.1.1 Storage

The organization of a relative file is shown in figure 17–1. Record positions are numbered, but not all of them contain data. The data used is that of table 17–1.

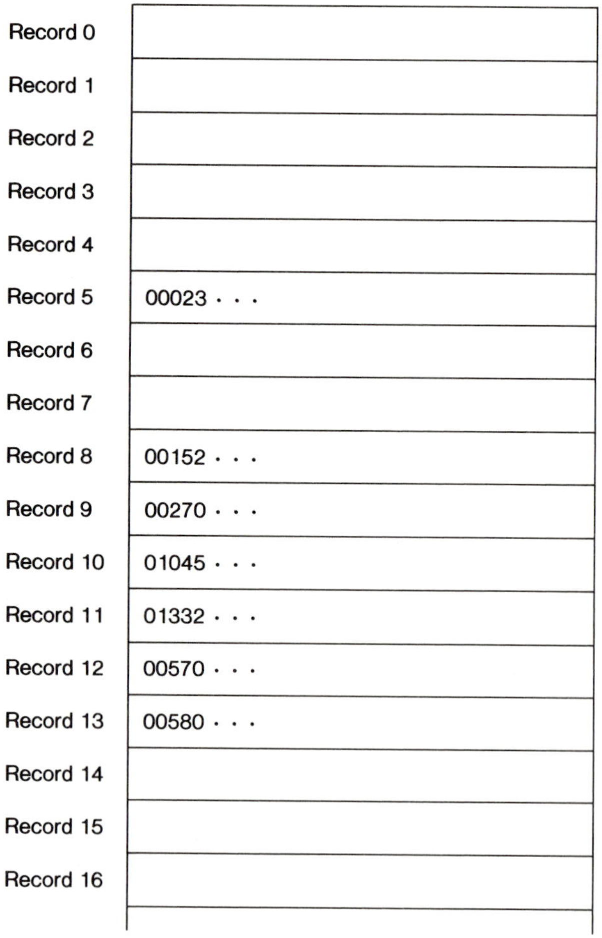

Record 0	
Record 1	
Record 2	
Record 3	
Record 4	
Record 5	00023 . . .
Record 6	
Record 7	
Record 8	00152 . . .
Record 9	00270 . . .
Record 10	01045 . . .
Record 11	01332 . . .
Record 12	00570 . . .
Record 13	00580 . . .
Record 14	
Record 15	
Record 16	

Figure 17–1

As you can see, the records are scattered through the file in an order different from the original order. The numbers shown as part of the records are the symbolic keys.

When a REGIONAL(1) file is created, it is important to allocate more file space than needed and to scatter the records evenly through the space. Unused record positions decrease the probability of attempting to store two records in the same position, and are also available when new records are to be inserted. The position in which each record belongs in the file can be calculated from the symbolic key. With REGIONAL files, duplicate keys are permitted. One way of storing records with duplicate keys is to place each extra record in the first available place beyond the position in which it belongs.

7.1.2 Keys

Keyed data is stored in a regional file in order by relative record number. However, the relative record number is not usually the same as the key of the data record. The key that identifies the data record is called a *symbolic key.* This is usually but not necessarily a unique key, for example, an account number. The key that indicates where the record belongs in the file is the *relative record key.* This is one form of storage key. The *home position* of a record is the position in the file with a relative record number equal to the relative record key, which is derived from the symbolic key. The following samples show some five-digit symbolic keys and different methods of deriving relative record keys from them.

	Relative record key			
Symbolic key	*Entire key*	*Last 2 digits*	*Sum of digits*	*Prime division*
00023	00023	23	5	23
00152	00152	52	8	55
00169	00169	69	16	72
00270	00270	70	9	76
00348	00348	48	15	57
00483	00483	84	15	95
00570	00570	70	12	85
01045	01045	45	10	75
01332	01332	32	9	71

Table 17–1

Table 17–1 shows that there are drawbacks and problems with the selection of a method for obtaining a record position from the symbolic key. If the entire key is used, the order of the records is preserved, but if only a few of the possible keys are assigned, there may be many unused record positions. The data of table 17–1 only uses 9 of 1332 possible record positions. However, if all the possible keys are assigned, there is no room for insertions. If the symbolic key is truncated or condensed, the resulting relative record keys may not preserve the original record order. Also, some of the numbers may be duplicates.

The method used to produce a relative record key from a symbolic key is known as a *hashing algorithm*. Almost any formula that gives values in the range of the file relative record numbers can be used. Ideally, the relative record keys produced should be scattered throughout the range of possible values, with no duplicates. Table 17–1 shows three different hashing algorithms applied to the same set of symbolic keys. Since what is best for one set of keys is not necessarily best for another, finding a good hashing algorithm for a set of data is a trial-and-error situation. Testing hashing algorithms is part of the design of a regional file system. Every program that uses a regional file must include the relative record key calculations.

Generally the prime division algorithm provides a good distribution of relative record keys for a random set of symbolic keys. The prime division method uses a prime number slightly less than the amount of space set aside for the file. In this example, the prime number is 97. Each symbolic key is divided by the prime number and the remainder is used as the relative record key.

The data of table 17–1 uses 9 of 100 possible record positions when the last two digits of the symbolic key are used as the relative record key. It uses 9 of 50 possible positions if the sum of the digits is used, and 9 of 98 possible positions when prime division is used, with 97 as the prime divisor.

The relative record key is not always the same as the relative record number for a record. In figure 17–1, the sum of digits method was used to position the data. Note that the record with the symbolic key 01332 has relative record key 9, but relative record number 11. That is, it is in position 11 although it belongs in position 9, its home position. The record in record position 9 also has 9 as its relative record key. The record with the duplicate key is stored after its home position.

Review questions

1. Indicate whether each of the following statements is true or false.

- **(a)** The relative record key is usually calculated from the symbolic key.
- **(b)** The relative record key always indicates where the record is in the relative file.
- **(c)** If symbolic keys are unique, so are relative record keys.
- **(d)** A REGIONAL file contains a predetermined number of record positions.
- **(e)** Records in a REGIONAL file are stored in consecutive positions.
- **(f)** The records in a REGIONAL file are in order by symbolic key.
- **(g)** The records in a REGIONAL file are in order by relative record number.
- **(h)** The relative record number is sufficient to identify a record.
- **(i)** A record is always stored in its home position.
- **(j)** The details of relative file handling are implementation-dependent.

2. A relative record key is produced from a symbolic key by using a (an) ____________________ algorithm.

3. More space than needed should be allocated for a REGIONAL file so that __________ and __________.

4. The lowest valid value of the relative record number is __________ on some computers and __________ on others.

5. A record with symbolic key 614 is to be added to table 17.1. Calculate its relative record key using
   (a) The last two digits.
   (b) The sum of digits.
   (c) Prime division by 97.

17.2 REGIONAL file declarations

Regional files can be used only for RECORD processing. They may be accessed using either sequential or direct access. Records may be inserted, deleted, or modified. The general form of the file declaration is:

```
DCL file_ name FILE [KEYED] [mode] [use] RECORD ENV(REGIONAL(1));
```

The mode may be SEQUENTIAL or DIRECT, and the use may be INPUT, OUTPUT, or UPDATE.

The file is declared as KEYED whenever the keys are being used in the record access. Keys must be used for direct access and for one form of skip-sequential access. The file may be created with or without the KEYED attribute, then later accessed using keys, provided that there is an efficient algorithm for locating specific records.

17.2.1 SEQUENTIAL processing

The use of regional files for sequential processing must take into consideration the unused record positions. When the file is first created, these positions are automatically filled with *dummy records,* which have '(8)1'B or some other special mark in the first byte. With some file management systems, these records as well as valid data records are retrieved by the system whenever they are requested; therefore the program must check for the presence of valid data as opposed to dummy records. With other systems, only valid data is retrieved and the KEY condition is raised when a dummy record is requested. All the examples in this chapter are written to check for inactive records. With a file management system that returns dummy records to the program, the inactive records include the dummy records. If dummy records are not retrieved, "inactive" refers to records that have been specially marked by the programmer.

UNKEYED

Following are examples of declarations of unkeyed sequential regional files:

```
DCL INFILE   FILE SEQL INPUT  RECORD ENV(REGIONAL(1));
DCL OUTFILE  FILE SEQL OUTPUT RECORD ENV(REGIONAL(1));
DCL MASTERF  FILE SEQL UPDATE RECORD ENV(REGIONAL(1));
```

These files may be used in exactly the same way as INDEXED or CONSECUTIVE sequential files. They may be processed by the programs of section 15.6 provided that inactive records are ignored.

KEYED

Following are examples of the declaration of regional files for sequential access using the KEYED option:

```
DCL IN_FILE   FILE KEYED SEQL INPUT  RECORD ENV(REGIONAL(1));
DCL OUT_FILE  FILE KEYED SEQL OUTPUT RECORD ENV(REGIONAL(1));
DCL MAST_FILE FILE KEYED SEQL UPDATE RECORD ENV(REGIONAL(1));
```

The KEYED attribute is used for creating the files sequentially when some of the record positions are skipped, or for retrieving the relative record numbers along with the records.

Sequential access is the most efficient way to create a regional file, provided that the records are in order by relative record key rather than by symbolic key. When a file is created sequentially, any unused positions are automatically filled with dummy records. Sequential access is the most efficient way of reading a file in order to copy it, but it is a poor way to obtain readable printed output because the symbolic keys usually are not in order.

17.2.2 DIRECT processing

When a file is declared as being used for direct processing, the KEYED attribute must be specified. The following declarations show the possibilities:

```
DCL IN_FILE   FILE KEYED DIRECT INPUT  RECORD ENV(REGIONAL(1));
DCL OUT_FILE  FILE KEYED DIRECT OUTPUT RECORD ENV(REGIONAL(1));
DCL MAST_FILE FILE KEYED DIRECT UPDATE RECORD ENV(REGIONAL(1));
```

With direct access, all input/output statements must include a key. The keys may be processed in any order. A REGIONAL file may be created, queried, or updated using direct processing. It is inefficient to use direct processing to list it or to process more than a few records.

To find a specific record in a regional file, you must know the values of the relative record key and the symbolic key. If there have been insertions and deletions to the file, there will be some records that are not in their home positions. Not only are records not stored in order by their symbolic keys, but when there are duplicates they are not stored in order by their relative record keys. The relative record key is used as the starting point for searching for a record. The symbolic key is used to identify the record. In practice, care is taken to ensure that all the records are close to their home positions. In theory, they could be very far away. Furthermore, when there is no room for a record near the end of the file, the overflow may wrap around to the beginning.

A file may be created using direct processing. Before any records are stored, the file must be filled with dummy records. On some systems, this is done by opening and then closing the file without writing any records. On other systems, this is done automatically when the file is first opened.

Review questions

1. Write a declaration for a REGIONAL file F, which is to be created from a source file that has been hashed and sorted on the relative record keys.

2. Write a declaration for a REGIONAL file G, which is to be created from an unsorted source file.

3. Write a declaration for a REGIONAL file H, which is to be updated on-line.

4. Write a declaration for a REGIONAL file I, which is to be updated from a transaction file that has been hashed and sorted on the relative record keys.

5. Complete each of the following statements.

(a) ______________ (direct/sequential) processing is used with a REGIONAL file when the file is to be copied.

(b) ______________ (KEYED/unkeyed) processing is used with a REGIONAL file when a specific record is wanted.

(c) A REGIONAL file generally ______________ (can/cannot) be listed in order by symbolic key.

(d) A record is located by using the ______________ (relative record key/symbolic key).

(e) A record is identified by using the ______________ (relative record key/symbolic key).

17.3 File availability

A regional file is made accessible by opening it and inaccessible by closing it.

17.3.1 OPEN statement

The general form of the OPEN statement is:

```
OPEN FILE (file_name) [mode] [use] [TITLE (title)];
```

The mode and use options of the OPEN statement are specified when the file declaration does not contain the necessary information. There is no access option, because the file must have RECORD access. The title option is used to associate the program file name with a file name known to the operating system.

17.3.2 CLOSE statement

The general form of the CLOSE statement is:

```
CLOSE FILE (file_name);
```

Closing a regional file that has been open for sequential output places dummy records in any trailing record positions and causes an end-of-file record to be written in the last physical position in the file.

Review questions

1. Indicate whether each of the following statements is true or false.
  (a) The OPEN statement makes a relative file accessible.
  (b) The TITLE option of the OPEN statement is not required.
  (c) The CLOSE statement makes a file inaccessible.
  (d) A relative file may be OPENed with the PRINT option.
  (e) A relative file may be OPENed as a STREAM file.

2. Write OPEN statements for a REGIONAL file that is to be created and listed in the same program.

3. Write OPEN statements for a REGIONAL file that is to be queried on-line and updated on-line in the same program.

4. The TITLE option of the OPEN statement associated the program file name with ________________ .

5. An end-of-file record is written to a REGIONAL file when the file is closed if it has been open for ________________ .

17.4 Record access

The input/output statements used with regional files are READ, WRITE, LOCATE, REWRITE, and DELETE. There are system-dependent variations in these statements. On some systems, the DELETE statement cannot be used with sequential update, and on other systems KEYTO is the only key option that can be used with sequential input.

17.4.1 Input statements

SEQUENTIAL INPUT

The general forms of the sequential input statements are:

```
READ FILE (file_name) INTO (var) [KEY (expression)];
READ FILE (file_name) INTO (var) [KEYTO (variable)];
READ FILE (file_name) SET (pointer) [KEY (expression)];
```

```
READ FILE (file_name) SET (pointer) [KEYTO (variable)];
READ FILE (file_name) IGNORE (expr);
```

The use of these statements is similar to their use with CONSECUTIVE and INDEXED files. Move-mode, locate-mode, and skip-sequential mode processing are available.

Move-mode processing The READ. . .INTO forms of the input statement are used for move-mode processing. The statement

```
READ FILE (MASTER) INTO (MAST_REC);
```

obtains the next record in sequence from the buffer and stores it in MAST_REC. The record obtained may be a valid or an inactive record. The ENDFILE condition is raised when the end-of-file record is read. This statement is used for sequential processing of REGIONAL files, the same way it is used for CONSECUTIVE files.

The following program segment shows the basic steps in the listing of a regional file, assuming there are no inactive records.

```
READ FILE (MASTER) INTO (MAST_REC);
DO WHILE (MORE_DATA);
  PUT SKIP LIST (MAST_REC);
  READ FILE (MASTER) INTO (MAST_REC);
END;
```

When the file contains inactive records, the basic steps in listing the file are as seen in the following program segment:

```
READ FILE(DATAF) INTO (DATA_REC);
DO WHILE (MORE_DATA);
  IF REC_TYPE ¬= INACTIVE
    THEN
      PUT SKIP LIST (DATA_REC);
  READ FILE (DATAF) INTO (DATA_REC);
END;
```

The same program segments can be used with CONSECUTIVE and INDEXED files.

The statement

```
READ FILE (MASTER) INTO (MAST_REC) KEYTO (REC_NO);
```

obtains the next record in sequence from the buffer and stores it in MAST_REC. The relative record number is stored in REC_NUM. The following program segment shows the basic steps in listing a file along with the positions of the records in the file.

```
READ FILE(MASTER) INTO (MAST_REC) KEYTO (REC_NO);
DO WHILE (MORE DATA);
  IF REC_TYPE ¬= INACTIVE
    THEN
      PUT SKIP LIST (REC_NO,MAST_REC);
  READ FILE (MASTER) INTO (MAST_REC) KEYTO (REC_NO);
END;
```

The computer stores the relative record number in REC_NO. Note that the relative record number is not necessarily the same as the relative record key and is not the same as the symbolic key. The ENDFILE condition is raised when the end-of-file record is read.

Keyed skip-sequential processing The statement

```
READ FILE (MASTER) INTO (MAST_REC) KEY (REC_NO);
```

obtains the record having its key equal to the value of REC_NO and stores it in MAST_REC. REC_NO must have a valid numeric value at the time this statement is executed. If it does not, the KEY condition is raised. If the key is in range, the record is always found, whether or not it is a dummy record, as there is a position for it. However, on many systems a dummy record is not retrieved and the KEY condition is raised. This is the only form of the input statement available with DIRECT processing.

The following example shows the basic steps in using the key to read and list a file selectively:

```
GET EDIT (REC_NO) (COL (1),A(8));
DO WHILE (MORE_KEYS);
  READ FILE (MASTER) INTO (MAST_REC) KEY (REC_NO);
  PUT SKIP LIST (MAST_REC);
  GET EDIT (REC_NO) (COL(1),A(8));
END;
```

A relative record number is obtained from an input stream for each record to be read from the indexed file. With DIRECT access, these keys may be in any order. It is assumed that the actual position of the record in the file is known. The KEY condition is also raised if there is a key for which no record can be found.

The following program segment shows the basic steps in locating a record using SEQUENTIAL access, assuming that there may be duplicate relative record keys. Therefore the record wanted may not be in its home position.

```
ON KEY (MASTER)              or          ON ENDFILE (MASTER)
  REC_NO = 0;                                REC_NO = 0;
GET EDIT (REC_KEY,SYMB_KEY) (COL(1),F(8),A(8));
REC_NO = REC_KEY;
DO UNTIL (MAST_KEY = SYMB_KEY | REC_NO = REC_KEY);
  READ FILE (MASTER) INTO (MAST_REC) KEY (REC_NO);
  REC_NO = REC_NO + 1;
END;
IF MAST_KEY = SYMB_KEY
  THEN
    PUT SKIP LIST (MAST_REC);
```

This program segment starts the search for the record wanted at the home position as given by the relative record key, REC_KEY. The search is sequential, checking each record for the correct value of the symbolic key. When the end of the file is reached, either the KEY condition or the ENDFILE condition is raised, depending on the implementation, to indicate that REC_NO is out of bounds. If the exception handler is used to restart the record number at zero, the search wraps around to the beginning of the file. When the record is missing, the entire file is searched. This program segment assumes that data is not stored in relative record position zero.

Locate-mode processing The READ. . .SET forms of the input statement provide locate-mode processing. The statement

```
READ FILE (MASTER) SET (P);
```

moves the file pointer down the buffer to the next record position and stores the memory address of that position in P, which must be a pointer variable. If there is a based variable associated with P, this statement superimposes the based variable on the record position in the buffer.

The statement

```
READ FILE (MASTER) SET (P) KEYTO (REC_NO);
```

moves the file pointer to the next record position, stores the memory address of that position in P, and stores the relative record number of the record in that position in REC_NO. The ENDFILE condition is raised when the end-of-file record is read.

Unkeyed skip-sequential processing (not in Subset G) The READ. . . IGNORE form of the input statement provides skip-sequential input processing. The statement

```
READ FILE (MASTER) IGNORE (9);
```

moves the file pointer ahead nine record positions without transmitting any data to the program. It is then ready to read the tenth record. The ENDFILE condition is raised when the end-of-file record is read.

17.4.2 Output statements

SEQUENTIAL OUTPUT

The general forms of the output statements for sequential access are:

```
WRITE FILE (file_name) FROM (var) [KEYFROM (expr)];
LOCATE based_var FILE (file_name) [KEYFROM (expr)] [SET (pointer)];
REWRITE FILE (file_name) FROM (var) [KEY (expr)];
DELETE FILE (file_name) [KEY (expr)];
```

Both move-mode and locate-mode processing are available. On some computers, keyed skip-sequential processing is also available.

Move-mode processing THE WRITE. . .FROM form of output provides move-mode processing. The statement

```
WRITE FILE (MASTER) FROM (MAST_REC);
```

causes the value of the record MAST_REC to be written to the buffer. When the buffer is full, the buffer is written to the file. On some systems, the ENDFILE condition is raised by an attempt to write beyond the end of the space allocated for the file. This use of the statement is identical with its use with CONSECUTIVE files.

The statement

```
WRITE FILE (MASTER) FROM (MAST_REC) KEYFROM (REC_NO);
```

causes the value of the record MAST_REC to be written to the file using the value REC_NO. The following program segment assumes that the relative record keys have already been calculated and a temporary file has been built and sorted. The relative record keys are in the records of the temporary file along with the symbolic keys. Skip-sequential processing is used to create the file. It is assumed that there are no duplicate relative record keys.

```
GET FILE (TEMP) EDIT (REC_NO,MAST_REC)) (COL(1),A(4),A(80));
DO WHILE (MORE_DATA);
  WRITE FILE (MASTER) FROM (MAST_REC) KEYFROM (REC_NO);
  GET FILE (TEMP) EDIT (REC_NOY,MAST_REC) (COL(1),A(4),A(80));
END;
```

When there are duplicate relative record keys, the duplicates must be identified and temporarily written to a work file. Then they are handled as insertions to the original file. The basic steps for doing this are shown in the following program segment:

```
GET FILE (TEMP) EDIT (REC_NO,MAST_REC)) (COL(1),A(4),A(80));
DO WHILE (MORE_DATA);
  IF OLD_KEY = REC_NO
    THEN
      PUT FILE (INSERTF) EDIT (REC_NO,MAST_REC) (COL(1),A,A);
    ELSE
      DO;
        WRITE FILE (MASTER) FROM (MAST_REC) KEYFROM (REC_NO);
        OLD_KEY = REC_NO;
      END;
  GET FILE (TEMP) EDIT (REC_NO,MAST_REC) (COL(1),A(4),A(80));
END;
```

The KEY condition is raised if the number is out of range.

These program segments may be used with SEQUENTIAL or DIRECT file access when the file is opened for OUTPUT or UPDATE.

LOCATE-MODE PROCESSING (not in Subset G)

The LOCATE output statement takes the following form:

```
LOCATE PTR_REC FILE (MASTER);
```

causes the file pointer to move to the next record position in the output buffer. The memory address of that position is stored in the pointer P. It sets aside the space required for the record description PTR_REC in the buffer, but does not store any data in the buffer. Notice that PTR_REC must be a based variable with an associated pointer. The ENDFILE condition is raised by an attempt to write beyond the end of the space allocated for the file.

The statement

```
LOCATE PTR_REC FILE (MASTER) SET (P);
```

moves the file pointer to the next record position in the output buffer, sets aside the space required for the record description PTR_REC at that position, and stores the memory address of the position in P. It does not store any data in the buffer. The ENDFILE condition is raised by an attempt to write beyond the end of the space allocated for the file.

When a key is used, the locate-mode statement takes the form

```
LOCATE PTR_REC FILE (MASTER) KEYFROM (REC_NO);
```

or

```
LOCATE PTR_REC FILE (MASTER) KEYFROM (REC_NO) SET (P);
```

The KEYFROM option is used when a file containing scattered dummy records is to be created.

UPDATE PROCESSING

REWRITE statement The REWRITE. . .FROM update statement provides move-mode processing. The statement has the forms:

```
REWRITE FILE (MASTER);
REWRITE FILE (MASTER) FROM (MAST_REC);
REWRITE FILE (MASTER) FROM (MAST_REC) KEY (REC_NO);
```

Without the FROM clause, the REWRITE statement causes the most recently read record to be written back to its previous position in the file. If the record has been changed, the new version replaces the old version.

The unkeyed form of the REWRITE. . .FROM statement causes the most recently read record to be replaced in the file by the record specified, in this example MAST_REC. When the KEY option is used, the statement replaces the record in the file having relative record number REC_NO with the record MAST_REC. The KEY condition is raised if there is no record with that record number.

Without the KEY clause, the REWRITE statement can be used only for processing of SEQL UPDATE files. With the KEY clause, the statement is used for either processing of SEQL UPDATE files or processing of DIRECT UPDATE files.

DELETE statement Both forms of the DELETE statement effectively remove a record from the file. The statement takes the forms:

```
DELETE FILE (MASTER);
DELETE FILE (MASTER) KEY (REC_NO);
```

When the KEY option is not used, the DELETE statement deletes the most recently read record of the file.

When the KEY option is used, it deletes the record from the file specified by REC_NO. If there is no record with that key, the KEY condition is raised.

The KEY clauses are nonstandard for sequential processing. On most systems the sequential updating statements are the same as for CONSECUTIVE files. The KEY option is required for direct processing.

Review questions

1. The I/O statement used in creating a file is ____________________.

2. The I/O statements used in changing a field of a record are ____________________ and ____________________.

3. The I/O statements used in replacing a record under sequential access are ____________________ and ____________________.

4. The I/O statement used in replacing a record under direct access is ____________________.

5. The ENDFILE condition is raised only if the processing is ____________________ and the I/O statement is ____________________.

6. The KEY condition is raised only if the ____________________ attribute is used.

7. The ____________________ clause is used to find a record at a particular location in the file.

8. The ____________________ clause is used to find the record number of the current position in the file.

9. The ____________________ clause is used to store a record in a particular place in the file.

10. Write a program segment that deletes the record for JOHN SMITH using as a hashing technique the sum of the alphabetic positions of all letters of the name, i.e., J is 10, O is 15, H is 8, ... The relative record key is 10 + 15 + 8 + ...

11. Write a program segment that counts the active records in a REGIONAL file.

12. Write a program segment that changes the name of MARY SMITH to MARY JONES on account 12345, assuming that the record number is found by the prime division method; that is, the relative key is the remainder when the account number is divided by 997.

17.5 File error conditions

The file error conditions have been discussed in detail in section 14.5. ENDFILE and KEY are the most common conditions for REGIONAL files.

All the file-processing error condition ON units must be identified with particular files. ON units for the same condition can be established for different files, and different ON units can be established for a single file.

ENDFILE CONDITION

The ENDFILE condition may be raised by SEQUENTIAL processing when there is an attempt to read beyond the end of the file. With regional files, the end of the file is the physical end of the allocated space, not the logical end of the data records. Any space after the last data record is filled with dummy records. With some file management systems, the ENDFILE condition is also raised if there is an attempt to write beyond the physical end of the allocated space. These situations are shown in table 17–2.

Statement	*Meaning of end file condition*
READ ...	Attempts to read beyond end of file
READ ... KEY ...	Key too large
WRITE ... KEYFROM ...	Key too large

Table 17–2

KEY CONDITION

The meaning of the KEY exception depends on the operation being attempted. On some systems, the READ, REWRITE, and DELETE statements raise the KEY condition when the file is KEYED and a record cannot be found, and the WRITE statement raises the KEY condition when the file already contains a record with that key. On other systems the KEY condition is raised in these situations only when DIRECT access is used. The KEY condition is also raised if a key is too small.

Table 17–3 shows the meaning of the KEY condition when it is raised during the execution of different types of statements.

Statement	*Meaning of key condition*
READ ... KEY ...	Invalid key, or key out of bounds [or record missing]
REWRITE ... KEY ...	"
DELETE ... KEY ...	"
READ ... KEYTO ...	Invalid key
WRITE ... KEYFROM ...	Invalid key, or key out of bounds [or duplicate key]
LOCATE ... KEYFROM ...	"

Table 17–3

The meaning of the KEY exception depends on the operation being attempted. Note that the keyword used in the key option indicates the error category.

The library function ONKEY may be used to print the value of an invalid key. This is shown in the following example:

```
ON KEY (DATA_FILE)
  BEGIN;
    PUT SKIP LIST ('INVALID KEY - ',ONKEY);
    KEY_ERROR = TRUE;
  END;
```

The different meanings of the KEY condition can be distinguished by looking at the value returned by the library function ONCODE. This is shown in the following example:

```
ON KEY (DATA_FILE)
  BEGIN;
    PUT SKIP LIST ('KEY ERROR - ',ONCODE);
    KEY_ERROR = TRUE;
  END;
```

The set of error codes is implementation-dependent and can be found in a reference manual for the particular version of PL/I used.

Review questions

1. On some systems, using SEQUENTIAL access, the ________________ condition is raised if a relative file key is too large. On others, the ________________ condition is raised.

2. Using DIRECT access, the ________________ condition is always raised when a key is out of bounds.

3. A relative record number will cause a key error if it is ________________.

4. The ENDFILE condition can be raised only if the REGIONAL file has the ________________ attribute.

5. The KEY condition can be raised only if the REGIONAL file has the ________________ attribute.

6. The library function ONKEY, used with the KEY condition, contains the value of ________________.

7. The library function ONCODE, used with the KEY condition, indicates ________________.

8. If the KEY condition is raised by a READ statement, using DIRECT access usually means that ________________.

9. If the KEY condition is raised by a WRITE statement, using DIRECT access usually means that ________________.

17.6 File maintenance

The following program segment shows the basic steps in creating a relative file using either SEQUENTIAL access or DIRECT access. With SEQUENTIAL access, the processing is skip sequential and the input records must be in order by relative record key.

```
ON KEY(MASTER)
  RECORD_FOUND = FALSE;

GET EDIT (REC_KEY,DATA_REC) (COL(1),A(8),A(80));
DO WHILE (MORE_DATA);
  RECORD_FOUND = TRUE;
  READ FILE (MASTER) INTO (MAST_REC) KEY (REC_KEY);
  IF REC_TYPE = INACTIVE | ¬RECORD_FOUND
    THEN
      REWRITE FILE (MASTER) FROM (MAST_REC) KEY (REC_KEY);
    ELSE
      WRITE FILE (INSERT) FROM (REC_KEY,MAST_REC);
  GET EDIT (REC_NO,MAST_REC) (COL(1),A(8),A(80));
END;
```

This program segment assumes that there may be duplicate relative record keys. Therefore, when a record is being stored, the file position must first be checked to see whether a record is already there. This can be done by reading the file and checking to see whether a dummy record is in that position. Using sequential access, it would be enough to compare the new relative record key with the previous relative record key. If the key is not a duplicate, the record can be stored. If there already was a record in the file position, the new record is written to a temporary file. When as many records as possible have been stored at their home positions, the temporary file is processed and the records placed using a record insertion routine.

With some systems, the dummy records are not returned by the READ statement. Instead of checking for dummy records, the KEY condition is used to determine whether there already is a record stored at that position. The following example creates a file for this situation:

```
ON KEY(MASTER)
  KEY_ERROR = TRUE;
GET EDIT (REC_NO,DATA_REC) (COL(1),A(8),A(80));
DO WHILE (MORE_DATA);
  KEY_ERROR = FALSE;
  WRITE FILE (MASTER) FROM (MAST_REC) KEY (REC_NO);
  IF KEY_ERROR
    THEN
      WRITE FILE (INSERT) FROM (REC_NO,MAST_REC);
  GET EDIT (REC_NO,MAST_REC) (COL(1),A(8),A(80));
END;
```

The program segment would be more portable if both types of checks were used.

With both sequential and direct output, when the file is closed, unused record positions are filled with dummy records and an end-of-file record is written at the end of the allocated file space.

A relative record file may be updated using either skip-sequential processing with a transaction file sorted on the relative record key, or direct processing with a sorted or unsorted transaction file. Sequential updating requires more than one pass if some of the records are not found at their home positions.

The file may be copied using sequential output, but as the records generally are not in order by symbolic key, most queries are processed using direct access.

Progressive overflow is only one way of handling duplicate keys. Sometimes the duplicate is placed in any available space, not necessarily the closest space, and the location of the overflow is stored in the home position. Sometimes a separate overflow area is used, similar to that used by INDEXED files.

Review questions

1. The ____________________ statement is used to insert a new record.

2. The ____________________ statement is used to replace a record.

3. The ____________________ and ____________________ statements are used to modify a record.

4. Write a segment of code to delete a record that has relative record key 12345 from file INFO, using
   (a) Sequential access.
   (b) Direct access.
   Assume that progressive overflow is used.

17.7 Examples using relative files

The programs in this section provide a representative sample of file maintenance techniques for relative/REGIONAL(1) files: creating files, updating files, and processing files.

17.7.1 Listing a file

Listing a regional file differs from listing a consecutive or indexed file in that the file may contain dummy or inactive records, which must be ignored. That is shown in this program.

```
LIST: PROC OPTIONS (MAIN);
/*********************************************************/
/*                                                       */
/* PROGRAM: LIST A REGIONAL FILE                         */
/* AUTHOR:  C ZIEGLER                                    */
/* VERSION: 07/17/84                                     */
/*                                                       */
/* PROGRAM DESCRIPTION                                   */
/* ---------------------------------------------------  */
/* THIS PROGRAM LISTS A REGIONAL FILE.                   */
/*                                                       */
/* INPUT: DATAF - COLS      1 RECORD TYPE                */
/*                     2 - 80 RECORD DATA                */
/*                                                       */
/* OUTPUT: SYSPRINT - LISTING OF VALID RECORDS           */
/*                                                       */
/*********************************************************/
DCL DATAF          FILE SEQL INPUT RECORD ENV (REGIONAL);
DCL 1 DATA_REC,
      5 REC_TYPE   BIT(8),
      5 DATA_INFO  CHAR(79);
DCL MORE_DATA      BIT(1),
    TRUE           BIT(1)     INIT('1'B),
    FALSE          BIT(1)     INIT('0'B);
DCL INACTIVE       BIT(8)     INIT ('(8)1'B);

ON ENDFILE (DATAF)
  MORE_DATA = FALSE;

MORE_DATA = TRUE;
OPEN FILE (DATAF);
READ FILE (DATAF) INTO (DATA_REC);
DO WHILE (MORE_DATA);
  IF REC_TYPE ¬= INACTIVE                 /* LIST ACTIVE RECORDS */
    THEN
      PUT SKIP LIST (DATA_REC);
  READ FILE (DATAF) INTO (DATA_REC);
END;
CLOSE FILE (DATAF);
END LIST;
```

17.7.2 Creating a file (skip-sequential processing)

The following example assumes that relative record keys have already been calculated and a temporary file has been built and sorted. The relative record keys are in the records of the temporary file along with the symbolic keys. Skip-sequential processing is used to build the file. All records with duplicate relative record keys are written to a second temporary file, to be treated as insertions. Duplicate keys can be detected by checking the sequencing of the keys. In a second and third pass over the new master file, each of these overflow records is stored in the first available place beyond its home

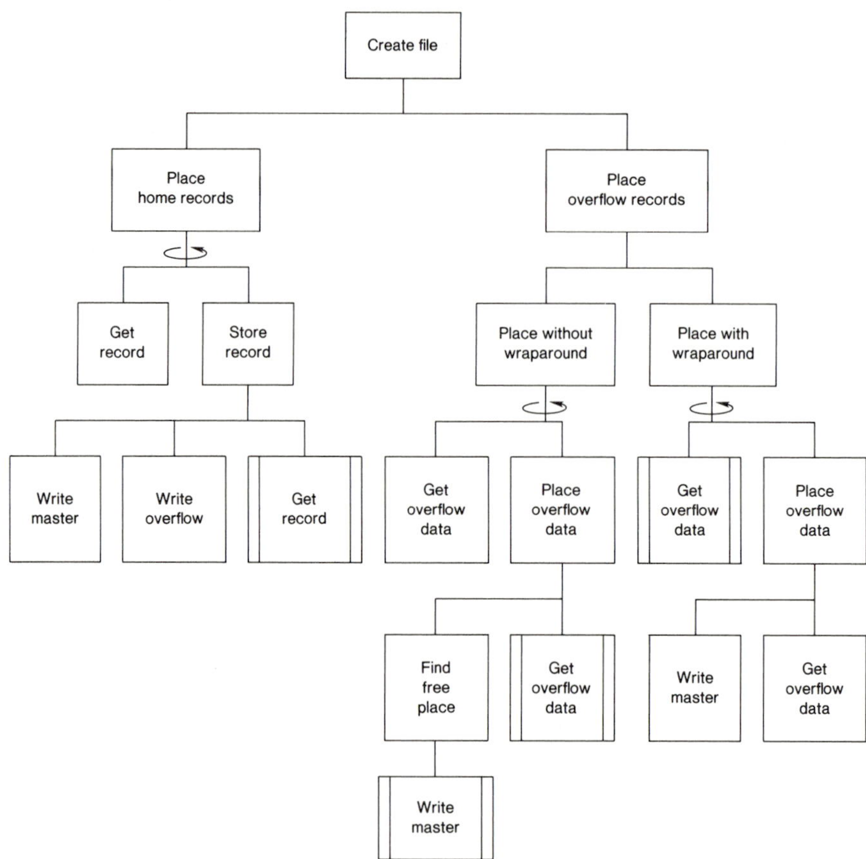

Figure 17–2

position. Two overflow passes are used because it is easier to treat wraparound to the beginning of the file as a separate case. The hierarchy chart for this program is shown in figure 17–2.

```
CREATE: PROC OPTIONS (MAIN);
/*************************************************************/
/*                                                           */
/* PROGRAM: CREATE A REGIONAL FILE                           */
/* AUTHOR:  C ZIEGLER                                        */
/* VERSION: 07/17/84                                         */
/*                                                           */
/* PROGRAM DESCRIPTION                                       */
/* -------------------------------------------------------- */
/* THIS PROGRAM CREATES A REGIONAL FILE USING SKIP           */
/* SEQUENTIAL PROCESSING                                     */
/*                                                           */
/* INPUT: TEMP - SORTED RECORDS                              */
/*                  COLS 1 -  2 RELATIVE RECORD KEY          */
/*                       3 -  7 SYMBOLIC KEY                 */
/*                       8 - 80 RECORD DATA                  */
/*         RECORDS IN ORDER BY RELATIVE RECORD KEY           */
```

```
/*                                                      */
/* OUTPUT: MASTERF - COLS       1 RECORD TYPE CODE      */
/*                              2 FILLER                */
/*                          3 - 7 SYMBOLIC KEY          */
/*                          8 - 80 RECORD DATA          */
/*                                                      */
/* TEMPORARY FILES: INSERTF - RECORDS WITH DUPLICATE    */
/*                            RELATIVE RECORD KEYS      */
/*                                                      */
/********************************************************/
DCL TEMP      FILE   INPUT  STREAM ENV(CONSECUTIVE),
    MASTERF   FILE   KEYED SEQL   RECORD ENV(REGIONAL),
    INSERTF   FILE   SEQL  RECORD ENV(CONSECUTIVE);
DCL 1  IN_REC,
       5  REC_KEY     PIC '99',
       5  SYMB_KEY    CHAR(5),
       5  DATA_INFO   CHAR(73);
DCL 1  DATA_REC,
       5  REC_TYPE    BIT(8),
       5  FILLER      CHAR(1),
       5  SYMB_KEY    CHAR(5),
       5  DATA_INFO   CHAR(73);
DCL MORE_DATA          BIT(1),
    MORE_MASTER        BIT(1),
    RECORD_FOUND       BIT(1),
    SPACE_FOUND        BIT(1),
    FILE_MAX           FIXED BIN    INIT(99),
    OLD_KEY            PIC '99',
    REC_NO             FIXED BIN;
DCL INACTIVE           BIT(8)       INIT ('(8)1'B),
    TRUE               BIT(1)       INIT('1'B),
    FALSE              BIT(1)       INIT('0'B);

/********************************************************/
/*                                                      */
/* FIRST PASS: PLACE FIRST RECORD OF EACH KEY VALUE     */
/*                                                      */
/********************************************************/
ON ENDFILE (TEMP)
  MORE_DATA = FALSE;
ON KEY (MASTERF)
  BEGIN;
    PUT SKIP LIST ('INVALID KEY - ',REC_KEY);
    WRITE FILE (INSERTF) FROM (IN_REC);
  END;

MORE_DATA = TRUE;
OLD_KEY = 0;
OPEN FILE (TEMP);
OPEN OUTPUT FILE (MASTERF),
     OUTPUT FILE (INSERTF);
GET FILE (TEMP) EDIT (IN_REC) (COL(1),A(2),A(5),A(73));
```

```
DO WHILE (MORE_DATA);
  IF REC_KEY = OLD_KEY
    THEN
      WRITE FILE (INSERTF) FROM (IN_REC);  /* DUPLICATE KEY      */
    ELSE
      DO;                                   /* NON-DUPLICATE KEY */
        DATA_REC = ' ';
        DATA_REC = IN_REC, BY NAME;
        WRITE FILE (MASTERF) FROM (DATA_REC) KEYFROM (REC_KEY);
        OLD_KEY = REC_KEY;
      END;
  GET FILE (TEMP) EDIT (IN_REC) (COL(1),A(2),A(5),A(73));
END;
CLOSE FILE (TEMP),
      FILE (MASTERF),
      FILE (INSERTF);

/*******************************************************/
/*                                                     */
/* SECOND PASS: PLACE OVERFLOW RECORDS                 */
/*                                                     */
/*******************************************************/

ON ENDFILE (INSERTF)
  MORE_DATA = FALSE;
ON ENDFILE (MASTERF)
  MORE_MASTER = FALSE;
ON KEY (MASTERF)
  SPACE_FOUND = TRUE;

MORE_DATA = TRUE;
MORE_MASTER = TRUE;
MASTER_EOF = FALSE;
SPACE_FOUND = FALSE;
OPEN UPDATE FILE (MASTERF),
     INPUT  FILE (INSERTF);
READ FILE (INSERTF) INTO (IN_REC);
REC_NO = REC_KEY;
DO WHILE (MORE_DATA & MORE_MASTER);
  DO UNTIL (SPACE_FOUND | REC_TYPE = INACTIVE
              | REC NO > FILE_MAX);   /* FIND AVAILABLE SPACE   */
    REC_NO = REC_NO + 1;
    READ FILE (MASTERF) INTO (DATA_REC) KEY (REC_NO);
  END;
  IF REC_NO <= FILE_MAX
    THEN
      DO;                           /* INSERT OVERFLOW RECORD */
        DATA_REC = ' ';
        DATA_REC = IN_REC, BY NAME;
        WRITE FILE (MASTERF) FROM (DATA_REC) KEYFROM (REC_NO);
        READ FILE (INSERTF) INTO (IN_REC);
        SPACE_FOUND = FALSE;
```

```
        IF REC_NO < REC_KEY
          THEN
            REC_NO = REC_KEY;
      END;
    ELSE
      MORE_MASTER = FALSE;
END;
CLOSE FILE (MASTERF);

/************************************************************/
/*                                                          */
/* THIRD PASS: PLACE OVERFLOW RECORDS WITH WRAPAROUND */
/*                                                          */
/************************************************************/
OPEN UPDATE FILE (MASTERF);
REC_NO = 0;
SPACE_FOUND = FALSE;
DO WHILE (MORE-DATA);
  DO UNTIL (SPACE_FOUND | REC_TYPE = INACTIVE | REC_NO = REC_KEY);
    REC_NO = REC_NO + 1;
    READ FILE (MASTERF) INTO (DATA_REC) KEYTO (REC_NO);
  END;
  IF REC_NO = REC_KEY
    THEN
      DO;
        PUT SKIP LIST ('FILE FULL ',IN_REC,' NOT STORED');
        MORE_DATA = FALSE;
      END;
    ELSE
      DO;                       /* INSERT OVERFLOW RECORD */
        DATA_REC = ' ';
        DATA_REC = IN_REC, BY NAME;
        WRITE FILE (MASTERF) FROM (DATA_REC) KEYFROM (REC_NO);
        READ FILE (INSERTF) INTO (IN_REC);
        SPACE_FOUND = FALSE;
      END;
END;
CLOSE FILE (MASTERF),
      FILE (INSERTF);
END CREATE;
```

The first pass places all the records that will fit in their home positions, using skip-sequential processing to find the record positions. Successive record keys are checked for duplicates. If a duplicate record key is found, the record is placed in the overflow file. At the end TEMP is closed and not opened again.

The second pass scans the positions beyond the home position for an available space. The insertion record is placed in the first available space beyond its home position. The insertion records are still in order by relative record key. This process is repeated until the end of the file is reached.

When an insertion record is found for which no space is available beyond the home position, the master file is closed and opened again to restart it at the beginning. In the third pass, the insertion records are placed wherever possible.

The decision tables for the three passes are:

Pass 1

TEMP-eof	Y	N	N	N
Key error	*	—	Y	N
New key = old key	*	Y	N	N
"Key error			X	
Write MASTERF				X
Write INSERTF		X	X	
Read TEMP		X	X	X
Repeat		X	X	X
Exit	X			

Pass 2

INSERTF-eof	Y	N	N	N
MASTERF-eof	—	Y	N	N
Space found	*	*	Y	N
Insert record			X	
Read MASTERF			X	X
Read INSERTF			X	
Repeat			X	X
Exit	X	X		

Pass 3

INSERTF-eof	Y	N	N	N
MASTERF full	*	Y	N	N
Space found	—	N	Y	N
"File full"		X		
Insert record			X	
Read MASTERF			X	X
Read INSERTF			X	
Repeat			X	X
Exit	X	X		

Slight modifications to this program would be necessary if there are no inactive records or if the file management system returns dummy records to the program.

17.7.3 Master file update (record insertion, modification, deletion)

The following decision table shows the complete master file update for regional files using direct processing and progressive overflow, under the assumption that no record is more than ten positions away from its home position. The transaction code indicates whether a record is to be inserted, modified, or deleted.

T_eof	Y	N	N	N	N	N	N	N	N	N	N
Code = insertion	*	Y	Y	Y	N	N	N	N	N	N	N
Code = modification	*	N	N	N	Y	Y	Y	N	N	N	N
Code = deletion	*	N	N	N	N	N	N	Y	Y	Y	N
Record_found	*	Y	N	N	Y	N	N	Y	N	N	—
Space_found	*	N	Y	N	N	Y	N	N	Y	N	—
"File full"				X							
"Invalid trans code"											X
"Record missing"						X			X		
"Duplicate record"		X									
Modify record					X						
Delete M_rec								X			
Insert record			X								
Read T_file		X	X		X	X		X	X		X
Search M_file		X	X		X	X		X	X		X
Repeat		X	X	X	X	X	X	X	X	X	X
Exit	X										

Before the operation on the file can be carried out, the transaction code must be checked for validity and a search conducted to find the record, if it is there.

The hierarchy chart of figure 17–3 differs from that of figure 16–4 in that

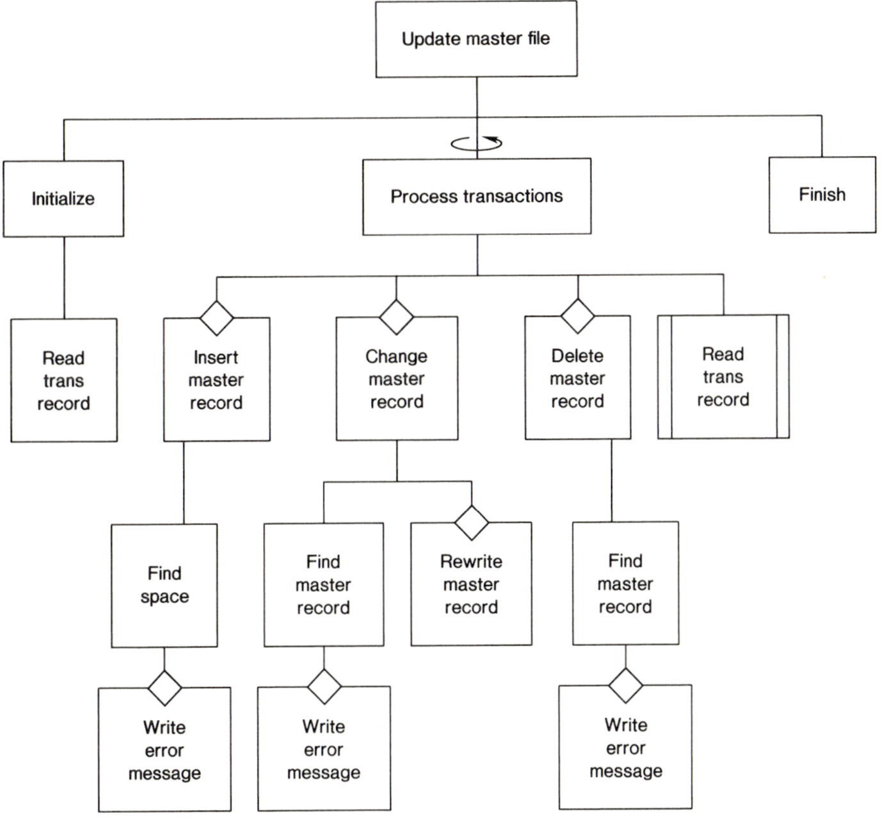

Figure 17–3

a search for either an empty position and/or a particular master record is needed.

The program to update the file follows. It updates the master record by subtracting an amount from the balance in the master record for each transaction.

```
UPDATE: PROC OPTIONS (MAIN);
/************************************************************/
/*                                                          */
/* PROGRAM: UPDATE A REGIONAL FILE                          */
/* AUTHOR:  C ZIEGLER                                       */
/* VERSION: 07/17/84                                        */
/*                                                          */
/* PROGRAM DESCRIPTION                                      */
/* ---------------------------------------------------      */
/* THIS PROGRAM UPDATES A REGIONAL DISK FILE.  IT           */
/* INSERTS RECORDS, MODIFIES RECORDS, AND DELETES           */
/* RECORDS USING DIRECT PROCESSING.                         */
/*                                                          */
/* INPUT: MASTERF - THE MASTER FILE                         */
/*                COLS      1 RECORD TYPE CODE              */
/*                      2 -  3 FILLER                       */
/*                      4 -  8 SYMBOLIC KEY                 */
/*                      9 - 16 ACCOUNT BALANCE              */
/*                     17 - 80 RECORD INFORMATION           */
/*        TRANSF - THE TRANSACTION FILE                     */
/*                COLS      1 TRANSACTION CODE              */
/*                             'I' FOR INSERTION            */
/*                             'D' FOR DELETION             */
/*                             'M' FOR MODIFICATION         */
/*                      2 -  3 RELATIVE RECORD KEY          */
/*                      4 -  8 SYMBOLIC KEY                 */
/*                      9 - 16 TRANSACTION AMOUNT           */
/*                      9 - 16 ACCOUNT BALANCE              */
/*                     17 - 80 RECORD INFORMATION           */
/*                                                          */
/* OUTPUT: MASTERF - THE UPDATED MASTER FILE                */
/*         SYSPRINT - ERROR MESSAGES                        */
/*                                                          */
/* CALLS: SEARCH_FILE                                       */
/*                                                          */
/************************************************************/
DCL MASTRF FILE KEYED DIRECT INPUT RECORD ENV(REGIONAL),
    TRANSF FILE        SEQL  INPUT RECORD ENV(CONSECUTIVE);
DCL 1  MASTER_REC,
       5  REC_TYPE      CHAR(1),
       5  FILLER        CHAR(1),
       5  SYMB_KEY      CHAR(5),
       5  ACCT_BAL      PIC'(6)S9V99',
       5  REC_INFO      CHAR(64);
```

```
DCL 1  TRANS_REC,
         5  TRANS_TYPE    CHAR(1),
         5  REC_KEY       PIC'99',
         5  SYMB_KEY      CHAR(5),
         5  ACCT_BAL      PIC'(6)S9V99',
         5  REC_INFO      CHAR(64),
      TRANS_AMT           PIC'(6)9V99'   DEF(ACCT_BAL);
DCL MORE_T                BIT(1),
    RECORD_FOUND          BIT(1),
    SPACE_AVAILABLE       BIT(1),
    TRUE                  BIT(1)      INIT('1'B),
    FALSE                 BIT(1)      INTI('0'B);
DCL REC_NO                FIXED BIN;

ON KEY (MASTERF)
  PUT SKIP LIST ('KEY OUT OF BOUNDS - ',REC_KEY);
ON ENDFILE (TRANSF)
  MORE_T = FALSE;

MORE_T = TRUE;
OPEN FILE (MASTERF),
     FILE (TRANSF);
READ FILE (TRANSF) INTO (TRANS_REC);
DO WHILE (MORE_T);                       /* FOR ALL TRANSACTIONS */
  CALL SEARCH_FILE;
  SELECT;
    WHEN (TRANS_TYPE = 'I')              /* PROCESS INSERTIONS   */
      SELECT;
        WHEN (RECORD_FOUND)
          PUT SKIP LIST ('DUPLICATE RECORD - ',REC_KEY);
        WHEN (SPACE_AVAILABLE)
          DO;
            MASTER_REC = ' ';
            MASTER_REC = TRANS_REC, BY NAME;
            WRITE FILE (MASTERF) FROM (MASTER_REC)
                        KEYFROM (REC_NO);
          END;
        OTHERWISE
          PUT SKIP LIST ('NO SPACE FOR - ',REC_KEY);
      END;
    WHEN (TRANS_TYPE = 'M')              /* PROCESS MODIFICATIONS */
      IF RECORD_FOUND
        THEN
          DO;
            MASTER_REC.ACCT_BAL = MASTER_REC.ACCT_BAL - TRANS_AMT;
            REWRITE FILE (MASTERF) FROM (MASTER_REC) KEY (REC_NO);
          END;
        ELSE
          PUT SKIP LIST ('RECORD NOT FOUND - ',REC_KEY);
    WHEN (TRANS_TYPE = 'D')              /* PROCESS DELETIONS     */
      IF RECORD_FOUND
```

```
        THEN
          DELETE FILE (MASTRF) KEY (REC_NO);
        ELSE
          PUT SKIP LIST ('RECORD NOT FOUND - ',REC_KEY);
    OTHERWISE
      PUT SKIP LIST ('INVALID TRANS CODE - ',TRANS_TYPE);
  END;
  READ FILE (TRANSF) INTO (TRANS_REC);
END;
CLOSE FILE (TRANSF),
      FILE (MASTERF);

SEARCH_FILE: PROC;
/***************************************************************/
/*                                                             */
/*  SEARCH FILE SEQUENTIALLY FROM HOME TO HOME + 10            */
/*  ON EXIT: REC_NO - POSITION WHERE RECORD FOUND              */
/*                    OR POSITION OF AVAILABLE SPACE           */
/*           RECORD_FOUND - STATUS FLAG                        */
/*           SPACE_AVAILABLE - STATUS FLAG                     */
/*                                                             */
/***************************************************************/
DCL INACTIVE    BIT(8)      INIT('11111111'B),
    FILE_MAX    FIXED BIN   INIT(99),
    NEW_REC_NO  FIXED BIN,
    K           FIXED BIN;
ON KEY (MASTERF)
  SPACE_FOUND = TRUE;

RECORD_FOUND = FALSE;
SPACE_AVAILABLE = FALSE;
REC_NO = REC_KEY - 1;
DO K = 1 TO 10 UNTIL (RECORD_FOUND);   /* SCAN UP TO 10 POSITIONS */
  IF REC_NO >FILE_MAX
    THEN
      REC_NO = 0;
  REC_NO = REC_NO + 1;
  READ FILE (MASTERF) INTO (MASTER_REC) KEY (REC_NO);
  IF SPACE_FOUND | REC_TYPE = INACTIVE
    THEN
      K = 10;                          /* AVAILABLE SPACE FOUND   */
    ELSE
      IF MASTER_REC.SYMB_KEY = TRANS_REC.SYMB_KEY
        THEN
          DO;
            RECORD_FOUND = TRUE;       /* RECORD FOUND            */
            K = 10;
          END;
END;
END SEARCH_FILE;
END UPDATE;
```

17.8 Summary

REGIONAL files may be used either KEYED or unkeyed, for sequential or direct processing. The three file operations of record insertion, modification, and deletion can be carried out under either sequential or direct access.

The KEYED attribute must be used for direct access. It may be used for sequential access, and should be used if only part of the file is being processed. With the KEYED attribute, the index is used. Otherwise the file is scanned sequentially from the beginning.

The uses of the various file types are:

SEQL INPUT	To write a report from a file.
SEQL OUTPUT	To create a file when the records are in relative record key order.
SEQL UPDATE	To update a file when there no duplicates.
DIRECT UPDATE	To retrieve a few selected records.
DIRECT OUTPUT	To create a file when the records are not in relative record key order.
DIRECT UPDATE	To update a file when there are few transactions or duplicate record keys in the file.

Table 17–4 shows the different possible combinations of file attributes and the input/output statements that may be used with each one.

File attributes	*Valid Operations*
SEQUENTIAL INPUT [KEYED]	READ ... INTO ... [KEY ...] READ ... INTO ... [KEYTO ...] READ ... SET ... [KEY ...] READ ... SET ... [KEYTO ...] [READ ... IGNORE ...]
SEQUENTIAL OUTPUT [KEYED]	WRITE ... FROM ... [KEYFROM ...] [LOCATE ... [KEYFROM ...] [SET ...]]
SEQUENTIAL UPDATE [KEYED]	READ ... INTO ... [KEY ...] READ ... INTO ... [KEYTO ...] READ ... SET ... [KEY ...] READ ... SET ... [KEYTO ...] READ ... IGNORE ... REWRITE ... [DELETE ...]
DIRECT INPUT KEYED	READ ... INTO ... KEY ...
DIRECT OUTPUT KEYED	WRITE ... FROM ... KEYFROM ...
DIRECT UPDATE KEYED	READ ... INTO ... KEY ... WRITE ... FROM ... KEYFROM ... REWRITE ... FROM ... KEY ... DELETE ... KEY ...

Table 17–4

The KEY, KEYFROM, and KEYTO clauses may be used only if the KEYED attribute is used.

17.9 Exercises

1. Write a program that merges two RECORD files, MASTER and NEW, which have records of the form:

Cols.		
	1-4	Student ID
	5-80	Student information

MASTER is a relative file with ID as the key field. NEW is a CONSECUTIVE file which has been sorted in ascending order on the ID field. Use ID as the relative record key. Insert the records from NEW in MASTER, using skip-sequential processing. Neither file contains duplicates, but there may be some IDs occurring in both files. If so, write the record in NEW to a printer file DUPL. Check on the accuracy of your program by printing the first 100 records from the original and the updated master files.

2. Write a program that prints a report from (a) a relative file, BOOK, which has the form:

Cols.		
	1-10	ISBN
	11-20	Library of Congress number
	21-40	Author
	41-60	Title
	61-64	Edition

and which uses ISBN as the symbolic key and the prime division hashing algorithm with prime 997; and (b) a CONSECUTIVE file CIRCUL, which has the form:

Cols.		
	1-10	ISBN
	11-20	Library of Congress number
	21-32	Copy
	33-42	Borrower
	43	Status ('C' checked out, 'O' overdue, 'L' lost, 'B' at bindery, 'S' shelved, 'X' unknown)

and is in ascending order by Library of Congress number. Assume that the file BOOK is correct and the relative record keys are unique. The file CIRCUL may contain duplicate key values. The report should list each BOOK record for which there are CIRCUL records, along with the CIRCUL records. If the status field does not contain a valid code, give it the code 'X'. The output should be readable. Use direct access.

3. Write a program that simulates a library card catalogue using (a) a relative file BOOK, which has the form:

Cols.		
	1-10	ISBN
	11-20	Library of Congress number
	21-40	Author
	41-60	Title
	61-64	Edition
	65-100	Description

and which uses the author's name as the key field; and (b) a CONSECUTIVE file QUERY, which has the form:

Cols.	1-20	Author

and has not been sorted. The records of BOOK are stored with the first two characters of the name, replaced by their position in the alphabet (A is 01, B is 02, . . .) as storage key. For instance, both JAMES and JANSEN are stored under 1001 for JA. For each author's name in QUERY, print all the records of books by that author. Assume maximum progressive overflow of ten positions in the file.

4. Write a driver routine and external procedures to create, update, and list a relative file. The original date is on a CONSECUTIVE file SOURCE, which has records of the form:

Cols.	1-5	Farm name
	6-12	Location
	13-15	Soil type
	16-20	Plant number
	21-30	Hybrid parentage
	31-80	Experimental information

The records are in ascending order by plant number. Build a relative file using the plant number as the symbolic key and the sum of digits hashing algorithm. Assume that the relative record keys are unique. One external subroutine should read plant numbers from the CONSECUTIVE file PLANT, which has records of the form:

Cols.	1-5	Plant number
	6-55	Experimental information

and should replace the experimental information stored in the record with the new information. Use DIRECT access. Another external subroutine should list the relative file. Print both the original file and the updated file.

5. Create a relative file using unkeyed sequential access by copying a CONSECUTIVE file SOURCE, which has records of the form:

Cols.	1-20	Name
	21-40	Address
	41-50	Telephone number

which are in order by telephone number. Count the number of records being stored in the file. Assume that the telephone numbers are unique. Read telephone numbers from a CONSECUTIVE file PHONE, which has records of the form:

Cols.	1-10	Telephone number

and use a binary search to look up the corresponding names and addresses in the relative file.

18
Teleprocessing and tasking

OBJECTIVE: To coordinate separate processes and service several terminals.

PL/I CAN BE USED to write programs for both batch and interactive processing. Batch applications take input from files on mass storage or from tape or cards. Output is sent to files on mass storage, tape, or printers. Those interactive applications that run as single-user jobs are similar. Input and output may be the same as in batch processing but input may also be taken from the CRT terminal that initiates program execution and output may be sent to that terminal. The default file names of SYSIN and SYSPRINT are assigned to the terminal by the JCL. Input may be either stream or variable-length records. Input transmission is initiated by a GET or READ instruction referring to SYSIN. The computer then waits for input followed by a carriage return, which acts as an end-of-line symbol for input. Output data is returned to the terminal. Output to be placed on a single line should be followed by a SKIP to return the carriage after displaying the data.

18.1 Teleprocessing (not in Subset G)

Application programs for use at more than one terminal can take several forms.

1. Each user can be provided with his or her own copy of the program to be run in an interactive mode. This copy is made available through the

operating system at the user's request. The user controls the processing, which is treated as a single-user job.

2. One program can be written to control several terminals. The computer operator initiates the processing, which is then controlled by the computer.

18.1.1 File organization

Technically, input from terminals to a multiuser application takes the form of *messages* rather than records. These messages are queued by the system in a storage buffer until they can be processed. The system *message control program* routes messages to and from terminals and programs, and controls the queuing of the messages. There is one queue for each terminal. In the application program these queues are associated with TRANSIENT files and accessed sequentially. They must be declared with the KEYED attribute, having the key identify the terminal. TRANSIENT is a file-access method rather than a method of file organization. The specific organization used is system-dependent. When a file is declared TRANSIENT, DIRECT and SEQUENTIAL access cannot be used.

A program handling terminals should have one transient file for input and one for output. The same transient file is associated with different queues by changing the key. The queues (terminals) may therefore be thought of as analogous to locations in a file holding values which are changed from outside the system.

18.1.2 File declarations

The general form of the declaration of a TRANSIENT file is:

```
DCL file_name FILE RECORD KEYED TRANSIENT BUFFERED
              ENV(teleprocessing);
```

The contents of the ENVIRONMENT clause are implementation-dependent.

Two types of files may be used to address terminals. CONSECUTIVE files may be used for input with a single terminal and in some circumstances with multiple terminals. However, if several terminals are being used for both input and output, TRANSIENT files are needed. The queues, keys, and message strings must all be declared as in the following example:

```
DCL IN_MSG    FILE RECORD KEYED TRANSIENT          /* INPUT FILE     */
                   BUFFERED ENV (teleprocessing),
    OUT_MSG   FILE RECORD KEYED TRANSIENT          /* OUTPUT FILE    */
                   BUFFERED ENV (teleprocessing),
    IN_DATA   CHAR(100),                           /* INPUT STRING   */
    OUT_DATA  CHAR(500),                           /* OUTPUT STRING  */
    TERM_KEY  CHAR(8);                             /* QUEUE ID       */

OPEN INPUT FILE(IN_MSG),
     OUTPUT FILE(OUT_MSG);
```

Messages are treated as variable-length records; therefore input and output variables must be large enough to contain the longest possible records. The maximum length is system-dependent.

18.1.3 File availability

TRANSIENT files are opened and closed like other files. Operating system commands are used to identify the terminals being addressed by each file.

18.1.4 Record access

Unlike ordinary files, the records in TRANSIENT files have no physical existence outside the dynamic storage of the input/output queues. Once they have been read or written, they are gone unless they are also stored in program variables. The end of the queue is detected not by an ENDFILE condition, since there may be more data to come which has not yet been keyed in, but by a PENDING condition. This signifies a wait for input. The programmer has the choice of waiting or of switching service to a different terminal by changing the value of the key, or of performing disk I/O or calculations.

In a message-based teleprocessing environment, the unit of transmission is the message even though the teleprocessing file is declared with the RECORD attribute. A message and a record are equivalent in this type of file.

Alternately the environment may be record-based, the unit of transmission being a record, which is part of a message. If short messages are being handled, the environment should be message-based. If long messages are expected, they must be broken into records and the environment declared as record-based. With this latter option, each record must contain an identification field which indicates the position of the record in the message. The system message control program can be set up for one or the other type of environment, but not both.

Table 18–1

Attributes	*Instructions*
TRANSIENT RECORD INPUT KEYED ENV (teleprocessing)	READ FILE (file_name) INTO (var) KEY (term) READ FILE (file_name) SET (ptr) KEY (term)
TRANSIENT RECORD INPUT KEYED ENV (CONSECUTIVE)	READ FILE (file_name) INTO (var) KEYTO (term) READ FILE (file_name) SET (ptr) KEYTO (term)
TRANSIENT RECORD OUTPUT KEYED ENV (teleprocessing)	WRITE FILE (file_name) FROM (var) KEYFROM (term) LOCATE var FILE (file_name) KEYFROM (term)

INPUT/OUTPUT OPERATIONS

A teleprocessing file can be accessed by READ, WRITE, and LOCATE instructions. The I/O statements used with various combinations of file attributes are given in table 18–1. Note that TRANSIENT files must be KEYED, must be RECORD files, and cannot be updated. The KEYFROM and KEY options are used to identify terminals.

18.1.5 File error conditions

The exception conditions that can be raised using TRANSIENT files are:

ERROR	Incorrectly identifying an input terminal
KEY	Incorrectly idenfifying an output terminal
PENDING	Attempting to read an empty queue
RECORD	Using too small a record size
TRANSMIT	Attempting to write when the queue is full

A READ issued for a TRANSIENT file causes an automatic wait for input. The PENDING condition is not really an error as it provides a way of testing for input.

Usually a program controlling many terminals will poll the terminals; that is, cycle through them checking for input. A PENDING condition is a signal to go on to the next terminal. This is shown in the following example:

```
ON PENDING (IN_MSG)
  BEGIN;
      K = K + 1;
      If K > LAST
        THEN
          K = 1;
      DATA_FOUND = FALSE;
  END;
 K = 1;
DO UNTIL (DATA FOUND);                /* POLL TERMINALS */
  TERM_KEY = TERM (K);
  DATA_FOUND = TRUE;
  READ FILE (IN_MSG) INTO (IN_DATA) KEY (TERM_KEY);
END;
```

If input is needed from a specific terminal, the PENDING condition is not necessary as the computer will wait for input if there is no ON unit. The only statement needed is:

```
READ FILE (IN_MSG) INTO (IN_DATA) KEY (TERM_KEY);
```

A second method of controlling the terminals is to process the input in the order it is received by the message control program. Terminals that need servicing interrupt the system. The program obtains data from the input queue by using it as a CONSECUTIVE file. The PENDING condition cannot be used. This is shown in the following example:

```
READ FILE (IN_MSG) INTO (IN_DATA) KEYTO (TERM_KEY);
DO WHILE (MORE);
 . . .
  WRITE FILE (OUT_MSG) FROM (OUT_DATA) KEYFROM (TERM-KEY);
  READ FILE (IN_MSG) INTO (IN_DATA) KEYTO (TERM_KEY);
END;
```

Input from terminals may be received in either a teleprocessing or a consecutive environment, but it may be transmitted only from a teleprocessing environment.

INTERACTIVE PROCESSING

As with standard files the TITLE option of the OPEN statement is used to relate a program file name to the queue identification established by the operating system. The queue names are system-dependent. The following example shows the computer prompting a user for data, then echoing the data and waiting for acknowledgment that it is correct.

```
DCL IN      FILE INPUT RECORD KEYED TRANSIENT
                 BUFFERED (teleprocessing),
    OUT     FILE OUTPUT RECORD KEYED TRANSIENT
                 BUFFERED (teleprocessing);
DCL PROMPT CHAR (11) INIT ('ENTER NAME _'),
    NAME   CHAR (30) VARYING,
    QUERY  CHAR (25) INIT ('IS NAME CORRECT (Y OR N)?'),
    REPLY  CHAR (1),
    TKEY   CHAR (8);
. . .

OPEN INPUT FILE (IN) TITLE ('Q1');
OPEN OUTPUT FILE (OUT) TITLE ('Q2');
TKEY = . . .
WRITE FILE (OUT) FROM (PROMPT) KEYFROM (TKEY);  /* PROMPT USER */
READ FILE (IN) INTO (NAME) KEY (TKEY);          /* GET INPUT   */
WRITE FILE (OUT) FROM (QUERY) KEYFROM (TKEY);   /* PROMPT USER  */
READ FILE (IN) INTO (REPLY) KEY (TKEY);         /* GET Y OR N  */
IF REPLY = 'Y'
  THEN
  . . .
CLOSE FILE (IN),
      FILE (OUT);
```

There are two basic methods employed in controlling multiple terminals.

1. Each terminal input can be independent of previous inputs, such as queries to a database that require a reply but do not require memory of previous queries.
2. Terminal I/O can be a dialogue that requires retention.

Independent inputs do not require work space for the terminal. A program can poll the terminals without retaining any memory of the processing except for entries written to a log file. Using independent inputs is an efficient way of controlling terminals. The example above does not use this method if the action taken in response to the reply uses the name that preceded it. An efficient dialogue, in which the computer must stay with one terminal for a while, is complex. Having a single work space for all terminals means that all but one must be shut out during the dialogue. This is undesirable since it results in an unnecessarily long response time at the other terminals.

Programming for interactive use involves a number of considerations which are not relevant to batch input.

1. Depending on the system, the input may not be echoed at the source; therefore it must be echoed by the program.
2. Data entered by on-line users may be fields of a formatted screen and therefore position-dependent, or it may be responses to questions.
3. At one extreme, the screen may be transmitted in its entirety. At the other extreme, characters may be transmitted one at a time. The choice depends on the characteristics of the terminal and on the program.

If the user is filling in a screen, the program and/or terminal must:

1. Display the formatted screen.
2. Display entries in the appropriate fields.
3. Validate the data.
4. Provide default values for fields.
5. Permit fields to be left empty.
6. Permit fields to be corrected.
7. Permit fields to be filled in any order.
8. Pick up values from the fields.
9. Ask for commitment of the data before acting on it.
10. Provide a way to terminate the input session.

When single-item responses are being input, the program must:

1. Prompt the user every time input is expected.
2. Acknowledge entries.
3. Provide a help function.
4. Provide a way to cancel input before acting on it.
5. Provide a way to omit input.
6. Provide a way to terminate the input session.

Since interactive I/O is very slow, throughput is helped by having intelligent terminals with screen-editing facilities. The simplest way to provide work space for each terminal is to set up separate tasks, two per terminal, one to process the input queue and one to process the output queue, which share a single work space.

Review questions

1. Indicate whether each of the following statements is true or false.
   (a) In interactive data entry, the end-of-line and end-of-file symbols are different.
   (b) When many terminals are controlled by a single program, there is one queue for each terminal.
   (c) When many terminals are controlled by a single program, there is one file for each terminal.
   (d) Teleprocessing can be record-oriented or message-oriented.
   (e) Each terminal is identified by a key.

2. Complete each of the following statements.
   (a) When a TRANSIENT file is used for single-user input, the ________________ (ENDFILE/PENDING) condition is raised when there is no data.
   (b) When a TRANSIENT file is used for multiuser input, the ________________ (ENDFILE/PENDING) condition is raised when there is no data.
   (c) When a CONSECUTIVE file is used for single-user input, the access is ________________ (SEQUENTIAL/TRANSIENT).
   (d) When a CONSECUTIVE file is used for multiuser input, the access is ________________ (SEQUENTIAL/TRANSIENT).
   (e) When the computer checks each terminal to determine whether it needs servicing, the system strategy is ________________ (polling/interrupt-driven).
   (f) When the computer waits for a terminal to indicate that it needs servicing, the system strategy is ________________ (polling/interrupt-driven).

3. A dialogue between computer and terminal is less efficient for multiuser applications than processing independent queries and responses because ________________.

18.2 Tasking (not in Subset G)

Tasks are programs or procedures that execute separately. Separate programs in separate job steps can be thought of as tasks, but usually what is meant is a procedure that is "spun off" or "initiated" or "attached" by another procedure, which starts it, then continues with its own processing. Such a procedure runs concurrently with its parent. Tasking is used in systems with more than one processor. It provides a way of making maximum use of the system resources for a single job by permitting the processors to execute parts of the program concurrently. Since channels are processors, the most common type of tasking is processing of input/output at the same time as computational processing. In multicomputer configurations and other forms of multiprocessing systems, several computations may be performed simultaneously on different processors.

A procedure may spawn any number of different tasks or may spin off several copies of the same task. Multiple copies of an internal procedure set up to handle different I/O devices or different terminals are run as tasks. Tasks must be written in such a way that they do not interfere with each other. If synchronization is needed, there are instructions that can be used to communicate between tasks by passing values back and forth. Also, data may be shared through global variables.

DECLARATIONS

Associated with tasks are variables known as EVENT variables, which are used in the synchronization of tasks. Both tasks and event variables can be declared explicitly or contextually.

TASK declarations The general form of declaration of a task is:

```
DCL task_name TASK;
```

A task is like a subprocedure except that when it is initiated, control does not transfer to it. Instead both the attaching (calling) and attached (called) tasks execute concurrently. A task is initiated by a CALL statement of the form:

```
CALL task_name [TASK] [EVENT(event_name)];
```

The word TASK is used in the CALL statement to declare it contextually when the TASK has not been declared explicitly. The EVENT option is used to contextually declare an EVENT variable.

EVENT declarations An EVENT variable is a flag that can be used to signal to one task the occurrence of a specific event in another task. An EVENT variable associated with a TASK signals the completion of the task. EVENT variables can also be declared explicitly. The form of declaration is:

```
DCL event-name EVENT;
```

The program segment

```
DCL READER TASK,
    READ_DONE EVENT;

CALL READER;
```

differs from the statement

```
CALL READER TASK EVENT (READ_DONE);
```

When the event variable READ_DONE is declared contextually, it is used to automatically signal completion of the task, and to associate the variable with the task. When the statement

```
CALL READER TASK EVENT(READ_DONE);
```

is executed, execution of the task READER is started, the event variable READ_DONE is set to incomplete, and the calling procedure continues execution. When the task exits, READ_DONE is set to complete. An event variable associated with a task is cleared automatically when the task is initiated and set automatically when the task is exited.

Separate declarations are used when event variables are to be explicitly set and cleared.

Tasks may be executed on a single processor as well as on separate processors. Since most computers cannot actually execute two programs at once, control switches back and forth between tasks according to some operating system formula. Since input and output are slow compared to calculations, subtasks are usually used to handle I/O so that the main processing can continue while the I/O takes place. In the case of I/O, a separate processor is often involved so that processing can in fact take place concurrently.

18.2.1 Task synchronization

Some synchronization of tasks is needed. A main program must not use data being provided by an input task until the input has been completed. Similarly, a main program that is filling an output buffer must not overrun the buffer but must wait until it has been partly emptied by an output task. This synchronization takes place by means of EVENT variables. A task can WAIT for an EVENT to occur.

Any procedure can be attached as a task and executed concurrently with its calling procedure. However, a calling procedure will terminate abnormally if it exits before all its attached tasks have been terminated. The calling procedure must therefore WAIT until all subtasks signal that they are finished. In the following example, the main program calls SUB, attaching it as a task and associating the event variable DONE with it.

```
MP: PROC OPTIONS (MAIN);
  . . .
CALL SUB TASK EVENT(DONE);
  . . .
WAIT (DONE);
  . . .
SUB: PROC;
  . . .
RETURN;
END SUB;
END MP;
```

The CALL statement automatically sets DONE to incomplete. The main program continues executing until the WAIT statement is reached, at which time it waits for the value of DONE to be set to complete. Meanwhile the subtask SUB is executing. The RETURN statement in it causes the associated event variable DONE to be automatically set to complete, and execution stops on both procedures.

WAIT STATEMENT

The WAIT statement has the form:

```
WAIT (event-name-list) [(num)];
```

It may reference any event name known to it. The scope of EVENT variables is similar to the scope of other types of variables. The effect of this statement is to cause the processing of a procedure to pause until the event named has completed. Completion takes place automatically if the event is associated with a task; otherwise it is signaled by explicitly setting the event variable to complete.

When two or more event names are used in the WAIT statement, the number option is used to indicate whether some or all of the events must occur before the procedure may continue.

Given the statement

```
WAIT (PUT_DONE);
```

the execution of the procedure pauses until the event PUT_DONE has occurred.

Given the statement

```
WAIT (GET_END,PUT_END) (2);
```

the execution of the procedure pauses until both of the events GET_END and PUT_END have occurred.

Given the statement

```
WAIT (A_FLAG,B_FLAG) (1);
```

the execution of the procedure pauses until one or the other of the events A_FLAG and B_FLAG have occurred.

SIGNALING EVENTS

Event variables may be explicitly set, cleared, and tested. This is done by using the function COMPLETION. This function equates the values of complete and incomplete, to '1'B and '0'B respectively.

```
IF COMPLETION(DONE)
```

tests whether the event DONE has occurred. The COMPLETION function can also be used as a pseudovariable to set the value of an event variable.

```
COMPLETION(AEV) = '1'B;
```

sets the event AEV to complete.

```
COMPLETION(AEV) = '0'B;
```

sets the event variable to incomplete.

In the following example, the task GET_REC reads a file and the task PUT_REC prints it.

```
DCL REC          CHAR(80),
    GET_DONE     EVENT,
    PUT_DONE     EVENT,
    TRUE         BIT(1)  INIT('1'B),
    FALSE        BIT(1)  INIT('0'B),
    COMPLETE     BIT(1)  INIT('1'B),
    INCOMPLETE   BIT(1)  INIT('0'B);

CALL GET_REC TASK EVENT(GET_END);
CALL PUT_REC TASK EVENT(PUT_END);
 . . .
WAIT(GET_END,PUT_END) (2);/* WAIT FOR BOTH TASKS TO FINISH */

GET_REC: PROC;              /* GET ONE RECORD AT A TIME      */
DCL MORE      BIT(1);
 . . .
READ FILE(SYSIN) INTO (REC);
DO WHILE (MORE);
  COMPLETION(GET_DONE) = COMPLETE;
  WAIT(PUT_DONE);          /* WAIT FOR RECORD TO BE WRITTEN  */
  COMPLETION(PUT_DONE) = INCOMPLETE;
  READ FILE(SYSIN) INTO (REC);
END;
END GET_REC;

PUT_REC: PROC;             /* PUT ONE RECORD AT A TIME       */
 . . .
DO WHILE (MORE);
  WAIT(GET_DONE);          /* WAIT FOR RECORD TO BE READ     */
  COMPLETION(GET_DONE) = INCOMPLETE;
  WRITE FILE(SYSOUT) FROM (REC);
  COMPLETION(PUT_DONE) = COMPLETE;
END;
END PUT_REC;
```

Notice that each task checks for the completion of the other task's I/O, then clears the other task's completion flag before starting its own I/O. When its own I/O is complete, it sets its own flag. The flags must be initialized in such a way that the priming READ is the first I/O operation. The calling procedure must wait for all of its attached tasks to complete before it exits.

18.2.2 Task communication

Tasks may share common data-storage areas. If the following two tasks are executed, it is likely that the value 3 will be printed, but this is not necessarily the case.

```
DCL X    FIXED BIN;
X = 0;
CALL A TASK EVENT(A_DONE);
CALL B TASK EVENT(B_DONE);
WAIT (A_DONE,B_DONE) (2);     /* WAIT FOR A & B TO FINISH */
PUT LIST(X);

A: PROC;
X = X + 1;
END A;

B: PROC;
X = X + 2;
END B;
```

When task A is attached it is placed in the queue of tasks waiting for processing. The same thing is done with task B. If A executes wholly before B or B wholly before A, the result will be 3. However, if the processor interleaves tasks, it is possible that task A picks up the value of X and is interrupted before it can increment the value and replace it. Therefore task B may pick up the value 0 and replace it with 2 before task A stores 1 in X. The main program waits until both A and B have finished.

Task A	*Task B*
Gets X (value 0)	
	Gets X (value 0)
	Adds 2
	Replaces X (value 2)
Adds 1	
Replaces X (value 1)	

Thus the final result may be 1. If the situation were reversed, the final result would be 2. Depending on operating system formulas, the processor may interleave statements at the machine language level.

Machine language instructions which are implemented by hardware cannot be broken in this fashion. However, most source language instructions require more than one machine language instruction to carry them out. In a high-level language, only the assignment of simple integer constants to variables is uninterruptable. Therefore, in a multiprocessing environment when tasks can interfere with each other, it is necessary to synchronize access to global variables by restricting possible interleaving. The statements X = X + 1 and X = X + 2 of tasks A and B above are *critical sections.* Their execution must be made mutually exclusive. This is done by starting task A, then task B. If the two tasks reach their critical sections at about the same time, whichever task reaches its critical section first turns control over to the other task, suspending operation. The other task returns control and waits until the first is out of its critical section.

The task synchronization at the beginning of the critical section is known as the *entry protocol.* For example,

In A:
```
A_BUSY = TRUE;
TURN = 'B';
DO WHILE (B-BUSY & TURN = 'B');   /* WAIT FOR B */
END;
```

In B:
```
B_BUSY = TRUE;
TURN = 'A';
DO WHILE (A-BUSY & TURN = 'A');   /* WAIT FOR A */
END;
```

Whichever task reaches its entry protocol first will be the task to enter its critical section first. The other task will be in a wait loop until the first one executes its exit protocol.

Clearing the busy flag at the end of the critical section is known as the *exit protocol.* For example,

In A: `A_BUSY = FALSE;`

In B: `B_BUSY = FALSE;`

The following example shows how this is used. Except for the protection offered by the entry and exit protocols, this example is the same as the one above.

```
MP: PROC OPTIONS(MAIN);
DCL X        FIXED BIN,
    A_BUSY BIT(1),
    B_BUSY BIT(1),
    TURN   CHAR(10);
DCL TRUE   BIT(1)    INIT('1'B),
    FALSE  BIT(1)    INIT('0'B);

A_BUSY = FALSE;                        /* A NOT BUSY       */
B_BUSY = FALSE;                        /* B NOT BUSY       */
TURN = 'A';                            /* START A FIRST    */
X = 0;
CALL A TASK EVENT (A_DONE);
CALL B TASK EVENT (B_DONE);
WAIT (A_DONE,B_DONE)(2);               /* WAIT FOR A & B   */
PUT LIST (X);

A: PROC;
A_BUSY = TRUE;                         /* ENTRY PROTOCOL   */
TURN = 'B';
DO WHILE (B_BUSY & TURN = 'B');        /* WAIT TURN        */
END;
X = X + 1;                             /* CRITICAL SECTION */
A_BUSY = FALSE;                        /* EXIT PROTOCOL    */
END A;
```

```
B: PROC;
B_BUSY = TRUE;                          /* ENTRY PROTOCOL     */
TURN = 'A';
DO WHILE (A_BUSY & TURN = 'A');         /* WAIT TURN          */
END;
X = X + 2;                              /* CRITICAL SECTION   */
B_BUSY = FALSE;                         /* EXIT PROTOCOL      */
END B;
```

(Refer to section 18.3.2)

The *entry protocol* is the set of instructions necessary to set up mutual exclusion protection of the shared variable. It is used to flag the task's need to access shared variables, then give priority to the other task. The critical section is the part of the program that must be protected to avoid interference between tasks. It involves updating of shared data areas. The *exit protocol* removes the protection.

If tasks A and B are interleaved, execution might proceed as follows.

MP	*A*	*B*
A_BUSY is false		
B_BUSY is false		
TURN is 'A'		
WAIT		
	A_BUSY is true	
		B_BUSY is true
		TURN = 'A'
		wait
	TURN is 'B'	
	wait	
		X = X + 2
		B_BUSY is false
		END
	X = X + 1	
	A_BUSY is false	
	END	
PUT LIST(X)		
END		

Or they may be interleaved in this way:

A_BUSY is false		
B_BUSY is false		
TURN is 'A'		
WAIT		
	A_BUSY is true	
	TURN is 'B'	
		B_BUSY is true
		TURN is 'A'
		wait
	X = X + 1	
	A_BUSY is false	
	END	
		X = X + 2
		B_BUSY is false
		END
PUT LIST(X)		
END		

Or in this way:

```
A_BUSY is false
B_BUSY is false
TURN is 'A'
WAIT
                    A_BUSY is true
                    TURN is 'B'
                    WAIT
                                        B_BUSY is true
                                        TURN is 'A'
                                        wait

                    X = X + 1
                    A_BUSY is false
                    END
                                        X = X + 2
                                        B_BUSY is false
                                        END
PUT LIST(X)
END
```

In these examples, control shifts from one task to another under control of the operating system. The shift may occur at any point: it may take place after the A_BUSY flag is set by task A, or it may take place after the TURN indicator is set by task A, or after task A enters a wait state. A task in an explicit wait state in a wait loop will continue to wait until conditions change. This limits the number of possible scenarios. In these examples, once one routine reaches the critical section, the other is locked out until the busy flag is cleared. In every case, the result is 3. The setting and clearing of flags are single machine-level operations. Therefore the synchronization assignments themselves are not interruptable.

DEADLOCK

Entry and exit protocols are designed to prevent deadlock. EVENT variables are used for the same purpose. *Deadlock* occurs if neither task can proceed. If the variable TURN were not used in the example above, it would be possible for each task to indicate intent to update the X value, then neither would be able to proceed, each waiting for the other to finish. With the variable TURN, this cannot occur. Every concurrent program must include safeguards against deadlock.

Deadlock may occur in accessing shared files as well as in accessing shared data storage areas. The same methods may be used in guarding file access. In addition, in some PL/I systems, the file declaration and commands can be used to prevent deadlock. The declaration

```
DCL MASTER FILE KEYED DIRECT UPDATE RECORD EXCLUSIVE ENV(INDEXED);
```

includes an EXCLUSIVE option which indicates that one task may lock another task out of either individual records of the file, or the entire file. To lock the entire file, the lock is set on the OPEN statement, as in:

```
OPEN FILE (MASTER) LOCK TITLE('MA');
```

When a locked file is closed, it is automatically unlocked. Individual records of an EXCLUSIVE file are locked by a READ statement, for example,

```
READ FILE(MASTER) INTO (REC) KEY (Q_KEY);
```

unless the UNLOCK option is used on the READ statement, for example,

```
READ UNLOCK FILE(MASTER) INTO (REC) KEY (Q_KEY);
```

WRITE and REWRITE statements cannot have the UNLOCK attribute. Any other users must be locked out of a record that is being replaced. The WRITE and REWRITE statements have the effect of automatically unlocking the record after the output has been completed.

The following example shows the interaction between a task that reads a file in response to queries and another task that revises a file.

```
DCL MASTER FILE KEYED DIRECT UPDATE RECORD EXCLUSIVE ENV(INDEXED);

CALL QUERY TASK;
CALL REVISE TASK;
 . . .

QUERY: PROC;
 . . .
OPEN FILE (MASTER) TITLE ('MA');
 . . .                                                  /***************/
                                                        /*             */
  READ UNLOCK FILE (MASTER) INTO (REC) KEY (Q_KEY);/* REPEAT        */
 . . .                                                  /*             */
                                                        /***************/
CLOSE FILE (MASTER);
 . . .
END QUERY;

REVISE: PROC;
 . . .                                                  /***************/
                                                        /* REPEAT      */
  WAIT(NO_QUERIES);                                     /*             */
  OPEN FILE (MASTER) LOCK TITLE('MA');                  /* LOCK FILE   */
  REWRITE FILE (MASTER) FROM (NEW_REC) KEY (R_KEY);/*             */
  CLOSE FILE (MASTER);                                  /* UNLOCK FILE */
. . .                                                   /*             */
                                                        /***************/
END REVISE;
```

or

```
REVISE: PROC;
 . . .
OPEN FILE (MASTER) TITLE('MA');
 . . .                                              /*****************/
                                                    /* REPEAT        */
  READ FILE (MASTER) INTO (REC) KEY (R_KEY);        /* LOCK RECORD   */
   . . .                                            /*               */
  REWRITE FILE (MASTER) FROM (REC) KEY (R_KEY);     /* UNLOCK RECORD */
 . . .                                              /*               */
                                                    /*****************/
END REVISE;
```

The QUERY procedure reads a specific record provided that neither the file nor the record are locked. If either are locked, it waits for the record to be available. The first version of the REVISE procedure waits until there are no tasks reading the file, then locks the file for its exclusive use. The second version of the REVISE procedure locks and unlocks single records. A procedure revising a record must lock out all other procedures revising the record. It may lock out procedures reading the record also, as in this example, because the current contents of the record are incorrect.

Review questions

1. Indicate whether each of the following statements is true or false.
- **(a)** Tasks are programs or procedures that execute concurrently.
- **(b)** Tasks can only communicate by passing values back and forth.
- **(c)** A lock is used in the synchronization of tasks.
- **(d)** Deadlock is a condition that occurs if neither of two tasks can proceed because of the other one.
- **(e)** An EVENT variable associated with a task is used to signal completion.
- **(f)** The main program must wait for all of its subtasks to complete.
- **(g)** Two tasks must not update a record at the same time.

2. When tasks share common variables, the statements that reference those variables are called ________________ .

3. Tasks synchronize their use of common variables through ________________ and ________________ protocols, which prevent ________________ .

4. To synchronize access to common variables by means of protocols, there must be a ________________ flag for each task and a switch to show which task ________________ .

5. An event has the value ________________ or ________________ .

6. File access can be synchronized if the file has the attribute ____________.

7. A task reading and rewriting a record must lock out any other tasks ____________ the record.

18.3 Examples of teleprocessing and tasking

In the single processor (or single processor plus I/O processor) computer configuration, the primary uses of tasking are to overlap computations and I/O processing, to overlap separate I/O operations, and to accommodate multiple users. The operating system interleaves the processing of batch jobs and the servicing of multiple terminals and devices.

18.3.1 Spooling data

Spooling the data moving from one set of devices or programs to another provides a classic example of tasking. The operating system uses spooling when it queues batch jobs from different sources or queues terminal I/O for an application program. Data is also spooled if the source and destination speeds or sizes do not match. In the following example, procedure IN obtains data from an input file and procedure OUT stores it in an output file. Since there may be delays in accessing file devices and the access speeds of devices differ, the data moving between the devices must be queued. The queue is maintained in the circular buffer BUFF. Procedures IN and OUT execute simultaneously, one building the queue, the other removing data from it.

```
SPOOLER: PROC OPTIONS (MAIN);
/*************************************************************/
/*                                                           */
/* PROGRAM: BUFFER DATA BETWEEN INPUT AND OUTPUT             */
/*          DEVICES                                          */
/* AUTHOR:  C ZIEGLER                                        */
/* VERSION: 07/17/84                                         */
/*                                                           */
/* PROGRAM DESCRIPTION                                       */
/* --------------------------------------------------------- */
/* THIS PROGRAM BUFFERS DATA OBTAINED BY AN INPUT            */
/* DEVICE AND SENDS IT TO AN OUTPUT DEVICE                   */
/*                                                           */
/* INPUT: IN_FILE                                            */
/*                                                           */
/* OUTPUT: OUT_FILE                                          */
/*                                                           */
/* PROCEDURES CALLED: IN, OUT                                */
/*                                                           */
/*************************************************************/
```

```
DCL (SPACE,DATA) EVENT,
    BUFF (1000)  FIXED BIN,
    IN_BUSY      BIT(1),
    OUT_BUSY     BIT(1),
    TURN         CHAR(3),
    KNT          FIXED BIN;
DCL TRUE         BIT(1)     INIT('1'B),
    FALSE        BIT(1)     INIT('0'B);
KNT = 0;
IN_BUSY = FALSE;
OUT_BUSY = FALSE;
TURN = 'IN';                        /* 'IN' MUST BE FIRST   */
COMPLETION(SPACE) = TRUE;           /* SPACE AVAILABLE      */
COMPLETION(DATA) = FALSE;           /* NO DATA AVAILABLE    */
CALL IN TASK EVENT (IN_DONE);
CALL OUT TASK EVENT (OUT_DONE);
WAIT (IN_DONE,OUT_DONE)(2);


IN: PROC;
/*********************************************************/
/*                                                       */
/* THIS PROCEDURE OBTAINS THE INPUT DATA                 */
/*                                                       */
/*********************************************************/
DCL IN_FILE FILE ENV(CONSECUTIVE);
DCL (NUM,NEXT)   FIXED BIN,
    MORE_DATA    BIT(1);

ON ENDFILE (IN_FILE)
  MORE_DATA = FALSE;

MORE_DATA = TRUE;
OPEN INPUT FILE (IN_FILE);
NEXT = 0;
GET LIST (NUM);
DO WHILE (MORE_DATA);
  WAIT(SPACE);
  NEXT = NEXT + 1;
  IF NEXT > 1000
    THEN
      NEXT = 1;
  BUFF(NEXT) = NUM;
  IN_BUSY = TRUE;                      /* ENTRY PROTOCOL    */
  TURN = 'OUT';
  DO WHILE (OUT_BUSY & TURN = 'OUT');
  END;
  KNT = KNT + 1;                       /* CRITICAL SECTION */
  IF KNT = 1000
    THEN
      COMPLETION(SPACE) = FALSE;
  COMPLETION(DATA) = TRUE;
```

```
  IN_BUSY = FALSE;                         /* EXIT PROTOCOL    */
  GET LIST (NUM);
END;
END IN;

OUT: PROC;
/*********************************************************/
/*                                                       */
/* THIS PROCEDURE CONTROLS THE OUTPUT                    */
/*                                                       */
/*********************************************************/
DCL OUT_FILE FILE ENV(CONSECUTIVE);
DCL NEXT     FIXED BIN;

OPEN OUTPUT FILE (OUT_FILE);
NEXT = 1;
DO WHILE (¬COMPLETION(IN_DONE) | KNT > 0);
  WAIT(DATA);
  PUT SKIP LIST (BUFF(NEXT));
  NEXT = NEXT + 1;
  IF NEXT > 1000
    THEN
      NEXT = 1;
  OUT_BUSY = TRUE;                      /* ENTRY PROTOCOL   */
  TURN = 'IN';
  DO WHILE (IN_BUSY & TURN = 'IN');
  END;
  KNT = KNT - 1;                        /* CRITICAL SECTION */
  COMPLETION(DATA) = FALSE;
  COMPLETION(SPACE) = TRUE;
  OUT_BUSY = FALSE;                     /* EXIT PROTOCOL    */
END;
END OUT;

END SPOOLER;
```

Keeping count of the number of items in the buffer is the simplest way to tell whether items are available for printing or space is available for more input. BUFF, KNT, SPACE, and DATA are global to both IN and OUT, therefore both may access them. KNT, SPACE, and DATA are used to control access of the buffer, so incrementing and decrementing the count are critical sections of the tasks and must be protected from interference. Rules for the scope of variables are the same for tasks as for other procedures. The variables NEXT are separate and local to the two procedures.

The task IN of this example will continue filling the buffer until the buffer is full or IN and OUT try to access the event variables or KNT at the same time. If the buffer is full, IN waits until there is space available to store more input. The buffer is recognized as full when KNT is 1000 and empty when KNT is 0. If IN and OUT both reach their critical sections at the same time, they simply take turns.

The statements COMPLETION and WAIT, along with the busy flags and turn indicator, are used to synchronize the tasks. COMPLETION sets an event flag while WAIT tests an event flag and causes a pause in the processing until the flag has been set.

The two events, DATA and SPACE, are set by the procedures IN and OUT respectively. DATA is used to signal that some data is available in the buffer. When OUT clears the buffer, it also clears the DATA signal, then waits until the signal has been set by IN. The signal SPACE is used by OUT to indicate that there is now space to store data in the buffer.

18.3.2 Multiple terminals

Tasks can be used to control separate terminals, providing work space for each. While one terminal is waiting for input, the operating system will switch control to a different task. Essentially, one copy of a task is attached for each terminal, as in the following example:

```
MP: PROC OPTIONS (MAIN);
 . . .
DO K = 1 TO LAST;
  CALL SUB(TERM(K)) TASK EVENT (EV(K));
END;
WAIT (EV)(LAST);
SUB: PROC(TKEY);
 . . .
END SUB;
END MP;
```

If the tasks do not share any common data, the only synchronization is the delay of the main program's termination until all the attached tasks have completed. In this example there are K concurrent tasks, one for each terminal.

When tasking is used to control multiple terminals, the execution is demand-driven rather than control-driven. The tasks synchronizing input from the terminals wait until it is available. The following example shows input from two terminals A and B being spooled to a common file. This technique would be used to capture on-line transactions which are to be run against a master file in batch mode later, after the time-sharing network has been shut down.

```
SPOOL: PROC OPTIONS (MAIN);
/************************************************************/
/*                                                          */
/* PROGRAM: SPOOL DATA FROM MULTIPLE INPUT DEVICES          */
/* AUTHOR:  C ZIEGLER                                       */
/* VERSION: 07/17/84                                        */
/*                                                          */
```

```
/* PROGRAM DESCRIPTION                                        */
/* ---------------------------------------------------------- */
/* THIS PROGRAM SPOOLS DATA OBTAINED FROM MANY                */
/* DIFFERENT INPUT DEVICES, ALL USING COPIES OF THE           */
/* SAME INPUT TASK                                            */
/*                                                            */
/* INPUT: MSG                                                 */
/*                                                            */
/* OUTPUT: OUT                                                */
/*                                                            */
/* PROCEDURES CALLED: IN, OUT                                 */
/*                                                            */
/************************************************************/

DCL OUT FILE  RECORD OUTPUT ENV(CONSECUTIVE);
DCL READY     EVENT,
    OUT_REC   CHAR(120),
    SYSTEM_UP BIT(1);

ON CONDITION (A)
  CALL IN TASK EVENT(READ);

OPEN FILE (OUT) TITLE ('F1');
DO WHILE (SYSTEM_UP | ¬ADONE | ¬BDONE);
  IF READY
    THEN
      DO;
        OUT_REC = ACCEPT(...);
        WRITE FILE (OUT) FROM (OUT_REC);
        COMPLETION (READY) = FALSE;
      END;
  SELECT;
    . . .

END;

IN:  PROC;
DCL MSG FILE INPUT KEYED RECORD TRANSIENT
        BUFFERED ENV (teleprocessing);
DCL MSG_BUFF CHAR(128),
    TKEY     CHAR(8),
    ON_LINE  BIT(1);

ON ENDFILE(MSG)
  ON_LINE = FALSE;

ON_LINE = TRUE;
DO WHILE (ON_LINE);
  WAIT (¬READ);
  READ FILE (MSG) INTO MSG_BUFF KEYTO (TKEY);
  IF ON_LINE
    THEN
      COMPLETION(READY)=TRUE;
```

```
END;
END IN;
END SPOOL;
```

The main program is activated from the operator's console. It is deactivated by a signal from the operator and completion of all the terminal processing tasks. The shutdown could include sending messages to the terminals indicating that the system is about to go down, then having the terminal processing programs take time out and shut down after about five minutes, rather than waiting for all the input to stop.

A single procedure is used for all the terminal input processing tasks. Duplicates of the procedure are spun off, distinguished only by the terminal key. The main task polls the terminals, checking each in turn to determine whether any input is waiting. If a terminal is ready, input is accepted from the input task for that terminal and spooled to the disk file. Each of the terminal tasks waits until transmission of its data to the controlling program and therefore to the disk has been completed before it reads another message from its input queue.

Rather than polling the terminals, the main procedure could provide on-demand processing for the terminals by using the signals from the terminal tasks to build a queue of service requests. The terminal input would be processed in the order the signals were received rather than in the order the terminals were polled. Having the main task provide the output to the disk rather than having all terminal tasks write to a shared disk file puts the input records on the disk more nearly in the order they are received than if each task wrote its own records. Also, it saves memory buffer space. Each task that writes must have its own disk buffer. If records are unblocked, which is inefficient, the whole system can only operate at disk speed. If records are blocked, the physical records would be written only when the buffers are full, affecting the physical order of the logical records on the disk. A block of records from one terminal would follow a block of records from another terminal. With one single task doing the writing, fewer buffers are needed and the logical records from the terminals are intermixed.

18.3.3 Reader-writer problem

When a disk file that must be updated is shared, the situation is termed the *reader-writer problem.* If two programs A and B are attempting to use the same file, as long as both are reading the file, the fact that at machine level the computer can only do one thing at a time provides enough synchronization. But if one or both users are trying to update the file, additional synchronization is needed. Updating a file requires two physical accesses, one to read, the other to write. This situation is analogous to the two accesses to retrieve and store a shared variable that is being updated. However, accessing the disk is much slower than accessing memory, so simultaneous access attempts are more likely. The system control program must allow only one user at a time to update a record. Otherwise, if the updates overlapped as follows, the first update would be lost when the second REWRITE was executed.

A reads record	B reads record
A rewrites updated record	B rewrites updated record

The record returned to the file by user B would not include the changes made by user A.

Depending on the software, when one user is updating a file, other users may be locked out of the file completely, or locked out at the record or field level. The PL/I language has file options that make it possible to lock other users out of a file but not out of a record or field. It is possible to use tasking to control lockout at the record level. The following program shows the synchronization of file access between two tasks A and B having separate input files. The input files contain record keys and codes indicating whether a record is to be updated or read. If the record is to be updated, the new information is included in the input file. The synchronization flags and turn variable have been replaced by events.

```
READWRI: PROC OPTIONS (MAIN, TASK);
/************************************************************/
/*                                                          */
/* PROGRAM: READER/WRITER PROBLEM                           */
/* AUTHOR:  C ZIEGLER                                       */
/* VERSION: 07/17/84                                        */
/*                                                          */
/* PROGRAM DESCRIPTION                                      */
/* ------------------------------------------------------- */
/* THIS PROGRAM CONTROLS ACCESS TO A FILE, ALLOWING         */
/* MANY READERS AT A TIME TO USE IT, BUT GIVING             */
/* EACH WRITER EXCLUSIVE USE.                               */
/*                                                          */
/* INPUT: A_FILE, B_FILE (TWO USER TRANSACTION FILES)       */
/*        MASTER                                            */
/*                                                          */
/* OUTPUT: MASTER                                           */
/*                                                          */
/* PROCEDURES CALLED: A, B (TWO USERS)                      */
/*                                                          */
/************************************************************/
DCL A_FREE   EVENT,
    B_FREE   EVENT,
    A_TURN   EVENT,
    B_TURN   EVENT,
    A_KEY    CHAR(8),
    B_KEY    CHAR(8);
  . . .
```

```
OPEN FILE(MASTER) TITLE('F1');
COMPLETION(A_FREE) = TRUE;
COMPLETION(B_FREE) = TRUE;
COMPLETION(A_TURN) = TRUE;
COMPLETION(B_TURN) = TRUE;
CALL A TASK EVENT (AEV);
CALL B TASK EVENT (BEV);
WAIT (AEV,BEV) (2);

A: PROC;
DCL A_FILE    FILE INPUT RECORD ENV (CONSECUTIVE),
    MASTER    FILE UPDATE DIRECT RECORD ENV(INDEXED);
DCL 1 A_REC,
      5 CODE        CHAR(1),    /* 'R' FOR READ, 'U' FOR WRITE */
      5 REC KEY     CHAR(8),
      5 INFO        CHAR(60);
DCL 1 MASTER_REC,
      5 FILLER      CHAR(4),
      5 MAST_KEY    CHAR(8),
      5 INFO        CHAR(60),
    MORE_DATA       BIT(1);
DCL TRUE            BIT(1)    INIT('1'B),
    FALSE           BIT(1)    INIT('0'B);

ON ENDFILE (A_FILE)
  MORE_DATA = FALSE;

MORE_DATA = TRUE;
OPEN FILE (A_FILE) TITLE ('A1');
READ FILE (A_FILE) INTO (A_REC);
DO WHILE (MORE_DATA);
  IF CODE = 'R'
    THEN
      DO;
        READ FILE (MASTER) INTO (MASTER_REC) KEY (REC_KEY);
        PUT SKIP LIST (MASTER_REC.INFO);
      END;
  IF CODE = 'U'
    THEN
      DO;
        A_KEY = REC_KEY;
        IF REC_KEY = B_KEY
          THEN
            DO;                                  /* ENTRY PROTOCOL   */
              COMPLETION(A_FREE) = FALSE;
              COMPLETION(A_TURN) = TRUE;
              COMPLETION(B_TURN) = TRUE;
              WAIT(B_FREE,A_TURN)(1);
            END;
                                                 /* CRITICAL SECTION */
        READ FILE(MASTER) INTO (MASTER_REC) KEY (REC_KEY);
        UNSPEC(FILLER) = FALSE;
```

```
        MASTER_REC.INFO = A_REC.INFO;
        MAST_KEY = REC_KEY;
        REWRITE FILE (MASTER) FROM (MASTER_REC) KEYFROM (MAST_KEY);
        COMPLETION(A_FREE) = TRUE;          /* EXIT PROTOCOL    */
      END;
  READ FILE (A_FILE) INTO (A_REC);
END;
RETURN;
END A;

B: PROC;                                    /* LIKE A           */
 . . .

END B;

END READWRI;
```

Procedure B is like procedure A. We assume there are no KEY errors. The initialization indicates that all records are available and that either task can have the first turn. In fact, both may run concurrently, accessing any records as long as both are just reading records. There is no wait in the part of the task that reads the file.

The block of instructions for CODE = 'U' is the critical section. At the machine level, updating is not a single operation. The entry protocol starts by indicating intent, clearing the A_FREE event to signify that A is busy. Then priority is given to the other task by setting the B_TURN event. A then waits to see whether task B is busy with the same record. If the B task is reading or updating a different record, the A task will proceed. If the B task is updating the same record, the B_FREE event is false, but A_TURN is true as B gives priority to A. The processing proceeds as shown below.

MP	*A*	*B*
A_FREE is true B_FREE is true A_TURN is true B_TURN is true WAIT		
	A_FREE is false A_TURN is false B_TURN is true WAIT	
		B_FREE is false B_TURN is false A_TURN is true WAIT
	A updates record A_FREE is true repeat	
		B updates record B_FREE is true repeat
END		

If the setting and clearing of flags by A and B is interleaved, it will not affect the processing. A WAIT instruction can be used in the tasks to do the waiting, rather than a DO loop, provided that event variables are used rather than ordinary flags. The explicit wait ensures that there will be no concurrent updates.

An alternate method is to use exclusive files and the LOCK option provided by PL/I. This is shown in the following version.

```
READWRI: PROC OPTIONS (MAIN,TASK);
/*************************************************************/
/*                                                           */
/* PROGRAM: READER/WRITER PROBLEM                            */
/* AUTHOR:  C ZIEGLER                                        */
/* VERSION: 07/17/84                                         */
/*                                                           */
/* PROGRAM DESCRIPTION                                       */
/* ------------------------------------------------------    */
/* THIS PROGRAM CONTROLS ACCESS TO A FILE, ALLOWING          */
/* MANY READERS AT A TIME TO USE IT, BUT GIVING              */
/* EACH WRITER EXCLUSIVE USE, USING THE PL/I 'LOCK'          */
/* OPTION ON AN 'EXCLUSIVE' FILE.                            */
/*                                                           */
/* INPUT: A_FILE, B_FILE (TWO USER TRANSACTION FILES)        */
/*        MASTER                                             */
/*                                                           */
/* OUTPUT: MASTER                                            */
/*                                                           */
/* PROCEDURES CALLED: READER, WRITER                         */
/*                                                           */
/*************************************************************/
DCL MASTER    FILE UPDATE DIRECT RECORD EXCLUSIVE
                 ENV(INDEXED);
DCL KNT       FIXED BIN,
    R_BUSY    BIT(1),
    W_BUSY    BIT(1),
    TURN      CHAR(1);

KNT = 0;
R_BUSY = FALSE;
W_BUSY = FALSE;
TURN = 'R';
 . . .
OPEN FILE (MASTER) TITLE ('F');
CALL READER(TKEY(I)) TASK EVENT (REV);
CALL WRITER(TKEY(J)) TASK EVENT (WEV);
WAIT (REV,WEV)(2);

READER: PROC(TKEY);
DCL TKEY      CHAR(8);
DCL R_FILE    FILE INPUT RECORD TRANSIENT
                 ENV(TELEPROCESSING);
```

```
DCL 1 R_REC,
      5 CODE       CHAR(1),    /* 'R' FOR READ, 'W' FOR WRITE */
      5 REC_KEY    CHAR(8);
DCL 1 MASTER REC,
      5 MAST_KEY   CHAR(8),
      5 INFO       CHAR(72);

OPEN FILE (R_FILE) TITLE ('D1');
READ FILE (R_FILE) INTO (R_REC) KEY (TKEY);
DO WHILE (REC_KEY ¬='QUIT');
  R_BUSY = TRUE;                              /* PROTECT CHANGE TO KNT */
  TURN = 'W';
  DO WHILE (W_BUSY & TURN = 'W');
  END;
  KNT = KNT + 1;
  R_BUSY = FALSE;
  READ UNLOCK FILE (MASTER) INTO (MASTER_REC) KEY (REC_KEY);
  PUT SKIP LIST (MASTER_REC.INFO);
  R_BUSY = TRUE;                              /* PROTECT CHANGE TO KNT */
  TURN = 'W';
  DO WHILE (W_BUSY & TURN = 'W');
  END;
  KNT = KNT - 1;
  R_BUSY = FALSE;
  READ FILE (R_FILE) INTO (R_REC) KEY (TKEY);
END;
RETURN;
END READER;

WRITER: PROC(TKEY);
DCL TKEY      CHAR(8);
DCL W_FILE    FILE INPUT RECORD TRANSIENT ENV(TELEPROCESSING);
DCL 1 W_REC,
      5 REC_KEY    CHAR(8),
      5 INFO       CHAR(72);
DCL 1 MASTER_REC,
      5 MASTER_KEY CHAR(8),
      5 INFO       CHAR(72);

OPEN FILE (W_FILE) TITLE('W1');
READ FILE (W_FILE) INTO (W_REC) KEY (TKEY);
W_BUSY = TRUE;                              /* PROTECT CHANGE TO KNT */
TURN = 'R';
DO WHILE (KNT) 0 & TURN ¬='W');
END;
KNT = 1;
CLOSE FILE (MASTER);
OPEN FILE (MASTER) LOCK TITLE ('D1');       /* LOCK ENTIRE FILE      */
W_BUSY = FALSE;
DO WHILE (REC_KEY ¬='QUIT');
  READ FILE (MASTER) INTO (MASTER_REC) KEY (MASTER_KEY);
 . . .
```

```
  READ FILE (W_FILE) INTO (W_REC) KEY (TKEY);
END;
W_BUSY = TRUE;                              /* PROTECT CHANGE TO KNT */
TURN = 'R';
DO WHILE (R_BUSY & TURN = 'R');
END;
KNT = 0;
CLOSE FILE (MASTER);
OPEN FILE (MASTER) TITLE ('D1');
W_BUSY = FALSE;
END WRITER;

END READWRI;
```

The OPEN statement with the lock option locks the entire file; therefore it must be used only when there are no active readers or writers. The critical sections of the task are the references to the shared variable KNT which tells how many active readers and writers are present. KNT must be protected while it is being updated. Also, control must not shift to the other task between the time KNT is tested and the master file is opened for exclusive use. Nothing would be gained by locking the entire file in order to update a single record. This method is used for batching updates.

If terminals are being used to both read and update data, the master program would activate several tasks—one to control the writing and one to control the reading. These in turn would activate tasks to handle input from separate terminals and handle output to them. The read and write tasks would not only control data transmission, they would check access rights. Not every terminal user would have permission to update the data set. Not every terminal user would have read access to the entire data set. Also, a balance would have to be maintained between on-line readers and writers. If the writers had to wait for all readers to finish, the updates might never take place. However, any lengthy update might cause a number of prospective readers to become discouraged and leave. Spooling the updates for off-line processing is one possible solution.

18.4 Summary

Tasking provides a way of overlapping the use of several processors executing instructions from the same program. It is used by the operating system in multiuser computer systems. In single-user computer systems it is used by application programs to increase turnaround time by improving the utilization of system resources. Usually the concurrent tasks handle I/O, such as accessing several disk files at the same time or servicing several terminals at the same time.

When tasks share data storage areas or files, data access must be synchronized. This can be done in three different ways:

1. By sharing program variables and guarding access to the critical sections of the tasks by means of entry and exit protocols.
2. By sharing EVENT variables and guarding access to the critical sections of the tasks through the use of the COMPLETION and WAIT functions.
3. By sharing access to an EXCLUSIVE file through the use of either record or file locks.

When tasks are used to service terminals, batch input may be spooled to a file for later processing, or the terminals may be accessed in an interactive mode using queries and responses, approximating a conversation. Terminals may be selected either by polling, which is program-controlled, or through the use of interrupts, which are terminal-controlled. When polling takes place, input and output to the terminal are available in TRANSIENT files, which use the terminal IDs as keys. When terminals are used only for input, a CONSECUTIVE file may be used.

18.5 Exercises

1. Assume that two INDEXED files are on two different devices. File STUDENT contains student information in the form:

Cols.		
	1-5	Student ID
	6-25	Name
	26-45	Address

File GRADES contains information of the form:

Cols.		
	1-5	Student ID
	6-13	Course ID
	14	Grade points
	15	Grade
	16-23	Course ID
	. . .	
	76-83	Course ID
	84	Grade points
	85	Grade

Write a program that reads a CONSECUTIVE file ID having records of the form:

Cols.	1-5	Student ID

and calls two tasks, one of which looks up the ID in the STUDENT file and the other in the GRADES file. The main program should combine the records and print a grade report for each student, including the total grade points and the grade point average.

2. Write a program that provides "phone" service between two terminals. Everything that is entered from either terminal should appear on both terminals, identified as to which terminal originated it.

3. Write a program that carries on a conversation with users at one or more terminals. The program should initiate each conversation by asking "How are you today?" Every time a terminal user replies, the program should extract one word of more than three characters from the reply and ask "Would you explain what you mean by '⟨word⟩'." Transcribe each conversation to a PRINT file.

4. The producer/consumer problem consists of an input procedure that fills a shared buffer with data and an output procedure that removes data from the buffer. Assume that the input procedure reads 80 character lines from a terminal, and the output procedure prints 132 character lines on a printer. Write the two procedures as tasks.

Appendix

Common character representations

Character	*BCD (6-bit)*	*octal*	*ASCII (7-bit)*	*hex*	*EBCDIC (8-bit)*	*hex*
A	010 001	21	100 0001	41	1100 0001	C1
B	010 010	22	100 0010	42	1100 0010	C2
C	010 011	23	100 0011	43	1100 0011	C3
D	010 100	23	100 0100	44	1100 0100	C4
E	010 101	25	100 0101	45	1100 0101	C5
F	010 110	26	100 0110	46	1100 0110	C6
G	010 111	27	100 0111	47	1100 0111	C7
H	011 000	30	100 1000	48	1100 1000	C8
I	011 001	31	100 1001	49	1100 1001	C9
J	100 001	41	100 1010	4A	1101 0001	D1
K	100 010	42	100 1011	4B	1101 0010	D2
L	100 011	43	100 1100	4C	1101 0011	D3
M	100 100	44	100 1101	4D	1101 0100	D4
N	100 101	45	100 1110	4E	1101 0101	D5
O	100 110	46	100 1111	4F	1101 0110	D6
P	100 111	47	101 0000	50	1101 0111	D7
Q	101 000	50	101 0001	51	1101 1000	D8
R	101 001	51	101 0010	52	1101 1001	D9
S	110 010	62	101 0011	53	1110 0010	E2
T	110 011	63	101 0100	54	1110 0011	E3
U	110 100	64	101 0101	55	1110 0100	E4
V	110 101	65	101 0110	56	1110 0101	E5
W	110 110	66	101 0111	57	1110 0110	E6
X	110 111	67	101 1000	58	1110 0111	E7
Y	111 000	70	101 1001	59	1110 1000	E8
Z	111 001	71	101 1010	5A	1110 1001	E9
0	000 000	00	011 0000	30	1111 0000	F0
1	000 001	01	011 0001	31	1111 0001	F1
2	000 010	02	011 0010	32	1111 0010	F2
3	000 011	03	011 0011	33	1111 0011	F3
4	000 100	04	011 0100	34	1111 0100	F4
5	000 101	05	011 0101	35	1111 0101	F5
6	000 110	06	011 0110	36	1111 0110	F6
7	000 111	07	011 0111	37	1111 0111	F7
8	001 000	08	011 1000	38	1111 1000	F8
9	001 001	09	011 1001	39	1111 1001	F9
b̸	110 000	60	010 0000	20	0100 0000	40
$	101 011	53	010 0100	24	0101 1011	5B
#			010 0011	23	0111 1011	7B

Character	*BCD (6-bit)*	*octal*	*ASCII (7-bit)*	*hex*	*EBCDIC (8-bit)*	*hex*
@					0111 1100	7C
+	010 000	20	010 1011	2B	0100 1110	4E
−	100 000	40	010 1101	2D	0110 0000	60
*	101 100	54	010 1010	2A	0101 1100	5C
/	110 001	61	010 1111	2F	0110 0001	61
∧			101 1110	5E	0101 1111	5F
!			010 0001	21	0100 1111	4F
&			010 0110	26	0101 0000	50
<	011 010	32	011 1100	3C	0100 1100	4C
=	001 011	13	011 1101	3D	0111 1110	7E
>	101 111	57	011 1110	3E	0110 1110	6E
.	011 011	33	010 1110	2E	0100 1011	4B
,	111 011	73	010 1100	2C	0110 1011	6B
:	001 001	11	011 1010	3A	0111 1010	7A
;	011 111	37	011 1011	3B	0101 1110	5E
(	111 100	74	010 1000	28	0100 1101	4D
)	011 100	34	010 1001	29	0101 1101	5D
'			010 0111	27	0111 1101	7D
_			101 1111	5F	0110 1101	6D
%	001 110	16	010 0101	25	0110 1100	6C
?			011 1111	3F	0110 1111	6F
[	001 111	17	101 1011	5B		
]	111 010	72	101 1101	5D		
"			010 0010	22		
\			101 1100	5C		
{			111 1011	7B		
}			111 1101	7D		
~			111 1110	7E		
|	101 101	55	111 1100	7C		
‘			110 0000	60		
a			110 0001	61		
b			110 0010	62		
c			110 0011	63		
d			110 0100	64		
e			110 0101	65		
f			110 0110	66		
g			110 0111	67		
h			110 1000	68		
i			110 1001	69		
j			110 1010	6A		
k			110 1011	6B		
l			110 1100	6C		
m			110 1101	6D		
n			110 1110	6E		
o			100 1111	6F		
p			111 0000	70		
q			111 0001	71		
r			111 0010	72		
s			111 0011	73		
t			111 0100	74		
u			111 0101	75		
v			111 0110	76		

Character	*BCD (6-bit)*	*octal*	*ASCII (7-bit)*	*hex*	*EBCDIC (8-bit)*	*hex*
w			111 0111	77		
x			111 1000	78		
y			111 1001	79		
z			111 1010	7A		
NUL			000 0000	00		
SOH			000 0001	01		
STX			000 0010	02		
ETX			000 0011	03		
EOT			000 0100	04		
ENQ			000 0101	05		
ACK			000 0110	06		
BEL			000 0111	07		
BS			000 1000	08		
HT			000 1001	09		
LF			000 1010	0A		
VT			000 1011	0B		
FF			000 1100	0C		
CR			000 1101	0D		
SO			000 1110	0E		
SI			000 1111	0F		
DLE			001 0000	10		
DC1			001 0001	11		
DC2			001 0010	12		
DC3			001 0011	13		
DC4			001 0100	14		
NAK			001 0101	15		
SYN			001 0110	16		
ETB			001 0111	17		
CAN			001 1000	18		
EM			001 1001	19		
SUB			001 1010	1A		
ESC			001 1011	1B		
FS			001 1100	1C		
GS			001 1101	1D		
RS			001 1110	1E		
US			001 1111	1F		
DEL			111 1111	7F		

Appendix

Library functions

ABS
ADD
ALLOCATION
ALL
ANY
ATAN
ATAND
ATANH
BINARY
BIT
BOOL
CEIL
CHAR
COMPLETION
COMPLEX
CONJG
COS
COSD
COSH
COUNT
DATE
DIM
DIVIDE
EMPTY
ERF
ERFC
EXP
FLOAT
FLOOR
HBOUND
HIGH
IMAG
INDEX
LBOUND
LENGTH
LINENO
LOG
LOG10
LOG2
MAX
MIN
MOD
MULTIPLY
NULL
NULLO
ONCHAR
ONCODE
ONCOUNT
ONFILE
ONKEY
ONLOC
ONSOURCE
POLY
PRECISION
PROD
REAL
REPEAT
ROUND
SIGN
SIN
SIND
SINH
SQRT
STRING
SUBSTR
SUM
TAN
TAND
TANH
TIME
TRANSLATE
TRUNC
UNSPEC
VERIFY

B.1 Common mathematical functions

Some of the most frequently used mathematical functions are given in Table B–1 and the following paragraphs.

Function	*Value returned*	*Error conditions*
ACOS(X)	Inverse (arc) cosine in radians 0 ≤ acos(x) ≤ pi	Error if abs (X) ≤ 1
ASIN(X)	Inverse (arc) sine in radians −pi/2 ≤ ASIN(X) ≤ pi/2	Error if abs (X) ≤ 1
ATAN(X)	Inverse (arc) tangent in radians −pi/2 < ATAN(X) < pi/2	
ATAN(X, Y)	Arctan (X/Y) in radians for Y > 0 pi/2 for Y = 0 and X > 0	Error if X = 0 and Y = 0
ATAND(X)	Arctan (X) in degrees −90 < ATAND (X) < 90	
ATAND(X, Y)	Arctan (X/Y) in degrees 180/pi * ATAN (X, Y)	Error if X = 0 and Y = 0
ATANH(X)	Hyperbolic tangent	Error if abs(X) ≥ 1
CEIL(X)	Smallest integer ≥ X	
COS(X)	Cosine, X in radians	
COSD(X)	Cosine, X in degrees	
COSH(X)	Hyperbolic cosine of X	
EXP(X)	e**X	
FLOOR(X)	Largest integer ≤ X	
LOG(X)	Natural logarithm	Error if X ≤ 0

Table B–1

Table B-1 *continued*

Function	*Value returned*	*Error conditions*
LOG10(X)	Common logarithm	Error if $X \leq 0$
LOG2(X)	Base 2 logarithm	Error if $X \leq 0$
SIN(X)	Sine, X in radians	
SIND(X)	Sine, X in degrees	
SQRT(X)	Square root	Error if $X < 0$
TAN(X)	Tangent, X in radians	
TAND(X)	Tangent, X in degrees	
TANH(X)	Hyperbolic tangent	
TRUNC(X)	If $X < 0$ then CEIL (X) else FLOOR (X)	

The ADD, MULTIPLY, and DIVIDE functions are described in detail in the following paragraphs to show the method used by PL/I to determine the precision of the results of arithmetic operations.

ADD FUNCTION (not in Subset G)

The ADD function is used to find the sum of two values. Its effect differs from that of the operator + in that the precision of the result can be specified. The general form of the function is:

```
ADD(expr,expr,precision)
```

The first two arguments represent the values to be added. The last specifies the precision to be used for the result, including the field width and the number of fractional digits. If either or both of the values are floating point, only the field width is specified.

Given

```
A = 15.372;
B = 185.62;
PUT LIST(ADD(A,B,6,2));
```

the value is 0200.99.

Given

```
X = 27;
Y = 985;
PUT LIST(ADD(X,Y,4));
```

the value is 1012.

The rule for the specification of precision for an addition (or subtraction) operation is as follows:

If X has precision (w_X, d_X)

Y has precision (w_Y, d_Y)

and the result has precision (w_{X+Y}, d_{X+Y})

then

$$w_{X+Y} = \max(w_X - d_X, w_Y - d_Y) + \max(d_X, d_Y) + 1$$

$$d_{X+Y} = \max(d_X, d_Y)$$

A fatal error occurs if the precision is underspecified and the most significant digits are lost.

MULTIPLY FUNCTION (not in Subset G)

The MULTIPLY function returns the product of two numbers. Its effect differs from that of the operator * in that the precision of the result can be specified. The general form of the function is:

```
MULTIPLY(expr,expr,precision)
```

The first two arguments are the values to be multiplied. The last argument is the precision to be used for the result, including the field width and the number of digits to the right of the point.

Given

```
A = 12.56;
B = 5.738;
PUT LIST(MULTIPLY(A,B,7,5));
```

the value is 72.06928.

The rule for the specification of the precision for a multiplication operation is as follows:

If X has precision (w_X, d_X)

Y has precision (w_Y, d_Y)

and the result has the precision $(w_{X \cdot Y}, d_{X \cdot Y})$

then

$$w_{X \cdot Y} = w_X + w_Y$$

$$d_{X \cdot Y} = d_X + d_Y$$

If the precision given for the result is such that the high-order digits of the result would be truncated, a fatal error occurs. If the precision is such that low-order digits would be truncated, the computer does so. No rounding of the answer takes place.

DIVIDE FUNCTION

The DIVIDE function returns the result of dividing its first argument by its second argument. The general form of the function is:

```
DIVIDE(expr,expr,precision)
```

Internally, the quotient is computed with the maximum number of digits allowed by the computer. It is then adjusted to have the proper precision.

Given

```
A = 158.65;
B = 17.275;
PUT LIST(DIVIDE(A,B,6,5));
```

the value is 9.18379.

Internally, if A and B are fixed-decimal numbers and the maximum number of decimal digits allowed is fifteen, the result has the form 000009 183791600. The rule for the specification of precision for a division operation is as follows:

If X has precision (w_X, d_X)

Y has precision (w_Y, d_Y)

and the result has precision $(w_{X/Y} \cdot d_{X/Y})$

then

$w_{X/Y} = 15$ (implementation dependent)

$d_{X/Y} = 15 - (w_X - d_X + d_Y)$

In the numeric example, the quotient has fifteen digits, the maximum. There are three integer digits from A and three from B, for a total of six. There are $15 - 6 = 9$ fractional digits. Enough space is provided for the largest possible answer. Usually this means that leading zeros are stored. If significant digits are truncated when the result is stored, a fatal error will occur.

If the second argument is zero, the ZERODIVIDE condition is raised.

ROUND FUNCTION

The ROUND functions rounds a given numeric value at a specified digit and returns the result. The general form of this function is:

```
ROUND(expr,num)
```

The first argument can be a constant, a variable, or any other expression. Its value is to be rounded. The second argument is a signed or unsigned decimal integer.

If num > 0 then round to the right of the decimal point
num = 0 then round at the decimal point
num < 0 then round to the left of the decimal point

This is shown in the following examples:

A = 1985.6283;	*Result*
B = ROUND(A,1)	1985.6000
B = ROUND(A,2)	1985.6300
B = ROUND(A,3)	1985.6280
B = ROUND(A,0)	1986.0000
B = ROUND(A,−1)	1990.0000
B = ROUND(A,−2)	2000.000

MOD FUNCTION

The MOD function can be used to produce a positive or zero remainder resulting from division of one number by another number. The general form of the MOD function is:

```
MOD(arg1,arg2)
```

The value returned by the function is the smallest possible nonnegative value p such that

$(\text{arg1} - p)/\text{arg2} = n$ is an integer

for most implementations. The value returned, when subtracted from arg1, gives a number evenly divisible by arg2. Arg1 and arg2 need not be integers. If arg1 is positive, the value returned is the true remainder, as shown by the following examples:

B = MOD(28,5)	Result is 3, the remainder
B = MOD(37,6)	1, the remainder
B = MOD(14.2,.3)	1, the remainder
B = MOD(−28,5)	2, not the remainder
B = MOD(−37,−6)	5, not the remainder
B = MOD(17,−5)	2, the remainder

If arg2 is zero, the ZERODIVIDE condition is raised.

MAX FUNCTION

The MAX function returns the value of the argument with the largest value. The function must have at least two arguments. In some systems it may have only two arguments. Its general form is:

```
MAX(arg1, arg2, arg3, . . . , argn)
```

If any of the arguments are positive, the result is the value of the greatest positive argument. If all arguments are negative, the result is the value closest to zero. In the following example,

```
A = 12.8;
B = 18.65;
C = 6.75;
D = -28.32;
E = -5.7;
F = MAX(A,B,C,D,E);
G = MAX(D,E);
```

the value assigned to F is 18.65 and the value assigned to G is −05.70.

MIN FUNCTION

The MIN function returns the value of the argument with the smallest value. By smallest is meant the value closest to zero if all the arguments are positive, or the most negative value if some of the arguments are negative. The MIN function must have at least two arguments. In some systems, it may have only two arguments. Its general form is:

```
MIN(arg1, arg2, arg3, . . . , argn)
```

In the following example,

```
W = 6.38;
X = -3.85;
Y = -12.75;
Z = 68.25;
R = MIN(W,X,Y,Z);
S = MIN(W,Z);
```

the value assigned to R is −12.75 while the value assigned to S is 06.38.

PROD FUNCTION (not in Subset G)

The PROD function computes the product of all elements of a one-dimensional array. It references the array by name. The following example shows the use of this function.

```
DECLARE X(5)   FIXED BIN,
        XPROD FIXED BIN;

XPROD = PROD(X);
```

The product computed is X(1)*X(2)*X(3)*X(4)*X(5). The values in the array are converted to FLOAT BIN before the fucntion is called. The function calculates their product and returns a FLOAT BIN value, which is then converted back to FIXED BIN for assignment to XPROD. Because the arithmetic is carried out in floating point, no overflow can take place during the calculation of the product, but the result returned may be too large to be placed in a FIXED BIN variable. The declaration

```
DECLARE XPROD FIXED BIN(31);
```

lessens the chance of a SIZE error, but at the expense of accuracy. FLOAT BIN variables only have six significant digits. Unreliable additional digits would be obtained by placing the value returned by the function in a storage area that accommodates more than six decimal digits.

If the product were to be calculated by a simple iterative DO loop rather than the function, the answer would be completely accurate. The PROD function should be used only for scientific programs which use floating-point numbers that are approximate rather than exact.

B.2 Common string functions

Some of the most frequently used string functions are given in Table B–2 and the following paragraphs.

Table B–2

Function	*Value returned*
CHAR(N[,L])	Character equivalent of numeric value of N
INDEX(S1,S2)	Location of S2 in S1
LENGTH(S)	Length of S
SUBSTR(S1,M[,N])	String of length N starting at position M in S1
VERIFY(S1,S2)	Position of first character in S1 that is not in S2

CHAR FUNCTION

The CHAR function converts numeric values into character strings. The general form of the function is:

```
CHAR(num,leng)
```

where num is the value to be converted. The second argument is optional. If it is present, it is an integer that specifies the desired length of the result. The following examples show the use of this function.

```
DCL NUM   FIXED DECIMAL (6);
DCL STRN CHAR(6);

NUM = 389547;
STRN = CHAR(NUM);                VALUE IS '389547'
NUM = 1854;
STRN = CHAR(NUM);                VALUE IS 'bb1854'
NUM = 116;
STRN = CHAR(NUM,4);              VALUE IS 'b116bb'-PADDED
STRN = CHAR(NUM,6);              VALUE IS 'bbb116'
STRN = CHAR(NUM,7);              VALUE IS 'bbbb11'-TRUNCATED
```

With the function call CHAR(NUM,4), the number is right-justified in a field of length 4 which is then assigned to STRN. With CHAR(NUM,7), it is right-justified in a field of length 7 which is then assigned to STRN. When necessary, the character value is truncated or padded with blanks.

Numbers can be converted to character strings without using the CHAR function, simply by assigning them to character variables. The advantage of using the function is that it gives the programmer control over the positioning of the digits in the result. The disadvantage is that the spacing of the result is implementation-dependent.

B.3 Functions used as pseudovariables

*COMPLETION(event-var)
*COMPLEX(num-var,num-var)
*IMAG(complex-var)
*LINENO(print-file)
*ONCHAR( )
*ONSOURCE( )
PAGENO(print-file)
*REAL(complex-var)
STRING(char-struct)
SUBSTR(string-var,num[,num])
UNSPEC(scalar-var)

*Not in Subset G

Pseudovariables are built-in functions which can be used to store a value in a memory location as well as to return a value. Their use depends on the context. When they are used on the left side of an assignment statement, a value is stored. When they are used on the right side of an assignment statement or in an output statement, they return values.

B.4 Common error condition functions

Some of the functions most frequently used in ON units are given in Table B–3 and the following paragraphs.

Table B–3

Function	*Value returned*
ONCHAR( )	Character raising CONVERSION condition
ONCODE( )	Error code
ONKEY( )	Key raising KEY condition
ONSOURCE( )	Character string raising CONVERSION condition

ONCHAR FUNCTION/PSEUDOVARIABLE (not in Subset G)

ONCHAR may be used only in an ON unit for a CONVERSION condition. When the condition is raised, the ONCHAR function may be used to access the illegal character that raised the condition. It returns a character string of length 1. It can also be used as a pseudovariable to change the illegal character. Both uses are shown in the following example:

```
DCL ONCHAR BUILTIN;

ON CONV
  BEGIN;
    BAD_CHAR = ONCHAR;
    ONCHAR = '0';
  END;
```

The first use of ONCHAR, on the right side of the assignment statement, returns the invalid character which is then stored in BAD_CHAR. The second use, on the left side of the assignment statement, temporarily replaces the bad character with a zero for the duration of the conversion operation.

ONSOURCE FUNCTION/PSEUDOVARIABLE (not in Subset G)

ONSOURCE may be used only in an ON unit for the CONVERSION condition. The length and value of the character string are obtained from the field being processed. ONSOURCE can be used as a pseudovariable to change the character string being processed. Both uses are shown in the following example:

```
DCL ONSOURCE BUILTIN;

ON CONV
  BEGIN;
    BAD_STR = ONSOURCE;
    ONSOURCE = '0';
  END;
```

Appendix

PL/I conditions

*AREA
[NO]CHECK
*[NO]CONVERSION
ENDFILE (file-name)
ENDPAGE (file-name)
ERROR
[NO]FIXEDOVERFLOW
KEY
*NAME
[NO]OVERFLOW
*PENDING
*RECORD
*[NO]SIZE
*[NO]STRINGRANGE
*[NO]STRINGSIZE
*[NO]SUBSCRIPTRANGE
*TRANSMIT
UNDEFINEDFILE
[NO]UNDERFLOW
[NO]ZERODIVIDE

*Not in Subset G

The most common of these conditions have been discussed in the text. Additional conditions are discussed in the following paragraphs.

CONVERSION CONDITION (not in Subset G)

The CONVERSION condition (abbreviated CONV) occurs when data must be converted from characters to another type and a character is found that cannot be converted. The condition is also raised when a character other than zero or one or a leading or trailing blank is to be converted to BIT and stored in a BIT string. Additionally, the condition is raised when a character other than a digit, decimal point, sign, or leading blank is part of a field to be converted to a numeric type, or when the characters in the field are not arranged in such a way as to represent a single number. Type errors such as these may occur during expression evaluation, assignment to a variable, input, or output. All STREAM input comes into the computer as characters. It is then converted, item by item, to the proper internal type. It leaves the computer as characters, too. The condition is raised on output if the internal bit pattern stored in a character or numeric variable cannot be interpreted as a valid value for the variable and therefore cannot be converted to output form.

The invalid bytes causing the CONVERSION error can be corrected within the ON unit by using the pseudovariables ONCHAR or ONSOURCE. Bytes are converted to or from characters one by one, from left to right. When an illegal byte is found, the condition is raised. On returning from the exception handler, the computer attempts the conversion a second time. If the invalid byte has not been altered, processing is terminated. Use of ONSOURCE permits the entire value to be printed or changed. ONCHAR contains the byte that raises the exception. The following examples show the raising and processing of this condition:

```
DCL STR                 CHAR(5),
    NUM                 FIXED DEC(5);
DCL (ONCHAR,ONSOURCE) BUILTIN;

ON CONVERSION
  BEGIN;
    PUT SKIP LIST('CONVERSION ERROR',ONSOURCE);
    ONCHAR = '0';                 prints 18K75
  END;

STR = '18K75';
NUM = STR;                        NUM is 18075
```

The CONVERSION condition is raised by the second assignment statement when the internal routine that converts character strings to numbers finds the character K. Control transfers to the exception handler, which uses the pseudovariable ONSOURCE to print an error message that exhibits the character string (18K75) being converted. The assignment of the character 0 to ONCHAR has the effect of replacing K with 0. Control returns to the assignment statement where the error occurred, the conversion is carried out, and 18075 is assigned to NUM. This correction allows the program to terminate normally. However, it is not clear that the value being assigned to NUM should have been 18075, so it is important to include in the output a message documenting the error that occurred.

In the following example,

```
DCL STR       CHAR(7),
    BTR       BIT(7);
DCL ONCHAR    BUILTIN,
    ONSOURCE  BUILTIN;

ON CONVERSION
  BEGIN;
    PUT SKIP LIST('CONVERSION ERROR',ONCHAR);
    ONSOURCE = '0000000';         prints X
  END;

STR = '011X110';
BTR = STR;                        BTR is '0000000'B
```

only the character (X) causing the conversion error is being printed in the error message. The entire source string is then being replaced by a string of zeros, the conversion is done again, and '0000000'B is assigned to BTR. Since STR had seven characters, seven zeros had to be assigned to ONSOURCE. If fewer zeros had been assigned in the exception handler, STR would have contained trailing blanks and the condition might have been raised again.

RULES FOR DATA TYPE CONVERSIONS

1. Arithmetic-to-character conversion:
   Arithmetic data items can be converted to character strings. The length of

the resulting character string depends on the precision of the arithmetic data. The decimal point, decimal fraction, whole part, and sign (if the number is negative) all appear as characters in the character string. Usually there are leading blanks as well.

2. Character-to-arithmetic conversion:
It is possible to convert character strings to arithmetic data if the character string contains only leading and trailing blanks and digits that form a valid number. There may also be a sign and a decimal point. No embedded blanks are allowed.

3. Arithmetic-to-bit conversion:
The magnitude of the arithmetic value is converted to a binary integer. The representation of the resulting binary integer is a bit string in memory, the length of which depends on the precision of the arithmetic data.

4. Bit string-to-arithmetic conversion:
The bit string is interpreted as a fixed-point binary number. The sign, base, and scale depend on the storage space used.

5. Character string-to-bit conversion:
This conversion is possible only if the character string contains just the characters 1 and 0. The character 1 becomes the bit 1 and the character 0 becomes the bit 0.

6. Bit string-to-character conversion:
A bit string is converted to character by using a character 1 for each bit 1 and a character 0 for each bit 0.

Table C–1 shows the type conversions that are always possible (Y), or possible when the source field has a value that can be interpreted as being of the target field type (?).

			Target	
		Numeric	*Bit*	*Character*
Source	Numeric	Y	Y	Y
	Bit	Y	Y	Y
	Character	?	?	Y

Table C–1 Valid type conversions

Those type conversions that are always possible may not give the result expected. The contents of the receiving field depend on the amount of space available as well as on the value of the source field.

Data types may be mixed in assignment statements, as in the following:

```
K = '5' + 3;          Result is 8
K = 3 + '110'B;       Result is 9
```

FIXEDOVERFLOW condition

The FIXEDOVERFLOW condition (abbreviated FOFL) is raised if the size of a fixed-point value exceeds the maximum permitted by the implementation. This can occur during input, from conversion of characters, or as a result of calculations. The following example shows several possibilities:

```
DCL (W,X,Y)  FIXED DEC(15),
    (A,B)    FIXED BIN(31),
    STR      CHAR(20);

W = 123456789012345;              15-digit number—OK
X = 10 * W;                       16-digit result—too large

A = 1000000;                      17-bit number—OK
B = A * A;                        33-bit result—too large

STR = '1234567890.123456789';     20 characters—OK
Y = STR;                          19-digit result—too large

X = (10 * W)/10;                  16-digit intermediate result—
                                     too large
```

In this example it is assumed that the implementation maximum for FIXED DECIMAL values is fifteen digits and for FIXED BINARY values thirty-one bits. The values of W, A, and STR can be stored in the space allocated for them. However, the results of the arithmetic and of the string conversion are too large for the implementation. The last assignment shows that this error is raised by an internal overflow rather than the inability to store the answer in the result field. In the last case, X is large enough to hold the fifteen-digit final result.

OVERFLOW CONDITION

The OVERFLOW condition (abbreviated OFL) occurs when the size of the exponent of a floating-point number exceeds the implementation maximum. In the following example it is assumed that a FLOAT DECIMAL number must be smaller than 10^{75}, a common limitation, and that a FLOAT BINARY number must be smaller than 2^{252}.

```
DCL (W,X,Y) FLOAT DECIMAL (6);

X = .832E65;
Y = .95E18;
W = X * Y / 0.1E10;               result is .79040E74
```

The result of the calculations is a valid FLOAT DECIMAL(6) number. It has fewer than six digits and an exponent smaller than seventy-five. However, overflow occurs during the multiplication of X and Y, as the result of that multiplication is .79040E83. In this example, the error condition is raised, not because of the size of the final result, but at an intermediate stage because arithmetic takes place from left to right.

UNDERFLOW CONDITION

The UNDERFLOW condition (abbreviated UFL) occurs when a floating-point number is too close to zero; that is, when the exponent of the number is smaller than the implementation minimum. Common limitations are that a FLOAT DECIMAL number may not be between -10^{-78} and $+10^{-78}$ and a FLOAT BINARY number may not be between -2^{-260} and $+2^{-260}$. Exponent underflow is not a fatal error. The system assumes that since the value is very close to zero, the number 0 may be used instead. No error message is written for this condition unless the program contains on ON unit for it.

```
DCL (W,X,Y) FLOAT DECIMAL(6);
    X = .59E-65;
    Y = .72E-23;
    W = X * Y;                result is 0
    Z = .23E01/W;             error
```

Underflow occurs in this example because the product of X and Y should have an exponent of -88, which is below the implementation minimum. While this is not treated as an error by the system, to continue the processing with division as shown above would cause a fatal error, as it is an attempt to divide by zero.

ZERODIVIDE CONDITION

The ZERODIVIDE condition (abbreviated ZDIV) is raised whenever division by zero is attempted. Mathematically, anything other than zero divided by zero is infinity and zero divided by zero is undefined. In either case, the result cannot be stored in a computer. The condition is a fatal error in the absence of an ON unit to handle it. After the processing of an ON unit, the program recovers and continues. This is shown in the following example:

```
DCL (K,N,M)  FIXED BIN;

ON ZERODIVIDE
  PUT SKIP LIST ('DIVISION BY ZERO');

N = 25;
M = 0;
K = N/M;                                   unpredictable result
```

SIZE CONDITION (not in Subset G)

The SIZE condition occurs when a numeric value is to be stored in a field that does not have space to the left of the point for all digits in the value. Since the point is aligned when the value is stored, the most significant decimal or binary digits are lost. This can occur during an assignment or during an output operation that assigns a value to a buffer field. Internally the value being stored is compared with the space available. The size of the location from which the value is being moved is not important. The following example shows several situations in which the SIZE condition would be raised:

```
DCL A FIXED DEC(5),
    B FIXED DEC(4),
    C FIXED DEC(6);

A = 12345;
C = 1234;
B = A;                      SIZE error
B = C;
PUT EDIT (A) (F(4));        SIZE error
```

In the assignment of C to B there is no SIZE error because the value stored in C is small enough to fit in B, even though the storage allocated to C is larger than the storage allocated to B.

The SIZE condition differs from the other arithmetic conditions discussed above in that the SIZE interrupt is normally disabled. The program should therefore explicitly enable it by establishing an ON unit for it, or by including it in the compiler parameters while a program is being debugged.

Appendix

D Statement formats

Declarations

* area-name AREA [(size)]

array-name (bounds-list) [type] [storage-class] [placement] [initial]

* event-name EVENT

$$\text{file-name FILE [KEYED]} \begin{Bmatrix} \text{[SEQUENTIAL]} \\ \text{DIRECT} \\ \text{TRANSIENT} \end{Bmatrix} \begin{Bmatrix} \text{[INPUT]} \\ \text{OUTPUT} \\ \text{UPDATE} \\ \text{PRINT} \end{Bmatrix} \begin{Bmatrix} \text{[STREAM]} \\ \\ \text{RECORD} \end{Bmatrix}$$

$$\text{ENVIRONMENT} \begin{Bmatrix} \text{(CONSECUTIVE)} \\ \text{(INDEXED)} \\ \text{(REGIONAL)} \\ \text{(teleprocessing)} \end{Bmatrix}$$

label-name LABEL

$$\text{locator-name} \begin{Bmatrix} \text{POINTER} \\ \text{OFFSET(area-name)} \end{Bmatrix} \text{[storage-class] [placement] [initial]}$$

$$\text{proc-name} \begin{Bmatrix} \text{BUILTIN} \\ \text{ENTRY [(arg-type-list)] [RETURNS(type)]} \end{Bmatrix}$$

remote-format-name: [name: . . .] FORMAT(format-list);

$$\text{var-name} \left\{ \begin{matrix} \begin{Bmatrix} \text{FIXED} \\ \text{FLOAT} \end{Bmatrix} \begin{Bmatrix} \text{DECIMAL} \\ \text{BINARY} \end{Bmatrix} \begin{Bmatrix} \text{REAL} \\ \text{COMPLEX} \end{Bmatrix} \\ \text{PICTURE 'spec'} \end{matrix} \right\} \text{[storage-class] [placement] [initial]}$$

$$\text{var-name} \begin{Bmatrix} \text{CHARACTER} \\ \text{BIT} \end{Bmatrix} \text{(length) [VARYING] [storage]}$$

1 struct-name [storage-class] [placement] [LIKE(struct-name)],

level-list

* task-name TASK

```
                   (BASED [(pointer-var)])
Storage-class is: { STATIC                 } {[INTERNAL]}
                  { CONTROLLED             } { EXTERNAL }
                   ([AUTOMATIC]            )

               (DEFINED(var-name) [POSITION(n)])
Placement is: {[AIGNED]                         }
               (UNALIGNED                       )
```

Initial is: INIT(value-list)

*Not in Subset G

Executable statement

ALLOCATE based-var [SET(pointer-var) [IN(area-var)]];

assignment

```
pseudovar  [ {,pseudovar }     ]
scalar-var [ {,scalar-var} ... ] = scalar-expr;

array-var  [,array-var...]  =  {array-expr; }
                               {scalar-expr;}

struct-var [,struct-var...] =  {struct-expr [,BY NAME];}
                               {scalar-expr;           }
```

CALL entry-name [(arg-list)] [TASK (task-name)] [EVENT (event-name)];

CLOSE FILE (file-name) [, FILE (file-name ...)];

DELETE FILE (file-name) [KEY (expr)];

```
FREE {controlled-var;                                }
     {[pointer-var ->] based-var [IN(area-var)];     }

GET {[STRING(char-name)]               } {LIST(input-list);              }
    {[FILE(file-name)] [SKIP[(n)]]     } {DATA(input-list);              }
                                         {EDIT(input_list) (format);     }

{GOTO } {label-const;}
{GO TO} {label-var;  }
```

LOCATE var FILE(file-name) [SET(pointer-var)] [KEYFROM(expr)];

OPEN [file attributes] FILE (file-name) [TITLE(title)] [PAGESIZE(n)]

[LINESIZE(n)] [...];

```
    ([STRING(char-name)]              ) (LIST(output-list);             )
PUT {                                 } {DATA(output-list);             }
    ([FILE(file-name)] [position]     ) (EDIT(output-list) (format);    )
```

Position is: [PAGE] [LINE(n)] [SKIP[(n)]]

$$\text{READ FILE(file-name)}\left\{\begin{array}{l}\left\{\begin{array}{l}\text{INTO (var)}\\ \text{SET (pointer-var)}\end{array}\right\}\left\{\begin{array}{l}\text{[KEY (expr)];}\\ \text{[KEYTO (expr)];}\end{array}\right\}\\ \text{IGNORE(expr);}\end{array}\right\}$$

RETURN [(expr)];

REVERT condition-name;

REWRITE FILE (file-name) [FROM(var)] [KEY(expr)];

*SIGNAL condition-name;

*WAIT (event-list);

WRITE FILE (file-name) FROM (var) [KEYFROM (expr)];

*Not in Subset G

Control structures

Block:

BEGIN;
  statement-list
END;

Exception handler:

ON condition
Block

Procedure:

$$\text{entry-name: PROCEDURE [(parameter-list)]}\left\{\begin{array}{l}\text{[OPTIONS(MAIN)];}\\ \text{[RECURSIVE] [RETURNS(type)];}\end{array}\right\}$$

  statement-list
END entry-name;

Repetition:

DO [scalar-var = expr TO expr [BY expr]] [WHILE(cond)] [UNTIL(cond)];
  statement-list
END;

Selection:

IF cond
  THEN
    statement
  [ELSE
    statement]

```
SELECT (var);
  WHEN(value)
    statement
  ...
  [OTHERWISE statement]
END;

SELECT;
  WHEN(condition)
    statement
  ...
  [OTHERWISE statement]
END;
```

Statement-list is:

```
statement
statement
. . .
```

Anywhere "block" is used, either a block or a simple statement may be used. Anywhere "statement" is used, either a control structure or a simple statement may be used.

Appendix

Answers to selected review questions

Section 1.1

1. memory, arithmetical / logical unit, input / output units

3. printer

5. to store the instructions being executed and the data being manipulated

7. System software manages the computer resources and makes them available to the user programs. Application software manages the data and makes it available to the user.

9. to translate PL/I programs to machine language before they can be executed

11. In a multiprogramming system several programs are in the computer memory at the same time but only one at a time is being executed. In a multiprocessing system, there are several processors, therefore several programs may be executed at the same time.

Section 1.2

1. The term "hardware" describes the physical components of a computer system. Software is the set of programs that are loaded into the computer memory to be executed. Firmware is the set of programs that are permanently installed in the equipment.

3. arithmetic operations, data transmission (input / output) operations, control operations

5. Move: "Move the vase to the piano."
Input: "Get some bread."
Output: "Put this in the closet."
Calculation: "Figure out how much I owe you."

7. Sequence: "Go to the store and buy some bread."
Decision: "If it is raining, take an umbrella."
Repetition: "Send an invitation to each person on this list."
Exception: "Be sure you read any footnotes."

Section 1.3

1. input

3. output

5. Bad data can cause incorrect output. At times it can even cause the computer system to break down.

7. the data and time as stored in the computer, counters, flags, or, in the calculation A + B + C, the partial sum A + B

Section 1.4

1. A program written in a high-level language (such as PL/I, which has not been compiled) is source code. The machine language program, which is the result of compilation, is object code.

3. A quality program should be able to detect bad data and respond appropriately.

5. the people who use the program and the people who maintain the program

Section 1.5

1. Its function can be described using an active verb.

3. The development starts with the top level of the chart which gives an overall view. The chart is then filled in from top to bottom, each level giving greater detail.

5. Statements that implement the basic control structures (sequence, decision, repetition, exception) and a way to modularize a program.

Section 2.1

1. Programs written in a standardized language are more easily moved from one computer system to another than programs which are not.

3. PL/I is a compiled language because PL/I programs are translated to machine languages by compilers. PL/I is a high-level language because it contains powerful built-in operations and high-level control structures.

5. Object code (machine language)

Section 2.2

1. false

3. a,c,e

5. to do something, to explain something, to identify something

7. semicolon (;)

9. computer, person reading the program

11. An IFTHENELSE structure provides two choices. A SELECT structure may provide any number of choices.

13. environment

15.

A>0	T	T	F
C*C=A*A+B*B	T	F	-
Calculate area	X		
Print A,B,C, area	X		
Print error msg		X	
Read A,B,C	X	X	
Repeat	X	X	
Exit			X

17. **(a)**

Get length, width, height	X
Calculate volume	X
Print length, width, height, volume	X

(b)

Fewer than 10 boxes	Y	N
Get length, width, height	X	
Calculate volume	X	
Print length, width, height, volume	X	
Repeat	X	
Exit		X

(c)

Length > 0	Y	-	-	N
Width > 0	-	Y	-	N
Height > 0	-	-	Y	N
Get length, width, height	X	X	X	
Calculate volume	X	X	X	
Print length, width, height, volume	X	X	X	
Repeat	X	X	X	
Exit				X

Section 2.3

1. algorithm
3. inside
5. a diamond-shaped entry point
7. Any module can be implemented as a PL/I control structure.

Section 3.1

1. In the procedure header

   ```
   MP: PROC OPTIONS(MAIN);
   ```

   the character string to the left of the colon is a name. The keyword PROCEDURE or PROC identifies the name as being a name of a procedure. The key clause OPTIONS(MAIN) indicates that the procedure is a main procedure and the place where program execution starts.

3. Exception handlers are blocks of code that tell what to do if an unusual situation or an error occurs.
5. PROC

Section 3.2

1. identifiers
3. 7, 31
5.

NASA150	external/internal	SHELL SORT	invalid
COST_IN_$	internal	#_PER_DOZEN	internal
MAXIMUMVAL	internal	PROCEDURE	internal
$VALUE	external/internal	AN5VA1	external/internal
MAX_VAL	internal	TOP. RATE	invalid
FLOW_	invalid	BASE_QUANTITY	invalid
7O'CLOCK	invalid	BANK_DEPOSIT	internal
@COST	internal	COST_OF_MATERIAL	internal

Section 3.3

1. type, storage needed
3. The value of a FIXED variable is written as an ordinary number. The value of a FLOAT variable is written in scientific notation using an exponent.

5. the total number of digits the number will contain, the position of the point

7. no

9. **(a)** 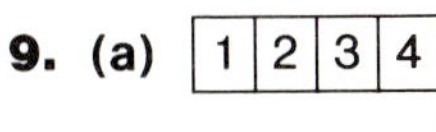

(b) error

(c) | 1 | 2 | 3 | 4 | 5 | 6 |

(d) error

(e) | 1 | 2 | 3 | 4 | 5 | 6 | 7 |

(f) | 1 | 2 | 3 | 4 | 5 | 6 | 7 | 8 |

(g) | 1 | 2 | 3 | 4 | 5 | 6 | 7 | 8 | 0 |

11. no; no

13. The computer can handle BINARY numbers more efficiently.

15. A large range of values is possible with FLOAT numbers.

17. DCL RATE FIXED DECIMAL (3.3) INIT (.075);

19. DCL HUNDRED FIXED BIN(15) INIT(100);

21. **(a)** | A | B | C | D | E | F | G | | | |

(b) | A | B | C | D | E |

(c) | A | B | C | D | E | F | G | / | / | / |

Section 3.4

1. +, −, *, /, **

3. **(a)** 34
(b) −32
(c) 15625

5. **(a)** 15
(b) 10
(c) 7

7. **(a)** 14.00
(b) 102.50
(c) 7.0

Section 3.5

1. (a) F
(b) T
(c) T
(d) F
(e) F
(f) T
(g) F

3. (a) F
(b) T
(c) F
(d) F
(e) F
(f) T

Section 4.1

1. stream, record

3. stream

5. edit-directed

7. list-directed, edit-directed

9. SYSIN is used for input, SYSOUT and SYSPRINT for output. Page formatting can be used with SYSPRINT, but not with SYSOUT.

Section 4.2

1. (a) T
(b) T
(c) F
(d) F
(e) T

3. A = 'XYZ'   B = 1.25000E+01;   C = −15.00   A = 'XYZ';

Section 4.3

1. (a) T
(b) T
(c) F
(d) T
(e) T
(f) T
(g) F

3. XYZ   1.25000E+01   −15.00   XYZ

Section 4.4

1. (a) F
(b) T
(c) F

3.

```
                  25          -17
              blank line
      ABC                      49
```

Section 4.5

1. (a) T
(b) F
(c) F
(d) T
(e) T
(f) T
(g) F
(h) F
(i) T
(j) T

3. PAGE, LINE, SKIP

5. Largest value is .99E+99, smallest value is −.99E+9

7. Largest value is 9.99E+99, smallest value is −9.99E+99

9.
```
GET EDIT (NAME,STREET,CITY,STATE,ZIP)
  (COL(1),A(20),A(10),A(10),A(5),A(5);
```

11. (a) F(6)
(b) F(12,4)
(c) E(13,6)
(d) F(10,5)
(e) B(8)

13. (6,2), (8,2)

Section 5.1

1. (a) T
(b) F
(c) T
(d) T
(e) T
(f) T

Section 5.2

1. (a) F
(b) T
(c) T
(d) F
(e) F

3. CTL/Z on a terminal

5. (a) CNT = 0;
(b) CNT = 1;
(c) CTN = 0;

Section 5.3

1. one or more

3. true

5. The condition is checked at the beginning of a DOWHILE loop and at the end of a DOUNTIL loop. A DOUNTIL loop is executed at least once, while a DOWHILE may not be executed at all. A DOWHILE loop repeats until the condition is false and a DOUNTIL loop repeats until the condition is true.

7. (a) Attempt to print data when the end-of-file has been reached. This can be avoided by using a priming read and reversing the order of the statements in the loop.
   (b) Attempting to get data when the end-of-file has already been reached. This can be avoided by using a DOWHILE loop.
   (c) Attempting to print data when there are fewer than nine values. This can be avoided by using a compound condition (CNT = 10 | EOF).

Section 5.4

1. (a) T
   (b) F
   (c) T
   (d) T
   (e) F
   (f) T

3.
```
IF X = Y
  THEN
    IF Y = Z
      THEN
        PUT SKIP LIST ('X, Y, Z, EQUAL');
```

5.
```
IF NAME_1 < NAME_2
  THEN
    IF NAME_3 < NAME_1
      THEN
        PUT SKIP LIST (NAME_3,NAME_1,NAME_2);
      ELSE
        IF NAME_3 < NAME_2
          THEN
            PUT SKIP LIST (NAME_1,NAME_3,NAME_2);
          ELSE
            PUT SKIP LIST (NAME_1,NAME_2,NAME_3);
  ELSE
    IF NAME_3 < NAME_2
      THEN
        PUT SKIP LIST (NAME_3,NAME_2,NAME_1);
      ELSE
        IF NAME_3 < NAME_1
          THEN
            PUT SKIP LIST (NAME_2,NAME_3,NAME_1);
          ELSE
            PUT SKIP LIST (NAME_2,NAME_1,NAME_3);
```

Section 5.5

1. (a) T
   (b) F
   (c) F
   (d) F
   (e) T
   (f) F

3.
```
SELECT;
  WHEN (A = B & B = C)
    PUT LIST ('EQUILATERAL');
  WHEN (A = B | A = C | B = C)
    PUT LIST ('ISOSCELES');
  OTHERWISE
    PUT LIST ('SCALENE');
END;
```

Section 5.6

1. Both parts are true.

3. '1' B

5. not ¬

7. (a) F
   (b) T
   (c) T
   (d) T

Section 5.7

1. (a) T
   (b) T
   (c) T
   (d) T
   (e) T
   (f) T
   (g) F
   (h) F

3. (a) 1
   (b) 10
   (c) 1, 2, 4, 7
   (d) adding J − 1 to I would make I equal to 11

5. The loop would not execute correctly if
   L is 0
   or J > K and L > 0
   or J < K and L < 0

7. `PUT EDIT ((I DO I = 1 TO 100 BY 10)) (COL(1),F(3));`

9. `PUT EDIT ((I DO I = 100 TO 1 BY -1)) (COL(1),F(3));`

Section 5.8

1. trap

3. raised

5. that the page is full

7. with the output statement

9. (a) An end-of-file exception handler is established which will not do anything when the condition is raised.
(b) One end-of-file exception handler is established which is later replaced by another exception handler.
(c) An end-of-file exception handler is established which will set two flags, MORE and EOF, when the condition is raised.
(d) An end-of-file exception handler is established which will set a single flag MORE_INFO when the condition is raised.
(e) End-of-file exception handlers are established for two different files, A and B.
(f) An end-of-page exception handler is established which will set a single flag when the condition is raised.

Section 6.1

1. (a) F
(b) T
(c) F
(d) F
(e) T
(f) F
(g) F

3. the blank

5. (a) THEbISbRED
(b) 6 ABCbbb
(c) 3 ABC
(d) 4

7.
```
PUT STRING (LINE_NUM) EDIT (N) (F(1));
```

9.
```
LAST_NAME  = SUBSTR(NAME,1,10);
FIRST_NAME = SUBSTR(NAME,11);
```

11.
```
TEXT = TRANSLATE(TEXT,'bb',',.');
DO UNTIL (TEXT = 'b');
  I = INDEX(TEXT,'b');
  IF I > 1
    THEN
      PUT SKIP LIST (SUBSTR(TEXT,1,I-1);
  TEXT = SUBSTR(TEXT,I+1);
END;
```

Section 6.2

1. (a) T
(b) F
(c) T
(d) F
(e) T
(f) F
(g) T

3.
```
SUBSTR(BSTR,5,1) = '1'B;
or BSTR = BOOL(BSTR,'00001'B,'1110'B);
or BSTR = BSTR | '00001'B;
```

5.
```
IF SUBSTR(BSTR,5,1) = '1'B
                           or BOOL(BSTR,'00001'B,'1000'B)
                           or BSTR & '00001'B
  THEN
    PUT LIST ('ON');
  ELSE
    PUT LIST ('OFF');
```

Section 7.1

1. (a) T
   (b) F
   (c) T
   (d) T
   (e) F
   (f) T
   (g) F

3. (a) valid
   (b) valid
   (c) valid
   (d) valid
   (e) invalid
   (f) invalid
   (g) valid
   (h) valid
   (i) invalid

5.
```
DCL TIME_OF_DAY  CHAR(9);
DCL T(2)         CHAR(2)  DEFINED (TIME_OF_DAY);
TIME_OF_DAY = TIME();
```

Section 7.2

1. (a)
```
DO I = 1 TO 10;
   GET LIST (A(I));
END;
```
   (b)
```
GET LIST ((A(I) I = 1 TO 10));
```
   (c)
```
GETLIST (A);
```

3.
```
GET LIST (X);
I = 0;
DO WHILE (MORE);
  I = I + 1;
  A(I) = X;
  GET LIST (X);
END;
```

5. (a)
```
PUTLIST (X);
```
   (b)
```
DO I = 1 TO 10;
   PUT LIST (X(I));
END;
```
   (c)
```
PUTLIST ((X(I) I = 1 TO 10);
```

Section 7.3

1.

(a)	(b)	(c)	(d)	(e)	(f)
0	1	3	3	−2	1
0	2	3	4	−1	−1
0	3	3	5	0	1
0	4	3	6	1	−1
0	5	3	7	2	1

3.

(a)	(b)	(c)	(d)
11 00	9 00	10 00	−9 00
13 00	9 00	5 50	−9 00
15 00	9 00	4 00	−9 00
17 00	9 00	3 25	−9 00
19 00	9 00	2 80	−9 00

5.
```
DO I = 1 TO 10 BY 2;
 A(I) = A(I) + 2;
END;
```

7.
```
DCL S (20) CHAR (1) DEFINED (STR);
DO I = 1 TO 10;
  CH = S(I);
  S(I) = S(11-I);
  S(11-I) = CH;
END;
```

Section 7.4

1. (a) T
(b) T
(c) F

3.
```
GET LIST (INCOME);
I = 6;
IF INCOME < 45000
  THEN
    DO;
      I = 1;
      DO UNTIL (INCOME < INCOME_TABLE(I));
        I = I + 1;
      END;
    END;
PUT LIST (TAX_RATE(I));
```

Section 7.5

1. b

Section 7.6

1. (a) 15 (b) 7 (c) 11 (d) 4

3. (a) 1 (b) 6 (c) −5 (d) −4

5.
```
DO X = 1 TO 10;
   Y = POLY(A,X);
  . . .
END;
```

Section 8.1

1. two

3. row-major

5.

	Lower bound First	Lower bound Second	Upper bound First	Upper bound Second	Number of Elements
(a)	1	1	3	4	12
(b)	2	3	6	7	25
(c)	−2	1	4	6	42
(d)	−3	−2	−1	4	21

7.
```
DCL STR(10,20) CHAR(20) INIT((200) (20)' ');
```

Section 8.2

1.
(a) `GET EDIT (ARR) (A(4));`
(b) `GET EDIT (ARR) (COL(1), A(4));`
(c) `GET EDIT (ARR) (COL(1), (4)A(4));`
(d)
```
GET EDIT (((ARR(I,J) I = 1 TO 3) J = 1 TO 4))
         (COL(1), (3)A(4));
```

3.
```
GET LIST (N);
I = 0;
DO WHILE (I <= 10 & MORE_DATA);
   I = I + 1;
   J = 0;
   DO WHILE (J < 12 & MORE_DATA);
      J = J + 1;
      NUM(I,J) = N;
      GET LIST (N);
   END;
END;
```

5. (a) 10 (b) 8 (c) 80 (d) 1

Section 8.3

1. (a) T
   (b) F
   (c) T
   (d) T
   (e) T

3. Is the original value of A(2,3) being used to multiply all of the values of A? If the results are not the same, is the arithmetic performed in row-major order in one and column-major order in the other?

Section 8.4

1. (a) plane
   (b) row
   (c) column
   (d) third
   (e) first

3.
```
PUT EDIT (SEAT(1,*,*)) (COL(1), (60)A(2));
PUT PAGE;
PUT EDIT (SEAT(2,*,*)) (COL(1), (60)A(2));
```

Section 9.1

1. main, sub

3. internal, external

5. (a) subroutine
   (b) function
   (c) internal
   (d) external

7. passing values through the parameter/argument lists

Section 9.2

1. (a) F
   (b) F
   (c) F
   (d) T

3. (a) A, B
   (b) A, B, C, D
   (c) A, B, D
   (d) none of these
   (e) A, B

4.
```
GET_ARR: PROC(X);     /* THIS PROCEDURE IS NOT ROBUST */
DCL X(20)  FLOAT BIN;
GET LIST (X);
END GET_ARR;
```

Section 9.3

1. (a) static
   (b) main procedure
   (c) lost
   (d) nested in
   (e) saved

Section 9.4

1. (a) type
   (b) reference
   (c) input
   (d) output (or input/output)
   (e) before
   (f) external

3. (a) T
   (b) T
   (c) T
   (d) F
   (e) F
   (f) T

Section 9.5

1. (a) inside
   (b) RETURNS clause
   (c) functions
   (d) functions
   (e) array

3.
```
SIGN: PROC (K) RETURNS (CHAR(1));
DCL K FIXED BIN;
IF K >= 0
  THEN
    RETURN('+');
  ELSE
    RETURN('-');
END SIGN;
```

5.
```
SUMSQ: PROC (VECT) RETURNS(FLOAT BIN);
DCL VECT(*) FLOAT BIN,
    SUM     FLOAT BIN,
    (L,H,I) FIXED BIN;
L = LBOUND(VECT,1);
H = HBOUND(VECT,1);
SUM = 0.0;
DO I = L TO H;
  SUM = SUM + VECT(I)*VECT(I);
END;
RETURN(SUM);
END SUMSQ;
```

Section 9.6

1. recursive

3. descent or call, ascent or return

5.
```
C: PROC(N,K) RECURSIVE RETURNS (FIXED BIN);
DCL (N,K) FIXED BIN;
IF K = 0
  THEN
    RETURN(1);
IF 1 <= K & K <= N
  THEN
    RETURN(C(N,K,-1)+C(N-1,K-1));
PUT SKIP LIST ('ERROR');
END C;
```

Section 9.7

1. (a) T
   (b) T
   (c) F
   (d) T

3. the occurrence of the condition associated with the ON unit

Section 10.1

1. master

3. disk, tape

5. input, output, processing

7. SYSIN, SYSOUT, SYSPRINT

Section 10.2

1. SYSPRINT, PRINT

3. (a) T
   (b) T
   (c) F
   (d) T
   (e) T
   (f) T
   (g) F

5. (a)
```
DCL MASTER FILE SEQL INPUT RECORD
        ENV(CONSECUTIVE);
```
   (b)
```
DCL TRANS FILE SEQL INPUT TRANSIENT
        ENV(teleprocessing);
```
   (c)
```
DCL REPORT FILE SEQL PRINT STREAM
        ENV(CONSECUTIVE);
```
   (d)
```
DCL TEMP FILE SEQL RECORD [or STREAM]
        ENV(CONSECUTIVE);
```

Section 10.3

1. (a) T
(b) F
(c) F
(d) T
(e) F
(f) T

3. (a) `OPEN FILE (REPORT) PRINT;`
(b) `OPEN FILE (TRANSACTION) INPUT;`

Section 10.4

1. SYSIN

Section 10.5

1. `SYSIN, INPUT`

3.
```
ON ENDFILE(SYSIN)
  MORE_DATA = '0'B;

ON ENDPAGE(SYSPRINT)
  PAGE_FULL = '1'B;
```

Section 11.1

1. (a) T
(b) T
(c) F
(d) T
(e) T
(f) T
(g) F

3. organization

5. LIKE

7.
```
DCL 1 PERSONAL_DATA,
      5 NAME        CHAR(20),
      5 AGE         CHAR(3),
      5 INCOME      FIXED DEC (7,2),
      5 EDUC        CHAR(50);
```

9.
```
DCL 1 CURRENT_TIME   DEF (NOW),
      5 HR   CHAR(2),
      5 MIN  CHAR(2),
      5 SEC  CHAR(2),
      5 MSEC CHAR(3);
```

Section 11.2

1. (a) T
   (b) F
   (c) T
   (d) T

3. (a) A.C is −81, A.D is 14.3
   (b) A.C is 14.3, A.D is −81
   (c) A.C is −162, A.D is 28.6
   (d) A.C is 28.6, A.D is −162

Section 11.3

1.
```
STRING(TODAY) = DATE( );
```

Section 11.4

1. (a)
```
GET EDIT(HEADING) (A(30),A(3));
```
   (b)
```
GET EDIT(STRING(HEADING)) (A(33));
```
   (c)
```
DCL HEADING_STR CHAR(33),
      1 HEADING          DEF(HEADING_STR),
        5 TITLE   CHAR(30),
        5 PAGENUM CHAR(3);

GET EDIT(HEADING_STR) (A(33));
```

3. (a)
```
PUT EDIT(HEADING) (A,A);
```
   (b)
```
PUT EDIT(STRING(HEADING)) (A);
```
   (c)
```
PUT EDIT(HEADING_STR) (A);
```
   (see declaration of answer 1(c) above)

5.
```
DCL 1 INVENTORY,
      5 PART_NO    CHAR(5),
      5 SUPPLIER   CHAR(20),
      5 COST       PIC'999V99',
      5 ON_HAND    PIC'99999';
```

7. XYZb̸
   XY
   Xb̸Yb̸Z

Section 11.5

1. (a) T
   (b) T
   (c) F
   (d) F
   (e) T
   (f) T
   (g) F
   (h) T

3.
```
DCL 1 SOIL_SAMPLE,
      5 SAMPLE_NO    CHAR(5),
      5 LOC_CODE     CHAR(5),
      5 DEPTH        PIC'99V999',
      5 ACIDITY      PIC'9V999',
      5 GRAIN_SIZE   PIC'V999';
```

Section 11.6

1. four

2. two digits

Section 12.1

1. control groups

3. control break

5. (a) T (b) T (c) F (d) T

Section 12.2

1. (a) change of value of a control field
(b) an interrupt
(c) ENDFILE
(d) ENDPAGE
(e) processing
(f) printing
(g) smallest
(h) footing
(i) heading

Section 12.3

1. hierarchy charts, flowcharts

3. program specifications, revision and maintenance history, record of testing and verification

5. (a) prints 5
3
pretty-printing, proper indentation and alignment would make it more readable.

(b) prints 10 11 12 13 14 15 16 17 18 19
Selecting user data names which are not keywords would make this easier to read.

(c) prints 175
Selecting user data names which are not commonly used for something else would make this easier to read.

(d) prints 1 2 3 4 5 6 7 8 9 10
Using standard control structures would make this easier to read.

(e) prints 420
This would be easier to read if the comments were not mixed in with the code.

Section 13.1

1. EXTERNAL, INTERNAL

3. AUTOMATIC

5. EXTERNAL

7. INTERNAL

9. (a) automatic
   (b) static
   (c) internal
   (d) automatic
   (e) global
   (f) description

Section 13.2

1. 5 8
   10 18

Section 13.3

1. automatic

3. based

5. FREE

7. 8 7 6 5

9.
```
DCL TITLE_REC     CHAR(60)     BASED(P),
    ARR_REC(10)   PIC'99999'   BASED(P);
```

Section 13.4

1. (a) T
   (b) T
   (c) F
   (d) T
   (e) T
   (f) T
   (g) T

Section 13.5

1. **(a)** unnamed
(b) named
(c) areas

Section 14.1

1. channel

3. main processor, channel

5. record, block

7. cards per minute

9. **(a)** T
(b) T
(c) F
(d) F
(e) T
(f) T
(g) F
(h) T

11. $\frac{10000}{1200} = 8.3$ minutes

Section 14.2

1. **(a)** physical
(b) physical
(c) nine
(d) character
(e) binary
(f) decreases
(g) increases
(h) increases

3. blocking factor

5. **(a)** $\left\lfloor \frac{47968}{560} \right\rfloor \times 15 \times 1770 = 2{,}256{,}750$ records

(b) $\left\lfloor \frac{47968}{1280} \right\rfloor \times 15 \times 1770 \times 100 = 98{,}235{,}000$ records

7. **(a)** $$\left\lfloor \frac{100000}{\left\lfloor \frac{47968}{560} \right\rfloor} \right\rfloor \times 16 + 100000 \times 8.4 + \frac{56000000}{3000000} = 858851 \text{ ms}$$
$$= 858.851 \text{ sec}$$

(b) $$\left\lfloor \frac{1000}{\left\lfloor \frac{47968}{1280} \right\rfloor} \right\rfloor \times 16 + 1000 \times 8.4 + \frac{56000000}{3000000} = 8848 \text{ ms}$$
$$= 8.848 \text{ sec}$$

Section 14.3

1. (a) T
   (b) T
   (c) T
   (d) F
   (e) T
   (f) T

Section 14.4

1. insert, delete, modify

3. deleted

5. sequentially, randomly

7. relative or regional

9. consecutive

Section 14.5

1. ENDFILE

3. ENDFILE, KEY

5. ENDFILE, KEY

Section 14.6

1. mass storage

3. magnetic tape

5. (a) DIRECT
   (b) DIRECT
   (c) CONSECUTIVE
   (d) CONSECUTIVE
   (e) REGIONAL

Section 15.1

1. CONSECUTIVE, SEQUENTIAL

3. mass storage

Section 15.2

1. (a) OPEN FILE (F) INPUT;
   (b) OPEN FILE (F) OUTPUT;
   (c) OPEN FILE (F) UPDATE;
   (d) CLOSE FILE (F);

3. end-of-file record

Section 15.3

1. READ, WRITE

3. move, locate, skip sequential

5. **(a)** move mode
(b) locate mode
(c) locate mode
(d) skip sequential
(e) update mode
(f) locate mode

Section 15.4

1. **(a)** T
(b) T
(c) F
(d) T

Section 15.5

1. disk

3. 5000

5. a status flag

7. modify, delete

Section 16.1

1. index, data, overflow data

3. the index must be created in that order

5. insertion

Section 16.2

1. CONSECUTIVE

3.
```
DCL IN_F FILE KEYED SEQL INPUT RECORD ENV(INDEXED);
```

5.
```
DCL INFO FILE KEYED DIRECT INPUT
     RECORD ENV(INDEXED);
```

Section 16.3

1. **(a)** T
(b) F
(c) F
(d) F
(e) F

3.
```
OPEN FILE (MASTER) INPUT;
. . .
OPENFILE(MASTER) UPDATE;
```

Section 16.4

1. The most recently read record is the one rewritten or deleted.
3. Check to see whether the record is in the file and raise the KEY condition if it is not there.
5. There is already a record in the file having the same key.

Section 16.5

1. SEQL INPUT
3. the bad key
5. the record is missing
7. the record is missing

Section 16.6

1. WRITE
3. READ, REWRITE
5. DELETE

Section 17.1

1. (a) T
   (b) F
   (c) F
   (d) T
   (e) F
   (f) F
   (g) T
   (h) F
   (i) F
   (j) T
3. records may be inserted, the number of duplicate relative record keys is reduced
5. (a) 14
   (b) 11
   (c) 32

Section 17.2

1.
```
DCL F FILE KEYED SEQL RECORD OUTPUT ENV(REGIONAL);
```

3.
```
DCL H FILE KEYED DIRECT RECORD UPDATE
      ENV(REGIONAL);
```

5. **(a)** sequential
(b) KEYED
(c) cannot
(d) relative record key
(e) symbolic key

Section 17.3

1. **(a)** T
(b) T
(c) T
(d) F
(e) F

3.
```
OPEN FILE (MASTER) INPUT;
  . . .
OPEN FILE (MASTER) UPDATE;
```

5. SEQL OUTPUT

Section 17.4

1. WRITE

3. READ, REWRITE

5. sequential, READ

7. KEY

9. KEYFROM

11.
```
CNT = 0;
READ FILE (F) INTO (F_REC);
DO WHILE (MORE_DATA);
  IF F_TYPE ¬= DUMMY
    THEN
      CNT = CNT + 1;
  READ FILE (F) INTO (F_REC);
END;
```

Section 17.5

1. ENDFILE, KEY

3. out of bounds

5. KEYED

7. the cause of the KEY error

9. there is already a record in the file with that key

Section 17.6

1. WRITE

3. READ, REWRITE

Section 18.1

1. (a) T
   (b) F
   (c) T
   (d) T
   (e) T

3. the computer must maintain a workspace for each dialogue

Section 18.2

1. (a) T
   (b) F
   (c) F
   (d) T
   (e) T
   (f) T
   (g) T

3. entry, exit, deadlock

5. complete, incomplete

7. modifying

Index